Dictionary of Literary Biography • Volume Fifty

Afro-American Writers Before the Harlem Renaissance

Dictionary of Literary Biography

1: *The American Renaissance in New England,* edited by Joel Myerson (1978)

2: *American Novelists Since World War II,* edited by Jeffrey Helterman and Richard Layman (1978)

3: *Antebellum Writers in New York and the South,* edited by Joel Myerson (1979)

4: *American Writers in Paris, 1920-1939,* edited by Karen Lane Rood (1980)

5: *American Poets Since World War II,* 2 parts, edited by Donald J. Greiner (1980)

6: *American Novelists Since World War II,* Second Series, edited by James E. Kibler, Jr. (1980)

7: *Twentieth-Century American Dramatists,* 2 parts, edited by John MacNicholas (1981)

8: *Twentieth-Century American Science-Fiction Writers,* 2 parts, edited by David Cowart and Thomas L. Wymer (1981)

9: *American Novelists, 1910-1945,* 3 parts, edited by James J. Martine (1981)

10: *Modern British Dramatists, 1900-1945,* 2 parts, edited by Stanley Weintraub (1982)

11: *American Humorists, 1800-1950,* 2 parts, edited by Stanley Trachtenberg (1982)

12: *American Realists and Naturalists,* edited by Donald Pizer and Earl N. Harbert (1982)

13: *British Dramatists Since World War II,* 2 parts, edited by Stanley Weintraub (1982)

14: *British Novelists Since 1960,* 2 parts, edited by Jay L. Halio (1983)

15: *British Novelists, 1930-1959,* 2 parts, edited by Bernard Oldsey (1983)

16: *The Beats: Literary Bohemians in Postwar America,* 2 parts, edited by Ann Charters (1983)

17: *Twentieth-Century American Historians,* edited by Clyde N. Wilson (1983)

18: *Victorian Novelists After 1885,* edited by Ira B. Nadel and William E. Fredeman (1983)

19: *British Poets, 1880-1914,* edited by Donald E. Stanford (1983)

20: *British Poets, 1914-1945,* edited by Donald E. Stanford (1983)

21: *Victorian Novelists Before 1885,* edited by Ira B. Nadel and William E. Fredeman (1983)

22: *American Writers for Children, 1900-1960,* edited by John Cech (1983)

23: *American Newspaper Journalists, 1873-1900,* edited by Perry J. Ashley (1983)

24: *American Colonial Writers, 1606-1734,* edited by Emory Elliott (1984)

25: *American Newspaper Journalists, 1901-1925,* edited by Perry J. Ashley (1984)

26: *American Screenwriters,* edited by Robert E. Morsberger, Stephen O. Lesser, and Randall Clark (1984)

27: *Poets of Great Britain and Ireland, 1945-1960,* edited by Vincent B. Sherry, Jr. (1984)

28: *Twentieth-Century American-Jewish Fiction Writers,* edited by Daniel Walden (1984)

29: *American Newspaper Journalists, 1926-1950,* edited by Perry J. Ashley (1984)

30: *American Historians, 1607-1865,* edited by Clyde N. Wilson (1984)

31: *American Colonial Writers, 1735-1781,* edited by Emory Elliott (1984)

32: *Victorian Poets Before 1850,* edited by William E. Fredeman and Ira B. Nadel (1984)

33: *Afro-American Fiction Writers After 1955,* edited by Thadious M. Davis and Trudier Harris (1984)

34: *British Novelists, 1890-1929: Traditionalists,* edited by Thomas F. Staley (1985)

35: *Victorian Poets After 1850,* edited by William E. Fredeman and Ira B. Nadel (1985)

36: *British Novelists, 1890-1929: Modernists,* edited by Thomas F. Staley (1985)

37: *American Writers of the Early Republic,* edited by Emory Elliott (1985)

38: *Afro-American Writers After 1955: Dramatists and Prose Writers,* edited by Thadious M. Davis and Trudier Harris (1985)

39: *British Novelists, 1660-1800,* 2 parts, edited by Martin C. Battestin (1985)

40: *Poets of Great Britain and Ireland Since 1960,* 2 parts, edited by Vincent B. Sherry, Jr. (1985)

41: *Afro-American Poets Since 1955,* edited by Trudier Harris and Thadious M. Davis (1985)

42: *American Writers for Children Before 1900,* edited by Glenn E. Estes (1985)

43: *American Newspaper Journalists, 1690-1872,* edited by Perry J. Ashley (1986)

44: *American Screenwriters,* Second Series, edited by Randall Clark (1986)

45: *American Poets, 1880-1945,* First Series, edited by Peter Quartermain (1986)

46: *American Literary Publishing Houses, 1900-1980: Trade and Paperback,* edited by Peter Dzwonkoski (1986)

47: *American Historians, 1866-1912,* edited by Clyde N. Wilson (1986)

48: *American Poets, 1880-1945,* Second Series, edited by Peter Quartermain (1986)

49: *American Literary Publishing Houses, 1638-1899,* 2 parts, edited by Peter Dzwonkoski (1986)

50: *Afro-American Writers Before the Harlem Renaissance,* edited by Trudier Harris (1986)

Documentary Series

1: *Sherwood Anderson, Willa Cather, John Dos Passos, Theodore Dreiser, F. Scott Fitzgerald, Ernest Hemingway, Sinclair Lewis,* edited by Margaret A. Van Antwerp (1982)

2: *James Gould Cozzens, James T. Farrell, William Faulkner, John O'Hara, John Steinbeck, Thomas Wolfe, Richard Wright,* edited by Margaret A. Van Antwerp (1982)

3: *Saul Bellow, Jack Kerouac, Norman Mailer, Vladimir Nabokov, John Updike, Kurt Vonnegut,* edited by Mary Bruccoli (1983)

4: *Tennessee Williams,* edited by Margaret A. Van Antwerp and Sally Johns (1984)

Yearbooks

1980, edited by Karen L. Rood, Jean W. Ross, and Richard Ziegfeld (1981)

1981, edited by Karen L. Rood, Jean W. Ross, and Richard Ziegfeld (1982)

1982, edited by Richard Ziegfeld; associate editors: Jean W. Ross and Lynne C. Zeigler (1983)

1983, edited by Mary Bruccoli and Jean W. Ross; associate editor: Richard Ziegfeld (1984)

1984, edited by Jean W. Ross (1985)

1985, edited by Jean W. Ross (1986)

Dictionary of Literary Biography • Volume Fifty

Afro-American Writers Before the Harlem Renaissance

Edited by
Trudier Harris
University of North Carolina at Chapel Hill

Associate Editor
Thadious M. Davis
University of North Carolina at Chapel Hill

A Bruccoli Clark Book
Gale Research Company • Book Tower • Detroit, Michigan 48226

Matthew J. Bruccoli and Richard Layman, *Editorial Directors*
C. E. Frazer Clark, Jr., *Managing Editor*

Manufactured by Edwards Brothers, Inc.
Ann Arbor, Michigan
Printed in the United States of America

Library of Congress Cataloging-in-Publication Data

Afro-American writers before the Harlem renaissance.

(Dictionary of literary biography; v. 50)
"A Bruccoli Clark book."
Includes index.
1. American literature—Afro-American authors—History and criticism. 2. American literature—Afro-American authors—Bio-bibliography. 3. Afro-American authors—Biography—Dictionaries. 4. Afro-Americans in literature. I. Harris, Trudier. II. Series.
PS153.N5A393 1986 810'.9'896 [B] 86-12121
ISBN 0-8103-1728-1

For
Hugh M. Gloster
J. Saunders Redding
Unareed Harris

Contents

Plan of the Series

. . . Almost the most prodigious asset of a country, and perhaps its most precious possession, is its native literary product–when that product is fine and noble and enduring.

Mark Twain*

The advisory board, the editors, and the publisher of the *Dictionary of Literary Biography* are joined in endorsing Mark Twain's declaration. The literature of a nation provides an inexhaustible resource of permanent worth. It is our expectation that this endeavor will make literature and its creators better understood and more accessible to students and the literate public, while satisfying the standards of teachers and scholars.

To meet these requirements, *literary biography* has been construed in terms of the author's achievement. The most important thing about a writer is his writing. Accordingly, the entries in *DLB* are career biographies, tracing the development of the author's canon and the evolution of his reputation.

The publication plan for *DLB* resulted from two years of preparation. The project was proposed to Bruccoli Clark by Frederick G. Ruffner, president of the Gale Research Company, in November 1975. After specimen entries were prepared and typeset, an advisory board was formed to refine the entry format and develop the series rationale. In meetings held during 1976, the publisher, series editors, and advisory board approved the scheme for a comprehensive biographical dictionary of persons who contributed to North American literature. Editorial work on the first volume began in January 1977, and it was published in 1978.

In order to make *DLB* more than a reference tool and to compile volumes that individually have claim to status as literary history, it was decided to organize volumes by topic or period or genre. Each of these freestanding volumes provides a biographical-bibliographical guide and overview for a particular area of literature. We are convinced that this organization—as opposed to a single alphabet method—constitutes a valuable innovation in the presentation of reference material. The volume plan necessarily requires many decisions for the placement and treatment of authors who might properly be included in two or three volumes. In some instances a major figure will be included in separate volumes, but with different entries emphasizing the aspect of his career appropriate to each volume. Ernest Hemingway, for example, is represented in *American Writers in Paris, 1920-1939* by an entry focusing on his expatriate apprenticeship; he is also in *American Novelists, 1910-1945* with an entry surveying his entire career. Each volume includes a cumulative index of subject authors and articles. The final *DLB* volume will be a comprehensive index to the entire series.

With volume ten in 1982 it was decided to enlarge the scope of *DLB* beyond the literature of the United States. By the end of 1985 twenty-one volumes treating British literature had been published, and volumes for Commonwealth and Modern European literature were in progress. The series has been further augmented by the *DLB Yearbooks* (since 1981) which update published entries and add new entries to keep the *DLB* current with contemporary activity. There have also been occasional *DLB Documentary Series* volumes which provide biographical and critical background source materials for figures whose work is judged to have particular interest for students. One of these companion volumes is entirely devoted to Tennessee Williams.

The purpose of *DLB* is not only to provide reliable information in a convenient format but also to place the figures in the larger perspective of literary history and to offer appraisals of their accomplishments by qualified scholars.

We define literature as the *intellectual commerce of a nation:* not merely as belles lettres, but as that ample and complex process by which ideas are generated, shaped, and transmitted. *DLB* entries are not limited to "creative writers" but extend to other figures who in this time and in this way influenced the mind of a people. Thus the series encompasses historians, journalists, publishers, and screenwriters. By this means readers of *DLB* may be aided to perceive literature not as cult scripture in the keeping of cultural high priests, but as at the center of a nation's life.

DLB includes the major writers appropriate to each volume and those standing in the ranks im-

*From an unpublished section of Mark Twain's autobiography, copyright © by the Mark Twain Company.

mediately behind them. Scholarly and critical counsel has been sought in deciding which minor figures to include and how full their entries should be. Wherever possible, useful references will be made to figures who do not warrant separate entries.

Each *DLB* volume has a volume editor responsible for planning the volume, selecting the figures for inclusion, and assigning the entries. Volume editors are also responsible for preparing, where appropriate, appendices surveying the major periodicals and literary and intellectual movements for their volumes, as well as lists of further readings. Work on the series as a whole is coordinated at the Bruccoli Clark editorial center in Columbia, South Carolina, where the editorial staff is responsible for the accuracy of the published volumes.

One feature that distinguishes *DLB* is the illustration policy—its concern with the iconography of literature. Just as an author is influenced by his surroundings, so is the reader's understanding of the author enhanced by a knowledge of his environment. Therefore *DLB* volumes include not only drawings, paintings, and photographs of authors, often depicting them at various stages in their careers, but also illustrations of their families and places where they lived. Title pages are regularly reproduced in facsimile along with dust jackets for modern authors. The dust jackets are a special feature of *DLB* because they often document better than anything else the way in which an author's work was launched in its own time. Specimens of the writers' manuscripts are included when feasible.

A supplement to *DLB*—tentatively titled *A Guide, Chronology, and Glossary for American Literature*—will outline the history of literature in North America and trace the influences that shaped it. This volume will provide a framework for the study of American literature by means of chronological tables, literary affiliation charts, glossarial entries, and concise surveys of the major movements. It has been planned to stand on its own as a vade mecum, providing a ready-reference guide to the study of American literature as well as a companion to the *DLB* volumes for American literature.

Samuel Johnson rightly decreed that "The chief glory of every people arises from its authors." The purpose of the *Dictionary of Literary Biography* is to compile literary history in the surest way available to us—by accurate and comprehensive treatment of the lives and work of those who contributed to it.

The *DLB* Advisory Board

Foreword

DLB 50, Afro-American Writers Before the Harlem Renaissance, is the first in a series of three volumes covering the work of black American authors up to 1955. The second volume addresses *Afro-American Writers from the Harlem Renaissance to 1940,* and the third treats *Afro-American Writers: 1940-1955.* During the early stages of Afro-American literary history, black writers were looked upon as being remarkable because they were able to write at all. Africans were brought to this country to be workers, not writers; if they somehow transcended their bonds, they became items of curiosity, like Phillis Wheatley, or examples in the argument for the abolition of slavery, as Frederick Douglass did. The idea of a literary tradition among Afro-Americans was a laughable proposition. However, Afro-Americans not only created a literary tradition, as the volumes in the *DLB* demonstrate, they brought it to a distinguished pinnacle by the middle of the twentieth century.

Those early voices found their literary models in the Bible, the classics, methodism, and neoclassicism. The poetry in the eighteenth and nineteenth centuries rings with the cadences of traditional forms and references. The very act of writing was more important than developing an aesthetic with a basis in Afro-American cultural forms, for it was indeed questionable—even to some of the writers—if black Americans had a culture. So the Jupiter Hammons and the George Moses Hortons and the Frances Harpers poured their complaints about slavery into formulaic molds that frequently made their efforts look stilted—and understandably so, for the forms were set for praising God, not for crying out against slavery.

When a few black writers at the turn of the century, such as Paul Laurence Dunbar and Charles W. Chesnutt, began to be appreciated as writers, the molds of expression were still not flexible enough to accommodate their presentation of black experiences; when they attempted frank forms of expression, they were censored. The limiting effect on Dunbar's career of the critics' perception that he was a dialect poet is legendary; Chesnutt was somewhat more successful in his attempts to break out of the constraints of the plantation tradition.

With the advent of the Harlem Renaissance shortly after World War I, and with the establishment of such black journals as the *Crisis* and *Opportunity,* black writers began to be freer in what they could publish. A parallel progression occurred in the treatment of subject matter. Langston Hughes, Zora Neale Hurston, and Jean Toomer were among the writers who led the way to indigenous forms in the black community. Folk music and poetry, along with an aura of superstition and uninhibitedness, began to permeate their works, leading to the "discovery" of the "primitive" black folks that occupied white writers of the Jazz Age, such as Waldo Frank and Carl Van Vechten.

The productivity of the writers in the 1920s clearly signaled that Afro-American authors had much to say and contribute to American literature. The Renaissance in that decade paved the way for the likes of Richard Wright and Gwendolyn Brooks, who became literary giants in the 1940s. Though still in touch with previous traditions, such as naturalism and formalist poetry, Wright and Brooks nonetheless continued the Renaissance trend of bringing a distinctively black flavor to their works. What they—together with the writers before them—managed to accomplish provided the strong foundation that supported the protest writers of the civil rights period and enabled contemporary writers to bring about their black arts revolution which, in turn, has led to a new appreciation of the Afro-American literary tradition.

To be a black writer in the United States prior to the 1920s was a lonely avocation. Certainly Phillis Wheatley was celebrated, after a fashion, in Boston, as George Moses Horton was on his visits to the University of North Carolina at Chapel Hill, but these poets are only two of the "long, long line" of "black and unknown bards" who sang "untaught, unknown, unnamed" and "stretched out upward, seeking the divine" inspiration of literary creativity in poetry, as well as in other genres.

This volume gives name to many of those unknown bards celebrated in James Weldon Johnson's poem, who, prior to the advent of the Harlem Renaissance, tried in their individual, isolated ways to break the bonds of slavery and Reconstruction. Familiar writers such as Wheatley, Horton, and

Frances Ellen Watkins Harper are treated here, as are less-well-known poets, such as James Madison Bell, James E. McGirt, and George Marion McClellan, who promoted their work through broadsides and self-published books and achieved regional readership in their day.

Many black writers included here took up their pens in the cause of abolition, whether in the form of slave narratives, as Olaudah Equiano and Frederick Douglass did; in fiction, slave narrative, and drama, as William Wells Brown did; or in poetry, as Charlotte L. Forten, Frances Harper, Jupiter Hammon, and many, many others did. Indeed, the possibility of freedom was frequently an inspiration to learning to read and write; Douglass and Brown recount in their narratives their identification with writing and reading books as a privilege of the free.

The writers included here also reflect the quest for a voice in Afro-American literature, a voice that would break out of the constraints of neoclassicism that Wheatley was forced into, and out of the Methodist hymnbooks that so confined Horton and Harper. The search for voice also included the use and later rejection of dialect forms, as in the works of Paul Laurence Dunbar, James D. Corrothers, and James Edwin Campbell. Though Dunbar preferred his poems in literary English, and Corrothers initially asserted he would never resort to dialect, both are perhaps best known for their dialect pieces. Dunbar was so identified with the dialect tradition as a result of William Dean Howells's praise of his dialect poems that he considered writing under an assumed name. The problem was, as James Weldon Johnson identified it later in his introduction to *The Book of American Negro Poetry* (1922), dialect evokes one of two responses from readers: pathos or humor. Therefore, it was too limiting to present the ranges of black American experience. The problem with dialect was not one that the poets in this volume solved, though, even with its limitations, dialect reached its most striking successes in Dunbar's poetry.

Some poets writing after the turn of the century chose not to attempt dialect poetry, establishing instead quieter, more individualized voices. Angelina Grimké turned more to feminist issues, and Fenton Johnson became the quintessential poet of despair. Joseph Seamon Cotter, Jr., was as introspective as Wheatley had been public.

Dialect was less problematic for black fiction writers, but it still smacked of stereotype and, often, caricature. William Wells Brown's depiction of some of the slaves in *Clotel; or, The President's Daughter* (1853) is a case in point; he too easily identifies dialect with uneducated, darker-skinned slaves and standard English with mulatto slaves, whether or not they were formally educated. But he sometimes forgets his own divisions and allows his mulattos to lapse into dialect, though that never occurs with Clotel. On the other hand, Charles W. Chesnutt has been praised for the authenticity of the dialect he uses in *The Conjure Woman* (1899). Nonetheless, his achievement was so shrouded by the negative connotations of dialect prevalent at the time that his talent in this area can only be appreciated in retrospect.

In his novels and short stories, Chesnutt also had to fight the battle against the stereotypes of black people perpetuated by proponents of the plantation tradition, who believed that slavery had been the best state for blacks and that freedom had only brought an increase in crime and lasciviousness. Thomas Dixon and Thomas Nelson Page were the most famous of the group that Chesnutt designed his works to combat. Sutton Griggs joined him in these efforts, but both were eventually forced to retreat in the face of unsympathetic or unavailable publishers.

These fiction writers also had to contend with how black characters should be presented in literature to achieve political objectives. Some, such as Martin Delany, Frank J. Webb, and many, many others, perpetuated the tradition of the tragic mulatto, that long-suffering creature in Afro-American literature usually designed to convey to white audiences how closely connected to them some black people were. The figure became a plea for acceptance that even Chesnutt could not resist drawing upon; it would take several decades into the twentieth century to eliminate this character's political focus from the literature (though lighter skinned black characters would take on other purposes). Other writers, like Sutton Griggs, used their novels and short stories to work out elaborate political arguments in fiction—whether blacks should assimilate, or migrate to Africa, or settle in an isolated portion of the United States. In the hands of such writers, fiction frequently became a tool for the expression of ideas central to the progress of the race as a whole.

Dramatists in this volume have not gained reputations comparable to the poets and fiction writers. William Wells Brown's *The Escape; or, A Leap for Freedom. A Drama in Five Acts* (1858) was never produced. Victor Séjour, writing over a span of years in the latter half of the nineteenth century, saw the bulk of his plays produced in Europe, especially France. Pauline Hopkins wrote *Slaves' Escape; or the Underground Railroad* in 1879 and produced it in Boston in 1880 with the help of her family's performing group. Early Afro-American literary history, therefore, is not the history of the development of stage dramas; plays were more frequently written to be read in the authors' homes or in churches.

Throughout their early history, Afro-American writers also wrestled with the place of religion in the lives of their people. How, Douglass and others asked, could a Christian country condone the horrors of slavery? Douglass was less willing to embrace such a contradictory faith than many of his fellow blacks, including Equiano, who were converted to Christianity in spite of their experiences during slavery. In many of their works, these writers portray the discrepancies in religious theory and practice that would be a recurring theme in black American literature well into the twentieth century.

This volume also presents a corollary history of the publishing outlets and efforts of early Afro-Americans. Frederick Douglass started his own newspaper, and James E. McGirt published *McGirt's Magazine*. William Stanley Braithwaite and Sutton Griggs started their own publishing companies and produced some of their own works through them, as did Pauline E. Hopkins. And Griggs, like Dunbar, sold copies of his books door to door. Oscar Micheaux went from peddling his own books to establishing his own film company, which he used to film adaptations of several of his novels. All of these endeavors testify to how resourceful black writers had to be in order to get their works to the reading public before more substantial and self-sustaining publishing outlets were established.

In all their efforts to write and publish, these early writers chronicle a determination on the part of black Americans to shape a literary tradition. Their achievements suggest that more and more of the "unknown bards" should be reclaimed and given a clear identity in the literary history to which they so valiantly contributed.

—Trudier Harris

Acknowledgments

This book was produced by BC Research. Karen L. Rood is senior editor for the *Dictionary of Literary Biography* series. Ellen Rosenberg Kovner was the in-house editor.

Art supervisor is Patricia M. Flanagan. Copyediting supervisor is Patricia Coate. Production coordinator is Kimberly Casey. Typesetting supervisor is Laura Ingram. The production staff includes Rowena Betts, David R. Bowdler, Joseph Matthew Bruccoli, Deborah Cavanaugh, Kathleen M. Flanagan, Joyce Fowler, Ellen Hassell, Pamela Haynes, Judith K. Ingle, Judith McCray, Mary Scott Sims, Joycelyn R. Smith, and Lucia Tarbox. Jean W. Ross is permissions editor. Joseph Caldwell is photography editor. James Adam Sutton did photographic copy work for the volume.

Walter W. Ross and Rhonda Marshall did the library research with the assistance of the staff at the Thomas Cooper Library of the University of South Carolina: Lynn Barron, Daniel Boice, Connie Crider, Kathy Eckman, Michael Freeman, Gary Geer, David L. Haggard, Jens Holley, Marcia Martin, Dana Rabon, Jean Rhyne, Jan Squire, Ellen Tillett, and Virginia Weathers.

We would like to acknowledge the invaluable assistance of Mary Yearwood, who researched materials at the Schomburg Center for Research in Black Culture, the New York Public Library.

Dictionary of Literary Biography • Volume Fifty

Afro-American Writers Before the Harlem Renaissance

Dictionary of Literary Biography

James Madison Bell

(3 April 1826-1902)

Keith E. Byerman
University of Texas

BOOKS: *A Poem: Delivered August 1st, 1862 . . . at the Grand Festival to Commemorate the Emancipation of the Slaves in the British West Indian Isles* (San Francisco: B. F. Sterett, 1862);

A Poem Entitled The Day and the War, Delivered January 1, 1864, at Platt's Hall at the Celebration of the First Anniversary of President Lincoln's Emancipation Proclamation (San Francisco: Printed by Agnew & Deffebach, 1864);

An Anniversary Poem Entitled The Progress of Liberty, Delivered January 1st, 1866 . . . at the Celebration of the Third Anniversary of President Lincoln's Proclamation (San Francisco: Printed by Agnew & Deffebach, 1866);

A Poem, Entitled The Triumph of Liberty, Delivered April 7, 1870 at Detroit Opera House, on the Occasion of the Fifteenth Amendment to the Constitution of the United States (Detroit: Tunis Steam Printing Co., 1870);

A Discourse Commemorative of John Frye Bell, Member of Hopkins High School, Hadley, attributed to Bell (Northampton, Mass.: Gazette Printing, 1874);

The Poetical Works of James Madison Bell (Lansing, Mich.: Press of Wynkoop, Hallenbeck, Crawford, 1901).

James Madison Bell

James Madison Bell, sometimes called the "Bard of the Maumee" for the region near Lake Erie with which he was associated, was a public, performing poet who devoted his artistic energies to the abolitionist cause and to versified analyses of post-Civil War America. In the rhetorical tradition of such well-known writers of the mid-nineteenth century as Ralph Waldo Emerson, William Cullen Bryant, and John Greenleaf Whittier, Bell used his poetry as oratory to support his beliefs and values. He mounted a rhetorical campaign to attack the institution of slavery and to defend black human rights.

Other than his birth in Gallipolis, Ohio, near the Maumee River, little is known of Bell's family or his early life. It is known that he moved to Cincinnati in 1842 and remained there until 1853, during which time he worked as a plasterer with his brother-in-law, George Knight, while he attended a high school set up for blacks. In 1847 he married Louisiana Sanderline with whom he had seven children. He and his family moved in 1854 to Canada West (Ontario), where he became actively involved with the antislavery movement. Bell allied himself with American abolitionist John Brown, whose radical views he adopted to the extent of enlisting men and raising funds for the 1859 raid on Harpers Ferry.

In 1860 Bell temporarily left his family and moved to San Francisco, where he remained during the entire period of the Civil War. He continued to make his living as a plasterer, but his real efforts were put into abolitionist activities. It was at this time that he wrote much of his poetry, which he delivered as orations for antislavery rallies. A number of the poems were written specifically for the anniversary of the Emancipation Proclamation or for 1 August celebrations, which marked the emancipation of slaves in the British West Indies. Several of his works were issued in pamphlet form. The first of these was probably *A Poem: Delivered August 1st, 1862.*

Bell's verse, both of this period and later, is characterized by iambic tetrameter lines, couplet or alternating rhymes, and conventional imagery and phrasing. *A Poem Entitled The Day and the War, Delivered January 1, 1864,* dedicated to John Brown, uses these conventions at length (over 700 lines) to describe slavery, the war, and the Emancipation Proclamation. First published with an "Argument," written by *Pacific Appeal* editor Philip A. Bell (not related), the poem opens with a statement of the hope for liberty brought by the Proclamation:

No longer need the bondman fear,
For lo! the good time's almost here,
And doubtless some beneath our voice
Shall live to hail it and rejoice:
For almost now the radiant sheen
Of freedom's glad host may be seen;
The ear can almost catch the sound,
The eye can almost see them bound,
As thirty million voices rise
In grateful peans to the skies.

Bell appeals to the North to persevere in the battle for freedom, while at the same time, he attacks those Europeans who claim neutrality yet in fact support the South. Their hypocrisy motivates the sarcasm Bell occasionally uses to break the seriousness of his theme:

Not intervene! And yet propose
To recognize the South when she
Discards the source of half her woes,
And sets her long bound captives free?
If this non-intervention is,
Then O may Jeff deliver us:
For better had we bow as his,
Than fall where nations reason thus.

The first part of the poem ends with a statement of the real ambitions of the Confederacy and an address to black soldiers fighting for the Union cause, a theme further developed in part two, a panegyric to the Massachusetts Fifty-fourth Regiment. The first black regiment of troops from that state, the Fifty-fourth was led by white officers, including one of Henry James's younger brothers, Garth Wilkinson James, under the command of Col. Robert Gould Shaw. On 28 May 1863 white Bostonians expressed their resistance to arming black troops by jeering at and attacking the Fifty-fourth as it proudly marched through the city. Bell compares the black soldiers to Alfred Lord Tennyson's Light Brigade, finding them equal in courage and sacrifice. In fact, he asserts, the task of the blacks is greater since even many of the Northerners they are defending doubt their ability:

Prejudged of slavish cowardice,
While many a taunt and foul device
Came weekly forth with Harper's sheet,
To feed that base, infernal cheat.

The history of the regiment is used to show how wrong the critics were and to encourage greater black participation in the war effort.

Part three of *The Day and the War* offers a vision of postwar America that requires a shift from an omniscient voice and expository style to a personal point of view and more lyrical language:

And here permit me to diverge
From real to fancy's flow'ry marge,
And sing of what I seemed to see
While there, enshrined in reverie.
The past, and what is yet to be
Reveal'd in blank futurity,
Swept like a phantom through my brain,
Of which some shadows still remain:
And to those shadows let me call
The eye and silent ear of all.

What is noteworthy here is the facility with which Bell—a black man with a limited education—mastered the literary traditions and poetic conventions of his day. Such mastery of convention was itself an argument for equality at a time when most whites, including many abolitionists, assumed that blacks were inherently incapable of acquiring even the rudiments of culture.

The vision offered in *The Day and the War* is of a peaceful, productive, and united nation:

And violets bloomed the banks along,
And the lark poured forth his matin song,
And the lowly cot and massive dome
Had each the air of a joyous home;
And temples rear'd their spires on high,
Pointing away to the clear blue sky;
And myriad souls had gathered there,
Whose grateful hearts went up in prayer
To the God of love, whose gracious hand
Had clothed in peace their bleeding land.

Bell prophesies the end of the war will fulfill the ideals of the nation by firmly establishing equality between the races; the result will be tranquillity between classes, between man and nature, and among religious groups.

For Bell, the means to this end is Abraham Lincoln, the subject of the last part of the poem. Lincoln's emancipation of the slaves has guaranteed his place for posterity:

His name shall grow a household word,
Where'er the human voice is heard;
And tribes and peoples yet unborn,
Shall hail and bless his natal morn.

Ending the poem with this praise of Lincoln, rather than with his vision, Bell reveals his political intent in this work. He had committed himself to a program for the future and sought to persuade his audience to support that program.

Just such a combination of idealism and political persuasion informs all of Bell's major poems, both those of the San Francisco period and those written and delivered after 1866, when he rejoined his family and moved to Toledo, Ohio. At the end of the war, he became very active in Republican politics, both in California and Ohio, where he was elected county delegate, and then delegate at large to the national convention in 1872. Although still working as a plasterer, he traveled around the country, lecturing to freedmen, giving readings of his poetry, and supporting party candidates until about 1890 when he settled down again with his family in Toledo.

Bell's significant poetry of the postwar period mainly updates the concerns expressed in *The Day and the War*. *An Anniversary Poem Entitled The Progress of Liberty* (1866), for example, takes into account the meaning of the ending of the war for the future. He eulogizes Lincoln, in largely the same terms he praised him in the earlier poem. He also advises the freedmen to use their newly gained liberty responsibly and warns the nation as a whole against placing too much trust in the ex-Confederates. He ends by hoping that Andrew Johnson will carry out the plans of Lincoln for reconstructing the nation.

When that hope failed to materialize, Bell attacked Johnson in a bitterly sarcastic poem, "Modern Moses, or 'My Policy' Man" (1868). The attack is directed as much against the character as against the policies:

But choose we rather to discant,
On one whose swaggish boast and rant,
And vulgar jest, and pot-house slang,
Has grown the pest of every gang
Of debauchees wherever found,
From Baffin's Bay to Puget Sound.

The regularity of rhythm and rhyme and the conventional imagery that so limits Bell's poetry elsewhere works to heighten the satire:

But as for *Mose*, he has been
And is to-day as free from sin
As that fond friend who kissed his Lord,
In presence of a Roman horde.

The same language that elsewhere seems trite works in this poem to show the distance between expectation and reality. While "Modern Moses . . ." is not as focused as it might have been, it nonetheless largely accomplishes a political purpose.

A Poem, Entitled The Triumph of Liberty (1870) is the third of the long poems dealing with the Civil War. Most of it repeats in very similar language the ideas of *The Day and the War* and *The Progress of Liberty*. The only significant achievement comes near the end of the work where Bell catalogues the praiseworthy aspects of the nation in a style reminiscent of Whitman:

And hail to thy Oceans, all dotted with sails,
Their white wings extended, inviting the gales;
And hail to thy Commerce, the pride of the world,
And hail to thy Standard so proudly unfurled;

And hail to thy Cities all teaming [*sic*] with life,
Where the interest of all is the center of strife.
And hail to thy Railroads and steam-driven trains,
That sweep through thy mountains and dash o'er thy
plains.

While Bell is clearly locked into a conventional poetics, he displays here a desire for inclusiveness that breaks the usual iambic pattern of his verse. While the anapestic pattern itself becomes predictable, it nonetheless reveals Bell's ability to vary his poetic forms.

Over half of the remaining poems in Bell's canon (there are only thirty-two poems in all) are shorter works that address the same themes as the political poems. Another smaller group of work consists of poems on religious subjects, such as the Garden of Eden story, the nature of evil, immortality, and creation. A few are tributes to religious leaders with whom Bell was acquainted. All of these provide versified statements of standard Protestant doctrine.

The remaining poems are mainly short pieces of an occasional sort, such as acrostics and wedding verse. The only nature poem in Bell's work is entitled "Descriptive Voyage from New York to Aspinwall" (1901). Though otherwise not remarkable, the poem does stand out for its rather straightforward depiction of the author's experience on the ship:

But while she reels thus to and fro
The sickest of the sick am I
And from my system would I throw
It's [*sic*] last contents, or even die.
Oh, of all sickness that's known or heard
Of sickness in its varied form,
The last of all to be preferred
Is sea sick-sickness in a storm.

Criticism of James Madison Bell's work has generally either emphasized its inspirational quality or its conventional poetics. Early readers, such as Bishop B. W. Arnett, who wrote the biographical introduction to the *Poetical Works* (1901), and who persuaded Bell to collect his poems, William Wells Brown, and, slightly later, Robert Kerlin, describe Bell as an eloquent and hopeful defender of black freedom and moral goodness. Later critics, including J. Saunders Redding and Eugene Redmond, have tended to be harsher in their evaluations; although they note the influence of the belletristic tradition on Bell's work, their consensus is that his writings are finally too conventional to allow him a major place in either American or Afro-American literature. Nonetheless it must be recognized that Bell was not as interested in the craftsmanship of his poetry as he was in the moral and political arguments that could be made through verse. He adopted whatever techniques would facilitate his goals as a spokesman against slavery and for black rights.

References:

Benjamin W. Arnett, "Biographical Sketch," in *The Poetical Works of James Madison Bell,* pp. 3-14;

Benjamin Brawley, *The Negro Genius: A New Appraisal of the Achievement of the American Negro in Literature and the Fine Arts* (New York: Dodd, Mead, 1937), pp. 70, 87-89;

Sterling A. Brown, *Negro Poetry and Drama* (Washington, D.C.: Associates in Negro Folk Education, 1937), pp. 9-10;

William Wells Brown, *The Rising Son* (Boston: A. G. Brown, 1873), pp. 504-505;

Robert Kerlin, *Negro Poets and Their Poems* (Washington, D.C.: Associated Publishers, 1923), pp. 32-37;

J. Saunders Redding, *To Make a Poet Black* (Chapel Hill: University of North Carolina, 1939), pp. 44-47;

Eugene B. Redmond, *Drumvoices: The Mission of Afro-American Poetry* (Garden City: Anchor/Doubleday, 1976), pp. 86, 94-97;

Joan R. Sherman, *Invisible Poets: Afro-Americans of the Nineteenth Century* (Urbana: University of Illinois, 1974), pp. 80-87.

William Stanley Braithwaite

(6 December 1878-8 June 1962)

Kenny J. Williams
Duke University

See also the B. J. Brimmer entry in *DLB 46, American Literary Publishing Houses, 1900-1980: Trade and Paperback.*

BOOKS: *Lyrics of Life and Love* (Boston: Turner, 1904);
The House of Falling Leaves (Boston: Luce, 1908);
The Story of the Great War (New York: Stokes, 1919);
Selected Poems (New York: Coward-McCann, 1948);
The Bewitched Parsonage: The Story of the Brontës (New York: Coward-McCann, 1950);
The William Stanley Braithwaite Reader, edited by Philip Butcher (Ann Arbor: University of Michigan Press, 1972).

OTHER: *The Book of Elizabethan Verse,* edited by Braithwaite (Boston: Turner, 1906; London: Chatto & Windus, 1908);
The Book of Georgian Verse, edited by Braithwaite (New York: Brentano's, 1909; London: G. Richards, 1909);
The Book of Restoration Verse, edited by Braithwaite (New York: Brentano's, 1910; London: Duckworth, 1910);
Anthology of Magazine Verse for 1913, edited by Braithwaite (Cambridge, Mass.: W.S.B., 1913);
Anthology of Magazine Verse for 1914 and Year Book of American Poetry, edited by Braithwaite (Cambridge, Mass.: W.S.B., 1914);
Anthology of Magazine Verse for 1915 and Year Book of American Poetry, edited by Braithwaite (New York: Gomme, 1915);
Representative American Poetry, edited by Braithwaite and Henry Thomas Schnittkind (Boston: Badger, 1916);
Anthology of Magazine Verse for 1916 and Year Book of American Poetry, edited by Braithwaite (New York: Gomme, 1916);
The Poetic Year for 1916: A Critical Anthology, edited by Braithwaite (Boston: Small, Maynard, 1917);
Anthology of Magazine Verse for 1917 and Yearbook of American Poetry, edited by Braithwaite (Boston: Small, Maynard, 1917);
The Golden Treasury of Magazine Verse, edited by Braithwaite (Boston: Small, Maynard, 1918);
Anthology of Magazine Verse for 1918 and Year Book of American Poetry, edited by Braithwaite (Boston: Small, Maynard, 1918);
Victory! Celebrated by Thirty-Eight American Poets, edited by Braithwaite (Boston: Small, Maynard, 1919);
Anthology of Magazine Verse for 1919 and Year Book of American Poetry, edited by Braithwaite (Boston: Small, Maynard, 1919);
The Book of Modern British Verse, edited by Braithwaite (Boston: Small, Maynard, 1919);
Anthology of Magazine Verse for 1920 and Year Book of American Poetry, edited by Braithwaite (Boston: Small, Maynard, 1920);
Anthology of Magazine Verse for 1921 and Year Book of American Poetry, edited by Braithwaite (Boston: Small, Maynard, 1921);
Anthology of Massachusetts Poets, edited by Braithwaite (Boston: Small, Maynard, 1922);
Anthology of Magazine Verse for 1922 and Yearbook of American Poetry, edited by Braithwaite (Boston: Small, Maynard, 1922);
Anthology of Magazine Verse for 1923 and Yearbook of American Poetry, edited by Braithwaite (Boston: B. J. Brimmer, 1923);
Anthology of Magazine Verse for 1924 and Yearbook of American Poetry, edited by Braithwaite (Boston: B. J. Brimmer, 1924);
Anthology of Magazine Verse for 1925 and Yearbook of American Poetry, edited by Braithwaite (Boston: B. J. Brimmer, 1925);
Anthology of Magazine Verse for 1926 and Yearbook of American Poetry, edited by Braithwaite (Boston: B. J. Brimmer, 1926);
Anthology of Magazine Verse for 1927 and Yearbook of American Poetry, edited by Braithwaite (Boston: B. J. Brimmer, 1927);
Anthology of Magazine Verse for 1928 and Yearbook of American Poetry, edited by Braithwaite (New York: Vinal, 1928);

Anthology of Magazine Verse for 1929 and Yearbook of American Poetry, edited by Braithwaite (New York: Scully, 1929);

Our Lady's Choir: A Contemporary Anthology of Verse by Catholic Sisters, edited by Braithwaite (Boston: Humphries, 1931).

Spanning more than fifty years, the work of William Stanley Braithwaite partially represents both the tragedy and the ambiguity of having been produced by an Afro-American writer in a pluralistic culture that does not always respect its own diversity. Yet, in spite of those forces which he could not control, Braithwaite became an important figure in American letters as he occupied a position for the advocacy of American poetry and criticism that has had few equals; however, his service in the cause of poetry in the United States has not been fully assessed. Given his importance in American literary circles, it is curious that so little has been written about him. Unfortunately, a great deal of his work is buried in little-read magazines and newspapers; but the introductions to his yearly anthologies, the essays in *The Poetic Year for 1916: A Critical Anthology* (1917), his biography of the Brontës, as well as the prefaces to his anthologies of Elizabethan, Georgian, and Restoration verse, give a clear indication of the evolution of his critical point of view as they record one of the most complete surveys of the history of American poetry. Perhaps one of the most telling estimates of him appeared on 30 November 1915 in the *Boston Transcript,* written after a reception had been given for him in New York. Praising Braithwaite for helping both poets and readers, the *Transcript* observed: "One is guilty of no extravagance in saying that the poets we have—and they may take their place with their peers in any country—and the gathering deference we pay them, are created largely out of the stubborn, self-effacing enthusiasm of this one man. In a sense their distinction is his own." Before his death, William Dean Howells, a leading figure in American criticism, referred to Braithwaite as "the most intelligent historian of contemporary poetry I know." More recently, Philip Butcher summarized the career of Braithwaite by noting that he was "a significant force in revitalizing poetry in America."

William Stanley Braithwaite

Beginning in 1905, Braithwaite's columns in the *Boston Evening Transcript* were primarily devoted to the evaluation of poets and poetry; then from 1913 to 1929 he collected and published outstanding examples of magazine verse which, accompanied by his reviews of contemporary writers, helped to create a wider audience for the so-called new poetry. While he supported the traditional in his own verse, he recognized, for example, the merit of Amy Lowell's work in a day when the Imagist movement and the experimental in poetry had not been fully accepted. Through his annual anthologies he became closely associated with such poets as Vachel Lindsay, Carl Sandburg, Edwin Arlington Robinson, Edgar Lee Masters, Robert Frost, and Wallace Stevens who became major figures in world literature. At the same time, he introduced many of the poets of the Harlem Renaissance to the American reading public. Yet, in spite of his active participation in the American literary scene during the first third of the twentieth century, Braithwaite has largely been ignored by literary historians, who apparently had difficulty understanding him. Even the poets who owed so much to him frequently forgot later in their careers their earlier reliance upon him. Nevertheless, the subsequent popularity of such anthologies and yearbooks as Edward J. O'Brien's annual collection of "best" short stories and Burns Mantle's "best" plays is due largely to Braithwaite having created an audience for that type of book. His work is also frequently dismissed by chroniclers and anthologists of Afro-American literature because either his race is unknown to them or his work is not "black" enough, and he has been condemned by those who failed to understand his approach to racial issues.

The range and scope of his interests reveal much about him. His great love for British literature is evident in many of the anthologies he edited as well as in several of his biographical studies. His own poetry reflects his fascination with the English romantic tradition. At the same time, his concern for black writers and his support of their publications revealed a commitment not always apparent to readers of his poetry. His acceptance of the credo of "art-for-art's-sake" as a guiding standard and his belief in the unity of the American experience led him to develop a view of literature and race relations which some supporters and detractors have found disconcerting. His insistence upon being part of the American scene was not predicated upon a view that race could or should be denied; rather, he felt race was simply a characteristic which did not have to be a motivating factor for one's life. Thus, he actually believed that the differences between races could be minimized and that the bitter conditions of black life should not be a major concern of art. Ultimately, appreciating Braithwaite means accepting not only the diversity of Afro-American literature but also assuming that blackness and whiteness are not in themselves determining artistic or evaluative criteria.

Born to Emma De Wolfe and William Smith Braithwaite in Boston on 6 December 1878, young William grew up in a home where the amenities of life were stressed. His father, who was from a distinguished West Indian family, considered being a British "gentleman" important. The Braithwaite children were educated at home partially because their father did not wish them to mingle with the other children in urban Boston. This life of presumed gentility came to an abrupt end with the death of the elder Braithwaite when William Stanley was eight. The family immediately found itself in financial straits although Emma Braithwaite worked to support the family. For four years William was able to attend school; but when he was twelve, his formal education ended because he had to work to help maintain the family. From that time on, Braithwaite began to teach himself.

Braithwaite's autobiography, "The House Under Arcturus" (serialized in *Phylon*, 1941-1942), chronicles his early life and records without bitterness the years of poverty. He tells of his apprenticeship at Ginn and Company which led not only to his becoming a typesetter but also to his introduction to literature. Apparently his employer, struck by Braithwaite's seriousness, initiated him into the world of books. The English romantic poets created in him a love for verse which became the driving force of his life. He recalled the day he was assigned to set the type for some of the poetry of John Keats, Robert Burns, and William Wordsworth as "a day of annunciation" because he was immediately transported "into a world of magical beauty." Soon he was writing his own poetry, much of which he put at the end of unused galley sheets as an exercise not only in typesetting but also of authorship. In time he became painfully aware of his own lack of formal education and turned to the Boston Public Library, which in effect became his university. "The deeper I read," he observed, "the more, and often discouragingly, I realized the difficulties confronting me"; but he was determined "to acquire the knowledge and to cultivate the faculties necessary in mastering an education for the pursuit of a literary career."

This career began shortly after his marriage in June 1903 to Emma Kelly, with whom he had

Portrait of Braithwaite used as frontispiece for Lyrics of Life and Love

seven children. In 1904 his first volume of poetry, *Lyrics of Life and Love,* was published, and he wrote some critical articles which appeared in *Colored American Magazine* of Boston. At this time he was also contributing verse to the *Voice of the Negro,* which was published in Atlanta, to *New Era,* and to *Crisis,* for which he became a frequent contributor in its early years. Like so many other writers, Braithwaite had the responsibility of getting subscribers for his book before the publisher would print it, and after it had been produced he had to sell and deliver the books. He appealed for subscriptions to such New Englanders as Julia Ward Howe, Thomas Wentworth Higginson, Edward Everett Hale, Thomas Bailey Aldrich, and Bliss Perry, prominent people who were not only fired by missionary zeal but were also associated with the genteel tradition in literature. Aware of William Dean Howells's efforts on behalf of Paul Laurence Dunbar, Braithwaite also appealed to him, but apparently his request was initially rejected, although the noncommittal Howells was pleasant.

When Braithwaite's *Lyrics of Life and Love* appeared in 1904, Dunbar was the acknowledged foremost black poet in the United States. The fact that Braithwaite's title resembles that of Dunbar's *Lyrics of Love and Laughter* (1903) may have been a coincidence or may reflect Braithwaite's desire to capitalize on the popularity of Dunbar; but there is little similarity in their poetry. Dunbar's standard English poems cover a wider range of subjects than those by Braithwaite, who used neither dialect nor the vernacular folksy language popularized by such writers as Dunbar and the midwestern authors who followed the lead of James Whitcomb Riley. Limited in subject and approach as Braithwaite's poems might appear, they are always wrought with technical precision. Several of the sixty-three poems which make up the first volume had already appeared in such journals as the *Christian Endeavor Herald, National Magazine,* and *Colored American Magazine.* The poems are generally short with an unusual focus upon the word "dream," which appears in six titles and is implied in fourteen others. The word is also highlighted in more than thirty-five of the poems. There is evidence, in these poems, of his growing interest in the sonnet as well as his tendency to address his verse to specific people. Two of the better poems in the collection center on his literary idol: "Keats Was an Unbeliever," in which Keats is represented as a divine "elect" who concretized "God's dream of life . . . Beauty," and "On a Pressed Flower in My Copy of Keats," a sonnet lamenting the paling of passion. Although it is clear that both Percy Bysshe Shelley and Keats served as his models, there is a darker strain in his work that is not imitative and which, in time, he was to develop more thoroughly. Braithwaite's poetry tends to employ an economy of image and language, demonstrated by the poem "Life and Death," in which the speaker refers to the ephemeral nature of life by stating that he "rented once a house of clay," which was illuminated "with pleasant thoughts/And Life 'twas named by Mystery." After spending many years in this "clay" dwelling, his body, he "moved into a fairer clime," where his "house was named anew—/For it was christened Death, by Time."

In 1906 Braithwaite was elected to the Boston Authors' Club with the support of Thomas Wentworth Higginson and Julia Ward Howe, and in 1908 his second volume of poetry was published. *The House of Falling Leaves,* like his first collection, was a mix of previously unpublished work and poems that had appeared in such journals as the *Voice, Century, American Magazine,* the *New England Magazine, Book News Monthly,* and *Christian Endeavor Herald.* The volume includes several sonnet sequences and twenty-two pieces dedicated to specific people. In "White Magic: An Ode Read at the Centenary Celebration of the Birth of John Greenleaf Whittier at Faneuil Hall, December 17, 1907," Braithwaite praises Whittier for sacrificing the muse of art in order to write about brotherhood. This poem is one of the few pieces in which Braithwaite expresses his belief in the distinctions between the social and aesthetic nature of literature, a notion which became more apparent in his critical essays as he began to accept the belief that literature had legitimate purposes outside the realm of aesthetics. Throughout *The House of Falling Leaves,* which is dedicated "to the memory of Frederic Lawrence Knowles," there is a sense of the New England locale which perhaps makes the volume more regional than Braithwaite had intended. Many of his scenes take place at twilight.

Although Braithwaite's poetry continued to appear in magazines and periodicals—for example, "Sandy Star" first appeared in the *Atlantic Monthly* (July 1909), "The Mystery" in *Scribner's* (October 1915)—it was not until 1948 that his next collection was published. (He had projected a volume entitled "The Five Wisdoms of Grainne, A Book of Poems" in 1917, but it never appeared.) Many pieces from *Selected Poems* (1948) had appeared in *Forum, Atlantic Monthly, Century, Scribner's,* and other nationally circulated journals. Taken together they show the growth of a mystical strain in his work and the lyrical idealism that marked so much of his poetry.

While several of the pieces in *Lyrics of Life and Love* are finely wrought without being particularly distinguished, and the poems in *The House of Falling Leaves* display an increasing sense of power and poignancy, *Selected Poems* demonstrates that Braithwaite was not simply an imitator, even though many of the poems show the influence of British poets. "Ascension" and "Myths of the Circumference," for example, illustrate the extent to which his interest in William Blake had influenced his writing, and his final poems show evidence of the erudition and density, popularized in the poetry of the American moderns, which render many pieces obscure to the average reader. Braithwaite's graceful lyrics, however, are often motivated by melancholy and the desire for mysteriousness, and he focuses upon dream sequences and explores events that occur while the poetic persona remains in a trancelike posture. The sense of life that pervades his work seems to come from some misty domain, and the dream-related sequences move him away from reality as many modern readers understand realism. The detachment so readily observed in his poetry is an isolation of his poetic persona from the ordinary world.

Braithwaite's poetry does not generally support in-depth analysis; rather it has a sort of surface fragility as it attempts to transmit something of the mystery of life and the awe of death. Occasionally his poetry deals with his fascinated contemplation of nature, and he wrote some simple didactic verse as well. "Thanksgiving," which seems to exemplify his philosophy of life, begins with the uncomplicated line: "My heart gives thanks for many things." He then proceeds to cite "strength to labor," "sleep," and "friends" as some of these "things."

Whether dealing with his mystical world or with his immediate surroundings, Braithwaite clearly selected subjects from a realm which did not include a consideration of the social and political issues of the nation. However, the restraint so commonly found in his work is a result of his view of the lyric rather than of his denial of race. As a body, his work raises the issue of the artistic responsibility of the Afro-American writer. For those who insist that there is something inherently "black" in the writings of Afro-Americans, the poetry of William Stanley Braithwaite stands as a refutation to a racial theory of literature. If his poems fail, they do so for reasons other than the lack of "racial fire."

James Weldon Johnson explained his mentor's lack of racial poetry by asserting in *The Book of American Negro Poetry* that "race has not impinged upon him as it has upon other poets." As early as 1924 the outstanding Shelley scholar, Newman Ivey White, observed in his *Anthology of Verse by American Negroes* that many of the poems in Braithwaite's *Lyrics of Life and Love* have "a technical finish well above average. Some are rather exquisite; many have a delicate beauty, but . . . there is no interest in racial questions at all, nor in much else that implies stress or conflict." He continued by noting that the poems in *The House of Falling Leaves* "have a somewhat pale and graceful estheticism with no feeling of 'mission' or racial self-consciousness." Three years later Countee Cullen declared in *Caroling Dusk: An Anthology of Verse by Negro Poets*—dedicated to William Stanley Braithwaite—that there is no such thing as "American Negro poetry." There is simply poetry written by American Negroes. Sterling Brown in his *Negro Poetry and Drama* (1937) asserted that Braithwaite's verse was not good but deemed him to be a critic who "was one of the pioneers in the poetry revival in America." J. Saunders Redding said in his *To Make a Poet Black* (1939) that Braithwaite's rejection of racially motivated poetry was "the most outstanding example of perverted energy that the period from 1903 to 1917 produced." But he also acknowledged that Braithwaite was a critic of "great sensibility." In *Black Poets of the United States* (1973), Jean Wagner maintained that Braithwaite's silence on racial matters "amounts to the rejection of his blackness" and noted the fact that while publishing anthologies of verse, including such specific collections as one of Massachusetts poets in 1922 and of Roman Catholic sisters in 1931, he did not publish an anthology of black poets. (Wagner either did not know of, or discounted, Braithwaite's abandonment of such a project when no financial backers would guarantee it.) In the meantime, Wagner drew the conclusion: "Braithwaite had not the least desire to be identified with the black world and what it stands for."

Although Braithwaite's poetry is not highly emotional, whether one can accept Louis Rubin's judgment that it exhibits "a thinness of feeling" is subject to question. Rubin's evaluation in his collaborative work with Blyden Jackson, *Black Poetry in America* (1974), once again raises the racial issue and perhaps unwittingly represents the application of the double standard in art. Rubin, for example, asserts that Braithwaite's "refusal as a poet to deal directly with his social identity is emblematic of a refusal in his poetry to confront any but obvious aspects of his own individuality. In suppressing his

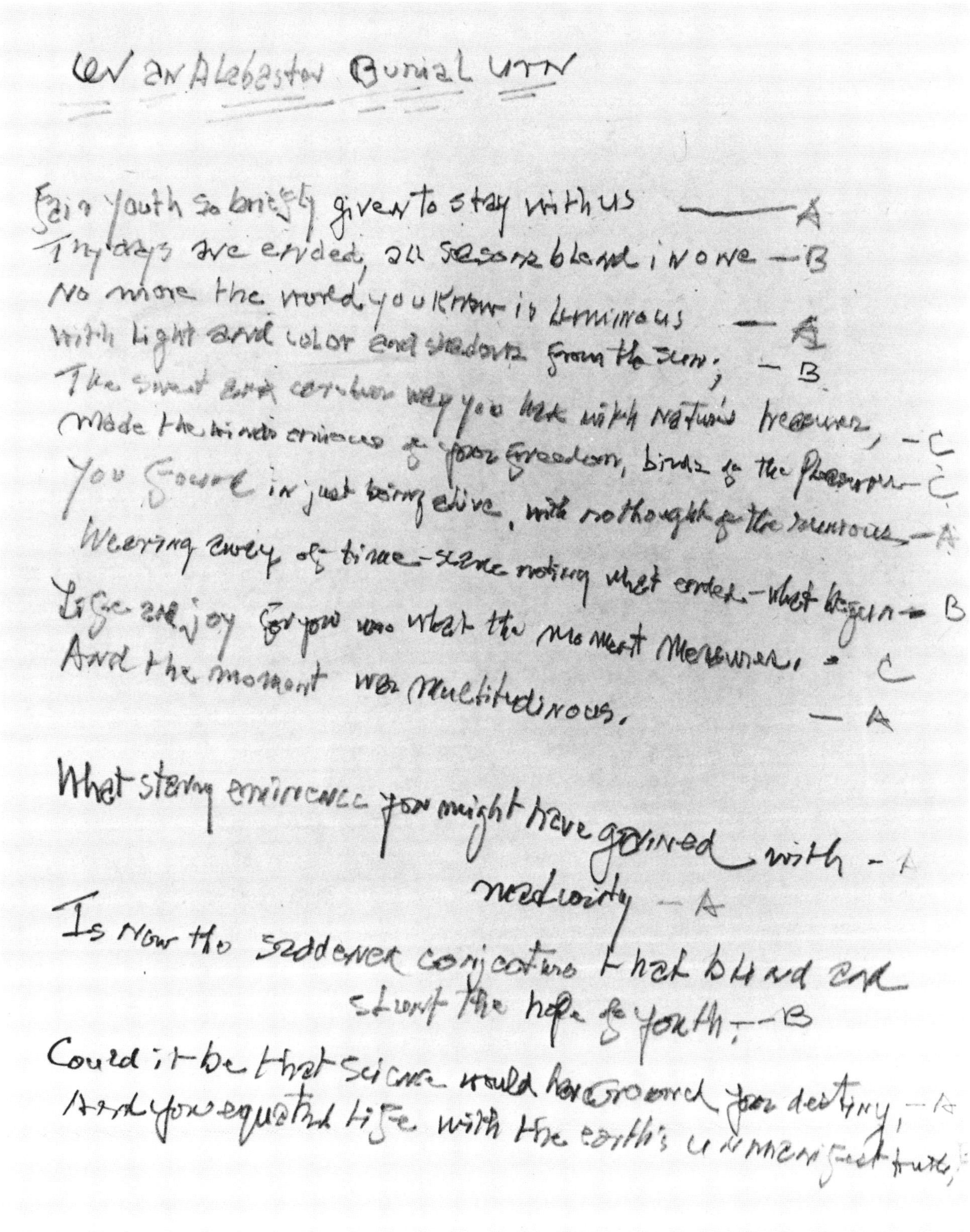
On an Alabaster Burial Urn

Fair youth so briefly given to stay with us — A
Thy days are ended, all seasons blend in one — B
No more the world you know is luminous — A
With light and color and shadows from the sun; — B
The sweet and careless way you had with nature's treasures, — C
Made the winds envious of your freedom, birds of the pleasures — C
You found in just being alive, with no thought of the ruinous — A
Wearing away of time — scarce noting what ended — what began — B
Life and joy for you was what the moment measures, — C
And the moment was multitudinous. — A

What stern eminence you might have gained with — A
mediocrity — A
Is now the saddened conjecture that blind and
stunt the hope of youth; — B
Could it be that science would have crowned your destiny, — A
And you equated life with the earth's unmanifest truth,

Working draft (William S. Braithwaite Collection, George Arents Research Library for Special Collections, Syracuse University)

blackness, he suppressed his human uniqueness. . . ." There is no concrete evidence to support the theory that he "suppressed" his blackness nor that he was oblivious to racial problems.

Despite its association with the abolition movement, Boston in the late nineteenth century was not a racial paradise when Braithwaite was growing up; neither was he blind to urban conditions that prevailed in twentieth-century Boston. Before condemning him for what he did not do, it is important to recognize that his life in Boston partially removed him from the centers of racial conflict as did his friendships and work on the *Boston Evening Transcript*. Furthermore, his own literary theory took him into another arena. He was not, however, so isolated that he was unaware of racial issues. Neither did he scorn the work of Afro-American artists. But he was convinced that social protest—valid though it was—was not the province of poetry. As a result, what Rubin and others may term the sterility of his verse was no more than his application of his belief in his right as a poet to determine his subject matter.

While he used traditional lyric forms in his own poetry, it is in his recognition of the avant-garde that he made a distinguished contribution to American literature. Consequently, in spite of the varying views of his poetry, there is general praise for his efforts on behalf of poetry in America, and it is in his role as an early Afro-American critic that one can best see his evolution as an artistic and racial spokesman. Literary criticism developed late in Afro-American literature. It was often the case that early historians made notice of writers in their work, but what seemed an early effort at literary criticism simply resulted in the presentation of biographical data. From the essays of such early-nineteenth-century writers as William Whipper, William Hamilton, and Maria Steward, one can discover the emphasis which they placed upon reading

William Stanley Braithwaite (William S. Braithwaite Collection, George Arents Research Library for Special Collections, Syracuse University)

and education; but seldom did these writers append anything remotely approximating literary criticism to their work outside of their acceptance of the classics. In his *The Black Man; His Antecedents, His Genius, and His Achievements* (1863), for example, William Wells Brown included Phillis Wheatley as one of the great figures of the past who ought to be remembered, but he made no attempt to critique her work. Later nineteenth-century writers and historians tended to repeat this pattern and often referred to writers without presenting critical views of their work. By the turn of the century and with the acceptance of Paul Laurence Dunbar by the white reading public, there was an embryonic development of "literary criticism" which coincided with the establishment of such journals as *Colored American Magazine, Voice of the Negro, New Era,* and eventually *Crisis.*

Among the first successful Afro-American critics was William Stanley Braithwaite, whose columns in the *Boston Transcript* after 1905 and his occasional contributions to the Negro periodicals, as well as his introductions to his many anthologies form perhaps the largest body of literary criticism by an Afro-American. W. E. B. Du Bois's assessment of Braithwaite as "the most prominent critic of poetry in America" was not an overstatement. Both William Dean Howells and Du Bois recognized what Harriet Monroe was to discover even before she established *Poetry: A Magazine of Verse* in 1912. Braithwaite's *Transcript* columns had been highly supportive of the cause of poetry and helped to create the poetic renaissance which swept the country during the first third of the twentieth century. His critical method was broad enough so that he was both willing and able to find that quality in a work which seemed lasting. Subordinating his own personal predilections and prejudices, he tended to focus his attention upon the younger poets who had not been "discovered" by the American reading public nor by the critical establishment. That he was often enthusiastic about what we might call "traditional" poetry should not obscure the fact that he had the ability not only to recognize new talent but also to be realistic about it.

The story of William Stanley Braithwaite is in part the chronicle of American poetry, which had reached at the turn of the century one of its lowest points. No one disputed its general sterility. The great American poets of the nineteenth century—Emily Dickinson, Walt Whitman, and Hart Crane—had died. Others who had made some contributions were no longer producing. The younger poets had few outlets and had not as yet captured the attention of the reading public. However, poetry was used extensively in magazines and newspapers, primarily as "fillers." In time, as he worked for the *Transcript* and continued reading new work, Braithwaite envisioned a magazine of verse. Apparently his proposal for an independent journal of poetry caused Harriet Monroe some concern in Chicago inasmuch as she was raising funds for a similar venture. She felt that he was trying to upstage her with the help of the eastern literary establishment, a notion which she continued to hold for a number of years. The truth of the matter, however, is that he had begun his interest in the assembling of poetic voices long before the idea of *Poetry* came to Monroe. Suffice it to say that both of their efforts were evidence of the nature of the poetic revival which swept the country in the days before World War I.

In the long run, Braithwaite's *Poetry Journal* was not particularly successful. Its first number came out in December of 1912 (two months after the appearance of Harriet Monroe's *Poetry*). The second number appeared in February 1913, and the magazine was issued for the five following months. The July 1913 issue was the last until February of 1914, and eventually it was taken over by others. It may well be that Braithwaite's time was so limited that he could not do justice to his magazine. Braithwaite was far more successful with his annual anthologies of magazine verse which began in 1913 and continued until 1929. While he supported the so-called "new poetry" movement in the United States, he was often in conflict with Harriet Monroe and the crowd associated with *Poetry*. In part both Braithwaite and Monroe simply became caught in the conflict between the eastern literary establishment and the growing group of midwestern writers who were not willing to accept the East as the arbiter of the nation's cultural life. Given the animosity which developed between Braithwaite and Monroe, it is significant to note that they both shared a similar commitment to the support of poetry in America. They demonstrated catholic tastes and were interested in promoting the cause of poetry without adopting a particular ideology. With the advent of the Imagist movement and its so-called relationship to the vers libre movement in France, Braithwaite was sorely taxed, not only because it violated the poetic traditions which he held dear but also because some of its strongest supporters were known for their strong antiblack attitudes. And no matter how broad he tried to be, he had difficulty supporting a theory that was being

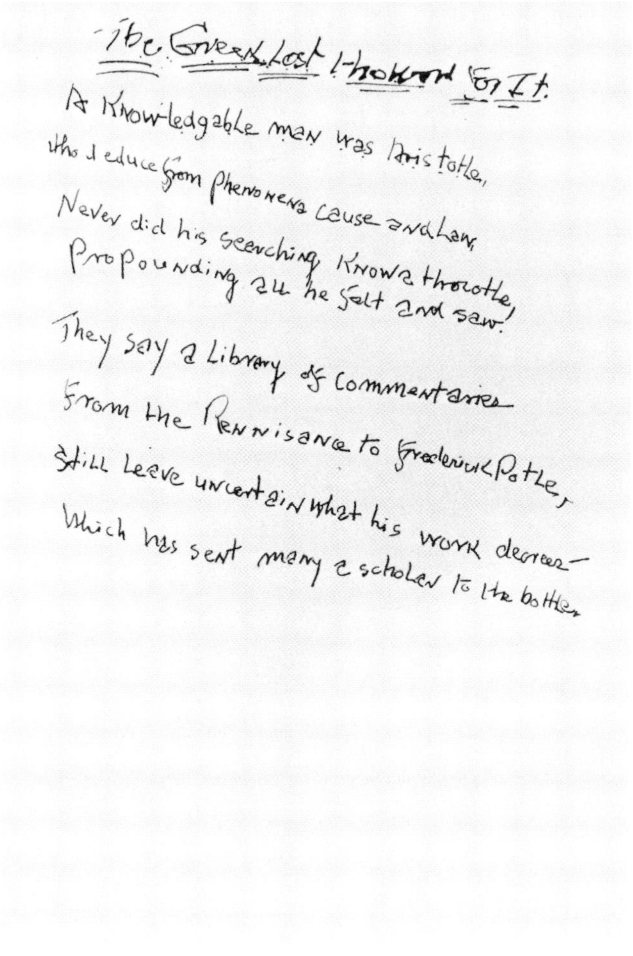

The Greek Lost Honored For It.

A Knowledgable man was Aristotle,
Who deduce from phenomena cause and law,
Never did his searching know a throttle,
Propounding all he felt and saw!

They say a library of commentaries
From the Renaissance to Frederick Potter,
Still leave uncertain what his work decrees—
Which has sent many a scholar to the bottle

Manuscript for a poem by Braithwaite (William S. Braithwaite Collection, George Arrents Research Library for Special Collections, Syracuse University)

touted by Ezra Pound and Conrad Aiken, even though he recognized the latter's ability as a poet. In the final analysis, that Monroe became associated with the Midwest and Braithwaite with the perceived traditionalism of New England was simply an accident of time and place.

While Braithwaite's anthologies were designed to reprint that verse which had appeared in selected magazines during the course of the year, they eventually became significant critical tools and Braithwaite himself soon became a powerful figure, literally a "king-maker" of poets. The anthologies began as outgrowths of his *Boston Transcript* annual survey which he had initiated in 1905. His reports had become quite influential by the time he began the anthologies, the prefaces to which formed a significant critical analysis of poetic movements and production in the United States. Thus it was, from the death of Whitman in 1892 to the founding of *Poetry* in 1912, that Braithwaite's voice was one of the few trying to advance the cause of poetry in the nation.

As early as 1915 he included "The White Witch" by James Weldon Johnson in the annual survey, and in the *Anthology of Magazine Verse for 1917* he noted among "first volumes by poets" in a "year [that] has been extremely rich," Johnson's *Fifty Years and Other Poems,* which he called "one of the lesser touched strings on the harp of life breaking into sound." Later in the same collection, he praised Johnson as giving "an intellectual virility to the treatment of racial problems and subjects hitherto unapproached. . . . He finds in humanity a kindred response to the common moods of experience, and the soul behind it breaks forth in many a finished bit of song." He also reviewed Georgia Douglas Johnson's *The Heart of a Woman and Other Poems* and praised her "lyric gift." In one of his few direct references to the race of a poet, he cited Waverly Turner Carmichael's *From the Heart of a*

Folk and noted: "Many have claimed the mantle of Paul Laurence Dunbar, but only upon the shoulders of . . . Carmichael has it fallen, and he wears it with becoming grace and fitness. For this poet, a veritable child of the Negro folk, gives expression to its spirit in mood and language more akin to the ante-bellum 'spirituel' than any writer I know. Like those 'black and unknown bards' he sings because he must, with all their fervid imaginativeness, symbolization, poignant strains of pathos, and philosophic humor." In the 1914 volume Braithwaite added the very useful biographical index that represented for most of the poets the first summary of their backgrounds, which included such details as the major poetic influences upon their work, but not the writers' racial identities. To survey his annual anthologies is to note his consistent inclusion of Afro-American writers, and he did so without apology or explanation.

In 1918 Braithwaite demonstrated his strong commitment to an honest and realistic judgment on racial matters. Citing Vachel Lindsay's *The Chinese Nightingale and Other Poems* among the "important volumes published during 1917-1918," he paid especial attention to the "Booker Washington Trilogy" which appears in Lindsay's book and observed, "except for the third member of the group, I care little for [it]; the significance of the tribute as a 'memorial' to the Negro educator is too detached in the symbolism to catch the imagination. And let me say here that in spite of what Professor Phelps and Professor Nelson Antrim Crawford have written about Mr. Lindsay's understanding and sympathy for the Negro, he neither understands nor represents them. I once heard Mr. Lindsay preface his reading of 'The Congo' with some reflections on the Negro race, and I saw immediately that he regarded it purely as a spectacle; that he drew little difference between the emotionalism of the aboriginal and the individual so interfused with other bloods and environments who was as far removed from the 'big, black bucks' as the poet himself."

Citing Countee Cullen as "an undoubtedly gifted poet of brilliant ability [who] is also an intensely racial singer," Braithwaite hoped in his 1924 anthology that the poet would not narrow "the fine powers he possesses [because] he stands at the threshold endowed to prove much, and if he looks deep enough into the heart and soul of man—America should by all counts give him that privilege—he has the power and should take the opportunity to solve much." In the same introduction Braithwaite praised James Weldon Johnson for the edition of *The Book of Negro Spirituals*, saying, "their beauty and pathos in the expression of religious aspirations are the most notable . . . of their kind in world literature." In view of his tendency to refrain, in his prefaces, from detailed analyses of individuals, unless they had made significant contributions to the development of American poetry, it is important to note Braithwaite's comments on both Cullen and Johnson.

The 1926 anthology, dedicated to the memory of Sidney Lanier, is the sesquicentennial volume in commemoration of the signing of the Declaration of Independence. It includes a series of essays by distinguished scholars and poets on the poetic achievement of each geographical sector of the United States, as well as essays on the nation's various ethnic and religious groups. Braithwaite felt that these elements were becoming part of the American mainstream, and he wanted to identify their contributions while they were still distinct. Alain Locke was invited to write the essay on Afro-

William Stanley Braithwaite (photograph by Carl Van Vechten; by permission of Joseph Solomon, the Estate of Carl Van Vechten)

American poetry. Central to his discussion was his explanation of the difference between "Negro poets" and "Negro poetry." He concluded that a great diversity exists in the work produced by Afro-Americans and that there was not a single "Negro poetry." Also included in the 1926 volume were practically all of the major poets now associated with the Harlem Renaissance.

The *Anthology of Magazine Verse for 1928* included still more work by the Harlem group, most of whom were no strangers by now to Braithwaite's annual listings and selections. There were poems by Lewis Alexander, Mae V. Cowdery, Countee Cullen, Waring Cuney, Langston Hughes, Georgia Douglas Johnson, and Effie Newsome. By 1929 it was apparent that the introductions to the anthologies served as an important history of American poetry and provided poetic preservation for those works which had originally appeared in short-lived journals and obscure magazines.

Although in time Harriet Monroe derisively referred to Braithwaite as "Sir Oracle" and the "Boston Dictator," while Alice Corbin Henderson called him "Amy Lowell's tool" and "a rotten prop," such name-calling did little to diminish his power in critical circles. Indeed he did seem on occasion to have tyrannical powers. Even when those poets who had reached the top with his help subsequently turned against him, he continued to be highly respected. Young poets as well as many established ones deemed it an honor to be included in his annual anthologies even though selection was predicated upon the poet's work having first appeared in one of the magazines surveyed by Braithwaite. But most of them knew that appearances in magazines alone would not suffice; hence, to be selected by Braithwaite was tantamount to a "nod of approval" from one whose opinion was considered to be of great importance.

By the time of the Harlem Renaissance, he had become extremely prominent not only in poetic circles but also in Afro-American culture. He had received the Spingarn Medal in 1918 and had established firm relationships with many of the well-known racial leaders. There were, however, some elements of the Harlem Renaissance which apparently worried him. While the writers of this period had opportunities that had been closed to those of earlier days, their work was often subjected to a double standard by those critics who came to view Afro-American literature as being exotic and primitive. The writers themselves often capitalized on this renewed interest in their culture and emphasized the "uniqueness" of their lives. Braithwaite was opposed to shifting criteria for creativity and criticism; as a result, he supported aesthetic rather than racial standards in the evaluation of literature. At the same time, he raised his voice sternly against white writers who superficially presented one-dimensional portraits of black life and who were—in his judgment—deliberately unjust. They were guilty, as he once said about Thomas Dixon, of carrying the image of the race "from caricature to libel." Even writers such as Eugene O'Neill who may have meant well were incapable of presenting "the immense paradox of racial life."

While he was issuing his annual anthologies, he was also contributing articles on every phase of Afro-American literature to such diverse journals as *Colored American Magazine, Forum, New Republic, Bookman, Opportunity, Independent, Crisis,* and *Phylon* in addition to his regular columns for the *Boston Transcript.* He never retreated from his belief in the multifaceted nature of black life and in the artistic capabilities of the Afro-American writer.

During this period when he was engaged in such demanding activities, he attempted to exist in the world of business. In 1921 he founded and served as editor in chief of the B. J. Brimmer Publishing Company. Before its bankruptcy in 1927 the firm had not only published some of Braithwaite's annual surveys but also such books as *Bronze: A Book of Verse* (1922) by Georgia Douglas Johnson and *Confusion* (1924), the first novel of James Gould Cozzens. Braithwaite actively sought manuscripts for his company during its existence, but he could not boost Brimmer's sales enough to prevent the company's collapse.

In 1935 Braithwaite was appointed Professor of Creative Literature at Atlanta University and remained there for ten years. During this time he led in the development of courses in Afro-American literature. His life in Atlanta brought him not only into the academic world but also gave him a firsthand experience in southern life, both of which must have presented some problems. In a situation which placed high priority upon academic credentials, he was made painfully aware—despite his accomplishments—of his limited formal education. Furthermore, he was fifty-seven when he began his teaching career and probably was not too inclined to change his life-style. Yet for ten years he gave guidance to a group of students who were able to benefit from his active familiarity with the development of the so-called mainstream of American literature, and his service on the editorial board of *Phylon* did much to enhance that journal.

Retiring from Atlanta University in 1945, Braithwaite moved to Harlem rather than to the Boston area which had been his home for over fifty years. By this time his anthologies had become American classics and had inspired similar collections of short stories and plays. Although the American Poetry Society gave a dinner in New York to commemorate the occasion of his eightieth birthday, it is apparent that his major contributions were important to only a select few. This period, however, is distinguished by the various commentaries he wrote for periodicals, *Selected Poems* (1948), and the 1958 anthology, which is but a shadow of his former work. Its significance rests in his chronicle of the poetic revival, in which he was extremely effective. He died on 8 June 1962.

That William Stanley Braithwaite is an enigma partially results from the ambiguous role often decreed for the Afro-American writer. That many think of him as "white" is indicative of the extent to which race has permeated a consideration of art. He is alternately condemned and ignored by those dedicated to the preservation of the past. But at a critical moment in our nation's literature, it was his voice which issued a clarion call for the support of American poetry. At the same time, he was one of the first to explore the role of the Negro in literature and to champion the cause of the Afro-American writer in places where he could be heard.

References:

Philip Butcher, Introduction to *The William Stanley Braithwaite Reader,* edited by Butcher (Ann Arbor: University of Michigan Press, 1972);

Butcher, "William Stanley Braithwaite and the College Language Association," *CLA Journal,* 15 (December 1971): 117-125;

Glenn Clairmonte, "The Cup-Bearer: William Stanley Braithwaite of Boston," *CLA Journal,* 17 (September 1973): 101-108.

Papers:

The major collection of Braithwaite's papers is located at Houghton Library, Harvard University. The Boston Public Library and the Schomburg Collection of the New York Public Library hold some letters, manuscripts, and documents relating to Braithwaite as do the libraries of Brown University, Columbia University, Dartmouth College, University of Delaware, Howard University, University of Illinois, Indiana University, and Princeton University. There are also letters at the Library of Congress, the Newberry Library in Chicago, the Huntington Library in San Marino, California, and the libraries of University of Arkansas, University of California, Berkeley, Colby College, University of Colorado, Duke University, Emory University, College of the Holy Cross, University of Iowa, University of Kentucky, Marietta College, Middlebury College, University of Minnesota, Northwestern University, University of Notre Dame, University of Pennsylvania, University of Pittsburgh, University of Rochester, Smith College, State University of New York at Buffalo, Syracuse University, Temple University, Texas College, Tufts University, Tulane University of Louisiana, University of Virginia, and Yale University.

William Wells Brown

Gregory L. Candela
University of New Mexico, Valencia

See also the Brown entry in *DLB 3, Antebellum Writers in New York and the South.*

BIRTH: near Lexington, Kentucky, probably fall 1814, to Elizabeth and George W. Higgins.

MARRIAGES: 1834 to Elizabeth (Betsey) Schooner (separated 1847, deceased 1851); children: Clarissa, Josephine. 1860 to Annie Elizabeth Gray; child: Clotelle.

DEATH: Chelsea, Massachusetts, 6 November 1884.

BOOKS: *Narrative of William W. Brown, A Fugitive Slave, Written by Himself* (Boston: Anti-Slavery

Office, 1847; enlarged, 1848; London: Charles Gilpin, 1849);

A Lecture Delivered before the Female Anti-Slavery Society of Salem, at Lyceum Hall, Nov. 14, 1847 (Boston: Massachusetts Anti-Slavery Society, 1847);

Three Years in Europe; or, Places I Have Seen and People I Have Met (London: Charles Gilpin, 1852); expanded as *The American Fugitive in Europe. Sketches of Places and People Abroad* (Boston: John P. Jewett/New York: Sheldon, Lamport & Blakeman, 1855);

Clotel; or, The President's Daughter: A Narrative of Slave Life in the United States (London: Partridge & Oakey, 1853); revised as *Clotelle: A Tale of Southern States* (Boston: J. Redpath/New York: H. Dexter Hamilton, 1864); revised as *Clotelle: or, The Colored Heroine; A Tale of the Southern States* (Boston: Lee, 1867);

St. Domingo: Its Revolutions and Its Patriots. A Lecture, Delivered before the Metropolitan Athenaeum, London, May 16 and at St. Thomas' Church, Philadelphia, December 20, 1854 (Boston: Bela Marsh, 1855);

The Escape; or, A Leap for Freedom. A Drama in Five Acts (Boston: R. F. Wallcut, 1858);

Memoir of William Wells Brown, an American Bondman. Written by Himself (Boston: Anti-Slavery Office, 1859);

The Anti-Southern Lecturer (London, 1862);

The Black Man; His Antecedents, His Genius, and His Achievements (New York: Thomas Hamilton/Boston: R. F. Wallcut, 1863; revised and expanded, 1863);

The Negro in the American Rebellion: His Heroism and His Fidelity (Boston: Lee & Shepard, 1867);

The Rising Son; or, The Antecedents and Advancement of the Colored Race (Boston: A. G. Brown, 1873);

My Southern Home: Or, The South and Its People (Boston: A. G. Brown, 1880).

OTHER: *The Anti-Slavery Harp; a Collection of Songs for Anti-Slavery Meetings. Compiled by William W. Brown* (Boston: Bela Marsh, 1848; Newcastle, U.K.: J. Blackwell, 1850).

PERIODICAL PUBLICATION: *Miralda; or the Beautiful Quadroon* (revised from *Clotel; or, The President's Daughter*), serialized in *Weekly Anglo-African* (1 December 1860-6 March 1861).

In a letter dated 2 July 1847, Edmund Quincy, a prominent Boston abolitionist, described the thirty-three-year-old William Wells Brown as "an extraordinary fellow. I do not know that his intellectual power is equal to that of [Frederick] Douglass, but he is of a much higher cast of character. There seems to be no meanness, no littleness, no envy or suspiciousness about him." William E. Farrison, Brown's biographer, notes that he was "a man of medium stature . . . was possessed of a melodious voice, a pleasing personality, and a wholesome sense of humor." Brown's particular genius lay in his down-to-earth, direct, and at times eloquent advocacy of abolitionism and, later, Christian temperance. His great talent was his ability to present dramatic, informed, and critical arguments for these major reforms, whether such arguments were given from a speaker's podium, in an essay, or in a novel. Brown was masterful at controlling a crowd, hostile or friendly; he was forthright in his opinions yet rarely dogmatic; he was single-minded in his commitment to abolish slavery and tireless in his speechmaking throughout the free states before and after the Civil War. Brown approached each challenge—escape from slavery, self-education, travel, lecturing, or writing—armed with a deep and sympathetic imagination, confident and persuasive manner, optimism, and courage. William Wells Brown, the first black American to publish a novel, play, travel book, full-length military study of Afro-Americans, and study of black sociology, was a pioneer.

Though Brown did not excel in any one of these groundbreaking efforts, his having been first to bridge the gap between black protest and black fiction is significant. Brown combined sensational elements from abolitionist tracts and speeches, testimonial slave narratives, and popular stage melodramas with a detached, often matter-of-fact, narrative point of view to shift attention onto slavery rather than sympathy away from the slave. This ironic formula, evident in Brown's autobiographical accounts, his novel, and his play, was adopted by many black novelists and dramatists who followed him.

Most of the information we have about his nineteen years as a slave comes from Brown's own memoirs and, most substantially, from his *Narrative of William W. Brown, A Fugitive Slave.* Written in 1846 and published in Boston in 1847, this popular slave narrative went through four almost identical editions and sold some ten thousand copies in only two years. In his prefatory letter to the work, Edmund Quincy testified to Brown's extensive knowledge of slavery and to the success of his narrative technique: "Your opportunities of observing the workings of this accursed system have been singularly great. Your experiences in the Field, in the House, and especially on the River in the service of the slave-trader, Walker, have been such as few individuals have had." Quincy "marvelled at . . . the simplicity and calmness with which [Brown described] scenes and actions which might well 'move the very stones to rise and mutiny.' "

Brown also used representative American figures to undercut slavery. For example, in one of his many autobiographical memoirs, Brown claimed that Daniel Boone was his maternal grandfather. This boast has proven unlikely, but Brown's version is illustrative of his persistent dramatization of a slave's undeniable connection, by blood and labor, to a nation that often refused to acknowledge either the human status or the contributions of its black population. Linking himself to a famous American frontiersman, Brown could make such connections concrete and more effectively cast doubts on the worn tenets of American justice and morality. Brown was after the same effect when he made the heroine of *Clotel; or, The President's Daughter: A Narrative of Slave Life in the United States* (1853) the slave daughter of Thomas Jefferson, author of the "Declaration of Independence." All of Brown's characters display the intimate, volatile, and ironic connections between black and white that signify what W. E. B. Du Bois called "a sort of seventh son, born with a veil, and gifted with second-sight in this American World." Brown used these characters to document the sordid facts of slavery, and romantic, even melodramatic literary forms, to portray the internal, black perspective, as well as the typical experience of the black in white society. The veil Du Bois refers to was, for Brown and those who followed him, the grinning black mask of servitude and irony.

The central fact about the world into which William Wells Brown was born in 1814 was the stark dividing line between those classified as Negroes and those who were not. Brown quickly learned this lesson under Dr. John Young of Kentucky, his first master, and relative of his father, George W. Higgins, a white slaveholder. When Brown was two years old, he and approximately forty other slaves were moved, with the rest of Young's property, from Kentucky to the Missouri Territory. The slaves included Brown's mother and her six other offspring, each of a different father. Brown had an early recollection of Young's overseer lashing his mother with a "negro-whip" because she was ten or fifteen minutes late for field work. He describes "the handle [of the whip as] about three feet long, with the butt-end filled with lead, and the lash six or seven feet in length, made of cowhide, with platted wire on the end of it." Brown's utter inability to aid his mother was only one hard lesson in a slave's education, which taught that housing, food, clothing, literacy, travel, and, above all, the freedom to pursue any of them were denied to the slave, except as they were meted out by whites.

Brown also learned that being considered property was not the most degrading aspect of slavery. Slaves could not have surnames, since the dignity, continuity, and strength conferred upon them by a family name would have undermined the system of slavery and clarified family ties between the races which frequently proved embarrassing. Thus, William's only possession was his Christian name, and it was taken from him when the Youngs adopted an infant nephew with the same first name. Since William the slave had a light complexion, the Youngs sought to prevent any confusion by renaming him Sandford.

In 1827, when his owner moved to St. Louis, Brown was forced to leave the relative security of service in Young's rural home. While William and his mother accompanied the doctor, three of his brothers and his sister remained on the farm. Two other brothers died during this period. Young hired William out to at least ten different employers over the next five years, and in 1833, which would become his last year of slavery, William was sold twice. This period of forced employment revealed to Brown slavery's full spectrum of cruelty, shaped the major beliefs of his mature years, convinced him that he must escape, and provided vivid materials for his abolitionist activities and major literary works.

One of his first employers (Brown received no wages) was Major Freeland, described in Brown's *Narrative* as the keeper of a public house or tavern, "a horse-racer, cock-fighter, gambler, and withal an inveterate drunkard." He often beat his servants "after which, he would cause a fire to be made of tobacco stems" in his smokehouse and would shut the imagined offender up in the shed to gag and suffocate him. Complaining to Young about his treatment did no good, and after some months of Freeland's tyranny, Brown tried to escape. Because he was only fourteen or fifteen years of age, he was probably more concerned with getting away from Freeland than making his way to a free state, but this first attempt gave Brown a brief respite from the major and opened for him the way to liberty. William Farrison observes that "Brown's experience with Freeland contributed a great deal to his abhorrence of intoxicants—an abhorrence that eventually made him an ardent temperance reformer."

Another, and for the most part positive, experience during this period of forced employment was Brown's work for Elijah P. Lovejoy in 1830. Lovejoy was then the editor and part-time owner of the newly founded *Saint Louis Times;* he was a kindly man, and Brown credits Lovejoy and his employment "in the printing office, for what little learning [he] obtained while in slavery." This six-month period came to an abrupt and violent end. For the offense of defending himself and protecting some printer's type from a gang of white boys, Brown was severely beaten by one of the boy's fathers. By the time he recovered from his injuries the position at the newspaper had been filled.

Brown's horrible beating was to prove a fortunate turning point, for experiences in the next year and a half convinced him to flee north. His next job, Brown's second on a Mississippi steamboat, was aboard the *Enterprise.* These few months in the summer of 1830 strengthened Brown's growing conviction that mobility was synonymous with freedom and security. As he recalls that time in his *Narrative,* "the situation was a pleasant one to me;—but in passing from place to place, and seeing new faces every day, and knowing that they could go where they pleased, I soon became unhappy, and several times thought of leaving the boat at some landing place, and trying to make my escape to Canada. . . ." Further heightening Brown's insecurity during his employment on the *Enterprise,* and reinforcing his determination to escape, was Brown's first contact with James Walker, a slave trader. Walker was impressed with the youngster's potential and, early in 1832, offered to purchase him from Young. Brown's master refused the offer but allowed Walker to hire Brown for a year, one which the author later called "the longest year I ever lived." Brown devoted one-quarter of his *Narrative* to the horrors of life under Walker, whom he called a "soul-driver," and he was to use scenes from this period in his most poignant and ironic writing. For example, his *Narrative* describes a distraught slave and mother, "who had been taken from her husband and children, and having no desire to live without them, in the agony of her soul jumped overboard, and drowned herself. She was not chained." Also, in one of the few instances of unaltered autobiography in his fiction, Brown devoted two chapters of *Clotel* to "Dick" Walker's slave trading activities. As Walker's unwilling assistant, he had to prepare slaves for sale in the "negro pens" of New Orleans, a business his *Narrative* describes in moving detail: "They were dressed and driven out into the yard. Some were set to dancing, some to jumping, some to singing. . . . This was done to make them appear cheerful and happy. My business was to see that they were placed in those situations before the arrival of the purchasers, and I have often set them to dancing when their cheeks were wet with tears." Brown's *Clotel* was the first novelistic account of such scenes, shaping the irony that is such a prevalent part of Afro-American literature, irony, as black author Paul Laurence Dunbar put it, that comes from behind "the mask that grins and lies."

Released from Walker's service in the spring of 1833, Brown was not relieved of the traumatic uncertainties of slavery. Short of funds, Young sold Brown's only sister to a man from Natchez, Mississippi, and decided to sell William also. Brown's mother, Elizabeth, was now the only other family member left in the St. Louis area. Brown was insecure about his immediate future, and he was terrified of losing the last link with his scattered family,

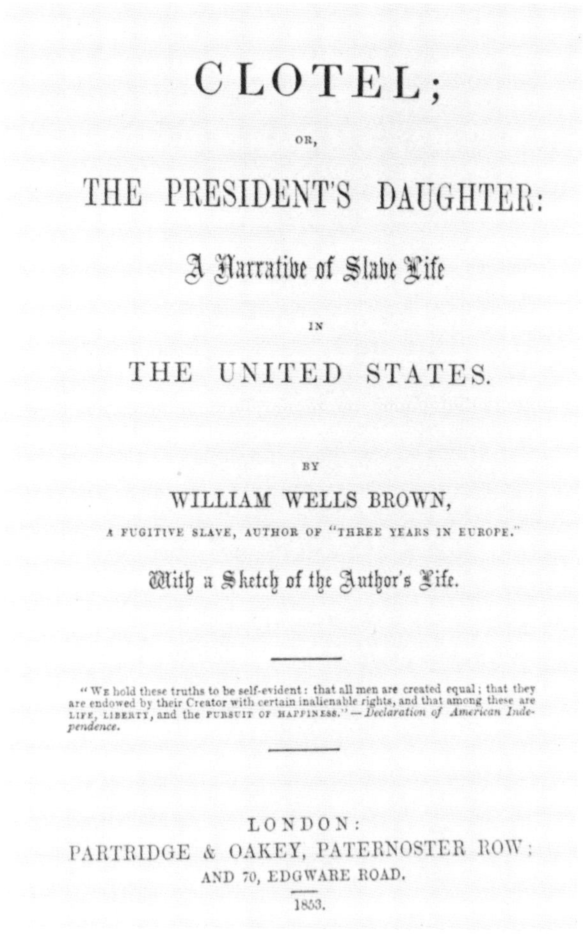

CLOTEL;

OR,

THE PRESIDENT'S DAUGHTER:

A Narrative of Slave Life

IN

THE UNITED STATES.

BY

WILLIAM WELLS BROWN,

A FUGITIVE SLAVE, AUTHOR OF "THREE YEARS IN EUROPE."

With a Sketch of the Author's Life.

"WE hold these truths to be self-evident: that all men are created equal; that they are endowed by their Creator with certain inalienable rights, and that among these are LIFE, LIBERTY, and the PURSUIT OF HAPPINESS."—*Declaration of American Independence.*

LONDON:
PARTRIDGE & OAKEY, PATERNOSTER ROW;
AND 70, EDGWARE ROAD.
1853.

Title page for the first edition of the first novel by a black American

so he persuaded his mother to escape with him. Fugitives for eleven days, they were caught in central Illinois and returned to St. Louis where Brown was sold to Samuel Willi, a merchant tailor, for $500; his mother suffered a worse fate—she was sold and transported to the Deep South. In one of the most moving scenes of his *Narrative,* Brown describes their final parting and his profound sense of guilt over a displacement that probably hastened his mother's death: "I walked on shore. The bell was tolling. The boat was about to start. I stood with a heavy heart, waiting to see her leave the wharf."

In October of 1833 Brown was sold to Enoch Price, a merchant and steamboat owner, for about $700. On Wednesday, 1 January 1834, while Price's steamboat, the *Chester,* was docked at Cincinnati, Ohio, William made his third bid for freedom. He hid by day and traveled by night, and on about the eighth day of his flight, starving and frostbitten, he fortunately happened on Wells Brown, a Quaker who shared his home with the exhausted and ill fugitive for twelve to fifteen days. William honored him by adopting his name. No longer Sandford the slave, nineteen-year-old William Wells Brown made his way to Cleveland to begin a new life in the Great Lakes region; he escaped on New Year's Day, 1834, closing out a year in which slavery was banned throughout the English Empire and William Lloyd Garrison of Boston established the American Anti-Slavery Society along with its abolitionist newspaper, *The Liberator.* Garrison's organization and newspaper were to play a pivotal role in making Brown an internationally famous orator and author.

After trying his hand as a waiter for twelve dollars a month, an enterprising barber, and a small-change banker who called himself "the Emperor of the West," Brown settled into stewarding for lake steamers. He held onto this seasonal job for the next nine years, until 1843. Meanwhile, with incredible energy, Brown began to teach himself how to read and write. With the same energy, but perhaps too much haste, he married Elizabeth (Betsey) Schooner in 1834. The couple lost their first-born daughter, but in 1836 they had their second, Clarissa. In the same year, the Brown family moved to Buffalo, and by that time, William had become a committed abolitionist.

In his capacity as a steward, Brown was able to conduct many fugitive slaves across the Great Lakes to freedom. Farrison tells us that Brown also "welcomed antislavery agents and lecturers into his home. He made his home a station of the Underground Railroad; and because many fugitive slaves passed through Buffalo on route to Canada, he frequently had stopover passengers to accommodate." In 1839 his favorite daughter, Josephine, was born, but Brown was never strictly a family man. In fact events between 1836 and 1843 drew Brown away from home and the Underground Railroad and toward the itinerant life of a lecturer committed to abolitionism. In this period, Brown continued to study, applying himself to English grammar, math, history, and literature.

By late summer 1843 Brown had clearly made a transition. During August "a national convention of colored citizens of the United States" was held in Buffalo; Brown was a member of the organizing committee for the convention and as such met Frederick Douglass and the Reverend Henry Highland Garnet, the two major speakers of the occasion. From this experience came other milestones in Brown's career, including the publication of his letter to the editor of the *National Anti-Slavery Standard* in the 26 September 1843 issue. Brown's first printed writing established his view, shared by the pacifistic Garrisonians such as Douglass, that abolitionism was not a political party but a grassroots movement aimed at turning the minds and hearts of Americans against slavery. No doubt this political philosophy influenced Brown to write sentimental fiction, such as *Clotel,* to speed the abolition of slavery.

In the fall of 1843 Brown gave up his steady work as a steward to become a full-time lecturer for the Western New York Anti-Slavery Society. He moved from one small town to another, seldom having a place to stay, depending for his sustenance on paltry contributions from often very unsympathetic crowds. Though we do not know the specifics, it was probably his decision to become a lecturer that spelled the end of Brown's first marriage. While Brown was away making speeches, Betsey formed a liaison with James Garrett, a family friend; this liaison, more than any other of the complications that no doubt led up to the affair, prompted the couple to separate for good in 1847.

In the meantime, Brown was launched into the national limelight by his appearance as a speaker before the tenth anniversary meeting of the American Anti-Slavery Society, held 7-10 May 1844 in New York City. Now thirty years old, he had been well prepared for such attention, having gained his experience as an antislavery agent and speaker on the toughest of circuits. His speaking engagements after the convention of 1844 continued to test his wit, commanding presence, and recuperative powers from both the psychological and physical wounds of prejudice. On a lecture tour of Ohio that summer, for example, Brown turned the tables on Jim Crow and saved some money in the process. As Farrison relates the incident, "one day on a train en route from Sandusky to Republic . . . Brown was ejected from one of the coaches, he said, because Negroes were not permitted to ride in the coaches with white people. . . . He chose to [ride in an open freight car] because he had an engagement in Republic a few hours later. As the train neared Republic . . . the conductor who had excluded him from the coaches came and asked for his fare—$1.25, as those in the coaches had paid. Brown refused to pay this amount. Instead he asked how much was the charge for the transportation of freight per hundred pounds. The conductor replied that it was 25¢; whereupon Brown nonplussed him by paying him only 37 1/2¢, Brown's weight being about 150 pounds." With some alteration for more humorous and ironic impact, Brown assigned this incident to a character named William in *Clotel.*

Brown was able to impress even the most hostile small-town crowds who were often whipped into antiabolitionist frenzies by local ministers. The best description we have of such a meeting is given by Alonzo D. Moore in his "Memoir of the Author" written for Brown's last historical work, *The Rising Son* (1873). In the winter of 1844 Brown spoke in Moore's hometown of Aurora, New York. "The coughing, whistling, stamping of feet, and other noises made by the assemblage, showed the prejudice existing against the anti-slavery cause. . . . This tumult lasted for half an hour or more, during which time unsalable eggs, peas, and other missiles were liberally thrown at the speaker." Angered by the crowd's rudeness and the rotten egg that caught him full in the face, Brown challenged the mob directly, calling them cowards; as Moore relates, this silenced the audience, and Brown then proceeded to move the listeners in his favor: "The intense interest connected with the various incidents [of his bondage and escape] as he related them, chained the audience to their seats, and for an hour and a half he spoke, making one of the most eloquent appeals ever heard in that section in behalf of his race."

However, in the increasingly emotional atmosphere of the 1840s created by the slavery question, Brown was not always able to manipulate a crowd. In Harwich, Cape Cod, for instance, he narrowly escaped death. Because antiabolitionist sentiments had risen to a high pitch among the townspeople, no one would allow the scheduled antislavery meeting to be held in any of Harwich's large buildings. Therefore, Brown and others organized the meeting in a grove outside the city. On a prearranged signal, a segment of the approximately 2,500 people present began a riot and attacked the speaker's platform. "Brown was picked up and thrown over the back of the platform 'down six or eight feet' and was then 'trampled on by the throng gathered there.' He escaped being killed only when the attention of his assailants was distracted. . . ."

Brown's escape from bondage in 1834 was the first of three watershed events in his life. Separation from Betsey Schooner and his move to Boston with his two daughters in 1847 was the second. Except for Brown's five-year sojourn in England and his itinerant habits, he made the Boston area his home for the remainder of his life. In those years, Boston was the intellectual center of the

NEGRO DENTISTRY. *Page* 130.

"BETTING" A NEGRO IN THE SOUTHERN STATES. *Page* 69.

Illustrations from the first edition of Clotel; or, The President's Daughter

A NEGRO HUNT IN THE SOUTHERN STATES. *Page* 137

THE DEATH OF CLOTEL. *Page* 218.

country as well as the birthplace and hub of abolitionism. Thus the area contained most of the nation's antislavery publishing activity. This move, then, also brought Brown to the immediate attention of the men and women who controlled both the movement and its presses: William Lloyd Garrison, Frederick Douglass, J. Elizabeth Jones, Wendell Phillips, Charles Lenox Remond, and Edmund Quincy. Within a very short time, Brown was a key member of this group as an organizer, speaker, and new author. His first major work, the *Narrative*, came out in 1847.

In its day Brown's slave narrative was one of the most popular of its kind. The split between his almost clinical point of view and the heartrending, melodramatic content (frequently a mixture of fact and fiction) stems ultimately from the black experience itself, as well as the author's conflicting impulses while writing about his life for a predominantly white audience. To survive, the black slave or freedman had to mask his profound anger with seeming contentment, passivity, supplication, or even humor no matter how he was provoked. Similarly, to gain support for abolitionism, Brown could not afford to alienate his readers through overt sarcasm, bitterness, or rage. To portray convincingly the actual horrors of slavery, he balanced gripping emotional scenes with his objective persona of the social historian or journalist.

In all of his work Brown displays the same detached narrative control over volatile subject matter. Even as an editor he exercised the right to remove too-highly-charged pieces. The first edition of his next significant publication, *The Anti-Slavery Harp; a Collection of Songs for Anti-Slavery Meetings* (1848), contained forty-eight selections, thirty-one of which he had culled from previous anthologies by other collectors. Only one piece, "Fling out the Anti-Slavery Flag," was composed by Brown; it was probably his first published attempt at poetry. John Greenleaf Whittier's "The Yankee Girl" and James Russell Lowell's "Stanzas on Freedom" were included in the volume. However, the two purely satiric works in *The Anti-Slavery Harp*, the anonymous "The Colonization Song" and John Pierpont's "Slaveholder's Address to the North Star," were dropped from the second edition of 1849 because they provoked anger. Yet Brown chose to retain the clearly ironic poem "Jefferson's Daughter," which had appeared in 1839 in *Tait's Edinburgh Magazine*. In fact, the sketchy sources for this "song" and the song itself—which was based on the alleged sale of Thomas Jefferson's slave daughter for $1000 dollars—inspired the central story of Brown's first and only novel, *Clotel*. The balance between sentiment and satire is evident here as well, although in the second edition of the novel, entitled *Miralda; or the Beautiful Quadroon* (1860), Brown removed one of the original version's keenest satires, the Reverend Hontz Snyder's sermon to Reverend John Peck's slaves.

In only two years Brown had published two popular and important books and had risen to national prominence as a speaker for abolitionism. On 18 July 1849 William Wells Brown began the third great sea change of his life: he sailed for Liverpool, England, on board the steamship *Canada*, an appropriate name for the vehicle that was to carry him to further liberation and a transformation of mind that would help him fulfill his destiny.

Brown gave two reasons for his journey: his desire to attend the Paris Peace Conference of 1849 as a delegate from Boston and to follow in the footsteps of his colleagues Charles Lenox Remond and Frederick Douglass by laying "before the people of Great Britain and Ireland the wrongs that are still committed upon the slaves and free coloured people of America." But there were other compelling reasons. Brown was increasingly anxious about his status as a fugitive, and he had good cause: his former master, Enoch Price, knew he was in Boston and had even sent Edmund Quincy a letter offering to sell Brown his freedom. In the late 1840s, slave bounty hunters were becoming bolder; indeed, only a year after Brown left the country, the U.S. Congress passed the Fugitive Slave Law (1850) and thus legitimized the kidnapping of fugitive slaves from anywhere in the country. In fact, this law forced Brown to remain in England four years longer than the year he had originally planned. Yet the most compelling reasons for the trip were Brown's insatiable curiosity and his wanderlust—his belief that movement itself was liberating.

Brown remained in Great Britain from 1849 to 1854 until he was forty years old. During this time, he traveled more than 25,000 miles, addressed more than 1000 public meetings, lectured at twenty-three institutions as well as before many antislavery, benevolent, and religious societies. He met Victor Hugo and was made an honorary member of the London club to which Charles Dickens belonged. He taught himself to read French, made "considerable progress," as he put it, in Latin, and took up the study of German. He helped to found and run, in 1852, a London newspaper, the *Anti-Slavery Advocate*, and he published four books. With the help of friends and through his lectures, publication of newspaper articles and books, Brown not only paid for the entire trip but sent both of his daughters to school in France and England. In 1854 eighteen-year-old Clarissa and fifteen-year-old Josephine would become schoolmistresses themselves in well-established English schools.

In 1852 Brown compiled letters he had written to friends and abolitionist newspapers in America, publishing them as an epistolary travel book, *Three Years in Europe; or, Places I Have Seen and People I Have Met.* The book ran to 344 pages, 312 of which were composed of twenty-three letters; all but two of these contained descriptions of the notable people, events, and places that Brown had observed or learned of during the prior two and a half years he had spent traveling through Europe. Letter 21 sketched the characters of twelve American reformers; but for the purposes of Brown's literary career, letter 22 was the most significant.

Titled "A Narrative of American Slavery," the "letter" was Brown's first attempt to write romance fiction. The story's hero is George Green, a nearly white mulatto slave who participated in Nat Turner's slave insurrection but is saved from hanging by a bit of stage melodrama: Mary, a slave in love with George, rescues the condemned man by changing clothes with him during a visit to his prison cell. He escapes to Canada, aided by a kindly Quaker in Ohio. After ten years and a number of improbable coincidences, the lovers are reunited in France. Brown claimed that the story was told to him in France by George Green himself, but clearly the tale, like so much of Brown's writing, is a mixture of the author's imagination, incidents from his own life, and accounts of other fugitive slaves that Brown gleaned from his work on the Underground Railroad and from abolitionist publications.

In fact, Brown transferred "A Narrative of American Slavery" directly into chapters 26-28 of his next and greatest contribution to black American literature: the novel *Clotel; or, The President's Daughter.* Originally published in London in November of 1853, *Clotel* was revised and republished in America under different titles for a period of fourteen years. From 1860 through 1861, it was serialized in the *Weekly Anglo-African* as *Miralda; or the Beautiful Quadroon.* In 1864 it reappeared as *Clotelle: A Tale of Southern States,* and in 1867 as *Clotelle: or, The Colored Heroine; A Tale of the Southern States.* The novel's plot (though the central story is often interrupted by digression and subplots which threaten to overwhelm it) concerns Currer, the slave mistress of Thomas Jefferson; Currer's daughters, Clotel and Althesa; and their children. Of these major characters, only Clotel's daughter Mary survives the novel's sensational and geographically scattered events.

Arthur Davis voices the general critical assessment of *Clotel* when he notes that Brown "tried to cram too many things into one work: antislavery lectures and verse; enough situations to supply at least five novels; newspaper accounts, . . . minstrel jokes and sketches; and every slavery anecdote he considered even remotely pertinent." Revised editions of the novel have less of this distracting material, although, as Davis says, they still have other weaknesses. Nonetheless, Brown's technique of bombarding the reader with a potpourri of materials and forms works to create a melodramatic tension. Brown presents the factual oppressions of slavery to the reader, then builds to an emotional climax through more subjective accounts of slavery's horrors. Chapter one illustrates Brown's ap-

Cover for the 1864 edition of Brown's 1853 novel

proach.

The chapter begins with what appears to be a factual argument meant "to show that the present system of chattel slavery in America undermines the entire social condition of man." Referring to authorities and citing excerpts from religious tracts, Brown argues that the legal system of slavery perverts marriage, "the foundation of all civilisation [*sic*] and culture—the root of church and state." As for the church, Brown states "that the ministers of religion, even in the so-called free states, are the mere echoes, instead of the correctors, of public sentiment." To appeal to that sentiment, the first narrative scene of the chapter focuses on a slave auction. Yet Brown still maintains his factual tone, placing in the text an advertisement for the auction which lists "several mulatto girls of rare personal qualities: two of them very superior." Those two are the daughters of Thomas Jefferson and Currer: Clotel, age sixteen, and Althesa, age fourteen.

Brown builds to the chapter's final scene, the actual sale, and his tone becomes less and less detached as he does so. Brown says that because Clotel was the most valuable slave that day, she was the last to be offered at the block. In one of the most compelling and ironic descriptions of a slave sale in literature, Brown first describes Clotel's purity of character and appearance, then takes us breathlessly through the auction process, contrasting Clotel's innocence with the vulgar, fast-paced bidding for human flesh: "Laughing, joking, sneering, smoking, spitting, and talking kept a continual hum and noise amongst the crowd; while the slave-girl stood with tears in her eyes. . . ." Playing melodramatic and ironic contrasts for their fullest impact, Brown next summarizes "a Southern auction, at which the bones, muscles, sinews, blood, and nerves of a young lady of sixteen were sold for five hundred dollars; her moral character for two hundred; her improved intellect for one hundred, her Christianity for three hundred; and her chastity and virtue for four hundred dollars more. And this, too, in a city thronged with churches. . . ." Two paragraphs after this blunt and shocking culmination, the chapter ends in the compressed but cathartic release of verse:

"O God! my every heart-string cries,
  Dost thou these scenes behold
In this our boasted Christian land,
  And must the truth be told?"

In this scene, Brown's increasingly metaphoric language works to move the reader from detachment to arousal of emotion to outrage.

Brown reserves his combination of sensational plot and ironic commentary especially for the leaders of the church. From personal experiences he knew that many northern clergymen obstructed abolitionism as staunchly as their southern counterparts; all argued the basic inferiority of the Negro. Brown was repeatedly frustrated by the clergy in communities where he spoke, and he was so angered by one Reverend John Peck of Rochester, New York, that he portrayed Peck in *Clotel* using his real name. The satire directed at Peck fills more pages in the novel and is much more overt than Brown's attack on Walker, the slave trader.

Peck's hypocrisy in *Clotel* is matched by the deception his slaves practice to survive. In no other work does Brown show such perception and skill in describing the mask of contentment slaves had to wear. For instance, when Peck dies, his slaves are respectfully subdued because they are in the presence of whites; yet later that night, they gather in the forest to celebrate his death in songs:

Hang up the shovel and the hoe—
Take down the fiddle and the bow—
Old master has gone to the slaveholder's rest;
He has gone where they all ought to go.

Thus, as disorganized and melodramatic as *Clotel* appears to be, it deserves more critical attention (particularly for its use of popular literary and dramatic forms) than simply as the first novel written by a black American.

After protracted negotiations between agents representing Enoch Price and William Wells Brown, the man who had liberated himself more than twenty years before, the author and lecturer was legally freed. Brown's papers were finalized on 7 July 1854; the price was $300. Under no further threat of reenslavement, Brown sailed for Boston in the fall of 1854 and, soon after his arrival, accepted a lecturer's position with Garrison's American Anti-Slavery Society. He returned to a nation fast approaching war and a radicalized abolitionist movement. This climate suited Brown, for before such ideas became acceptable to antislavery groups, he had broken with the Garrisonians and endorsed slave uprisings and military intervention by the North as a means to end slavery. Soon after his return, he reinforced this view by composing and delivering a lecture featuring Toussaint L'Ouverture, the black Haitian revolutionary; the lecture was published as a pamphlet entitled *St. Domingo: Its Revolutions and Its Patriots* (1855).

In 1856 Brown, a revolutionary in his own right, became the first black American to write a play. Brown wrote at least two plays: the first, a satire aimed at clergyman Dr. Nehemiah Adams and called "A South-Side View of Slavery," was never published and has been lost; the other, the first published play by a black American, was entitled *The Escape; or, A Leap for Freedom* (1858). Neither play was ever produced, but Brown read them at his lectures to enthusiastic reviews. Yet as Brown himself wrote in the preface to *The Escape,* "as I never aspired to be a dramatist, I ask no favor for [the play], and have little or no solicitude for its fate."

The five-act drama centers on Glen and Melinda, two slaves who marry in secret, are abused by their master, Dr. Gaines, and finally escape to Canada. Most interesting about the play are its hyperbolic language, comedy, and satire. Although the characters, themes, and plot are drawn from Brown's life and other abolitionist materials, what

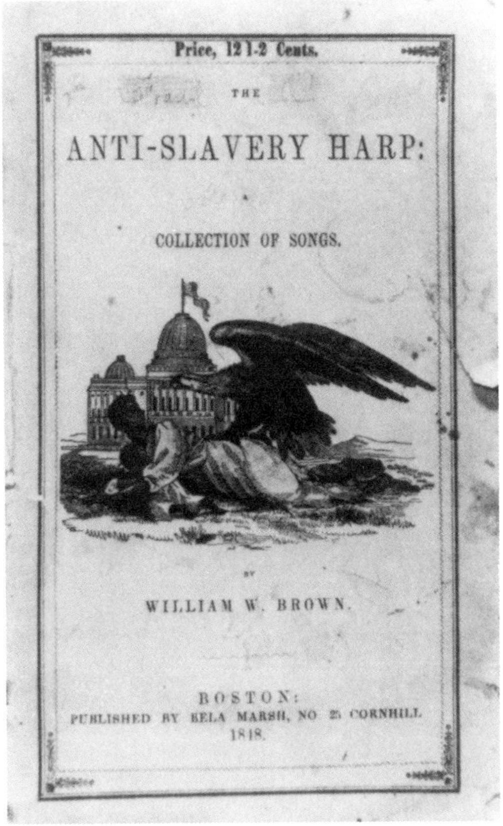

Cover for the anthology edited by Brown (courtesy of Glen Carrington Collection, Moorland-Spingarn Research Center, Howard University)

Brown does with these materials is unique and important for black literature. The play's melodramatic framework reveals the anger behind the mask of contentment and obedience. As Glen exclaims, "Oh! there is a volcano pent up in the hearts of the slaves of these Southern States that will burst forth ere long." Perhaps the passage was inspired by lines from Josiah Henson's narrative (with which Brown was undoubtedly familiar) published in Boston, 1849: "A blow at one white man is a blow at all; is the muttering and upheaving of volcanic fires, which underlie and threaten to burst forth and utterly consume the whole social fabric." Brown's use of this metaphor on the eve of the Civil War proved prophetic, and both passages are still applicable.

Much of the comedy is quite good. One scene—in which Cato mistakenly pulls the wrong tooth from an ailing fellow slave—is expanded from a scene in *Clotel* which, in turn, was taken from Brown's experiences as a medical assistant to his first master, Dr. Young. The major black characters in the play, including Cato and Glen, are either self-deprecating, comic, or idealized versions of the author's personality. The play's dramatic and verbal irony is especially directed at Dr. Gaines (loosely based on Young) and, of course, at the play's parson, Mr. Pinchen. Dick Walker, the same man depicted in *Clotel* and based on James Walker of Brown's *Narrative,* makes his appearance, and Brown's irony shows Pinchen to be of the same ilk as the slave trader. In act 2, scene 2, both men discuss a trip down the river to Natchez, Mississippi, the speculator to buy and sell slaves, the preacher to hold a camp (revival) meeting. Pinchen asks, "What kind of niggers sells best in the Orleans market, Mr. Walker?" The trader replies, "Why, field hands. Did you think of goin' in the trade?" The ever diffident parson responds, "Oh, no; only it's a long ways down to Natchez, and I thought I'd just buy five or six niggers, and take 'em down and sell 'em to pay my travellin' expenses. . . ."

The novel and the play, then, are extensions of Brown's autobiography; characters are composites or representative types that simultaneously played upon popular stereotypical views of black character and refuted them. Brown set the pattern for early black fiction, of using autobiography yoked with melodramatic techniques to reach a wide audience, and to reveal a volatile black consciousness divided by the double standard of American racism.

Betsey Schooner had died in 1851 or 1852, and in 1860 Brown married twenty-five-year-old

William Wells Brown

Annie Elizabeth Gray in Cambridgeport, Massachusetts. The couple had two children: the first, a boy, died soon after his birth in 1861; the second, Clotelle, was born in 1862 but survived only eight years. In the dozen years after his marriage, Brown first lectured concerning the war and the new era that would follow the abolition of slavery. After the Civil War, Brown switched his attention to temperance work and medicine, which he had been practicing since his early work under Dr. Young and during his stay in England. By 1864 Brown was actively treating patients and had begun to use the title M.D. after his name. It was also in this period that Brown's interest shifted from literature to socio-historical writings.

His first major historical work, *The Black Man; His Antecedents, His Genius, and His Achievements,* was published in 1862 (though the date of imprint and copyright is given as 1863). After a short memoir by the author, the book is composed of two major sections. Part one, "Antecedents," argues for the freeing of black slaves and the benefits of abolition to the nation and is prefaced by a comparison between Anglo-Saxon and African civilizations. Part two, which forms the bulk of *The Black Man,* is composed of fifty-three biographical sketches, mostly of noteworthy black Americans and Haitians. The book went through two editions with four printings overall; the last printing appeared in 1865. Brown's style is clear and direct, but *The Black Man* is full of inaccuracies. However, the book is a credit to Brown's energy as well as his determination to lift the black American out of obscurity and to refute negative racial myths.

Brown's next historical work was *The Negro in the American Rebellion: His Heroism and His Fidelity* (1867). Although there had been previous sketches concerning the participation of Afro-Americans in the Revolutionary War and the War of 1812, *The Negro in the American Rebellion* was the first treatment of blacks' roles during the Civil War, and it attempted to cover Afro-American participation in all three wars. This book was not popular, and, unfortunately, the many unsold copies of it were burned in the great Boston fire of 1872. Much of *The Negro in the American Rebellion* is a compilation of other sources; however, sections which can hardly be called objective historical accounts are of great value for the study of black literature. For example, Brown satirically dissects President Andrew Johnson: "Intensely in love with himself, egotistical, without dignity, tyrannical, ungrateful, and fond of flattery, Mr. Johnson was entirely unprepared to successfully resist the overtures of the slaveholding aristocracy, by whom he had so long wished to be recognized."

Although Brown was deeply involved in temperance work by the 1870s, he had time to compile and compose his last, longest, although not his best historical book. In his preface, Brown described *The Rising Son; or, The Antecedents and Advancement of the Colored Race* (1873) this way: "After availing himself of all the reliable information obtainable, the author is compelled to acknowledge the scantiness of materials for a history of the African race." Brown's full life and his lack of time for thorough research are the more likely causes for the "scantiness" of factual matter, but in the book's biographical section, Brown again helped preserve the individual histories of some one hundred Afro-Americans, many of which would otherwise have been lost. Finally, though the book's general organizational plan was based on *The Black Man,* the earlier study is much better written; its style is clearer and more forceful.

Brown's last book, *My Southern Home: Or, The South and Its People* (1880), is the best single example we have of his various strengths as a writer and collector. Typically, for the first part of the work's

261 pages, Brown reused his old abolitionist materials, historical writings, and realistic and romanticized fictions to tell about slave life. The second section of *My Southern Home* is an account of his trip to the South in the winter of 1879 to 1880. Brown's commentary here, on the growing despair and oppression of southern blacks, is a direct forerunner of W. E. B. Du Bois's magnificent work, *The Souls of Black Folk* (1903). Like Du Bois, Brown had an eye for sociological detail and the skill to see and present such data in dramatic and often idealized terms, and he filled his book with black slave and folk songs, saving them for posterity.

Reviewing the life of William Wells Brown, one is struck by the various roles he played: slave, fugitive, steamboat steward, antislavery activist and speaker, essayist, newspaperman, novelist, playwright, historian, sociologist, doctor, temperance reformer. The sheer variety is even more stunning in the face of the fact that Brown did not learn to read or write until he was in his early twenties. Brown was the first to bring popular forms of entertainment and abolitionist propaganda into prose fiction which more clearly exposed and destroyed the false arguments for slavery than historical narratives could have, and which began a tradition in black fiction whose authors rejected social realism. Although Brown took on the role of husband and father too, his ethical commitments never allowed him much time for a family. It is almost as if his flight from nineteen years of slavery never ended, but simply turned into one crusade after another. Brown was a constant traveler until he was forced to stop because of the increasing ailments associated with a tumor of the bladder that led to his death on 6 November 1884 at seventy years of age.

Biography:

William Edward Farrison, *William Wells Brown: Author and Reformer* (Chicago & London: University of Chicago Press, 1969).

References:

Robert A. Bone, *The Negro Novel in America,* revised edition (New Haven: Yale University Press, 1965);

Arthur Davis, Introduction to *Clotel; or, The President's Daughter* (New York: Collier-Macmillan, 1970);

William Edward Farrison, "Brown's First Drama," *CLA Journal,* 2 (December 1958): 104-110;

Vernon Loggins, *The Negro Author: His Development in America to 1900* (New York: Columbia University Press, 1931);

Jean Fagan Yellin, *The Intricate Knot: The Negro in American Literature 1776-1863* (New York: New York University Press, 1971).

Papers:

Small collections of Brown's papers are located at Butler Library, Columbia University; the Schomberg Center for Research in Black Culture of the New York Public Library; George Arents Research Library at Syracuse University; Enoch Pratt Free Library in Baltimore, Maryland; Boston Public Library; Houghton Library, Harvard University; and the Historical Society of Pennsylvania.

James Edwin Campbell

(28 September 1867-26 January 1896)

Lorenzo Thomas
University of Houston/Downtown College

BOOKS: *Driftings and Gleanings* (Charleston, W. Va.: Privately published, 1887);
Echoes from the Cabin and Elsewhere (Chicago: Donohue & Henneberry, 1895).

OTHER: "Negro Serenade" and other poems, in *The Book of American Negro Poetry*, edited by James Weldon Johnson (New York: Harcourt, Brace, 1922), pp. 64-71;
"Ol' Doc' Hyar," "When Ol' Sis' Judy Pray," in *The Negro Caravan*, edited by Sterling A. Brown, Arthur P. Davis, and Ulysses Lee (New York: Dryden, 1941), pp. 316-318.

James Edwin Campbell (courtesy of Schomburg Center for Research in Black Culture, the New York Public Library, Astor, Lenox and Tilden Foundations)

Recognized as the first Afro-American writer to publish a collection of black dialect poems, and described by French critic Jean Wagner as "the most interesting of Dunbar's contemporaries," James Edwin Campbell remains a little-known but fascinating figure. Campbell, writing in the last two decades of the nineteenth century, created charming and eloquent poems that several critics suggest might have served as models for Paul Laurence Dunbar's most popular pieces. Certainly Campbell, a successful educator, helped to popularize Dunbar's early efforts in his region, and both poets shared true mastery of a black theatrical tradition that combined carefully recorded folk idioms, ageless comedy, and moral instruction. Unlike the works of such white southern writers as Joel Chandler Harris and Harry Stillwell Edwards, Campbell's dialect pieces cannot be dismissed as caricature. Campbell's untimely death at the age of twenty-eight and Dunbar's enormous celebrity at the turn of the century have served to obscure his contribution to the black American literary canon, making him, in critic Joan R. Sherman's apt term, an "invisible" poet. "Had he not died young," wrote the editors of *Negro History Bulletin* in 1938, "he would have undoubtedly left a more lasting impression in the literary world."

James Edwin Campbell was born 28 September 1867 in the town of Pomeroy, Ohio. He received an education that acquainted him with the work of William Shakespeare and other classics of literature, and he graduated from Pomeroy High School in 1884. As was the custom of the period, Campbell spent the next two years teaching in a rural school near Gallipolis, Ohio (a town settled by French peasants who responded to an early real estate scam with which the Revolutionary War poet Joel Barlow was unwittingly involved). In 1887 Campbell traveled across the Ohio River to the new state of West Virginia, where he had been invited to head the staff of the *Pioneer,* a black newspaper with statewide distribution. As in Ohio, Campbell supported himself by teaching and by 1890 had become principal of the Langston School at Point Pleasant, where he supervised the construction of a five-story school building.

In March 1891 the state legislature approved plans for a land grant university for black students. Campbell was appointed principal of the new West Virginia Colored Institute (now West Virginia State University) and also became involved in organizing the black state's teachers association. Carter G. Woodson described Campbell as "an orator with gifts not to be despised" and suggested that he was chosen to head the new school because a member of the state board of regents had been impressed by one of Campbell's speeches. Campbell had many opportunities to exercise his gift as he traveled the state exhorting young black men and women on the farms and in the coal mines to consider furthering their education.

Woodson recalled one such speech that he attended when he was a teenaged coal miner. Campbell, he writes, "appeared and made one of his forceful speeches, diplomatically urging upon these people to forsake . . . unbecoming ways and to apply themselves to the development of their minds. His words had immediate effect, and numbers of miners changed in a right-about face, straightened up . . . and attended the West Virginia Colored Institute." Campbell's oratory certainly inspired the young Woodson, who returned to school and, in 1920, served as dean at the institute.

Campbell did not, however, enjoy a long tenure in his post. When he was elected president of the black West Virginia Teachers Association at its 1893 meeting, it is possible that his activist politics created problems with the regents of the institute. He resigned his position at the end of the spring semester in 1894 and moved to Illinois to resume his journalistic career, this time with the *Chicago Times-Herald.* He had attended the Columbian Exposition there in 1893 which afforded him an opportunity to visit with Dunbar, James D. Corrothers, and other writers. In 1895 Campbell traveled to Ohio to spend Christmas with his parents. Perhaps suffering from tuberculosis, James Edwin Campbell died of pneumonia in January 1896 at his parents' home in Pomeroy.

Clearly the move to Chicago refocused Campbell's poetic interests and led him to compile *Echoes from the Cabin and Elsewhere,* which was published in October 1895. It is a collection of poems written over a decade, skillfully arranged in a pleasing and dramatic sequence.

Echoes....
From The Cabin
AND Elsewhere
BY JAMES EDWIN CAMPBELL.
CHICAGO, 1895.

Title page for the poetry collection Campbell dedicated "in loving thought of the lights and shadows of his days" to the "Negro of the Old Regime" (courtesy of Schomburg Center for Research in Black Culture, the New York Public Library, Astor, Lenox and Tilden Foundations)

Like Dunbar, Campbell wrote in both standard English and dialect, and Eugene Redmond feels that "it is in the dialect poems that he shows his power, complexity and originality." Dialogues in black rustic dialect, a comical turn on classical pastoral poetry, were first popularized in the 1840s in minstrel shows performed by white actors in blackface. By the late 1850s several successful black minstrel troupes also traveled across the country. Minstrelry was, according to musicologist Sheldon Harris, "a valuable part of American history and the primary source of entertainment in the period. Audiences may have been segregated but the humor was enjoyed by both black and white and was seen as regional or American humor." Ernest Hogan, Bob Cole, Bert Williams, and other black minstrel artists were also determined to use the popular format to present something more than derogatory images. Redmond suggests that some of their shows were "designed to destroy 'stereotypes' fostered by white minstrels." Similarly, Campbell—dedicating his book "To the Negro of the Old Regime . . . in loving thought"—saw his work as an appreciative extension of the Afro-American oral tradition and attempted to utilize dialect poetry and minstrel conventions as vehicles for the expression of ideas concerning racial progress.

Campbell's dialect poems open the collection and are arranged in the form of the traditional minstrel show's satirical first part; beginning with a modern version of a folktale ("Ol' Doc' Hyar"), we are then invited to enjoy the comic and tragic incidents of Uncle Ephraim Brown's family and neighbors at Mill Creek Dam. The second part of the book—equivalent to the minstrel show's second act, known as the Olio—presents poems in standard English that touch upon classical, philosophical, amatory, and sentimental themes. All of the poems, Richard Linthicum notes in his introduction to Campbell's collection, "are adapted to musical interpretation."

Campbell is a didactic poet but a subtle and entertaining one, and he is drawn to the retelling of standard motifs and simple allegories, such as Br'er Rabbit tales and "Jack and the Beanstalk." Campbell's treatment usually does not add mythic depth to these pieces because his primary interest is audience recognition of the story's broad outline. "Ol' Doc' Hyar," for example, presents the archetypal trickster as a country physician who really doesn't care whether or not his patients get well:

> "Ef pashons git well ur pashons git wu's,
> Money got ter come een de Ol' Hyar's pu's;
> Not wut folkses does, but fur wut dee know
> Does de folkses git paid"—an' Hyar larfed low

Similarly the character of Uncle Eph attempts to live by his wits, but his ploys are not always successful. "The Church Rally" shows Uncle Eph at his best, using his questionable talents to benefit the church building fund. Each family hosts a fundraising event, but Uncle Eph waits until the deadline and announces a possum supper at which he delights in watching his neighbors:

> spen'in de quarters an' de dimes
> Dey raise at cake-walks, fes'buls, dem fan-drills an'
> sich times;
> For wen ur man am hongry he hab no fuchah plan;
> Hit allus so, from Esau cla'r down ter Brudder Mann.

Of course, Uncle Eph is acclaimed on Sunday as the deacon who raised the most money for the new church.

"Uncle Eph Backslides" is a perfect minstrel skit including set-up monologue, a drunken card game accompanied by male chauvinist bravado, and the inevitable comic dissembling when Uncle Eph's devout wife returns home. The poem also includes a delightfully unscrupulous song in which one is warned not to steal—not because stealing is wrong, but because one might get caught.

Campbell's poems in standard English are also written in classical forms on standard themes: a sonnet entitled "Richard III"; and landscape philosophy (such as "Twice the Maple Blushes") in stanzas reminiscent of Thomas Hardy. But the same devotion to models also informs dialect poems, such as "Uncle Eph—Epicure" and "Song Of The Corn" which attempt to redact Latin and Greek classical models such as Virgil's *Georgics* and Hesiod's *Works And Days* for those who eat roast possum and cornpone. The dialect homage to the classics is, as in the case of the ironically titled "Uncle Eph—Epicure," more successful than the standard English exercises. One of Campbell's poems celebrating the bohemian life in Chicago, "Saturday Night At Heinrich's," is notable for espousing interracialism in the midst of Dionysiac revelry: "Here's to all the brown-eyed maids,/Blue-eyed, black-eyed and all shades;/Drink and sing the night away—/Day for work and night for play!" It is the same interracial theme in other poems such as "The Pariah" that has interested some critics.

Joan R. Sherman has suggested that the popularity of dialect poetry such as Campbell's, in the last quarter of the nineteenth century, paralleled a sociopolitical "movement from a militant to an upward-bound and down-home life style in response to societal pressures." It should be noted, however, that militancy has been conceived in different ways. It is clear that, though chided by J. Saunders Redding for providing theme music for "Negro monkeyshines," James Weldon Johnson and other early-twentieth-century poets who brought dialect poetry to Broadway felt that their efforts were of serious—indeed militant—value on a cultural level. Composer Will Marion Cook, who collaborated with Dunbar on the 1898 hit musical *Clorindy; or the Origin of the Cakewalk,* expressed the Afro-American artist's point of view clearly. "Negroes," Cook wrote, "were at last on Broadway, and there to stay. Gone was the uff-dah of the minstrel! Gone the Massa Linkum stuff! We were artists and we were going a long, long way."

Campbell's contribution to dialect verse certainly influenced writers like Dunbar and Johnson and seems, on careful reading, quite in keeping with Cook's idea that the popular style presented artists with an opportunity to express the true meaning of the lives experienced by the masses of black people. It is doubtful, considering Campbell's circuit-riding activities in the black communities of West Virginia, that he (as Dunbar sometimes did) addressed his dialect verse to a white audience. The poems were devised for entertaining and didactic purposes and tailored to the tastes of a black audience that could still actually touch the experience of slavery.

Campbell's finest and most touching poem speaks directly to this audience, though some critics have not entirely understood the poem's significance. A moving and effective allegory, "Linkum," is a dramatic monologue that gives testimony to Dunbar's assertion, in "Sympathy," that there are those who "know why the caged bird sings."

"Linkum," a dialect version of "Lincoln," again features the character of Uncle Eph. He talks about his youngest son who died at the age of ten, rescuing a baby from a fire. The boy was pleasant and gifted:

> He so perlitely mannahed—he *gempman,* dats ur fac'.
> Fur *chile* kin be ur gempman ez well ez folks dat's
> grown,
> An' hit was so wit Linkum, hit des bred in de bone.
> Yit *spite* ob all his goodness he wa'n' no stupid
> chile—
> He roun' de house ur singin' an' whis'lin all de
> w'ile.
> An' saiks how he *could* whis'le! No red bu'd sing so
> cl'ar;
> He could des morck ur pa'tridge twel pa'tridge come
> right dar.

Entrusted with the care of a wealthy white woman's baby, Helen, Linkum is distracted by the music of a traveling minstrel show and dashes off to watch the company's parade down Main Street. A fire breaks out in the house while he is gone, and he rushes back to save the infant:

> De fiah bells wuz janglin', de crowd wus rushin'
> roun',
> De smoke hed filled de sta'rway—hit drove de *bes'*
> man down.
> De women all wuz screamin', an' men ur shoutin' loud,
> W'en lak ur flash ob lightnin' ur boy to' froo de
> crowd.
> Right up de blazin' sta'rway; right froo de smoke an'
> flame,
> Arter dat sleepin' baby—He put dem men ter shame!
> He wropped her in ur blankit an' down de blazin' sta'r
> He brung dat blessed baby

Having rescued the child, the boy dies from burns and "de stranglin' smoke."

"Linkum" is the sort of piece an elocutionist might use as an encore. In Campbell's day the audience for poetry was found at any Sunday dinner, church social, or school assembly where someone skilled in dramatic interpretation was present and prepared to recite. Even Dunbar's popularity among black audiences depended more on that tradition than on the circulation of his books. Over the years, "Linkum" has been highly appreciated, although often misinterpreted. The French critic Jean Wagner sees the poem as a slyly worded celebration of interracial love disguised as a sentimental depiction of stereotypical black devotion to white masters. "And Campbell does not nearly dare to create this tableau, a really audacious action in 1895," Wagner writes, "he actually imagines bonds of affection" between the black boy and the white girl. While Campbell's poem does suggest a certain quality of human caring and the responsibility we share for each other's lives that transcends race or political custom, "Linkum" can only be understood if we can imagine it in the context of its historical period. Certainly the name of the boy, the idea of his self-sacrifice to save someone else's baby, would have evoked for Campbell's audience the martyred president, Abraham Lincoln, and the price he paid—assassination by the hand of the southerner John Wilkes Booth—for emancipating the slaves.

Campbell reverses the historical color scheme in "Linkum" but the allegory is still communicated. The poem's final line is the young boy's epitaph (commissioned a decade later by the girl he rescued): "DE ONE DAT SABED ALL UDDERS, HISSE'F HE COULDN'T SABE." The line would certainly elicit a chorus of quietly thoughtful amens and sober nods of deep understanding from any of Campbell's audiences of rural church deacons and schoolteachers.

"Throughout history," W. E. B. Du Bois wrote in *The Souls of Black Folk* (1903), "the powers of single black men flash here and there like falling stars, and die sometimes before the world has rightly gauged their brightness." The statement might be an appropriate epitaph for James Edwin Campbell.

While Dunbar also died young, he managed to achieve a vast body of work and international recognition; but Campbell's work, until quite recently, has been almost ignored. Anyone who has read Campbell's poems will, however, realize that it is not really antiquarianism that draws contemporary critics to a reconsideration of his work. The humble and extraordinary lyrics of *Echoes from the Cabin and Elsewhere* continue to reward the reader with an unforgettable brightness and charm.

The essence of James Edwin Campbell's work is an energetic optimism that very accurately reflects the generally hopeful and cautiously militant temperament of black Americans at the end of the nineteenth century. His work expresses, through lucid poetic figures, another aspect of the "double consciousness" of the black American in white society described by Du Bois. His view would have been immediately grasped by his audience. In "Before The Fire," Campbell pictures himself seated at "the wide-mouthed hearth" on an inclement evening. It is a standard sentimental turn. But only Campbell would use the moment to meditate upon the allegory of the cave in Plato's *Republic* and create a moving testament to the hopes to which he devoted his own life: "From centuries of prison dark—/A spirit moves each flame I see,/A sunbeam's soul is in each spark." Those who read the poet's lines understand that each spark is meant to light a better way.

References:

"Negro Poets, Singers in the Dawn," *Negro History Bulletin*, 2 (November 1938): 9-10, 14-15;

Eugene Redmond, *Drumvoices: The Mission of Afro-American Poetry* (Garden City: Anchor/Doubleday, 1976), pp. 87-89, 111-113, 116;

Joan R. Sherman, *Invisible Poets: Afro-Americans of the Nineteenth Century* (Urbana: University of Illinois Press, 1974), pp. 186-192;

Jean Wagner, *Black Poets of the United States*, translated by Kenneth Douglas (Urbana: University of Illinois Press, 1973), pp. 129-138;

Carter G. Woodson, "Early Negro Education in West Virginia," *Journal of Negro History*, 7 (January 1922): 23-63;

Woodson, "J. E. Campbell: A Forgotten Man of Letters," *Negro History Bulletin*, 2 (November 1938): 11.

Charles Waddell Chesnutt

William L. Andrews
University of Wisconsin-Madison

See also the Chesnutt entry in *DLB 12, American Realists and Naturalists*.

BIRTH: Cleveland, Ohio, 20 June 1858, to Anne Maria Sampson and Andrew Jackson Chesnutt.

MARRIAGE: 6 June 1878 to Susan Perry; children: Ethel, Helen Maria, Edwin, Dorothy.

AWARDS AND HONORS: Spingarn Medal, 1928.

DEATH: Cleveland, Ohio, 15 November 1932.

SELECTED BOOKS: *The Conjure Woman* (Boston & New York: Houghton Mifflin, 1899; London: Gay & Bird, 1899);

Frederick Douglass (Boston: Small, Maynard, 1899; London: Kegan Paul, Trench & Trubner, 1899);

The Wife of His Youth and Other Stories of the Color Line (Boston & New York: Houghton Mifflin, 1899);

The House Behind the Cedars (Boston & New York: Houghton Mifflin, 1900);

The Marrow of Tradition (Boston & New York: Houghton Mifflin, 1901);

The Colonel's Dream (New York: Doubleday, Page, 1905; London: Constable, 1905);

The Short Fiction of Charles W. Chesnutt, edited by Sylvia Lyons Render (Washington, D.C.: Howard University Press, 1974).

OTHER: "The Disfranchisement [*sic*] of the Negro," in *The Negro Problem: A Series of Articles by Representative American Negroes of To-day*, by Booker T. Washington and others (New York: James Pott, 1903), pp. 79-124.

PERIODICAL PUBLICATIONS: "What Is a White Man?," *Independent*, 51 (30 May 1889): 5-6;

"The Future American: A Complete Race-Amalgamation Likely to Occur," *Boston Evening Transcript*, 1 September 1900, p. 24;

"Superstitions and Folk-Lore of the South," *Modern Culture*, 13 (May 1901): 231-235;

"Peonage, Or the New Slavery," *Voice of the Negro*, 1 (September 1904): 394-397;

"Race Prejudice: Its Cause and Its Cure," *Alexander's Magazine*, 1 (July 1905): 21-26;

"Woman's Rights," *Crisis*, 10 (August 1915): 182-183;

"The Negro in Art: How Shall He Be Portrayed?," *Crisis*, 33 (November 1926): 28-29;

"Post-Bellum—Pre-Harlem," *Colophon*, 2, no. 5 (1931).

Charles Waddell Chesnutt

Charles W. Chesnutt was the first important Afro-American writer of fiction to enlist the white-controlled publishing industry in the service of his social message, touching a significant portion of the white American reading audience with his indictment of American racism. His writing, which appeared during the nadir of Afro-American sociopolitical fortunes, made him a literary advocate for the interests of Afro-Americans with whom he most identified, namely, middle-class mixed-race Americans like himself and working-class blacks of the small-town South, whom he had known from his youth in eastern North Carolina. For this role Chesnutt has been most often remembered and most widely praised. However, he is being increasingly recognized as a literary innovator whose mastery of his craft, especially in the short story, enabled him to place a distinctive personal signature on his public message. Just as Afro-Americans gained from Chesnutt's sensitive analysis and portrayal of their social, economic, and political situation, so American literature was advanced by Chesnutt's literary experiments with the folktale and the novel of miscegenation. Ambitious for national recognition and the financial independence that he believed would accompany literary success, Chesnutt tried his best to find a literary formula that would make him a best-selling popular writer who, nevertheless, would be taken seriously as a thoughtful commentator on social problems. He failed to win an enduring audience for his work in his own time. However, he succeeded in laying the groundwork for twentieth-century literary treatments of the American color line in techniques and metaphors that have still not lost their suggestiveness or validity.

Charles Waddell Chesnutt was born in Cleveland, Ohio, two years before the beginning of the Civil War. His parents, Andrew Jackson and Anne Maria Sampson Chesnutt, were members of antebellum North Carolina's free Negro class, a predominantly middle-class group that included racially mixed individuals. In 1856 Chesnutt's parents had emigrated from their homes in Fayetteville seeking refuge from increasingly oppressive laws against free blacks. They met on a wagon train going north and married in Cleveland in 1857. Charles's father worked as a horse-car conductor until the Civil War, when he enlisted in the Union Army as a teamster. He left his wife with three small boys to raise. By the time he returned in 1866,

Charles, the eldest, had completed two years in the Cleveland public schools. Anne Maria Chesnutt, who had clandestinely taught slaves in North Carolina, felt the city was a good place to raise a family, but her husband wanted to return to Fayetteville where his aging father promised to help set him up in a grocery business. The family resettled in Fayetteville in 1866. When he was not working in the store, young Charles attended the normal school for blacks founded by the Freedman's Bureau in 1865. During this period the Chesnutts had three more children, and in 1871 Anne Maria died. At the age of fourteen Charles took a position at the school as pupil-teacher in order to help with family expenses. His formal education came to an end within the year. He taught briefly in Spartanburg, South Carolina, and then became a full-time teacher in a black school in Charlotte, North Carolina. In what little spare time he had, Chesnutt educated himself further. He taught himself algebra, studied Latin, and read in American history, but the classics of English and European literature were his first love. He began to keep a journal in the summer of 1874, in which he commented on his reading, practiced composition, and ruminated on the idea of the literary life.

Seven-year-old Chesnutt (left) and his brother Lewis (courtesy of Cleveland Public Library)

In 1877 Chesnutt returned to Fayetteville to become a teacher of reading and writing and assistant principal at the normal school. He courted a colleague, Susan Perry, daughter of a prosperous barber in the town, and married her in 1878. For two years they lived with the Perrys, and during this time, in addition to his studies in literature, foreign languages, and music, Chesnutt took up stenography as a way to escape the life in Fayetteville that felt increasingly restrictive to the new family man. His appointment as principal of the normal school in 1880 did not relieve his restlessness. Even the most accomplished Afro-American in the postwar South was still a "nigger," whereas a black man with a skill like stenography might advance himself and provide well for his family in the North. An Afro-American whose features barely distinguished him from whites, the young principal felt his mixed racial heritage was a special social liability in the South. He confided to his journal early in 1881, "I occupy here a position similar to that of Mahomet's Coffin [alleged to be suspended in mid-air]. I am neither fish, flesh, nor fowl—neither 'nigger,' white, nor 'buckrah.' Too 'stuck-up' for the colored folks, and, of course, not recognized by the whites." In the North, he believed, a man would be judged by his ability alone; there, he could live down any prejudice by hard work and perseverance.

Chesnutt intended his particular ticket to a new life in the North to be legal stenography, but when he resigned his position at the normal school in the spring of 1883, he had begun thinking in earnest of pursuing a literary career. In March 1880 he had noted somewhat enviously the attention and the profits that Albion Tourgée, a former judge in Reconstruction North Carolina, was earning as a result of the publication of his autobiographical novel, *A Fool's Errand* (1879). Chesnutt reasoned that if a Yankee carpetbagger with a limited knowledge of southern blacks and racial conditions could make such a mark in the North, then Chesnutt, who had an insider's view of the same subjects, could write as good a book about the South. Chesnutt became convinced that he had an obligation to write. Literary success seemed the best way for him to prove his worth to the world and to achieve for his family the best advantages in life.

In addition, literary work appealed to the crusader in Chesnutt, who believed that if his pen could educate whites out of their "subtle almost indefinable feeling of repulsion toward the Negro," he could strike a telling blow against "the unjust spirit of caste" that had hindered him, his fellow Afro-Americans, and the "moral progress" of white America as a whole. Leaving his growing family, Chesnutt moved to New York City in the summer of 1883 where he worked as a stenographer and reporter for the New York *Mail and Express.* After six months he decided to move to the city of his birth and in 1884, with his family, he settled in Cleveland. Starting as a bookkeeper for the Nickel Plate Railroad Company, Chesnutt was transferred, within a year, to the company's legal division, where he worked as a stenographer. He also began studying law.

Chesnutt's literary career, according to Sylvia Render, began with the 1872 publication of a short story in a local newspaper. Chesnutt's second start was in 1885, when he published his first substantive short story, "Uncle Peter's House," for the S. S. McClure newspaper syndicate. This story and many of his comedic early tales reflect the regional and local color trends that were popular during the late 1800s. Most of Chesnutt's literary labor of that period went into the writing of such humorous sketches and mildly sentimental or didactic squibs for home journals, Sunday supplements, and humor magazines. Having passed the Ohio state bar in 1887, he joined a Cleveland law firm, supporting his family as a court reporter while waiting for his legal practice to grow.

Through his friendship with George W. Cable, the most politically liberal southern literary figure of his time, Chesnutt began writing commentary for the perusal of an association of progressive southerners known as the Open-Letter Club. In one unpublished essay, "An Inside View of the Negro Question," Chesnutt called for an end to all forms of segregation in the South, the immediate granting of equal political and civil rights to blacks, and a genuine biracial partnership in the rebuilding of the South. Cable was impressed by Chesnutt's thinking and his writing. He tried to help Chesnutt get a short story entitled "Rena Walden" into the *Century Magazine;* he was instrumental in the publication of his protégé's first essay, "What Is a White Man?," in the *Independent* in 1889. Cable wanted Chesnutt to become his secretary, but the latter found the court reporting business he had set up too remunerative to put aside. He had also begun to taste success as a short story writer for some of the best American magazines. The tragic fate of a "mixed-blood" like the fictional Rena Walden in the postwar South might not appeal to editors like Richard Watson Gilder of the *Century,* but Thomas Bailey Aldrich of the *Atlantic Monthly* had accepted three less controversial local color stories from the aspiring author. Their setting, the "down-eastern" North Carolina that Chesnutt knew so well, was ripe for literary exploitation, given the rising popularity of southern regional writing. Moreover, by featuring an ex-slave raconteur named Uncle Julius, who could spin wonderful tales about times "befo' de Wah," Chesnutt followed in the tradition of "plantation writers" like Joel Chandler Harris and Thomas Nelson Page who had made their fame writing entertaining stories in Negro dialect. But Chesnutt's first *Atlantic* story, "The Goophered Grapevine" (August 1887), was singular in two respects. Stemming from an oral tale his father-in-law's gardener had told him, Chesnutt's story presented the lore of "conjuration," black hoodoo beliefs and practices, to a white reading public largely ignorant of black folk culture. More important, Uncle Julius displayed a shrewdness and self-interest in adapting his conjure stories to outwit his white employer and secure his own economic advantage. This was a side of Afro-American character local color readers were not accustomed to seeing.

Chesnutt was pleased with Uncle Julius as his entrée into the literary world, but he did not plan to be a local color magazine writer for long. He told Tourgée in an 1889 letter that Julius was "about used up" as a persona and that henceforth he wanted to move out of "the realm of superstition" and dialect and into the "realm of feeling and passion." "The Sheriff 's Children," which the *Independent* published in the fall of 1889, marks this shift in Chesnutt's work. In its emphasis on the consequences of miscegenation, racial hatred, mob violence, and moral compromise in the postwar South, this story was the germ of much of Chesnutt's later protest fiction as well as his first significant study of the mulatto in American life. In "The Sheriff 's Children," the spurned illegitimate son of a North Carolina aristocrat and his slave mistress returns to remind his father of his failure of paternal duty. But the Sheriff 's plans to atone for years of indifference are stymied by his son's suicide, a gesture of hopelessness amply justified by the climactic ironies of the story.

In "The Sheriff 's Children" and "Rena Walden" Chesnutt wrote frankly about the origins, aspirations, and social and psychological dilemmas of

The normal school in Fayetteville, North Carolina, where Chesnutt was successively pupil, teacher, and principal, was on the top floor of this building (courtesy of Cleveland Public Library)

mixed-bloods in the postwar South. Gilder's squeamish reaction to what he termed the "brutality" of Rena and the "lack of mellowness" and humor in the depiction of her life made Chesnutt despair of getting honest fictional discussion of life along the color line into genteel literary magazines. He began to hope for the publication of his short stories in book form and he devoted himself during most of the 1890s to polishing his skills, exploring new literary material, and building a body of short fiction from which a salable book might be taken. In 1897 Walter Hines Page, a senior member of the Houghton Mifflin firm, asked to see all the short fiction that Chesnutt had written. He concluded that his company would be interested in bringing out a collection of Chesnutt's conjure stories if the author would add to his original stock in this genre. Within six weeks of Page's request, Chesnutt sent him a half-dozen new conjure stories. The editor winnowed down the nine stories Chesnutt gave him into a volume of seven stories which opens with "The Goophered Grapevine," Chesnutt's initial conjure tale, and concludes with "Hot-Foot Hannibal," which the *Atlantic* published separately in 1899 as an advertisement for the collection. In March of that year, Charles Chesnutt had his first book, *The Conjure Woman,* under Houghton Mifflin's imprint.

The Conjure Woman was favorably received as a dialect book with a difference. Although the vogue of this kind of regional writing was waning, the character of Uncle Julius, the peculiar blend of realism and fantasy in his plantation reminiscences, and the dramatic byplay between himself and the whites who hear, judge, and record his tales, all pleased Chesnutt's reviewers. It was clear that the author had not tried to romanticize slavery or the slaveholders of the Old South. Unlike the norm of plantation fiction, *The Conjure Woman* evoked a world of mean-spirited, penny-pinching masters

Charles Waddell Chesnutt in 1883 (courtesy of Cleveland Public Library)

whose preoccupation with profit competes with their slaves' resourcefulness in preserving their families and their essential dignity and human identity. Through the magic of conjuration, slaves in "Sis' Becky's Pickaninny," "Mars Jeems's Nightmare," and "Hot-Foot Hannibal" are able to resist successfully the power wielded by their would-be exploiters. There are also tragic stories like "The Conjurer's Revenge" and "The Gray Wolf 's Ha'nt" in which hoodoo power is put to vengeful purposes in internecine struggles between slaves and free blacks. Employing universal folk motifs like metamorphosis and the trickster figure (Uncle Julius), as well as materials specific to the folk beliefs of southern blacks, Chesnutt added a depth to his literary adaptations of folklore not found in the work of writers like Joel Chandler Harris. The black author's ironies are subtle and complex, whether they stem from his explicitly revisionistic image of the Old South or his implicit debunking of the complacent materialism and rationalism of the Progressive Era. By pitting the narrator of *The Conjure Woman,* a literal-minded Ohioan to whom Julius is merely a reciter of quaint "fairy tales," against his wife, who gradually comes to accept the metaphoric truth of Julius's stories, Chesnutt quietly launched his campaign to challenge the social and aesthetic premises on which genteel literary realism had been founded.

Chesnutt did not wait for the reviewers' verdict to come in before urging Houghton Mifflin to publish another of his books. He had much to say about upwardly mobile freemen in the contemporary rural South and urban North, but he had had very little success in placing his stories on these subjects. However, he felt the times were more propitious. "The Wife of His Youth," a story that illuminated the manners and mores of the mulatto subculture in northern metropolitan areas, had drawn an unusual amount of attention since its appearance in the *Atlantic* in 1898. After *The Conjure Woman* came out, word gradually began to spread that this new voice of racial realism belonged to an Afro-American, a fact that Chesnutt had asked his publishers not to mention in their advertising because he wanted his work to be judged on its literary merit alone. Growing public curiosity about Chesnutt, together with the evident popular appeal of *The Conjure Woman,* and the potential audience that "The Wife of His Youth" had uncovered, convinced Houghton Mifflin to announce in September 1899 that plans were afoot for a new collection of Chesnutt stories.

Of the nine stories that make up the contents of *The Wife of His Youth and Other Stories of the Color Line,* only one addresses the antebellum era. "The Passing of Grandison" echoes the Uncle Julius stories in picturing the slave as a trickster who feigns loyalty to his master as a strategem to win freedom for himself and his family. It is a clever burlesque of stylized southern romantic fiction and a sophisticated variation on Chesnutt's characteristic themes of mask-wearing and hoaxing. However, the contemporary color line was the main issue in Chesnutt's second book of stories, and the social, psychological, and moral questions he addressed, required literary techniques different from those applied in the more formulaic conjure stories.

The fundamental social issue, as well as the unifying theme, in most of the stories of *The Wife of His Youth* is miscegenation in America. "The Wife of His Youth," "A Matter of Principle," and, to a lesser extent, "Her Virginia Mammy" analyze with both irony and pathos the racial prejudices of light-skinned, middle-class Afro-Americans in "Groveland," Ohio. Many of Chesnutt's fictional models in these stories were people he knew from his own membership in the Cleveland Social Circle, an exclusive society of upwardly mobile mulattoes who were reputed to discriminate against anyone with complexions darker than their own. "The Wife of His Youth" tells how a leader of the "Blue Veins" triumphs over his class, if not caste, prejudices by acknowledging after decades of separation his dark-skinned plantation wife. In a less pathetic and more satirical case, Chesnutt deflates the racial pretensions of Cicero Clayton, protagonist of "A Matter of Principle," by showing how this mulatto's "principle" of dissociation from all dark-skinned Negroes spoils his daughter's chance for marriage to a light-skinned congressman. In "Her Virginia Mammy," Chesnutt broke with American social mores and literary tradition in his unhysterical depiction of the betrothal of a Boston Brahmin to a Groveland woman unaware of her black ancestry. Despite his recurring use of the theme of the mulatto's predicament, Chesnutt had no desire to be identified as a literary exponent of racial intermixing or "social equality" for its own sake, as "Uncle Wellington's Wives" clearly illustrated. In this exemplum, Chesnutt argued that southern blacks like Wellington, who think that prestige and equality in the North can be had by marrying a white woman, are foolishly deluded. Meaningful and lasting assimilation into the American mainstream, Chesnutt believed, depended on education, preparation, and application, and he used Uncle Wellington's unhappy experiment in northern social equality to underline the necessity of the middle-class work ethic for blacks who wished to get ahead.

However, when Chesnutt turned to the southern scene in stories like "The Sheriff 's Children" and "The Web of Circumstance," he focused on racial problems that resisted his faith in the ameliorative powers of traditional rugged individualism. In "The Web of Circumstance," a former slave tries to pull himself up by his bootstraps via a philosophy of self-help, but a combination of adverse circumstances, racism, and betrayal leave him broken and degraded at the end of the story. His violent death threatens to conclude *The Wife of His Youth* on a despairing note until the narrator adds a prayer for patience and hope in the last paragraph of the book. In such stories as these Chesnutt's own pessimistic reaction to the rise of white supremacist attitudes and the eclipse of black opportunity in the "New South" of the 1890s was manifest. He could not maintain the mask of comic imperturbability that he wore as narrator in stories about the "Blue Veins" like "A Matter of Principle." The urbane Clevelander could play the ironist when surveying isolated examples of color consciousness among mulattoes of his own set. But when the North Carolina expatriate looked southward, where a systematic and cancerous racism threatened the entire social organism, he found it difficult to accommodate his sense of the enormity of the problem and the difficulty of its solution to the forms and techniques of genteel realism. He tried sermonizing, sentimentalizing, and sensationalizing his case studies in southern racial realities. His goal was to find ways to dramatize contemporary racial problems so that they could be seen in the clarifying light of purely ethical considerations, apart from custom, prejudice, or past traditions.

Chesnutt's children, Ethel, Edwin, and Helen, in 1888 (courtesy of Cleveland Public Library)

The Wife of His Youth and Other Stories of the Color Line did not set particularly well with its reviewers or the public. Prominent editors and critics like William Dean Howells and Hamilton Wright Mabie felt Chesnutt's craftsmanship and original subject matter proved him to be a literary realist of the first order. Other reviewers were troubled by Chesnutt's concentration on such cheerless topics as segregation, mob violence, legalized discrimination, and, most obviously, miscegenation, which a few felt Chesnutt was advocating outright. Houghton Mifflin hoped to capitalize on the volume in the Christmas book trade, but by the middle of January 1900, the publisher could report only a little more than a thousand copies sold. Chesnutt could not afford to worry over what this indifferent showing might mean, having closed his court reporting business on 30 September 1899 in order to pursue what had been his lifelong dream, a career as a full-time author. With a comfortable middle-class style of life to maintain and two daughters enrolled at Smith College, Chesnutt could not take this step lightly. But by living frugally on his savings and his modest royalties, he felt he could afford to test the literary waters for two years to see if writing would keep him and his family afloat financially. In addition to his short story collections, he had also written a schoolroom biography of Frederick Douglass for the Beacon Biographies series published by Small, Maynard and Company in Boston. None of these books was likely to make much money for their author, but Chesnutt thought them all useful ways of spreading his name and creating a potential audience for novels he hoped to publish soon.

In late 1899 Chesnutt put two novel manuscripts, "Rena Walden" and "The Rainbow Chasers," into the hands of his editors at Houghton Mifflin. The latter story was an undistinguished novel of entertainment involving white characters only; it seems to have been tailored to appeal to the tastes of the popular reading market, a group Chesnutt felt he needed to reach if he was to be a commercial success. "Rena Walden" was the product of ten years of rethinking, expanding, and revising the story he had shown to Gilder; its subject and theme were probably closer to Chesnutt's heart than anything else he would ever write. On 24 March 1900 Houghton Mifflin rejected "The Rainbow Chasers" but accepted "Rena Walden" with the provision that it be published under the title *The House Behind the Cedars*. Chesnutt knew that the twin subjects of his first novel, miscegenation and passing for white, were too controversial to give the book much chance for a wide sale. But, as he confided to his publisher, he hoped that his "problem novel" would "raise some commotion" for him as an up-and-coming writer who understood such issues, not just as a matter for polemical discussion but also because of "the element of human interest involved."

Chesnutt stated the plot of *The House Behind the Cedars* succinctly: it is "a story of a colored girl who passed for white." The first half of the novel describes the attempt of Rena Walden, product of an illicit union between an antebellum southern gentleman and his light-skinned slave concubine, to assimilate into white upper-class society in a South Carolina town. Her brother, John, who has successfully passed into the white world some years earlier, introduces his demure sister to George Tryon, a Carolina blueblood, who courts her fervently. However, untoward circumstances reveal Rena's background to Tryon, who breaks off the match. In the second half of the story, Rena seeks fulfillment among her "own people" by becoming a country schoolteacher. Increasingly harassed by Tryon and a lecherous mulatto principal, Rena tries to return to the safety of her mother's home but dies as a result of fatigue and exposure.

Cover for Chesnutt's first book

The prospect of racial intermixing as a result of the putative freedom extended to blacks by the 14th and 15th Amendments was an issue that many late nineteenth-century fiction writers, pundits, and politicians discussed. Charles Chesnutt was virtually alone among novelists of his time in treating racially mixed characters like John and Rena Walden as persons who had a morally and socially defensible argument, if not a natural right, to be accepted as white. Such people as the Waldens, who were, like Chesnutt, seven-eighths white, were black only by a "social fiction," Chesnutt declared in a series of articles he wrote for the Boston *Transcript* in the late summer of 1900. So long as white bigotry and Jim Crow legislation barred otherwise aspiring and deserving mulattoes from access to the American Dream, people like the Waldens would be forced to take a clandestine route to dignity and opportunity across the color line.

Chesnutt did not write *The House Behind the Cedars* to advocate miscegenation; he depicted in conventional fashion the tragic consequences of his heroine's attempt to pass for white. He did want to create in his white readers an awareness of and responsiveness to the social, economic, and psychological rationale for mulatto assimilation into mainstream American life. In pursuit of this aim, Chesnutt dispassionately detailed the antebellum conditions that created the liaison between Molly Walden and her white lover, the alien status of the "bright mulatto" class in postwar "Patesville" (Fayetteville), where the Waldens grew up, and the reasons why traditional racial stereotypes and moral categories could not be applied to the Waldens or what they did. Chesnutt did not try to idealize John Walden, but he made sure that Rena's brother was no degenerate, as popular mythology judged the mixed-blood to be. As a result, John Walden became one of the few convincingly portrayed mulattoes in late nineteenth-century American fiction. The characterization of his sister departed less from the literary convention of the "tragic mulatto," but in his attempt to arouse sympathy for his heroine, Chesnutt never had Rena indulge in self-hatred or disgust toward what most whites would have judged as her "tainted" blood. Chesnutt personally detested the implication of most fiction dealing with the mulatto—that people like himself were social invalids who, having no self-respect, tried to become white in order to hide their shame over mixed ancestry. Many years earlier, Chesnutt had decided not to pass for white, though he could have done so, because he was unwilling to deny his past, his family, or the people among whom he had grown up. Yet he knew other mixed-bloods who had chosen the white world, and he could sympathize with them. *The House Behind the Cedars* was his literary memorial to these people, to what he termed their "courage" as well as the often tragic outcome of their strivings. The novel traces the source of their misfortune not to their supposedly "tainted" blood or to the immutable laws of God but to the unjust customs and unreasoned prejudices of man.

Chesnutt's first novel had a modest sales record, but critics and reviewers judged it successful insofar as its restrained and judicious treatment of an often-sensationalized social question was concerned. As a novel of purpose, the book was remarkably subdued and unpolemical; its artfulness lay primarily in the disarming way the mulatto and his social options were characterized. The concessions it made to literary clichés and popular sentiment, especially in its conclusion, were the price Chesnutt had to pay to get this, his favorite literary child, before the American reading public. No sooner had *The House Behind the Cedars* appeared than both Houghton Mifflin and Harpers requested a second novel from Chesnutt. Chesnutt was convinced that the time was ripe for a problem novel on a major racial issue of immediate concern. For two years he had been gathering information about the Wilmington, North Carolina, race riot of 1898, in which more than a score of black people had been killed and the town government overthrown by a cadre of white supremacists. In February 1901 he set out on a kind of fact-finding mission to Wilmington and the Cape Fear region of North Carolina, where he had not visited for seventeen years. He lectured and gave readings in Fayetteville, Charlotte, and Greensboro. He spent enough time at both Tuskegee Institute and Atlanta University to write favorable articles about each. By the time he returned home, Chesnutt felt prepared to write a book about the New South which he hoped would be as influential and as widely selling as *Uncle Tom's Cabin* had been about the Old.

On 27 October 1901, Houghton Mifflin published Chesnutt's magnum opus, *The Marrow of Tradition.* It incorporates his most sweeping image of the small-town South and his most probing analysis of the causes and the effects of the South's racial and social situation. The novel contains the largest and most diverse cast of characters, the most complicated plotting, and the most problematic themes that Chesnutt would ever ponder in one literary work. The main thread of action knits together the lives of two families in "Wellington," North Carolina: the Carterets, who represent the New South aristocracy, and the Millers, a mixed-blood couple who embody Chesnutt's idea of the progressive

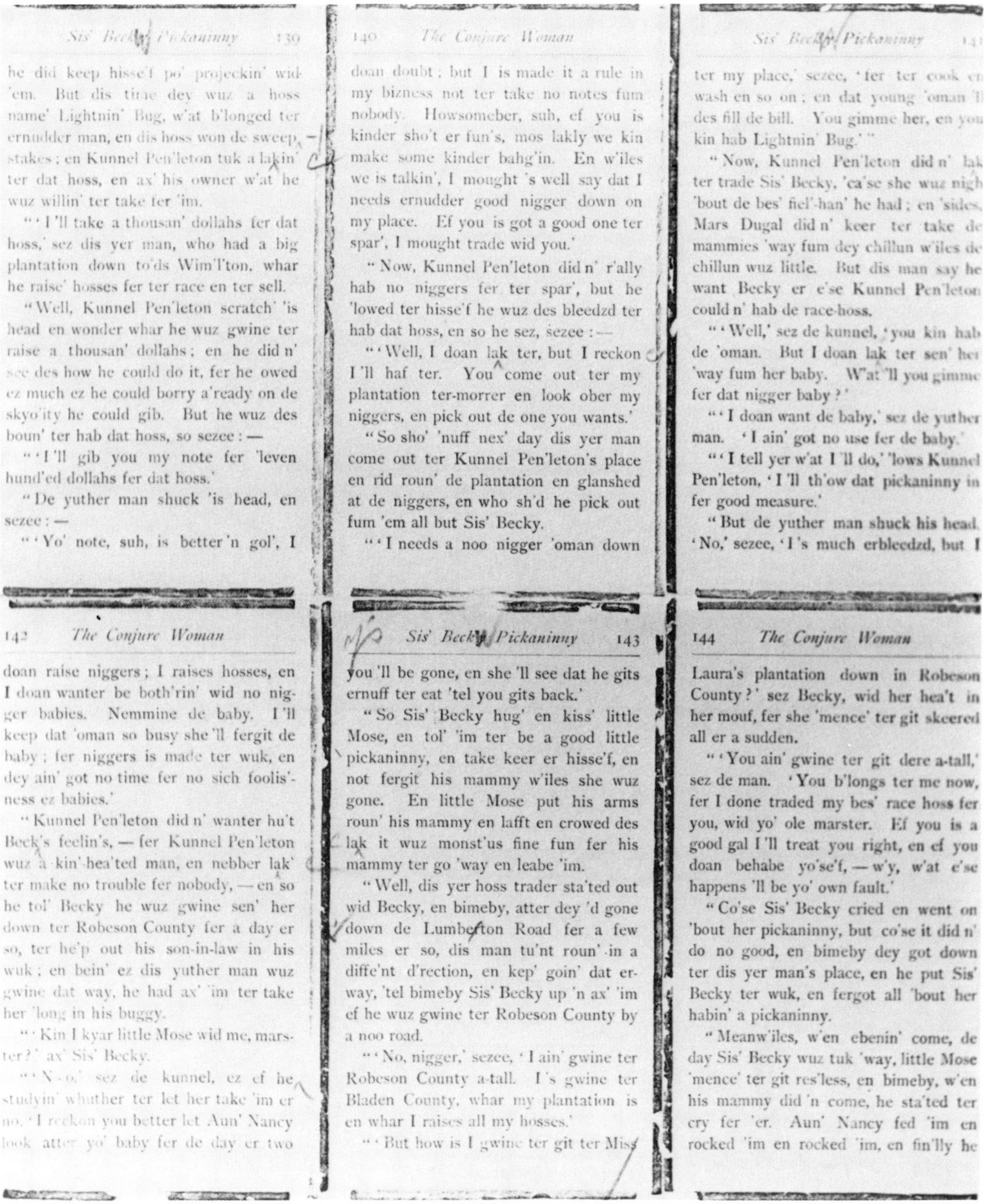
Sis' Becky's Pickaninny 139

he did keep hisse'f po' projeckin' wid 'em. But dis time dey wuz a hoss name' Lightnin' Bug, w'at b'longed ter ernudder man, en dis hoss won de sweep-stakes; en Kunnel Pen'leton tuk a likin' ter dat hoss, en ax' his owner w'at he wuz willin' ter take fer 'im.

"'I'll take a thousan' dollahs fer dat hoss,' sez dis yer man, who had a big plantation down to'ds Wim'l'ton, whar he raise' hosses fer ter race en ter sell.

"Well, Kunnel Pen'leton scratch' 'is head en wonder whar he wuz gwine ter raise a thousan' dollahs; en he did n' see des how he could do it, fer he owed ez much ez he could borry a'ready on de skyo'ity he could gib. But he wuz des boun' ter hab dat hoss, so sezee: —

"'I'll gib you my note fer 'leven hund'ed dollahs fer dat hoss.'

"De yuther man shuck 'is head, en sezee: —

"'Yo' note, suh, is better'n gol', I

140 The Conjure Woman

doan doubt; but I is made it a rule in my bizness not ter take no notes fum nobody. Howsomeber, suh, ef you is kinder sho't er fun's, mos lakly we kin make some kinder bahg'in. En w'iles we is talkin', I mought 's well say dat I needs ernudder good nigger down on my place. Ef you is got a good one ter spar', I mought trade wid you.'

"Now, Kunnel Pen'leton did n' r'ally hab no niggers fer ter spar', but he 'lowed ter hisse'f he wuz des bleedzd ter hab dat hoss, en so he sez, sezee: —

"'Well, I doan lak ter, but I reckon I'll haf ter. You come out ter my plantation ter-morrer en look ober my niggers, en pick out de one you wants.'

"So sho' 'nuff nex' day dis yer man come out ter Kunnel Pen'leton's place en rid roun' de plantation en glanshed at de niggers, en who sh'd he pick out fum 'em all but Sis' Becky.

"'I needs a noo nigger 'oman down

Sis' Becky's Pickaninny 141

ter my place,' sezee, 'fer ter cook en wash en so on; en dat young 'oman 'll des fill de bill. You gimme her, en you kin hab Lightnin' Bug.'"

"Now, Kunnel Pen'leton did n' lak ter trade Sis' Becky, 'ca'se she wuz nigh 'bout de bes' fiel'-han' he had; en 'sides, Mars Dugal did n' keer ter take de mammies 'way fum dey chillun w'iles de chillun wuz little. But dis man say he want Becky er e'se Kunnel Pen'leton could n' hab de race-hoss.

"'Well,' sez de kunnel, 'you kin hab de 'oman. But I doan lak ter sen' her 'way fum her baby. W'at 'll you gimme fer dat nigger baby?'

"'I doan want de baby,' sez de yuther man. 'I ain' got no use fer de baby.'

"'I tell yer w'at I 'll do,' 'lows Kunnel Pen'leton, 'I 'll th'ow dat pickaninny in fer good measure.'

"But de yuther man shuck his head. 'No,' sezee, 'I's much erbleedzd, but I

142 The Conjure Woman

doan raise niggers; I raises hosses, en I doan wanter be both'rin' wid no nigger babies. Nemmine de baby. I'll keep dat 'oman so busy she 'll fergit de baby; fer niggers is made ter wuk, en dey ain' got no time fer no sich foolis'-ness ez babies.'

"Kunnel Pen'leton did n' wanter hu't Becky's feelin's, — fer Kunnel Pen'leton wuz a kin'-hea'ted man, en nebber lak' ter make no trouble fer nobody, — en so he tol' Becky he wuz gwine sen' her down ter Robeson County fer a day er so, ter he'p out his son-in-law in his wuk; en bein' ez dis yuther man wuz gwine dat way, he had ax' 'im ter take her 'long in his buggy.

"'Kin I kyar little Mose wid me, mars-ter?' ax' Sis' Becky.

"'N-o,' sez de kunnel, ez ef he studyin' whether ter let her take 'im er no, 'I reckon you better let Aun' Nancy look atter yo' baby fer de day er two

Sis' Becky's Pickaninny 143

you 'll be gone, en she 'll see dat he gits ernuff ter eat 'tel you gits back.'

"So Sis' Becky hug' en kiss' little Mose, en tol' 'im ter be a good little pickaninny, en take keer er hisse'f, en not fergit his mammy w'iles she wuz gone. En little Mose put his arms roun' his mammy en lafft en crowed des lak it wuz monst'us fine fun fer his mammy ter go 'way en leabe 'im.

"Well, dis yer hoss trader sta'ted out wid Becky, en bimeby, atter dey 'd gone down de Lumberton Road fer a few miles er so, dis man tu'nt roun' in a diffe'nt d'rection, en kep' goin' dat er-way, 'tel bimeby Sis' Becky up 'n ax' 'im ef he wuz gwine ter Robeson County by a noo road.

"'No, nigger,' sezee, 'I ain' gwine ter Robeson County a-tall. I 's gwine ter Bladen County, whar my plantation is en whar I raises all my hosses.'

"'But how is I gwine ter git ter Miss

144 The Conjure Woman

Laura's plantation down in Robeson County?' sez Becky, wid her hea't in her mouf, fer she 'mence' ter git skeered all er a sudden.

"'You ain' gwine ter git dere a-tall,' sez de man. 'You b'longs ter me now, fer I done traded my bes' race hoss fer you, wid yo' ole marster. Ef you is a good gal I'll treat you right, en ef you doan behabe yo'se'f, — w'y, w'at e'se happens 'll be yo' own fault.'

"Co'se Sis' Becky cried en went on 'bout her pickaninny, but co'se it did n' do no good, en bimeby dey got down ter dis yer man's place, en he put Sis' Becky ter wuk, en fergot all 'bout her habin' a pickaninny.

"Meanw'iles, w'en ebenin' come, de day Sis' Becky wuz tuk 'way, little Mose 'mence' ter git res'less, en bimeby, w'en his mammy did 'n come, he sta'ted ter cry fer 'er. Aun' Nancy fed 'im en rocked 'im en rocked 'im, en fin'lly he

Page proofs for The Conjure Woman *corrected by Chesnutt (courtesy of Cleveland Public Library)*

New Negro. As editor of Wellington's white newspaper, Philip Carteret pursues an editorial policy of Negro defamation while conspiring with other reactionaries to take over the town's government. Eventually his efforts lead to a race riot in which Dr. Adam Miller's son is killed. Then, Carteret is forced to request Miller's professional attention for his own ill child; Miller at first refuses, recalling the many social slights the Carterets have shown him and his wife (who is Mrs. Carteret's half-sister). The riot has also destroyed the hospital that symbolizes Miller's progressive approach to the race problem in Wellington. After reconsidering his position, however, Miller puts vengeance aside and resumes his role as Wellington's healing agent.

Several subplots and a dozen significant though minor characters enable Chesnutt to present a wide spectrum of southern racial opinion and class identity. Appearing in the novel are an old-fashioned black "mammy," a fawning "white man's nigger," an "ideal old aristocrat" and his loyal black retainer, a "degenerate aristocrat," a former Klan leader who is poor white trash, a beautiful southern belle, a vengeful black resistance fighter, a young, Quaker-born southern liberal; all play rather predictable parts as demonstration vehicles for general truths and opinions about the southern social scene. Chesnutt's predilection for pairing characters with their foils, for balancing types with antitypes dramatizes his perception of the turn-of-the-century South as poised on the edge of a historical watershed. An optimist, Chesnutt liked to pronounce "the present anti-Negro legislation" as "but a temporary reaction," to be reversed inevitably by the steady evolution of white and black in America toward a higher type of civilization and a finer type of citizen. But he could not ignore daily evidence suggesting that the post-Reconstruction South was steadily sliding backward toward its now-discredited traditions. In the writing of southern apologists like Thomas Nelson Page and Thomas Dixon, these old traditions—especially white supremacy, black subjugation, and the aristocratic monopoly of power—were given a literary face-lift, so that unreconstructed Dixie could pose as the "redeemed" and "reconciled" New South. One of the major purposes of Chesnutt's second novel was to tear away the New South's mask of progressivism to reveal the corrupt marrow of its guiding traditions and principles. In an atmosphere of intimidation and violence, naked power politics, and ever-widening racial polarization, the South had little chance of reforming itself, Chesnutt believed, unless the national conscience could be galvanized in support of the region's embattled progressive forces. These forces are symbolized by Miller. "There's time enough, but none to spare," Miller is told at the close of the novel as he enters Carteret's house on his mercy mission. This was the sum of *The Marrow of Tradition*'s urgent plea for moral action from white America.

Hoping for sales of twenty to thirty thousand, Chesnutt was very disappointed to learn from his publisher that *The Marrow of Tradition* had sold fewer than five thousand copies in the first two months after publication, despite an energetic advertising campaign. He knew the book would be controversial; he expected an outcry from southern critics. But he did not anticipate the division that developed among northern reviewers, who could not agree on whether Chesnutt had been fair to the South and on whether he was a social realist or just a bitter pessimist. Even a previously supportive William Dean Howells was unsettled and ambivalent about the novel. The fact that few complained about the book's workmanship or the power of its writing led Chesnutt to conclude that his subject matter and moral thesis were what had doomed the book. "I am beginning to suspect," he told his publishers, "that the public as a rule does not care for books in which the principal characters are colored people, or written with a striking sympathy with that race as contrasted to the white race." He also admitted to Houghton Mifflin that his friends had advised him not to write any more race problem novels for a while since they felt in his latest book he had drawn "perilously near" the "line between zeal and fanaticism." For the present, his goal of supporting his family with his pen seemed unreachable. Thus, in 1902 Chesnutt reopened his court reporting business.

Chesnutt had not renounced his literary ambitions; he had only placed them in temporary abeyance. While he rebuilt his financial base, he continued to write in his spare time. His public comments on racial conditions were confined to essays, the most important of which was "The Disfranchisement [*sic*] of the Negro," which appeared in a collection, *The Negro Problem: A Series of Articles by Representative American Negroes of To-day* (1903). While two of his fellow contributors to this symposium, Booker T. Washington and W. E. B. Du Bois, argued their opposing solutions to the problem—the Tuskegee plan of industrial training versus the Du Bois program of higher education for the "talented tenth," the best black minds, Chesnutt urged full restoration of the right of suffrage as the only lasting guarantee of black advancement.

Characteristically he refused to ally himself finally to either the "Bookerite" or the "Anti-Bookerite" faction in Afro-American leadership, preferring not to become identified as a spokesman for either camp since he had philosophical affinities with both. In 1903 Chesnutt wrote "Evelyn's Husband," a novel of entertainment centering on a love triangle among a group of white, upper-class Bostonians. It did not find a publisher. Like "The Rainbow Chasers," this new bid for commercial success in a mode completely removed from the racial scene had little to recommend it. Its rejection placed Chesnutt in something of a dilemma. He had been able to publish serious problem novels about racial conditions in the South, but there seemed little hope of their appealing to the public at large. He had tried to rectify this situation by writing entertaining noncontroversial novels about the romantic adversities of whites in the North, but he could not get them past an editor. In the winter of 1903-1904, Chesnutt decided to return to the short story, a form he knew well and one that had brought him his first recognition. The result was "Baxter's Procrustes," the author's best-crafted work of short fiction and the last story he would publish in the *Atlantic.*

Although "Baxter's Procrustes" is another of Chesnutt's nonracial stories, it has much in common with his earlier conjure and color line stories. Like the Uncle Julius tales, "Baxter's Procrustes" is a hoax story. Its protagonist, an enigmatic dilettante and sometime writer named Baxter, is a con artist and trickster like Julius. Baxter's victims are the members of the Bodleian Club, an all-male organization of well-heeled bibliophiles whose ostensible love of literary classics is rooted in the dollar-consciousness that makes fine books a wise investment. Baxter contrives a strategem that exposes the misplaced priorities of his fellow-Bodleians. In the process, Chesnutt satirizes the Bodleians' self-delusions as he had satirized the social pretensions of another exclusive society, the Groveland Blue Veins. Like the Blue Veins, the Bodleians were patterned after a social club in Cleveland that Chesnutt identified with, though not without an awareness of their excesses and foolish prejudices. Cleveland's Rowfant Club, a fraternity of white, upper-class book lovers and collectors founded in 1892, undoubtedly recognized themselves when they read "Baxter's Procrustes" in the June 1904 issue of the *Atlantic.* Two years earlier they had denied the author membership in their club because of the racial prejudice of a few of the Rowfanters. Chesnutt created Baxter as his means of unmasking those Rowfanters who claimed to respect culture and humane letters but who actually cared much more for appearances. The tone of the story and its deft ironies showed that it had been conceived as a literary riposte, not an exercise in revenge. In 1910 Chesnutt authorized and accepted a second nomination for membership in the club, and he took an active part in it in subsequent years.

In the spring of 1904 Chesnutt completed a draft of a new race problem novel, *The Colonel's Dream,* which he immediately offered to Houghton Mifflin. The firm thought well of the manuscript but did not wish to commit themselves to another of Chesnutt's race novels, having suffered a net loss on the Afro-American author's four previous books. Walter Hines Page, a senior partner in the then recently formed Doubleday, Page and Company, was willing to publish the book, but he requested much revision and development of the story before he felt it was ready for the public. Chesnutt was compliant; he hoped that with Page's guidance he might yet write a novel of purpose about the South that would rescue his literary reputation. In this new book, Chesnutt tried to enhance white identification with his protagonist by making him a white man, an enlightened ex-Confederate officer who has made himself rich as a northern manufacturer without losing his aristocratic sense of *noblesse oblige.* Colonel French's return to his native North Carolina for health reasons reintroduces him to the land of his birth, now languishing in a social, cultural, and economic depression. Like many other heroes of economic novels during the Progressive Era, French optimistically sets about reforming the inadequate, often exploitative systems of education and production in his region. Resistance steadily mounts from Bill Fetters, a corrupt economic and political boss whose control over blacks and poor whites has reduced both classes to virtual servitude. In the end, the Colonel gives up his dream in despair and, with the handful of other forward-looking southerners in the novel, returns to the North.

The Colonel's Dream was the final volume of what might now be termed Charles Chesnutt's New South trilogy. Each of the previously published novels tests out a certain means of alleviating the caste consciousness and racial injustice that Chesnutt believed was endemic in the South. In *The House Behind the Cedars,* the strategies of the Waldens are shown to be very risky, often self-defeating ways of gaining social rights and opportunities. In *The Marrow of Tradition,* both violent resistance and diplomatic accommodation are

Cover for Chesnutt's first novel, which was published in 1900

weighed as alternatives for southern blacks. At the end of the novel, neither alternative proves itself capable of stopping the rise of institutionalized racial repression in the postwar South.

The Colonel's Dream asks whether white philanthropy, cooperative enterprise, and the pursuit of enlightened self-interest between whites and blacks could raise the socioeconomic prospects of everyone in the New South, thus creating a climate in which racial justice might wax and thrive. These were panaceas proposed by many observers of the southern scene in the late nineteenth and early twentieth centuries. In articles, speeches, and letters, Chesnutt personally subscribed to several of Colonel French's programs for combatting the social and economic ills of the New South. His hero sponsors an industrial school on the Tuskegee model, employs blacks in the rebuilding of a textile mill, attacks black peonage in the courts, and tries to soothe white suspicions and fears with reasoned appeals to fair play and good business. Yet, for all his moderation and well-intentioned progressivism, French is a loser largely because he fails to realize until the end of the novel that piecemeal reforms in education, economics, and civil rights cannot cure the fundamental moral and intellectual blight of racism. Fetters's barbaric retaliation on his idealistic campaign reveals to French that "the very standards of right and wrong had been confused by the race issue." "A new body of thought must be built up," French concludes, but he never discovers a way to do this. Neither did Chesnutt, except in the creation of novels like *The Colonel's Dream.* His last race problem novel was the most undeluded and thoroughgoing exposé of the New South myth in the literature of his day. Much of his analysis of the region's problems has been borne out by subsequent historical investigation, qualifying Chesnutt as one of the precursors of twentieth-century southern literary realism; but, it is unlikely that he took much comfort from the few reviewers who praised his "almost Flaubertian" detail in recording the ugly facts of southern mill-town life. Those critics who commented on the book at all felt it was too pessimistic and unpleasant to recommend to their readers. Consequently, in 1905 Chesnutt, like his hero in *The Colonel's Dream,* took his leave of the New South in literature as he had done twenty years before in life.

After it became clear to Chesnutt that the last of his problem novels would not spark any new interest in the issues he cared most about, he tried a new literary tack in 1906. He copyrighted a four-act play entitled "Mrs. Darcy's Daughter" and tried to find a producer for it in New York. No one was interested in Chesnutt's genteel melodrama of crime and detection, however. Like his other non-racial works, the play was well-written insofar as it conformed to the conventions of its genre, but it lacked originality. After *The Colonel's Dream,* Chesnutt became involved in social and political activities that drew his attention away from literature because he had to devote time to writing speeches, position papers, and argumentative prose. He joined the Committee of Twelve, founded by Booker T. Washington for the purpose of preparing speeches and circulating printed matter that treated black people sympathetically in order to correct public misinterpretation of their cause. This seeming alliance with the Tuskegeean did not prevent Chesnutt from supporting the rival Niagara Movement or from serving on its central committee. He continued to stress in public statements and private correspondence the necessity of predicating the reform of southern racial conditions on restoration of the suffrage to blacks of that region. In several articles and speeches he foresaw the ultimate solution to the American race problem in the intermarriage and amalgamation of blacks and whites into one undifferentiated race. He was suspicious of what he termed the "new doctrine—that of Race Integrity" among blacks, judging it as merely another way of perpetuating the color line. In his more philosophical moods Chesnutt felt that racial separation would inevitably disappear as the melting pot principle in America took its inexorable course. In the meantime, he fought caste consciousness and color barriers wherever he found them, whether in anti-intermarriage bills, Cleveland settlement houses, army training methods in the South, or popular films, such as *The Birth of a Nation* (1915).

In the decade that followed the publication of *The Colonel's Dream,* Chesnutt became established as a leading citizen of Cleveland. He became a member of the Chamber of Commerce, the City Club, and the Rowfant Club; he presided over the Cleveland Council of Sociology and served on the General Committee of the National Association for the Advancement of Colored People. His revived court reporting business flourished. He lived affluently, sending his son Edwin to Harvard, and his youngest daughter Dorothy to Western Reserve University. He suffered a mild stroke in June 1910, but his illness did not prevent him from making his second trip abroad two years later. Still, his stamina for after-hours literary work decreased as the business and community activities and social causes that absorbed him displaced his ambition for literary recognition. Between publication of *The Colonel's Dream* and the end of World War I, Chesnutt published only three negligible short stories. His writing appeared most often in local Cleveland outlets and in the Afro-American periodical press, especially the *Crisis,* whose editor, W. E. B. Du Bois, was always pleased to publish a writer he admired so much.

The 1920s saw some belated recognition come to Chesnutt for his pioneering literary labors at the turn of the century. In 1921 the black filmmaker Oscar Micheaux bought the rights to *The House Behind the Cedars;* with a happy instead of tragic ending, the film version of the novel played for black theater audiences in the early 1920s. The Chicago *Defender* serialized Chesnutt's first novel in 1922, putting the book back in print for the first time in over fifteen years. Another film company paid for the right to produce *The Marrow of Tradition,* but nothing came of these plans. Chesnutt kept his eye on the rise of the new Harlem school of writers, whom he welcomed in theory but often scolded in practice. He told a 1926 *Crisis* symposium on "The Negro in Art: How Shall He Be Portrayed?" that there should be no boundaries on subject matter in race literature. Black writers should feel free to write about "Negro characters in the underworld, so long as they do it well." The dean of Afro-American writers hoped that the New Negro movement in literature would not forget to record "the real romance, the worthy ambition, the broad humanity" of black folk in all social classes. But when he read books like Claude McKay's *Home to Harlem* (1928) and Wallace Thurman's *The Blacker the Berry* (1929), he found much to condemn in their failure to portray anything "noble" or "heroic" in either the black lower classes or the mulatto middle classes. With Du Bois and William Stanley Braithwaite, Chesnutt fought a rear-guard action in the 1920s against the aesthetic and social iconoclasts of the Harlem Renaissance. At the beginning and end of the decade, he wrote novels extolling the virtues of ostensibly mixed-blood heroes who, on discovering they are actually white, choose to remain "Negroes" rather than compromise themselves morally by accepting wealth and position in the more favored caste. The publishers who rejected "Paul Marchand, F. M. C." in 1921 judged the story foreign in setting, characterization, and theme to the social realities of Jazz Age America. In "The Quarry," Chesnutt updated his plot to the 1920s, introduced a number of topical allusions to current racial issues, and tried to sound less Victorian in his treatment of sex and the fast life among contemporary blacks. Still, as Houghton Mifflin told him in 1930, the manuscript sounded too much like a thesis novel headed by a high-minded hero with whom few could identify, white or black. From a clear-sighted, often ironic analyst of the embryonic mulatto middle class at the turn of the century Chesnutt had evolved into a somewhat tunnel-visioned literary apologist for the entrenched "talented tenth" in the 1920s. When he took up his pen as a belletristic writer, he could not seem to get beyond his well-worn themes and motifs—the "tainted" past, the stolen birthright, the undeservedly wronged mulatto, and the moral problem of his divided racial heritage and loyalties. At the heart of "Mrs. Darcy's Daughter," "Paul Marchand, F. M. C.," and "The Quarry," as well as Chesnutt's last published story, "Concerning Father" (*Crisis,* May 1930), lies the tragedy of Rena Walden, which Chesnutt tried to resolve comically in almost all the writing of his last twenty-five years. His failure to reach an artistic resolution of the mixed-blood's divided identity, except through what amounts to exercises in literary avoidance and wish-fulfillment, lends support to the notion of Chesnutt as ultimately a frustrated and in many ways unfulfilled writer.

Charles Chesnutt's literary triumphs were real, however, and not inconsiderable. In 1928 the NAACP awarded him its Spingarn Medal for his "pioneer work as a literary artist depicting the life and struggles of Americans of Negro descent, and for his long and useful career as scholar, worker, and freeman of one of America's greatest cities." The next year Houghton Mifflin reprinted *The Conjure Woman* in a handsome deluxe edition that put Chesnutt back in print thirty years after he had first become an author. When he died on 15 November 1932, he was a neglected but by no means forgotten literary figure, especially in black America, where his books had become classics. A year before his death, Chesnutt reckoned some of the gains and losses of his artistic career in "Post-Bellum—Pre-Harlem," an essay in literary autobiography that appeared in the fifth issue of the *Colophon* (1931). He accepted the fact that literary fashion had passed him by, but he took pride in pointing out how far Afro-American literature and the attitude of the white American literary world had come since the days when he first broke into print. Once he had been virtually the only representative of black America to write seriously about the Negro in fiction. He had devoted most of his artistic efforts to reorienting the literary and social consciousness of his era toward what he perceived as the real issues of race in America, not the pseudo-issues raised by most of his white literary contemporaries. He had lived to see the field of

Chesnutt in his study at 9719 Lamont Avenue, Cleveland (courtesy of Cleveland Public Library)

Afro-American fiction crowded with bold and talented writers who enjoyed a public following far greater than any he had ever known. Chesnutt could have claimed an important role in preparing the public mind in America for the advent of the New Negro author of the 1920s, for in a basic sense, the new movement followed his precedent in unmasking the false poses and images of their era in order to refocus public attention on the reality of race experience in their America.

Almost singlehandedly, Charles Chesnutt established a truly Afro-American literary tradition in the short story and the novel. He was the first to make the broad range of Afro-American experience his artistic bailiwick and to consider practically everything therein to be worthy of treatment. Because of this conviction, he initiated Afro-American belletristic writing about many aspects of the post-Civil War black experience. Chesnutt not only surveyed the literary topography of Afro-American life; he also assayed some of its richest sociopsychological veins. Because he was concerned with finding literary modes appropriate to his materials, he left his successors examples of the uses of ironic distance in an Afro-American fiction of manners, a sense of the romance of black folk culture, a concept of tragedy for a people heretofore regarded as merely grotesque or pitiable, and a recognition of the genuinely comic potential for the black writer as manipulator and hoaxer, instead of sentimental entertainer of his white audience. This was a rich artistic legacy for twentieth-century Afro-American literature. In his own era, Chesnutt's achievement can be summed up more succinctly: it was he who taught white America for the first time to respect a black fiction writer as a critical realist, even if this meant it could not embrace him as a literary native son.

Biographies:

Helen M. Chesnutt, *Charles Waddell Chesnutt: Pioneer of the Color Line* (Chapel Hill: University of North Carolina Press, 1952);

Frances Richardson Keller, *An American Crusade: The Life of Charles Waddell Chesnutt* (Provo: Brigham Young University Press, 1978).

References:

William L. Andrews, *The Literary Career of Charles W. Chesnutt* (Baton Rouge: Louisiana State University Press, 1980);

Andrews, "William Dean Howells and Charles W. Chesnutt: Criticism and Race Fiction in the Age of Booker T. Washington," *American Literature,* 48 (November 1976): 327-339;

Richard E. Baldwin, "The Art of *The Conjure Woman,*" *American Literature,* 43 (November 1971): 385-398;

Robert Bone, *Down Home: Pastoral Impulse in Afro-American Short Fiction* (New York: Putnam's, 1975);

Curtis W. Ellison and E. W. Metcalf, Jr., *Charles W. Chesnutt: A Reference Guide* (Boston: G. K. Hall, 1977);

Donald B. Gibson, "Charles W. Chesnutt: The Anatomy of a Dream," in *Politics of Literary Expression: A Study of Major Black Writers* (Westport, Conn.: Greenwood, 1981), pp. 125-154;

J. Noel Heermance, *Charles W. Chesnutt: America's First Great Black Novelist* (Hamden, Conn.: Shoe String Press, 1974);

Robert E. Hemenway, " 'Baxter's Procrustes': Irony and Protest," *CLA Journal,* 18 (December 1974): 172-185;

Hemenway, "The Functions of Folklore in Charles Chesnutt's *The Conjure Woman,*" *Journal of the Folklore Institute,* 13, no. 3 (1976): 283-309;

William Dean Howells, "Mr. Charles W. Chesnutt's Stories," *Atlantic Monthly,* 85 (May 1900): 699-701;

Julian D. Mason, "Charles W. Chesnutt as Southern Author," *Mississippi Quarterly,* 20 (Spring 1967): 77-89;

Sylvia Lyons Render, *Charles W. Chesnutt* (Boston: Twayne, 1980);

Robert P. Sedlack, "The Evolution of Charles Chesnutt's *The House Behind the Cedars,*" *CLA Journal,* 19 (December 1975): 125-135;

Eugene Terry, "Charles W. Chesnutt: A Victim of the Color Line," *Contributions to Black Studies,* 1, no. 1 (1977): 15-44;

John Wideman, "Charles W. Chesnutt: *The Marrow of Tradition,*" *American Scholar,* 42 (Winter 1972-1973): 128-134.

Papers:

The Charles Waddell Chesnutt Collection of the Erastus Milo Cravath Memorial Library, Fisk University, contains Chesnutt's unpublished journals, letters, and novels. The Library of the Western Reserve Historical Society in Cleveland also contains a significant number of Chesnutt manuscripts and letters.

James D. Corrothers

(2 July 1869-12 February 1917)

Richard Yarborough
University of California, Los Angeles

BOOKS: *The Black Cat Club* (New York & London: Funk & Wagnalls, 1902);
In Spite of the Handicap (New York: Doran, 1916).

PERIODICAL PUBLICATIONS:
POETRY
" 'Way in de Woods, an' Nobody Dar," *Century,* 57 (April 1899): 959;
"A Dixie Thanksgivin'," *Century,* 59 (November 1899): 160;
"Me 'N' Dunbar," *Colored American,* 3 (July 1901): 163-164;
"An Awful Problem Solved," *Colored American,* 6 (November 1903): 793-795;
"Paul Laurence Dunbar," *Century,* 85 (November 1912): 56;
"The Negro Singer," *Century,* 85 (November 1912): 56;
"At the Closed Gate of Justice," *Century,* 86 (June 1913): 272;
"The Dream and the Song," *Century,* 87 (January 1914): 398;
"In the Matter of Two Men," *Crisis,* 9 (January 1915): 138;
"The Black Man's Soul," *Crisis,* 10 (October 1915): 304, 306;
"An Indignation Dinner," *Century,* 91 (December 1915): 320.
FICTION
"A Man They Didn't Know," *Crisis,* 7 (December 1913): 85-87; 7 (January 1914): 136-138;
"At the End of the Controversy," *American Magazine,* 77 (March 1914): 36-41.

Critical studies of Afro-American literature at the turn of the century generally focus on the work of Charles W. Chesnutt, W. E. B. Du Bois, and Paul Laurence Dunbar. As a result one black author who has been undeservedly relegated to footnotes in such scholarship is James D. Corrothers. Not only was Corrothers among the most celebrated and widely published black poets of his day, but he also produced short stories, numerous magazine and newspaper articles, an autobiography, and a book of fictional sketches. Moreover, his career vividly reveals how black writers striving for a broad audience in late-nineteenth- and early-twentieth-century America had to cope with the racial stereotypes which shaped the expectations of white editors and readers alike.

James David Corrothers was born in Cass County, Michigan, on 2 July 1869, to Maggie and James Richard Carruthers (he changed the spelling of the family name while in grade school). The first of several tragic personal losses Corrothers was to experience, Maggie's death in childbirth led to a protracted struggle for custody between his father and his paternal grandfather, who was taking care of him. At one point, the conflict became so heated that an aunt was driven to hide James in the woods for a night lest his father succeed in carrying him away. Eventually, Corrothers's grandfather managed to adopt the youngster outright, and the two settled in South Haven, Michigan.

Without question, the elder Carruthers was the dominant force in the shaping of James's values and tastes. An upright, devout man of Cherokee, Scotch, and Irish extraction, he imbued his young charge with a deep-seated religious faith and a fierce sense of pride. Furthermore, through his dignity, industriousness, and honesty, he set an example that would guide his grandson for the rest of his life. James was especially struck by the high regard in which the local residents, both black and white, held the older man.

Corrothers's treatment in the predominantly white South Haven community played a key role in his development as well. On the one hand, he felt that being raised in "an atmosphere of pure speech" prevented him from picking up black dialect or stereotypically black behavior patterns. On the other, he argues in his autobiography that this lack of extensive early contact with Afro-Americans handicapped him in his dealings with what he termed "the unschooled Negro." In addition, as the sole black student, Corrothers had to fight nearly every boy in his class, and he was often punished unfairly by his teachers. Instead of embittering him, however, these experiences formed the foundation for the relatively conservative and optimistic position on the race question he held as an adult. That is, because his forbearance, academic excellence, and ability to defend himself gradually won him respect, he came to believe that even the harshest oppression might be overcome.

Around 1883 Corrothers moved to Muskegon, Michigan, where, in a desperate struggle to support himself and his grandfather, he worked long hours in local lumber mills and was occasionally forced to sleep in factory boiler rooms or outdoors in freezing weather. Unfortunately, the relatives on whom he depended to help care for his grandparent were far less dedicated than he. In fact, they threatened to put the elderly man in a poorhouse, and he mysteriously disappeared soon thereafter.

Now totally on his own, Corrothers befriended an Irish sailor and shipped to Chicago, where he was duped out of what little money he had. Nevertheless, he managed to make his way to his mother's relatives in Ohio, and with their assistance, he settled in a small Indiana town named Liberty. There he spent his days working in a hotel; at night he "laboured at self-improvement" by reading whatever literature he could find. Henry Wadsworth Longfellow, John Greenleaf Whittier, Alfred Lord Tennyson, Thomas Gray, Oliver Goldsmith, Heinrich Heine, and Robert Burns were among his favorite authors; but he was particularly impressed by the Hoosier poetry of James Whitcomb Riley. In the initial stages of Corrothers's own writing career, the great popularity of Riley's dialect verse would suggest to him that the folk voice of the Afro-American might be both an artistically valid and a commercially rewarding mode of literary expression.

In the mid-1880s Corrothers moved to Springfield, Ohio, where he encountered not only an influential role model in the poet-minister Albery A. Whitman, perhaps the town's most celebrated black resident, but also a group of supportive peers in the Young Men's Republican Club. The secretary of the organization was Emmett J. Scott, who would later become one of Booker T. Washington's closest aides; Corrothers was the club's poet. Most importantly, it was while he lived in Springfield that "The Deserted School House," probably his first published poem, appeared in a local newspaper. An amateurish piece obviously influenced by Goldsmith's "The Deserted Village," it is of interest primarily because it reveals that his earliest efforts were not in black dialect.

Hoping to market a book of campaign songs that he composed for the 1888 presidential election, Corrothers gathered his meager savings and moved to Chicago. His venture failed, however, and he worked as a pantryman on a lake steamer until the violence and vulgarity of his fellow black employees drove him to find a job as a bootblack when the ship laid up in Chicago. One afternoon, the noted writer Henry Demarest Lloyd visited the barbershop where Corrothers was employed. Taking an immediate interest in the well-spoken, literate young man who was polishing his shoes, Lloyd soon arranged for the publication of Corrothers's "The Soldier's Excuse" in the *Chicago Tribune.* Another nondialect poem, this piece about a quick-witted Yankee soldier evinces the sentimen-

Corrothers, at about ten years old, with an aunt

tality and cheery good humor that characterize much of his later verse.

Corrothers's friendship with Lloyd also resulted in his being hired as a porter in the *Tribune* offices; and when he was subsequently asked to compose an article on the progress made by the Chicago black community, he jumped at the chance. Working in his spare time, he spent several weeks interviewing wary members of the local Afro-American bourgeoisie, including the noted heart surgeon Dr. Daniel Hale Williams. To Corrothers's considerable dismay, however, the story that finally appeared differed radically from the one he had submitted, for a white reporter had revised his material to fit the conventions of comic black portraiture current in the popular media of the day. Humiliated, Corrothers felt obliged to apologize personally to his enraged interviewees. To make matters worse, he discovered that the reporter had received fifteen dollars while he was paid nothing for his efforts. When he angrily confronted the editor, he was fired.

Corrothers's ambitions received more positive reinforcement at the first meeting of the National Afro-American League, called by T. Thomas Fortune in Chicago in early 1890. Corrothers took part in the convention's literary program and was lauded as "the coming poet of the race." Then, in the fall, he entered a preparatory school affiliated with Northwestern University, which he attended off and on through 1893. Although he worked as a cabdriver, a groundskeeper, and even a boxing instructor in order to support himself, Corrothers could not have continued his studies without the backing of an aunt, Henry Lloyd, and the world-famous reform leader Frances Willard, whom he had met when he addressed the Evanston branch of the Woman's Christian Temperance Union. Like Lloyd, Willard provided Corrothers with both friendly advice and sorely needed funds; she financed not only his education in the North but also his first trip south, where he studied briefly at Bennett, a black North Carolina college.

During this same period, Corrothers encountered a number of aspiring black artists, many of whom were drawn to the Chicago area by the 1893 Columbian Exposition, an event made especially attractive by the magnetic presence of Frederick Douglass. The relationships that developed between Corrothers and, among others, the poets Paul Laurence Dunbar and James E. Campbell provided him with an important sense of intellectual community. These were young men wrestling with problems similar to his own, and the awareness that he was not alone surely strengthened his dedication to goals that American society at large told him were unattainable.

In 1894, shortly after marrying Fanny Clemens, Corrothers resolved to make journalism his profession. He had published material in local papers previously, but it was not until his wife sold one of his articles to the *Chicago Daily Record* for three dollars that he was ever paid for his writing. Despite his best efforts, however, income from the "space work" he managed to pick up proved to be skimpy and uncertain, and he had to move furniture and wait on tables for a living.

Corrothers's first major break as a journalist came early in 1896, when he found himself in the middle of winter with neither money nor marketable news. In desperation, he concocted a story about a self-taught black poetaster named Sandy Jenkins, to whom he attributed "De Carvin'," a comic rendering of a razor fight in dialect verse. To his surprise, the editors of the *Chicago Evening Journal* published it, even in the face of his confession that it was untrue. Further, they urged him to produce additional sketches about Jenkins and gave him a book in dialect to study because of his admitted ignorance of the form. In 1899 Corrothers commented on his initial reluctance to produce such work:

> Just about then, . . . I think I was the most conceited negro that ever lived. Why, I was a great race man, always talking about the abuse my people received and thinking that anything that referred to them was a slur. I would have no more written verse in negro dialect than fly. I thought it would demean me.

His change in attitude was partially due to the current vogue of dialect poetry in general and to Dunbar's popularity in particular; in his autobiography, Corrothers recalls, "[H]ere was splendid material which I had overlooked, and which all Negroes but Dunbar had allowed to go begging." It is also likely

Corrothers at twenty. Fearing he would never make a career of writing, he considered becoming a "professional pugilist."

that driven by pressing economic considerations, Corrothers put his squeamishness aside and wrote what he must have suspected would sell. Regardless, his success was short-lived, and by the fall of 1896 he again found himself struggling to support his family.

About two years earlier, Corrothers had decided to enter the Methodist ministry, but the ignorance and improprieties of many black preachers convinced him that he could not, at that time, join their ranks. Now, as he bitterly contemplated the degree to which some clergymen unscrupulously exploited their followers, he suddenly realized that "the cause of righteousness needed honest men." This thought struck him like "a sunburst," and he immediately committed himself to becoming the exemplary leader he felt that blacks lacked. Tragically, his wife Fanny died of consumption soon after he received his first assignment; Richard, the youngest of their two children, succumbed about a month later. Entrusting his remaining son, Willard, to his wife's relatives in Baltimore, the disconsolate Corrothers proceeded alone to the A. M. E. Church in Bath, New York.

Ironically, the beginning of Corrothers's career as a full-time minister led directly to his rise to celebrity as a popular poet, for he decided to give dialect verse a serious try primarily because he found it difficult to live on his preacher's salary. Early in 1899, Corrothers sent the following melancholy meditation in dialect to *Century:*

" 'Way in de Woods, an' Nobody Dar"

De ole owl libs in a lonely place—
'Way in de woods, an' nobody dar;
Eyes lak sunflowers in his face—
'Way in de woods, an' nobody dar;
Sets an' broods alone, alone,
Set an' sigh an' moan an' moan,
When de silvah moon goes down—
'Way in de woods, an' nobody dar.
. . . .
'Way down in mah Southe'n home,—
'Way in de woods, an' nobody dar.
Dar's de place I longs to roam—
'Way in de woods, an' nobody dar.
Oh, mah lub wid eyes ob coal,
Listen tel mah story's tole;
Owl's a-hootin' in mah soul—
'Way in de woods, an' nobody dar.

When, to his surprise, Richard Watson Gilder accepted the poem, Corrothers realized that his work would sell.

The next few years were busy ones for Corrothers. After serving as the private secretary of the powerful Bishop Alexander Walters, he headed a pastorate in Red Bank, New Jersey. Then, following a brief, unsuccessful second marriage, he was assigned to a bankrupt church in Hackensack, New Jersey, which he quickly rehabilitated. Despite these demands, however, he wrote steadily during this period, and his poetry appeared in print with increasing frequency.

In the spring of 1902, Funk and Wagnalls published Corrothers's first book, *The Black Cat Club*. Based largely on the dialect material he had produced for the *Chicago Evening Journal*, this collection of sketches relates the adventures of Sandy Jenkins and his eight sidekicks, whom Corrothers portrays as the bickering, superstitious, boisterous black buffoons of popular dialect comedy. To the extent that many of the stories that the club members tell are variations or even literal transcriptions of actual folktales, Corrothers taps a vein of genuine Afro-American folk expression. His ear for slang and his ability to incorporate aspects of the black oral poetic tradition into Sandy's verse are also noteworthy. However, *The Black Cat Club* more consistently displays Corrothers's indulgence in the slapstick tactics of stereotypical darky humor. At one point, for example, a raucous debate over the respective merits of courage and common sense degenerates into a razor-fight, during which the combatants go tumbling out of a second-story window. Furthermore, in revising the original sketches for publication in book form, Corrothers decided to impose a plot on the loosely organized set pieces. As a result, a totally improbable love story begins to emerge about halfway through the volume; and by the end, Sandy has entered the catering business and married into a proper, middle-class black family. Almost all of the other club members have reformed as well. Although such radical plot developments possibly justify classifying the book as a novel, Corrothers's strategy is ultimately self-defeating as he vacillates between broad, cartoonish farce and belated attempts at psychological realism. The grossly exaggerated caricatures that illustrate the text simply exacerbate the problem. Funk and Wagnalls touted *The Black Cat Club* as proof that Corrothers was "undoubtedly the coming star in that quarter of the literary firmament that has until recently been in Ethiopian darkness," and the Afro-American author William Stanley Braithwaite praised the book's "quaint humor and delightful situations." Overall, however, the critical response was mixed, and in his autobiography Corrothers described the book as "a very poor one" and expressed regret that it was ever published.

Henry Demarest Lloyd, who was Corrothers's mentor and friend

Several months after *The Black Cat Club* appeared, Corrothers became embroiled in a controversy that marked the low point of his life. Apparently Bishop Walters accused him of improper behavior in his relationship with a young female member of his congregation; Corrothers was further charged with plotting to ruin the bishop's name. Acquitted in open court, he was, nevertheless, expelled from the denomination. Forced to leave his home and without a regular income, he moved to New York City, where he worked as a janitor and as an entertainer in white churches and halls. He was even offered a vaudeville job, which he rejected as unbecoming to a minister. Finally the blow that, in Corrothers's own words, "hurt deepest in all this period of sadness" came when his landlady sold the trunk that he had left as security until he earned enough money to pay the rent. He thereby lost not only mementos of his deceased wife and child but also precious manuscripts, pictures, and letters.

As it had several years earlier, religion played a key role in the reordering of Corrothers's world. Around 1904 he became a Baptist, and he was officially ordained after effectively heading two congregations in Michigan. Gratified by the church leaders' willingness to overlook malicious reports about his past, Corrothers reentered the ministerial service with a new dedication and confidence. In addition, his marriage in 1906 to a New York music teacher named Rosina B. Harvey gave his domestic life a stability and a security that it had lacked since the death of his first wife.

The publishing history of Corrothers's poetry, like that of Paul Laurence Dunbar's, reflects the demands of the editors with whom he dealt as well as the concessions he made to those demands. Dunbar distinguished between his conventional English poetry and that written in black dialect by the phrase "Majors and Minors," the title of his second volume. To his chagrin, he discovered that white editors were interested primarily in his dialect verse. Similarly, it is hardly coincidental that most of Corrothers's dialect poems appeared in white periodicals and newspapers and resemble those works popularized in the late nineteenth century by plantation tradition writers who were busy propagating the myth of the Old South. With their comic use of black stereotypes and nostalgic recollection of a bucolic southern past, pieces like "De Rabbit's Foot" and "Ghoses" might well have been produced by Irwin Russell, Joel Chandler Harris, or Ruth McEnery Stuart. The first two stanzas of "A Dixie Thanksgivin' " typify Corrothers's generally perfunctory approach in composing such poems:

Hollerdays hab come once mo'—
  Hyar it am Thanksgivin'!
Ole man gittin' stiff an' so'e—
  Hahdly make a livin'.
But, sah, when Thanksgivin' come,
Honey, I ain't nevah glum;
'Ca'se ma dinnah 'll sho be some—
  Bress de good Thanksgivin'!

Bes'es' white folks in dis town
  Sont a turkey to me!
'N' evahthaing to go aroun'—
  Dat's de way dey do me.
Lucy Ann's a-comin' down
Fuh to bake it nice an' brown;
Den we'll 'vite de preachah roun'—
  No time to be gloomy!

In contrast, a number of Corrothers's dialect poems—especially those carried in *Colored American* magazine—demonstrate his ability to overcome the more debilitating restrictions of that verse form. "An Awful Problem Solved," for example, is a biting, allegorical indictment of racial prejudice presented as the dream of a disarming black folk narrator. "Me 'N' Dunbar," another of Corrothers's finer efforts, opens this way:

One day when me 'n' Dunbar wuz a-hoein' in de co'n,
Bofe uv us tried an' anxious foh to heah de dinnah-ho'n,—
Him in his fiel', an' me in mine, a-wo'kin' on togeddah,
A-sweatin' lak de mischief in de hottes' kine o' weddah,
A debblish notion tuck me 't Paul wuz gittin' on too fast;
But, thainks I: "Wait untwel he git 'mongst all dem weeds an' grass,
'N' I'll make him ne'ly kill his se'f, an' den come out de las'."

Tuck off ma coat, rolled up ma slebes, spit on ma han's an' say:
"Ef God'll he'p me—'n' not he'p him—I beats ma man today!"
S'I: "Paul, come on, le's have a race! . . .

The key to this poem is Corrothers's absolutely inspired use of a black folk voice to render the friendly rivalry between Dunbar and himself as a race between two farmers laboring in adjoining fields.

In his nondialect poetry, the bulk of which appeared in black publications, Corrothers is freed from the stifling conventions of the plantation tradition. Unfortunately, he also leaves behind much of the invigorating concreteness and humor of the Afro-American folk materials. As a result, several of these poems manifest the saccharine, ornate style of popular magazine verse. Only his attempt to confront the discrepancies between the American dream and the nightmarish oppression of blacks in the United States prevents his nondialect work from crumbling under the weight of mawkish sentiment and ponderous, florid diction. Although such disjunctions between promise and reality often lead the speaker in Corrothers's verse to religious doubt and insecurity, the majority of his poems on this topic end with a reaffirmation of his faith in God and in a better future to come. Even the most notable exception, "The Snapping of the Bow," stands out not because Corrothers's hope is shaken, but because the poem's sanguine resolution depends exclusively upon a faith in the black's Af-

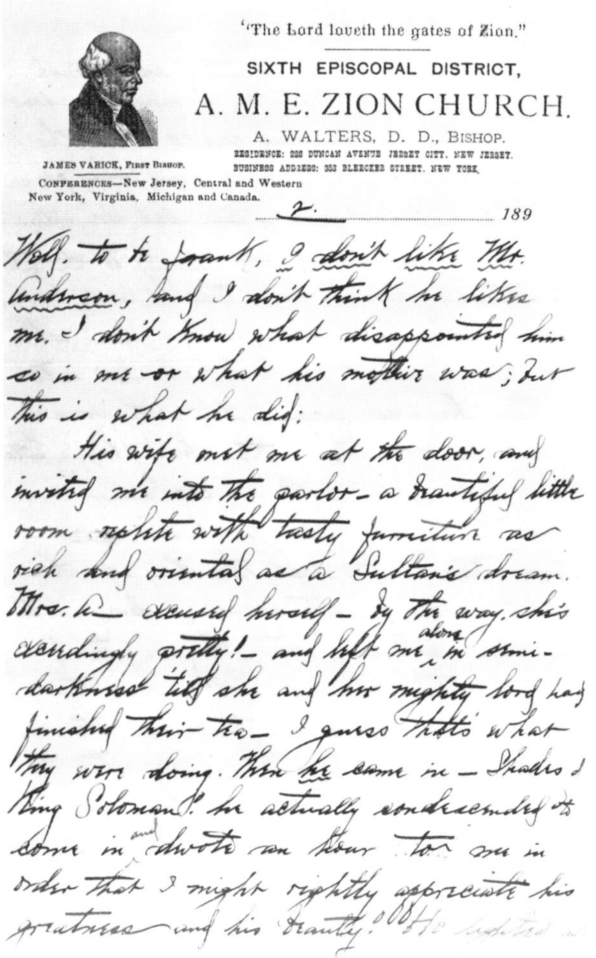
"The Lord loveth the gates of Zion."

SIXTH EPISCOPAL DISTRICT,

A. M. E. ZION CHURCH.

A. WALTERS, D. D., BISHOP.

RESIDENCE: 238 DUNCAN AVENUE JERSEY CITY, NEW JERSEY.

BUSINESS ADDRESS: 353 BLEECKER STREET, NEW YORK.

JAMES VARICK, FIRST BISHOP.

CONFERENCES—New Jersey, Central and Western New York, Virginia, Michigan and Canada.

2. 189

Well, to be frank, I don't like Mr. Anderson, and I don't think he likes me. I don't know what disappointed him so in me or what his motive was; but this is what he did:

His wife met me at the door, and invited me into the parlor—a beautiful little room replete with tasty furniture as rich and oriental as a Sultan's dream. Mrs. A— excused herself—by the way, she's exceedingly pretty!—and left me alone in semi-darkness till she and her mighty lord had finished their tea—I guess that's what they were doing. Then he came in—Shades of King Solomon! he actually condescended to come in and devote an hour to me in order that I might rightly appreciate his greatness and his beauty!" He ...

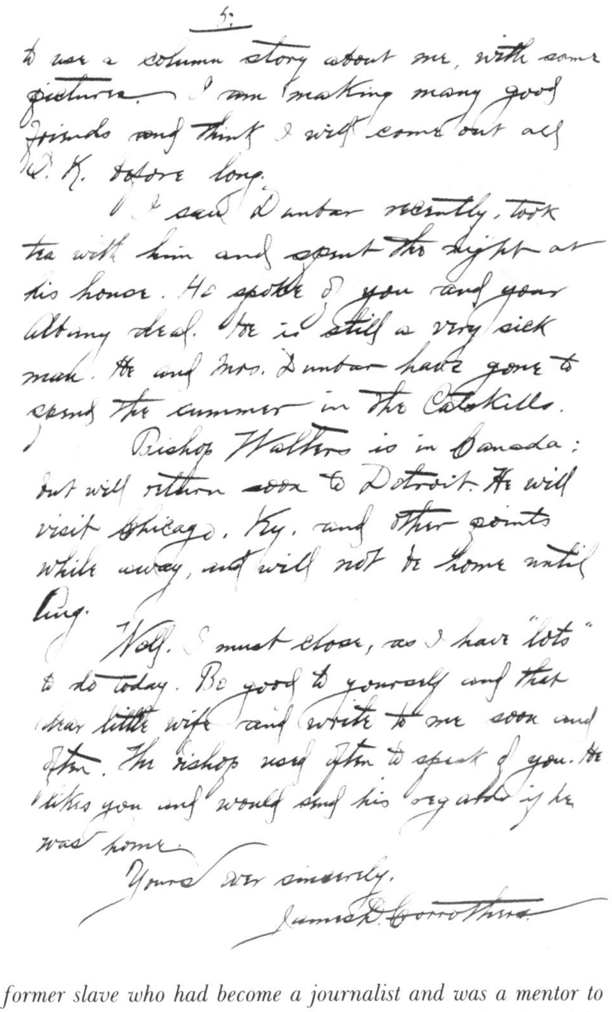
5.

to run a column story about me, with some pictures. I am making many good friends and think I will come out all O.K. before long.

I saw Dunbar recently, took tea with him and spent the night at his house. He spoke of you and your Albany deal. He is still a very sick man. He and Mrs. Dunbar have gone to spend the summer in the Catskills.

Bishop Walters is in Canada; but will return soon to Detroit. He will visit Chicago, Ky. and other points while away, and will not be home until Aug.

Well, I must close, as I have "lots" to do today. Be good to yourself and that dear little wife and write to me soon and often. The Bishop used often to speak of you. He likes you and would send his regards if he was home.

Yours ever sincerely,

James D. Corrothers

Pages from an 1899 letter Corrothers wrote to John E. Bruce, a former slave who had become a journalist and was a mentor to many black writers. Charles Anderson was a black government official with whom Bruce had founded the New York Chronicle *(courtesy of Schomburg Center for Research in Black Culture, the New York Public Library, Astor, Lenox and Tilden Foundations).*

rican heritage, which is expressed in symbolic terms similar to those used by Claude McKay in "Africa" and "America." The resemblance is most striking in the final stanza of Corrothers's poem:

> But, on the plain there rose
> A phantom of the silent sphinx—the grim,
> Spell-casting thought of some deep master dead.
> And lo! beside its ancient, crumbling base,
> Napoleon, fresh from mighty deeds of war,
> Halted his band, and spoke in tones of awe.—
> All this I saw, and dreamed that yet—aye, yet!—
> The race might rise that built the awful thing
> That holds its secret still in Egypt's sands.

This work exemplifies how consistently Corrothers's optimism led him to counsel patience in the face of personal suffering in general and racism in particular, both of which threatened to undermine his belief in a just God.

For a number of reasons, Corrothers published little between 1907 and 1911. First, the demand for dialect verse had cooled. Moreover, the black magazines that had carried his writing either changed editorial policy or ceased publication altogether. Finally, his ministerial and family responsibilities demanded a great deal of his time and energy. During this relatively dormant period, Corrothers's views on his craft underwent dramatic growth, which he attributed primarily to the impact that Swinburne had upon him:

> The beauty of Swinburne's verse was a revelation to me. It taught me new possibilities and delights in verse-making. The beauty, fervour, and fire; the divinely sad music, the mystery and masterfulness of Swinburne's beautiful poetry enthralled and enraptured me. Trees became my teachers, and the winds spoke to me. I strung my harp anew, and began singing in the pure joy of things.

Deciding to focus less on dialect verse and instead to strive for a "higher class" of literature, Corrothers felt that he was now, as he put it, "working for my *race,* as well as for myself and family." *Century*'s acceptance in 1912 of "Paul Laurence Dunbar" and "The Negro Singer," two nondialect pieces on which Corrothers had labored diligently, seemed to validate his decision, and he soon achieved a degree of success as great as, if not greater than, that which marked his literary activities at the turn of the century. By 1913 he had moved with his wife and two sons, Willard and Henry, to Philadelphia, where he was reported to have given up the ministry for writing.

Although some of Corrothers's poetry published after 1910 suffers from the same flaws evident in his previous work, his range of themes has broadened to include both the inadequacy of language to capture beauty and also the problematic role of the black artist in a white world. "The Negro Singer," for instance, examines the apparent anomaly that is the Afro-American poet:

> O'er all my song the image of a face
> Lieth, like shadow on the wild, sweet flowers.
> The dream, the ecstasy that prompts my powers;
> The golden lyre's delights bring little grace
> To bless the singer of a lowly race.
> Long hath this mocked me. . . .

However, unlike another sonnet on the same topic, Countee Cullen's "Yet Do I Marvel," Corrothers's poem ends on a note of confidence and secure pride in his art ("So shall men know me, and remember long,/Nor my dark face dishonor any song"). Moreover, in such widely anthologized works as "The Black Man's Soul," "In the Matter of Two Men," and "At the Closed Gate of Justice," Corrothers protests racial prejudice with a new power and forthrightness. Ironically, "An Indignation Dinner," one of his most famous poems from this period and probably the last he published, is in dialect and appeared in a slightly different version fifteen years earlier. Corrothers's career as a popular poet had come virtually full circle.

Besides poetry and journalism, Corrothers produced several pieces of short fiction, perhaps the strongest of which are "A Man They Didn't Know," a two-part story carried in *Crisis* in 1913-1914, and "At the End of the Controversy," published in 1914. Although overwritten and melodramatic, "A Man They Didn't Know" deals imaginatively with the allegiance of Afro-Americans to the country that so oppresses them. As the story opens, the president is foolishly ignoring indications that the Japanese, with Mexican cooperation, are about to invade the United States. The defection of Afro-American troops to Mexico and increasing black demands for civil rights only serve to heighten the tensions. Among the black leaders with whom the president meets in a last-ditch effort to resolve the crisis is Rev. Grant Noble, the aptly named protagonist whose selfless advice and patriotic action save the nation. Like Sutton E. Griggs's novel *Imperium in Imperio* (1899), Corrothers's story is designed to move the reader in two

"Seated in a big arm-chair, Sandy Jenkins read his poetry."
(See page 41.)

Frontispiece and title page for Corrothers's first book, which draws heavily from Afro-American oral traditions

ways: first, it warns white America that the unjust treatment of blacks may well lead to rebellion and armed conflict; second, it contends that although the majority of Afro-Americans still love their country, racial catastrophe can be averted only if the courageous and loyal black no longer remains "a man they [whites] didn't know."

The more realistically executed "At the End of the Controversy" again involves Grant Noble, but here the parallels between the protagonist and Corrothers himself are quite explicitly drawn. The story begins with the minister's attempt to refute a bigoted white's claim that blacks are selling their votes and therefore do not deserve suffrage. The focus quickly shifts, however, to a frequent source of bitterness in Corrothers's life—the widespread jealousy, underhandedness, and ignorance he saw among blacks—and by the conclusion of the piece, Noble's congregation has rewarded his dedication and honesty by voting him out of the church. A recent widower, Noble now finds himself and his young son homeless, much like Corrothers did in 1902. The hero's final words are a prayerful admonition to his people to awaken from their benighted condition.

Convinced that Afro-Americans "needed religious training along the higher lines," Corrothers joined the Presbyterian church and, in mid-1915, was appointed to a parish in West Chester, Pennsylvania. Comfortable with his congregation, secure in his faith, and surrounded by his loving family, he could write a year before his death, "I envy no man." On 12 February 1917 he suffered a stroke and died at the age of forty-seven.

In 1901 John Livingston Wright commented, "In the career of James D. Corrothers we have a story of struggle, athletics, adventure, and a romance more remarkable than that in many novels." Published in 1916 by George H. Doran Company, *In Spite of the Handicap* effectively conveys the rich-

Rosina B. Harvey Corrothers

ness and inherent drama of that story. At first glance, Corrothers's autobiography is, as the title implies and as Ray Stannard Baker observed, "a book singularly without rancor." Corrothers's message throughout is that perseverance and moral uprightness almost invariably lead to success, and he emphasizes the degree to which the help and sympathy of whites made his way easier. His depiction of blacks, however, suggests that Baker's characterization of *Handicap* demands amendment, for as Rebecca Chalmers Barton points out, it is the Afro-American who often "becomes a convenient whipping post for his negative feelings." The disappointment Corrothers experienced in his contact with the black masses and the unconscionable treatment he received at the hands of some of his fellow churchmen seem to have left the most painful memories of all.

Throughout his career, Corrothers's poetry met with generally favorable critical response, and toward the end of his life, *Crisis* could quite justifiably rank him with William Stanley Braithwaite as "the greatest of living Negro American poets." Yet, with the turning away from dialect verse by black authors in the twentieth century, he quickly fell from favor. That *The Black Cat Club* and *In Spite of the Handicap* are the only readily available books by Corrothers has contributed further to the neglect with which his work has been treated. Several usually reliable sources cite two volumes of his poetry—*Selected Poems* (1907) and *The Dream and the Song* (1914); however, none provides a publisher or a place of publication. If the books did, in fact, appear, they met with no major critical response and had extremely limited distribution.

As a result of these factors, although several major anthologies of Afro-American literature include two or three samples of Corrothers's poetry, his accomplishments continue to be overshadowed by the more distinguished productions of his good friend Dunbar. With the noteworthy exceptions of Eugene B. Redmond's discussion of Corrothers in *Drumvoices*, Abby Arthur Johnson and Ronald Maberry Johnson's brief comments on his work in their study of Afro-American magazines, and James Robert Payne's essay comparing Griggs's fiction with that of Corrothers, contemporary literary commentators have ignored him altogether. However, the recent trend of reassessing pre-Harlem Renaissance texts suggests the likelihood that the place of James D. Corrothers in the Afro-American literary canon will eventually be adjusted. The critical consensus may, in the final analysis, judge him to have been an ambitious and historically significant talent, but not one of the first rank. Nonetheless, as Sterling Brown observed, "Corrothers' poetry does have some personal distinction"; and in according his writing the attention it merits, scholars will learn a great deal about the complex, precarious situation of the black author in the United States at the turn of the century.

References:

Ray Stannard Baker, Introduction to *In Spite of the Handicap*, p. 8;

Rebecca Chalmers Barton, *Witnesses for Freedom: Negro Americans in Autobiography* (New York: Harper, 1948), pp. 18-23;

Sterling Brown, *Negro Poetry and Drama* (Washington, D.C.: Associates in Negro Folk Education, 1937);

Abby Arthur Johnson and Ronald Maberry Johnson, *Propaganda and Aesthetics: The Literary Politics of Afro-American Magazines in the Twentieth Century* (Amherst: University of Massachusetts Press, 1979), pp. 6, 13, 40;

James Weldon Johnson, ed., *The Book of American Negro Poetry* (New York: Harcourt, Brace, 1931), pp. 72-80;
"A New Negro Poet," *Southern Workman*, 28 (December 1899): 508-509;
James Robert Payne, "Griggs and Corrothers: Historical Reality and Black Fiction," *Explorations in Ethnic Studies*, 6 (January 1983): 1-9;
Eugene B. Redmond, *Drumvoices: The Mission of Afro-American Poetry* (Garden City: Anchor/Doubleday, 1976), pp. 115-118;
John Livingston Wright, "Three Negro Poets," *Colored American*, 2 (April 1901): 410.

Joseph Seamon Cotter, Sr.

(2 February 1861-14 March 1949)

A. Russell Brooks

BOOKS: *A Rhyming* (Louisville, Ky.: New South, 1895);
Links of Friendship (Louisville, Ky.: Bradley & Gilbert, 1898);
Caleb, the Degenerate, A Play in Four Acts; A Study of the Types, Customs and Needs of the American Negro (Louisville, Ky.: Bradley & Gilbert, 1903);
A White Song And A Black One (Louisville, Ky.: Bradley & Gilbert, 1909);
Negro Tales (New York: Cosmopolitan, 1912);
Twenty-fifth Anniversary of the Founding of Colored Parkland or "Little Africa," Louisville, Ky. (Louisville, Ky.: Cole, 1934);
Collected Poems of Joseph S. Cotter, Sr. (New York: Henry Harrison, 1938);
Sequel to "The Pied Piper of Hamelin" and Other Poems (New York: Henry Harrison, 1939);
Negroes and Others At Work And Play (New York: Paebar, 1947).

Joseph Seamon Cotter, Sr.'s birth year marked the start of the Civil War, and he lived past the flowering of Afro-American culture in the 1920s and 1930s. Over the course of his career, this self-educated writer published five books of poetry, one each of drama and fiction, and a miscellaneous collection of tales, short plays, poems, and brief prose items consisting mainly of aphorisms, proverbs, and jokes. Some of his poetry has appeared in anthologies and periodicals, and his single full-length play, the second published by an Afro-American, is included in a collection of early black drama. A poet whose life circumstances prevented him from attaining his full powers, Cotter nonetheless enjoyed the distinction and popular acclaim which came from his roles as a revered Louisville educator and community leader, popular storyteller at church and school functions. He was also known for his promotion of story-telling contests, an activity that grew into a movement of national consequence, earning him a place in *Who's Who in America* in 1919. Although he was essentially a local poet, his vision was universal; though never a slave, he experienced the aftermath of slavery, and while his works seldom dealt with the hardships suffered by blacks during the period of adjustment following the war, some of his earlier poetry has an aura of the antebellum plantation. His early work endorsed friendly relations between the races and an ethic of hard work but discouraged political involvement by blacks. A portion of Cotter's early poetry was written in imitation of Paul Laurence Dunbar's dialect poetry, which Cotter, like Dunbar, considered secondary to his work in standard English. At no time did he confine himself to purely regional themes. In the period of the Harlem Renaissance the new black voice served to broaden Cotter's perspective on racial matters and to give his poetic imagination greater scope.

Joseph Cotter was born in Nelson County, a few miles from Bardstown, Kentucky. His father was sixty-year-old Micheil J. Cotter, a Scotch-Irishman who is said to have been fond of books. Joseph's mother, Martha Vaughn, was the freeborn daughter of an African slave and Fleming Vaughn, son of an Englishman and a Cherokee Indian, who had bonded Martha out, along with six other children. At the time she became pregnant she worked

as a nurse for the Cotter family, and she returned to her maternal great-grandfather's farm to have her son. She eventually found herself at Federal Hill in Bardstown, where Stephen Foster is said to have written "My Old Kentucky Home." Much of his love of books Cotter owed to his mother who figured powerfully in determining Joseph's personal outlook and intellectual and cultural inclinations. She frequently carried a hidden book and stole moments from work to read. Her strong dramatic instinct often led her to make up little plays and act out the characters. When Cotter was four months old, Martha Vaughn moved him to Louisville, where he remained for the rest of his life. In order to help support his mother he was forced to leave school when he was eight; but his education nevertheless had had a fortuitous beginning, for he had been taught to read before he was four years old.

Aside from picking up rags in the streets, Cotter's first job was in a Louisville brickyard, where he was ostracized and taunted by the other boys. To ward off this persecution, he tried telling stories to the boys and sometimes to the men, thus initiating an avocation that considerably enhanced his professional and literary pursuits and made him widely known even beyond Kentucky. Until he reached the age of twenty-two he managed to survive through a variety of other jobs: as a distillery worker, a teamster on the levee, and a prizefighter. While engaging in this last undertaking he met a prominent Louisville educator, William T. Peyton, who convinced him to stop fighting and return to school.

After a short period of remediation and two Louisville night school sessions of five months each, he was qualified to teach. Thomas G. Watkins of the editorial staff of the *Louisville Courier-Journal,* who knew him during those early years, wrote that he "was wholly self-taught in English literature and composition." Efforts have been made to track down the source of a report that in his seventies Cotter began studying on the college level and within two years attended two colleges and a university. The report is unconfirmed and probably erroneous.

Cotter taught in Cloverdale, near Louisville, from 1885 to 1887 and in a private school for the next two years. When he began his Louisville public school career as a teacher at Western Colored School in 1889, he immediately began looking for a wife, one who was nearly the color of his mother "and a few years older than myself," he wrote, "so that she might be able to keep me straight." He found Maria F. Cox, an intelligent woman a few years his elder, who had taught and served as a principal, and in 1891 they married. Maria and Joseph Cotter had three children: Florence Olivia, born in 1893, who died of tuberculosis in 1914; Joseph, Jr., born in 1895, who began a career as a poet but died young of tuberculosis in 1919; and Leonidas, born in 1899, who died a year later.

In 1891 Cotter organized a black community in Parkland, an outlying section of Louisville, which was known as "Little Africa." "It is a part of the city," he wrote, "where the word 'segregation' breeds no terror and conjures up no law suits." In light of this forthright acceptance of racial coexistence, it is surprising that his first two books of poems dwell so slightly on the subject.

Cotter's first volume, *A Rhyming* (1895), was dedicated to his wife and included five ballads, all using the traditional form of four- and three-stress lines with alternating rhymes; commendatory and inspirational lyrics of different rhythms and stanzaic forms; and a variety of humorous pieces. Conventional and bookish diction in several poems shows the strong influence of early English lyrics. In one piece, the speaker, while sailing out on the "briny sea," is lonely for Mary and wonders if she is thinking of him as she trips "across the lea" or while in the lighted banquet hall she enjoys the company of the "youthful and gay." Lily, in another poem, is one of the prettiest little maids that ever tripped along. She sings "a rustic lay" and lives in a "cot beneath a rocky hill." But this artificial style and content by no means dominate the collection. In "The Bachelor," a ballad told in a rugged manner, a sad but raving old man tells a curious, taunting boy why he never married: as he crept on hands and feet to peep through a crack in a ruined cottage to see the witches reputed to be living there, an unbearable weight suddenly came down on his back, and ever since he has found no pleasure in being near a woman.

In "Man Does Not Know," the poet wrestles with man's limitations in the face of divine inscrutability and his own inability to master nature or to predict the future. The poem employs what was to be in all of Cotter's poetry collections his favorite rhythmic effect, the extra unaccented syllable coming after the rhyming syllable, most frequently in alternating lines: "Man does not know. He daily looks *around* him/And tries to master earth and air and skies;/But some mysterious power has firmly *bound* him/Unto a place from which he may not rise." The volume contains a sonnet addressed to Oliver Wendell Holmes, whose "God-like" wit presents the truth to us "as through a twist." Already in this first book Cotter evidenced near mastery of the tight Italian sonnet form, with only two corresponding sounds rhyming at the ends of eight successive lines in the octave and complementing rather than obstructing the lyrical quality of the passage (except for the flawed rhythm of the third line, which omitted a needed syllable):

> Who can hold up the intellect and say:
> "From here to there scampers a vein of wit
> With laughing humor beside of it
> Assisting cold philosophy to play
> The game of thinking?" Not a single ray
> That boldly shines therefrom will e'er admit
> Of close analysis. So bit by bit
> We fall to guessing out the mind's true way
> Of forming wholes.

A Rhyming also contains "Description of a Kentucky School House," which no doubt came from Cotter's bleak months in the one-room schoolhouse at Cloverdale before he began teaching in the city schools. The building was only "a few boards; yet the trustees called it a house," he wrote. On one side "the floor and ground meet," but on the other side there is nothing but ground. Seats are boards, and the stove no longer provides heat.

The hand of the amateur shows too clearly in some of the poems in *A Rhyming*. Conscientiously testing a variety of artistic forms, Cotter introduced an element of artificiality into many of the poems. Nonetheless, although critics have not commented specifically on Cotter's early volumes, Paul Laurence Dunbar noticed the "ease and beauty" with which Cotter wrote in a number of meters.

Cotter's second poetry collection, *Links of Friendship* (1898), contains four of five ballads, a narrative poem, and several lyrics from *A Rhyming*. Among the new pieces are two eulogies, some children's poems, humorous verses, and several pieces specifically about blacks, one of which is in dialect and was the result of a visit from Dunbar, who was then a rising young poet (although not yet catapulted to fame by a review by William Dean Howells). Dunbar had visited Cotter's home in 1894, and during his stay, he had read some of his dialect poems. He later honored the occasion in a poem entitled "After a Visit to Kentucky," in which he said his fellow Ohioans had no right to talk about hospitality "Tell you be'n down there to see." Cotter responded with "Answer to Dunbar's 'After a Visit,' " probably his first attempt at dialect. He twitted his Ohio friend, who had written of plantation life, for knowing little about the South. In fact, he said, he had tried to help him understand the true nature of Southern hospitality:

> Fur it might stir up your feelings
> To the righteous point of wrath
> As you brood o're what you lost, sir
> By not stayin' with us longer.

Cotter became one of the lesser imitators of Dunbar's dialect poetry, although he did not always share Dunbar's points of view. For example, in answer to Dunbar's "A Choice," a poem that lauds "the spirit wine of a singing line," Cotter wrote "Answer to Dunbar's 'A Choice,' " saying that the world was in such need of reform that poets should "wed stern facts to song" (an injunction which, fortunately, he himself often failed to heed).

Tributes to great people abound in *Links of Friendship,* and although many of them are too general to be effective, Cotter can also be quite pointed. He writes, for example, of "Little men of fluent tongue" who try to imitate Frederick Douglass but end up underrating him when they learn they are not his equals. Robert Burns's sins soiled his reputation, but he blew "so clear and pure a blast," "Its echo warrants censure's banishment." Cotter occasionally used black vernacular, as opposed to dialect. A boy in "Six in Deportment" is chided by his fellows for low marks on his report card: "That thing don't say you're going to pass,/You know you done been giving sass." Several humorous poems in the volume are written in standard English, notably "The Devil and the Higher Critics" and "A Just Reward." Cotter obviously thought much of his "Sequel to 'The Pied Piper of Hamelin,' " for he ran it in three of his collections, using it for the title poem of one. For narrative skill, lively movement of verse, and appropriate phrasing and diction, it has hardly been surpassed by any of his other poems. After the Piper and children in Browning's poem disappeared through an opening in Kuppenberg's Hill, another race of rats (in Cotter's poem) "outnumbering all the hosts of Caesar" swarmed in: "With rats for mayor and rats for people,/With rats in the cellar and rats in the steeple,/With rats without and rats within/Stood poor, deserted Hamelin." Robert T. Kerlin wrote of "Sequel" in the *South Atlantic Quarterly* (1921) that it "surpasses the original—Browning's—that is, in rushing rhythms and ingenious rhymes. It is an incredible success. . . . Its content, too, is worthy of the metrical achievement." We see in *Links of Friendship* an advance, though not marked, over the previous volume: less of the conventional, stilted eighteenth-century diction, particularly in the new pieces, more humor, and a generally more relaxed mood.

Cotter founded the Paul Laurence Dunbar School in Louisville in 1893, and he had served as its principal until 1911, when he became the principal for the Samuel Coleridge-Taylor School. He remained there until his retirement in 1942. Information about Cotter's professional and civic activities during the 1890s is limited, but we do know that throughout virtually his entire adult life he was a respected leader in a variety of projects relating to community uplift and race betterment.

In 1903 Cotter's four-act blank verse play *Caleb, the Degenerate* was published. The play endorsed many of the views that had been expressed by Booker T. Washington in his 1895 Atlanta Exposition speech. Washington had urged blacks to start at the practical end of the socioeconomic ladder to establish themselves in American culture and to better their relations with white people. He looked down upon attempts by Afro-Americans to establish themselves in politically powerful positions. In his preface to *Caleb* Cotter advised his fellow blacks against participating in politics and heeding solicitations of advocates for a return to Africa; and he recommended that they concentrate instead on industrial training and "clean, intelligent leadership," since to do otherwise would be "dangerous for the present."

The play is written predominantly in blank verse, with a few rhymes interspersed and several short scenes in prose. The black man is depicted "as he is today," rising intellectually and spiritually but plagued by unprecedented depravity among a certain class—"not due to anything innate" but "the result of unwise, depraved leadership and conditions growing out of it." Caleb, an unscrupulous, blasphemous, brutal villain, is tutored and nurtured by a disreputable minister-politician, Rahab, who induces Caleb to believe that his own evil is the result of his mother's sinfulness. Rahab causes Caleb to murder his own father, and in a grotesque moment the two of them stand grinning over the corpse as they divide the money they received from a medical student in payment for it. Rahab teaches Caleb to hate work and instills in him the notion that the ideal gentleman eats and wears only what he has picked up, borrowed, or stolen. Also under Rahab's influence is Dude, a positive, upright, young man who is encouraged to vote and participate in politics and in the back-to-Africa movement. To offset Rahab's destructive leadership are the Bishop and Olivia, his adopted daughter, who together run Industrial School, the Working Room of which is the setting for a number of rather skillfully arranged scenes with boys on one side and girls on the other going through symbolic movements—the girls sewing in unison and the boys moving saws in like manner—as the Bishop strikes the anvil, proclaiming, "That sound is the password to Negro enfranchisement." The good leaders win out in the end. At the last rising of the curtain, we see Olivia holding checks totaling $100,000 which she collected from Boston philanthropists. Dude, who has eschewed his former Rahab-instilled ideas, is there in uniform, standing erect and holding a large American flag. Except for one or two short scenes, the play is hardly actable, and it is not known if it was ever produced. Portions of the dialogue, especially in the opening scenes, are stilted and pretentious ("What now? . . . "A word, perchance"), but a few pleasant surprises await the persevering reader: for example, several passages written in imitation of John Milton's use of the epic simile. Arthur P. Davis, remarking that *Caleb* was the second play published by an American black, called it "another very bad closet drama." James Hatch and Ted Shine believe critics have failed to recognize in the character Caleb a representation of the black experience in America.

After the Civil War, the black man was at least free to vote, but in the 1880s and 1890s and the early years of the twentieth century, he was being disenfranchised, forced into involuntary labor under the peonage system, confined to plantations by means of vagrancy laws, and lynched. Kentucky was not a plantation state, but the situation there was bad enough. Only once or twice, and then briefly, did Cotter indicate awareness of these deplorable conditions; rather he sounded the note of racial cooperation, mutual good will, and tolerance; yet the racial content of *A White Song And A Black One* (1909) exceeds by far that of his previous work. In the opening poem, Cotter glowingly praised the South, whose strength when pitted against the disruptions and destruction of war "Renewed the mansion, vivified the farm,/Kept timid hearts from growing desolate/By teaching valor through a missing arm." The book is equally divided between "A White Song" and "A Black Song." In the White section, there are poems in a variety of stanzaic and metrical arrangements treating southern attitudes and conditions, childhood, and the teaching of children. Only one poem, "The Sequel to 'The Pied Piper of Hamelin,' " had appeared earlier.

Neither the North nor the South, says Cotter in "Grant and Lee," bears the burden of guilt for the Civil War; it "took root in the nation's heart," and our song of peace is sung "With regret for the bond and hope for the free,/And a God-like love for Grant and Lee." In another poem, his long-suffering South needs only one weapon, the "love and faith and poise" of "Marse" Henry Watterson. In one of the dialect pieces, Joel mourns for Uncle Remus, but here Cotter slyly intends irony: "Specs de Lawd gwine to call us brudders/When He sees us face to face." A few poems relate to children, and they are among the best in the book. "The Sequel" is repeated here, and it is preceded by a poem addressed to President Taft's young son on being sent a copy of "The Sequel."

The Black half of the book, with fourteen dialect poems out of twenty-two, fully establishes Cotter as a disciple of Dunbar in the use of that medium. He used dialect effectively in relating humorous incidents and situations. The speaker in "Reporting the Sermon" is telling his drinking buddy about the preacher's sermon, when the preacher shows up too late to enjoy more than the last drops from a bottle as the two buddies spy on him from behind the weeds: "Ef you 'spouse de temp'rence cause,/We's gwine be both jedge and laws." And sometimes Cotter lets dialect point up the faults of his fellow blacks, as in "The Loafing Negro," "The Don't Care Negro," and "The Vicious Negro." When Cotter wanted to bring to his people the message that hard work is the best policy, he employed standard English, as in this distillation of Booker T. Washington's speech before the National Negro Business League: "What deeds have sprung from plow and pick!/What bank-rolls from tomatoes!/No dainty crop of rhetoric/Can match one of potatoes."

Afro-American fiction had fallen on lean days since the death of Dunbar in 1906 and public discovery of Charles W. Chesnutt's racial identity had all but put an end to publication of his tales in white journals. A few minor writers like George McClellan, James McGirt, and Cotter were managing to get some of their stories into print; but they had little impact on the literary scene, which needed the new Negro renaissance to bring about the cultural emancipation of Afro-Americans, such as Jean Toomer, Langston Hughes, and Claude McKay. Cotter's *Negro Tales* (1912) was one of four collections of fiction by blacks to appear between 1906 and 1922, when William Pickens published his *The Vengeance of the Gods*. Aside from items in newspapers, Cotter's fictional output is limited almost entirely to *Negro Tales*. Only ten of the items are "Negro," in that they are either about blacks or are tales that were current in the black community; four of them are written in dialect. Seven of the pieces written in standard English are not "black" pieces. The book includes a variety of styles and genres, ranging from a long medieval-like tale, to stories with fairy-talelike elements, to rustic comedy and unified narratives approximating the modern short story.

The collection gets off to a poor start with the diffuse and pointless "Caleb," incorrectly named in the preface "a short version" of the play *Caleb, the Degenerate,* with whose action and characters it has too little in common, except for portions of the stilted, pretentious, and stichomythic dialogue ("She must be buried" . . . "I must be married"). The second story, "Rodney," could have been omitted because of similar defects in dialogue and structure, but it does have a theme: the despised half-white child. (Cotter was himself more than half-white, and it is hardly surprising that at times he broached the subject of the unhappy consequences of mixed blood.) The precocious Rodney's father said to him on their first and last meeting together that his "fine head of hair" was a disgrace to him. The silly and absurd conversations in the tale and its slight action hardly give adequate support to the theme. "Tesney, the Deceived," also about illegitimacy, is a small improvement over "Rodney."

Several stories in *Negro Tales* have natural dialogue and characters and unified plots, including "Regnan's Anniversary," about a man late for his wedding because on his way home he was chased into a pond by two rival gangs of boys; "A Rustic Comedy," in which an old, miserly couple is visited by three strangers they suspect of plotting to steal their money; and "Kotchin' De Nines," which concerns a man whose dream about living in a rich house leads him to become poorer than he was at first. Three short dialect pieces come near the end of the volume. Two are jokes, and one—a brief episode entitled "Observation"—is a skillful rendering through dialogue of a woman's skeptical observations of a professor who came to talk her into sending her son to his school. Some of the stories in *Negro Tales* have merit, but except for its historical importance, it is generally ignored by black literary scholars.

Eighteen years following the twenty-fifth anniversary celebration of the 1891 founding of Little Africa in Louisville's Parkland area, Cotter published his first work in many years: *Twenty-fifth Anniversary of the Founding of Colored Parkland or "Little Africa"* (1934). A slight work, it nevertheless bears considerable importance in furnishing a rare close-up view of Cotter in his local habitat. The nineteen-page pamphlet contains two unsigned newspaper articles relating to the celebration and one article by Cotter, together with a collection of commendatory letters from prominent Louisville citizens. The itinerant orator Roscoe Conkling Simmons, whom black American schoolchildren had heard deliver one or more orations, was the main speaker in the large tent provided for the anniversary event; he spoke on Booker T. Washington. Cotter devoted his speech to some of the aims of the celebration: to put up mailboxes, lay cinder walks, level the streets, and provide other improvements. He wrote in his article that the settlement had gone a long way—"from William McGowan's Sunday School to six churches, from John Thomas' broken-legged mule to Charley Cook's automobile; from chasing rabbits over the territory by the writer to telling the story of Negro families settled thereon." His "creed," written for the Parkland Improvement Club, said, in part: "Let us lose ourselves in the welfare of our children. Let us remember that the child is the only force that raises or lowers a community. Society has its ebb and flow in the cradle and school room. He who steals or kills may be reformed behind prison bars, but he who fails to educate his children libels posterity."

By 1938, having completed fifty years of service in the Louisville public schools, Cotter dedicated his next book, *Collected Poems,* "To the Boards of Education, superintendents, supervisors and co-workers, who have made this long service possible." Of the seventy-three poems in the book, thirty-eight had already appeared in one or more of the previous volumes. Only four of the dialect poems were new—the only ones written for publication since *A White Song And A Black One.* Of the new poems in standard English, fewer are about race relations, fewer defend southern ways, and fewer praise various individuals. More of them deal with natural beauty, abstract reasoning, and the art of writing poetry. Several earlier poems treating race and region are included in the volume, and they obscure signs of Cotter's growth as a poet reaching out to a larger world and attempting to bring greater variety to his poetic skills. The selections include several sonnets, each of which implicitly relates certain aspects of nature to the human condition: the poet would be lifted up by June breezes, "Coaxing elixir from the swelling bud," to where "Life's toil wins peace from strife and love from care"; the buzzard sails early in the morning, seeming to scorn "all that's low and vulgar," but his quest ends when he sights a "rotten carcass." In previously published sonnets, Cotter showed a fondness for the Italian form, which he used with remarkable success, but in these sonnets he turns to the more flexible English model.

The poetic craft as a subject for poetic treatment enjoys greater prominence in this collection. In "Style" Cotter wrote: "Plain words come forth as clear and free/As notes from a chirping linnet;/And every sentence carelessly/Holds a thought within it." It was the "haunting word" of Shakespeare's sonnet that opened up for him a new world, and, "Now all that may be felt or seen or heard/I bring to you embedded in a word." The new works in *Collected Poems* scarcely touch on race, but when they do, they are among Cotter's strongest expressions on the subject. For instance, in "Babe on Babe," his first published free-verse poem and his only one on lynching, the narrator speaks to God and asks for assurance that God hears the little black baby alone in the cabin crying while his "father's dead body/Is part of yon charred tree." "The Negro Preacher," "The Negro Woman," and "The Negro Child" are praise poems. The author of *Collected Poems* is still engrossed in the ways of black and white folks, still eager to advise hard work for his people and careful relations with the dominant race. The new poems taken together, however, reveal a poet of larger view and greater skill.

Only one year elapsed between publication of *Collected Poems* and that of *Sequel to "The Pied Piper of Hamelin" and Other Poems* (1939). Twenty-five of the sixty poems were previously published, including three of the six in dialect. Six of Cotter's seven published free-verse poems are included in the volume. The book is divided into three parts—Childhood, Biography, and Miscellaneous, with "A Poem" in free verse opening the first section:

> Baby is a poem—
> A lyric in its coo and laugh,
> An elegy in its cry,
> An epic in its dreams,
> And punctuated by its toes and fingers.

The title poem, printed in two previous collections, is not so much about children as their delight. "The Door-Sill" recounts a toddler's confrontation with "life's first mystery" as he toddles from his mother's chair to the door-sill and beyond. "My Lad" uses stereotypes to build the image of the Arab child sitting in a gutter dreaming great dreams. Three delightful poems published earlier are also included: "Mr. Goody's Goat," "Six in Deportment," and "Johnny's Dream of Santa Claus," which occupied a full page (with pictures) in the rotogravure section of the *Louisville Courier-Journal* during the 1926 Christmas season.

The Biographical section of *Sequel* carries poems addressed to or in commemoration of fellow teachers, ministers, black leaders, and white friends. Although many of these poems are generalized tributes, others have a special interest—the one about W. E. B. Du Bois, for instance. An enthusiastic follower of Booker T. Washington in his advocacy of industrial education as the best means of survival and advancement for the black race, Cotter nevertheless admired the distinguished scholar Du Bois, proponent of a liberal education for the "Talented Tenth" (the sector of the Afro-American population Du Bois thought should be groomed to lead), who for a number of years engaged Washington in debates on the subject. After Washington died in 1915, Cotter thought of Du Bois as the black race's greatest leader; and in a free-verse poem, "The Race Welcomes Dr. W. E. B. Du Bois As Its Leader," he implied that Du Bois's was, after all, the better philosophy:

> To work with your hands
>   Is to feed your own mouth
> And maybe your neighbor's;
>   To work with your mind
> Is to unleash the feet of millions.

Cotter's abiding love of children spilled over from the section on Childhood to the Biography section, for several of the poems addressed to leaders are primarily about children. In a touching poem on his son Joseph's death in 1919, he asks, "Is it eternity's farewell,/Or just a span's good-bye?"

The Miscellaneous section opens with a ballad, "The Tragedy of Pete," perhaps Cotter's most popular poem. It won third place out of 1,276 entries in *Opportunity*'s second annual literary contest in 1926, and in that year it appeared in William Stanley Braithwaite's annual *Anthology of American Magazine Verse*. It is written in the manner of the folk-ballad, later made popular by Sterling Brown and Julius Lester:

> There was a man
>   Whose name was Pete,
> And he was a buck
>   From his head to his feet.

After he killed the drunken driver who caused his girlfriend's death, Pete welcomed death "From his head to his feet." "The Wooded Path" laments people's penchant for taking the easier path in life. When Countee Cullen published his anthology of black poetry, *Caroling Dusk* (1927), he stressed, in his introduction, the absence of poems in dialect. Cotter's dedication of his dialect poem "Christmas Turkey" to Cullen is, therefore, somewhat surprising. The speaker recounts the turkey's life from before it was hatched, and his tale is so tedious that his fellow diners lose their appetites, while he has the turkey all to himself. Cotter insured the quality of the volume by balancing the new poems with many of the best already published, including "The Bachelor," "Answer to Dunbar's 'After a Visit,'" "The Strange Man," and "Prologue to a Supposed Play." In the quality of the poetry and the attractive physical layout of the book, *Sequel* is easily Cotter's most presentable work. If he were known by it alone, his reputation as a writer would be considerably higher than it is.

In 1942 Cotter retired from his principalship of the Samuel Coleridge-Taylor Elementary School after thirty-one years there and fifty in the Louisville public school system. He had served as director of the Louisville Colored Orphans Home Society and had been active in the National Association for the Advancement of Colored People, the Kentucky Negro Educational Association, the Story-Tellers League, and the Authors League of America. Two years before his death, when he was seen less often at educational and civic gatherings, he prepared a casual collection of miscellaneous items, entitled *Negroes and Others At Work And Play* (1947). It contains several half-page ruminations, made up largely of previously unpublished proverbs, aphorisms, and other wise sayings; several tales, two of which—"A Town Sketch" and "Kotchin' De Nines"—had been printed in *Negro Tales;* seven poems, all new except one; two very poor one-act plays; and three songs to which he wrote the words and music. Entries relating to blacks and "others" are about evenly divided, but the latter never seem to refer specifically to whites.

The tales range from "Another Cinderella," a short fairy tale with a labyrinthine plot, to "One Strange Night," in which a practical joke is played on a man after he helps carry a trunk through a long, dark hall into a little room in a large building. A slight drama, "The Chastisement," though hardly long enough for one scene, packs much plotless action into small space. A father pursues his son with a cowhide for the same bad habits that he himself is guilty of, only to end up giving in to him. The dialogue is stilted and artificial. "Caesar Driftwood" is written in much the same undramatic style, but it does have a plot. Caesar, who never appears in the play because he does not exist, is expected to storm in any minute to murder Mary's brother who, against Caesar's will, wants to marry Caesar's sister; but Caesar never shows up, for as it turns out in the discovery scene at the end, he is no more than an invention of the postman. Five of the seven poems are praise pieces about blacks; for example, the black man in "The True Negro" "moves by walking, not by stumbling"; in "Walnut Street" he is moving up, urging others to get out of his way. In "Fourth Avenue of Yesteryear," white people in their finery promenade along a street, subsequently monopolized by blacks, and "little Negroes traipsing on/Had thoughts they dare not utter." "Psalm of the Zoot-Suit" is written in the bop mood of Langston Hughes's urban blacks: "A zoot-suit swirls,/A zoot-suit swings—/And, believe it or not,/It almost sings." In a poem handling a more modern subject, God is asked, in "The A-Bomb," to "show man that his learned trick/Makes Hell jazz step and Heaven sick." On the whole, *Negroes and Others* is an anticlimactic consummation of Cotter's long career. Several very good pieces fail to redeem the book from two defective short plays and a miscellany of ephemeral prose items borrowed from his scrapbooks.

Cotter for the most part has fared rather well at the hands of literary historians, although some critics dismiss him without actually having read his work. His poems have found their way into a large number of anthologies of early-Afro-American poetry, the notes and biographical sketches of which have generally accorded Cotter a respectable, though not prominent, role in the development of early-twentieth-century black literature. Although he published some drama and prose fiction, his contribution in those areas has been almost exclusively historical rather than literary. Most of his best poems are about children, and he was widely known and loved for his promotion of various projects involving children, especially the story-telling contests which he initiated in the Louisville public libraries. Though his writings never won him high recognition during his life, they remain an enduring legacy.

Biography:

Ann Allen Shockley, "Joseph S. Cotter, Sr.: Biographical Sketch of a Black Louisville Bard," *CLA Journal,* 18 (March 1975): 327-340.

References:

Hugh M. Gloster, *Negro Voices in American Fiction* (Chapel Hill: University of North Carolina Press, 1948);

James V. Hatch, ed., *Black Theater, U.S.A.: Forty-Five Plays by Black Americans, 1847-74* (New York: Free Press/Macmillan, 1974);

Robert T. Kerlin, "A Poet from Bardstown," *South Atlantic Quarterly,* 20 (July 1921): 213-221;

Eugene B. Redmond, *Drumvoices: The Mission of Afro-American Poetry* (Garden City: Anchor/Doubleday, 1976);

Joan R. Sherman, *Invisible Poets: Afro-American Writers of the Nineteenth Century* (Urbana: University of Illinois Press, 1974);

John Wilson Townsend, "Kentucky's Dunbar: Joseph Seamon Cotter," in *Lore of the Meadowlands* (Lexington, Ky.: J. L. Richardson, 1911), pp. 23-27.

Papers:

Unpublished works dating from the period 1920 to 1934 are housed in the Western Branch of the Louisville Free Public Library.

Joseph Seamon Cotter, Jr.

(2 September 1895-3 February 1919)

James Robert Payne
New Mexico State University

BOOK: *The Band of Gideon and Other Lyrics* (Boston: Cornhill, 1918).

PERIODICAL PUBLICATIONS: "On the Fields of France," *Crisis*, 20 (June 1920): 77;
"Out of the Shadows: An Unfinished Sonnet-Sequence," *AME Zion Quarterly Review*, 31, no. 3 (1920): 54-59;
"Poems," *AME Zion Quarterly Review*, 32, no. 2 (1921): 56-57.

Joseph Seamon Cotter, Jr. (photograph by Evans Studio, Louisville, Kentucky)

The poetry of Joseph Seamon Cotter, Jr., was a promising harbinger of the 1920s renaissance in black American literature. Innovative in technique and theme, Cotter's poems address universal concerns as well as protest the treatment of black Americans in the World War I era. In addition to his poetry, Cotter tried his hand at play writing before his untimely death at twenty-three.

Joseph Seamon Cotter, Jr., was born on 2 September 1895, in Louisville, Kentucky, son of Maria F. and Joseph Seamon Cotter. The senior Cotter, a well-known Louisville poet and educator, wrote proudly that his son had been born at home in the room in which, at Thanksgiving the year before, family friend Paul Laurence Dunbar had read his poems for the first time in the South. Cotter, Sr. had worked himself up from laborer to high school principal and nationally known poet and was able to offer his son advantages he himself had not known in youth, such as access to a private library at home. Young Cotter's older sister, Florence Olivia, taught her brother to read when he was very young, and the boy was especially fond of the poetry in his father's collection. Florence Olivia Cotter was an important friend to her brother. They attended Fisk University together, and she was a positive influence on Cotter's ultimate emergence as poet. Another significant childhood friend was Abram Simpson, who went on to become the youngest black captain in the First World War. The friendship with Simpson was no doubt a factor which helped to stimulate Cotter's writing of war poetry.

After graduating second in his class from the Louisville Central High School in 1911, Cotter enrolled at Fisk, where Florence was already a student. In the midst of Cotter's second year at the university, Florence wrote home that her brother was ill with tuberculosis. Cotter was sent home and put under good medical care. For the remainder of his life he fought the disease that was then a prime killer of black Americans. Soon Florence too was home with tuberculosis. Within a year, on 16 December 1914, she was dead. It was the poignancy of Florence's death that motivated Cotter's first poem, "To Florence." Cotter was to have only a little over four years as a poet; he died 3 February 1919. Within his short lifetime and despite his affliction, Joseph Seamon Cotter, Jr., established himself as one of the young, modern American poets of genuine promise and achievement.

Although the body of work of Joseph Seamon Cotter, Jr., is relatively small, it is marked by bold diversity and range in technique and theme. While on the one hand Cotter is noted as one of the earlier black American poets to experiment with techniques associated with the new American poetry of the period, some of his finest writing employs traditional forms, most notably exemplified by the sonnet sequence "Out of the Shadows." Cotter wrote effectively of nature, religious faith, love, and death and of the situation of Afro-America in his time. Cotter's book, *The Band of Gideon and Other Lyrics* (1918), reflects his varied strengths in both the traditional and newer poetic styles.

In five stanzas the title poem presents the Old Testament protector of the Israelites figured across the heavens:

> The band of Gideon roam the sky,
> The howling wind is their war-cry,
> The thunder's roll is their trump's peal,
> And the lightning's flash their vengeful steel.

Cotter effectively adapts detail and language from the account of Gideon in Judges, as is seen most notably in the powerful refrain: "And they cry aloud/With each strong deed,/'The sword of the Lord and Gideon.' " Cotter's style and language in "The Band of Gideon" have reminded some readers of the sermon style of the traditional southern black preacher. More particularly, it could be said that black readers of his time would be in a good position to appreciate Cotter's celebration of the righteous and militant Gideon. Following his military success against external enemies of his land, Gideon had to face rejection from some of his fellow Israelites, who denied his simple requests for assistance (Judges 8: 4-9). In 1918 black Americans fought successfully against the enemies of their land under the idealistic slogan "to make the world safe for democracy," only to face, like Gideon and his men, denial from many of their fellow countrymen. The last stanza, recalling Gideon's righteous, punishing anger, in effect serves as a prophecy for what may come to the unjust of Cotter's own land.

The BAND *of* GIDEON

And Other Lyrics

By JOSEPH S. COTTER, Jr.

THE CORNHILL COMPANY
BOSTON

Title page for Cotter's only book

Cotter's versatility is demonstrated in the two free-verse poems following the technically traditional "The Band of Gideon." Unadorned statements in everyday American idiom, "The Mulatto to His Critics" and "A Prayer" clearly reflect the newer American poetic style of the period that was beginning to supplant the genteel and plantation styles of Cotter, Sr.'s generation. "A Prayer" is a highly personal statement of the poet's desire for the power to evoke in language the stages of life that he will not be able to undertake fully because of his illness. "A Prayer" is one of a number of such subjective, sometimes elusive poems in *The Band of Gideon* which explore questions of religious faith (as in "The Goal"), love (as in "Is This the Price of Love?"), relationships to nature ("Ego"), and death ("To Florence").

"The Mulatto to His Critics" is the first of a group of poems which express Cotter's positive identification with the Afro-American community and which in effect give a description of the state of the community in the period. One of Cotter's most quoted poems, "The Mulatto to His Critics" suggests the style of Walt Whitman in its rhythms and catalogue style. Listing his various ethnic heritages, the poet observes: "Thru my veins there flows the blood/Of Red Man, Black Man, Briton, Celt and Scot." He goes on to conclude that it is his black heritage which he values most. Thus, the Whitman-like catalogue of ancestral peoples gives way to a strong affirmation of black identity. This affirmation recurs throughout *The Band of Gideon,* especially in the group of poems of black American experience among which many readers have found Cotter's strongest efforts.

At the very center of *The Band of Gideon* appear four of Cotter's most important poems: "And What Shall You Say?," "Is It Because I Am Black?," "O Little David, Play on Your Harp," and "Sonnet to Negro Soldiers." All four articulate important aspects of the poet's feelings about black identity. Through the series of free-verse statements and concluding question which form "And What Shall You Say?," Cotter projects a black man who asks a white to stand with him before their God. The black man declares that he can say to God that he does not hate, does not desire what is not his, and does not mock other peoples. Turning to the white man, he asks simply, "And, brother, what shall you say?" "The longer one thinks of it, the deeper the question presses in," observed one critic, who regards this as Cotter's strongest poem. "Is It Because I Am Black?," closely related in technique and theme to "And, Brother, What Shall You Say?," is comprised of a series of short, direct questions which highlight patronizing white attitudes toward black Americans. Both poems are noteworthy for their articulate and uncompromising stance of black pride.

Perhaps "O Little David, Play on Your Harp" was ahead of its time with its stringent critique of white America's racial prejudice. Although it is one of Cotter's most fully accomplished poems, "O Little David" has received little critical mention. "O Little David" presents details of the horrors of world war and other devastating events and culminates with a declaration that blacks suffer like wartime victims. Although written in free verse and thereby technically associated with the new poetry of the period, "O Little David" has beginning and ending refrain stanzas which evoke traditional Judeo-Christian attitudes, as in the line "O Little David, play on your harp" or in "Of the Prince of Peace and the God of Love." The sentimental appeal of the framing stanzas is harshly undercut by the internal imagery of the poem, in which "A seething world . . . gone stark mad" is "Blinded with the ashes/Of her millions of dead." Personifying the "arrogant pride and greed" that fuel the horrors of war, Cotter creates a "World-creature" who commits terrifying deeds, including pogroms in Russia, atrocities in Belgium under the Germans, and finally, "in every land," he says, "Are black folk scourged;/Their only crime—/That they dare be men."

Thus, in 1918 Cotter placed the "scourge" of blacks into a world context, on a plane with then-recent atrocities against the Jews in Czarist Russia and against the Belgians under the Kaiser; he thereby reveals a very modern, unflinching perspective of the criminal nature of bigotry.

Cotter placed "Sonnet to Negro Soldiers" just after "O Little David" in *The Band of Gideon,* giving it fourth and final position in the set of poems at the center of his book. W. E. B. Du Bois thought highly enough of "Sonnet to Negro Soldiers" to feature it in the special June 1918 "Soldiers' Number" of the NAACP journal, the *Crisis.* In the opening octave the speaker establishes the bravery of the black World War I soldiers in fighting "Against man's wrong to man—for such full well/They know." In the succeeding quatrain the speaker suggests that the black war experience serves as a sign of the coming overthrow of prejudice. The closing couplet prophesies that "though through blood it be," the soldiers' fight against injustice "breaks this day their dawn of Liberty." In addition to the tough-minded theme of Afro-Americans achieving freedom by fighting for it, "Sonnet to Negro Soldiers" is noteworthy for its incorporation of features of both the Italian and English sonnet forms.

Cotter's posthumous publications include the one-act play "On the Fields of France," carried in the *Crisis,* and two series of poems in the *AME Zion Quarterly Review.* The play presents a poignant encounter between two dying American World War I officers, one white, one black. Cotter's sonnet sequence "Out of the Shadows," in the third issue of the *Zion Quarterly* for 1920, definitely merits wider readership than the specialized nature of the journal has afforded. The nineteen love poems in the English sonnet style conclude with a moving evocation by the dying poet of the child he might have shared with his beloved but for his affliction, the child "That never was, nor is, nor e'er shall be." Cotter's last posthumously published poems, which filled two pages of the second *Zion Quarterly* for 1921, range in form from the traditional Italian sonnet to free verse. Like *The Band of Gideon,* the miscellany includes poems of love and black pride as well as expressions of the poet's personal predicament. Taken together, the final group of poems is strongly indicative of Cotter's broad talent and versatility.

The talents of Joseph Seamon Cotter, Jr., unfolded rapidly during his brief career. His work, almost from the beginning, exhibits the technical virtuosity and wide-ranging thematic concern which we usually associate with writers older than Cotter. Cotter received critical recognition in his day as one of the bright rising stars appearing at the close of the war. That judgment was sound, but a full and fair assessment of Cotter in recent years has been severely hampered by the fact that a significant portion of his work is largely inaccessible.

References:

Joseph S. Cotter, Sr., "Joseph S. Cotter, Jr.," in *Caroling Dusk: An Anthology of Verse by Negro Poets,* edited by Countee Cullen (New York: Harper & Row, 1927), pp. 99-100;

L. H. Hammond, *In the Vanguard of a Race* (New York: Council of Women for Home Missions, 1922), pp. 162-176;

Eugene B. Redmond, *Drumvoices: The Mission of Afro-American Poetry* (Garden City: Anchor/Doubleday, 1976), pp. 155-169;

Ann Allen Shockley, "Joseph S. Cotter, Sr.: Biographical Sketch of a Black Louisville Bard," *CLA Journal,* 18 (March 1975): 327-340.

Papers:

Manuscript material of Joseph Seamon Cotter, Jr., is housed at the Louisville Free Public Library, Western Branch.

Martin Robinson Delany

(6 May 1812-24 January 1885)

Carol P. Marsh-Lockett
Georgia State University

SELECTED BOOKS: *The Condition, Elevation, Emigration, and Destiny of the Colored People of the United States* (Philadelphia: The author, 1852);

The Origins and Objects of Ancient Freemasonry: Its Introduction into the United States and Legitimacy among Colored Men (Pittsburgh: W. S. Haven, 1853);

Political Destiny of the Colored Race on the American Continent in *Proceedings of the National Emigration Convention of Colored People Held at Cleveland, Ohio the 24th, 25th and 26th of August, 1854* (Pittsburgh: The author, 1854);

Official Report of the Niger Valley Exploring Party (New York: Hamilton, 1861);

University Pamphlets: A Series of Four Tracts on National Polity (Charleston, S.C.: Republican Book & Job Office, 1870);

Principia of Ethnology: The Origin of Races and Color, with an Archaeological Compendium of Ethiopian and Egyptian Civilization (Philadelphia: Harper & Brother, 1879).

OTHER: Introduction to *Four Months in Liberia*, by William Nesbitt (Pittsburgh: Privately printed, 1855).

PERIODICAL PUBLICATION: *Blake; or the Huts of America*, serialized in *Anglo-African*, January-July 1859; *Weekly Anglo-African*, 23 November 1861-April 1862.

Martin Robinson Delany

Martin Robinson Delany was the first black American to espouse black nationalism and the first black American Pan-Africanist. A man whose political views were far ahead of his time, he was committed not only to the abolition of slavery but also to the total elevation of black people. An individual of many callings, Delany was a family man, a writer and editor, a practicing physician, a lecturer, an African explorer, the first black major in the United States Army, a trial justice, an ethnologist, and a Reconstruction political activist, who never wavered in his fierce pride in blackness and Africa. Delany's views, evident in his writings and lectures, often alienated him from both black and white Americans who, at best, espoused only an accommodationist philosophy. Notably Delany's *Blake; or the Huts of America* (1859) was the third novel written by a black American and the first by a black American to be issued in the United States.

Martin Delany was born free in Charles Town, Virginia (now West Virginia) to Pati Delany, daughter of a Mandingo prince, and Samuel Delany, descended from the Golah tribe in Africa. His grandmother made him aware of his African heritage; from her, Delany learned that his grandfather's name was Shango, the name designated to the supernatural power in Yoruba culture. His sensitivity to the problems of being black in America may have been reinforced by events that touched his own life. One such incident occurred before Delany was ten, when his father was imprisoned for protecting himself from a white man who was trying to beat him. As a child Delany learned of the impediments to the social and educational advancement of blacks. In spite of an 1819 law that prohibited black children from being educated, the Delany children received rudimentary education from a white man. When the authorities discovered that they were literate, Delany's mother was found guilty of violating the law. She fled to Chambersburg, Pennsylvania, where Delany continued his formal education. In 1831, the year of the Nat Turner rebellion in Southampton, Virginia, Delany left Chambersburg for Pittsburgh where he worked as a barber and studied under a black man, the Reverend Lewis Woodson, employed by blacks to teach their children who were barred from attending public schools. Here, he also began his study of medicine under Dr. Andrew N. McDowell.

Delany's Pittsburgh years saw the beginnings of his political activities. He joined the Abstinence Society and became the executive secretary of the Philanthropic Society, an organization which helped free blacks to flee north. He also joined a black vigilante brigade which protected Pittsburgh's black communities against white attacks. In 1839 Delany visited the southern states of Louisiana, Texas, and Arkansas and witnessed the viciousness of slavery. This tour, in fact, may have inspired the essential plot of *Blake; or the Huts of America.*

Delany's views and experiences also touched his family life. In 1843 he married Catherine A. Richards. This union ultimately produced thirteen children, four of whom died in infancy. Delany's sense of himself and his blackness can be seen in the names they received: Toussaint L'Ouverture, Alexander Dumas, Faustin Soluque, Rameses Placido, Charles Lenox Remond, Saint Cyprian, and Ethiopia Halle Amelia. From 1847 Delany also edited the *Mystery*, one of the earliest black newspapers. This publication he viewed as a forum for defending the rights of black people. For example, in the paper, he attacked a black man, Tom "Fiddler" Johnson, for assisting slave catchers in Pennsylvania. This attack subsequently led to Delany's being sued for libel, found guilty, and fined $150 with $25 in court costs. Because this fine was so excessive—one of the highest in Pennsylvania's history up to that date—his attorney, William E. Austin, local newspapers, and abolitionists sought public support against the court's decision. They petitioned Gov. Francis R. Shunk to intervene in the case. Shunk rescinded the fine but not the court costs. Delany, however, was undaunted by the incident and earned a reputation as a "fearless" black leader. Eventually, being the sole proprietor of the *Mystery* proved to be a financial hardship for him. Therefore, in 1847 he gave up the editorship and sometime later joined forces with Frederick Douglass to become coeditor of the *North Star,* which was published in Rochester, New York. Delany remained in Pittsburgh as its western agent and correspondent. At the same time, he lectured extensively on such topics as the abolitionist cause and temperance while he also solicited subscriptions for the *North Star.* Delany remained with Douglass until 1849 when ideological differences led to the dissolution of the partnership. Douglass reported the dissolution in a spring 1849 issue of the *North Star.* Indeed, Delany's nationalist outlook clashed with Douglass's accommodationist views, which held that the well-being of blacks lay within the structure of a racially integrated American society. The result was Douglass's public disavowal of any responsibility for what he perceived as Delany's tactless and caustic comments.

Delany's activities during the 1850s and the 1860s were characterized by his interests in science and Pan-Africanism (specifically emigration). Pursuing an interest in medicine, he applied in the fall of 1850 for admission to the Berkshire Medical School in Pittsfield, Massachusetts. He was highly recommended by physicians and clergymen but was denied entry because he did not plan to practice medicine in Liberia under the auspices of a colonization society, as was expected of him. In the same term, he sought application and was enrolled in the Harvard University Medical School along with two other black students. Unfortunately, their presence caused such a rift in the student population that the faculty of the medical school voted not to allow them to return for second term in 1851. He then returned to Pittsburgh, began to practice medicine, and became further involved in politics. At this time he openly espoused the idea of emigration. As a continuation of his Pan-Africanist views, he represented Pittsburgh blacks at a meeting of black emigrationists in Toronto in 1851. Out of this meeting came a call for the formation of a black emigrationist society.

In 1852 he published his first polemical work, *The Condition, Elevation, Emigration, and Destiny of*

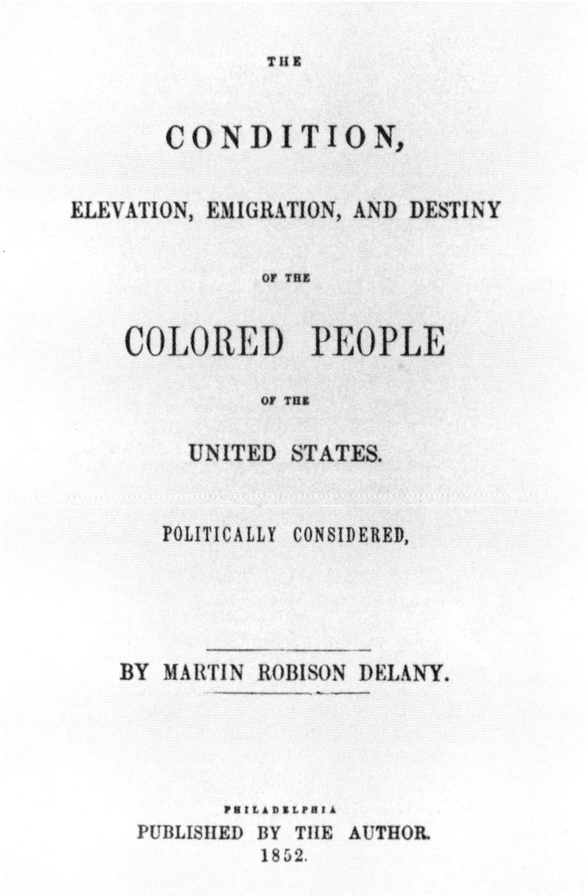

THE

CONDITION,

ELEVATION, EMIGRATION, AND DESTINY

OF THE

COLORED PEOPLE

OF THE

UNITED STATES.

POLITICALLY CONSIDERED,

BY MARTIN ROBISON DELANY.

PHILADELPHIA
PUBLISHED BY THE AUTHOR.
1852.

Title page for Delany's first controversial sociopolitical tract

the Colored People of the United States. In this work Delany expresses the notion that the United States had not fulfilled her obligation to her black citizens and that Afro-Americans were thus obligated to aspire to be educationally and economically self-reliant. He advocates the emigration of free blacks to Central America and the creation of a black country that could use economic and political pressure to defeat American slavery. When it was published, *Condition* received mixed reviews from abolitionist newspapers. In 1852 William Lloyd Garrison's *Liberator* praised the writing but found fault with the sentiment of the work. Similarly, *Frederick Douglass's Paper* found *Condition* an excellent book but asserted that Delany's proposals left readers as perplexed as they were before they read the book. The harshest criticism, however, came from the *Pennsylvania Freeman,* which attacked Delany's presentation of the facts, saw the work as detrimental to the credibility of Delany and the race, and suggested that it should never have been published.

Attacks on *Condition,* however, did not deter Delany from addressing controversial issues. In 1853 he delivered his treatise on black freemasonry in the United States before his own St. Cyprian Lodge, No. 13 and subsequently consented to its publication in Pittsburgh. The tract, *The Origins and Objects of Ancient Freemasonry: Its Introduction into the United States and Legitimacy among Colored Men* (1853), is the only historical document on the issue. Based on Delany's ethnological studies, it is grounded in the principle that all wisdom began with blacks in Africa. His purpose was to prove that freemasonry was founded in the earliest Egyptian and Ethiopian civilizations for the purpose of bettering the government of man. From this premise, he argues that to deny blacks access to freemasonry is to deny black heritage. Finally he continues the theme set forth in *Condition* when he links the origins and establishment of freemasonry to the issue of the elevation of the black race. This tract received little attention at the time of its publication and since then seems to have been largely ignored.

Delany continued his advocation of self-elevation and voluntary emigration of free blacks when he issued a call for a National Emigration Convention which met in Cleveland in August 1854. Here he attacked the American Colonization Society and delivered his famous nationalist speech, "Political Destiny of the Colored Race on the American Continent." This address, which has been reproduced in Congressional records, is one of the earliest recorded statements of black nationalism. In it Delany openly rejects the idea that blacks can live and prosper only under North American white oppression and that the United States is the government that can provide the greatest progress and improvement for blacks. In true nationalist and Pan-Africanist spirit, he attacks the notion that blacks are incapable of self-government and puts forth, as a viable alternative, emigration to the West Indies and Central and South America. Delany's public advocacy of emigration during this period was particularly timely, for 1850 witnessed the enactment of the Fugitive Slave Law; and it thus appeared to him that equality and justice for blacks were impossible.

In 1856 Delany left the United States for Chatham, Canada West, where he practiced medicine and specialized in chronic diseases and diseases of women and children. In 1859 he wrote a scientific article, "The Attraction of the Planets," which appeared in the short-lived *Anglo-African* magazine. He continued to lecture and be politically active and had a small involvement in founding a black communal experiment at Dawn Institute. He also met John Brown in Chatham at a meeting that is believed to have laid the groundwork for the later uprising at Harper's Ferry, Virginia. At this time, Delany also completed his only novel, *Blake; or the Huts of America,* which he had begun writing in 1852. Although the novel fell victim to publication difficulties, it began to appear serially in the *Anglo-African* magazine in the winter of 1859; but it did not appear in its entirety until it was published in the *Weekly Anglo-African* in 1861 and 1862.

Delany's *Blake* is an important American novel because of the penetrating insights it offers into the system of slavery. Moreover, in the body of black American literature, it gives the first fully developed portrayal of a West Indian character in the protagonist, Henricus Blacus, later known as Blake. The novel is clearly more topical and more nationalistic in theme than William Wells Brown's *Clotel; or, The President's Daughter* (1853) or Frank Webb's *The Garies and Their Friends* (1857). The novel sets the figure of the ideal docile Christian, mulatto slave against the idea of emigration to Liberia, subjects Harriet Beecher Stowe, whom Delany resented, had already forwarded in *Uncle Tom's Cabin* (1852). The plot departs from the stock slave narrative, which includes the broken slave family, the escape, and the journey to the North.

In this two-part novel, Henricus Blacus is stolen from his home and enslaved in the Red River Region of Louisiana, where he is renamed Henry Holland and where he marries a mulatto slave, Maggie, the daughter of her owner, Col. Stephen Franks. Maggie is sold to the wife of a northern judge, whereupon Henry vows to retrieve her. Henry escapes and travels throughout the South, observing slavery and encouraging the slaves to unite in a mass rebellion. He then returns to the Franks plantation and helps several slaves to escape to Canada. Henry next sails as a manservant to Cuba, where he finds Maggie, buys her freedom, and subsequently reunites her with the rest of her family. Operating now as Blake, he becomes the general of a force of black insurrectionists; and with the help of his friend and distant cousin, Placido, a militant Cuban poet, he plans to overthrow the Cuban government and to prevent the United States's annexation of Cuba.

In *Blake* Delany expresses a militancy which was rare for his time and which would not gain popularity until the 1960s. Indeed, in the novel he advocates slave rebellion and attacks the economic system of slavery. He also attacks the weaknesses in the thinking of black people that contributed to the perpetration of slavery. He shows, for example, that many slaves were overly committed to the same Christianity that was used to rationalize slavery. He also demonstrates that some black people had erroneous concepts of their relationship to the slaveholding society. One instance in the novel occurs when Tib, a drunkard, reveals to the masters the plot for a slave insurrection. There are also portraits of vicious black slave owners and of the members of the Brown Society, a misguided group of mulattoes.

Except for cursory commentary on the first three chapters of *Blake* in the *Anglo-African* magazine, there was practically no contemporary critical response to *Blake,* and the novel received no further critical attention until the 1930s. Nevertheless, scholars agree that the novel represents the culmination of Delany's thinking about slavery and the status of free blacks.

Between 1859 and 1861, the period during which *Blake* was not being printed, Delany was out of North America. Following up on the idea of emigration, he and Robert Campbell, a Jamaican, traveled to the Niger Valley in Africa to investigate the possibilities of black American settlement. Initially the prospect seemed hopeful. They planned to establish a colony which would spread Christianity throughout West Africa and which would export cotton to England and thus undermine the economy of the slave-holding southern states. In December 1859 Delany and Campbell signed treaties at Abekuta with a group of native chiefs.

Optimistic about the success of the project, Delany returned to Canada in 1861, and he completed the *Official Report of the Niger Valley Exploring Party,* which was simultaneously published in London and in Canada. Delany had begun work on the book while en route from Africa to England. The report is largely journalistic, and in it Delany recounts the inception of the settlement project and many of his experiences and observations in Africa. As a result of the publication of this report, Delany received many invitations to speak in the northern states.

Delany's optimism, however, was short-lived. In February 1861 the treaties were revoked due to British intervention. In addition, because of the growing number of emigration societies in America and missionary opposition in Africa, Delany's scheme began to lose support, and the dream eventually died. During this period, Delany was also involved in an incident which brought him international attention and the United States embar-

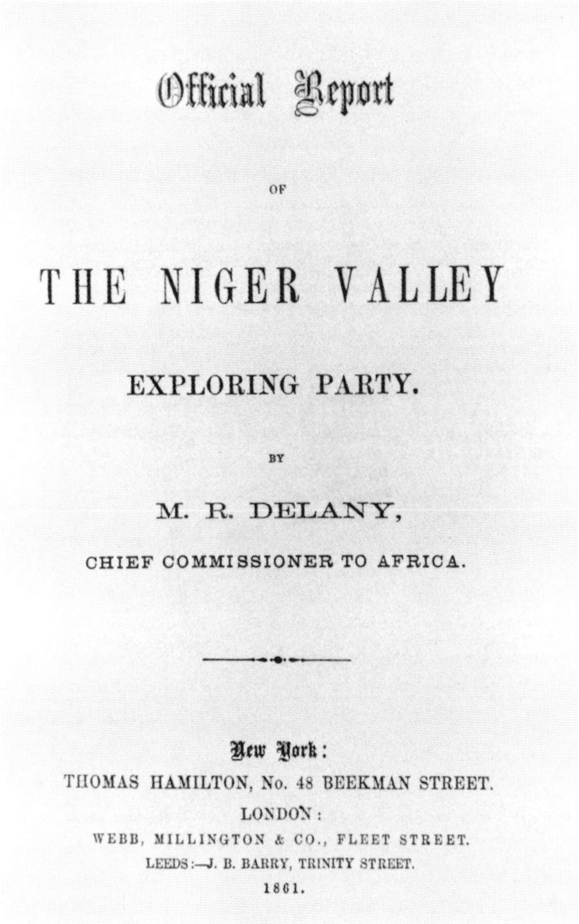

Official Report

OF

THE NIGER VALLEY

EXPLORING PARTY.

BY

M. R. DELANY,

CHIEF COMMISSIONER TO AFRICA.

New York:

THOMAS HAMILTON, No. 48 BEEKMAN STREET.

LONDON:

WEBB, MILLINGTON & CO., FLEET STREET.

LEEDS:—J. B. BARRY, TRINITY STREET.

1861.

Delany's evaluation of the Niger Valley as the possible site for a black settlement

rassment. In England during the summer of 1860 Delany was a delegate to the International Statistical Congress. Lord Henry Brougham, acknowledging Delany's presence, announced that there was a black man among the delegates. Delany, addressing Prince Albert, responded by assuring Lord Brougham that he (Delany) was foremost a man. Delany's statement has been as enthusiastically applauded by historians as it was then. But it was the cause of the withdrawal of the American delegation headed by Judge August B. Longstreet, who considered the incident an offense offered to the United States, to her delegation, and to himself. The incident brought Delany to the attention of the London and the American presses. It increased his international stature and fostered support for him in England and Scotland.

Support for the emigration scheme, however, was not forthcoming in America. After his failure to implement the plan, Delany lectured throughout the United States on Africa until the middle of 1863, when he became involved in domestic politics. He recruited black soldiers to fight against the Confederate forces, and in February 1865, after conversations with President Lincoln and Secretary of War Stanton, he was commissioned as the first black major in the United States Army. He was then assigned to South Carolina, where he was first a recruiter and then a Freedman's Bureau official. In his work for the Freedman's Bureau, he continued to have a nationalist perspective, aiming to obtain land for freedmen and reiterating his old theme of black self-sufficiency.

Delany's military career ended in 1868, but he remained active in South Carolina during the Reconstruction period. He continued to advocate the rights of freedmen and engaged in several political activities. Particularly noteworthy are his unsuccessful bid to become lieutenant governor in 1874 and his appointments in 1875 and 1876 as a Charleston County trial justice. In 1876, however, he lost this office.

Toward the end of his career, Delany's interest in Africa revived. He made two unsuccessful bids for a ministerial post in Liberia. He also made a final attempt to implement his emigration plan when, in 1878, he became treasurer of the Liberian Exodus Joint Stock Steamship Company. The group purchased a ship, the *Azor*, but the maiden voyage was a disaster.

Delany spent his final years lecturing and campaigning for John Dezendorf, a white Republican. In 1879 he wrote his final work, *Principia of Ethnology: The Origin of Races and Color with an Archaeological Compendium of Ethiopian and Egyptian Civilization*, which was published in Philadelphia by Harper and Brother. Here he asserted the racial superiority of pure-blooded Africans over mulattoes. It has been noted that this theme stands in opposition to racist arguments, such as that set forth in Thomas Carlyle's "Occasional Discourse on the Nigger Question," the subject of which was West Indian blacks, and the theses of such Americans as Dr. Samuel G. Morton of Philadelphia, who forwarded an argument for "Negro Inferiority" based on "cranial difference." Dedicated to the Earl of Shaftesbury, who had been particularly supportive of Delany, the work is based on the Hametic thesis that from Noah's three sons, Shem, Ham, and Japheth, the races evolved. Japheth settled in the Northwest to begin the white race; Shem in Asia, where he began the yellow race; and Ham, the darkest of the three, in Africa, where he and his sons began the establishment of the most advanced civilization in the pre-Christian world. Against this thesis, Delany discusses the chemistry of blood and holds that the blood of all three races is "rouge" but appears in different concentration in the three races.

The bulk of *Principia of Ethnology* is given to Delany's proof of the intellectual, economic, political, and social ascendancy of the early Ethiopian and Egyptian empires under the descendants of Ham. As evidence he cites phenomena from the life and culture of Africa, including the construction of the pyramids and the negroid features of the Sphinx, neither of which has been duplicated even by modern society. He also points to the alphabet, which was originally Ethiopian, and the science of letters, the political system, and the religion of the Israelites, all of which, according to Delany's Biblical documentation, were derived from Africa. Moreover, he refers to the historian Lucian, who stated that the Ethiopians invented astronomy and astrology. Finally, Delany holds that the Garden of Hesperides was not a myth and was, in fact, located in the heart of Ethiopia.

This African superiority, Delany holds, could only serve as positive motivation to nineteenth-century, black Americans. He submits, further, that black Americans were in a position to look to other civilizations, emulate their desirable aspects, and reject the undesirable. In line with this thought, Delany discusses the nineteenth-century Yoruba, who, he felt, most closely approximated the ancient ideal Africans. In support of this notion, he points to their delegation of labor which kept women in the home and thus preserved the most desirable social structure.

Finally, Delany addresses the issue of miscegenation, a fear of which loomed large in nineteenth-century America. In the work, Delany shows that blacks disapproved as strongly of racial mixture as did whites, but he also asserts that if, by the nineteenth century, three races still prevailed, there was no danger of the loss of racial distinctiveness.

Delany then concludes the work with a hope for the fulfillment of a prophecy made in the psalms: "Princes shall come out of Egypt; Ethiopia shall soon stretch forth her hands unto God." This was, in fact, his life's wish for black America. Delany, however, was not to see the realization of his wish. Weakened by a lifetime struggle for the rights of his people and argument in behalf of the merits of the Pan-African perspective, Delany joined his family in Xenia, Ohio, in 1884. There he succumbed to a lung infection and died on 24 January 1885, two years before the birth of the West Indian Pan-Africanist Marcus Garvey.

Critical perspectives on Delany's life and work have shifted over the decades. Because Delany did not see himself as primarily a verbal artist, and because his first obligations were political and humanitarian, there was no visible growth in his art. For this reason he received little attention until the 1920s, when his work received limited attention in studies of black American life and culture. In the 1930s and the 1940s, interest in Delany increased, but not his popularity. During these years, critics paid special attention to *Condition* and *Blake*. Benjamin Brawley recognized Delany's talents and pronounced *Condition* his best work. Vernon Loggins assessed Delany's writing as "crude" literature but "interesting sociology." Sterling Brown judged *Blake* an imitation of *Uncle Tom's Cabin,* but he felt its strength lay in the descriptions of the areas which Delany had visited. Hugh Gloster, on the other hand, acknowledged Delany's creation of an "ideal" black character and the sympathetic treatment of the black masses but dismissed the novel as abolitionist propaganda.

Most of the attention given to Delany in the 1950s came from historians. In 1958, however, Robert Bone acknowledged Delany's departure from the traditional conventions of the abolitionist novel in *Blake*. With the flowering of black nationalism in the 1960s and 1970s came a revival of interest in Delany's life and works. During this period Delany's major works were reprinted, and since then critical attention has been given to his attitude toward abolition and emigration. Significantly, most of the text of *Blake* has been discovered and republished, and the novel has been given positive treatment as literature, as critics address Delany's vision of the black experience and his literary techniques. Similarly, *Condition* has received critical attention and has been heralded as one of the most important black prose pieces of its era.

What will become of interest in Delany's reputation remains to be seen. Scholarship on him was handicapped when his papers and artifacts from his travels were lost in a fire at Wilberforce University on 14 April 1865. As a black man engaged in a lifetime of protest, Delany had no room to espouse the notion of art for its own sake; indeed his craft was a vehicle for protest. But it is precisely in response to Delany's commitment to the elevation of his people, as well as his recognition of the ultimate power of the written word that recent scholars have finally begun to confirm his reputation as a man far ahead of his time and an important contributor to the literature and thought of black America.

Bibliography:

Curtis W. Ellison and E. W. Metcalf, Jr., *William Wells Brown and Martin R. Delany: A Reference Guide* (Boston: G. K. Hall, 1978), pp. 155-234.

Biographies:

Frank A. Rollins (Frances E. Rollin Whipper), *Life and Public Services of Martin R. Delany* (Boston: Lee & Shepherd, 1868);

Dorothy Sterling, *The Making of an Afro-American: Martin Robinson Delany, 1812-1885* (Garden City: Doubleday, 1971).

References:

Howard H. Bell, "The Negro Emigration Movement, 1849-1854: A Phase of Negro Nationalism," *Phylon*, 20 (1959): 132-142;

William Montogue Cobb, "Martin Robinson Delany," *Journal of the National Medical Association*, 44 (1952): 232-238;

Cyril E. Griffith, *The African Dream: Martin R. Delany and the Emergence of Pan-African Thought* (University Park & London: Pennsylvania State University Press, 1975);

Melvin Bert Rahmming, "The Evolution of the West Indian's Image in the Afro-American Novel," Ph.D. dissertation, University of Oklahoma, 1978;

Victor Ullman, *Martin R. Delany: The Beginnings of Black Nationalism* (Boston: Beacon Press, 1971).

Frederick Douglass

Russell K. Hively

See also the Douglass entries in *DLB 1, The American Renaissance in New England,* and *DLB 43, American Newspaper Journalists, 1690-1872.*

BIRTH: Tuckahoe, Maryland, probably February 1817, to Harriet Bailey.

MARRIAGES: 15 September 1838 to Anna Murray (deceased, 1882); children: Lewis, Frederick, Rosetta, Charles Remond, and Annie. 24 January 1884 to Helen Pitts.

DEATH: Anacostia Heights, Washington, D.C., 20 February 1895.

SELECTED BOOKS: *Narrative of the Life of Frederick Douglass, an American Slave. Written by Himself* (Boston: Published at the Anti-Slavery Office, 1845; Dublin: Webb & Chapman, 1845); enlarged as *My Bondage and My Freedom,* introduction by Dr. James M'Cune Smith (New York: Miller, Orton & Mulligan, 1855); enlarged again as *The Life and Times of Frederick Douglass, Written by Himself,* introduction by George L. Ruffin (Hartford, Conn.: Park, 1881); republished as *The Life and Times of Frederick Douglass, from 1817-1882, Written by Himself,* introduction by the Right Hon. John Bright, M.P., edited by John Lobb (London: Christian Age Office, 1882); revised as *Life and Times of Frederick Douglass, Written by Himself,* introduction by Ruffin (Boston: De Wolfe, Fisk, 1892);

Farewell Speech of Mr. Frederick Douglass, Previously to Embarking on Board the Cambria, *upon His Return to America, Delivered at the Valedictory Soiree Given to Him at the London Tavern, on March 30, 1847. Published, by Order of the Council of the Anti-Slavery League, from the Short-hand Notes of Mr. W. Farmer* (London: Ward, 1847);

Lectures on American Slavery (Buffalo, N.Y.: Reese & Co's Power Press, 1851);

Oration, Delivered in Corinthian Hall, Rochester, by Frederick Douglass, July 5th, 1852 (Rochester, N.Y.: Printed by Lee, Mann, 1852);

The Claims of the Negro Ethnologically Considered. An Address before the Literary Societies of Western Reserve College, at Commencement, July 12, 1854

Courtesy of Library of Congress

(Rochester, N.Y.: Printed by Lee, Mann, 1854);

The Anti-Slavery Movement. A Lecture by Frederick Douglass, before the Rochester Ladies' Anti-Slavery Society (Rochester, N.Y.: Press of Lee, Mann, 1855);

Address by Frederick Douglass, and Poem by A. C. Hills Delivered at the Erection of the Wing Monument, at Mexico, Oswego Co., N.Y., September 11th, 1855 (Syracuse, N.Y.: J. G. K. Truair, 1855);

Two Speeches by Frederick Douglass: One on West India Emancipation, Delivered at Canadaigua, Aug. 4th, and the Other on the Dred Scott Decision. Delivered in New York, on the Occasion of the Anniversary of the American Abolition Society, May 1857 (Rochester, N.Y.: C. P. Dewey, printer, 1857);

Eulogy of the Late Hon. Wm. Jay, by Frederick Douglass, Delivered on the Invitation of the Colored Citizens of New York City in Shiloh Presbyterian Church, New York, May 12, 1859 (Rochester, N.Y.: Press of A. Strong & Co., 1859);

U.S. Grant and the Colored People. His Wise, Just, Practical, and Effective Friendship Thoroughly Vindicated by Incontestable Facts in His Record from 1862 to 1872. Words of Truth and Soberness! He Who Runs May Read and Understand!! Be Not Deceived, Only Truth Can Endure!!! (Washington, D.C., 1872);

Address Delivered by Hon. Frederick Douglass, at the Third Annual Fair of the Tennessee Colored Agricultural Association on Thursday, September 18, 1873, at Nashville, Tennessee (Washington, D.C.: New National Era and Citizen Print., 1873);

Oration by Frederick Douglass, Delivered on Occasion of the Unveiling of the Freedmen's Monument in Memory of Abraham Lincoln, in Lincoln Park, Washington, D.C., April 14th, 1876. With an Appendix (Washington, D.C.: Gibson Brothers, printers, 1876);

John Brown. An Address by Frederick Douglass, at the Fourteenth Anniversary of Storer College, Harper's Ferry, West Virginia, May 30, 1881 (Dover, N.H.: Morning Star Job Printing House, 1881);

The 21st Anniversary of the Emancipation of Slavery in the District of Columbia: An Address (Washington, D.C.: National Republican, 1883);

Three Addresses on the Relations Subsisting between the White and Colored People of the United States (Washington, D.C.: Gibson Brothers, printers, 1886);

The Race Problem; Great Speech of Frederick Douglass, Delivered before The Bethel Literary and Historical Association in the Metropolitan A.M.E. Church (Washington, D.C.: N.p., 1890);

Lecture on Haiti. The Haitian Pavilion Dedication Ceremonies Delivered at the World's Fair in Jackson Park, Chicago, Jan. 2d, 1893 (Chicago, 1893);

Address by Hon. Frederick Douglass, Delivered in the Metropolitan A.M.E. Church, Washington, D.C., Tuesday, January 9th, 1894, on the Lessons of the Hour. In Which He Discusses the Various Aspects of the So-Called, but Mis-Called, Negro Problem (Baltimore: Press of Thomas & Evans, 1894);

Why is the Negro Lynched? By the late Frederick Douglass (Bridgewater: Printed by J. Whitby & Sons, 1895);

Negroes and the National War Effort, an Address by Frederick Douglass, foreword by James W. Ford (New York: Workers Library Publishers, 1942);

Frederick Douglass: Selections from His Writings, edited by Philip S. Foner (New York: International Publishers, 1945);

The Frederick Douglass Papers: Series One: Speeches, Debates, and Interviews. Volume I: Eighteen-Forty-One to Eighteen-Forty-Six, edited by John W. Blassingame (New Haven: Yale University Press, 1979).

Champion of the suppressed people of the world, Frederick Douglass was an escaped slave who rose to become the United States Minister to Haiti and a counselor to four presidents. A man with no formal education who spoke at universities all over the world, Douglass, who as a youngster slept in an animal pen, eventually became wealthy enough to afford the home of his dreams.

Frederick Augustus Washington Bailey was born in Tuckahoe, Maryland, which he once described as "a small district of country, thinly populated, and remarkable for nothing I know of more than the worn-out sandy, desert-like appearance of its soil." He calculated his birth date to have been in February 1817; later in life, he celebrated it on 14 February. His mother, Harriet Bailey, was a literate slave; his father is presumed to have been a white man. During the first few years of his life he was raised by his grandparents, Betsey and Isaac Bailey. "My only recollections of my own mother are of a few hasty visits made in the night on foot, after the daily tasks were over. . . . Of my father I know nothing. Slavery had no recognition of fathers, as none of families." Betsey Bailey was held in high esteem by her owner, and her only job was the raising of the youngsters whose mothers were working in the fields.

Douglass's master was Capt. Aaron Anthony, who owned several farms in Tuckahoe and was chief clerk and butler on the home plantation of Col. Edward Lloyd. After a few years Douglass was marched from his grandmother's cabin to the main plantation where he was put into a breeding pen with dogs and pigs, where the smaller children were kept. Some of the children in the pen with Douglass were his brothers and sisters. They were called "pigs," and their main fare was corn mush,

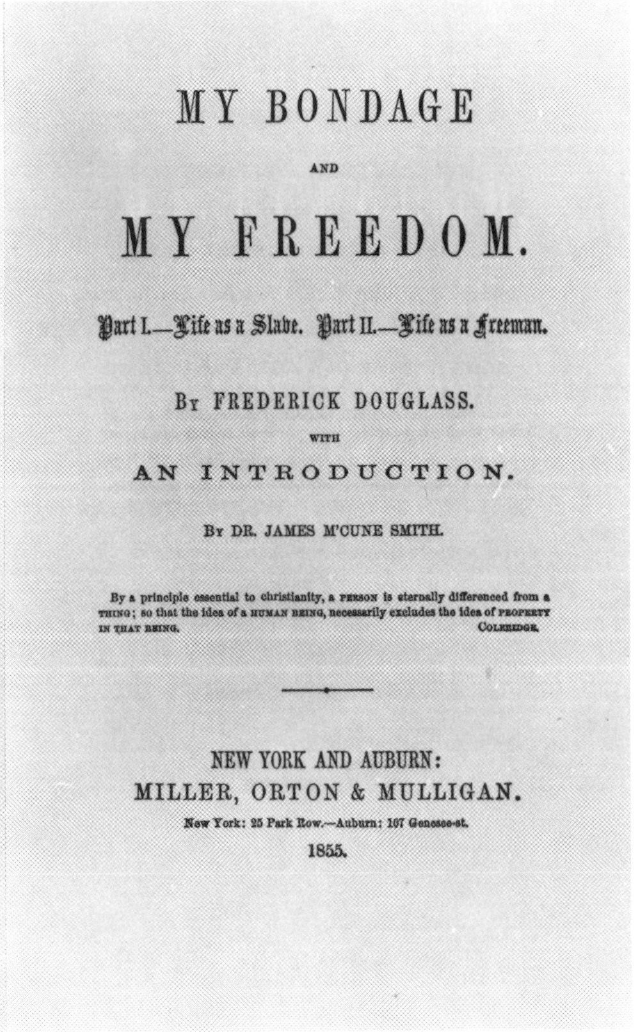
MY BONDAGE

AND

MY FREEDOM.

Part I.—Life as a Slave. Part II.—Life as a Freeman.

BY FREDERICK DOUGLASS.

WITH

AN INTRODUCTION.

BY DR. JAMES M'CUNE SMITH.

By a principle essential to christianity, a PERSON is eternally differenced from a THING; so that the idea of a HUMAN BEING, necessarily excludes the idea of PROPERTY IN THAT BEING. COLERIDGE.

NEW YORK AND AUBURN:
MILLER, ORTON & MULLIGAN.
New York: 25 Park Row.—Auburn: 107 Genesee-st.
1855.

Frontispiece and title page for Douglass's second autobiography

which they dipped from a trough with oyster halves or pieces of old shingle. Frederick's overseer in the pen was a devoted woman called Aunt Katy. The young Bailey had one long tow-linen cloth shirt which hung to his knees. He wore this garment day and night, and it was washed once a week.

Frederick's first work was to serve as errand boy to Lucretia Auld, a daughter of Colonel Lloyd. In January 1826 he was sent to Baltimore, Maryland, to Hugh Auld, brother-in-law of Lucretia, to care for the Aulds' "bright-eyed and beloved boy Tommy." Although Frederick was picked on by the boys in the city and he disliked being locked away from the out-of-doors, he was treated by Hugh's wife Sophia with dignity. Freddy (her nickname for him) became like a stepbrother to little Tommy. Hugh Auld was not as congenial, but he was completely wrapped up in his shipbuilding and left Frederick under the care of his wife. At young Bailey's request Sophia began teaching him how to read. He soon learned the alphabet and could spell words three and four letters long. When Sophia told her husband of Frederick's accomplishment, he forbade her from teaching the boy anymore. He told her, "If you give a nigger an inch, he will take an ell. . . . If he learns to read the Bible, it will forever unfit him to be a slave."

Frederick invented his own ways of learning to read. Having earned a little money by blacking boots for some gentlemen, he purchased a copy of the *Columbian Orator,* which he used not only to improve his reading but to learn the principles of freedom from the speeches included in the book. He soon began to read the daily newspaper, the *Baltimore American,* and learned of the abolition movements in the North. This new knowledge fueled his desire to be free.

When Frederick was put to work running errands for the workers in the shipyards, he saw the carpenters writing the location of certain boards on the new ships. The boy traced the markings and in this manner taught himself to write. He often tricked neighborhood boys into writing contests as a way to get them to aid in his lessons. Later, when Tommy was going to school, Frederick was frequently left at home alone, and he used Tommy's books to practice his reading and writing skills.

In 1833 he returned to St. Michaels, Maryland, and to Thomas Auld, his new owner after Colonel Anthony's death. Young Bailey, who was beginning to show signs of independent thinking, was put in charge of "Mr. Thomas's" horse, an outlaw that constantly ran away. Neither the horse nor the boy were broken by beatings, and on 1 January 1834 Bailey was placed in the care of Edward Covey, a man paid to break disrespectful slaves. Covey enjoyed sneaking up on the slaves to see if he could catch them doing anything worthy of a beating. For his stealthiness, he earned the nickname "the snake." Covey put Bailey to work in the fields, where he was an awkward hand. He was beaten three days after he arrived and for over one year was beaten at least once a week with either a stick or a piece of cowskin.

Once, after Covey beat him unmercifully, Bailey fled to his master's store and begged for mercy, but Auld sent him back. When he reached the Covey farm, "the snake" jumped out from bushes along the driveway. Bailey became frightened and ran into the woods. He was rescued by Sandy, a neighbor's slave who was an African believed to possess some magical powers. Sandy gave the boy a pinch of soil from Africa along with much advice. Bailey regained his courage and returned to Covey's where, surprisingly, he was treated well. The next morning he was ordered to work in the barn. Covey sneaked in and attacked the boy who, for the first time, fought back. They reportedly tousled for nearly two hours; no one would help Covey subdue his slave. Covey lost the battle but still gave orders, saying, "Now you scoundrel, go to your work. I would have not whipped you so hard, if you had not resisted." Bailey's resistance was a turning point in his life: "When a slave cannot be flogged, he is more than half free." His days of service with Covey ended on Christmas Day 1834.

For the next year Bailey worked for William Freeland, who lived three miles from St. Michaels. He was not mistreated there and eventually began to teach reading to the other slaves with books borrowed from the big house, including James Fenimore Cooper's *The Last of the Mohicans* (1826).

In 1836, with five others, Henry Harris, John Harris, Sandy Jenkins, Charles Toberts, and Henry Bailey, Frederick Bailey began forming a scheme for escape. They planned to steal a canoe and row up the Chesapeake Bay to the North. Frederick wrote passes for each of them, and they planned to escape on Easter eve. Their escape was thwarted, and they were dragged fifteen miles behind horses to jail. Bailey was never convicted but was sent back to Hugh Auld in Baltimore.

There Bailey was hired out by Auld to William Gardiner to learn to caulk ships, but the white workers refused to work with Bailey because he was black, and he was forced to quit. He then went to work for Walter Price and received the highest caulker's wages, up to $9 a week, which he was forced to turn over to Auld. Having to hand over his money convinced Bailey he had to escape. He first acquired partial freedom by hiring himself out and paying a weekly fee to Auld. This arrangement required him to live on his own and provide his own keep. Once, when he did not make a payment on time, he was called back to Auld's care.

On Monday, 3 September 1838, with the moral and financial support of freedwoman Anna Murray, he left Baltimore and slavery. He obtained papers resembling those of a free sailor, and he boarded a train in disguise. After a one-day stopover in Philadelphia, he reached New York. "I soon found that New York was not quite so free or so safe a refuge as I had supposed, and a sense of loneliness and insecurity again oppressed me most sadly." He feared being recaptured by the many slave hunters in New York, and he was lucky to befriend a sailor who took him to David Ruggles, the secretary of the New York Vigilance Committee and the local underground railroad agent. While Bailey was hiding with Ruggles, Anna Murray came from Baltimore, and they were married 15 September 1838 by Presbyterian minister J. W. C. Pennington. Ruggles relocated the newlyweds to New Bedford, Massachusetts. They sailed on the *John W. Richmond* to their new home.

Frederick Augustus Washington Bailey had stopped using his two middle names when he was in Baltimore. He called himself Frederick Johnson while in flight, but when he arrived in New Bedford he discovered there were many Johnsons. He took the name Douglass from a character in Sir Walter Scott's *Lady of the Lake*.

On the fifth day after his arrival, he put on working clothes and went to find employment. On his walk to the docks, he saw a large pile of coal in front of a house. He went to the door and asked the matron if he could bring in the coal. When asked what wages he wanted, he replied, "I will leave that to you." When the job was finished, he received two silver half dollars, his first earnings as a free man. He worked at various jobs, most frequently loading ships. In time he obtained employment in a brass foundry. When Douglass began working on the docks, he discovered the major difference between the North and the South: in the North they used animal and machine power; in the South they used slave power.

After living in New Bedford for a few months, he was approached by a young man who asked him to subscribe to William Lloyd Garrison's *Liberator*. Douglass said the "paper took a place in my heart second only to the Bible." In summer of 1841

Anna Murray Douglass (courtesy of Moorland-Spingarn Research Center, Howard University)

Douglass attended an antislavery convention that was held in Nantucket under the direction of Garrison and his friends. William C. Coffin, who had heard Douglass speak to some friends at a church in New Bedford, sought Douglass out and asked him to say a few words at the convention. Douglass spoke of some of the things he had seen as a slave. In response to his speech, a contemporary wrote, "your whole soul was fired." At the close of the convention, John A. Collins, the general agent of the Massachusetts Anti-Slavery Society, solicited Douglass to become an agent for his organization. Although he feared he might be discovered by his owners, he agreed to act as an agent for a three-month period. "Fugitive slaves were rare then, and as a fugitive slave lecturer, I had the advantage of being a 'bran new fact.'" His strong, pleasant speaking voice helped turn the three months into four years.

During his four years of work for the society, Douglass suffered from many prejudices. When his troupe traveled on trains, he was forced to ride in the Negro or Jim Crow car. Sometimes his white campaigners would join him, but he felt they should take advantage of the accommodations they had.

Once when Douglass was scheduled to talk in Grafton, Massachusetts, he discovered that no one had advertised he was to speak. To summon an audience, he borrowed a dinner bell from the hotel and went through the streets crying, "Notice! Frederick Douglass, recently a slave, will lecture on American slavery at the Grafton Common, this evening at 7 o'clock." This notice produced a large audience.

Eighteen forty-three was a year of intense activity for the New England Anti-Slavery Society. Sometimes the speakers were met by mobs and "evil smelling eggs," but they went forward. In Pendleton, Indiana, Douglass's group was speaking when they were attacked by a mob. In the melee he broke his hand but continued on his speaking engagements.

In 1845 he wrote the stories of his life as he had been telling them in his orations. The result was *Narrative of the Life of Frederick Douglass, an American Slave.* This simple narration became a best-seller on two continents and was translated into both French and German. It was a small volume of 125 pages selling for fifty cents with introductions by Garrison and Phillips. The book came off the press in May 1845. "Considered merely as a narrative," read a review in the *New York Tribune,* "we never read one more simple, true, coherent, and warm with genuine feeling. It is an excellent piece of writing, and on that score to be prized as a specimen of powers of the black race, which prejudice persists in disputing."

After his *Narrative* was published Douglass, for fear of being recaptured, fled to England. He was given a second-class cabin ticket but in time had almost free run of the *Cambria.* Only once was there trouble, and that was when he was going to speak about slavery on invitation of the ship's captain. Some passengers from Georgia attempted to prevent his speaking but were rewarded for their efforts by being put into irons. Douglass spent two years lecturing in England, Ireland, Scotland, and Wales, and he corresponded with abolitionist newspapers in America. He found the British "knew nothing of the republican Negro-hate prevalent in our glorious land."

Douglass's friends in England corresponded with an attorney and found out Capt. Thomas Auld would take £150 ($750) for Frederick Douglass's

Cover for 1845 songbook dedicated to fugitive slaves, featuring Douglass's portrait (courtesy of Library of Congress)

freedom. The papers releasing Douglass were signed on 13 November and 5 December 1846. He sailed to America in the spring of 1847 as a free man.

Upon his return he moved with his family to Rochester, New York, where he began a newspaper with $2,174 given him by English friends. The *North Star,* a joint effort, with Martin Robinson Delany initially serving as the other editor, dedicated to "Universal Emancipation," was known as a good journalistic paper working for the abolition of slavery by using peaceful political methods. Douglass and Delany chose Rochester as the home of the *North Star* so that it would not interfere with the New England *Liberator* and the *Anti-Slavery Standard,* two established papers. Delany left the *North Star* after only a brief tenure there. The weekly paper had several thousand subscribers, but the editor often had difficulty meeting "pecuniary engagements." In 1851 the title was changed to *Fred-*

erick Douglass's Paper to distinguish it from the many papers with "star" in their titles.

The paper was typical of antislavery publications of the day. Unpaid correspondents reported on local and regional abolitionist activities, and articles were culled from other periodicals and reprinted in *Frederick Douglass's Paper.* Appropriate verse, book reviews, and novel serializations were run alongside articles on woman suffrage and job training for blacks.

In June 1858 Douglass initiated *Douglass' Monthly,* an abolitionist magazine aimed at circulation in the British Isles. This periodical succumbed for lack of funds. To historians' dismay the files of *Frederick Douglass's Paper,* from 1848 until it folded in mid-1860, were destroyed by fire on 2 June 1872, after Douglass had been invited to send the volumes to Harvard University.

Apart from the journal, Rochester provided Douglass with a range of experiences. While publishing and editing his paper, Douglass also was the Rochester Station agent for the underground railroad. Once he had eleven fugitives under his roof.

Ironically, while Douglass was concerned with racial inequities in society, his oldest daughter was segregated from the rest of the girls at Tracy Seminary, where she was enrolled as a student. Douglass tried to force the school to integrate but failed.

During the 1850s Douglass worked with many abolitionists, including Sojourner Truth. In March 1853, a year after *Uncle Tom's Cabin* was published, Douglass was summoned to Harriet Beecher Stowe's home in Andover, Massachusetts, to counsel her on additional upcoming plans to help the American slaves. Douglass revamped and republished his autobiography, calling it *My Bondage and My Freedom* (1855). In this version he inserted more of his philosophies and feelings than he had in the first *Narrative.*

In the early Rochester days, Douglass had been introduced to John Brown, and he had later visited the Browns in Springfield, Massachusetts. During the time of the bloody Kansas Wars and the Missouri Compromise, Brown continued to visit with Douglass in Rochester. Douglass had strong feelings about what was happening in the United States, and he expressed his thoughts in his newspaper. On 16 October 1859 John Brown and eighteen followers attacked the arsenal at Harper's Ferry. They held the ground for nearly thirty hours but did not succeed in getting all the neighboring slaves to join in the battle as planned. They did collect fifty blacks to their ranks, but the insurrection was put down by Robert E. Lee and his United States soldiers. The riot by Brown roused very strong feelings among the American citizens, especially in the South. The survivors of the raid were executed, and the public called for prosecution of Brown's friends and allies, including Frederick Douglass.

Douglass, who at that time had a speaking engagement in Philadelphia, first fled to Hoboken, New Jersey. He telegraphed home, instructing his son Lewis to "secure all the important papers in my high desk." These papers were correspondence between Douglass and Brown. The governor of Virginia sent a request to Pres. James Buchanan asking that Douglass be brought to Virginia for trial. Douglass, in the meantime, had sneaked back to his home and on to Canada, six hours before the agents arrived at Rochester. On 31 October 1859 Douglass wrote a letter to the editor of the *Rochester Democrat and American* explaining his position in regard to Brown's raid and his reasons for leaving the country. Douglass had been against the plan and had argued with Brown about it. Douglass said he had felt the raid would "rouse the country."

On 12 November 1859 Douglass boarded the steamer *Scotia* for England to avoid arrest for complicity. The English knew of Harper's Ferry and Douglass's implication in the raid, and consequently he was in great demand and readily engaged in speaking engagements about American slavery. After six months Douglass learned of his daughter Annie's death and immediately boarded the first steamer for America and Rochester. He was at home for over a month before anyone realized he was not in England.

The state of Virginia had executed all the raiders by this time, and Brown had acted with such dignity that he had become a martyr. The investigation by Congress of Brown's supporters faltered because Brown had implicated no one, and because the great political battle between Abraham Lincoln, Stephen A. Douglas, and John C. Breckinridge was taking over the spotlight of the day. Douglass initially opposed Lincoln's cautious policies, but he supported Lincoln after the president issued the Emancipation Proclamation.

Because Douglass did not support the policy of enforced slavery, still a law in the North, he did everything possible to assure the war effort would not only preserve the Union but also free all slaves. The Federal Union would not allow blacks to be members of the military. Douglass argued that the use of blacks for all the support work for the Southern forces freed the whites to fight, thus helping the Confederate cause. Blacks were first used by

The shop in Rochester, New York, where North Star *and* Frederick Douglass's Paper *were printed*

the Northern forces as waiters, then laborers. Finally they were put into uniform, albeit a different one from the rest of the soldiers.

In time Governor Andrew of Massachusetts received permission from Abraham Lincoln to raise two black regiments, the 54th and the 55th. On 2 March 1863 Douglass used his magazine to make a plea for support to all black citizens of the North. Douglass's two sons Charles and Lewis were among the first men from New York to volunteer for service in the Massachusetts regiments. In time Frederick Douglass, Jr., became an army recruiter in the Mississippi Valley.

The Southerners would not treat captured black soldiers as equals; and when a black soldier was captured, he was either shot or sold off into slavery. Douglass went to Washington to meet with Lincoln to discuss solutions for this demoralizing situation. Douglass was after three things: equal pay for black soldiers, assurance of equal treatment from Jefferson Davis for black prisoners of war, and equal recognition for honors in battle. Lincoln assured Douglass that equal pay and equal recognition for bravery would be forthcoming, but the third request would be difficult to accomplish.

On 1 January 1863 the Emancipation Proclamation went into effect, changing the direction of the fight for black equality. The proclamation caused unrest for many Northerners, especially in New York. Many antidraft riots broke out because whites felt they were being asked to fight the war for the blacks and not for the preservation of the Union.

During the war Douglass was summoned by Lincoln several times. Once he was asked to organize a system to get free Southern slaves to the Union lines and freedom. The war ended before the plan was completed.

One incident which impressed Douglass about Lincoln happened in one of their meetings. While Douglass was in Lincoln's office discussing some matter, Lincoln's secretary announced twice that Governor Buckingham of Connecticut was waiting. Lincoln replied, "Tell Governor Buckingham to wait, for I want to have a long talk with my friend Frederick Douglass." Douglass worked hard to see that Lincoln was re-elected, and he attended Lincoln's inauguration; he was one of the first blacks to attend an inauguration as a guest. He was not impressed with Vice-Pres. Andrew Johnson and felt Johnson was not a friend of the Afro-American.

With the Civil War over, Douglass believed that his work of twenty-five years, nearly his entire adult life, was completed. He had seen freedom for the slaves and an end to the great war, but he continued speaking to various groups because he knew that the struggle for freedom was not yet won, except in law. In practice the black was looked down upon. The free black man had, Douglass said, "neither money, property, nor friends. He was free from the old plantation, but he had nothing but the dust road under his feet. He was free from the old quarters that once gave him shelter, but a slave to the rains of summer and to the frosts of winter. He was, in a word, literally turned loose, naked, hungry, and destitute, to the open sky."

On 7 February 1866 Douglass and a delegation met with Pres. Andrew Johnson to talk about the reconstruction of the South and how the Negro fit into the reconstruction plans. They were not well received. Douglass, in a later letter to Johnson, admitted that relationships between blacks and whites in the South were not and would not be good for a while. Douglass's biggest concern was getting suffrage for the blacks. He was also much opposed to the colonization approach advocated by President Johnson, through which blacks were to be settled in their own country or state.

In September 1866 the National Loyalist's Convention was held in Philadelphia and Douglass was elected to represent Rochester at this meeting. It was unusual for a black man to be elected from a city of 60,000 whites and 200 blacks. His election caused great stress among the other delegates, as well. On the train to the convention he was asked not to participate because his attendance might alter the votes of some of the members. "You might as well ask me to put a loaded pistol to my head and blow my brains out, as to ask me to keep out of this convention," he responded. His attendance influenced Ulysses S. Grant to favor the right to vote for American blacks. After the adoption of the 14th and 15th amendments into the Constitution, Douglass's friends tried to convince him to run for political office, possibly the Senate. He declined and later stated that he "never regretted that I did not enter into the arena of congressional honors."

Douglass contributed pieces to the leading periodicals of his day, including the *Washington Evening Star, Harper's Weekly, Woman's Journal,* and *London Times.* After attempting to retire to yard work at his home, he joined another newspaper venture, the *New National Era,* in Washington, D.C. In time he became the paper's owner and turned it over to his sons Lewis and Frederick. It never really succeeded and folded in 1874.

During this period Douglass became involved with "The Freedman's Savings and Trust Company," known as "Freedman's Bank." The men who set up the bank were mostly former preachers who wanted a bank for the freed slaves to help teach them "sobriety, wisdom, and economy, and to show them how to rise in the world." In time Douglass was solicited by the trustees of the organization to take over as president. Four months later the organization failed. Douglass lost a sizeable part of his savings and livelihood.

Douglass's career shifted from journalism to politics during this period. President Grant appointed him to the Council of the District of Columbia. Douglass served only a short time because of other commitments; his son Lewis filled out the term. On Declaration Day 1871 he was asked to deliver a speech to the "Unknown Loyal Dead" at Arlington for President Grant and "the great multitude of distinguished people." In April 1872 Douglass presided over the "national convention of colored citizens" in New Orleans. At this time the Republican party was split and the convention was to decide where the black vote was to be cast. The convention ended up supporting Grant and Wilson. Douglass was an avid campaigner for the Republican party for the rest of his life. Douglass participated in the ceremonies on the occasion of the unveiling of Lincoln's Monument in Washington, D.C., on 4 April 1876. He found it "one of the most interesting incidents of [my] life."

President Hayes appointed Douglass United States Marshall of the District of Columbia. Many members of Congress opposed this appointment mainly because Douglass was responsible for "introducing the aristocratic citizens of the republic" at the White House, as official greeter to the many guests.

A new cause now taken up by Frederick Douglass was his opposition to the black northern migration. Douglass believed that the South needed black labor to renew the country's economic structure, and he felt blacks should be a part of the renewal and not flee from it.

When Capt. Thomas Auld was eighty years old and on his deathbed, he invited Frederick Douglass to come to the old plantation and visit. It

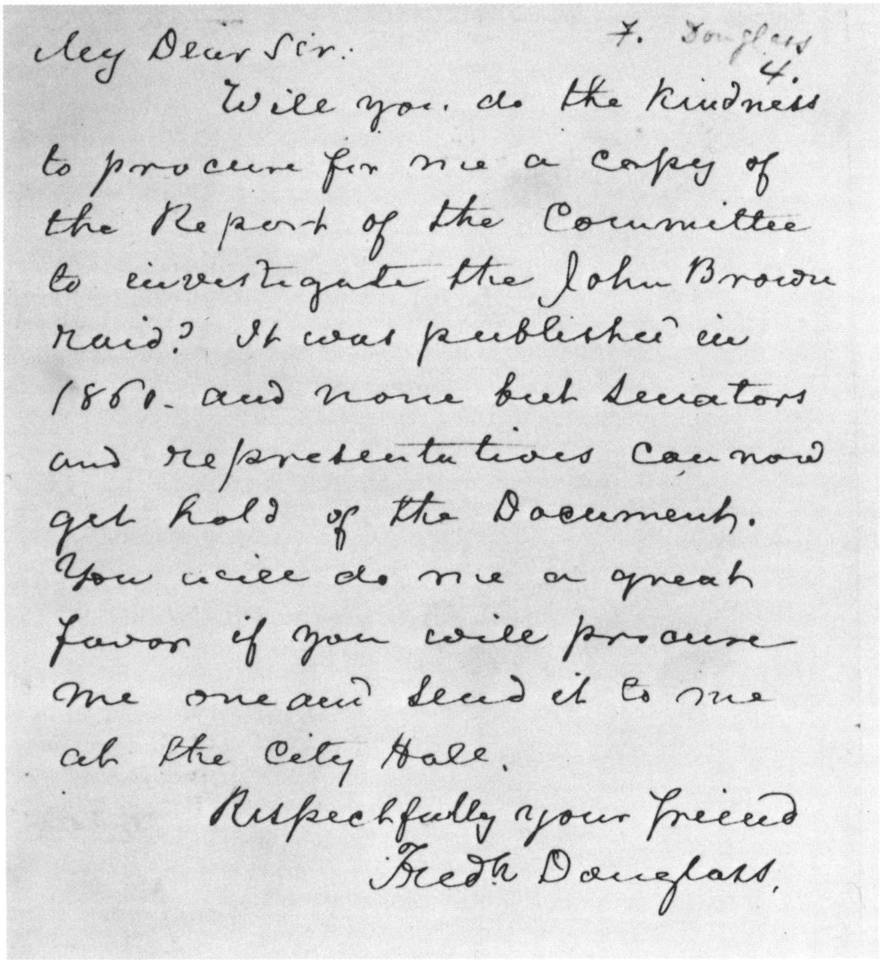

F. Douglass
4.

My Dear Sir:

Will you do the kindness to procure for me a copy of the Report of the Committee to investigate the John Brown raid? It was published in 1860 and none but Senators and representatives can now get hold of the Document. You will do me a great favor if you will procure me one and send it to me at the City Hall.

Respectfully your friend
Fredk Douglass.

Undated request for the findings of an investigation of the Harper's Ferry raid; Douglass had been under suspicion for complicity with John Brown (courtesy of Schomburg Center for Research in Black Culture, the New York Public Library, Astor, Lenox and Tilden Foundations)

had been over forty years since the two men had met. "But now that slavery was destroyed, and the slave and master stood upon equal ground, I was not only willing to meet him and was very glad to do so." In this meeting Douglass learned that he had erred in his *Narrative* when he had accused Auld of turning Douglass's grandmother Bailey "out to die like an old horse." Auld had not even inherited Betsey Bailey, but he did rescue her after reading Douglass's accusations in the *Narrative.* On this trip Douglass also visited the Lloyd mansion and other places from his childhood. He was amazed how time had changed things. He was treated as a welcome guest in the same places he had been a slave over forty years before.

In the 1880s Douglass was once asked to speak at Storer College, a school created to educate black students. He delivered a speech on John Brown. On the platform with Douglass sat the Hon. Andrew J. Hunter, the prosecuting attorney for the state of Virginia, who had conducted the Brown case and had consigned the abolitionist to the gallows. Hunter congratulated Douglass on his speech and commented that Robert E. Lee would also have liked it.

When James A. Garfield was elected and inaugurated into office, Douglass as marshall was the escort for both the outgoing and incoming presidents. Douglass was very fond of Garfield and was grieved at his assassination six months later.

Garfield did not reappoint Frederick Douglass to the marshall's office, although he had promised to do so. Instead, he appointed Douglass to the office of Recorder of Deeds for the District of Columbia, a position Douglass preferred to that of marshall. The job was exacting but had no social

Frederick Douglass

duties attached to it; Douglass was free to write or lecture as he wished. Another benefit of the job for Douglass was financial. The Office of the Recorder was supported by fees, and because of the rapid growth and strong financial atmosphere in Washington at the time, the recorder's income had "risen to a larger sum than that of any office of the national government except that of the President of the United States." The money he earned permitted him to buy the home of the Douglasses' dreams. When they had first married and were on their way to New Bedford, they had seen a large house on a hill. Douglass promised someday to buy one like it for Anna. They had lived in Anacostia Heights at Cedar Hill for only one year when Anna Murray Douglass died on 4 August 1882.

The same year they moved to Anacostia Heights, Douglass had republished his autobiography for a third time. He called the newest version *The Life and Times of Frederick Douglass* (1881). He brought his life up to date, and he expanded the philosophy and ideas section.

Douglass served five years as recorder, the last one under Pres. Grover Cleveland, and he married his white secretary, Helen Pitts, in late January 1884. This marriage across color lines raised a fuss from many people, but President Cleveland treated the couple as equals and invited them to the receptions and gatherings with no reservations. Douglass said of the marriage, "They would have had no objection to my marrying a person much darker in complexion than myself, but to marry one much lighter, and of the complexion of my father rather than my mother, was, in the popular eye, a shocking offense, and one for which I was to be ostracized by white and black alike."

On 15 September 1886 the Douglasses went on a tour of Europe. Douglass wanted to visit the British Isles and Europe, where he had not ventured before. He was impressed by the historical aspects of "the country lying between Paris and Rome," and he was delighted to discover people with black features as he traveled eastward and southward. Douglass found many areas of interest because of his previous readings. He visited the prison of which Alexander Dumas had written and he visited Genoa where Christopher Columbus was born, as well as the rock from which Edmond Dantes was hurled. Douglass was not impressed with the religious monuments and humorously noted "some curiosity in seeing devout people going to the black statue of St. Peter—I was glad to find him black, I have no prejudice against his color—and kissing the old fellow's big toe, one side of which has been nearly worn away by these devout and tender salutes. . . ."

Douglass believed that the African race had started in Egypt and he was anxious to visit there. He climbed to the top of the highest pyramid like a normal tourist, but he was most impressed when he thought how he was retracing the very steps of great men like Paul and Demosthenes.

The Douglasses took an entire year to travel and returned to America to become involved in the next election. Although he was not a delegate, he was called upon to speak from the Republican platform. Benjamin Harrison won the election.

In 1889 Harrison appointed Frederick Douglass to the office of Minister Resident and Counsul-general to the Republic of Haiti and chargé d'affaires to Santo Domingo. He served at these posts for two years and was condemned for not obtaining certain concessions from the Haitians. The biggest concession was to get a naval base for the United States Navy at Mole, St. Nicolas. The United States newspapers claimed because Douglass was a black man serving a predominately black nation his sympathy was with his race and not his nation. Douglass refuted this claim in an article in the *North American Review* in September and October 1891.

Helen Pitts Douglass

From 1891 until his death in 1895, Douglass retired to Anacostia Heights. Although retired, he never rested. He fought against prejudice and the lynching of blacks in the South, and he continued to work for racial equality under the law. Once when he was asked how he felt when he was jeered or hooted at by hecklers because of his color, Douglass answered, "I feel as if an ass had kicked, and hit nobody."

On the afternoon of 20 February 1895, Douglass died of heart failure.

Biographies:

Frederic May Holland, *Frederic* [sic] *Douglass: The Colored Orator* (New York: Funk & Wagnalls, 1895);

Charles W. Chesnutt, *Frederick Douglass* (Boston: Small, Maynard, 1899);

Shirley Graham, *There Was Once a Slave* (New York: Julian Messner, 1947);

Benjamin Quarles, *Frederick Douglass* (Washington, D.C.: Associated Publishers, 1948);

Philip S. Foner, *The Life and Writings of Frederick Douglass,* 4 volumes (New York: International Publishers, 1950-1955);

Foner, *Frederick Douglass* (New York: Citadel Press, 1964);

Quarles, ed., *Frederick Douglass* (Englewood Cliffs, N.J.: Prentice-Hall, 1968);

Booker T. Washington, *Frederick Douglass* (New York: Haskell House, 1968);

Arna Bontemps, *Free at Last: The Life of Frederick Douglass* (New York: Dodd, Mead, 1971);

Nathan Irvin Huggins, *Slave and Citizen: The Life of Frederick Douglass* (Boston: Little, Brown, 1980);

Diopkon J. Preston, *Young Frederick Douglass: The Maryland Years* (Baltimore: Johns Hopkins University Press, 1980).

Papers:

Some of Douglass's papers, including his diary, are housed at the Frederick Douglass home museum, Cedar Hill, Washington, D.C. Yale University and the Library of Congress house other Douglass documents.

W. E. B. Du Bois

Addison Gayle, Jr.
Bernard M. Baruch College of the City University of New York

See also the Du Bois entry in *DLB 47, American Historians, 1866-1912.*

BIRTH: Great Barrington, Massachusetts, 23 February 1868, to Alfred and Mary Burghardt Du Bois.

EDUCATION: B.A., Fisk University, 1888; B.A., 1890; M.A., 1891; Ph.D., 1896, Harvard University; University of Berlin, 1892-1894.

MARRIAGES: 1896 to Nina Gomer (deceased 1950); children: Burghardt, Yolande Du Bois Williams. 14 February 1951 to Shirley Graham.

AWARDS AND HONORS: Minister Plenipotentiary and Envoy Extraordinary to Liberia, conferred by President Calvin Coolidge, 1923; LL.D. from Howard University, 1930; Spingarn Medal from NAACP, 1932; LL.D. from Atlanta University, 1938; Litt.D., Fisk University, 1938; L.H.D., Wilberforce University, 1940; elected to the National Institute of Arts and Letters, 1943; Lenin International Peace Prize, 1958; honorary degrees from Charles University, 1958 (Prague), Humboldt University, 1958 (Berlin), Moscow University, 1959.

DEATH: Accra, Ghana, 27 August 1963.

SELECTED BOOKS: *The Suppression of the African Slave-Trade to the United States of America, 1638-1870,* volume 1 of Harvard Historical Studies (New York & London: Longmans, Green, 1896);

The Conservation of Races (Washington, D.C.: American Negro Academy, 1897);

The Philadelphia Negro: A Social Study (Philadelphia: University of Pennsylvania, 1899);

The Souls of Black Folk: Essays and Sketches (Chicago: McClurg, 1903; London: Constable, 1905);

The Negro in the South, His Economic Progress in Relation to His Moral and Religious Development; Being the William Levi Bull Lectures for the Year 1907, by Du Bois and Booker T. Washington (Philadelphia: Jacobs, 1907);

John Brown (Philadelphia: Jacobs, 1909);

The Quest of the Silver Fleece (Chicago: McClurg, 1911);

The Negro (New York: Holt, 1915; London: Williams & Norgate, 1915);

Darkwater: Voices From Within the Veil (New York: Harcourt, Brace & Howe, 1920; London: Constable, 1920);

The Gift of Black Folk: The Negroes in the Making of America (Boston: Stratford, 1924);

W. E. B. Du Bois (courtesy of Archives, University Library, University of Massachusetts/Amherst)

Dark Princess: A Romance (New York: Harcourt, Brace, 1928);

Africa: Its Geography, People and Products (Girard, Kans.: Haldeman-Julius, 1930);

Africa: Its Place in Modern History (Girard, Kans.: Haldeman-Julius, 1930);

Black Reconstruction: An Essay Toward a History of the Part Which Black Folk Played in the Attempt to Reconstruct Democracy in America, 1860-1880 (New York: Harcourt, Brace, 1935);

Black Folk, Then and Now: An Essay in the History and Sociology of the Negro Race (New York: Holt, 1939);

Dusk of Dawn: An Essay Toward an Autobiography of a Race Concept (New York: Harcourt, Brace, 1940);

Color and Democracy: Colonies and Peace (New York: Harcourt, Brace, 1945);

The World and Africa: An Inquiry into the Part Which Africa Has Played in World History (New York: Viking, 1947);

In Battle for Peace: The Story of My 83rd Birthday (New York: Masses & Mainstream, 1952);

The Ordeal of Mansart (New York: Mainstream, 1957);

Mansart Builds a School (New York: Mainstream, 1959);

Worlds of Color (New York: Mainstream, 1961);

Selected Poems (Ghana: Ghana University Press, 1964?);

The Autobiography of W. E. B. Du Bois: A Soliloquy on Viewing My Life From the Last Decade of Its First Century, edited by Herbert Aptheker (New York: International Publishers, 1968);

W. E. B. Du Bois Speaks: Speeches and Addresses, edited by Philip S. Foner (New York: Pathfinder Press, 1970);

W. E. B. Du Bois: The Crisis Writing, edited by Daniel Walden (Greenwich, Conn.: Fawcett, 1972);

The Emerging Thought of W. E. B. Du Bois: Essays and Editorials From "The Crisis," edited by Henry Lee Moon (New York: Simon & Schuster, 1972);

The Education of Black People: Ten Critiques, 1906-1960, edited by Aptheker (Amherst: University of Massachusetts Press, 1973).

OTHER: *Atlanta University Publications,* nos. 3-18, edited by Du Bois (Atlanta: Atlanta University Press, 1898-1914);

Haiti, in *Federal Theatre Plays,* edited by Pierre de Rohan (New York: Random House, 1938);

An Appeal to the World: A Statement on the Denial of Human Rights to Minorities in the Case of Citizens of Negro Descent in the United States of America and an Appeal to the United Nations for Redress, edited by Du Bois (New York: National Association for the Advancement of Colored People, 1947).

PERIODICAL PUBLICATIONS: "Strivings of The Negro People," *Atlantic Monthly,* 80 (August 1897): 194-198,

"The Negro and Crime," *Independent,* 51 (18 May 1899): 1355-1357;

"The Atlanta Conferences," *Voice of the Negro,* 1 (March 1904): 85-90;

"Credo," *Independent,* 57 (6 October 1904): 787;

"The Souls of White Folk," *Independent,* 69 (18 August 1910): 339-342;

"Negro In Literature And Art," *Annals of the American Academy of Political and Social Science,* 49 (September 1913): 233-237;

"Editing *The Crisis,*" *Crisis,* 58 (March 1951): 147, 213;

"I Take My Stand," *Masses and Mainstream,* 4 (April 1951): 10-16.

"Every intellectual," writes Ignazio Silone, "is a revolutionary," and though this may not be generally true, in the case of W. E. B. Du Bois, the observation is both accurate and fitting. The internationally known scholar and writer, born in Great Barrington, Massachusetts, was one of America's few Renaissance men, contributing to the artistic, social, literary, and political environment of his time as have few men before or since. His dedication to principle and unswerving devotion to truth for over fifty years earned him the praise and scorn of his fellow countrymen, black and white. When he died on the eve of the March on Washington in 1963, he was lauded from the platform by the executive secretary of the NAACP; yet in 1966, three years later, he was excoriated by soon-to-be-President of the United States, Richard M. Nixon, because a group of idealistic, progressive, young Americans had established clubs on the nation's campuses bearing his name. These dual attitudes—praise and scorn—were constants throughout his life and although, in the latter stages of his career, the scorn seemed excessive, he bore it with that stoic determination that so marked his character. Writing of one trying experience—indictment and trial as a subversive—in 1951, during the infamous McCarthy era, he revealed his attitude toward the numerous crises of his long life: "It was a bitter experience and I bowed before the storm. But I did not break."

If there is something in Du Bois that Americans have come to identify as New England temperament, the stubborn Yankee, spiritual descendant of Henry David Thoreau and Washington Irving, it may well be because Du Bois's character was formed in the same New England clime. Certainly his description of his hometown, written in an essay, "The Pageant Of Seven Decades," rivals some of Thoreau's descriptions in *Walden:* "The town and its surroundings were a boy's paradise... there were mountains to climb and rivers to wade and swim, lakes to freeze and hills for coasting. There were orchards and caves and wide green fields; and all of it was the free property apparently of the children of town." Such poetic visions of their hometown were uncommon to most blacks in America in the 1800s, but Du Bois's family, though not middle-class, was unlike that of most blacks. His mother, Mary Burghardt, whom he describes as descending from Dutch-African stock, was a proud woman who encouraged her only son toward hard work and study. His respect for her, evidenced in numerous autobiographical sketches, was perhaps engendered by her condition: she was a single parent, whose husband Alfred Du Bois had fled almost simultaneously with the birth of their son. Aided now and then by relatives, a close-knit group whom Du Bois was to refer to as "The Du Bois Clan," she inculcated her son with her own New England virtues. She died on the eve of his entrance into college, and her death was both an occasion for grief and a moment for renewal of determination.

This sense of determination had begun to manifest itself earlier, when Du Bois had suddenly realized that here, in this arcadian setting, he was somewhat different from others. The realization was long in coming and exploded with force in a classroom where, during the customary exchange of greeting cards, a white female student refused to accept his. The refusal was registered "preemptorily with a glance. Then it dawned upon me with certain suddenness that I was different from the others . . . shut out from their world by a vast veil." Though he concluded with angry defiant words, "I had, thereafter, no desire to tear down that veil, to creep through," these are sentiments recollected and garnished in the tranquillity of later years. For here was the first serious stressful moment of his life, one that fired his determination and imbued his character with such anger that he was propelled forward with almost a singular objective: "That sky was bluest when I could beat them at a foot race or even beat their stringy heads . . . the worlds I longed for, and all their dazzling opportunities were theirs, not mine. But they should not keep these prizes, I said; some, all, I would wrest from them." When he journeyed to the black belt in 1885 to become a student at Fisk University, the wresting time had begun.

Those were memorable years spent in Tennessee at the all-black college founded for the sons and daughters of emancipated slaves, and Du Bois, whose nurturant years were spent in a predominantly white world, was "deliriously happy" in a setting that was black. At Fisk he began writing and public speaking, and, paying obeisance as always to his mother's tutelage, he excelled among his classmates, graduating with honors in 1888. Perhaps the most important days at Fisk were spent during the summer, when he left the campus to trek out into the hillsides, into the shanties and wood-shack homes of Tennessee's black inhabitants, seeking work as a teacher. Here he glimpsed, despite appalling poverty, a grandeur and heroism that he

W. E. B. Du Bois at the age of nineteen (courtesy of Schomburg Center for Research in Black Culture, the New York Public Library, Astor, Lenox and Tilden Foundations)

was later to describe eloquently in the essay "On The Meaning Of Progress." He recalled few such memorable events during his tenure at Harvard, however, where he entered with the junior class in 1888. He remembered the animosity of fellow white students, the friendship and guidance of such influential teachers as William James, Albert Bushnell Hart, George Santayana, and Frank Tausig, and the accolades which greeted his commencement speech on Jefferson Davis as he graduated cum laude with a B.A. degree. "Du Bois, the colored orator," wrote a commentator in *Washington,* a leading periodical, "was the star of the occasion."

A master's degree was awarded to him in the spring of 1891, and though he would not receive his Ph.D. until 1896, he had achieved more education than most young men in America. Still, he felt unprepared to cope "with the new and extraordinary situations then developing in America." To do so meant more education and this meant, in his mind, training abroad: "Any American scholar who wanted preferment went to Germany to study . . . I wanted then to study in Germany. I was determined that any failure on my part to become a recognized American scholar must not be based on any lack of modern training." With this idea in mind, aided by a fellowship from the Slater fund, in the fall of 1892, he enrolled at the University of Berlin.

Like Tennessee before, Berlin provided him with experiences that would last throughout his life. Here more than ever before, he felt the dilemma of being black in America. As he traveled across the continent, sat in classrooms presided over by the intellectuals of the time, formed enduring relationships with whites of both sexes, he experienced for the first time a world unbounded by color restrictions. Not surprisingly then, years after his first experiences abroad he writes with nostalgia, anger, and sarcasm: "As a student in Germany, I built great castles in Spain and lived therein. I dreamed and wandered and sang; then after two long years I dropped suddenly back into 'nigger' hating America."

He came back to America in 1894, one year before Booker T. Washington, addressing an exposition in Atlanta, was to assume the mantle of "Leader of the Negro People." At that moment, however, Washington was principal of Tuskegee Institute, a black college in Alabama, and his was one of the offers the young scholar received as he began the search for work. In his autobiography, published posthumously in 1968, Du Bois asks sarcastically what the meaning of his life might have been had the offer from Tuskegee arrived before he had accepted the one from Wilberforce College. The small denominational college in Ohio needed a professor of Greek and Latin, and Du Bois took up his duties there in 1894, imbued, he later remembered, with notions of what a university should be. Whether any black university at the time could have met his criteria is doubtful; certainly Wilberforce did not, and his tenure there was somewhat disillusioning. He was chastised by the presiding bishop for refusing to lead students in a prayer and became involved in a patronage dispute concerning the college and the bishop's son. More important, he was denied his request to add sociology to his curriculum, a refusal that led him to conclude that the college was not interested in a scholarly, systematic analysis of "The Negro Problem." Thus he willingly accepted an offer to conduct a sociological study of blacks for the University of Pennsylvania in 1896, the year in which he married Nina Gomer and saw the publication of his dissertation *The Suppression of the African Slave-Trade to the United States of America.*

He arrived in Philadelphia to fulfill his mandate, "the study of the social conditions of the Colored People of the Seventh Ward of Philadelphia." What had not been possible at Wilberforce was now offered at the University of Pennsylvania, the chance to test one of his major theories concerning race in America. "The Negro problem," he wrote, "was in my mind a matter of systematic investigation and intelligent understanding. The world was thinking wrong about race, because it did not know. The ultimate evil was stupidity. The cure for it was knowledge based on scientific investigation." Almost single-handedly, he sought to provide such knowledge in his study *The Philadelphia Negro* (1899).

The book represented the first systematic study of a large number of blacks in any major city in America. Du Bois studied the racial history of his subjects as well as the history of the city itself. He studied every conceivable group in the community and concentrated on such categories as crime, employment, and education. In the conclusion, he offered stern suggestions to blacks throughout the country: "Simply because the ancestors of the present inhabitants of America went out of their way barbarously to mistreat and enslave [blacks] . . . gives those blacks no right to ask that the civilization and morality of the land be seriously menaced for their benefit . . . a nation may rightly demand even of a people it has consciously and intentionally wronged, every effort

Speakers at Harvard's 1890 commencement, at which Du Bois (seated, right) received his B.A. (courtesy of Archives, University Library, University of Massachusetts/Amherst)

and sacrifice possible on their part towards making themselves fit members of the community within a reasonable length of time. . . ."

The study abounds with such statements and differentiates the early Du Bois from the latter, the conservative from the radical, who, at this point in his career, is philosophically close to Booker T. Washington in the belief that blacks were unwilling conspirators in their own plight and that through hard work and application their conditions might be readily improved. Thus upon the shoulders of the victim, he placed much of the blame for poverty, crime, and lack of progress.

His statements, however, were undercut by the irony of his own situation. He was accomplished, hardworking, diligent; yet, his studies completed, he was not offered a faculty position at the University of Pennsylvania. Thus, because he was black and for no other reason, after one and a half years at Pennsylvania, he was on his way to accept a position as professor of economics and history at Atlanta University, a black college. Later, he wrote, "I was going to study the facts, any and all facts, concerning the American Negro and his plight. . . ." He would transfer to Atlanta the methodology he had perfected at the University of Pennsylvania, and his claim that he had developed "during the years 1897 to 1910 . . . a program of study of the problems affecting the American Negro" was justified. University studies concerning blacks were in progress before he arrived at Atlanta, but these, some under the auspices of Tuskegee and Booker T. Washington, concentrated mainly on blacks in agriculture. Under Du Bois's direction, however, the Atlanta conferences became, in effect, a sociological laboratory, a series of "scientific investigation[s]" into social conditions, primarily for social ends. The conferences resulted in the publication of eighteen monographs dealing with such subjects as "Morality Among Negroes in Cities," "The Negro In Business," "The Negro Church," and "The Negro American Family." With these studies, Atlanta became, for years, a resource bank of sociological data for colleges and public and private institutions.

His work at Atlanta was not without some difficulty. He enjoyed cordial relations with President Horace Bumstead, but this relationship would become somewhat strained as a result of Du Bois's increasing criticism of the policies of Washington. Funds to expand and continue his conferences and studies would suffer for the same reason. Yet in 1900 he was the conscientious scholar, using his laboratory to investigate, analyze, measure. He regularly wrote articles for such periodicals as *World Work* and the *Atlantic Monthly* and in addition to making his first attempt at an *Encyclopedia of African People,* he was elected a member of the American Association for the Advancement of Science. Then, suddenly, cataclysmically, the relatively quiescent life of the social scientist was transformed forever: "I had been studying the American Negro Problem," he writes, "And at the time when these studies were most successful, there cut across this plan which I had as a scientist, a red ray which could not be ignored."

The "red ray" was a metaphor for the circumstances surrounding Sam Hose, an illiterate black, far removed from the environs of Atlanta University. He was charged with having murdered and raped his landlord's wife, a white woman. The facts, however, as Du Bois learned them, were somewhat different. Hose appeared to have acted in self-defense. Armed with these new facts, Du Bois drafted a statement and started for the office of Joel Chandler Harris, editor of the *Atlanta Constitution.* He related the incident in his autobiography: "On the way news met me: Sam Hose had been lynched, and they said that his knuckles were on exhibition at a grocery store. . . . Two considerations thereafter broke in upon my work and eventually disrupted it: first, one could not be a calm, cool, and detached scientist, while Negroes were lynched, murdered, and starved; and secondly, there was no such definite demand for scientific work of the sort I was doing. . . ." In fact the demand seemed to be exactly the opposite of what Du Bois was pursuing at Atlanta, and it was not simply the white world of the early twentieth century that desired no scientific evidence to invalidate the racist machinery of caste distinction; gradually, it became clear to Du Bois that such scholarship was not wanted by influential members of the black world either.

Whether this was altogether true of Booker T. Washington is not clear, but what is indisputable is that to speak of the black world after 1895 was to speak first and foremost of Booker T. Washington, and few programs could be pursued with adequate financial support without Washington's tacit approval. The man, born a slave in 1856, managed through virtue of hard work and application to become principal of Tuskegee Institute, and after 1895 became, in the eyes of whites north and south, the accepted leader of black people. His support rested largely on statements he issued at the Atlanta Exposition of 1895 which affirmed the validity of the caste system. He belittled efforts by blacks to gain the right to vote, spoke of the virtues of segregation, and suggested second-class citizenship for America's blacks: "In all things that are purely social we can be as separate as the five fingers, yet one as the hand in all things essential to mutual progress. . . ."

If, as one newspaper later remarked, there were tears in the eyes of blacks in the audience during Washington's speech, Du Bois was not among those so moved. In fact, he lagged behind many black intellectuals, whose opposition to Washington was instantaneous. Not only did he not oppose Washington seriously but he praised aspects of the Atlanta Exposition address. When he did speak out, his opposition was reasoned and calculated, and the two men enjoyed, for some time, cordial, if increasingly strained, relations. In 1902, one year before publication of *The Souls of Black Folk,* Washington, in a letter, commended Du Bois upon his work at Atlanta: "Constantly putting such facts before the public cannot but help our cause greatly in the long run." Efforts were made to entice Du Bois from Atlanta to Tuskegee, and several meetings between the two men were held toward this goal.

Du Bois's reticence concerning overt criticism of the Tuskegan notwithstanding, chances of a rapprochement were impossible. Though he had accepted much of Washington's program as early as 1890, incidents such as those involving Sam Hose convinced him of its shortcomings. When Du Bois published *The Souls of Black Folk* in 1903, it became apparent to Washington and his supporters, if not to the author himself, that the two men were diametrically opposed. And this, despite the fact that the book is not that of an adversary, but of a member of an opposition seeking to be loyal. One of the essays, "On Mr. Booker T. Washington and Others," written especially for the book, illustrates this point:

> So far as Mr. Washington preaches Thrift, Patience, and Industrial training for the masses, we must hold up his hand and strive

An 1895 photograph of Du Bois, his son, Burghardt, who died young, and his wife Nina (courtesy of University Library, University of Massachusetts/Amherst)

> with him . . . glorifying in the strength of this Joshua called of God and of man to lead the headless host. But so far as Mr. Washington apologizes for injustice, North or South, does not rightly value the privilege and duty of voting, belittles the emasculating effects of caste distinctions and opposes the higher training and ambition of our brighter minds . . . we must unceasingly and firmly oppose [him.]

The careful, cool, and detached scholar was still in evidence in this influential collection of essays but for the most part his commentary upon men and events bore the unmistakable mark of personal observations and passionate experience. Included among the fourteen essays were autobiographical ones, those that assailed the caste system and those that delineated the dilemma of black folk as few essays have before or since: "One ever feels his twoness—An American, a Negro; two souls, two thoughts, two unreconciled strivings; two warring ideals in one dark body, whose dogged strength alone keeps it from being torn asunder." Here, clearly revealed, was an intellectual of stature and depth, a formidable potential foe of the policies and programs of Washington. Now, finally, the intellectuals who had opposed the Tuskegan from the beginning had an able champion, and Du Bois's articulate and impassioned voice began to be respected in black America.

It soon became impossible for him to straddle the fence between outright opposition and loyal criticism. He was to discover that Washington considered all criticism destructive, whether from radicals or conservatives, and using the vast resources of the Tuskegee Machine, moved swiftly to demolish it. Du Bois was witness to one dramatic example in the case of William Monroe Trotter. The fiery editor of the *Guardian Magazine* had been a staunch Washington critic from the beginning and some of the most vitriolic attacks on the Tuskegan had come from his pen. Du Bois was not enamored of Trotter's approach, but he considered him a dedicated defender of the race and, above all, a man entitled to have his say. When Washington

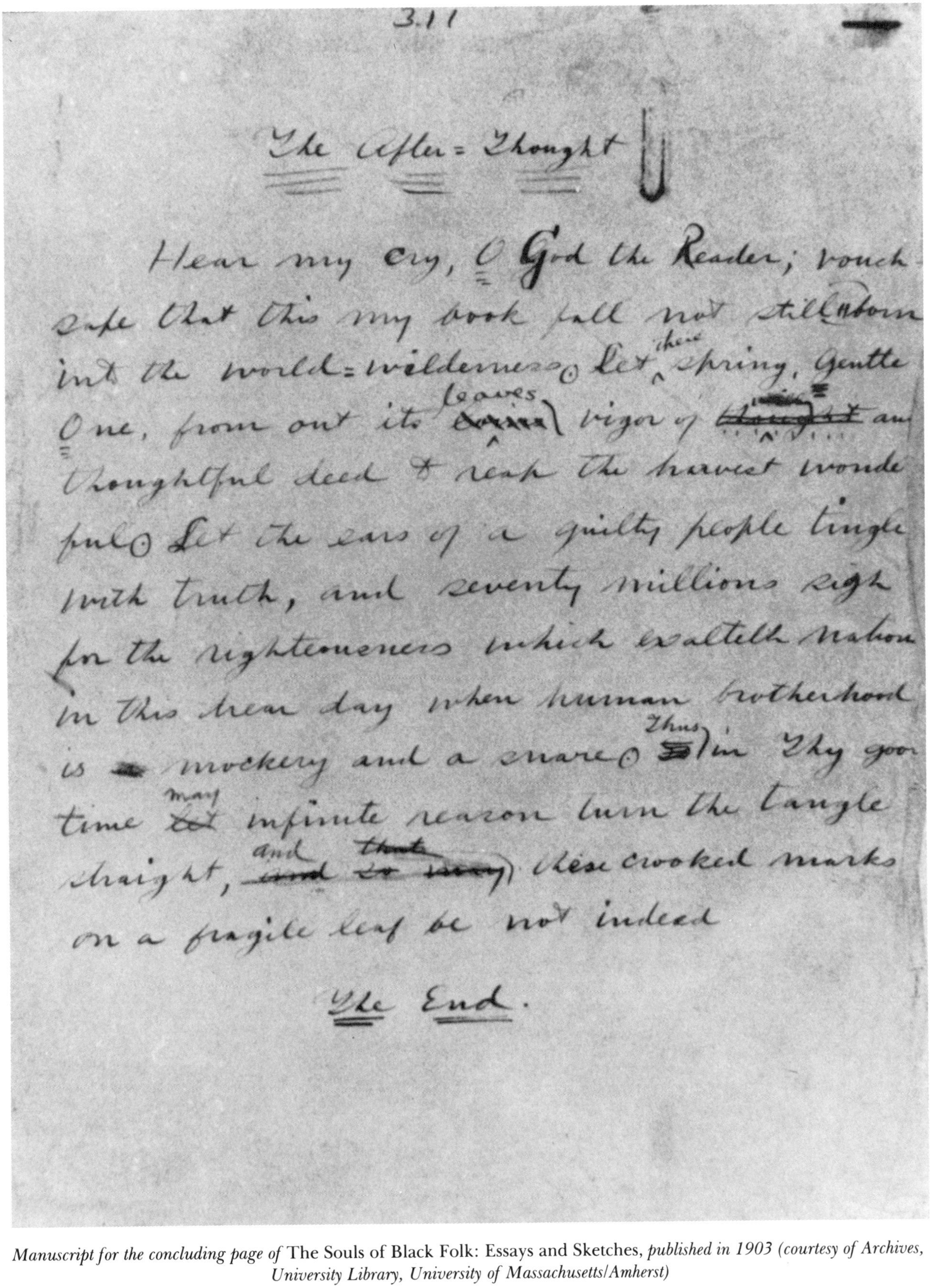

3.11

The After-Thought

Hear my cry, O God the Reader; vouchsafe that this my book fall not still-born into the world-wilderness. Let there spring, Gentle One, from out its leaves vigor of thought and thoughtful deed & reap the harvest wonderful. Let the ears of a guilty people tingle with truth, and seventy millions sigh for the righteousness which exalteth nations in this drear day when human brotherhood is mockery and a snare. Thus in Thy good time may infinite reason turn the tangle straight, and these crooked marks on a fragile leaf be not indeed

The End.

Manuscript for the concluding page of The Souls of Black Folk: Essays and Sketches, *published in 1903 (courtesy of Archives, University Library, University of Massachusetts/Amherst)*

uncharacteristically addressed an urban, northern, black audience and Trotter rose to speak, he was subdued, and arrested. The incident moved Du Bois to words and action: "When Trotter went to jail, my indignation overflowed. I did not always agree with Trotter. . . . But he was an honest, brilliant, unselfish man, and to treat as a crime that which was at worst mistaken judgement was an outrage. I sent out from Atlanta in June 1905 a call to a few selected persons for organized determination and aggressive action on the part of men who believe in Negro freedom and growth." The call resulted in the formation of the Niagara Movement.

The first all-black protest movement in black history, though short-lived, was composed of men and women from fourteen states, most of whom opposed Washington. Their platform advocated voting rights, higher education for blacks, freedom of the press and speech, and first class citizenship. In 1906, in a symbolic gathering, the group met at Harper's Ferry, the scene of John Brown's abortive revolutionary attempt to free slaves, twice more in 1907 and 1908, and was finally eclipsed by a new organization that absorbed many of its members, the National Association for the Advancement of Colored People.

Opposition to Washington's policies had helped to create the Niagara Movement. The NAACP, on the other hand, had a genesis altogether different. In Springfield, Illinois, in 1908, one of the worst race riots in American history occurred. Over fifty thousand militia were brought in to quell the disturbance; two blacks were lynched, four whites killed and over seventy people injured. A white writer, William English Walling, was so appalled by the events that together with Mary White Ovington, a white social worker, and Oswald Garrison Villard, grandson of the abolitionist newspaperman William Lloyd Garrison, he issued a call for "a national conference for the discussion of present evils . . . and the renewal of the struggle for civil and political rights." From this conference sprang the formal organization, chartered in 1910, with one black officer, W. E. B. Du Bois, who became the association's director of publicity and research.

For what can only be described as over two tumultuous decades, Du Bois served the NAACP in this capacity. The only prominent black among the hierarchy for many years, the leading black intellectual of his day, and a man of unswerving principle, he founded the association's official organ, *Crisis* magazine, and became, for black people, the voice of the association. The magazine that began with a circulation of 1000 in 1910, by 1918 was being read by over 100,000 subscribers. All topics of interest to blacks were covered within its pages: politics, education, culture, art, science. But the most favored sections were the editorials in which the editor, like a Lycurgis, tutored and sometimes cajoled his flock. He inveighed against lynching, disenfranchisement, crimes by and against blacks, and used the pages of the *Crisis* as a fulcrum for the black literary revival known as the Harlem Renaissance.

When Americans went to war in 1914, in a controversial article, Du Bois urged blacks to "close ranks" and support the government. After the war, he journeyed to Europe to investigate the wartime treatment of blacks abroad and reported his findings of rampant racism and discrimination by the armed services in the pages of the *Crisis*. From 1919 to 1927, he was the leading architect of four Pan-African conferences, and he reported these attempts at international liaison between blacks in the magazine's pages. He pinned a denunciatory article on Booker T. Washington when the Tuskegan died in 1915 and took note of the Garvey movement when, under the auspices of a Jamaican black, the mass movement organization began its extraordinary rise in America.

After corresponding with Booker T. Washington, Marcus Aurelius Garvey, who founded the Universal Negro Improvement Association in Jamaica, set out for America in 1915 to meet Washington, who had died earlier in the same year. Garvey stayed on and created an American branch of his organization, appealing primarily to impoverished and uneducated blacks. In less than five years the organization's membership numbered in the hundreds of thousands, and money was available to enable Garvey to attempt many questionable ventures. Through his magazine, the *Negro World*, Garvey openly espoused segregationist policies and attacked the integrationist NAACP and its leadership. Du Bois, who was having his own disagreements with the middle-class leadership of the NAACP, was initially positive toward Garvey. In an editorial in 1920, he wrote that Garvey was "an extraordinary leader of men. Thousands of people believe in him. He is able to stir them with singular eloquence and the general run of his thought is of a high plane."

By 1923 Garvey's business ventures had led to his indictment and arrest by the federal government. As a result, he increased his attack upon the Negro leadership. Some prominent blacks, among

The founding members of the first black protest organization in America, the Niagara Movement. Massachusetts representative E. B. Jourdain and Pennsylvania representative George W. Mitchell are not pictured (courtesy of Archives, University Library, University of Massachusetts/Amherst).

them members of the NAACP, demanded that he be tried immediately. Though no evidence exists to prove that Du Bois was among them, in the *Crisis* of February 1923, he wrote some of the strongest invective of his journalistic career and in the 24 May issue called Garvey, "the most dangerous enemy of the Negro race in America and the world." Du Bois's confrontations with officials in the NAACP, however, are well-documented, and these were of a much more serious nature than those involving Garvey.

At the center of this ongoing conflict was Du Bois's control of the *Crisis* magazine, which enabled him to espouse policy, oftentimes antithetical to that of the organization itself. In the January 1934 issue of the magazine, he wrote in the editorial, "Segregation": "The thinking colored people of the United States must stop being stampeded by the word segregation. The opposition to racial segregation is not or should not be any . . . unwillingness of colored people to work with each other, to cooperate with each other, to live with each other." In its entirety, the essay, besides being in opposition to the NAACP's stand on integration, illuminated an important shift in his own thinking, brought about by daily events in America and by experience gleaned from travels throughout the world.

In 1924 he admonished blacks to fight for America, declaring that to do so would produce dividends in racial progress in America. Instead, during the Depression years, black progress diminished as whites looked out for the welfare of other whites. The efforts to pass an antilynching bill failed in the Congress of the United States, and the economically hard-hit black population gained less than whites from the programs enacted by the

Du Bois (right) in the Crisis *office, circa 1914 (courtesy of the Collection of Milton Meltzer)*

Roosevelt Administration. After his initial trip to Europe when the war ended, Du Bois had traveled extensively in western Europe and Africa, and he had become more extensively involved with the Pan-African conferences and had been a first-hand witness to the Communist experiment in Soviet Russia. The combination of these experiences led him to conceive of black economic cooperatives organized and manned by blacks, underpinned by a quasi-voluntary, segregationist, superstructure.

To propound this theory, he used the pages of the *Crisis,* often attacking such officials as Walter White in invectives once used to assault the personal character of Garvey. But the *Crisis* magazine was no longer self-supporting and could not be kept as Du Bois's personal vehicle with the acquiescence of the NAACP governing board. During the Depression, circulation dropped considerably and both the magazine and Du Bois's salary were sustained by the NAACP. The organization moved, therefore, in 1934 to exercise censorship over the editorials of the uncompromising editor. The result was that Du Bois tendered his resignation on 11 June 1934, and severed over two decades with the nation's oldest civil rights organization.

At age sixty-six he left the NAACP with an enviable record of accomplishment behind him. In addition to his editorials and articles for the *Crisis* and other magazines, he had lectured widely in America and abroad and published a variety of books. In 1909 he published *John Brown,* a biography of the Kansas hero which he called his best book. *The Quest of the Silver Fleece* (1911) was a novel in which Du Bois dramatized the economic conflict between southern planters and northern capitalists during Reconstruction. In 1915 he published *The Negro,* a history of African and black Americans, presenting a compendium of facts concerning black people throughout the world. *The Gift of Black Folk* (1924) was a book detailing contributions of blacks to civilization, and he published his second novel, *Dark Princess,* in 1928. The book deals with the international conditions of black people and the worldwide ramifications of racism. His intellectual credentials were unassailable when, accepting an offer from his friend John Hope, who became president of Atlanta University in 1929, Du Bois returned to the school to chair its department of sociology.

He was determined, he later wrote, to resume his role as the dispassionate scholar, and though this was difficult, due to his own activist temperament, between 1935 and 1940 he authored *Black Reconstruction* (1935), *Black Folk, Then and Now* (1939), and *Dusk of Dawn* (1940). In 1941, he held the first of a series of conferences looking forward to "a long time program of Negro economic stabilization after the war." In 1944 he founded *Phylon* magazine, a scholarly journal of "comment and research on world race problems."

Black Reconstruction is a revisionist interpretation of the Reconstruction period. Written with his usual passion and eloquence, Du Bois sought to interpret Reconstruction from a black and Marxist perspective and acknowledged for the first time in American history the impressive role played by blacks in the period. *Black Folk, Then and Now,* like the earlier *The Negro,* traced the continuity between blacks in Africa and America and illustrated varying lines of racial kinship, and *Dusk of Dawn* was his first complete autobiography. Here, in lyrical terms, he presented his life metaphorically and wrote what can only be called a dissertation on race. In 1941, after having gathered the black presidents of the land grant colleges together, he outlined his plan of economic redevelopment and admonished the presidents "that the chief studies of the Negro's condition today are not being done by Negroes and Negro colleges."

His attempts at formulating and carrying out his economic proposals with the aid of the presidents of the land grant colleges came abruptly to an end, however, when he was summarily retired from Atlanta University. After the death of John Hope, Du Bois's relations with both the new president of Atlanta University, Rufus Clement, and Spellman College's President Florence Reed became strained. Enmity, enviousness, and pettiness all seem to have motivated the sudden decision to retire Du Bois, since he was past the age of retirement when he was hired. More likely his forced retirement rested upon his involvement with the presidents of the land grant colleges, his economic program, and his worldwide reputation. Equally as surprising as his dismissal from Atlanta was his being restored to service by the NAACP.

Two close friends of Du Bois, Arthur Spingarn and Louis Wright, his personal physician, learned of his dismissal by Atlanta. Without consulting the seventy-six-year-old Du Bois, the two men approached his old adversary, executive secretary Walter White. They arranged a "deal" whereby Du Bois would return, presumably for the

W. E. B. Du Bois (courtesy of National Portrait Gallery, Smithsonian Institution)

rest of his life, to the organization he helped found and in the event White became dissatisfied with him or his performance, he could be terminated. Du Bois's old friends sought protection for their friend in his later years, and White believed that Du Bois would offer prestige and stature to the organization and invaluable help to him as a speechwriter. Thus, in 1944 Du Bois returned to the NAACP as director of special research.

In 1945 he attended the sixth session of the Pan-African Conference in England, a session which included future President of Ghana, Kwame Nkrumah. In the same year, Du Bois worked on proposals for the United Nations Commission on Human Rights, publishing a book, *Color and Democracy: Colonies and Peace*, about his efforts and the organization in general in 1945. However, the possibility of coexistence with White was remote from the outset. Accusations were made early against Du Bois for appearing before a congressional committee without White's consent. Later he was accused of interfering in a school desegregation case as a result of remarks made during a speech. The conflict that led to his expulsion, however, concerned the presidential campaign of 1948. Though the NAACP claimed neutrality during the campaign, White openly campaigned for the election of the Democratic candidate, Harry Truman. When Du Bois privately advocated the candidacy of the Progressive party standard bearer, Henry Wallace, he was upbraided by White. Du Bois's counteraccusations against White concerning Truman led the secretary to exercise the option granted earlier by Du Bois's friends. For the second time he was removed from the NAACP.

"I would have been hailed with approval, if I had died at age fifty," he recalled later. "At seventy-five my death was practically requested." Yet some of the most tumultuous years of his life lay in the future. After expulsion from the NAACP, he became honorary vice chairman of the Council of African Affairs, at a time when the political atmosphere was dense with charges and countercharges of subversion, Communist association, and conspiracy. The role of the organization was to disseminate information pertaining to Africa. Shortly after Du Bois accepted the vice presidency, the Council was cited by the Attorney General of the United States as a "subversive" organization. Greater consequences of a personal nature, however, confronted Du Bois when he became chairman of the Peace Information Center in 1950.

The avowed aim of the Center was to tell "the people of the United States what other nations were doing and thinking about war." In this connection the Center issued peace-grams and collected signatures on a petition to abolish the atomic bomb. It sponsored its chairman at meetings abroad, so that Du Bois appeared at conferences in Paris, Mexico City, and Prague. Early on the Center was denounced by Secretary of State Dean Acheson as a front for the Soviet Union's propaganda machine, a statement that elicited from Du Bois a summary of his own long involvement with peace, accompanied by questions as to whether or not the sole sponsor of peace in the world was the Soviet Union. In 1951 Du Bois, along with other officials of the Center, was indicted for being an unregistered "agent of a foreign principal."

Concurrent with the indictment, Du Bois received a request from the American Labor party, petitioning him to run for the United States Senate as a representative from New York. Hesitant at first, he relented when assured that his candidacy would help that of the progressive congressman from New York, Vito Marcantonio, who faced a difficult reelection fight. His campaign was vigorous and hardhitting and though he lost, as expected, he used the platform to further his advocacy of peace, and his untiring effort undoubtedly helped Marcantonio. During this period, his first wife, Nina Gomer, died, and in 1951 shortly before arraignment by the government, Du Bois married Shirley Graham, a longtime associate. Together, on 8 November 1951, they sat in the federal courtroom in Washington. Du Bois writes of the episode: "nothing has so cowed me as that day . . . when I took my seat . . . as an indicted criminal. I was not a criminal. I had broken no law, consciously or unwittingly." His own judgment concerning his guilt or innocence was validated by the court, which on the first day of trial, acquitted the scholar and his associates.

Innocent or no, his passport was still the property of the United States government and remained so for sometime, prohibiting him from accepting invitations abroad. Nor did acquittal alter his status among those he believed would be his constituency and defenders in his fight against governmental oppression, the black community. The black churches, the black press, the black educational institutions, and the NAACP were mostly silent during and after the period of his struggle. In his autobiography, he expresses his discontent and pain: "the federal government took a determined stand to insure my destruction. . . . The central office of the NAACP refused to let local branches invite me or sponsor any lectures. . . . I found new friends and a wider world than ever before—a world with no color line. I lost my leadership of my race. . . . The colored children ceased to hear my name." In his own recollection of his trial and indictment, which he described in *In Battle for Peace* (1952), he noted one group that supported him during his terrible ordeal and paid tribute to "the communists of the world for their help in my defense."

For whatever the reasons, "the communists of the world" became his ardent supporters and, with progressives in America, his constituency. The organs of the more conservative black press closed to him, he wrote widely for such left-wing periodicals as the *National Guardian*. From 1958 to 1959, his passport, after court action, was finally released by the government, and he traveled extensively throughout Eastern Europe and Asia. He received an honorary degree from Prague University and had audiences with the leaders of the Soviet Union and the People's Republic of China. In 1958 he was awarded the International Lenin Prize by the

Du Bois and Shirley Graham at their wedding on 27 February 1951 (courtesy of Archives, University Library, University of Massachusetts/Amherst)

U.S.S.R. In 1961, at the age of ninety-three, he made application for and accepted membership in the Communist party of the United States. Later, during the same year, he accepted an invitation from Prime Minister Nkrumah of Ghana and became a resident of that African nation; shortly before his death in 1963, he renounced his American citizenship altogether, dying as a citizen of Africa.

These actions during the last years of his life do not, as commentators on Du Bois and his biographers assert, amount to either a betrayal of "his" country or his race. Few Americans have defended their right to citizenship as vociferously as Du Bois. In 1903 he extolled an imaginary white audience: "Your country? How come it's yours? Before the Pilgrims landed we were here. . . . Actively we have woven ourselves with the very warp and woof of this nation. . . . Could America have been America without her Negro people?" And few blacks have written so passionately and devotedly about their kinsmen: "Especially do I believe in the Negro Race: in the beauty of its genius, the sweetness of its souls, and its strength in that meekness which shall yet inherent this turbulent earth." Yet, the country and the race to which he had given so much offered him little in return. He could and did eventually forgive black people, for he was cognizant of their powerlessness and concerns with their own personal survival. Forgiving the country, however, was another matter altogether.

"I may be a romantic," he once said, "but I am not a damn fool." In time, the pragmatist in him consumed the romantic regarding the American society, and he realized what many young blacks were beginning to realize on the eve of his death: that the American Dream would not come true for black Americans, and that at this stage of history, one should demand that the nation which asks loyalty from its citizens return loyalty in kind. In articles and lectures near the end of his life, and in his own symbolic exile, Du Bois raised such questions, and the younger, brighter members of the black community, his intellectual heirs, continue to raise them with increasing urgency and consistency.

Letters:

The Correspondence of W. E. B. Du Bois, edited by Herbert Aptheker, 3 volumes (Amherst: University of Massachusetts Press, 1973-1978).

Biographies:

Rayford Logan, *W. E. B. Du Bois* (New York: Hill & Wang, 1971);

Virginia Hamilton, *W. E. B. Du Bois: A Biography* (New York: Crowell, 1972);

W. M. Tuttle, ed., *W. E. B. Du Bois* (Englewood Cliffs, N.J.: Prentice-Hall, 1973).

References:

J. Max Barber, "The Niagara Movement At Harpers Ferry," *Voice of the Negro,* 3 (7 October 1905): 22-24;

Franklin E. Frazier, "The Du Bois Program in the Present Crisis," *Race,* 1 (1935-1936): 11-13;

Julius Lester, ed., *The Thought And Writings Of W. E. B. Du Bois: The Seventh Son* (New York: Random House, 1971);

Elliott M. Rudwick, *W. E. B. Du Bois: Propagandist of the Negro Protest* (New York: Atheneum, 1969).

Papers:

Papers of W. E. B. Du Bois are at the University of Massachusetts, Amherst.

Paul Laurence Dunbar

Doris Lucas Laryea
North Carolina State University

BIRTH: Dayton, Ohio, 27 June 1872 to Joshua and Matilda Glass Burton Murphy Dunbar.

MARRIAGE: 6 March 1898 to Alice Ruth Moore (separated 1902).

DEATH: Dayton, Ohio, 9 February 1906.

SELECTED BOOKS: *Oak and Ivy* (Dayton, Ohio: Press of United Brethren Publishing House, 1893);
Majors and Minors (Toledo, Ohio: Hadley & Hadley, 1896);
Lyrics of Lowly Life (New York: Dodd, Mead, 1896; London: Chapman & Hall, 1897);
Folks from Dixie (New York: Dodd, Mead, 1898; London: Bowden, 1898);
The Uncalled: A Novel (New York: Dodd, Mead, 1898; London: Service & Patton, 1899);
Lyrics of the Hearthside (New York: Dodd, Mead, 1899);
The Strength of Gideon and Other Stories (New York: Dodd, Mead, 1900);
The Love of Landry (New York: Dodd, Mead, 1900);
The Fanatics (New York: Dodd, Mead, 1901);
The Sport of the Gods (New York: Dodd, Mead, 1902); republished as *The Jest of Fate; A Story of Negro Life* (London: Jarrold, 1902);
Lyrics of Love and Laughter (New York: Dodd, Mead, 1903);
In Old Plantation Days (New York: Dodd, Mead, 1903);
The Heart of Happy Hollow (New York: Dodd, Mead, 1904);
Lyrics of Sunshine and Shadow (New York: Dodd, Mead, 1905);
The Life and Works of Paul Laurence Dunbar, edited by Lida Keck Wiggins (Naperville, Ill. & Memphis, Tenn.: J. L. Nichols, 1907);
The Complete Poems (New York: Dodd, Mead, 1913);
The Best Stories of Paul Laurence Dunbar, edited by Benjamin Brawley (New York: Dodd, Mead, 1938);
The Paul Laurence Dunbar Reader, edited by Jay Martin and Gossie H. Hudson (New York: Dodd, Mead, 1975).

OTHER: "Representative American Negroes," in *The Negro Problem: A Series of Articles by Representative American Negroes* (New York: James Pott, 1903), pp. 189-209;
"The Tuskegee Song," in *Selected Songs Sung by Students of Tuskegee Normal and Industrial Institute* (Tuskegee, Ala.: Tuskegee Institute, 1904), p. 3.

PERIODICAL PUBLICATIONS: "Of Negro Journals," *Chicago Record,* 22 June 1894;
"Some London Impressions," *Chicago Record,* 14 April 1897;
"England as Seen by a Black Man," *Independent,* 48 (16 September 1897): 4;
"Our New Madness," *Independent,* 50 (15 September 1898): 469-471;
"The Race Question Discussed," *Toledo Journal,* 11 December 1898;
"The Negroes of the Tenderloin: Paul Laurence Dunbar Sees Peril for His Race in Life in the City," *Columbus* (Ohio) *Dispatch,* 19 December 1898;
"The Hapless Southern Negro," *Denver Post,* 17 September 1899;
"Negro Life in Washington," *Harper's Weekly,* 44 (13 January 1900): 32;
"Is Negro Education for the Negro Hopeless?," *Philadelphia Times,* 10 June 1900;
"The Leader of His Race," *Saturday Evening Post,* 174 (9 November 1901): 15;
"Negro Society in Washington," *Saturday Evening Post,* 174 (14 December 1901): 9;
"The Fourth of July and Race Outrages: Paul Laurence Dunbar's Bitter Satire On Independence Day," *New York Times,* 10 July 1903;
"Is There a Slump in Poetry?," *Literary Digest,* 30 (18 March 1905): 391.

Paul Laurence Dunbar, one of the most popular American poets of his time, was also the first black poet to attain national and international recognition. Booker T. Washington called him the "Poet Laureate of the Negro race," and William Dean Howells lauded him as a Negro dialect poet who studied the Afro-American "objectively and represented him as he found him to be, with humor, with sympathy, and yet with what the reader must instinctively feel to be entire truthfulness." He was a master craftsman not only in his use of dialect but in his standard English poems and in much of his fiction. He captured the humor, pathos, and hopeful spirit of a resolute and struggling people in and out of slavery. His skillful handling of rhythm, satire, narrative, and irony places him among the best poets this country has produced.

Dunbar was born in Dayton, Ohio, to Joshua and Matilda Glass Burton Murphy Dunbar, former Kentucky plantation slaves, who had taught themselves to read and write. Joshua, who was born in 1816, worked as plasterer on a large plantation until he escaped to Canada by the Underground Railroad. During the Civil War, he enlisted in the Fifty-fifth Massachusetts Regiment, Company F, under Col. Norwood Penrose Hallowell, and fought in the Union army. After the war he settled in Dayton, where he had lived earlier.

Paul Laurence Dunbar

Dunbar's mother was born a slave on the plantation of David Glass near Shelbyville, Kentucky, circa 1844, and she worked as a house servant until the end of the Civil War. As a young woman, she married R. Weeks Murphy, a slave on a nearby plantation, and they had two sons, William and Robert. Following emancipation and Murphy's death (apparently during the war), she and her sons moved to Dayton to be near relatives, and in 1871 she married Joshua Dunbar. When Paul was only one and a half years old, Matilda and Joshua separated, and in 1876 they were divorced. Joshua died when Paul was twelve, and the Murphy boys moved to Chicago. Matilda built a strong bond of affection and understanding between herself and her son that was nurtured throughout his life. She taught him to read, and she shared his interest in literature. When Paul was younger, Matilda and Joshua told him stories of their slave experiences that he later would draw upon as he composed many of his dialect poems and plantation stories.

During his senior year in school, Dunbar, the only black in his class, was president of his class, editor in chief of the *High School Times,* president of the Philomathean Society (a literary club), and class poet, writing the class poem and delivering it at graduation in June 1891. Already he had earned recognition in Dayton for his poems, which had begun appearing in the *Dayton Herald* as early as 8 June 1888, and for his ambition in founding the *Dayton Tattler,* a black newspaper printed by his friend and classmate Orville Wright. The first issue appeared 13 December 1889, but the paper folded after about six issues because its advertising revenues failed to cover printing costs.

Following his graduation Dunbar entertained the notion of attending Harvard University to study law, but, aware that his mother's scant earnings as a washerwoman were insufficient to pay his college tuition, he applied for work at newspapers, law offices, and other businesses in Dayton, only to be turned away because of his color. Despite his journalistic experience and creative ability, he was denied all but menial employment.

He went to work in the Callahan Building for four dollars a week as an elevator operator. Between calls, he wrote poems and articles that were published in several midwestern newspapers, although he received little or no pay for them. In the elevator he reread his favorite poets: Alfred Tennyson, William Shakespeare, John Keats, Percy

Bysshe Shelley, Edgar Allen Poe, Henry Wadsworth Longfellow, James Russell Lowell, and the regionalist James Whitcomb Riley. Dunbar's biographer Virginia Cunningham suggests that Riley influenced the homely quality of Dunbar's verse, with his "nostalgia for the good old days, love of childhood, a twinkle in one eye and a tear in the other." Dunbar especially imitated Riley's Hoosier dialect and his humor in poems such as "The Ol' Tunes," "A Banjo Song," "The Old Homestead," and "A Drowsy Day."

Not only was Dunbar writing poems at this time but he began writing short stories. For six dollars he sold his first story, "The Tenderfoot," a Western tale, to the Kellogg Newspaper Company, a syndicate firm. "Little Billy," another Western, soon followed. Neither tale added to his reputation, nor did they appear later in his volumes of short stories. Dunbar became convinced that he could get published, however, and that if his works were good enough, he might profit financially.

In June 1892 the Western Association of Writers met in Dayton, and three days before the convention Helen M. Truesdale, a member of the association and Dunbar's former English teacher, asked him to give a welcoming address. For the occasion he composed a twenty-six-line poem, which so stirred the audience that he was invited by James Newton Matthews to become a member. Later, Matthews became one of Dunbar's patrons and friends.

Shortly after the convention, Dunbar began experimenting with Negro dialect verse, later becoming the first black American poet to gain national praise for dialect verse, although both white and black writers had used it before. One of his early dialect poems, "Goin' Back," establishes the plantation motif that became a major theme in his work. It is the monologue of a former slave, now residing in the North, who looks with nostalgia to antebellum plantation life as he waits to board a train for a visit to Kentucky. The dialect poems sold, as did Dunbar's poems in standard English, giving him the assurance that poetry could make him famous.

When a letter that Matthews wrote about Dunbar was published in a Mason, Illinois, newspaper and was reprinted in papers across the country, it caught the attention of James Whitcomb Riley, who wrote to Dunbar on 27 November 1892, addressing him as "my chirping friend" and calling his poem "A Drowsy Day" "a superior one." The encouragement from Matthews and Riley furnished Dunbar the confidence he needed to get a volume of poems published. At the suggestion of Orville Wright, he collected fifty-six poems and took them to William Lawrence Blacher, the business manager of the United Brethren Publishing House in Dayton, who agreed to print them for $125, allowing Dunbar to pay him in installments from the proceeds of book sales. Dunbar called his first collection *Oak and Ivy.*

The book came off the press in December 1892, but was dated 1893. Five hundred copies were printed and sold for one dollar a copy, and within two weeks Dunbar had sold enough books to reimburse Blacher for the printing costs. The volume contained the poet's first dialect poems—"A Banjo Song," which had first appeared in the *Chicago News Record,* and "Goin' Back." In the standard English "Ode to Ethiopia" he affirms his racial loyalty and pride by citing the contributions blacks had made in the building of America and of their achievements during Reconstruction. He tells blacks: "Be proud, my Race, in mind and soul," because they have "the right to noble pride/. . ./No other race, or white or black,/When bound as thou wert, to the rack,/So seldom stooped to grieving." One of his favorite poems in the volume was "Life": "A Crust of bread and a Corner to sleep in,/A minute to smile and an hour to weep in,/A pint of joy to a peck of trouble,/And never a laugh but the moans come double;/And that is life." Some of the best poems in the collection are "The Ol' Tunes," "A Drowsy Day," "October," "A Career," and "Sympathy," a poem in which he laments, "I know why the caged bird sings, ah me,/When his wing is bruised and his bosom sore,/When he beats his bars and he would be free." "Sympathy" is perhaps Dunbar's most-anthologized poem after "We Wear the Mask."

In early 1893 Dunbar met Charles A. Thatcher, a Toledo lawyer who became a longtime patron and friend. Hearing of Dunbar's strong desire for a college education, Thatcher offered to pay part of his college expenses and to solicit contributions from other philanthropists, but Dunbar's commitment to becoming a successful poet—after the reception of *Oak and Ivy*—forced him reluctantly to reject the offer. Thatcher later rescued Dunbar when severe financial difficulties arose, lending him money to pay bills and move his mother from Chicago back to Dayton after their sojourn there. Thatcher used his influence, nevertheless, to give the poet literary exposure in Toledo and in other parts of the state by arranging for him to give poetry readings at which Dunbar was able to sell copies of his book and widen his audience.

In the late spring of 1893, Dunbar left Dayton for Chicago in hopes of furthering his writing career, securing more meaningful employment, and thereby, improving his financial situation. This move brought him into contact with other black writers and artists with whom, for the first time in his life, he could discuss his poetic and literary aims. Chief among his new acquaintances was Frederick Douglass, who had been appointed Consul General to the Republic of Haiti, and who gave him work as a clerk at the Haitian Pavilion at the World's Columbian Exposition. In Chicago he met Angelina Grimké, Ida B. Wells Barnett, Hallie Brown, Mary Church Terrell, Alexander Crummell, Rebekah Baldwin, and Wendell Dabney, and he established close friendships with the poets James D. Corrothers and James Campbell, the first black poet to use dialect consistently in his work. His closest friend in Chicago was Richard B. Harrison, an actor who teamed up with him to give dramatic readings and to sell his book. He met composer Will Marion Cook, who would later set "A Negro Love Song" and many of his other poems to music. The Chicago experience provided the poet additional opportunity to write. When the fair was over, he returned to Dayton and ruefully resumed his job as elevator operator.

In 1894 Dunbar suffered critically from financial difficulties, yet he managed to write and survive through the pecuniary assistance of Henry A. Tobey, a Toledo psychiatrist who bought copies of *Oak and Ivy* and who generously sent him money at different points in his life. Tobey offered Dunbar $500 to cover the tuition at Harvard, but Dunbar declined because this sum was not enough to pay college tuition and make mortgage payments on the family house. Fortunately, his financial woes were lessened when in 1895 *Century* magazine published three poems: "A Negro Love Song" (in the April issue), "Curtain" (in May), and "The Dilettante" (in July). Other popular magazines and newspapers, such as the *New York Times,* the Chicago magazine, *Blue and Gray,* and the *Independent,* also began publishing his poems.

In the spring of 1895 Dunbar fell in love with Alice Ruth Moore when he saw a picture of her in the *Boston Monthly Review.* He began corresponding with this poet from New Orleans, who was also a short-story writer and teacher. During their two-year epistolary romance, they shared each others' works, and in June 1895, while serving as temporary editor of the small black newspaper the *Indianapolis World,* Dunbar published one of Alice's legends of old New Orleans.

Meanwhile, fully determined to help promote Dunbar's career, Tobey collaborated with Charles Thatcher in sponsoring the publication of a second volume of poems with the book's profit to go to the poet. Tobey arranged for Hadley and Hadley Printing Company in Toledo to print and bind the little volume Dunbar called *Majors and Minors,* in an edition of 1,000 copies. The date of its publication was 1895, but it did not appear until 1896. It contains ninety-three poems, some of which had appeared in *Oak and Ivy,* that treat love, nature, race, melancholy, death, and other subjects. At this early stage in his development Dunbar experimented with a diversity of styles, themes, and forms—from the simple language of his dialect poems to the eloquent and more polished diction of the poems in standard English—demonstrating his poetic maturity through his mastery of technically complex poetic forms. *Majors and Minors* includes some of his most serious and most joyful poems and many of the verses that proved most popular at his readings. "When Malindy Sings," inspired by his mother's spontaneous outbursts of singing, became one of his most popular poems.

Tobey brought the volume to the attention of actor James A. Herne, who recognized the genius of its author and notified William Dean Howells, the renowned novelist and critic, of its publication. Howells's review of *Majors and Minors* in the 27 June 1896 issue of *Harper's Weekly* won Dunbar an important place in the literary history of the United States. Howells compared Dunbar with Robert Burns and praised his ear for the southern dialects of blacks and whites. Howells said that in the treatment of his material Dunbar was "able to bring us nearer to the heart of primitive human nature in his race than anyone else has yet done." Finally, Howells noted that he "sometimes fancied that the Negro *thought* black and *felt* black, that they were racially so utterly alien and distinct from ourselves that there could never be common intellectual and emotional ground between us, and that whatever eternity might do to reconcile us, the end of time would find us as far asunder as ever. But this little book has given me pause in my speculation. Here in the artistic effect, at least, is white thinking and white feeling in a black man; and perhaps the human unity, not the race unity, is the precious thing, the divine thing after all." In the review, Howells categorized Dunbar as a dialect poet, a label of which the poet was never able to rid himself. Howells was especially effusive in his praise for "The Party," a dialect poem depicting the antics of blacks on a plantation and reflecting the epitome of the

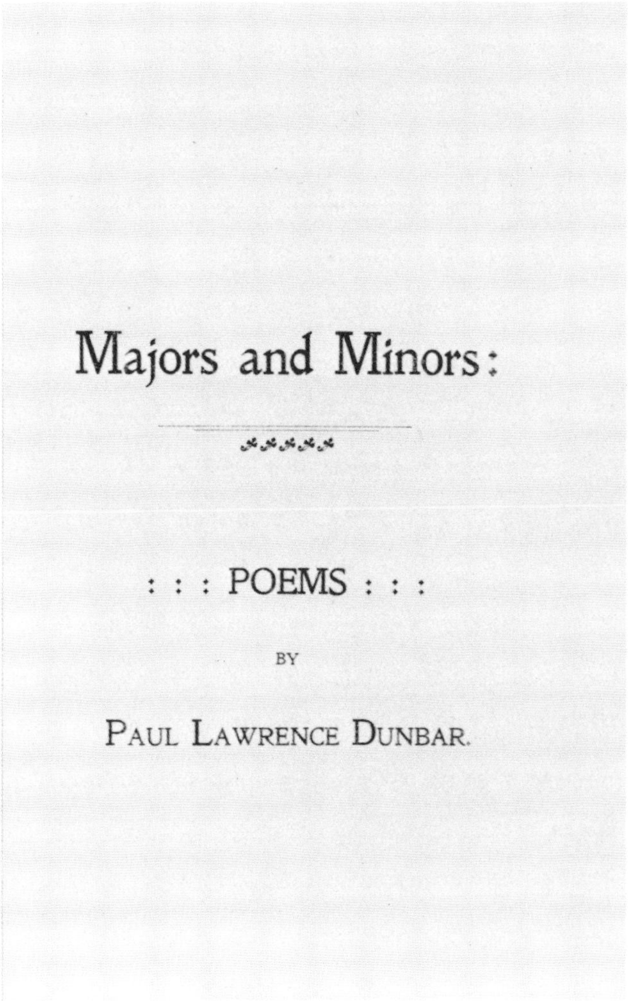

Majors and Minors:

: : : POEMS : : :

BY

PAUL LAWRENCE DUNBAR.

Frontispiece and title page for Dunbar's second volume of poetry

"happy darky" stereotype:

> Dey had a gread big pahty down to Tom's de othah night;
> Was I dah? You bet! I nevah in my life see sich a sight;
> All de folks f 'om fou' plantations was invited, an' dey come,
> Dey come troopin' thick ez chillun when dey hyeahs a fife an' drum.

Full of exaggerated manners, the black party goers prance and preen for each other's benefit. They have no cares and concerns; indeed, they are hilariously funny in their dancing, and even churchgoers are tempted to lose their religion:

> Jigs, cotillions, reels an' breakdowns, cordrills an' a waltz er two;
> Bless yo' soul, dat music winged 'em an' dem people lak to flew.
> Cripple Joe, de old rheumatic, danced dat flo' f 'om side to middle,
> Th'owed away his crutch an' hopped it; what's rheumatics 'ginst a fiddle?
> Eldah Thompson got so tickled dat he lak to los' his grace,
> Had to tek bofe feet an' hol' dem so's to keep 'em in deir place.
> An' de Christuns an' di sinnahs got so mixed up on dat flo',
> Dat I don't see how dey'd pahted ef de trump had chanced to blow.

Howells's praise of such a poem established the pattern for what was expected from Dunbar, for what his primarily white audiences most wanted to read.

Dunbar had higher regard for the sixty-nine poems written in standard English than for his dialect poems, and he demonstrated this preference by grouping them at the beginning of the book under the heading "Majors," and the twenty-four dialect poems at the end under "Minors." Some years later Alice Moore Dunbar wrote that "it was in the pure English poems that the poet expressed *himself*. He may have expressed his racial identities in the dialect poems; they were to him the side issues of his work, the overflowing of a life apart from his dearest dreams."

Later in 1896 Thatcher and Tobey arranged for Dunbar to meet Maj. James B. Pond, a professional manager who had arranged tours for Mark Twain, Frederick Douglass, George Washington Cable, James Whitcomb Riley, and other writers. Pond immediately prepared for Dunbar to visit New York City, where he negotiated contracts for a series of public readings and a contract with Dodd, Mead to become Dunbar's publisher. That December Dodd, Mead brought out *Lyrics of Lowly Life* (1896), which became his best-selling book, introducing him to a national audience and enabling him to devote himself entirely to literature. The publishers were so sure of the book's success that they paid Dunbar $400 in advance and later agreed to pay him a regular monthly income on the understanding they would publish his later works. His reputation increased as groups demanded his poetry readings and newspapers sought out his articles.

Lyrics of Lowly Life, dedicated to his mother, as his other books had been, and to William Dean Howells, who wrote an introduction—contains 105 poems, of which 97 had been published in *Oak and Ivy* and in *Majors and Minors.* Although Dunbar would write three more collections of poetry, none would surpass the achievement of *Lyrics of Lowly Life.*

In February 1897, with his literary reputation firmly established in the United States, Dunbar sailed for London on a reading tour under the management of Major Pond's daughter Edith. In New York, on the eve of his departure, he finally met Alice Ruth Moore at a reception given for him by Victoria Earle Matthews and attended by Booker T. Washington and other prominent people. He and Moore became engaged the same evening.

In London he arranged through Chapman and Hall publishers for an English edition of *Lyrics of Lowly Life,* which appeared in 1897. John Hay, the U.S. Ambassador to Great Britain, scheduled a reading before some of London's most prominent citizens, and he introduced Dunbar to Samuel Coleridge-Taylor, a black musician who befriended Dunbar and set some of his lyrics to music; Dunbar also wrote the libretto for Coleridge-Taylor's operetta *Dream Lovers* (1898). Dunbar established a friendship with well-known journalist Henry M. Stanley, and for a while he stayed with one of his old friends, Alexander Crummell, and began work on *The Uncalled* (1898), a partly autobiographical novel. By this time Dunbar had become the first black American poet to achieve both national and international acclaim. Despite his popularity, he failed to achieve the financial success he had hoped for in England, largely because the celebrations surrounding Queen Victoria's Diamond Jubilee had made poetry readings seem less attractive. His London experiences inspired him to write a poem, "The Garret," and an article, "England as Seen by a Black Man," which appeared in the *Independent* on 16 September 1897.

After spending six months in England, he returned to New York. Through the assistance of Col. Robert G. Ingersoll, he began work on 1 October as an assistant clerk in the reading room at the Library of Congress in Washington, D.C., with an annual salary of $720.

Dunbar's Washington years (1897-1899) were among his most productive, economically successful, and spiritually rewarding. His secret marriage to Alice Ruth Moore—which they kept secret because of her family's objections to his dark skin and to his work in minstrel shows—took place on 6 March 1898. Despite his poor health and the demands of his job, he energetically turned out seven articles (many voiced his racial protest), a musical, two collection of short stories, two volumes of poems, and the novel he had started in London; he also gave innumerable readings. His royalties, fees, and annual salary furnished him the first financial stability he had ever known. In recognition of his achievements, Atlanta University bestowed upon him an honorary Master of Arts degree on 5 June 1899.

The first work that came out of this two-year period was *Folks from Dixie,* a collection of short stories published in April 1898, illustrated by E. W. Kemble, as many of his books were, and dedicated to his patron and friend, Henry A. Tobey. By the end of 1899, it had sold more than four thousand copies, and the J. Bowden Company in London had brought out an edition. Four years would pass before he would publish another collection of poems. Apparently Dunbar turned to fiction to present an enlarged perception of the tragic dilemma of the black American. Prose helped to free him of the yoke that bound him as a dialect poet. He had accommodated his dialect poems to the tastes of his white reading public, but he was also conscious of his black audience and the need to rekindle and reinforce their awareness of the need for solidarity, pride, and above all, dignity.

There were twelve stories in *Folks from Dixie,* five set before emancipation and seven during post-Reconstruction. Dunbar collected the materials for this volume from stories told him by his mother and by freedmen living in Washington, D.C. Although most of them are plantation tales, the second story, "The Ordeal at Mt. Hope," introduces into Dunbar's fiction racial protest against the Jim Crow laws that were implemented and rigidly enforced to prevent blacks from becoming first-class citizens. Dunbar infuses into the story of the Reverend Howard Dokesbury portions of the diverse economic and political philosophies of Booker T. Washington and W. E. B. Du Bois; he traces discrimination against blacks in America and points out that, historically, the black man's plight arose from his association with whites and that this association shaped the world within which he has lived. Dunbar dismisses the belief held by many whites that blacks are shiftless and lazy, and he attacks the grim reality of the system of slavery with little attempt to assume an accommodative spirit.

One of the best stories in *Folks from Dixie* is "Jimsella," Dunbar's first treatment of black migration to the North. Jim and Mandy Mason, who have left the South for New York, discover that while they, and others like them, may enjoy certain social privileges there that they could not enjoy in the South, they cannot secure property, business opportunities, or satisfactory income because of their lack of the necessary skills for jobs in industry and because of their color. Dunbar's antipathy for the city, a major concern in some of his fiction, was shaped by his own experiences and by his observations of transplanted southern blacks in cities such as Dayton, Chicago, New York, and Washington, D.C. He saw the demoralizing effects of racism upon the black urban population. Another post-Reconstruction story, "At Shaft 11," exposes the corruption within labor unions and confirms that labor, when constructively organized, could be one of the major factors in eradicating economic inequality, but when they bar blacks from membership, their action is self-defeating.

Folks from Dixie received generally favorable reviews. The reviewer for *Outlook* (7 May 1898) said Dunbar was "eminently successful in catching the salient traits of southern life, white as well as his own race," and the reviewer for the *Bookman* (7 June 1898) considered the collection "the first expression in national prose fiction of the inner life of the American Negro." Some reviewers pointed to the loose construction of the stories, but the reviewer for *Nation* (21 July 1898) predicted that Dunbar would become a truer chronicler of the folks from Dixie than he had shown in this work.

Dedicated to Alice Dunbar, Dunbar's first novel, *The Uncalled,* appeared in the May 1898 issue of *Lippincott's Monthly* magazine. In September of that year, it was published by Dodd, Mead. Although by mid-1899 three thousand copies had been sold in the United States and editions had been published in Canada and England, it was not as well-received as Dunbar had hoped. Reviewers condemned its lack of local color as well as its loosely constructed and implausible plot, found its characters—all white—unrealistic, and differed over the reason Dunbar chose to write about whites rather than blacks. Some critics believed it was for commercial reasons, while others suggested he had not developed enough within himself to write a realistic protest novel about black people.

Set in Dexter, Ohio, *The Uncalled* has characters and themes reminiscent of Nathaniel Hawthorne's classic *The Scarlet Letter* (1850). Dunbar's novel focuses on Frederick Brent, who becomes the ward of Hester Prime, a deeply religious spinster, after his father has become a drunkard and abandoned his family. Convinced, along with the rest of the townspeople, that Freddie will be like his father, Hester rears Freddie strictly by the Calvinistic teachings of her church and insists that he study for the ministry. Eliphalet Hodges, who marries Hester, is less rigid, however, and encourages the young boy to be self-reliant.

Upon graduation from a seminary he returns home to be the respected pastor of Dexter Baptist Church and later becomes engaged to Elizabeth Simpson, whose father is pastor emeritus of the church. However, he frequently goes against the puritanical regulations of the church, and, when the churchgoers insist that he denounce a woman who has given birth to an illegitimate child, he resigns his post, breaks his engagement to Elizabeth, who has sided with her father and the townspeople, and journeys to Cincinnati. There, he accidentally meets his father, who now calls himself the "California Pilgrim," since he has undergone a spiritual regeneration. Concealing his identity, Freddie learns of his father's plans to return to Dexter to be reunited with his family. In Dexter, the father takes a room by chance in the home of Eliphalet and Hester Hodges and becomes fatally ill, and the Hodges send for Freddie. He returns full of bit-

Cover for the first edition of Dunbar's 1898 novel

terness, but he forgives his father when he learns of his critical condition. After leaving Dexter once more for Cincinnati, he writes the Hodges of his membership in the Congregational church and of his engagement to another young woman, Alice. The story ends when the Hodges arrive for the couple's wedding. The work was important for Dunbar personally because it represented his own meditation over his mother's insistence that he become a minister; however, the novel failed to heighten his literary reputation.

After working about a year and a half at the Library of Congress, Dunbar resigned on 31 December 1898 to devote himself to his literary career and readings. Dunbar had been in delicate health since childhood, but now his health was rapidly failing. He had developed a persistent cough, but he traveled constantly, reciting his poems and giving lectures. His visit to Tuskegee, Alabama, to attend an annual conference on Negro farmers at the invitation of Booker T. Washington was his first physical contact with the South although he had used it as the subject for numerous poems and stories. He wrote the words for the Tuskegee Institute school song, keeping in mind the tune of "Fair Harvard."

A collection of poems, *Lyrics of the Hearthside,* appeared in 1899, sold well, and received favorable reviews. *Lyrics of the Hearthside* contained 110 poems, including thirty-seven grouped under "Humor and Dialect," which Dunbar placed at the end of the book as he had done with the dialect poems in *Majors and Minors.* The range of the poems in this volume illustrates the mature craftsmanship of the poet who presents his broadened perception of art in such poems as "Love's Apotheosis," and "Love," which is a sonnet.

In May 1899, while en route to a poetry recital in Albany, New York, at which Governor Theodore Roosevelt had planned to introduce him, Dunbar fell ill; he later developed pneumonia. For a month he lay near death in a New York City apartment, but his spirit was enlivened by his many visitors, including Howells. After doctors diagnosed his underlying ailment as tuberculosis and advised him to move to the mountains, he took Alice to the Catskills for several weeks in hope of recovering. There he wrote an article on the Negroes in Washington, D.C., for *Harper's Weekly,* and several poems and short stories.

In September 1899, at the request of his doctors, the Dunbars left Washington, and along with Dunbar's mother, journeyed to Colorado, where they settled in Harmon, a small town near Denver. He carried letters of introduction from Henry Tobey to friends in Denver and Colorado Springs. For the next few months he contributed stories to the *Denver Post,* the *Independent, Lippincott's* and the *Saturday Evening Post.* Some of his poetry appeared in *Century* and *Harper's Weekly.* His special focus at this time, however, was the writing of a Western novel.

By Christmas, Dodd, Mead had published a selection of eight poems from earlier books in an illustrated volume of 125 pages with photographs taken by the Hampton Institute Camera Club of simple, southern, black people in natural settings. Alice Morse decorated each page with light green designs. Dedicated to Bishop Henry C. Potter and friends who had been kind to Dunbar during his illness, *Poems of Cabin and Field* (1899) includes "The Deserted Plantation," "Hunting Song," "Little Brown Baby," "Chris'mus is A-Comin'," "Signs of the Times," "Time to Tinker 'Roun'," "Lullaby," and "A Banjo Song." By the middle of 1900, the book had sold five thousand copies. Reviewers praised these dialect pieces, noting especially Dunbar's sensitive appreciation of nature and human character, his immense sense of humor, and his artistic ability. Over the years Dodd, Mead brought out more illustrated editions of poems from Dunbar's previously published books. After *Poems of Cabin and Field,* these volumes of selections include: *Candle-Lightin' Time* (1901); *When Malindy Sings* (1903); *Li'l Gal* (1904); *Howdy, Honey, Howdy* (1905); and the posthumously published *Joggin' Erlong* (1906).

At the turn of the twentieth century, Dunbar was America's most notable black poet, and he was quite prosperous. *Lyrics of Lowly Life* alone had sold over twelve thousand copies, and there was a constant flow of requests for his works from such magazines as *Atlantic Monthly, Harper's, Lippincott's,* and *Century.* On 15 January 1900, in recognition of his literary accomplishments, he was invited to become a member of the Executive Council of the American Social Science Association. By 1900 Dunbar had also made inroads into a theater career. Ernest Hogan, the comedian who had starred in *Clorindy; or, the Origin of the Cakewalk* (produced in 1898), a musical comedy for which Dunbar had written the book and lyrics, also starred in *Uncle Eph's Christmas* (1900), a one-act musical sketch for which Dunbar had written lyrics in collaboration with Will Marion Cook. "Uncle Eph's Christmas" had been a part of a vaudeville program at the Boston Music Hall but had received very bad reviews, particularly from blacks who objected to Dunbar's stereotyping and his use of minstrel imagery and dialogue. One reviewer went so far as to call him "the Prince of the Coon Song Writers." Dunbar, fearing for his literary reputation, had wished to disassociate himself from the show, but he continued writing musical lyrics for the rest of his career. In early 1900, Dunbar made a few reading appearances in the East and parts of the Midwest, and he and Alice returned to Harmon in March.

In May 1900, just prior to his return to Washington, D.C., for another two-year stay, Dunbar published *The Strength of Gideon and Other Stories,* which contained twenty short stories that treated an assortment of themes, including racial protest. "The Ingrate," one of his best stories, is based on what he knew about his father's slave experiences and of his escape from slavery by the Underground Railroad. "The Finish of Patsy Barnes" and "Silas Jackson" address the black migration theme. There were also three stories that focused on black politicians, and two about lynching. "The Tragedy at Three Forks," written at a time when lynchings were quite frequent in the South and other parts of the country, focuses on Jane Hunster. A poor white girl, she is envious of Seliny Williams, who also is white, because Seliny's father is wealthier than hers. Seeking revenge against Seliny, who has embarrassed her at a party, Jane burns the Williams's house and barns. When two black men are arrested and jailed for the crime, the prosecuting attorney forces them to accept the blame. They are denied a trial by jury and are hanged for a crime they did not commit.

The longest short story Dunbar ever wrote is also in *The Strength of Gideon.* Divided into four parts, "One Man's Fortune" gives a rather lengthy yet realistic picture of the experiences of Bertram Halliday, a young black college graduate crippled in employment by racism and prejudice, and it chronicles the corrupt practices of white politicians. Much of Dunbar's own personal experiences of racial discrimination in employment went into his development of Halliday's character. In the story Dunbar demands equal treatment of blacks, and he strongly roots his social protest in the accepted values of American society. He does not argue for the destruction of the white power structure, but for an open society for blacks. He regards capitalism as one of the primary causes of racial discrimination and prejudice, and he suggests the need for unity among blacks as the solution for collectively eliminating the major difficulties oppressing them.

"A Council at State" offers a rather vivid picture of the unscrupulous methods of a white party boss and his black deputy. Luther Hamilton, a powerful and corrupt politician, finds it "pleasant and more profitable simply to boss his party" because such a position gives him power and patronage and yet places him under no obligation to constituencies. His greatest pleasure is silencing troublesome dissenters by ruining their careers, driving them out of public life, and forcing their businesses into insolvency. He particularly enjoys harassing black politicians who oppose his political tactics.

Working closely with Hamilton is a black woman who is the only female political spy in Dunbar's fiction. Miss Kirkman, a thirty-year-old mulatto—shrewd, aggressive, and deceitful—is motivated by her desire for financial and social security. Her tragedy is that she does not wish to be black, yet she is constantly and firmly rejected as a social equal by her white associates, who see her as a convenient mediator between the two races. As a political spy, her duty is to disrupt a black political meeting, the purpose of which is to denounce the administration for showing hostile sentiments to-

The Strength *of* GIDEON *and* OTHER STORIES

By PAUL LAURENCE DUNBAR
Author of "Lyrics of Lowly Life," "Folks from Dixie," "Poems of Cabin and Field," etc.
With illustrations by E. W. KEMBLE

New York: DODD, MEAD & COMPANY Mcm.

Frontispiece and title page for the first edition of Dunbar's collection

ward blacks. To achieve her objective, she contacts various blacks and encourages them to reduce their opposition. One of her victims is her own fiancé, Joseph Aldrick, whom she threatens not to marry unless he takes a more conservative stance. In similar fashion throughout the story, rebellious sentiment is undercut by concessions made to preserve the security of one's employment or the possibility of social and political elevation. As he does several times in his fiction, Dunbar suggests in one passage that for blacks to obtain justice and equality in America, they must abandon traditional Uncle Tomism and passive resistance. Instead they must adopt violence, which clearly speaks to white America of the deeply rooted anger and dissatisfaction of blacks.

Most early reviewers of *The Strength of Gideon* pointed to Dunbar's crisp style, the quick action of the stories, and his effective use of humor and pathos. Others said he was at his best when he expressed the character, dialect, feeling, and sentiment of southern blacks. In general, the public warmly received stories such as "Viney's Free Papers," set before emancipation. "The Case of Ca'line," a humorous kitchen monologue, and "The Fruitful Sleeping of the Rev. Elisha Edwards." The reviewers did not comment on the social, economic, and political protest in stories such as "The Finish of Patsy Barnes," "Mr. Cornelius Johnson, Office-Seeker," and "An Old-Time Christmas." However, recent critics have accorded a number of such protest stories the literary respect they rightfully de-

"MAMMY PEGGY CAME MARCHING IN LIKE A GRENADIER."

UNCLE ISHAM DYER EXHORTS.

JIM.

HIS BROTHER AND SISTER.

Illustrations by Edward Windsor Kemble for the first edition of The Strength of Gideon and Other Stories

serve, and they point to the collection as a demonstration of Dunbar's development as a writer who possessed keen insight into the racial problems of his times and who used his stories to denounce racism. According to Peter Revell, the "unevenness of Dunbar's short story writing has perhaps caused these stories to be underrated by critics. . . . But Dunbar deserves credit for his attempts to extend the range of the black short story into a wide variety of locales, into various social levels and to use an extensive range of character types."

Later in October of 1900 Dunbar's second novel, *The Love of Landry,* appeared. Most critics agree that this is not Dunbar's best novel. Like those of *The Uncalled,* the characters are not drawn from the rich materials of the black experience. However, Addison Gayle, Jr., wrote in his biography of Dunbar that it is a "remarkable accomplishment" of a "poetic spirit seeking escape, seeking release from the bars and cages of life, of a dying soul attempting to lessen the impact of pain upon the still living." *The Love of Landry* is a short romantic Western tale written while Dunbar convalesced in Colorado. Its plot is slight: Mildred Osbourne, the heroine, comes West to regain her health. She falls in love with cowboy Landry Thaler, and they marry after he saves her during a cattle stampede. One of Dunbar's Denver friends, Maj. William Cooke Daniels, a young merchant and millionaire who frequently sent his carriage for Dunbar, furnished suggestions for the Western mannerisms and customs in the novel, and his stories of cattle stampedes were invaluable. In appreciation of Daniels's assistance, Dunbar dedicated the work to him.

Dunbar's next novel, *The Fanatics* (1901), was the first work to come out of his second Washington stay. It was published in March 1901 and dedicated to Edwin H. Keen, an English friend. Dunbar devoted much time toward its development and was extremely disappointed at its poor reception. As early as September 1899, while he was still in Colorado, he had begun plans for this historical account of the sectional strife in America at the outbreak of the Civil War. Though he rather realistically and objectively captures the spirit of the times, he often fails to furnish accurate historical details. His shallow, incomplete, and unrealistic treatment of many of the black characters is a disappointment, as is his monumental effort to reconcile all parties in the conflict. His sympathies are with the escaped slaves, but he admires the northern copperheads; he respects their courage in voicing their beliefs in a region unsympathetic to their sentiments.

The novel concerns not only sectional chauvinism during the Civil War era, but it also mirrors the conflicts within the lives and thoughts of the main characters, who are white. Two prominent Dorbury, Ohio, families, the Van Dorens and the Waterses, hold dissimilar political views. Bradford Waters sympathizes with the Union, while Stephen Van Doren, a copperhead, sympathizes with the Confederacy. Each finds equal support for his views from the community. Adding to the tension between the two families is the engagement of Bradford's daughter Mary to Robert Van Doren, Stephen's son. When escaped slaves enter town, the two families resolve some of their differences in the common cause of keeping the blacks from settling there. One of the major ironies of *The Fanatics* is the attitude and behavior of the older citizens who are zealous supporters of the Union but do not support the abolition of slavery. The novel shows that Dunbar saw racial injustice not as a regional problem but as a general trend in America.

After the appearance of *The Fanatics* and following a string of strenuous readings, Dunbar, suffering from physical and mental exhaustion, went South in April 1900 to Jacksonville, Florida, where he spent six weeks recuperating in the home of his old friend James Weldon Johnson. By this time he had started drinking heavily to ease his cough and to quench his pain. Although his writing had slackened, he composed several poems and gave a few reading recitals.

Dunbar's last novel, *The Sport of the Gods,* appeared in the May issue of *Lippincott's* magazine and was published by Dodd, Mead in 1902. The English edition, published later that year, was titled *The Jest of Fate; A Story of Negro Life.*

The novel reveals Dunbar's genuine effort to show the forces that prevented black Americans from charting their own destinies, suggesting that by organizing a legal system that denies blacks justice and equal job opportunities—and by generally ignoring the needs of the black man in their political decisions—white Americans set themselves up as "protective guardians" of Afro-Americans.

The plot of the novel follows a straight line of action. Berry Hamilton, the hardworking, thrifty black butler who has remained with his employer, Maurice Oakley, "through thick and thin," is wrongly accused of stealing money from Maurice's weak and dissipated younger brother, Francis. Although no evidence supports the charge against him and Berry consistently proclaims his innocence, he is given a ten-year sentence at hard labor, and his wife, Fannie, and two children, Joe and

Kitty, are ostracized by both blacks and whites. Unable to find employment, dispossessed by the Oakleys, and robbed of $500 by the police, the Hamiltons are forced to migrate north. In New York, instead of improving economically and socially, they experience physical, mental, and moral decay. The city is "cruel and cold and unfeeling," and corrupt. It is an environment that forces its people to prey upon each other. Nowhere are the characters free agents. Joe is quickly corrupted by the night life, and later he becomes an alcoholic and a murderer. Insincere blacks succeed in spoiling Kitty's character and enticing her onto the vaudeville stage as a dancer and singer. Meanwhile, Fannie is led to believe that Berry's prison sentence automatically grants her a divorce; consequently, she is duped into marrying a man who beats her and reduces her to abject poverty.

In the meantime, in the South, Maurice Oakley has been visited by troubles which weaken him physically and mentally. His brother Francis confesses that he invented the story of the theft and that Berry is innocent. Upon his release from prison after serving five of the ten years (four years of which Maurice Oakley knew of Berry's innocence), Berry travels to New York and discovers his family ripped apart and totally debased by the grim "sport of the gods." Following the murder of Fannie's "husband," Berry remarries her, and they return to Virginia.

Unlike some of Dunbar's short stories that describe scenes of happy black people on southern plantations, *The Sport of the Gods* becomes social criticism in its exposure of blacks as prey to a white racist society. Maurice Oakley, the genteel southern white liberal, espouses the negative racial attitude that blacks as a race are incapable of intellectual and moral advancement. As a social critic, Dunbar condemns racial injustice and stereotyping, and argues that blacks have the same hopes, human feelings, and sensibilities as whites and ought to be seen as human kin, not as fearsome criminals and beasts.

The novel further develops Dunbar's vision of the new black man, which he first developed in the strong-limbed twenty-year-old, ragged, barefoot son of a contraband slave he had depicted in *The Fanatics*. In Berry Hamilton, he sees the emergence of this new black man, full of pride and dignity, who recognizes his right to be free and independent, a man struggling against ignorance and white oppression in an effort to offer his children the "best education in town" and his family a "neat cottage." In his concept of this new black man, Dunbar touches upon an idea that is treated more fully by writers of the Harlem Renaissance, who stressed a new black awareness in America nearly twenty years after the appearance of Dunbar's novel.

The Sport of the Gods, Dunbar's major achievement in fiction, was reviewed in the leading newspapers and magazines across the country. Some critics called the story powerful and poignant reality, full of strength, vigor, and timelessness; yet, a few, such as the *Minneapolis Tribune* reviewer, regretted that Dunbar, "whose exquisite darkey stories have delighted the nation, should employ his strength with prose of the sort" found in the book. The *New York Times* reviewer said the New York scenes were the work's strongest part and called the "delineations of the southern gentleman" its weakest. The novel is widely considered to be the first major protest novel by a black American writer and the first significant novel to describe the life of blacks in Harlem.

In January 1902, Dunbar was invited to Charleston, South Carolina, to give a poetry recital.

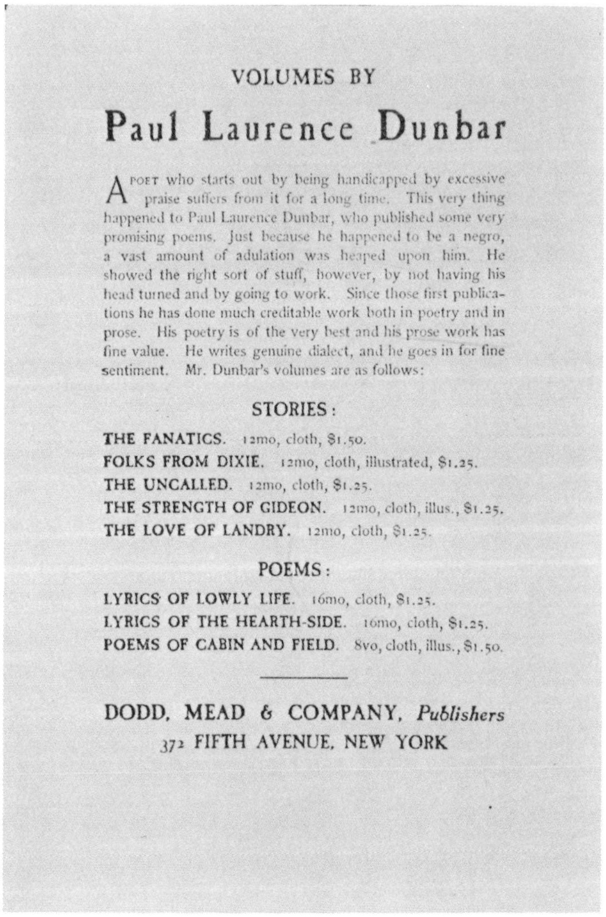

Advertisement in the 1901 edition of The Uncalled

When he returned to Alice Moore in Washington, D. C., they quarrelled as they had done many times before. Under pressure from her family, who objected to Dunbar's blacker complexion, his lack of a college education, and his mother's menial job, Alice, who had become increasingly intolerant of Dunbar's persistent drinking and his moodiness, asked Dunbar to leave. He boarded a train for New York and never returned to Washington.

In New York he wrote three lyrics, "On Emancipation Day," "That's How the Cake-Walk's Done," and "Happy Jim" for *In Dahomey.* Will Marion Cook set the pieces to music, and the show played in Boston, New York, and in England, where it had a command performance at Buckingham Palace in celebration of the Prince of Wales's birthday. After *In Dahomey* Dunbar, who still hoped to achieve a reunion with Alice, living first in Chicago, succumbed to the pressure of the separation and failing health; his creative impulse decreased considerably, and he suffered a nervous breakdown followed by pneumonia. By late autumn, however, with P. R. Reynolds as his literary agent, he was well enough to serve as guest editor of the *Chicago Tribune* and to resume his travels and readings.

Despite his weariness and illness, in 1903 he completed *Lyrics of Love and Laughter,* a collection of short stories, *In Old Plantation Days,* and two articles: "Representative American Negroes" and "The Fourth of July and Race Outrages," inspired by the race riots in Wilmington, North Carolina.

Lyrics of Love and Laughter illustrates the poet's full maturity. Dedicated to a friend, Catherine Impey, it includes "The Poet," in which Dunbar laments being praised only as a dialect poet: "He sang of life, serenely sweet,/With now and then, a deeper note./. . ./He sang of love when earth was young,/And love, itself, was in his lays./But ah, the world, it turned to praise/A jingle in a broken tongue." Some of the poems, such as "To a Violet Found on All Saint's Day," allude to his relentless physical and mental pain and suffering. Others reflected his experiences in the Catskills ("Keep a Song Up on de Way," "Joggin Erlong," "Whip-poor-will And Katy-Did"), in Colorado ("In the Morning," "Dat Ol' Mare O' Mine," "Spring Fever," "A Warm Day in Winter"), and in New England ("Ballade," "To Let," "To sell"). The long stanzaic poem "The Haunted Oak" treats the theme of lynching. The volume also carries tributes to Abraham Lincoln, Frederick Douglass, Robert Gould Shaw, and Booker T. Washington. It received praise both for the dialect and the nondialect pieces.

In early autumn of 1903, Dunbar left Chicago and returned to Dayton to the home he had bought his mother. Declining health and an unsuccessful reunion with Alice continued to weaken and sadden the poet. In September Dodd, Mead published his *In Old Plantation Days,* dedicated to George H. Lorimer, editor of the *Saturday Evening Post,* "out of whose suggestion these stories were born and by whose kindness they first saw the light." Illustrated by B. Martin Justice, the twenty-five stories are set on Master Stuart Mordaunt's plantation during the time of slavery. Most of the stories give brief accounts of life in the cabins. The slaves appear loyal to their masters, and the masters are benevolent and paternalistic toward them. Such romantic depictions of slavery, coupled with his dialect poems, caused critics for several decades after his death to group Dunbar among writers of the plantation tradition—with writers such as Joel Chandler Harris and Thomas Nelson Page. He was labeled an Uncle Tom by many black scholars and accused of destroying the dignity of black people. Hugh Gloster, for example, saw his fiction as a means of perpetuating the plantation mentality of white America. However, in the 1960s and 1970s black scholars such as Darwin T. Turner and Addison Gayle, Jr., pointed to the literary skill displayed in presenting both elements of accommodation and protest in the stories, and Dunbar's standing as a writer rose. Sometimes a story, such as "Mr. Groby's Slippery Gift," which seems to fit perfectly into an idyllic and romantic treatment of slave life, may ironically focus on the miseries and discontentment among the slaves. As a writer of ironic prose fiction, Dunbar was handicapped by a white reading public, but he devised subtle means to voice his criticism of racism in America and at the same time to get his work published. Not all the stories, however, show elements of protest. "Aunt Tempe's Triumph" is about a forceful and clever house servant, and two stories, "The Walls of Jericho," the most humorous in the volume, and "How Brother Parker Fell From Grace," portray the black plantation preacher.

The collection was a commercial success because it provided the kind of entertainment Dunbar's white audience wanted. The reviewer for the *New York Times* (31 October 1903) expressed the sentiment of most readers of *In Old Plantation Days,* saying these stories were good because they "tend to the encouragement of good feelings between races—black and white. . . . Dr. Thomas Nelson Page himself does not make 'ole Marse' and 'ole Miss' more admirable nor exalt higher in the slave the qualities of faithfulness and good humor."

The Heart of Happy Hollow (1904), Dunbar's last collection of short fiction, contains sixteen stories and sketches treating a variety of experiences in Happy Hollow, a place "wherever Negroes colonise in the cities or villages, North or South . . . wherever laughter and tears rub elbows day by day, and the spirit of labour and laziness shake hands."

The first story in the book returns to a theme Dunbar had employed in 1900. "The Scapegoat" condemns the corrupt practices of those philanthropists and politicians who use blacks to help them win elections, and it attacks those blacks who willingly participate in any conduct, legal or illegal, that keeps other blacks from increasing their social, economic, and political clout. A shrewd, influential black, who has lifted himself from bootblack to barbershop owner and operator of a private law firm, Robinson Asbury, the main character, is the one man who understands the racial attitudes and political corruption of party leaders, while he is concurrently fully aware of the joys and frustrations of black ghetto dwellers, whose economic status has been determined by politicians unfamiliar with and unsympathetic to their plight.

Dunbar's revelation of the corruption in American politics reaches its peak after a close election which Asbury's party wins. The defeated argue that their opponents won mainly through fraudulent tactics. Perceiving the sudden impulse of reform among the people, Asbury's party members find a scapegoat: Asbury.

Two other stories in the collection develop the theme of the confidence man, which Dunbar introduced in "Aunt Mandy's Investment" in *Folks from Dixie*. In "The Mission of Mr. Scatters," set in Miltonville, Kentucky, the title character is a shrewd, keen-witted, artful master of guile, who seduces and intrigues his listeners with his eloquence and physical appearance. Arrested for swindling the townspeople of their money, he is acquitted after a powerful speech in which he persuades the court that his actions served the worthwhile purpose of teaching "the darkies" not to trust men they do not know.

"The Promoter," set in the North during the Reconstruction, is more than an illustration of criminal conduct in the service of survival, for it shows Dunbar's interest in the confidence man himself and in the forces that motivate him to swindle others. Revealing the proficiency with which the mulatto Jason Buford exercises his profession, the story explores Buford's own response to his experience and captures the quality of Buford's existence in a world full of hatred and racism.

"A Defender of Faith" continues the black migration theme of *Folks from Dixie* and in *The Strength of Gideon*. The only one of Dunbar's stories to describe the physical environment of a northern ghetto and the plight of the poor, it is also the only story to use small children as central characters.

The more popular of Dunbar's two stories on lynching is "The Lynching of Jube Benson," which is included in the volume. The story focuses on Dr. Melville's guilt over having wrongfully accused his loyal servant Jube Benson of having murdered a white woman, whose last words were "That black." Seconds after Jube had been lynched, Jube's brother had dragged in Tom Skinner—"The worst white ruffian in the town"—whose scratched face was smeared with dirt and blackened in order that he might appear black. Melville immediately recognized his mistake and was the first to attempt to resuscitate Jube. Some critics condemn the story because the ending fails to denounce lynching emphatically. But Melville had learned from the experience to protest continuously the injustice of killing a person before his guilt had been established.

Li'l Gal, an illustrated volume of Dunbar's poems published by Dodd, Mead in late October 1904, contains only one poem, "Clarity," that had not appeared in other collections. Apparently the lady in that poem is Alice; the poet reaffirms his love for her and alludes to the pain caused by their separation.

Lyrics of Sunshine and Shadow, which came out in May 1905, contains seventy-eight poems treating such themes as love, sorrow, death, and nature. Dunbar had always wanted children, and the tenderness he had for them can be observed in poems such as "A Boy's Summer Song," "Johnny Speaks," "The Plantation Child's Lullaby," "Puttin' the Baby Away," "The Fisher Child's Lullaby," and "The Farm Child's Lullaby." In general, though, the poems in this volume are weak.

Howdy, Honey, Howdy, another of Dunbar's illustrated volumes, appeared in October 1905 and was favorably received. Comprised almost exclusively of dialect verse, the volume includes "A Death Song," which later would become Dunbar's epitaph: "Lay me down beneaf de willers in de grass,/Whah de branch'll go a-singin' as it pass./An' w'en I's a-layin' low,/I kin hyeah it as it go/Singin', 'Sleep, my honey, tek yo' res' at las'."

By the end of 1905, the poet's health had failed, and on 9 February 1906 he died at his home in Dayton, Ohio. Dunbar's last book, *Joggin' Erlong* (1906), published posthumously, contains nineteen previously collected poems, as well as "Sling Long," the last poem Dunbar wrote.

Paul Laurence Dunbar was a poet of genuine imagination who rose to literary fame despite nearly insurmountable obstacles. His fast rise as a widely read poet in little more than a decade is a remarkable phenomenon, especially because of the adverse racial atmosphere in which he lived and wrote, his lack of formal education, financial security, and good health. His poems and stories picture the hopeful, sensuous, and joyous side of working-class black life as well as its sorrows and disillusionments. Few American poets before him attracted such a wide, diversified group of readers and held them for such a long, unbroken period of time. He lifted the black oral tradition to the height of art and looked at his people objectively and with pride.

Twentieth-century critical assessment of Dunbar's poetry largely has followed the course established by William Dean Howells's review of *Majors and Minors,* in which he maintained that Dunbar's genius lay in his dialect verses. James Weldon Johnson said that in these dialect poems Dunbar "not only carried his art to the highest point of perfection, but he made a contribution to American literature unlike what anyone else had made, a contribution which, perhaps, no one else could have made." A modern critical shift toward according Dunbar's standard English poems the recognition they deserve began in 1971 with Allen Fox's article, "Behind the Mask: Paul Laurence Dunbar's Poetry in Literary English," which located the poet's significant contribution to American poetry in his standard English poems rather than in his dialect verse. Darwin Turner in "Paul Laurence Dunbar: The Poet and the Myths" argues that Dunbar's poetic accomplishments have been overlooked because scholars have too often relied upon myths about him, rather than critically examining his works.

Critical reception of Dunbar's fiction has followed a similar course. To Saunders Redding, Dunbar's stories depicted "Negroes as folksy, not-too-bright souls, all of whose concerns are minor, and all of whose problems can be solved by the emotional and spiritual equivalent of sticks of red peppermint candy." According to Sterling Brown, Dunbar's last volume of short stories repeated "the Thomas Nelson Page formula. . . . The harshness of Reconstruction and of Dunbar's own time is . . . conventionally neglected in his other volumes of short stories." In fact Brown claimed that "Dunbar's fiction veers away from anything more serious than laughter or gentle tears. . . . Dunbar in fiction must be considered as one who followed the leader, not as a blazer of new trails." Finally, Robert Bone wrote of Dunbar that whenever he had "something to say which transcended the boundaries of the plantation tradition, he resorted to the subterfuge of employing white characters, rather than attempting a serious literary portrait of the Negro. The effect of his work, therefore, was simply to postpone the main problem confronting the Negro novelist."

Dunbar's fiction, however, deserves reevaluation because much of it is devoted to racial protest against the social, economic, and political conditions of blacks that prevailed in America during the latter half of the nineteenth century and the opening of the twentieth. Dunbar's early stories more often show attitudes of accommodation than of protest, but this approach may have been the only practical way to get them published. Once he became an established writer, he seems to have felt freer to modify his accommodation and to express more openly his condemnation of American racism and prejudice.

Unlike such plantation writers as Harris and Page, whose black men find themselves confused and troubled as freedmen, Dunbar's black man emerges as a new man fully capable of devising the means by which he can ameliorate his social and economic paralysis. Dunbar's depictions depart from the myth that blacks were contented with slavery and that they did not know what to do with freedom once they obtained it. The unwillingness of Dunbar's freedman to remain a laborer or a tenant on the plantation is evident in the behavior of Jeremiah Anderson in "The Wisdom of Silence," Howard Dokesbury in "The Ordeal at Mt. Hope," Bertram Halliday in "One Man's Fortune," and Berry Hamilton in *The Sport of the Gods.* When Dunbar's new blacks are confused and troubled, their condition is mainly attributable to their frustration with white racism in America—not because they lack intellectual capability, or because they are inefficient or dishonest.

In his fiction Dunbar created a skillful mix of accommodation and protest, producing stories designed to offend neither black nor white readers. Seen from this perspective, Dunbar's stories show him to be a skilled spokesman for the racial complexities of his times.

Interviews:

"Solutions of Negro Problem Seen From Two Sides: Bishop H. C. Morrison and Paul Laurence Dunbar Discuss A Subject That is Brought to Notice by Murders in Illinois," *Denver Daily News,* 24 September 1899;

Gilberta S. Whittle, "Paul Dunbar," *A.M.E. Church Review,* 18 (April 1902): 320-327;

Lida Keck Wiggins, "Den of a Literary Lion," *Voice of the Negro,* 3 (January 1906): 50.

Bibliographies:

E. W. Metcalf, *Paul Laurence Dunbar: A Bibliography* (Metuchen: Scarecrow Press, 1975);

M. Thomas Inge, Maurice Duke, and Jackson R. Bryer, eds., *Black American Writers: Bibliographical Essays,* volume 1 (New York: St. Martin's Press, 1978).

Biographies:

Benjamin Brawley, *Paul Laurence Dunbar: Poet of His People* (Chapel Hill: University of North Carolina Press, 1936);

Virginia Cunningham, *Paul Laurence Dunbar and His Song* (New York: Dodd, Mead, 1947);

Jean Gould, *That Dunbar Boy* (New York: Dodd, Mead, 1958);

Addison Gayle, Jr., *Oak and Ivy: A Biography of Paul Laurence Dunbar* (Garden City: Anchor/Doubleday, 1971).

References:

Davis W. Clark, ed., *Paul Laurence Dunbar Laurel-Decked* (Boston: Paul Laurence Dunbar Scholarship Fund, 1909);

Mrs. Paul Laurence Dunbar (Alice Ruth Moore Dunbar Nelson) and others, *Paul Laurence Dunbar: Poet Laureate of the Negro Race* (Philadelphia: Reverdy C. Ransom, 1914);

Allen Fox, "Behind the Mask: Paul Laurence Dunbar's Poetry in Literary English," *Texas Quarterly* (Summer 1971);

Sara S. Fuller, *The Paul Laurence Dunbar Collection: An Inventory to the Microfilm Edition* (Columbus: Ohio Historical Society, 1972);

James W. Johnson, ed., *The Book of American Negro Poetry* (New York: Harcourt, Brace, 1922);

Victor Lawson, *Dunbar Critically Examined* (Washington: Associated, 1941);

Doris M. Lucas, "Patterns of Accommodation and Protest in the Fiction of Paul Laurence Dunbar," dissertation, University of Illinois, Urbana, 1973;

Jay Martin, ed., *A Singer in the Dawn: Reinterpretations of Paul Laurence Dunbar* (New York: Dodd, Mead, 1975);

Peter Revell, *Paul Laurence Dunbar* (Boston: Twayne, 1979);

James B. Stronks, "Paul Laurence Dunbar and William Dean Howells," *Ohio Historical Quarterly,* 67 (April 1958): 95-108;

Darwin T. Turner, "Paul Laurence Dunbar: The Rejected Symbol," *Journal of Negro History,* 52 (January 1967): 1-13;

Jean Wagner, *Black Poets of the United States: From Paul Laurence Dunbar to Langston Hughes,* translated by Kenneth Douglas (Urbana: University of Illinois Press, 1973), pp. 73-125.

Papers:

The largest collection of Dunbar's papers is located at the Ohio Historical Society in Columbus, Ohio. It includes a sizeable collection of his prose and poetry manuscripts and several song lyric manuscripts. The Schomburg Collection of the New York Public Library houses a collection of his papers available on microfilm as *The Life and Works of Paul Laurence Dunbar* (St. Paul, Minn.: 3M Company, 1969). Additional letters are scattered among other collections at Houghton Library at Harvard University.

Olaudah Equiano (Gustavus Vassa)

(circa 1745-31 March 1797)

Wilfred D. Samuels
Prairie View A&M University

See also the Equiano entry in *DLB 37: American Writers of the Early Republic.*

BOOK: *The Interesting Narrative of the Life of Olaudah Equiano, or Gustavus Vassa, the African, Written by Himself,* 2 volumes (London: Printed & sold by the author, 1789; New York: Printed & sold by W. Durell, 1791).

Editions: *Equiano's Travels: The Interesting Narrative of the Life of Olaudah Equiano or Gustavus Vassa the African,* abridged and edited by Paul Edwards (New York: Praeger, 1967; London: Heinemann, 1967);

The Life of Olaudah Equiano or Gustavus Vassa, The African, 1789: In two volumes with a New Introduction, 2 volumes, edited by Paul Edwards (London: Dawsons of Pall Mall, 1969).

The slave narrative, a genre the genesis of which can be dated from the early seventeenth century, is primarily associated with the biographical and autobiographical sketches of former North American bondsmen and bondswomen of African descent. This genre reached the height of its popularity in the midnineteenth century with Frederick Douglass's *Narrative of the Life of Frederick Douglass, An American Slave* (1845) and Booker T. Washington's *Up From Slavery; An Autobiography* (1901). Of these two well-known books, Douglass's carefully constructed autobiography is considered, by such experts as Stephen Butterfield, "the finest example of the slave autobiography as a literary art form." Yet a number of eighteenth-century slave narratives continue to attract critical attention; among these, Olaudah Equiano's *The Interesting Narrative of the Life of Olaudah Equiano, or Gustavus Vassa, the African* (1789), according to critic Paul Edwards, is "the most remarkable of the 18th century" books by black writers.

In *The Negro Author* (1931) Vernon Loggins places Equiano's narrative among such landmarks of eighteenth-century black writing as the poetry of Phillis Wheatley and the almanacs of Benjamin Banneker. Loggins found Equiano's book of even greater significance than Washington's or Douglass's because "At the time it was published, in 1789, few books had been produced in America which afford such vivid, concrete, and picaresque narrative." After noting that the slave narrative provides the "spirit and vitality and the angle of vision responsible for the most effective prose writing by

Olaudah Equiano

Black Americans," Arna Bontemps, in his introduction to *Great Slave Narratives* (1969), called Equiano's work "the first truly notable book in the genre."

Equiano's declaration from the outset that he was writing his memoirs at the request of friends; his announced hope that through his work he would become "an instrument of [his] suffering countrymen"; and the polemical character of the slave narrative obscure the forty-four-year-old Ibo's autobiographical intentions and his literary innovations. Equiano is fundamentally concerned with coherently shaping his past in order to gain insight into the long-range significance of his life. Consequently, although through narration and description he succeeds in recreating some sense of the slave trade during the eighteenth century, Equiano ends up reconstructing, as Roy Pascal says the autobiographer inevitably does, "the movement of a life, or a part of a life, in the actual circumstances in which it was lived."

What is significant about the autobiographical form of Equiano's slave narrative is that autobiography, as a genre, was in its infancy during the eighteenth century and thus had not achieved stature as a bona fide literary form. According to Wayne Shumaker, before the mideighteenth century, "the prestige of autobiography was not great enough to make the writing of personal life seem, as it is today, quite natural and normal." In fact, he argues, self portraiture "was thought well-bred only when it had admonitory or historical values or explained the conduct which through public misunderstanding had brought the moral conduct of the writer into doubt."

By the mideighteenth century, however, there was a noticeable movement away from what had been the consistently objective and resolutely impersonal narratives to a more introspective analysis. Autobiographies seemed more concerned with self-analysis, psychological individuality, and intellectual and emotional analysis. These interests were due in part to religious concerns of the authors who, for example, may have been concerned with the immediacy of the spiritual self and the repentance of sins, or who may have accepted the journal of autobiography as "almost a requirement of faith." But another body of conversion literature, which merged the spiritual and secular, that had been written by individuals who stood on the fringe of the established church, was becoming visible.

The popularity of Equiano's *Interesting Narrative of the Life* was due to its spiritual elements and reader interest in the private lives of public figures. Without a doubt, Equiano seems to place his religious concerns at the center of his work. The crux of his narrative is related more to his spiritual freedom than his physical freedom; the text is even framed with his portrait, in which he holds a Bible conveniently turned to Acts 4:12: "For there is no other name under heaven by which we must be saved." An eighteenth-century reader would have realized at once that Equiano's focus was his effort to make straight "the crooked paths" of a "sinful" life. In fact, midway through the narrative, Equiano includes a lengthy discourse on his conversion to Methodism.

Equiano was an Ibo born in the Essaka region, northeast of the Niger River, in the interior of Nigeria. At the age of eleven, he was kidnapped with his sister by local raiders. Carried west and south

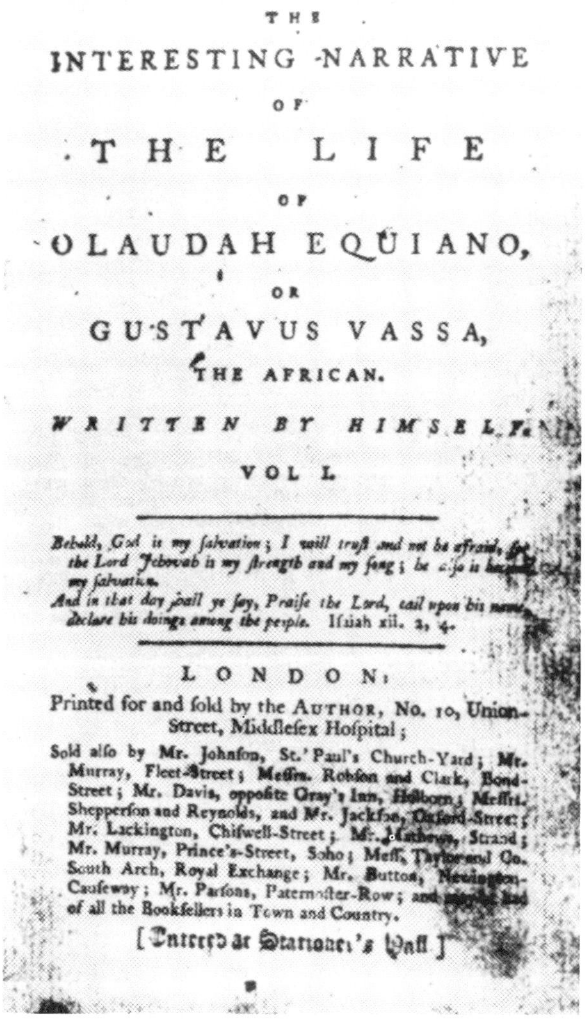
THE
INTERESTING NARRATIVE
OF
THE LIFE
OF
OLAUDAH EQUIANO,
OR
GUSTAVUS VASSA,
THE AFRICAN.
WRITTEN BY HIMSELF.
VOL I.

Behold, God is my salvation; I will trust and not be afraid, for the Lord Jehovah is my strength and my song; he also is become my salvation.
And in that day shall ye say, Praise the Lord, call upon his name, declare his doings among the people. Isaiah xii. 2, 4.

LONDON:
Printed for and sold by the AUTHOR, No. 10, Union-Street, Middlesex Hospital;
Sold also by Mr. Johnson, St. Paul's Church-Yard; Mr. Murray, Fleet-Street; Messrs. Robson and Clark, Bond-Street; Mr. Davis, opposite Gray's Inn, Holborn; Messrs. Shepperson and Reynolds, and Mr. Jackson, Oxford-Street; Mr. Lackington, Chiswell-Street; Mr. Mathews, Strand; Mr. Murray, Prince's-Street, Soho; Mess. Taylor and Co. South Arch, Royal Exchange; Mr. Button, Newington-Causeway; Mr. Parsons, Paternoster-Row; and [illegible] of all the Booksellers in Town and Country.
[Entered at Stationer's Hall.]

Title page for the first edition of Equiano's autobiography

across a large river, probably the Niger, by tribal Africans who spoke a different language, Equiano was brought to the coast and sold to British slavers sailing to the American continent. In his narrative he recounts his departure from his African homeland, the horrors of the voyage, and his multifarious experiences with slavery in the West Indies, North America, the British Isles, and England, his adopted home.

Equiano begins his twelve-chapter, two-volume work with an introduction to the manners and customs of his Essakan community, including descriptions of the social, political, and economic systems of eighteenth-century, traditional Ibo life. His culture was built on simple manners and few luxuries, and although it was one in which slavery was practiced and polygamy was a way of life, adultery was condemned, and slaves were often treated as members of the community. In his review of Ibo life, Equiano draws many religious and cultural analogies between his people and the Jews and expresses the belief "that the one people had sprung from the other."

During a century when even other black writers spoke of slavery with hushed voices, in laying bare the horrors of slavery that confronted him with each step he took away from his father's home, Equiano raises his voice loudly against it, examining and criticizing the arguments and rationalizations of the proslavery camp. In order to "assemble a weight of evidence against slavery that would crush it in every aspect before the court of world opinion," as Charles Nichols tells us the slave narrative would do, and to make the atrocities of slavery the central theme of his work, Equiano addresses the gamut of the dehumanizing experiences of enslavement, from the separation of families to the deaths of those who chose suicide over slavery.

Feeling fragmented by his own separation from community, and later from his sister, Equiano tells us that he began his term in slavery "in a state of distraction not to be described. I cried and grieved continually; and for several days did not eat anything but what they forced into my mouth." As witness to the "wretchedness of slavery" Equiano interrogates his audience with irony: "Are the dearest of friends and relations, now rendered more dear by their separation from their kindred, still to be parted from each other, and thus prevented from *sharing the gloom of slavery,* with the small comfort of being together, and mingling their *sufferings* and *sorrows?* Why are parents to lose their children, brothers their sisters, or husbands their wives? Surely this is a new refinement in cruelty."

Equally violent for Equiano were the inhumane conditions which the Africans were made to endure while on board the slave ships that brought them to the New World. In graphic detail he describes the stench that permeated the ship's hold: "the closeness of the space, and the heat of the climate added to the number in the ship which was so crowded that each had scarcely room to turn himself, almost suffocating us. This produced copious perspirations, so that the air soon became unfit for respiration, from a variety of loathsome smells, and brought on a sickness among the slaves, of which many died—thus falling victims to the improvident avarice . . . of their purchasers." Later when the slave ships reached the West Indies to disperse their human cargo, and when the still-unsold Equiano, called variously Jacob or Michael, reached Virginia, he witnessed further atrocities, including rapes and mutilations. As chattel, slaves were often "branded with the initials of their master's name; and a load of heavy iron hooks hung about their necks. Indeed, on the most trifling occasions, they were loaded with chains; and often instruments of torture were added. . . . I have seen a Negro beaten till some of his bones were broken, for only letting a pot boil over." Equiano reported seeing a Virginia cook muzzled. The "poor creature was cruelly loaded with various kinds of iron machines; she had one particularly on her head, which locked her mouth so fast that she could scarcely speak; and could not eat or drink." In his report of a slave who was hung and then burnt for trying to poison a cruel overseer, Equiano wrote: "thus, by repeated cruelties are the wretched driven to despair, and then murdered because they still retain so much of human nature about them as to wish to put an end to their misery, and retaliate on their tyrants."

Equiano's own experiences would be mostly those of an indulgently treated African slave-servant. Even in Africa, his first masters purchased him more for companionship than for labor. In Virginia, he was secured by "one Mr. Campbell," who was his only New World master to put him in the field for "a few weeks weeding grass, and gathering stones in a plantation." This apprenticeship in manual labor was short-lived; Campbell sold Equiano to Michael Henry Pascal, a former lieutenant in the Royal Navy, who commanded a merchant ship. Pascal had become fond of Equiano and purchased him as "a present to some friends in England."

Pascal renamed Equiano Gustavus Vassa, after the sixteenth-century Swedish king. Equiano resisted the name, and when he insisted upon being called Jacob, he was hit. He finally submitted, but returned to using an African name when he bought his freedom in 1766. Equiano's life en route to England aboard Pascal's *Industrious Bee* was eased by the friendship he established with Richard Baker, a teenaged American sailor. Serving as his companion and tutor, Baker was instrumental in Equiano's acculturation into Western civilization. In one of the most poignant passages in Equiano's *Narrative,* he expresses his desire to read like Pascal and his friend Richard Baker. "I had often seen my master and Dick employed in reading, and I had a great curiosity to talk to the books as I thought they did, and so to learn how all things had a beginning: for that purpose I have often taken up a book and have talked to it and then put my ears to it, when in hopes it would answer me; and I have been very much concerned when I found it remained silent." By 1759 Equiano was fluent in English.

From the time they landed in England Equiano was preferentially treated. In Falmouth, where Pascal took the slave first, the servants of the master with whom Equiano boarded waited on him as one of the family. In Guernsey he was again boarded with a beneficent family. Their kind treatment caused the now-pampered slave to become confused about his role and to attempt to "change" his color by washing his face until his cheeks would become rosy like his white playmate's. "[B]ut it was all in vain," he wrote; "and now I began to be mortified at the difference in our complexions."

After spending two years at sea with Pascal, Equiano returned to England where he was sent to wait on Pascal's cousins, the Guerin sisters (perhaps the individuals for whom he had originally been purchased as a gift). The sisters encouraged his personal development by sending him to school for a formal education, and they saw to his spiritual well-being by having him baptized. But Pascal, who was then serving under Admiral Boscawen during the Seven Years' War, soon took him to sea again.

In 1757, when Equiano had arrived in England with Pascal, Great Britain was engaged in a full-fledged war with her colonial rival, France. Pascal was assigned as captain to the *Namur,* which served as flagship in the fleet of Admiral Boscawen, and Equiano served with him. Ironically, in this war for dominance over a part of West Africa that was not very far from his own homeland, in order to control such "commodities" as African slaves, Equiano found an avenue for rising above the "blood stained gates of slavery," to find meaning and dignity while still enslaved. He wants his readers to believe that he was able to find in the Seven Years' War an avenue for regaining the power, valor, honor, and respect, in short, the humanity of which he had been robbed with his abduction into slavery. In his tale, Equiano fashions himself as a protagonist who, had he been left to traditional African experiences, could easily have risen to heroic stature, since, as he seems to suggest throughout the narrative, traditional African communal life was associated with that which is heroic and ideal.

On the surface of his narration of the war Equiano takes the role of the eyewitness observer, the on-the-scene correspondent reporting with precision land and sea engagements between the British and the French. Naturally, he provides the most detail about those battles involving the *Namur.* Perhaps no battle was more important to Boscawen (and, indeed, to Equiano) than his successful gun battle with the French fleet at Gibraltar in August 1759.

After dramatically and suspensefully reporting this significant engagement, Equiano reveals his view of his own role in the battle; more than a mere servant or slave, he sees himself as a heroic fighter. "My station during the engagement was on the middle deck, where I was quartered with another boy, to bring powder to the aftermost gun.... Happily I escaped unhurt, though the shots and splinters flew thick about me during the whole fight.... At this station my gun-mate ... and I ran a very high risk, for more than a half hour, of blowing up the ship.... We were also, from our employment, very much exposed to the enemy's shots; for we had to go through nearly the whole length of the ship to bring the powder."

In the tradition of the African folk-trickster Anansi, who is sometimes caught in the traps that he sets for others, Equiano can be glimpsed for a moment behind the facade of his tale. Undoubtedly he is aware of the possibly indignant reaction of his audience to his work, were they to conclude that he had overstepped the bounds of his subservient social role; but a proud Equiano cannot refrain from revealing the fact that he had covertly assumed the role of the chivalrous warrior from the very beginning.

By the age of fourteen and after three years in and around England, Equiano was relatively comfortable in his situation. "I was so far from being afraid of anything new which I saw that after I had been some time in the ship," he says, "I even began to long for an engagement. My griefs, too,

Illustration for the second volume of the first edition of Equiano's narrative

which in young minds are not perpetual, were now wearing away, and I soon enjoyed myself pretty well. . . ." His active participation in maritime experiences, British life, and strong friendships gave him a competence in the language and culture that led him not only to absorb the British spirit and to imitate its manners but also to conclude that Pascal did not have the right to hold him in bondage. Although Pascal treated him "with the greatest kindness," Equiano desired above all his freedom. Determined that Equiano should remain enslaved, Pascal sold him to Captain Doran, who took the disappointed youth to Montserrat in the West Indies where, as a "prisoner without hope," he was sold to Robert King, a Philadelphia merchant.

Convinced that Equiano was not a "common slave," King placed him in a trusted position as shipping and receiving clerk and, recognizing his diverse talents, he soon called upon Equiano to serve him as barber, currier of his horses, and even manager of his vessels. He also assigned Equiano to assist Capt. Thomas Farmer, manager of one of King's vessels who carried cargo throughout the West Indies and the southern part of the American colonies. For nearly four years, this assignment provided Equiano with the opportunity to travel to new and different places, where he continued to witness firsthand the atrocity and barbarity of slavery which he would later record in his narrative. During this period he was "filled with the thoughts of freedom," and through his entrepreneurial skills, he amassed the forty pounds necessary to purchase his freedom from King.

On 11 July 1766 Equiano purchased his papers of manumission, and as a freeman he continued his travels in the West Indies and America. Only a month after he was freed, in Savannah, Georgia, Equiano had a physical altercation with a slave whose master boarded the ship the next day to demand satisfaction. Equiano refused to go ashore with him because, he said, he was "much embarrassed, and very apprehensive of a flogging at the least." Later, working himself into a rage, he reports he "would sooner die like a free man, than suffer [himself] to be scourged by the hands of ruffians, and [his] blood drawn like a slave." However, he went into hiding instead and was only released from the threat of a constable's warrant for

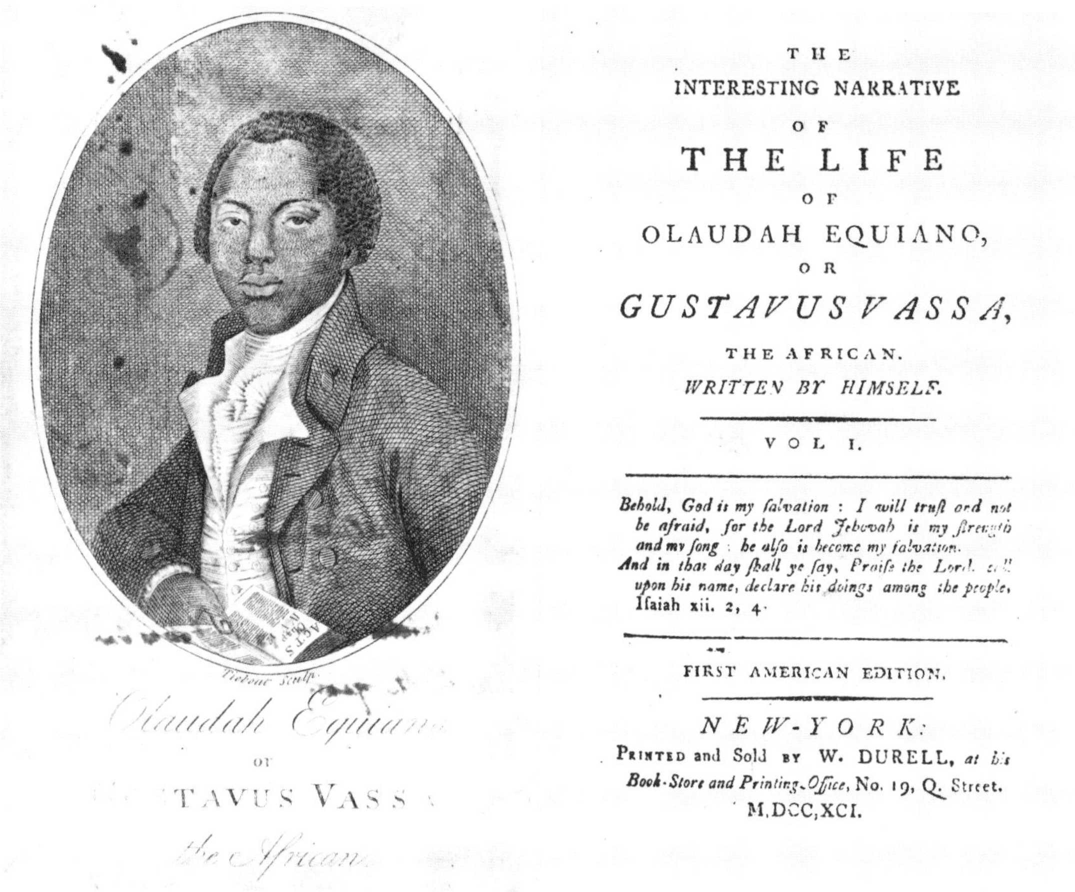

THE
INTERESTING NARRATIVE
OF
THE LIFE
OF
OLAUDAH EQUIANO,
OR
GUSTAVUS VASSA,
THE AFRICAN.
WRITTEN BY HIMSELF.

VOL. I.

Behold, God is my salvation : I will trust and not be afraid, for the Lord Jehovah is my strength and my song : he also is become my salvation.
And in that day shall ye say, Praise the Lord, call upon his name, declare his doings among the people.
Isaiah xii. 2, 4.

FIRST AMERICAN EDITION.

NEW-YORK:
PRINTED and Sold BY W. DURELL, *at his Book-Store and Printing-Office,* No. 19, Q. Street.
M,DCC,XCI.

Frontispiece and title page for the first volume of the American edition of Equiano's autobiography (courtesy of the John Carter Brown Library, Brown University)

his arrest by the intercession of his captain.

Equiano traveled to the West Indies but a short time later returned to America sailing under William Phillips, captain of a merchant ship whose cargo included slaves. With Phillips, Equiano returned to Savannah, where he was again nearly retaken into slavery when he broke a curfew for blacks. A few days later he was nearly kidnapped by two white men he met on a road. "I took a final leave of Georgia," Equiano narrates at the opening of chapter nine, "for the treatment I had received in it disgusted me very much against the place; and when I left it . . . I determined never more to revisit it."

Equiano soon returned to England. There he dedicated himself to a rigorous program of self-improvement which included being trained and employed as a hairdresser and receiving instruction in the French horn and arithmetic. Driven by a desire to secure a larger income and to travel in the manner of a cultured gentleman, Equiano worked for a time for Dr. Charles Irving, a scientist whose experiments with the purification of salt water were widely known. He later traveled to Italy, Turkey, Portugal, and the Mediterranean, where he was engaged in such diverse activities as studying architecture, attending the grand opera, visiting churches, and savoring the finest foods and wines that he could find. In 1773 Equiano joined Dr. Irving once again; this time, however, he sailed with Irving's expedition to the Arctic in quest of a passage to India. The harrowing voyage, vividly recounted in Equiano's narrative, included encounters with killer whales and "sea horses," and the boat nearly sank after it struck an iceberg. Equiano's seafaring life eventually returned him to America, specifically to New York and Pennsylvania, where he spent extended periods of time, met with black leaders, and explored the diverse denominational practices of several religious sects. He eventually became a Methodist.

Returning finally to London, he became actively involved in the British plan to colonize Sierra Leone and was appointed commissary for Stores for the Black Poor, an emigrationist group that aimed at returning blacks to Africa. Among the first emigrants, he spoke out against the mismanagement of funds and supplies he had witnessed en route, as well as the inhumane treatment of the emigrants, and he was dismissed from the colonizing party. In 1788 he petitioned the Queen of England on behalf of his enslaved fellow Africans. By the time his autobiography appeared in 1789, Equiano was deeply involved in the abolitionist movement in England. After marrying Susanna Cullen of Ely at Soham Church, Cambridgeshire, in April 1792, Equiano fathered two daughters, Ann Maria and Johanna. He died 31 March 1797. In Equiano's own words, his "life and fortune [were] extremely checkered, and [his] adventures various."

From the beginning, *The Interesting Narrative of the Life,* which would experience some fifteen editions, was well received and reviewed in the leading journals of the time. The *Monthly Review* commentator wrote: "We entertain no doubt of the general authenticity of this very intelligent African's interesting story; though it is not improbable that some English writer has assisted him in the compilement, or, at least, the correction of his book: for it is sufficiently well written." But for the reviewer from *Gentleman's Magazine,* "The memoirs, written in a very unequal style, place the writer on a par with the general mass of men in subordinate stations of civilized society, and prove that there is no general rule without an exception."

In the final analysis, Equiano's narrative must, to a great degree, be perceived as the mold from which much early black fiction was first cast, particularly since it is apparently one of the first records to shape the experiences of the black African diaspora during slavery. Like the modern alienated hero in black fiction, Equiano remains above all in his narrative an exile. In his response to life, Equiano epitomizes the black fictional character whose quest is for wholeness and meaning in a world that often does not offer aggregation or fulfillment.

References:

Houston Baker, *The Journey Back* (Chicago: University of Chicago Press, 1981);

John Blassingame, *The Slave Community* (New York: Oxford University Press, 1972);

Arna Bontemps, ed., *Great Slave Narratives* (Boston: Beacon, 1969);

Benjamin Brawley, *Early Negro American Writers* (Chapel Hill: University of North Carolina Press, 1953);

Stephen Butterfield, *Black Autobiography in America* (Amherst: University of Massachusetts Press, 1974);

Philip Curtin, ed., *Africa Remembered* (Madison: University of Wisconsin Press, 1967);

Charles H. Nichols, "O Wasn't That a Wide River," in *Many Thousands Gone: The Ex-Slaves' Account of Their Bondage and Freedom,* edited by Nichols (Leiden, Netherlands: E. J. Brill, 1963);

James Olney, *Metaphor of Self* (Princeton: Princeton University Press, 1973);

Roy Pascal, *Design and Truth in Autobiography* (London: Routledge & Kegan Paul, 1960);

Sidone Smith, *Where I'm Bound: Patterns of Slavery and Freedom in Black American Autobiography* (Westport, Conn.: Greenwood Press, 1974);

Robert Stepto, *From Behind the Veil: A Study of Afro-American Narrative* (Urbana, Ill.: University of Illinois Press, 1979).

Papers:

Equiano's papers and first editions of his works are held at: The Schomburg Collection, New York Public Library; Library Company, Philadelphia; Ridgeway Brothers, Philadelphia; Boston Public Library; Yale University; Harvard University; Atlanta University; Hornby Collection, Liverpool City Library.

Charlotte L. Forten

(17 August 1837-23 July 1914)

Trudier Harris
University of North Carolina at Chapel Hill

BOOK: *The Journal of Charlotte L. Forten,* edited by Ray Allen Billington (New York: Dryden, 1953; London: Collier-Macmillan, 1961).

OTHER: "A Parting Hymn," in *The Black Man, His Antecedents, His Genius, and His Achievements,* by William Wells Brown (New York: Hamilton/Boston: Wallcut, 1863);

Émile Erckmann and Alexandre Chatrian, *Madame Thérèse; or, The Volunteers of '92,* translated by Forten (New York: Scribners, 1869).

PERIODICAL PUBLICATIONS: "To W. L. G. on Reading His 'Chosen Queen,'" *Liberator* (16 March 1855);

"Glimpses of New England," *National Anti-Slavery Standard* (19 June 1858);

"The Two Voices," *National Anti-Slavery Standard* (15 January 1859);

"The Wind Among the Poplars," *National Anti-Slavery Standard* (2 April 1859);

"The Slave-Girl's Prayer," *Liberator* (3 February 1860);

"Letter," *Liberator* (12 December 1862);

"Interesting Letter from Miss Charlotte L. Forten," *Liberator* (19 December 1862);

"Life on the Sea Islands," *Atlantic Monthly,* 8 (May 1864): 587-596; 8 (June 1864): 666-676;

"Personal Recollections of Whittier," *New England Magazine,* 8 (June 1893): 468-476.

Charlotte Forten, abolitionist, poet, champion of liberal causes, and descendant of famous personages, was born free in Philadelphia in 1837. Unwavering in her opposition to slavery and in her desire to devote her life to the education of black people, Forten is important to Afro-American literary history for her poetry as well as her prose. In an age when the majority of the black writers were producing autobiographies and narratives of their lives as former slaves, Forten kept a journal that illuminates the growth of a young black woman who was unique in her dedication to the progress of her people. Her own freedom did not provide a bed of ease for Forten; rather, she used it to further the cause of freedom for the masses of blacks. Her journal recounts her commitment and gives us a rare glimpse into a world where contact with the famous was as casual as attending a lecture and where politics and life were synonymous.

Born to Robert Bridges and Mary Wood Forten on 17 August 1837, Charlotte Forten was destined to be distinguished, radical, and uncompromising toward injustice. Her grandfather was James Forten, a free black man born in 1766. He was educated in the school of Anthony Benezet, a Quaker abolitionist, before he became a powder boy aboard a Philadelphia privateer during the Revolution. After the war, he went to England to escape color prejudice. Renewed in abolitionist spirit, he returned to Philadelphia to become a community and national leader. He became a sailmaker and earned a fortune of $100,000 for an invention to handle sails. He was involved in a number of abolitionist activities, including signing a petition to modify the Fugitive Slave Act of 1793, opposing a ban on free blacks coming into Pennsylvania, and advocating citizenship in America over colonization in Africa. According to Forten's twentieth-century editor, Ray Allen Billington, James Forten's "stout advocacy of racial equality helped convince William Lloyd Garrison that colonization was an evil, thus laying the basis for the rise of abolitionism." James Forten was apparently a principal financial backer of Garrison's Anti-Slavery Society and the *Liberator,* the society's periodical. It was in her grandfather's home on Lombard Street and under the influence of his "reforming zeal" that the young Charlotte spent her early youth, during the first five years of which her grandfather was still alive.

James Forten's several sons and daughters continued his abolitionist work. All of them were prominent in their work, the daughters inspiring a poem by John Greenleaf Whittier entitled "To the Daughters of James Forten." Robert Bridges Forten, father of Charlotte, was also a sailmaker. He showed his father's spirit by addressing antislavery meetings and keeping Charlotte at home rather than allowing her to attend the segregated schools of Philadelphia; she was educated by tutors until he sent her to Salem, Massachusetts, in 1854. There was no discrimination in schools there, and Charlotte could live with a family friend, Charles Lenox Remond, himself a famous orator in the mold of Frederick Douglass. Robert Bridges Forten was so disgusted with the racial climate in the United States that he left for Canada while Charlotte was in school in Salem; he also briefly sought a more congenial environment in Britain. He returned, however, to fight in the Union Army. When he died of erysipelas in 1864, he was buried in Philadelphia with full military honors, the first time a black man had been so honored in America. Charlotte's mother died when the child was very young, and little mention is made of her in the biographical material on Charlotte.

In addition to her father and grandfather, another strong early influence on Forten was Robert Purvis, husband of her father's sister Harriet. Purvis signed the original declaration of the American Anti-Slavery Society, and he worked extensively with Garrison until the Civil War. He also founded the Vigilance Committee of Philadelphia, which aided fugitive slaves in their bids for freedom. Purvis's farm in Byberry, fifteen miles from Philadelphia, became Charlotte's second home after her mother's death. From her uncle and cousins, she "heard the doctrines of radical abolitionism from morning until night."

By the time Forten went to Salem and began her journal in 1854, she was already steeped in the tradition that forced her to see the world from the perspective of color. For approximately eleven years of her life, with a few lapses during that period, Forten kept a journal of her activities. The journal provides the basis for the detailed information of her school years and of her teaching in the early 1860s in the Port Royal area of South Carolina. The journal reflects the growth of a sensitive young woman who was, at times, almost too concerned about the nature of slavery and the evils of mankind. It also shows a young black woman who manages to get a strikingly complete education in a period when few black people were able to go to elementary school, and certainly not to normal school, as Forten did.

The journal begins in 1854 with Forten at the Higginson Grammar School in Salem, Massachusetts. Her father had requested that she come home at least twice in the next school term, but Forten and her teachers persuaded him to allow her to stay. Although some of the journal entries cite slights she received from whites in the area, overall she seemed well adjusted and at home with students and teachers, socializing more, however, with the teachers. Forten was in Salem in an auspicious time, for by making trips to Boston and neighboring areas, she was able to meet most of the outstanding abolitionists of the day. She also made trips to New York to visit her brother Henry.

She begins her journal with an account of an escaped slave, Burns, who was captured in Boston, tried, and forcibly returned to his master. Forten uses the occasion to lament the failure of freedom on northern soil, especially in a state like Massachusetts, which was so saturated with the spirit of revolution and the refusal to cast human beings into bondage. She is particularly critical of the ministers, indicting them as supporters of slavery because they would not defend Burns. At times, her hatred of slavery led her to question her own Christianity and almost to question God.

Forten followed the Burns case with great interest and wailed to her journal when the man's fate was sealed. Her reaction to Burns had many spiritual parallels in the numerous antislavery lectures she attended and in her great admiration for Wendell Phillips and William Lloyd Garrison, both of whose lectures she attended and both of whom she met and held discussions with during her school years; in later years, she would correspond with Phillips. She also heard lectures by Henry Ward Beecher, Ralph Waldo Emerson, Charles Sumner, and William Wells Brown, the famous Afro-American novelist and lecturer. Brown stayed for a brief period in the same house in Salem in which Forten lived, and each time he passed close to Salem on the lecture circuit in 1855 and 1856, she managed to hear him. Forten joined the Salem Female Anti-Slavery Society with Brown's daughter Josephine.

Forten's strong abolitionist sentiments did not prevent her from enjoying life as a schoolgirl. She went on long walks for exercise with women from her school, traveled extensively in the New England area, played the piano, took German and French, and kept up with the latest fashions in sewing. She also went to the theater, noting in her journal that she saw *Hamlet* in March of 1856. Dedicated to the art of reading, Forten seems to have spent many hours in perusing histories, autobiographies, novels, and poetry. She read Charles Dickens's *Hard Times* shortly after it was released in 1854, Elizabeth Barrett Browning's poetry, Thomas Macaulay's *History of England* (1848) (which sent her into rap-

Freedmen's schools in Beaufort, South Carolina, circa 1862, similar to the one on nearby St. Helena Island where Forten taught (courtesy of the South Carolina Historical Society)

tures for that country), Phillis Wheatley's poetry, works by Nathaniel Hawthorne and Harriet Beecher Stowe, and Mattie Griffiths's *The Autobiography of a Female Slave* (1857), in addition to the standard fare of the Bible, the *Liberator,* and the *Atlantic Monthly* (in one year she read more than a hundred books). She couched her pursuits in racial terms, perhaps intending to show through excessive example that blacks were capable of learning and excelling. Always she strived to learn more, and always she fell short of her own exacting standards; she was, as Billington correctly asserts, always "overcritical" of herself.

In areas beyond self-criticism, her evaluations were appropriate. Like Frederick Douglass, she was critical—and commented on it year after year—of the celebration of the Fourth of July in a country where a large percentage of the citizens were not free. Yet she joined in other festivals, including those in Boston at Christmas each year.

Forten extended her writing from private journal entries to public poetry for the first time in 1855, when she penned "To W. L. G. [William Lloyd Garrison] on Reading His 'Chosen Queen,' " which was published in the *Liberator* on 16 March of that year. She praised Garrison for his dedication to the cause of liberty, suggesting by analogy that his championing of truth was like that of a knight in service to a queen. She was embarrassed when one of her aunts saw the poem, and resolved: "If ever I write doggerel again I shall be careful not to sign my own initials." It was the first of fourteen poems that she would publish.

In a less political vein, her poetic inspiration continued in "A Parting Hymn," which she wrote for the examination ceremony at Higginson Grammar School and which William Wells Brown published in *The Black Man* in 1863:

When Winter's royal robes of white
From hill and vale are gone
And glad voices of the spring
Upon the air are borne,
Friends who have met with us before,
Within these walls shall meet no more

Forth to a noble work they go:
O, may their hearts keep pure,
And hopeful zeal and strength be theirs
To labor and endure,
That they an earnest faith may prove
By words of truth and deeds of love.

The poem introduced the themes of commitment and endurance that characterized Forten's later works.

Upon graduation from Higginson, Forten enrolled in the one-year program at Salem Normal School, from which she graduated in July 1856. She was asked to write a poem for the graduation exercises. Despite feelings of modesty, which references to her writing would evoke for the remainder of her life, she wrote the poem, and it was used in the ceremony. It was later published in an issue of the *Liberator.* With her usual belief in aspiration to as much learning as one could acquire, Forten penned an inspirational piece, "Poem," which brought regional recognition to the nineteen-year-old:

In the earnest path of duty,
    With the high hopes and hearts sincere,
We, to useful lives aspiring,
    Daily meet to labor here.

No vain dreams of earthly glory
    Urge us onward to explore
Far-extending realms of knowledge,
    With their rich and varied store;

....

Not the great and gifted only
    He appoints to do his will.
But each one, however lowly,
    Has a mission to fulfill.

Knowing this, toil we unwearied,
    With true hearts and purpose high;—
We would win a wreath immortal
    Whose bright flowers ne'er fade and die.

An occasional piece of more passion than talent, "Poem" continued Forten's emphasis upon responsibility and labor for higher causes. After this effort, Forten "produced a succession of sentimental poems and essays," culminating in several "poetic effusions," such as "The Two Voices" (1859), "The Wind Among the Poplars" (1859), and "The Slave-Girl's Prayer" (1860). "The Two Voices" depicts, in twenty-four quatrains, the plight of an individual, obviously modeled on Forten, who is torn between a sense of responsibility to the struggle for abolition and who is herself so victimized by the injustices of racism that she is frequently drawn toward giving up the struggle. One voice, perhaps that of despair, counsels that "Thou canst find a haven only/In the quiet of the grave." The persona prays for death and instead finds a second voice, one that admonishes her to follow a higher calling:

"Knowing that to strive and suffer,
With a purpose pure and high,
In a holy cause is nobler
Than ingloriously to die.

"Sweet the grave's unbroken quiet
To thy aching heart would be;
But, believe, to live for others
Is a higher destiny."

While its call to struggle is worthy, the poem borders on doggerel, and the "ah, woe is me" brand of sentiment is more suggestive of affectation than true dilemma. With its appeal to God for guidance, the poem also evokes an aura of the conversion, hymnbook brand of poetry characteristic of slave narratives and some of the work of Frances Ellen Watkins Harper.

"The Wind Among the Poplars," while slightly shorter, is even more strikingly sentimental. It is a dialogue between two women, Clare and Bertha, in which, upon Clare's invitation to Bertha to leave her reading and go for a walk "among the poplars," Bertha explains why that seemingly pleasant activity is so painful to her. Her beloved had sailed far away and promised to return, only to be drowned at sea; it was during a walk among the poplars that the intuition of his death came to her. The wind in the trees became a premonition of death:

Ah, my heart, too, too prophetic!
'Twas in truth a funeral knell;
In the storm, my Clare, he perished,
He whom I had loved so well.
So the wind among the poplars
Hath a mournful sound to me,
For it moaneth to me ever
Of that loved one, lost at sea.

Romantic, self-indulgent, and escapist, the poem is far removed from the sentiments Forten expressed in her journal. The focus on death, however, is a theme that runs through her early poetry, and she frequently mentions in her journal a longing for the peace of the grave. Death as an escape is also the desire of the slave in "The Slave-Girl's Prayer." After her family and friends are sold away, the girl prays for death, threatening to commit suicide to escape her horrible circumstances if God does not honor her request and strike her dead.

Forten had already begun her teaching career, in June 1856, as the first black teacher at the all-white Epes Grammar School of Salem, but her work would shortly be interrupted by the ill health that plagued her for several years. In May 1857 she was forced to return to Philadelphia for recuperation. Weakened from lung fever, but not entirely incapacitated, Forten was able to make excursions into the city and to visit friends and family. In her journal, she recounts one instance in which, on an outing, she was refused admission to an ice cream saloon. Such prejudice renewed her determination to fight injustice wherever she found it. She was soon heartened by returning in August 1857 to Boston and Salem, where Whittier visited her before she began teaching again in September. In addition to the renewed effort at teaching, she returned to studying French, but was forced to discontinue the lessons for lack of funds.

In December 1857 she noted in her journal that she sent a story to *Home Journal* and was waiting anxiously to hear its fate; however, no such publication or story has been found. Forten's teaching and writing were again interrupted when illness forced her to resign and return to Philadelphia in March 1858; the *Salem Register* wrote a long piece on her tenure as a teacher. She completed an essay in May entitled "Glimpses of New England," which, to her "great astonishment," was published in the 19 June 1858 issue of the *National Anti-Slavery Standard;* Billington calls the piece "a description of Salem and the surrounding countryside." The usually modest Forten was perhaps made more insecure about her writing when one of her former acquaintances complained about "Glimpses." The woman, Forten confided to her journal, "has burst out most *venomously* upon my poor 'Glimpses'—accusing them of being pro-slavery, and heaven knows what all. I *pity* her."

Now teaching in Philadelphia, Forten found herself lonely at times and so weakened by illness that she maintained she "would gladly lay me down and rest in the quiet grave," a rather romantic longing that she echoes in other entries. Still, she followed abolitionist news and stories of runaway slaves. She celebrated when a slave who had escaped to Philadelphia was released after being captured and tried in April 1859. Shortly thereafter, on 7 May 1859, Forten stopped writing in her journal and did not resume entries until 1 January 1860; during this interval, she returned to Salem. The entry on 1 January 1860 preceded a more extensive gap, this time until 22 June 1862, during which time she became ill with lung fever and re-

Melba Moore portraying Charlotte Forten in the 1985 American Playhouse *production of "Charlotte Forten's Mission: Experiment in Freedom" (photograph by Shep Morgan)*

cuperated in Philadelphia.

During her illness someone read her Diana Mulock's *Life for a Life* (1861), a journal which Mulock personified as "Unknown Friend." Perhaps out of guilt for having neglected her own journal, Forten decided to personify it as well, calling it "A" (for *ami inconnu*). In Salem in 1862, she recounted to "A" visits from Whittier and his sister; she maintained an extended correspondence with Whittier for years. He advised her to apply to Port Royal for a teaching position.

Port Royal, South Carolina, was of national interest at this time because of events connected to the Civil War. In 1861 President Lincoln had decided to close Southern coasts from Virginia to Texas in an effort to prevent supplies from reaching Confederate troops. Union soldiers were dispatched to capture certain ports, and it was decided that Port Royal should be taken first. A successful sea attack on 7 November 1861 pushed the Southern white owners of island plantations into retreat and left the Sea Islands and the Port Royal district in Northern hands. The ten thousand slaves who were left behind became freedmen by default, and it was left to the Union to decide what should be done with them. From this set of circumstances evolved the conception of the Port Royal experiment, as it became popularly known, whereby the War Department, in conjunction with teachers and abolitionists from the North, set out to prove that the freedmen could be educated and become self-determining and that they could fight for the Union cause. Teachers like Forten gave them the opportunity to learn, and Civil War battles, combined with the sporadic attempts of the displaced Southern whites to reclaim their property, gave them the chance to show their bravery.

Forten followed Whittier's advice and applied to go to Port Royal under the auspices of the Boston Educational Commission. When she did not hear

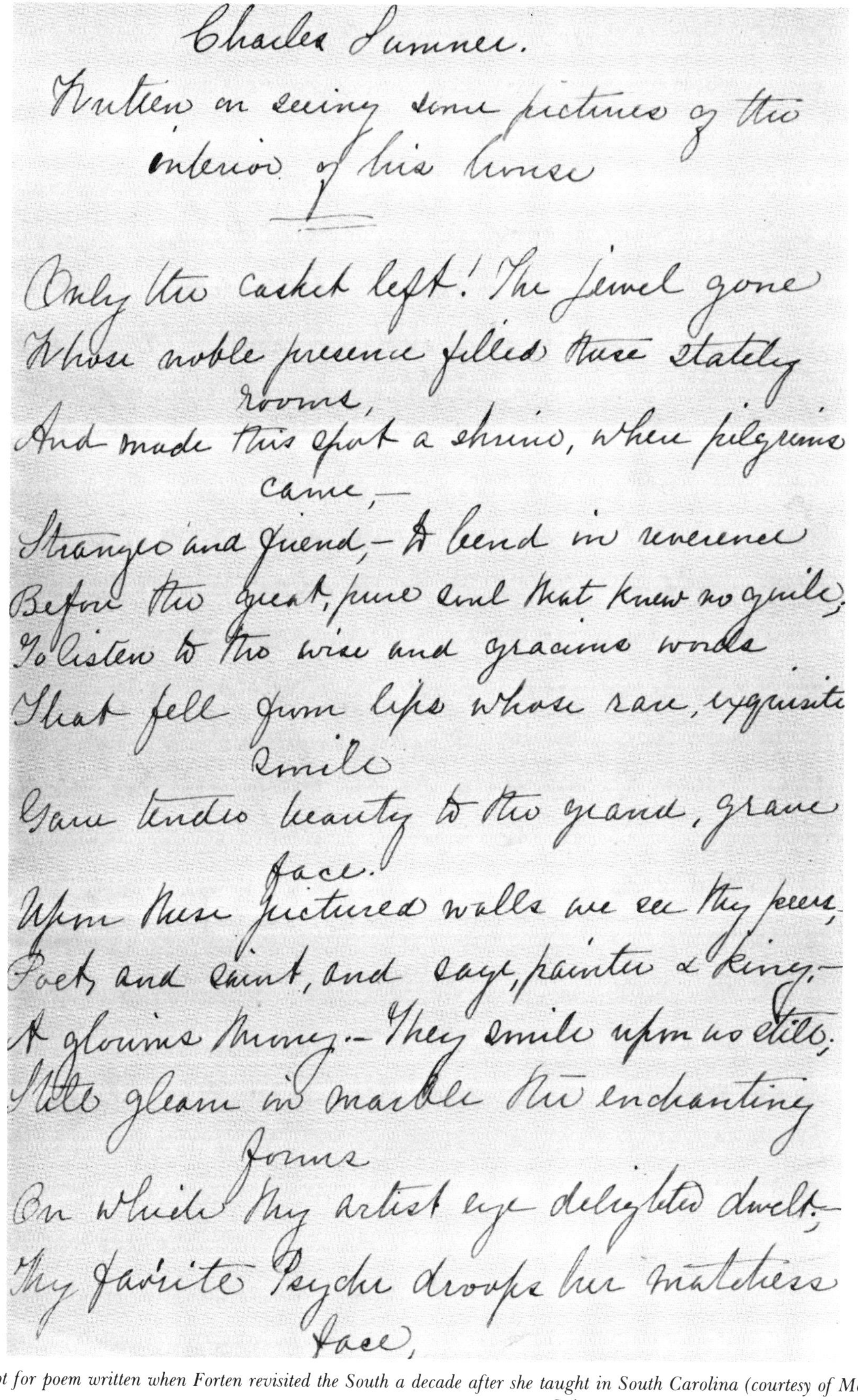

Charles Sumner.

Written on seeing some pictures of the interior of his house

Only the casket left! The jewel gone
Whose noble presence filled these stately rooms,
And made this spot a shrine, where pilgrims came,—
Stranger and friend,—to bend in reverence
Before the great, pure soul that knew no guile;
To listen to the wise and gracious words
That fell from lips whose rare, exquisite smile
Gave tender beauty to the grand, grave face.
Upon these pictured walls we see thy peers,—
Poet, and saint, and sage, painter & king,—
A glorious throng.—They smile upon us still;
Still gleam in marble the enchanting forms
On which thy artist eye delighted dwelt;—
Thy favorite Psyche droops her matchless face,

Manuscript for poem written when Forten revisited the South a decade after she taught in South Carolina (courtesy of Moorland-Spingarn Research Center, Howard University)

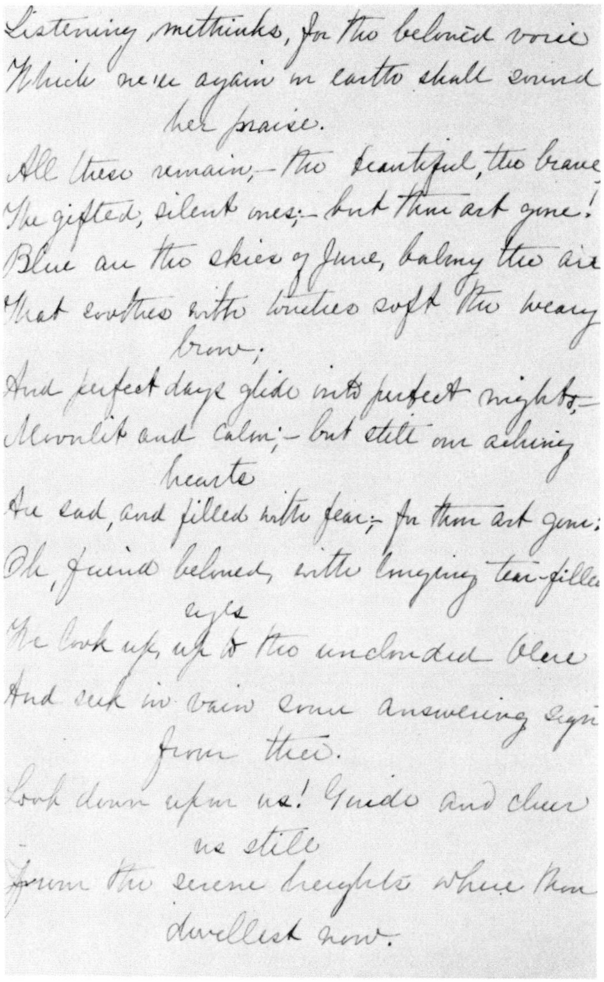

Listening, methinks, for the beloved voice
Which never again on earth shall sound
her praise.
All these remain;—the beautiful, the brave
The gifted; silent ones;—but thou art gone!
Blue are the skies of June, balmy the air
That soothes with touches soft the weary
brow;
And perfect days glide into perfect nights,—
Moonlit and calm;—but still our aching
hearts
Are sad, and filled with fear;—for thou art gone!
Oh, friend beloved, with longing tear-filled
eyes
We look up, up to the unclouded blue
And seek in vain some answering sign
from thee.
Look down upon us! Guide and cheer
us still
From the serene heights where thou
dwellest now.

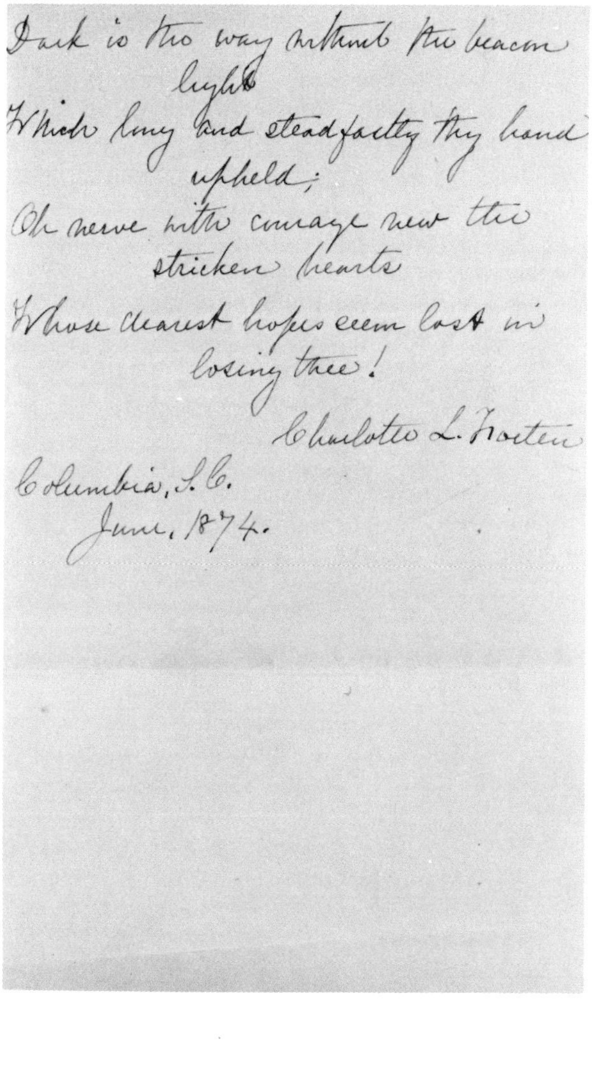

Dark is the way without the beacon
light
Which long and steadfastly thy hand
upheld;
Oh nerve with courage new the
stricken hearts
Whose dearest hopes seem lost in
losing thee!
Charlotte L. Forten
Columbia, S.C.
June, 1874.

from them, she returned to Philadelphia and obtained a teaching assignment through J. Miller McKim, a family friend and organizer of the Port Royal Relief Association of Philadelphia.

The next few years of Forten's life provide some of the most interesting details for contemporary readers. Her association with the famous Port Royal experiment, designed to show through education and training that blacks were not destined for bondage, was the culmination of her belief that blacks could become just as educated as whites if given the opportunity. Her work also put her in touch with other abolitionist spirits, including McKim, Thomas Wentworth Higginson, and Harriet Ware, all of whom were interested in the status of the freedmen on the islands once the "Secesh" had conceded that territory to the Union Army.

Forten's journal and articles on sea island life provide details and a sympathetic perspective on the cultural folkways and the former slaves she met. For example, she constantly notes in her journal the talents for singing among the blacks with whom she came into contact; indeed, she comments upon that assumed innate ability so much that she, liberal though she was, ran the risk of stereotyping other black people even as she professed appreciation of their singing skills. She also showed a gap between herself and the island blacks by initially responding to the songs as "strange" and "wild"; very quickly, however, she grew to love them and to be disappointed when she did not hear singing. Forten was not alone in her interest in the music of the sea islands. Out of this period came one of the first efforts to record indigenous Afro-American cultural forms. In 1864 William Allen, Charles Ware, and Lucy McKim Garrison (daughter of J. Miller McKim) published *Slave Songs of the United States,* collected from blacks in the Port Royal area. That volume remains one of the most informative about the process of creation and transmission of Afro-American songs.

Forten traveled by boat to Port Royal, arriving in Hilton Head and from there went on to Beaufort and St. Helena. She assumed a teaching position there with Laura M. Towne and Ellen Murphy, both northern white women; Towne founded the school that became famous as the Penn school. Forten's teaching responsibilities went relatively well, and she still had plenty of time for consort with the abolitionists, including the surgeon of the local regiment, Dr. Seth Rogers, whom she had met in Massachusetts during one of her bouts of lung fever and with whom she had extensive contact. Her continued contact with Whittier resulted in a hymn that he composed for her schoolchildren. She also had the opportunity to meet Harriet Tubman, who had settled for a brief time in Beaufort, South Carolina. She described her adventures in letters she wrote back to the North, two of which were published in the *Liberator* (12 and 19 December 1862).

The threat of attack from Southern soldiers was constant, so that by 1863 Forten and the other teachers had their own guns for protection. Ever busy, Forten served briefly in a hospital and dressed wounded soldiers. She also desired to go to Florida with Dr. Rogers and others on a Union campaign, but the fort they planned to visit was attacked and lost before the party left South Carolina. Shortly thereafter, during the period from 31 July to 16 October 1863, Forten was forced to return north for health reasons. Once again, however, she returned to teaching duties in the South despite health problems.

Her teaching in Port Royal was indeed unusual, for all of the other northern teachers who came south with their missionary zeal were white; they were also far healthier than Forten. For these reasons, perhaps, Forten's life has been of interest to education historians as well as to others.

Forten made the last entry in her journal on 15 May 1864 after a lapse of several months. Her father had died suddenly in April, providing perhaps a partial reason for the lapse. Later in May, Forten left Port Royal and sailed to New York, thereby bringing to an end her share in that famous experiment.

For the next twelve years, Forten taught in the schools of Philadelphia and lived a rather quiet existence; she also lived briefly in the Boston area. She continued her reading and gained a "modest reputation" as a writer. She published "Life on the Sea Islands" in the May and June 1864 issues of the *Atlantic Monthly,* and wrote on a variety of other subjects for the *Christian Register,* the *Boston Commonwealth,* and the *New England Magazine.* She also translated Émile Erckmann and Alexander Chatrian's 1863 *Madame Thérèse; or, The Volunteers of '92,* which was published in 1869; Forten apparently saw parallels to the American Civil War in this novel about internal conflict in France in 1793. She published "Personal Recollections of Whittier" in the June 1893 issue of the *New England Magazine.*

In the mid-1870s Forten moved to Washington, D. C., where, in 1877, she met the man she would later marry. On 19 December 1878, Forten married the Reverend Francis J. Grimké, thirteen years her junior and a mulatto offspring of the

Francis James Grimké (courtesy of New York Public Library)

famous South Carolina Grimkés that produced the abolitionist sisters Angelina and Sarah. Grimké, who would become a famous clergyman, distinguished in his own right, provided a kindred spirit for the socially active Forten. Their only child, Theodora Cornelia, was born 1 January 1880 but died six months later.

Together, the Grimkés "worked with equal vigor for racial equality"; they also "shared a love of music, art, and literature that made their home a social and cultural center." They lived in Jacksonville, Florida, between 1885 and 1889, then returned to Washington, where Charlotte Grimké worked as a clerk in the Treasury Department and served as a trustee and secretary of the Westborough Insane Hospital. Five years before her death, she became an invalid. After more than three decades of marriage and many more of social activism, Charlotte Forten Grimké was bedridden for the last thirteen months of her life, trying to fight the lung fever that took her life on 23 July 1914.

Her legacy of commitment to equality and civil rights is perhaps more significant than her literary accomplishments, but it is the telling, through her journal, of those struggles that gives her a place in literary history. Sections of the journal continue to be anthologized in volumes on Afro-American literature, giving students and scholars a chance to see inside the incisive, probing mind of Charlotte L. Forten Grimké. A 25 February 1985 *American Playhouse* production indicates the current trend of interest in Forten's life and work. In "Charlotte Forten's Mission: Experiment in Freedom," Melba Moore played Forten, who did not leave the fate of thousands of poor and illiterate black children solely up to nonblacks. In spite of poor health and possible rejection from the very blacks she wished to help, she pursued her goal, eventually winning their respect and admiration and educating hundreds of children in the process. A woman with a dream, Charlotte Forten strove to give it life in spite of the numerous strikes against her; for her vision and her accomplishment of that dream, she is remembered well.

References:

Anna Julia Cooper, ed., *Life and Writings of the Grimké Family,* 2 volumes (N. p., 1951);

James M. McPherson, Introduction to *Two Black Teachers During the Civil War,* by Forten and Lewis C. Lockwood (New York: Arno Press, 1969), pp. i-vi;

Polly Longsworth, *I, Charlotte Forten, Black and Free* (New York: Crowell, 1970);

Joan R. Sherman, *Invisible Poets: Afro-Americans of the Nineteenth Century* (Urbana: University of Illinois Press, 1974).

Papers:

Charlotte L. Forten Grimké's manuscripts are in the Moorland-Spingarn Research Center of Howard University.

Sutton Elbert Griggs

(1872-1930)

Betty E. Taylor Thompson
Texas Southern University

BOOKS: *Imperium in Imperio* (Cincinnati: Editor, 1899);
Overshadowed (Nashville: Orion, 1901);
Unfettered (Nashville: Orion, 1902);
The Hindered Hand: or, The Reign of the Repressionist (Nashville: Orion, 1905);
The One Great Question . . . (Nashville: Orion, 1907);
Pointing the Way (Nashville: Orion, 1908);
Needs of the South (Nashville: Orion, 1909);
The Race Question in A New Light (Nashville: Orion, 1909); enlarged as *Wisdom's Call* (Nashville: Orion, 1911);
The Story of My Struggles (Memphis: National Public Welfare League, 1914);
How to Rise (Memphis: National Public Welfare League, 1915);
Life's Demands; or, According to the Law (Memphis: National Public Welfare League, 1916);
The Reconstruction of a Race (Memphis: National Public Welfare League, 1917);
Light on Racial Issues (Memphis: National Public Welfare League, 1921);
Guide to Racial Greatness; or, The Science of Collective Efficiency (Memphis: National Public Welfare League, 1923);
The Negro's Next Step (Memphis: National Public Welfare League, 1923);
Kingdom Builders' Manual: Companion Book to Guide to Racial Greatness (Memphis: National Public Welfare League, 1924);
Paths of Progress; or, Co-operation Between the Races (Memphis: National Public Welfare League, 1925);
Triumph of the Simple Virtues, or the Life Story of John L. Webb (Hot Springs, Ark.: Messenger, 1926?);
The Winning Policy (Memphis: National Public Welfare League, 1927).

The novels, pamphlets, and political tracts of Sutton Elbert Griggs contain the seeds of black nationalism, and black Americans today who espouse black beauty, pride, militancy, and separatism are the ideological successors of Sutton E. Griggs, one of the most neglected black writers of the period between the Spanish American War and World War I. During the period of disenfranchisement of the black American, when Thomas Nelson Page and Thomas Dixon aided antiblack legislation by writing works which showed the black person as a vicious beast and an irresponsible degenerate, Griggs wrote novels glorifying black people and demanding racial justice.

Griggs's novels have been virtually ignored by major black and white critics, with the exceptions of Hugh M. Gloster, Robert Bone, and, recently, Robert E. Fleming and Campbell Tatham. His work has been left out of most anthologies, with the notable exception of Arthur P. Davis and J. Saunders Redding's *Cavalcade* (1971). In addition, his works have been criticized for their melodramatic style, fantastic episodes, and thematic inconsistencies; however, as new scholarship examines the contributions of blacks to the body of American literature, it is inevitable that Griggs's works will undergo reevaluation and a new scholarly criticism of his writing will continue to emerge.

Griggs demonstrates his wide reading and his familiarity with world history and literature, politics, government, and philosophy in his political tracts and pamphlets. Influenced by the romantic poets, he exhibits in his novels a predilection for the melodramatic. His all-consuming interests in uplifting his race and eliminating racial injustice overwhelm his novels and form the bases for their plots, characterizations, and themes.

Sutton Griggs spent his entire life in the South and devoted his adulthood to religious and civic matters. He was born in Chatfield, Texas, in 1872 and received his elementary education in Dallas, Texas. He attended Bishop College in Marshall, Texas. Little is known about his personal life, his parents, friends, or other associations; his primary concerns in his writings were his political philosophy and religious career. In 1893 Griggs completed the theological course at Richmond Theological Seminary (later part of Virginia Union University). He was ordained a Baptist minister and served his first pastorate in Virginia. His ministerial duties also took him to Tennessee and Texas. Griggs held his longest ministerial office at Tabernacle Baptist Church in Memphis, Tennessee, and his last duty was in Houston, Texas, where he went to establish the National Religious and Civic Institute, sponsored by the Baptists in Houston. He also served as the Secretary of the Education Department of the National Baptist Convention in Nashville, Tennessee. He died in Houston, Texas, in 1930.

Apart from numerous political and philosophical tracts, Sutton Griggs was the author of five racially militant novels and two full-length political tracts which directly reflect the themes, ideals, and philosophy found in the author's fiction. In *Wisdom's Call* (1911) and *Guide to Racial Greatness* (1923), both written after the publication of his five novels, Griggs expressed the same ideas he had voiced in his fiction. His three most significant novels are *Imperium in Imperio* (1899), *Unfettered* (1902), and *The Hindered Hand: or, The Reign of the Repressionist* (1905). *Overshadowed* (1901) and *Pointing the Way* (1908) demonstrate the same themes, literary style, and philosophy, but with less technical and literary skill. Among the primary themes found in the works of Griggs are the effects of lynching and mob action, slavery and repression on black and white people, the impracticality of migration to Africa, the unprotected state of the black female, political, economic, and labor problems of black people, and the mulatto "problem." In contrast to Charles W. Chesnutt's and Frances Harper's main characters, who always had very light complexions, many of Griggs's major characters have dark pigmentation. Most of Griggs's mulatto characters also show an intense racial pride and as much zeal as his strong-willed, darker characters.

Griggs's own determination and racial pride fueled his efforts to publish his racially militant literature and to put his works into the hands of the common black people: the black working class and the black student. *The Story of My Struggles* (1914) is a pamphlet by Griggs in which he relates the hardships he endured to get his works published and distributed to a black audience. In the preface to the work, he states that the unsettled questions concerning the Negro include the conditions under which he is willing to live and the kind of treatment he can expect if he does nothing to change his situation. Griggs reported that all of his novels were financial failures in spite of helpful reviews and announcements in the news media by influential persons; therefore, on behalf of his own publishing company, he resorted to selling his works door to door. His major customers were poor, and his ideas and concerns were directed toward raising their level of achievement and their standing in society. Hugh Gloster maintains that precisely because Griggs's novels were only sold by direct appeal, they were read widely and circulated among blacks more than the books of Charles Chesnutt or Paul Laurence Dunbar. *The Story of My Struggles* also tells of Griggs's founding of the Public Welfare League, the aims of which included organizing for the common good of all black people, developing the talents of blacks, and shaping a friendly public for the race. Some of his works were published under the name of this organization.

Hugh Gloster and Robert Bone, the first critics to address Griggs's work and to give him a significant place in the development of the Afro-American novel, give somewhat contrasting views of Griggs as a novelist. In the 1940s, and again in the 1960s and 1970s, Gloster describes Griggs, the writer of the first political novel by an American Negro, as the most outspoken among the glorifiers and defenders of his race. In comparing Griggs with Chesnutt, Gloster points out that both novelists exploit the themes of miscegenation, prejudice, and oppression, but he maintains that Chesnutt was the better writer in his handling of plot, characterization, and diction. Bone, on the other hand, points out in *The Negro Novel in America* (1965) what he considers to be Griggs's vacillation between the poles of militancy and accommodation, especially in *Pointing the Way,* and he asserts that the novelist's vacillation reflects the peculiar political dilemma of the Negro intellectual during the period. He also calls attention to Griggs's reliance on white people of quality to solve the race problem. In 1973 Robert Fleming called for a new evaluation of Griggs by contemporary scholars because he believed that Griggs's works, especially his most important novel, *Imperium in Imperio,* had been carelessly and callously handled by earlier critics.

Imperium in Imperio, Griggs's most critically acclaimed novel, is a political and propagandistic work. The most important features of the novel are its description of a black government within the United States and its picture of a newly self-respecting and determined black people. It contains the themes and philosophical ideas found in all of the author's other works, as well as all of the technical and literary faults which critics have enumerated.

Griggs uses an authorial persona called Sutton Griggs to introduce the first person narrative of Berl Trout, a confessed traitor. Trout expresses

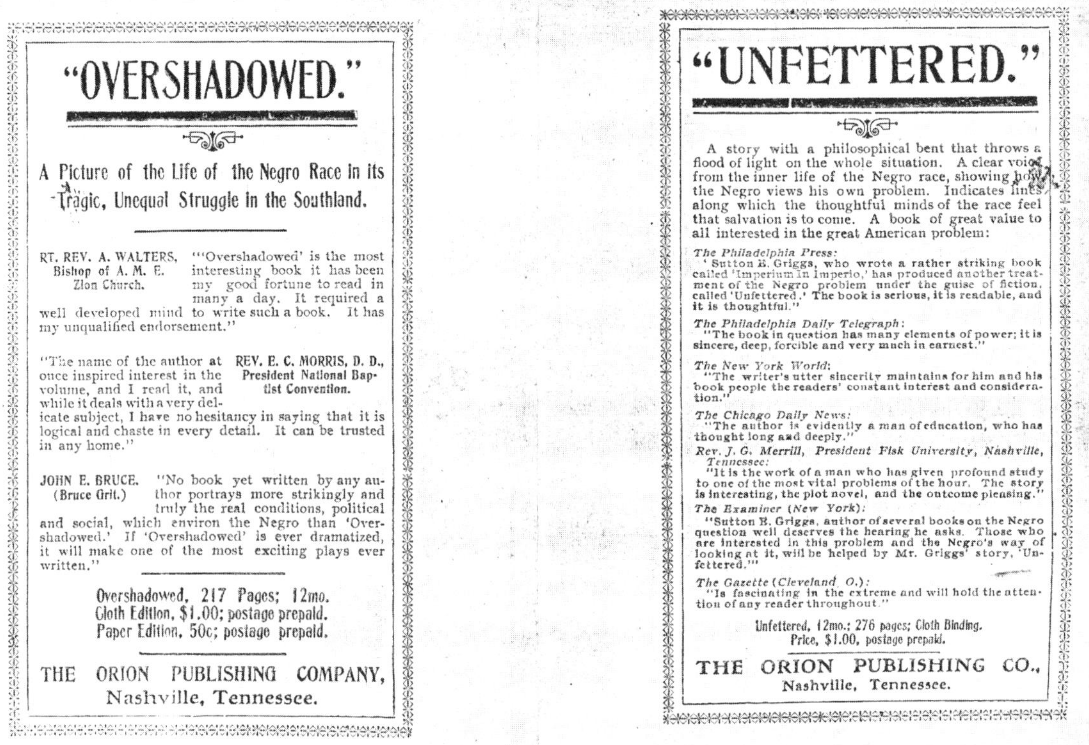

"OVERSHADOWED."

A Picture of the Life of the Negro Race in its Tragic, Unequal Struggle in the Southland.

RT. REV. A. WALTERS, Bishop of A. M. E. Zion Church. "'Overshadowed' is the most interesting book it has been my good fortune to read in many a day. It required a well developed mind to write such a book. It has my unqualified endorsement."

"The name of the author at once inspired interest in the volume, and I read it, and while it deals with a very delicate subject, I have no hesitancy in saying that it is logical and chaste in every detail. It can be trusted in any home." REV. E. C. MORRIS, D. D., President National Baptist Convention.

JOHN E. BRUCE. (Bruce Grit.) "No book yet written by any author portrays more strikingly and truly the real conditions, political and social, which environ the Negro than 'Overshadowed.' If 'Overshadowed' is ever dramatized, it will make one of the most exciting plays ever written."

Overshadowed, 217 Pages; 12mo.
Cloth Edition, $1.00; postage prepaid.
Paper Edition, 50c; postage prepaid.

THE ORION PUBLISHING COMPANY,
Nashville, Tennessee.

"UNFETTERED."

A story with a philosophical bent that throws a flood of light on the whole situation. A clear voice from the inner life of the Negro race, showing how the Negro views his own problem. Indicates lines along which the thoughtful minds of the race feel that salvation is to come. A book of great value to all interested in the great American problem:

The Philadelphia Press:
"Sutton E. Griggs, who wrote a rather striking book called 'Imperium In Imperio,' has produced another treatment of the Negro problem under the guise of fiction, called 'Unfettered.' The book is serious, it is readable, and it is thoughtful."

The Philadelphia Daily Telegraph:
"The book in question has many elements of power; it is sincere, deep, forcible and very much in earnest."

The New York World:
"The writer's utter sincerity maintains for him and his book people the readers' constant interest and consideration."

The Chicago Daily News:
"The author is evidently a man of education, who has thought long and deeply."

Rev. J. G. Merrill, President Fisk University, Nashville, Tennessee:
"It is the work of a man who has given profound study to one of the most vital problems of the hour. The story is interesting, the plot novel, and the outcome pleasing."

The Examiner (New York):
"Sutton E. Griggs, author of several books on the Negro question well deserves the hearing he asks. Those who are interested in this problem and the Negro's way of looking at it, will be helped by Mr. Griggs' story, 'Unfettered.'"

The Gazette (Cleveland, O.):
"Is fascinating in the extreme and will hold the attention of any reader throughout."

Unfettered, 12mo.; 276 pages; Cloth Binding.
Price, $1.00, postage prepaid.

THE ORION PUBLISHING CO.,
Nashville, Tennessee.

Advertisements at the end of The Hindered Hand *for two of Griggs's novels*

his willingness to face a humiliating death since he feels that his objectionable actions have been understood by God and will be understood eventually by mankind; however, the novel itself offers no such hope. Trout is untrustworthy and his confession is confusing, but the persona Griggs insists that we trust Trout.

The story centers on the lives of two black men, Belton Piedmont, and a mulatto, Bernard Belgrave. The contrasting social origins of the two men are traced from the time they meet as boys in a small school for black children in Winchester, Virginia. Belton is poor and smart; Bernard is also intelligent but has a beautiful mother who has an ample, mysterious (since Bernard is mulatto—not so mysterious) source of income. Griggs creates a melodramatic contrast between the picture of Belton's poor, uneducated mother sending her ill-clothed son to school, and that of Bernard, dressed quite adequately, being escorted to school by his beautiful mother. Both boys emerge from the school as honor students, but Belton is denied the highest honors for his graduation oration because of discrimination, while the white teachers and judges favor Bernard for his obvious white parentage. Subsequently, Belton is helped by a white benefactor to go to college. In a characteristically didactic passage which supports the critical observation that Griggs inserts accommodationism into a militant framework, Griggs notes that this act of philanthropy will influence Belton's entire life.

In a miraculous episode that highlights the indomitable black man, Belton goes to Louisiana as a voting-rights activist, and he is hanged, but not killed, by a lynch mob. The mob also shoots him, but the bullet does not penetrate Belton's skull. He is cut down unconscious and escapes before being dissected by a villainous white doctor who considers having a well-formed, handsome "nigger" to dissect one of the greatest boons of his career.

Bernard's emotionally shattering experience revolves around the death of his sweetheart, the beautiful, black Viola Martin. Viola, who has subscribed to the theory that miscegenation robs the black race of its strength, commits suicide, ostensibly to prevent further damage to the race by conjoining with the half-white Bernard. In a suicide note she tells him: "Study the question of the intermingling of the races. If miscegenation is in reality destroying us, dedicate your soul to the work of separating the white and colored races. Do not let them intermingle. Erect moral barriers to separate them. If you fail in this, make the separation physical; lead our people forth from this accursed land. Do this and I shall not have died in vain. . . ." Viola's letter influences Bernard's decision to join the Imperium, a separate state, within the United States, formed and governed by blacks. Contrary to expectations, Bernard becomes the uncompromising militant black nationalist, while Belton becomes the conservative assimilationist. The Imperium declares Bernard to be its first president because of his brilliance as a lawyer. From the beginning, though, his radical commitment to the Imperium, like his dream of marrying Viola, is doomed.

Griggs's notion of a separate black state is embellished through the character of Belton, who points out the flaws in the United States Constitution and judicial system and their failure to protect the black man. Belton outlines the way in which the Imperium must answer these failures through a court that debates every racial issue tried in a United States' court.

In some ways Bernard echoes Belton's ideas. After a white mob murders a black man, Bernard makes a fiery appeal to the Imperium to retaliate by conquering Texas and Louisiana: "Seven million eyes are riveted upon you, hoping that you will be brave and wise enough to take such action as will fully atone for all the horrors of the past and secure for us every right due to all honorable, loyal, law-abiding citizens of the United States." In Bernard's call to war, Griggs establishes his sympathy for radical, black militancy. Bernard concludes, "Let us then at all hazards, strike a blow for freedom. If it calls for a Thermopylae be free. If contending for our rights given to us by God, causes us to be slain, let us perish on the field of battle, singing as we pass out of the world, 'Sweet Freedom's' song though every word of this soul-inspiring hymn must come forth wrapped in our hearts' warm blood." Bernard's speech is not far away from some of the militant rhetoric of the civil rights movement of the 1960s. Ironically Belton, who repudiates Bernard's violent plan, is killed for resigning from the Imperium. In the novel nothing comes from the plans for war, because they are exposed by Berl Trout. As the novel begins with Trout's traitorous declaration, it ends with his comments on his impending execution by the Imperium.

Griggs's seeming vacillation between extreme militancy and violence, symbolized by Bernard's commitment to war, and the accommodationist position, demonstrated by Berl Trout, and Belton, through his resignation, caused critics to castigate Griggs for thematic inconsistency. Perhaps Griggs's religious orientation prevented him from extolling violence as the only way for the black man to receive racial justice in America. Nevertheless, by presenting the workings of the Imperium in elaborate detail, Griggs may have hoped to demonstrate to a society which was placing more and more discriminatory restrictions on blacks the injustice of these restrictions. Through Belton and Bernard, Griggs demonstrates the dangers of restraining brilliant minds which could better serve constructive purposes in society, if allowed.

Unfettered, like *Imperium in Imperio,* was dismissed by early critics, such as Sterling Brown, as being a hodgepodge of trite and pompous prose because of its idealized characters and long dissertations on race and politics. In *Unfettered* all the hostility and violent hatred that the South unleashed on the black man is exposed in Griggs's characteristically melodramatic style. Griggs stated that the aim of the novel was to lead the reader into the inner life of the Negro and expose the aspirations of the race. He said, "Those who come to these pages in quest of pen pictures of either angels or demons, are not likely to find what they seek, for our story has to do with human beings simply." Nevertheless, the reader will find stereotyped portraits of good and virtuous black men and women and evil, vicious whites in the novel. Furthermore, *Unfettered* has as its sequel "Dorlan's Plan," a fifty-six-page dissertation on the race problem. The plan, including the foreword by Griggs, is supposed to be authored by Dorlan Worthell, a major character in the novel. Although *Unfettered* contains Griggs's typical fantastic episodes, minor plots, and abundance of varied characters, its value is that it portrays the realistic and difficult problems of black people during the early twentieth century.

Unfettered begins when Morlene, a beautiful mulatto girl of mysterious descent, and Aunt Catherine, an old, faithful, black servant, are turned out of the Dalton estate after the death of its benevolent owner. The elder Dalton had provided for the care of Morlene and Aunt Catherine, but they are immediately dispossessed by his nephew and heir, Lemuel Dalton, the villainous white man. Lemuel Dalton subsequently meditates on the character differences between the young Morlene and the old servant: "Now, I like that plucky spirit manifested by the girl. Give me, every time, the haughty sufferer, too proud to crouch beneath the lash even when its sting is keenest. I want none of your whining suppliants. A plague on these Negroes who meet injury with woe-begone expressions."

Lemuel then has a fight with Harry Dalton, against whom Lemuel has carried a grudge since childhood. Harry, a black man whose family were former slaves, still lives and works on the Dalton property. Harry is badly wounded by a shot from Lemuel's gun. Morlene nurses Harry through his illness and agrees to marry him out of pity. After Harry's sister is killed by a group of young white drunks, Harry and Morlene flee to the city, where Morlene meets Dorlan Worthell, a political leader and a courageous, young, black man, described by Griggs as an "ebony-like Apollo."

Harry is eventually persuaded by a white Republican politician to murder Dorlan, but Morlene informs Dorlan and then deserts Harry. Harry Dalton is eventually and conveniently killed in a fantastic and heroic manner after repenting his attempted murder of Dorlan. Morlene agrees to marry Dorlan, but only if he can submit a plan to "unfetter" the Negro. "Dorlan's Plan" calls for the organization of the Negro into an effective political group, points out the need for education beyond the elementary school level, and admonishes the Negro not to rely too heavily on the Republican party.

Dorlan is a mouthpiece for Griggs's opinions and political ideals, but one cannot refute the essential wisdom of Griggs's thinking. His political opinions were humane and have been supported by political and social history. Dorlan's plan calls for six reforms to aid the black race:

> 1. The Negro must become the owner of the soil he tills.
> 2. He must be placed above the conditions of dire necessity that causes him to resort to the credit system. . . .
> 3. Provisions must be made whereby he may secure modern appliances with which to farm.
> 4. He must be educated. . . .
> 5. He must be taught to keep fully posted upon the important happenings in the commercial world bearing upon his interests.
> 6. The Negro must join hands with the students of the agricultural problem in general, ready to avail himself of any new developments of value that may arise.

Even though *Unfettered* is didactic, episodic, and sentimental, the ideas expressed for the betterment of an oppressed people are essentially well thought-out and pragmatic.

In *The Hindered Hand,* Griggs openly attacks his favorite enemy: Thomas Dixon, author of such works as *The Leopard's Spot: A Romance of the White Man's Burden-1865-1900* (1902). He refers to Dixon's novel as one written for the express purpose of discrediting the black race. *The Hindered Hand* presents the black man as a capable, intelligent human, hindered by the oppressive, brutal, and prejudiced American society. Gloster pointed out that the novel also treats the themes of miscegenation and injustice and the Negro's consideration of open revolt and immigration to Africa.

The story centers around a couple with light complexions, the Seabrights, and their three children, two of whom can pass for white. Tiara, the dark Seabright daughter—who is courted by the dark-skinned Ensal—is separated from her family because the other members pass for white in order to gain positions of respect in their community. Their purpose is to help change the opinions of the white community toward the black race, but their efforts lead to tragedy. The Crumps, a family who befriend Tiara, meet the worst tragedy, for Foresta Crump and her husband are tortured and burned by a white mob in Mississippi where they have ironically run to escape racial injustice. The Crumps are persecuted because of the very thing Griggs tried to promote in his political tracts: education and intelligence. An investigator asks a white native if the mob action against the educated Crumps was caused by one crime, and the investigator is answered in the following manner: "That's all rot about one crime. . . . The truth of the matter is the real 'one Crime' that paves the way for a lynching whenever we have the notion, is the crime of being black." In his own time Griggs saw many lynchers set free by prejudiced juries, and he has the same thing happen in the novel. The murderers of the Crumps are set free, and the young white prosecuting attorney becomes a political outcast for demanding justice.

The pessimism of the novel is embodied in the character of Eunice Seabright, Tiara's sister, who eventually goes mad because of the racial situation. When her husband Earl attempts to bring her out of her grief and madness by giving her

290 THE HINDERED HAND.

Eunice so quietly, so intelligently, that hopes sprang up in Earl's breast.

Stooping, he kissed his wife, saying:

"I can't say, my darling; but it will surely come in time."

"Time!" shrieked Eunice. "Same old thing! Time! Bah! We shall all die in 'time.' Earl, are you turning against me, coming to me with that old word 'time?' Ah! Earl, are you a Southerner? Time! Earl, can't you persuade the people to let justice do now what they are waiting for 'time' to do?"

Jumping up she whirled round and round until from sheer exhaustion she fell into her weeping husband's arms.

"O thou of little faith, counterpart of my own darker days, Eunice, awake! Awake! The currents are forming that will sweep the caste spirit out of the political life of the nation. Awake, my Eunice! Awake!" plaintively spoke the grief-stricken husband to the unheeding ears of his wife.

While hope thus wrestles with despair, we visit another parlor.

* * * * * *

In the parlor of Tiara's home Ensal sat awaiting the coming of the girl that he had loved so long and so ardently, on whom he had now called for the purpose of asking her to link her destiny with his.

"Without any pretense at delivering any one of the many thousand little preliminary speeches framed for the occasion, Ensal bent forward and kissed Tiara."

(290-291.)

Pages from The Hindered Hand; or, The Reign of the Repressionist *(1905)*

hope about the racial situation, she demands to know when the things he has spoken of will come to pass. When Earl answers "in time," Eunice explodes: "Time! . . . Same old thing! Ah! Earl are you a Southerner? Time! Earl, can't you persuade the people to let justice do now what they are waiting for time to do?" Griggs uses Eunice to show his disgust for the words used throughout American history to pacify black people.

Although Tiara and Ensal get together at the end of the novel, the reader feels no triumph. In fact, the reader feels as if Ensal has failed because he and Tiara make plans to leave for Liberia. *The Hindered Hand* does not show a cringing and subservient black race, but a people thwarted by injustice. In an appendix at the end of the novel, Griggs explains that the situations of violence pictured in the novel are not mere fiction but are based on real facts.

Overshadowed and *Pointing the Way* also paint a dismal picture of race relations and show the black man hindered in all areas of American life. Interracial love affairs and the lust of white men for black women cast a shadow over the lives of the black characters in these novels.

Overshadowed, which was Griggs's second novel, surveys the national scene with hopelessness. Protagonists Erma Wysong and Astral Herndon find themselves in Richmond, Virginia, enduring hardships caused by an intolerable racial situation. The racially mixed Erma is preyed upon by the lascivious white villain John Benson Lawson, who is eventually punished. In this novel of miscegenation, incest, and moral degeneracy, blacks suffer horribly, but at least some whites have to face justice. One white character loses his mind; another receives a jail sentence. Although Erma and Herndon finally marry and have a son, they are not to have happiness, for none of Griggs's black heroes and heroines simply rides off into the sunset. Erma's brother, John, surprisingly arrives one night after having escaped from a chain gang where he was sent for the murder of a prejudiced white master workman. John dies as a result of exposure, and Erma dies of shock and grief, a little too quickly. Herndon then considers immigration to

Africa but decides against it because freedom is "overshadowed" there, too. He decides to bury his wife in midocean where there is no racial prejudice. In this novel Griggs examines the world black situation and finds that, just as in the United States, there is miscegenation, insanity, unjust imprisonment, unjust courts, and unstable black employment everywhere. Griggs, like Du Bois, attacks the accommodationist philosophy of Booker T. Washington. After listening to a speech by Washington, Erma persuades her brother to confess to the murder. That confession ultimately leads to his death.

While *Overshadowed* presents one of the gloomiest pictures of race relations found in any novel of Sutton Griggs, *Pointing the Way* is less tragic. The novel also concerns interracial relationships and racial politics, but it is less militant and less violent than the author's other novels. Bone calls *Pointing the Way* an accommodationist work when he compares it to Griggs's other work. It is a confusing novel with an abundance of major characters and two major plots. The major characters include Letitia Gilbreth, the spinster daughter of a white man and his former slave mistress; her niece Clotille; Baug Peppers, a mulatto lawyer to whom Clotille is engaged; Conroe Driscoll, the dark-skinned man whom Clotille loves; Eina, a beautiful girl of English, Spanish, and Indian blood; and Seth Molair, a white attorney who admires Eina and explains to her about race and southern society. In one subplot, when Eina first comes to Molair's office on business, he goes through great pains to surreptitiously find out her race; he finally asks Eina about her heritage. Then Molair goes into great detail to explain to Eina the advantages of being white since she finds herself in the unique position of being able to "choose" her race. He informs her that once she fraternizes socially and openly with one race, she will be confined to that race forever.

In another plot of the novel, Letitia Gilbreth believes that it is a crime for two dark-skinned people to marry since every newborn dark child prolongs the agony of the black race. Letitia maintains that all light-skinned blacks should marry within the race until the black race is whitened; therefore, she chooses mulatto Baug Peppers as a husband for her niece Clotille. When Clotille marries Conroe, Letitia goes mad and tries to disinherit Clotille, but she is prevented from it by Molair. The lawyer tries to dissuade Letitia from disinheriting her niece, because he does not wish to have any members of the black race enter the white race; Letitia angrily retorts: "Who wants to always be a problem? Who wants someone else to always have his foot on your neck? America hasn't got enough of the grace of God in her heart to treat a black man as she would a white man. Her life is a living lie, And I want every drop of the despised blood sucked into her veins. I want her to eat up the race she hates."

All the characters seek to cure Letitia of her madness by giving her hope for the future of the black race. After Conroe takes a position in the fire department because Letitia favors firemen, both he and Letitia lose their lives during a fire. Clotille, who has not been disinherited, is urged to do something for black people with her inheritance, and Baug Peppers makes an inconclusive bid for black suffrage in the Supreme Court. At the end, the racially mixed Baug and Eina finally marry, and Clotille is left with Conroe's black, healthy son.

Pointing the Way suggests that justice for black people might be found in court action, although nothing really positive comes from such action in the novel. Griggs's feeling that court action might be a positive solution for the injustices suffered by blacks is expressed in his nonfiction works, as well. In his political treatises Griggs calls for legal action, along with a number of other civic and educational solutions, to relieve the plight of the Afro-American. In *Needs of the South* (1909), *The Race Question in A New Light* (1909), *Wisdom's Call* (1911), and *Guide to Racial Greatness; or, The Science of Collective Efficiency* (1923), Griggs pointedly discusses the problems of miscegenation, mob violence, black suffrage, and inadequate employment opportunities for blacks.

In *Needs of the South,* Griggs states that the greatest hindrance to the political power of the South is its restricted vision concerning the political rights of blacks, especially in regard to equal voting rights. During his time it was felt to be politically impossible to elect a democratic southerner to the Presidency, and Griggs felt that extending voting rights to blacks would allow that political phenomenon to occur.

In the more sociological tract, *The Race Question in A New Light,* Griggs talks about "the unprotected spot," by which he means the helpless black women and children who have no hope of civic, political, or social protection. Griggs, pointing to Pasteur's germ theory of disease, notes that a small germ can feed upon and destroy the whole body. He says that, in like manner, the seemingly small and unimportant black woman and child will eventually cause a social disease which will infect the rights of an entire society. Griggs concludes that society cannot afford to overlook even the smallest

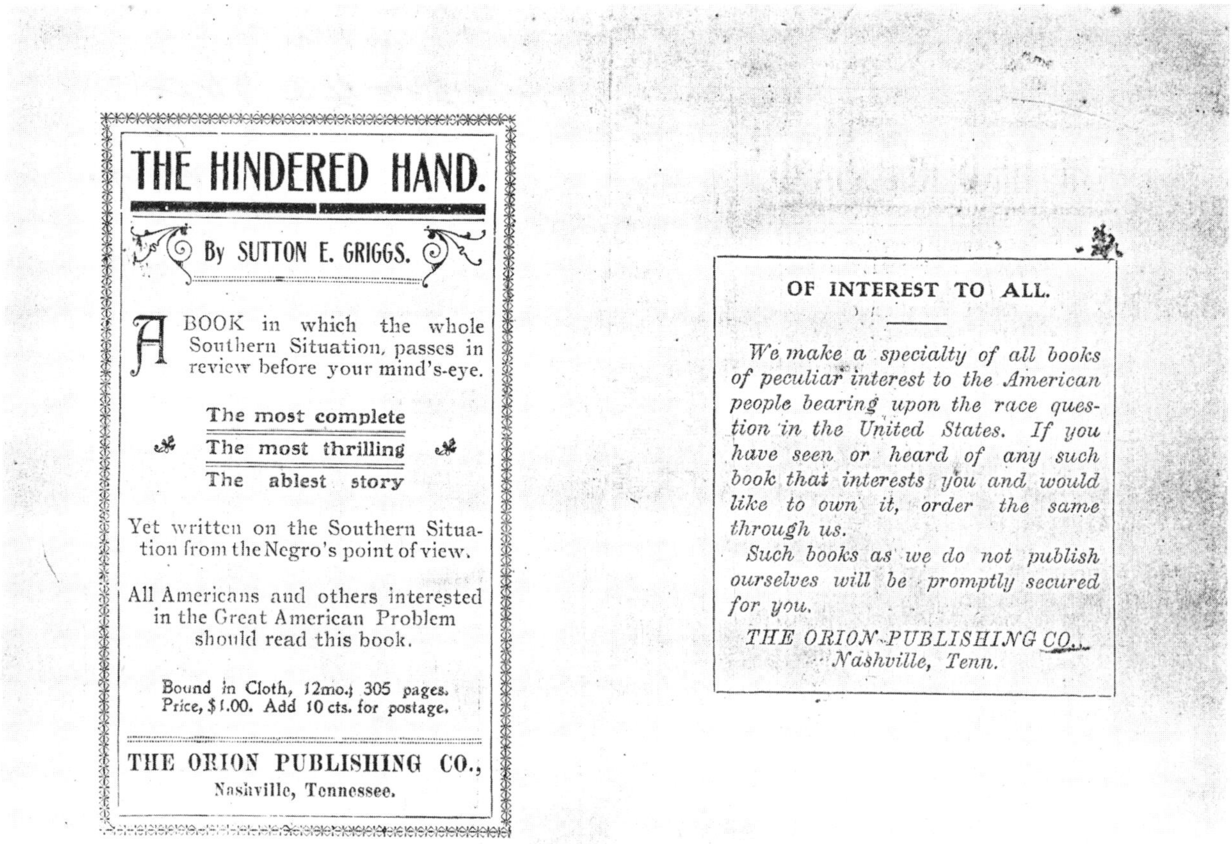

Advertisements from The Hindered Hand *for the novel and for Griggs's publishing company*

and most helpless part of its constituency. In Griggs's important novels this idea is reinforced through the fate of Foresta Crump and Beulah Dalton, both of whom are viciously murdered by white mobs for no reason other than they are simply unprotected black females.

In *Wisdom's Call,* one of Griggs's longest political works, the black is compared to a toothless dog which has more stones thrown at him because he has no teeth. *Wisdom's Call* combines *The Race Question in A New Light* with new chapters: "A Luxury of Great Price," "A Better System for Making Men," "The Preservation of the Two Races," and "The Spirit of a People." Griggs directs his attention to two specific themes found also in his novels: the wisdom, capability, and intelligence of many black people; and the problem of miscegenation. Griggs calls attention to the ability of black people to understand and discern the character and honesty of whites:

> Moreover the Negro's judgment of the qualities of mind and heart of the various grades of white men is very good. It is interesting to know that the Negroes have their white neighbors clearly classified and any one proposing to have dealings with them can find out before hand almost to the utmost detail just what to expect. The terrible shadow of a possible annihilation that has hung like a pall over the Negro race has caused an enforced study of the white man that makes the Negro a good judge of that race.

Griggs concludes that the black voter's political judgment will therefore be sound. As to the preservation of two separate races, black and white, a question which he feels is of primary importance to the southern white, Griggs states: "So long as human passions are what they are—and we can never hope to subvert them to American ideas of altruism—the black and white streams will intermingle."

Finally in *Guide to Racial Greatness; or, The Science of Collective Efficiency* Griggs attempts to give society a guide to follow in order to solve the many

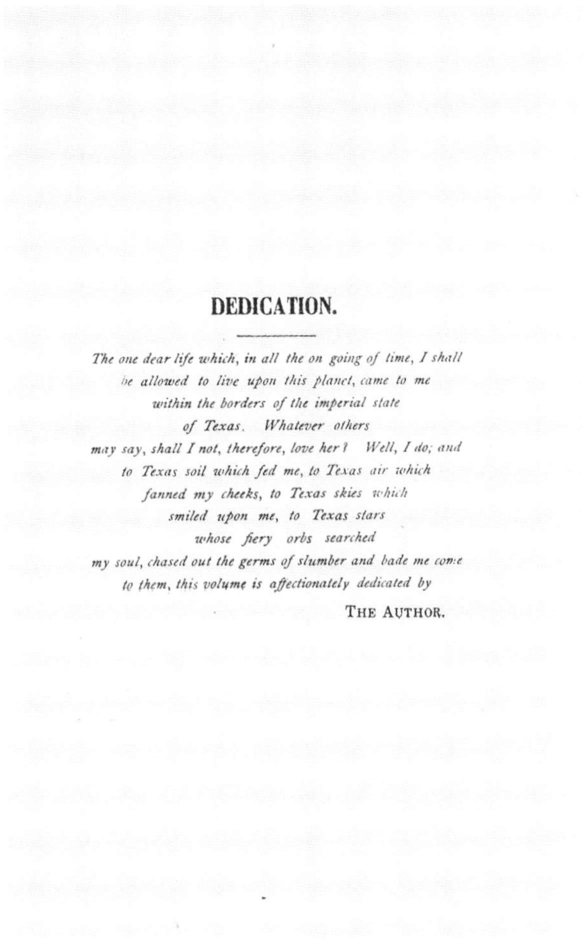

DEDICATION.

The one dear life which, in all the on going of time, I shall be allowed to live upon this planet, came to me within the borders of the imperial state of Texas. Whatever others may say, shall I not, therefore, love her? Well, I do; and to Texas soil which fed me, to Texas air which fanned my cheeks, to Texas skies which smiled upon me, to Texas stars whose fiery orbs searched my soul, chased out the germs of slumber and bade me come to them, this volume is affectionately dedicated by

THE AUTHOR.

Dedication in Wisdom's Call *(1911)*

racial problems outlined in his fiction and nonfiction. This book was written toward the end of Griggs's life, and we may suppose that he had assessed fully the racial problems of the United States and come to some definite conclusions. First, Griggs defines collective efficiency by asserting that it "points the way to successful collective action in domains other than political." Griggs hopes that collective efficiency will point the way for those groups that lagged behind socially and offer them a way to change. He even gives a warning to those who refuse collective efficiency, saying that if the guide is not followed, those lagging groups will disintegrate. Obviously, Griggs is addressing his guide to black people and has completely put aside any subterfuge of fiction. In summarizing the elements of collective efficiency, Griggs advocates renunciation of the self in favor of the needs of the group. Griggs did not believe in individualism, and these admonishments are, in fact, those of a minister and a social reformer.

Griggs's novels may be classified as political because of his advocacy of pride in blackness and the necessity of fighting against racial injustice. He was an advocate of voting rights for blacks, but he did not forget the need for economic and job stability for blacks. A zealous political and social philosopher and a fiery propagandist, Griggs's determination to reach a black reading audience molded his life. Melodramatic though his style is, the scenes of brutality, violence, and mob action in the South that he depicted were based upon actual events which took place during his lifetime. Griggs's sentimental characterizations, verbosity, and fantastic episodes are at times overwhelming, but not significantly different from the immensely popular soap opera plots that capture enormous audiences in contemporary society. Always serious, Griggs sought to wake up the American public to the atrocities performed against black people throughout the South. For their thematic structure and their social ideas, his works predate the principles of the Black Aesthetic of the 1960s and 1970s, and like those later writers, Griggs intended his work to be a teaching tool for his people, guiding them to a better life and a consciousness of their possibilities.

References:

Robert Bone, *The Negro Novel in America* (New Haven: Yale University Press, 1965);

Arthur P. Davis and J. Saunders Redding, *Cavalcade: Negro American Writing From 1760 to the Present* (Boston: Houghton Mifflin, 1971);

Robert E. Fleming, "Sutton E. Griggs: Militant Black Novelist," *Phylon,* 34 (March 1973): 73-77;

Hugh M. Gloster, *Negro Voices in American Fiction* (Chapel Hill: University of North Carolina Press, 1948; revised edition, New York: Russell & Russell, 1965);

Gloster, "Sutton E. Griggs, Novelist of the New Negro," *Phylon,* 4 (Fourth Quarter 1943): 335-345;

"In Memoriam: Dr. Sutton E. Griggs," *Mission Herald,* 36 (February 1933): 9-10;

Campbell Tatham, "Reflections: Sutton Griggs' *Imperium in Imperio,*" *Studies in Black Literature,* 5 (Winter 1974): 7-15;

Patricia Dianne Watkins, "Sutton E. Griggs: The Evolution of a Propagandist," M.A. thesis, Howard University, 1970.

Angelina Weld Grimké

(27 February 1880-10 June 1958)

Michael Greene
North Carolina A&T State University

BOOK: *Rachel: A Play in Three Acts* (Boston: Cornhill, 1920).

PLAY PRODUCTIONS: *Rachel,* Washington, D.C., Myrtilla Miner Normal School, 3 March 1916; New York, Neighborhood Theater, 1921.

OTHER: "The Black Finger," in *The New Negro: An Interpretation,* edited by Alain Locke (New York: Boni, 1925);

Countee Cullen, ed., *Caroling Dusk,* includes poems by Grimké (New York: Harper, 1927), pp. 35-46;

Otelia Cromwell, Lorenzo Dow Turner, and Eva B. Dykes, eds., *Readings from Negro Authors,* includes poems by Grimké (New York: Harcourt, Brace, 1931), pp. 24-26;

Robert T. Kerlin, ed., *Negro Poets and Their Poems,* revised and enlarged edition, includes poems by Grimké (Washington, D.C.: Associated, 1935), pp. 152-156;

Sterling Brown, Arthur P. Davis, and Ulysses Lee, eds., *Negro Caravan,* includes poems by Grimké (New York: Dryden, 1941);

Langston Hughes and Arna Bontemps, eds., *Poetry of the Negro, 1746-1949,* includes poems by Grimké (Garden City: Doubleday, 1949), pp. 54-58;

Arna Bontemps, ed., *American Negro Poetry,* includes poems by Grimké (New York: Hill & Wang, 1963);

Richard K. Barksdale and Keneth Kinnamon, eds., *Black Writers of America: A Comprehensive Anthology,* includes poems by Grimké (New York: Macmillan, 1972);

Arnold Adoff, ed., *Poetry of Black America: Anthology of the Twentieth Century,* includes poems by Grimké (New York: Harper & Row, 1973), pp. 15-16;

Michael W. Peplow and Arthur P. Davis, eds., *New Negro Renaissance: An Anthology,* includes poems by Grimké (New York: Holt, Rinehart & Winston, 1975);

"A Mona Lisa," "At April," "To Keep the Memory of Charlotte Forten Grimké," and "For the Candle Light," in *Black Sister: Poetry by Black American Women, 1746-1980,* edited by Erlene Stetson (Bloomington: Indiana University Press, 1981), pp. 60-63.

PERIODICAL PUBLICATIONS: "To Keep the Memory of Charlotte Forten Grimké," *Crisis,* 9 (January 1915): 134;

"To the Dunbar High School," *Crisis,* 13 (March 1917): 222;

"The Closing Door," *Birth Control Review,* 3 (September 1919);

"The Black Finger," *Opportunity,* 1 (September 1923): 343;

"Little Grey Dreams," *Opportunity,* 2 (January 1924): 20;

"Dusk," *Opportunity,* 2 (April 1924): 99;

"I Weep," *Opportunity,* 2 (July 1924): 196;

"A Biographical Sketch of Archibald H. Grimké," *Opportunity,* 3 (February 1925): 44-47;

"Death," *Opportunity,* 3 (March 1925): 68.

Angelina Weld Grimké has often been considered interesting only as a literary footnote—a transitional figure standing somewhere between the writers of the genteel tradition and those of the Harlem Renaissance. Some readers confuse her with Angelina Grimké Weld, her great-aunt, for whom she was named. Grimké's output was small, and she made little effort to establish a literary reputation; her poetry has never even been collected. She wrote her play, *Rachel* (1920), to express her concern with society's racial problems, but she did not pretend to have solutions. Her best energy went into her poetry, which was not written for posterity but for the satisfaction of exercising her craftsmanship and for the need to express her personal anxieties. Her best work is not only sensitive and skillful but is also a reflection of how a complex, unhappy personality found its creative outlet.

The daughter of Archibald Henry and Sarah Stanley Grimké, Angelina Weld Grimké was born

Angelina Weld Grimké (courtesy of the Collection of Mary O. H. Williamson, Moorland-Spingarn Research Center, Howard University)

in Boston in 1880, a member of the distinguished biracial Grimké family, some members of which were important in the abolitionist movement and active in civil rights into the twentieth century. Grimké's paternal great-grandparents were wealthy South Carolina slaveholder, Revolutionary War veteran, and notoriously severe judge John Faucheraud Grimké and Mary Smith, descended from one of the first landgraves of South Carolina, daughter of one of the wealthiest bankers in the Charleston area. Two of their children, Angelina and Sarah Moore Grimké, became Quaker abolitionists and suffragists in the 1830s. Angelina married abolitionist Theodore D. Weld and wrote *Appeal to the Christian Women of the South* (1836), *Letters to Catherine E. Beecher, in Reply to An Essay on Slavery and Abolitionism* (1838), and *Letter from Angelina Grimké Weld to the Womens Rights Convention* (1852); Sarah Grimké wrote *An Epistle to the Clergy of the Southern States* (1836) and *Letters on the Equality of the Sexes, and the Condition of Women* (1838).

Angelina Weld Grimké's paternal grandfather was Henry Grimké, another of John and Mary Grimké's children. Unlike his sisters, Henry Grimké was not an abolitionist. After the death of his white wife, by whom he had three children, he took one of his slaves, Nancy Weston, as his mistress and fathered three sons, Archibald Henry, Francis, and John. Henry Grimké died when Nancy was pregnant with John and on his deathbed asked one of his white sons, Montague, to care for his black mistress and children as though they were members of the family. Montague ignored his father's request. Francis escaped, was caught, sold, and finally freed. He became a minister and later married black poet and essayist Charlotte Forten. Archibald escaped. In 1868 Angelina Weld saw his name in the *Anti-Slavery Standard* and wrote to ask him if he were one of her brother's former slaves. After Archibald responded that he was in fact her nephew, he was taken into the Grimké family fold and was educated in Charleston public schools and at Lincoln University.

Supported by his aunts, Archibald attended Harvard Law School, earned his LL.B. degree in 1874, and became a prominent practicing lawyer, diplomat, author, editor, and executive of the National Association for the Advancement of Colored People; he served as president of the Washington, D.C., chapter for ten years and later as vice-president of the national organization. He was president of the American Negro Academy from 1903 to 1916. In a 1925 biographical sketch of her father Angelina Weld Grimké wrote, "he has the satisfaction of knowing that his life is open to the inspection of any man; that he has been a consistent and uncompromising fighter, all his life, for the welfare of his race as he has seen it; that the fight has been a good one, a clean one and above board. . . . and that if all men do not love him, they respect him. Pleasant, pleasant thoughts these."

Grimké's mother, Sarah, was white, the daughter of Mary Stanley and Methodist minister M. C. Stanley. Sarah's parents opposed her interracial marriage. Perhaps their resistance influenced Sarah's decision to leave Archibald Grimké in 1883. She took her daughter with her but four years later brought Angelina back to her father. Sarah Stanley Grimké never saw her daughter again. She died in 1898, having written a small number of metaphysical tracts, including *Personified Unthinkables, An Argument Against Physical Causation* (1884).

Angelina Weld Grimké's relationship with her father was very close, and she had a privileged life as a child. She was often cared for in the home of her aunt Angelina Weld, and Theodore Weld provided for her education in his will. Light-skinned and relatively unconscious of racial issues, she was protected from direct experience of the condition of most blacks of the period. By the time she wrote *Rachel* (produced in 1916) and her short story "The Closing Door" (1919), Grimké had become more aware of the problems of racial discrimination; and the intensity with which her characters react to racial hatred seems to suggest that Grimké's awareness of the problems must have come abruptly after her protected childhood.

Grimké attended a variety of upper-class, liberal schools, including Carleton Academy in Northfield, Minnesota, and Cushing Academy in Ashburnham, Massachusetts; she graduated from the Boston Normal School of Gymnastics in 1902. In 1902 she began teaching English in Washington, D.C., first at the Armstrong Manual Training School and then, from 1916, at Dunbar High School. During the summers she took courses at Harvard University. Some of her better-known writings were produced during her years in Washington when she was part of the coterie of black artists, writers, and scholars doing creative work there.

Grimké had been writing from the time she was a young girl; nonetheless, only a small portion of her work was published during her lifetime: a few short stories, her play *Rachel,* some reviews and general nonfiction pieces, but mainly brief praise poems and lyrics which appeared occasionally in the pages of the *Gazette* ("To Theodore Weld on His 90th Birthday," 1893), the *Boston Transcript* ("Longing," 1901; "El Beso," 1909), and in the *Crisis* and *Opportunity* in the first two decades of the twentieth century, including "To Keep the Memory of Charlotte Forten Grimké" (*Crisis,* 1915), "To the Dunbar High School" (*Crisis,* 1917), and "The Black Finger" (*Opportunity,* 1923). Her poetry was anthologized in the 1920s by some of the leading figures of the New Negro Renaissance: Alain Locke (*The New Negro,* 1925) and Countee Cullen (*Caroling Dusk,* 1927), and white critic Robert T. Kerlin (*Negro Poets and Their Poems,* 1935). At her death in 1958, most of her work still remained unpublished, and analytical critiques by commentators such as Gloria T. Hull imply that Grimké did not avidly pursue her writing career because her energies were invested in her emotional problems.

Hull has suggested that Grimké experienced unhappiness over her sexual identity and believes that her inner turmoil was the most profound determinant of the sad tone of her work. In several poems and in her diaries Grimké expressed the frustration that her lesbianism created; thwarted longing is a theme in several poems. She apparently did have a youthful relationship with a Mamie Burrill, but later in life she suppressed her desires. Her more mature years were especially unhappy, partly because of the death of her father in 1930. Hull says that after Archibald Grimké's last illness, "the strains of neurosis and paranoia in [Angelina's] personality became more pronounced—to the extent that she was threatening to exhume and rebury him. . . . She moved from Washington, D.C. to New York, ostensibly for her writing. But she produced nothing—and, in Arna Bontemps' words, 'spent the last years of her life in quiet retirement in a New York City apartment.' "

Archibald Grimké

One of Grimké's most interesting works is her play, *Rachel,* performed on 3 and 4 March 1916, sponsored by the NAACP in Washington at the Myrtilla Miner Normal School. The program included the announcement: "This is the first attempt to use the stage for race propaganda in order to enlighten the American people relating to the lamentable condition of ten millions of Colored citizens in this free republic." The play received mixed reactions and was even criticized by some members of the sponsoring NAACP as propaganda. Although it was published in 1920, it has still received little comment, positive or negative. Frederick Bond, in *The Negro and the Drama* (1940), dismisses it in one sentence: "Lacking in the fundamental principles of drama, the piece is preposterous, and will hardly meet the approval of an audience." Alain Locke and Montgomery Gregory, in *Plays of Negro Life* (1927), however, call it "apparently the first successful drama written by a Negro and interpreted by Negro actors." The play was included in the James V. Hatch anthology, *Black Theater, U.S.A.: Forty-five Plays by Black Americans, 1847-1974* (1974), where its historical importance and its emotional impact are stressed.

Rachel may strike most modern readers as a historical footnote, a sentimental play with a Victorian, moralistic underpinning, or, perhaps, a "problem" play with no suggested solution. However, given its 1916 context, and making allowances for the fact that it is difficult to stage, it emerges as a sensitive but painful work.

The play is set in New York, and all three acts take place in the tenement apartment of Mrs. Loving, a seamstress. She is worried because her teenaged daughter, Rachel, is late coming home. As the play begins, Rachel comes in, explains that she met a little boy, Jimmy, on the stairs and was so charmed by him that she lost track of time. John Strong, a young man, comes by to pick up some sewing for his mother; he has a college degree but works as a waiter because no jobs are available for blacks in his profession; he appears only briefly in this act, but is obviously interested in Rachel. Tom Loving, Rachel's brother, comes home; he also goes to school and works at a menial job. He finds home a warm haven from name-calling whites and low pay. The central focus of the act is on Mrs. Loving's decision to tell Tom and Rachel about their father, who had been a crusading newspaper editor. Ten years earlier, she reveals, he had been killed by a lynch mob, along with Tom and Rachel's half brother. Tom's reaction is anger at "those devils with white skins." Rachel, however, whose deepest instinct is her love of small children, responds by thinking of the future black children will face: "Then, everywhere, everywhere, throughout the South, there are hundreds of dark mothers who live in fear, terrible, suffocating fear, whose rest by night is broken, and whose joy by day in their babies on their hearts is three parts—pain. . . . And so this nation—this white Christian nation—had deliberately set its curse upon the most beautiful—the most holy thing in life—motherhood! Why—it—makes—you doubt—God!"

The second and third acts take place a week apart, but four years later. Tom Loving, now looking for a permanent job, is offered a place as a waiter by John Strong, and he broods over the system that denies him opportunity: "I hear people talk about God's justice—and I wonder. . . . It seems our educations aren't of much use to us: we aren't allowed to make good—because our skins are dark. . . . And, in the South today, there are white men. . . . Look at us—and look at them. We are destined to failure—they, to success. Their children shall grow up in hope; ours, in despair. Our hands are clean;—theirs are red with blood—red with the blood of a noble man—and a boy. They're nothing but low, cowardly, bestial murderers. The

Grimké's great-aunt, Angelina Grimké Weld (courtesy of the Garrison Papers, Sophia Smith Collection, Smith College Library)

scum of the earth shall succeed.—God's justice, I suppose."

In the second act, Rachel receives two shocks: Mrs. Lane, who is looking for an apartment, tells of the humiliations and cruelties at school that have made her little girl, Ethel, withdrawn and frightened; and little Jimmy, who has become Rachel's adopted son since his parents died of smallpox, tells her of being stoned by white boys who screamed "nigger" at him. In agony over her inability to change the world's cruelty, Rachel seizes the roses that John Strong has just sent her and stamps on the buds in her frustration, declaring that she cannot touch them because she is accursed and may not love or bring little children into such a world. As the act ends, she collapses on the floor, while "the laughter of the children shrills loudly through the window."

The last act, a week later, finds a convalescent Rachel playing with Jimmy, but in agony because of her inability to keep him from nightmares. John Strong proposes, but she rejects him, vowing to spend her life caring for black children but not bringing any into the world herself. As the play ends, she runs to comfort Jimmy, who is weeping in the next room. The last stage direction reads, "The light in the lamp flickers and goes out. . . . It is black. The terrible, heart-breaking weeping continues."

A modern audience might find the play's sense of futility objectionable. Instead of confronting experience, Rachel withdraws from it, martyring herself. She resolves to spend her life comforting and teaching children, but the impulse springs more from a desire to protect them from knowledge of the world's hatred than from a commitment to change or even cope with the white world. Her brother can respond only with futile anger. The suitor, John, tries to be philosophical, but he expresses no hope for anything better than his table-waiting job. The playwright's response to the world seems to be to shrink away in isolation from man and from God. The fact that a later generation encountered its problems with a face thrust forward does not invalidate Grimké's depiction of the ways in which some blacks in 1916 reacted. For her characters, as for many of her generation, the diagnosis of the ills of society does not lead to a prescription. As a result, the painfulness of the play is almost unbearable.

Another problem *Rachel* presents for a modern audience is its sentimentality. Although other dramas of that period were often just as sentimental, the play sometimes seems extreme: in the happier events of the play the dialogue is saccharine, even cloying; and the poignancy in scenes between Rachel and the children sometimes tends to get drowned in a bath of love. On a psychological level, perhaps, Rachel's naiveté leads her to smother those around her with love, and the intensity of her emotional idealism makes her painfully vulnerable.

Angelina Grimké was not a practiced playwright, and she often lacked the sense of verbal restraint and of staging that more training could have given her. Nevertheless, the play's intensity and Grimké's ability to make Rachel's vulnerability matter force the reader to become involved in her own disillusioning recognition that the world does not love as she is capable of loving. Another strength of the play arises from the fact that Grimké is a poet who uses language with sensitivity. Some of the speeches rise to eloquence, while others are emotionally fevered; and some of the best passages, such as the long tale Rachel shares with the children about the search for a land of laughter, are lyrical and moving.

It was apparently Grimké's genuine conviction that black children should not be brought into this painful world, judging by the evidence of her short story "The Closing Door," in which a pregnant black woman hears of her brother's lynching (ironically, this story was published in the *Birth Control Review*). After her child is born, the protagonist goes mad and kills it. The traumatic situation has obvious affinities with the story told in *Rachel.* The play, however, does control the hysteria Grimké felt on the subject and builds the idea into a plausible drama, whereas the story is less successful at containing her emotion.

Where Grimké's drama and fiction are broadly delineated, her poetry is subdued and enigmatic. In "The Black Finger," probably her best-known poem, she describes a cypress tree seen "Slim and still,/Against a gold, gold sky" as "A black finger/Pointing upwards" and asks, "Why, beautiful, still finger, are you black?/And why are you pointing upwards?" Grimké's poetry is delicate, quiet, and personal. Racial and social concerns are largely absent; in most of the poems the reader would be unaware of the poet's race. There are fewer calls for action and less social anger than one would expect from the author of *Rachel.* Nonetheless, even Grimké has an occasional warning, as in "Beware Lest He Awakes," a 1902 poem published in the *Boston Pilot.* In this piece the young Grimké cautions the reader that the abused black man may one day actively avenge himself. In a similarly subtle, threatening poem, "Tenebris," a tree's shadow is depicted as a "huge and black" hand that "plucks and plucks/At the bricks" of the white man's house. Other poems, including "At April," the dialect poem "Lullaby," and "Trees," allude to the tragic plight of the Afro-American even when the ostensible subjects are the play of girls, the sleeping child, or the beauty of natural setting. But the majority of Grimké's poems deal with subjects that evoke other kinds of pain. Vividly imagistic, they are often modest in subject and muted in tone.

Many of Grimké's poems are love poems, through which run themes of isolation and poignant longing. In several pieces, the persona's intense yearning is followed by rejection, or by death. Some of the poems express the persona's desire to be contained within another person, even, in one poem, cupped permanently in the palm of a lover's hand. Frequently Grimké couches her subjects in images drawn from nature. Her depictions of nature's beauty are invariably sharpened by her awareness of its evanescence. These elements coalesce in several of the poems, such as in this excerpt from the first part of "A Mona Lisa": "I should like to poise/On the very brink/Of the leaf-brown pools/That are your shadowed eyes;/I should like to cleave/Without sound,/The glimmering waters,/Their unrippled waters,/I should like to sink down/And down/And down. . . ./And deeply drown." The highly visual imagery makes the lines intensely sensual. It is typical of Grimké, also, that she depicts no consummation of the imagined relationship, unless death itself be considered a satisfaction.

Angelina Weld Grimké

Several love poems, such as "El Beso," speak of the persona's rejection by the beloved. Natural images are grouped together for the purpose of reinforcing the themes of loneliness and pain. In the poem the persona describes being lured to the loved one's mouth, and at the moment of the kiss she experiences "madness, madness,/Tremulous, breathless, flaming,/The space of a sigh." But the moment is followed by "regret—your sobbing;/ And again quiet—the stars, Twilight—and you." Frequently Grimké creates meaning in her poems by juxtaposing a pattern of images to a single statement that seals the mood and completes the poem, as in the four-line poem "Dusk," where "Twin stars through my purpling pane" are "a yellowing moon" and the dusk itself. Sometimes Grimké tells, or at least implies, a story with a sequence of images, as in "For the Candle Light," which juxtaposes the images of a day in which the "sky was blue" and "each daisy white, so white" with a night in which "the gray skies grayly cry," and "in a book for the candle light," is a "daisy dead and dry." Grimké has a funereal sensibility, and her favorite images often unexpectedly combine death with unrelated images. Grass, for example, in one poem is "a mothering green finger" over a grave; in another, "Grass Fingers," she revels in lying in the grass, touched by "Elusive, delicate grass fingers," but concludes that "Soon I shall be too far beneath you,/For you to reach me, even,/With your tiny, timorous toes."

Grimké's poetry has affinities with the work of other black poets like Jessie Redmon Fauset, Anne Spencer, Georgia Douglas Johnson, Countee Cullen, and William Stanley Braithwaite—poets who frequently tended to avoid racial subjects and dialects, focusing instead on the subjects of a more genteel tradition. Grimké seems to have been more influenced by romantic, Victorian, and even Edwardian writers than by her contemporaries in New York and Washington. The etched quality of her imagery, the way she used images to tell a story, her association of love and death, and the enervated loneliness of her verse suggest the Pre-Raphaelites, particularly the Rossettis, as we see in "A Winter Twilight":

A silence slipping around like death,
Yet chased by a whisper, a sigh, a breath;
One group of trees lean, naked and cold,
Inking their crests 'gainst a sky green-gold;
One path that knows where the corn flowers were;
Lonely, apart, unyielding, one fir;
And over it softly leaning down,
One star I loved ere the fields went brown.

Grimké's subjects and tonality suggest the sentimental morbidity of several of the late Victorian and Edwardian poets. The association of love and death and the enervated loneliness of her verse are reminiscent of the work of Christina Rossetti, Ernest Dowson, and some of the verse of Thomas Hardy. Her work suggests that she may have read many of the late Victorians, for whom style frequently was substance; Grimké's work also bears resemblance to the Imagist poems of H. D. (Hilda Doolittle), Edna St. Vincent Millay, and Amy Lowell. She could be as satisfied as any doctrinaire Imagist by a whole poem made of a concentrated image pattern, as in her four-line poem "Dawn":

Grey trees, grey skies, and not a star;
    Grey mist, grey hush;
And then, frail, exquisite, afar,
    A hermit-thrush.

"More vivid imaging of objects," said Robert T. Kerlin, introducing some of her poems in his 1935 anthology, "has not been done in verse by any contemporary. This, too, in stanzas that suggest in their perfection the work of the old lapidaries."

Grimké's poetry probably gets much of its sadness from the conflicts of her emotional life. Hull comments that Grimké had to suppress much of her poetic impulse and to resist publishing some of her work. Several of the published poems, which most readers would presume at first to be written for a lover of the opposite sex, contain lines that suggest a woman as object rather than a man, as in the reference to "the long brown grasses/That are your lashes" in "A Mona Lisa," or "your curls so shiny and sweet" in "When the Green Lies Over the Earth." Some of her unpublished poems are much more explicitly lesbian, with lines like "If I might taste but once, just once/The dew/Upon her lips." The most important implication of this for an evaluation of Grimké's poetry is that she lived a life of suppression, both personal and creative. One should not be surprised, thus, that images of deprivation and unfulfillment and a preoccupation with death and thwarted love fill her poetry, or that her poetic output was limited until the emotional instability of her later years dried up her output completely. Hull says that her lesbianism ultimately "meant, finally, that you stopped writing altogether, dying, no doubt, with your real gifts stifled within—and leaving behind (in a precious few cases) the little that manages to survive of your true self in fugitive pieces."

Grimké has received little critical attention. Her play, *Rachel,* is moving and often eloquent, but presents problems of staging and suffers from a defeatism that is unlikely to appeal to modern audiences. Grimké's delicate poems, on the other hand, exhibit a craftsmanship and an intensity that warrant much more attention than they have received. Her poetry has a melancholy, muted beauty that is a fitting memorial to her life.

References:

Gerald Bradley, "Goodbye, Mister Bones," *Drama Critique,* 7 (Spring 1964): 83-84;

Gloria T. Hull, " 'Under the Days': The Buried Life and Poetry of Angelina Weld Grimké," in *Conditions: Five* (Black Women's Issue), edited by Lorraine Bethel and Barbara Smith (1979): 17-25;

Ernest R. McKinney, "*Rachel:* A Play by Angelina W. Grimké," *Competitor,* 1 (1920): 51-52.

Papers:

Private papers, letters, diaries, scrapbooks, and manuscripts of Angelina Weld Grimké are housed at the Moorland-Spingarn Research Center, Howard University, Washington, D.C.

Jupiter Hammon

(17 October 1711-died between 1790 and 1806)

Sondra A. O'Neale
Emory University

See also the Hammon entry in *DLB 31, American Colonial Writers, 1735-1781.*

BOOKS: *An Essay on the Ten Virgins* (Hartford: Printed by Hudson & Goodwin, 1779);

A Winter Piece: Being a Serious Exhortation, with a Call to the Unconverted: and a Short Contemplation on the Death of Jesus Christ (Hartford, Conn.: Printed by Hudson and Goodwin?, 1782);

An Evening's Improvement: Shewing the Necessity of beholding the Lamb of God, To Which is Added, A Dialogue, Entitled, The Kind Master and Dutiful Servant (Hartford: Printed by Hudson & Goodwin?, circa 1783);

An Address to the Negroes in the State of New-York (New York: Printed by Carroll & Patterson, 1787).

Collection: *America's First Negro Poet: The Complete Work of Jupiter Hammon of Long Island,* edited by Stanley Austin Ramsom, Jr. (Port Washington, N.Y.: Kennikat Press, 1970).

Jupiter Hammon, the first black writer to publish in America, has been one of the least understood and most undervalued writers among those in the tradition that he engendered. Facts about his life are hidden in the lost records of slavery; and his cries for freedom, veiled in biblical language, are further obscured by modern unfamiliarity with that context. A slave all his long life, Hammon nonetheless distinguished himself as a preacher among his people, as a well-known folk, religious, and occasional poet in rural New York, and as an essayist who was invited to speak to and publish for both black and white audiences. Hammon's extant works are extensive, considering that he was a slave with little formal education and no sustained support from the abolition movement, such as that which Phillis Wheatley and Olaudah Equiano would later enjoy. Evidence indicates that he wrote much more than the four poems, two essays, and a sermon that have survived. His work includes the first and most comprehensive statement of black theology and the earliest antislavery protests by a black writer in American literature.

Hammon's themes of race, slavery, and religion were tied to the social disintegration and alienation African slaves in America were experiencing in a white society. He realized that his first task was to give the slaves in his audience a new sense of ethnic and class identity. Thus he addressed them as "brethren," "Africans by nation," "ancient people," or "Ethiopians," and usually as "servants" instead of as "slaves." These terms are fraught with serious biblical implications for white Christians, for they challenge the white colonists' commitment to religious principles. Using biblical analogies, Hammon reminds whites and encourages blacks to follow God's commandment to show empathy for the poor, the stranger, and social outcasts, especially those rejected because of race. In employing traditional iconography, Hammon resisted the image of Christ as master and chose instead to depict him as God's bondservant and as man's savior and redeemer. He also drew analogies between the plight of American slaves and that of the Jews before and during their exodus from Egypt (an analogy white Puritans had often used in speaking of themselves). Always subtly attacking the eighteenth-century theology that was employed to make slavery morally acceptable in a "Christian" society, Hammon addressed the deceptive equation of the color "black" with evil, which led to the justification of slavery on the grounds that black people were inherently evil. Instead he defined this philosophy and the practice of slavery itself—whether as personal habit or institutional oppression—as satanic in nature and origin.

Because there is a dearth of historical information about slavery in the North and because twentieth-century readers are for the most part unfamiliar with the biblical myth and idiom underlying eighteenth-century thought, Hammon's writings have frequently been ignored or misunderstood. The poet couched his antislavery protests in biblical symbols because the Bible was the cultural reference of his times and because slave supporters contorted a few of its verses to justify the enslavement of blacks. Hammon's modern detractors, in asserting that he failed to attack slavery, demonstrate their unfamiliarity with this context.

Rigidly enforced slavery was the financial foundation of colonial life—in the North as well as in the South. Northern colonial slave codes, of which New York, Hammon's home state, had the most stringent, strictly controlled the slave community. Marriage was discouraged. Most black females were shipped to southern colonies or to the Caribbean because of their low utility in the northern economy and to prevent black family development. The male-to-female ratio among blacks was about ten-to-one in the northern colonies. Existing families were often summarily separated to accommodate slave sales. The only difference in slave conditions between the North and the South was that northern commercial interests required some literate slaves to serve as clerks and artisans, and therefore a higher percentage of northern blacks were allowed to obtain educational and industrial skills. Jupiter Hammon was one slave who was so privileged.

Hammon lived through four successive generations of "owners" in the wealthy Lloyd family, one of the important spokes in the autocratic wheel of the slave economy. As the representatives of British aristocracy on Long Island, with strong ties to Old and New England, the Lloyds imported slaves for sales first to their New York neighbors and then throughout New England. They prospered greatly from an exchange of human commodities and from the living derived from their acreage in Oyster Bay, Long Island, which was originally "purchased" from Indians for "three coats, three shirts, two cuttoes, three hatchets, three hoes, two fathom of wampum, six knives, two pair of stockings and two pair of shoes."

Although the Lloyds' scant records of their slaves' lives make certainty impossible, Hammon's mother and father probably arrived with the first shipment of slaves to the Oyster Bay estate in the summer of 1687. Among these arrivals, the one most closely associated with Hammon in the records was a rather militant slave whom the Lloyds named "Opium," who tried to escape several times through the years. The Lloyds kept only two servants for their entire life spans: Opium, who from all indications was Hammon's father, and Hammon himself. Hammon's mother was probably a slave named Rose, who was sold when the boy was quite young.

John Lloyd, the younger son of the plantation founder, was born in the same year as Jupiter Hammon. Growing up with him and his older brother, Henry (two years their senior), Hammon may have shared in some of their private tutelage. In addition, Hammon may have received some education from the Society for the Propagation of the Gospel, the missionary arm of the Church of England, which came to Oyster Bay in 1726, primarily to reach African slaves, native Indians, and unchurched whites.

The Lloyd manor house, which still stands on Long Island (photograph by Carl Anderson through the courtesy of the Lloyd Harbour Historical Commission)

Lloyd family records indicate that in 1730, when he was about nineteen years old, Jupiter nearly died from a goutlike disease. In 1733, having bought a Bible from Henry Lloyd, Hammon underwent a religious awakening that eventually led to a career as a writer and preacher who, aware of the limitations of his slavery, was nonetheless able to wage subtle war against the slave system. Having attended both the Congregational assembly in Huntington, Long Island, and the Anglican church in Stamford, Connecticut, Hammon quoted both Congregational and Anglican preachers in his works, but his self-formulated assumptions are more akin to the doctrine of Arminianism, the belief that Christ died for all people and that anyone can exercise free will to choose salvation. However, those colonists most supportive of Hammon's work were the Quakers—more liberal in social outreach than other colonial Protestants—who exerted influence on Hammon's conversion, intellectual growth, and commitment to writing as a tool for emancipation. After Hammon's death the Quakers republished his 1787 prose work *An Address to the Negroes in the State of New-York* with a dedication indicating years of fond association.

On Christmas Day 1760, Hammon's first poem, a broadside titled *An Evening Thought. Salvation by Christ, with Penetential Cries,* became the first work by a slave to be published in the Western hemisphere during modern times. Ostensibly about spiritual conversion and Christian growth, "safe" topics for a black man who lived during the religious revivals of the eighteenth century, the twenty-two-stanza poem is written in the call-and-response mode and the meter still familiar in Negro spirituals. For Hammon and most blacks during the Great Awakening, the concept of salvation was never a solely spiritual one; they yearned for salvation from all life's problems, especially slavery. Underlying the poem's insistence that Christ offers his salvation to "every one" of "every Nation" of "all the World," rather than just to a chosen few, is a message of escape for more than just the soul. Thus the poem's line "redemption now to every one" thematically expresses the interrelatedness of a slave's theology to his quest for freedom.

The Lloyd manor was used as a base for British troops during the Revolutionary War, but Joseph Lloyd, who supported the colonial revolt, fled to Hartford when British troops overran Long Island, taking Hammon and all others in the household with him. Hammon's literary career thrived in Hartford, where his next three extant works were published: a 1778 broadside poem dedicated to Phillis Wheatley; and his first prose sermon, *A Winter Piece* (1782), to which he attached "A Poem for Children with Thoughts on Death."

While in Hartford, Hammon learned of the child prodigy, Phillis Wheatley, who was also a slave. In his poem dedicated to her, Hammon joins two of his most enduring themes. First, like all eighteenth-century Christians, he wrestles with the sovereignty of God in the affairs of men. The essential aim of the words "That thou a pattern still might be/to youth of Boston town" is to remind his fellow writer of the burden of their prophetic call to report the truth despite the constraining circumstances of their enslavement. Hammon is reminding Wheatley that they too may die, like those Africans who did not survive the Atlantic passage; but from the Christian context of death and judgment established in the poem, black writers must answer specifically to God for the fulfillment of their obligation to raise their voices against injustice.

Second, in the poem to Wheatley and in his next work, *A Winter Piece,* Hammon equates the black experience in America to that of the Samaritans in Palestine. Both groups were racial and religious outcasts among a dominant people who felt themselves to be God's elite. In his broadside *An Address to Miss Phillis Wheatley,* Hammon tells the poetess "to drink Samaria's flood," and in *A Winter Piece* he quotes the entire section of Christ's meeting with the Samaritan "woman at the well," recorded in the gospel of John. In that narrative, one of Hammon's favorite scriptural references, Christ addresses a Samaritan woman who was morally suspect, even within her own outcast class. Yet Christ, revealing himself as the Messiah (an admission he never made to Jews), speaks extensively to her about her position in society and her relation with God and promises her deliverance. Because it transgressed social mores, the conversation was, of course, condemned by Jewish religious leaders. In most of his poems and essays Hammon sets the Samaritan narrative before his slave audiences to illustrate Christ's primary concern for those who have been rejected and oppressed by established society.

In *A Winter Piece,* Hammon also equates the colonial slaves to biblical publicans (from the Greek term "tax-gatherer"), another ostracized class in Christ's time. Israelites labeled publicans traitors to national freedom, accusing them not only of collecting taxes for the Roman Empire, but also of levying additional surcharges for their own pockets. The Pharisees criticized Jesus because he often dined with publicans, whom these Pharisees considered gross sinners. In *A Winter Piece* Hammon cites an occasion when Christ recognized a penitent publican as more acceptable to God than a self-righteous Pharisee. From a religious context, Hammon is equating colonial slaveholders, who trust in their religious election, to the smug Pharisees; and he is promising that Africans can find as much acceptance with God as publicans did with Jesus.

Because in *A Winter Piece* and his other prose works Hammon urges slaves to accept Christ and enter the church "mainstream" through baptism and communion, twentieth-century critics have charged that he was so concerned with religion that he ignored slavery. Actually, Hammon was directly challenging colonial slave laws and the conscience

AN

Evening THOUGHT.

SALVATION BY CHRIST,

WITH

PENETENTIAL CRIES:

Compoſed by Jupiter Hammon, a Negro belonging to Mr Lloyd, of Queen's-Village, on Long-Iſland, the 25th of December, 1760.

SALVATION comes by Jeſus Chriſt alone,
The only Son of God;
Redemption now to every one,
That love his holy Word.
Dear Jeſus we would fly to Thee,
And leave off every Sin,
Thy tender Mercy well agree;
Salvation from our King.
Salvation comes now from the Lord,
Our victorious King;
His holy Name be well ador'd,
Salvation ſurely bring.
Dear Jeſus give thy Spirit now,
Thy Grace to every Nation,
That han't the Lord to whom we bow,
The Author of Salvation.
Dear Jeſus unto Thee we cry,
Give us thy Preparation;
Turn not away thy tender Eye;
We ſeek thy true Salvation.
Salvation comes from God we know,
The true and only One;
It's well agreed and certain true,
He gave his only Son.
Lord hear our penetential Cry:
Salvation from above;
It is the Lord that doth ſupply,
With his Redeeming Love.
Dear Jeſus by thy precious Blood,
The World Redemption have:
Salvation comes now from the Lord,
He being thy captive Slave.
Dear Jeſus let the Nations cry,
And all the People ſay,
Salvation comes from Chriſt on high,
Haſte on Tribunal Day.
We cry as Sinners to the Lord,
Salvation to obtain;
It is firmly fixt his holy Word,
Ye ſhall not cry in vain.
Dear Jeſus unto Thee we cry,
And make our Lamentation:
O let our Prayers aſcend on high;
We felt thy Salvation.
Lord turn our dark benighted Souls;
Give us a true Motion,
And let the Hearts of all the World,
Make Chriſt their Salvation.
Ten Thouſand Angels cry to Thee,
Yea louder than the Ocean.
Thou art the Lord, we plainly ſee;
Thou art the true Salvation.
Now is the Day, excepted Time;
The Day of Salvation;
Increaſe your Faith, do not repine:
Awake ye every Nation.
Lord unto whom now ſhall we go,
Or ſeek a ſafe Abode;
Thou haſt the Word Salvation too
The only Son of God.
Ho! every one that hunger hath,
Or pineth after me,
Salvation be thy leading Staff,
To ſet the Sinner free.
Dear Jeſus unto Thee we fly;
Depart, depart from Sin,
Salvation doth at length ſupply,
The Glory of our King.
Come ye Bleſſed of the Lord,
Salvation gently given;
O turn your Hearts, accept the Word,
Your Souls are fit for Heaven.
Dear Jeſus we now turn to Thee,
Salvation to obtain;
Our Hearts and Souls do meet again,
To magnify thy Name.
Come holy Spirit, Heavenly Dove,
The Object of our Care;
Salvation doth increaſe our Love;
Our Hearts hath felt thy fear.
Now Glory be to God on High,
Salvation high and low;
And thus the Soul on Chriſt rely,
To Heaven ſurely go.
Come Bleſſed Jeſus, Heavenly Dove,
Accept Repentance here;
Salvation give, with tender Love;
Let us with Angels ſhare.

FINIS.

Hammon's first poem, the first work known to be published by a slave in the modern Western world (courtesy of the New-York Historical Society)

of the Christian church. To seventeenth- and eighteenth-century New England whites, baptism meant political enfranchisement and economic empowerment. When a small number of blacks publicly confessed conversion and sought the privilege of baptism, baffled colonists changed the laws to deny blacks that social advantage.

With communion, however, northern blacks had some support among whites. Stoddardism, named after a liberal Calvinist, Solomon Stoddard, was the accepted doctrine on communion in the middle colonies by the mid-eighteenth century. Stoddard had enraged more conservative Calvinist clergymen by advocating that persons of good moral character could share in communion even though they had not exhibited what Calvinists considered to be the outward evidence of grace. This reform widened church fellowship for blacks throughout the colonies. As with baptism, conservative colonists resisted "integrated" communion service, following the advice of Cotton Mather; but before the burgeoning of black churches throughout the colonies in the nineteenth century, such separation of the races was not feasible. Thus, every time Hammon encouraged slaves to seek full participation in the sacred rites, he was challenging white evangelicals to follow the deepest spirit of Christian brotherhood. Such testing was thoroughly in line with New England expectations of Christian piety and with the apostles' directive that love is the only evidence of true Christianity.

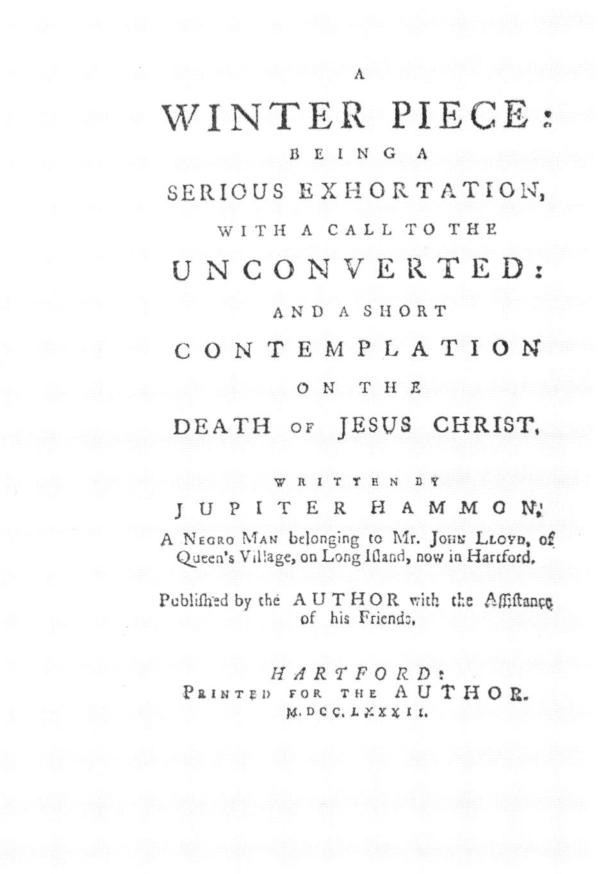
A

WINTER PIECE:

BEING A

SERIOUS EXHORTATION,

WITH A CALL TO THE

UNCONVERTED:

AND A SHORT

CONTEMPLATION

ON THE

DEATH OF JESUS CHRIST,

WRITTEN BY

JUPITER HAMMON,

A Negro Man belonging to Mr. John Lloyd, of Queen's Village, on Long Iſland, now in Hartford.

Publiſhed by the AUTHOR with the Aſſiſtance of his Friends.

HARTFORD:

Printed for the AUTHOR.

M.DCC.LXXXII.

Title page for Hammon's first prose sermon

In "A Poem for Children with Thoughts on Death" Hammon once more enjoins whites to be as thoughtful of black children as they are of their own. Children were of special interest to colonists, and the question of their predetermined salvation, based on their parents' election or rejection, was a major theological debate. The issue was especially crucial if a child died before adulthood, and it was often discussed in elegies, as in this poem. Anglicans and Puritans believed that their offsprings' salvation, and thus a legacy of social rule, was assured in their own election. In the choiceless manner, the doctrines of original sin and predestination would condemn the children of the unsaved, particularly unsaved blacks and lower-caste Englishmen, to perdition along with their parents.

Hammon was angered by this oversight, and in some of his most unsubtle remarks to whites, he castigated them for what he saw as their sinful neglect of slave children, whom they insisted upon rearing with a slave mentality in a "so-called Christian land."

After the Revolutionary War, which, in "A Dialogue, Entitled, 'The Kind Master and Dutiful Servant' " (published in *An Evening's Improvement*, 1783), he charged was God's judgment against the white hierarchy, Hammon returned to Oyster Bay with the Lloyds. The Lloyds' ledgers indicate that he maintained a private garden, worked as a clerk in the community store, and often acted as a banker by holding funds for the younger Lloyd sons. There is no evidence that Hammon had a wife or children; rather, like most black males in northern slavery, he remained alone. By the time of the Long Island resettlement he was over seventy years old but could still say with confidence, "I can do almost any kind of work." Obviously slavery's forced responsibilities greatly impeded Hammon's creativity and his publication plans. He was past retirement age when the move to Hartford enabled him to publish *An Address to Miss Phillis Wheatley* eighteen years after the appearance of his first broadside in 1760. Hammon was "upwards of seventy" when he wrote *An Address to the Negroes in the State of New-York* (1787) and *An Evening's Improvement* (circa

1783). Only when his usefulness as a slave had diminished did the Lloyds grant him enough free time to write and to make arrangements for printing his work.

Hammon has received his greatest criticism because of a statement prompted by his newfound "freedom" in old age. In *An Address to the Negroes in the State of New-York* he said: "Now I acknowledge that liberty is a great thing, and worth seeking for, if we can get it honestly; and by our good conduct prevail on our masters to set us free, yet I should be glad if others, especially the young Negroes, were to be free; for many of us who are grown up slaves, and have always had masters to take care of us, should hardly know how to take care of ourselves; and it may be more for our own comfort to remain as we are. That liberty is a great thing we may know from our own feelings and we may likewise judge so from the conduct of the white people in the late war. How much money had been spent, and how many lives have been lost to defend their liberty! I must say that I have hoped that God would open their eyes, when they were so much engaged for liberty, to think of the state of the poor blacks, and to pity us. He has done it in some measure, and has raised us up many friends; for which we have reason to be thankful, and to hope in his mercy."

Rather than encouraging blacks to acquiesce to their bondage, Hammon was commenting on his personal circumstances and on two prevailing social phenomena. First, as the eighteenth century progressed, an increasing number of masters "emancipated" elderly slaves such as Hammon when these servants were no longer able to work. Ejected from the only homes that most of them had known, and lacking established families, work opportunities, or available organized state aid, most of these former slaves were reduced to begging and vagrancy. As a result, ordinances were passed making owners responsible for their former slaves and requiring them either to post bonds for their emancipated charges or to provide them a monthly stipend. Hammon was seventy-six when *An Address to the Negroes in the State of New-York* was published. His statement reflects his belief that the Lloyds had some obligation to provide food and shelter in his retirement; yet there is no evidence that the Lloyds were willing to pay the expensive bond or to give him a monthly stipend, as their records show that neither they nor their neighbors had ever done so for any other slave.

Second, the aged poet was advocating a plan of gradual emancipation, one that New York Quakers had often suggested to the state legislature as a compromise settlement to end slavery. However, in New York, the largest slaveholding state north of Maryland, the state legislature felt that slavery was required for economic reasons. It was 1799 before the state of New York adopted the precise plan that Hammon suggested. Younger blacks were declared free when they reached adulthood. New York slaves were not fully manumitted until 1821, making the state the last in the North to end slavery totally. Ironically, the statements for which critics have so denigrated Hammon may have been—through Quaker dissemination of his address as a responsible slave's counter to proslavery hypotheses—his greatest contribution to the cause of freedom.

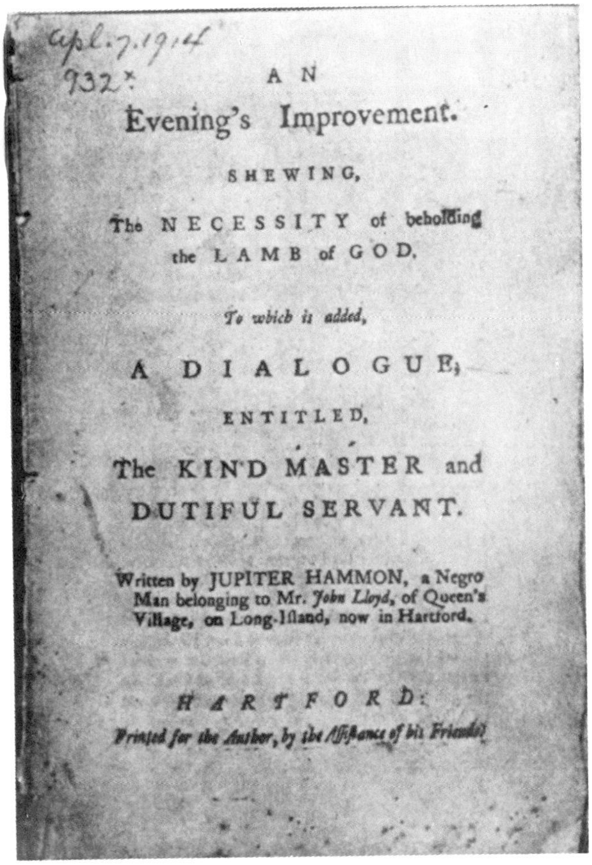
AN
Evening's Improvement.
SHEWING,
The NECESSITY of beholding
the LAMB of GOD.
To which is added,
A DIALOGUE,
ENTITLED,
The KIND MASTER and
DUTIFUL SERVANT.
Written by JUPITER HAMMON, a Negro Man belonging to Mr. John Lloyd, of Queen's Village, on Long-Island, now in Hartford.
HARTFORD:
Printed for the Author, by the Assistance of his Friends.

Title page for the sermon in which Hammon promised his fellow slaves, "if we love God, black as we be, and despised as we are, God will love us" (courtesy of the New-York Historical Society)

In *An Address to the Negroes in the State of New-York,* as in all of his works, Hammon offered judgment in the afterlife as the slave's only hope for vindication. For him, life was reduced to the slave's struggle to be free from his oppression, at least

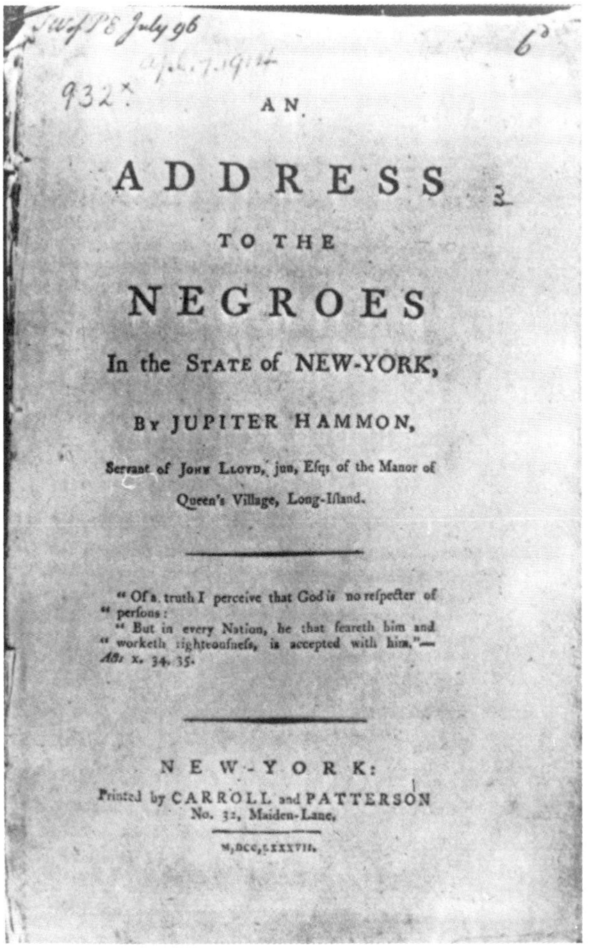
AN
ADDRESS
TO THE
NEGROES
In the STATE of NEW-YORK,
BY JUPITER HAMMON,
Servant of JOHN LLOYD, jun, Efq; of the Manor of Queen's Village, Long-Ifland.

"Of a truth I perceive that God is no refpecter of "perfons:
"But in every Nation, he that feareth him and "worketh righteoufnefs, is accepted with him."— Acts x. 34. 35.

NEW-YORK:
Printed by CARROLL and PATTERSON
No. 32, Maiden-Lane,
M,DCC,LXXXVII.

Title page for Hammon's last book

spiritually, even if physical freedom was not possible. Hammon did not expect to see the end of physical bondage during his lifetime. Instead, he believed that the only way the slave or free black could escape the effects of racism was through death. He preached that those slaves who did not accept Christ had succumbed to the slaveowners' attempts to force them into a lack of spiritual and moral awareness. Those who did discover faith would awaken after death to a transformation that would lift the veil of color. (Hammon implies elsewhere that pigmentation would be obvious in the spirit world.) Drawing his pronouncements from biblical theology, he urgently pressed blacks to display superior moral behavior (advice that again has been called "tomish") precisely because he believed that earthly oppression and the inherent sinfulness of slavery as an institution guaranteed the slave his place in heaven.

Hammon discussed sin and blackness in all of his essays. But in *An Evening's Improvement* he exposed and then reconciled several separate yet interdependent definitions of sin in ways that absolved any racial guilt. When he says to his African audience, "It is not we only that are unworthy," he is speaking of the curse of Ham (Genesis 9), its possible connection to African racial identity and the preordination of slavery, and the burden of guilt that eighteenth-century white theologians tried to lay on black shoulders. While the Lloyds gave Hammon a name to identify him with both Ham and the Roman god Jupiter, nowhere does the poet ever accept the Anglo-European theory that Africans descended from Ham or that they were recipients of an ancient curse. Instead, he reiterates Galatians 3:13: Christ's sacrifice, if accepted, eradicates this and all other curses to which mankind might be heir. He is also trying to render ineffective the colonial philosophy that blacks, as Ham's descendants, inherited a peculiar depravity predisposing them to be slaves. Moreover, he insists that all men, not just Africans, are fallen through Adam's sin, and that all can be saved through sincere and absolute conversion. Like the words in the Negro spiritual ("everyone that talks about heaven ain't goin' there"), Hammon's use of Matthew 7:21—"Not every one that saith unto me, Lord, Lord, shall enter into the kingdom of heaven; but he that doeth the will of my Father which is in heaven"—is another direct confrontation of white hypocrisy. Hammon judges Christians by their support of slavery as an institution.

Always when he spoke to Africans about their sin, Hammon emphasized individual acts for which he believed all men would stand in judgment. He thus urged blacks to repent of individual transgressions. He did not offer the same opportunity for repentance to their master, however, or to his white readers, because he posited that they had heard the gospel and then, through their lack of love, had individually and collectively decided to reject it.

Because of an entry in the Lloyds' account books, Hammon is known to have been alive in 1790. But, based on eulogistic language in a 1806 Quaker reprint of *An Address to the Negroes in the State of New-York,* he is thought to have died by that time. As yet, neither the exact date of his death nor the place of his burial has been determined.

Modern readers who assert that he had no regard for the plight of slaves are ill-informed about biblical typology and even less cognizant of the constraints of an oppressive society on a slave who tried to write about his victimization. In his prose, Hammon urged blacks to learn and become literate so that they could read the Bible for themselves. Only then could they understand his coded messages about their enslavement. His topics were not so veiled, however, that knowledgeable whites in his more biblically conscious society would have missed them. In haste to apply twentieth-century expectations to Hammon's works, modern critics have not always clearly understood his codes, his themes, and his commitment to black American freedom. Continuing reevaluation of his life and work in light of not only that biblical code but other contemporary frameworks will undoubtedly enhance modern views of his prominence as the founder of black American literature.

Biographies:

Oscar Wegelin, "Was Phillis Wheatley America's First Negro Poet?," *Literary Collector* (August 1904);

Wegelin, Biography of Hammon, in *Jupiter Hammon: American Negro Poet, Selections from His Writings and a Bibliography,* edited by Wegelin (New York: Printed for C. F. Heartman, 1915);

Charles A. Vertanes, "Jupiter Hammon: Early Negro Poet of Long Island," *Nassau County Historical Journal,* 18 (Winter 1957): 4.

References:

Bernard W. Bell, "African-American Writers," in *American Literature 1764-1789: The Revolutionary Years,* edited by Everett Emerson (Racine: University of Wisconsin Press, 1977), pp. 171-193;

Benjamin Brawley, "Jupiter Hammon," in *Early Negro American Writers: Selections with Biographical and Critical Introductions,* edited by Brawley (Chapel Hill: University of North Carolina Press, 1935), pp. 21-30;

Sidney Kaplan, "Jupiter Hammon," in *The Black Presence in the Era of the American Revolution: 1770-1800* (Greenwich, Conn.: New York Graphic Society, 1973), pp. 171-176;

Vernon Loggins, *The Negro Author: His Development in America to 1900* (Port Washington, N.Y.: Kennikat Press, 1964);

Ronald B. Miller, Review of *America's First Negro Poet: Jupiter Hammon of Long Island,* edited by Stanley A. Ransom, Jr., *New York History,* 55 (1974): 483;

Sondra A. O'Neale, "Jupiter Hammon and his Works: A Discussion of the First Black Preacher to Publish Poems, Sermons, and Essays," *Journal of the Interdenominational Theological Center,* 9 (Spring 1982): 99-113;

Thomas L. G. Oxley, "Survey of Negro Literature, 1760-1929," *Messenger* (February 1927): 37-39;

R. Roderick Palmer, "Jupiter Hammon's Poetic Exhortations," *CLA Journal,* 18 (September 1974): 22-28;

Stanley Austin Ransom, Jr., Introduction to *America's First Negro Poet: The Complete Works of Jupiter Hammon of Long Island,* edited by Ransom (Port Washington, N.Y.: Kennikat Press, 1970);

J. Saunders Redding, "The Forerunners: Jupiter Hammon, Phillis Wheatley, George Moses Horton," in his *To Make A Poet Black* (Chapel Hill: University of North Carolina Press, 1939), pp. 3-18;

Carolyn Reese, "From Jupiter Hammon to LeRoi Jones," *Changing Education,* 1 (Fall 1966): 30-34;

William H. Robinson, *Early Black American Poets* (Dubuque, Iowa: Wm. C. Brown Company, 1969).

Frances Ellen Watkins Harper

Maryemma Graham
University of Mississippi

BIRTH: Baltimore, Maryland, 24 September 1825.

MARRIAGE: 22 November 1860, to Fenton Harper; child: Mary.

DEATH: Philadelphia, Pennsylvania, 22 February 1911.

BOOKS: *Forest Leaves* (N.d.);
Poems on Miscellaneous Subjects (Boston: Printed by J. B. Yerrinton & Son, 1854; enlarged, Philadelphia, 1855; enlarged again, Philadelphia: Merrihew & Son, 1871);
Moses: A Story of the Nile (Philadelphia: Printed by Merrihew, 1869; enlarged, Philadelphia: Privately printed, 1889); enlarged again as *Idylls of the Bible* (Philadelphia: Privately printed, 1901);
Poems (Philadelphia: Printed by Merrihew & Son, 1871);
Sketches of Southern Life (Philadelphia, 1872; enlarged, Philadelphia: Merrihew & Son, 1887);
The Sparrow's Fall and Other Poems (N.p., 1890?);
Iola Leroy; or, Shadows Uplifted (Philadelphia: Garrigues Brothers, 1892);
The Martyr of Alabama and Other Poems (N.p., 1894?);
Atlanta Offering, Poems (Philadelphia: Privately printed, 1895);
Poems (Philadelphia: Printed for the author by George S. Ferguson, 1895; enlarged, 1898; enlarged again, 1900);
Light Beyond Darkness (Chicago: Donohue & Henneberry, n.d.).

OTHER: "The Slave Mother," in *The Black Man, His Antecedents, His Genius, and His Achievements,* edited by William Wells Brown (New York: Hamilton/Boston: Wallcut, 1863);
"Duty to Dependent Races," in *Transactions of the National Council of Women of the United States Assembled in Washington, D.C., February 22-25, 1891* (Philadelphia: Lippincott, 1891), pp. 86-91;
"Woman's Political Future," in *World's Congress of Representative Women,* edited by May Wright Sewall (Chicago: Rand McNally, 1894), pp. 433-437.

PERIODICAL PUBLICATIONS: "The Two Offers," *Anglo-African,* 1 (September 1859): 288-291; 1 (October 1859): 311-313;
"The Colored Woman of America," *English Woman's Review* (15 January 1878): 10-15.

Known as the "Bronze Muse" to her broad audience, Frances Ellen Watkins Harper was the major black woman poet of the nineteenth century. She achieved high distinction and great popularity as an antislavery orator and poet who turned to the causes of temperance and woman suffrage after the Civil War. A trained seamstress, Harper gave up an early career in the domestic arts, choosing instead to earn her living as a public lecturer, which she did until she was nearly eighty, when she officially retired. Her significance lies in her involvement in the major movements of the latter nineteenth and early twentieth century, and her writing resonates with the social, moral, political, and racial causes to which she dedicated herself.

Harper was a remarkably independent woman and an ambitious writer of poetry and fiction; she wrote *Iola Leroy* (1892), the second of a handful of novels written by American black women in the nineteenth century, and "The Two Offers" (1859), probably the first short story published by an Afro-American female writer. An accessible and popular author, Harper read from and sold her collections at public gatherings, a practice which was common among activist writers in her day. Her works, especially *Poems on Miscellaneous Subjects* (1854) and *Sketches of Southern Life* (1872), were consistently reprinted during her lifetime, and her essays and articles appeared frequently in journals and periodicals of the late nineteenth century. When she died, however, her collections went out of print and her importance as one of the chief advocates for the rights of blacks and women at national and international conferences was just beginning to be recognized.

(courtesy of Schomburg Center for Research in Black Culture, the New York Public Library, Astor, Lenox and Tilden Foundations)

The only child of free black parents in the slave state of Maryland, Frances Ellen Watkins was born in Baltimore, probably in 1825, although the records on file at the Pennsylvania Department of Health give 1824 as the year of her birth. When her mother died, Frances was three or four years of age; she went to live with her aunt and attended the school for free blacks that was owned by her uncle, William J. Watkins, a self-educated minister and craftsman and a firm abolitionist whose writings appeared frequently in the *Liberator*. After she had completed her early education, she found a position in a Baltimore bookshop, which made available to her all of the popular literature of the period. She took full advantage of her position and read widely, preparing herself for her career as a writer and social reformer. As was the custom for young working women of the time, the teenaged Frances roomed with a Baltimore family who trained her in the domestic arts and strongly encouraged her reading and writing. She came to be considered well educated for a nineteenth-century black woman.

Although the date cannot be verified, Frances Ellen Watkins published her first volume of poetry in about 1845. No copies of *Forest Leaves* have been found, but there are several references to it in early historical documents and there are indications that Underground Railroad agent William Grant Still, who became Watkins's longtime correspondent and friend, had assisted her in circulating a published volume before 1854. The widely circulated 1854 publication, *Poems on Miscellaneous Subjects*, may have included many if not all of the verses from *Forest Leaves;* certainly they were included in later collections, particularly those published in the 1890s. In 1850 Frances Watkins took a job at Union Seminary near Columbus, Ohio, as an instructor of domestic science. The move to Union was significant for she was joining, as its first woman teacher, the faculty of a new school for free blacks founded in 1847 by the African Methodist Episcopal Church.

Watkins was not in Ohio long before she began questioning whether her position as a teacher was compatible with her growing interest in social issues. Biographer Lawson Scruggs, in *Women of Distinction* (1893), records Watkins's letter to a friend in which she expresses her concerns: "What would you do if you were in my place? Would you give up and go back and work at your trade? There are no people that need all the benefits resulting from well-directed education more than we do. The condition of our people, wants of our children and the welfare of our race demand the aid of every helping hand, the God speed of every Christian heart. It is a work of time, a labor of patience, to become an effective school-teacher, and it should be a work of life in which they who engage should not abate heart or hope until it is done. And after all, it is one of woman's most sacred rights to have the privilege of forming the symmetry and rightly adjusting the mental balance of an immortal mind." Her conflict between teaching and the desire to be more actively involved with the antislavery issue grew.

Frances Watkins moved to Little York, Pennsylvania, a town on the Underground Railroad, and taught one more year before two events caused her to shift her interests away from a teaching career. First, she met William Grant Still, the black abolitionist and composer from Philadelphia who was widely known for his work with the Underground Railroad. Still, a skillful orator, had a remarkable impact upon Watkins and would later describe in his book on the Underground Railroad the impact that Watkins herself had on the many audiences she addressed. The second event which influenced her decision to join the antislavery movement occurred in 1853, when her home state of Maryland, although a free state, passed a law that permitted the capture of blacks entering the state, whether slave or free. Once captured, they could be remanded to chattel slavery and sold. Watkins began to hear of individual tragedies resulting from the enforcement of this law; they affected her deeply and caused her to strengthen her resolve to fight such abrogations of human rights.

In 1853 Watkins relinquished her teaching position and although she was a Unitarian all her life, she never severed her connection with the African Methodist Episcopal Church. She frequently promoted the interests of the AME church in her work. In 1854 she moved into the Underground Railroad Station in Philadelphia under Still's tutelage, and she joined the abolitionist movement formally by delivering her initial antislavery lecture in New Bedford, Massachusetts. This first lecture, entitled "Education and the Elevation of the Colored Race," reflected her concern for social and political reform as well as the need for moral uplifting, dual themes that would influence all of her writing. Watkins began traveling as a lecturer for the Maine Antislavery Society. For two years she lectured throughout that state, and her popularity grew quickly. She was recognized as both a scholar and an articulate and effective orator. For the next four years, she lectured on behalf of abolitionist causes throughout Massachusetts, Pennsylvania, New York, New Jersey, Ohio, Delaware, Vermont, Michigan, and Canada where responses to her were enthusiastic. The *Liberator* regularly carried entries about her speeches as did other papers supportive of the antislavery cause.

From the beginning, Watkins included readings from her own poetry in her lectures. *Poems on Miscellaneous Subjects* received the full endorsement of the abolitionist movement and was published with William Lloyd Garrison's preface. Generally well considered, Watkins's poems were even compared, in an article in the *Portland Daily Press* Scruggs reports, with the works of Emily Dickinson. In style and form, Watkins reflected the influence of popular poets of the period, especially Henry Wadsworth Longfellow, John Greenleaf Whittier, and Felicia Dorothea Hemans. And except for *Moses: A Story of the Nile* (1869) one finds that her poetic language and technique are routinely similar. Her poetic voice was nonetheless strong and powerful, and the comparison to Dickinson suggests the positive reception her literary writings were given by an audience that knew her primarily as a lecturer.

Poems on Miscellaneous Subjects, first published in 1854 and enlarged twice, proved to be her most popular book. The second enlargement (1871) is called the twentieth edition. This version collected twenty-six poems and three prose essays, "Christianity," "The Colored People of America," and "Breathing the Air of Freedom," which, while reflecting the same themes as the poems, were more forward-looking. If the poetry concentrates on the evils of slavery, then the essays prophesy the larger moral and social concerns which would become more visible in her later writings and public lectures. The poems in the collection touch on religion, social and moral reform, and love and death, but antislavery poetry dominates the volume.

Watkins's poetry is generally narrative, written in the distinctly oral style of the folk ballad. She made frequent use of familiar biblical themes and imagery. It is Watkins's preference for the rhymed quatrain, most often with an *aabb* or *abcb* pattern, that links her to nineteenth-century writers of sentimental poetry in the genteel tradition. Watkins grew adept at working in this popular, conventional style. While her choice of form permitted few technical innovations, Watkins was extremely successful in producing highly lyrical poetry well-suited to her abolitionist themes as well as to social and moral uplift. Watkins's poetry is best known for its directness, its simplicity, and its rhythmic quality. Using vivid imagery, she echoed features of the slave narrative, those nonfiction and fiction accounts of the tribulations of freedmen and women or escaped slaves. Benjamin Brawley and Vernon Loggins, early critics of Afro-American literature, agreed that Watkins was principally responsible for popularizing what became known as the first Negro poetry of protest in the midnineteenth century.

Watkins's remarkable power and dramatic appeal as a poet come from her strong, rhetorical, oral style. William Robinson in his collection *Early Black American Poets* (1969) includes Watkins in his discussion of "orator poets," along with Lucy Terry, Jupiter Hammon, George Moses Horton, James Whitfield, and James Madison Bell. According to Robinson, their poetry derives from the rich oral tradition so pervasive in Afro-American culture and is both thematically and technically different from the more formalist poetry of such writers as Phillis Wheatley, Ann Plato, George McClellan, and Cordelia Ray and from the more decidedly romantic poetry of John Boyd, Albery Whitman, and the Creole poets Armand Lanusse and Victor Séjour.

The oratorical ease which characterized her poetry can be seen in the ballad "Eliza Harris," which appeared in *Frederick Douglass's Paper,* 23 December 1853, before being included in *Poems on Miscellaneous Subjects.* Apparently derived from *Uncle Tom's Cabin,* this poem is the prototype for Watkins's numerous poems focusing on female figures. It does not show the maturity of later work, but, as these lines demonstrate, it is a solid achievement of her apprentice years:

> The bloodhounds have miss'd the scent of her way;
> The hunter is rifled and foil'd of his prey;
> Fierce jargon and cursing, with clanking of chains,
> Make sounds of strange discord on Liberty's plains.

The poem captures the intensity and immediacy of a slave escape in language that is vivid and emotionally charged.

More characteristic of the style and structure of Watkins's poetry is her popular "Bury Me in a Free Land," first published in the *Liberator* in 1864 and again in Lydia Maria Child's *Freedmen's Book* (1866) before Watkins included it in *Poems* (1871):

> Make me a grave where'er you will,
> In a lowly plain, or a lofty hill;
> Make it among earth's humblest graves,
> But not in a land where men are slaves.

Considered her best antislavery poem, "Bury Me in a Free Land" is especially inspiring because of the poet's total empathy with the fate of the slaves whose cause she champions. According to correspondence between Still and Watkins, the poet was in poor health and had actually begun to think that she would die before her life's work was completed. Each stanza builds in dramatic intensity as Watkins describes the agony she experiences. Her request not to be buried "in a land of slaves," which appears at the end of both the first and last stanzas, is both an indication of her recognition of the possibility of an early death as well as her commitment to struggle. According to critic Melba Joyce Boyd, this poem shows Watkins's maturation as a poet, in its correlation between slavery as living death and the narrator's "real" death, a "more sophisticated use of imagery" than in earlier poems, according to Boyd:

> I could not rest if I heard the tread
> Of coffle gang to the shambles led,
> And the mother's shriek of wild despair
> Rise like a curse on the trembling air.
>
> . . . .
>
> If I saw young girls from their mothers' arms
> Bartered and sold for their youthful charms,
> My eye would flash with a mournful flame,
> My death-paled cheek grow red with shame.
>
> . . . .
>
> I ask no monument, proud and high,
> To arrest the gaze of the passers-by;
> All that my yearning spirit craves,
> Is bury me not in a land of slaves.

As "Bury Me in a Free Land" suggests, Watkins's best poems have an intrinsic mass appeal, which endeared Watkins to her audiences, and made her one of the most popular poets between Phillis Wheatley and Paul Laurence Dunbar.

Eighteen fifty-nine was an important year for Watkins. The short story, "The Two Offers," appeared in the September and October issues of the short-lived *Anglo-African,* a black periodical. In the tale, Watkins departs from what is otherwise a traditionally romantic plot by having her protagonist question the wisdom of choosing marriage over social commitment. By 1859 over 12,000 copies of her poetry collection had been sold, and her work had been frequently published in the *Liberator, Frederick Douglass's Paper,* and other popular antislavery publications. During this year, Watkins reportedly gave away much of her personal savings and income, earned mainly through her speeches, to aid fugitive slaves. Perhaps the most significant event to occur in 1859 was the wide distribution of Watkins's sympathetic letter to slave insurrectionist John Brown, written while he was imprisoned and under sentence of death for his raid at Harper's Ferry.

It is not known when Watkins met Fenton Harper, a widower from Cincinnati, whom she married in 1860. At thirty-five, Frances Ellen Watkins Harper seemed disposed toward retirement from public life. She and her husband settled on a farm near Columbus where Harper continued to write, probably working on new poems and the manuscript for *Moses.* Details from this period in her life are quite sketchy, but a child, Mary, was born to the Harpers and Fenton Harper died in 1864.

After her husband's death, Harper gave up farm life and resumed her lecturing. Following emancipation, she went South for the first time, traveling and lecturing, using her own earnings and living among the people she met. She shared her observations and reports of her experiences through her lectures and writings, and she created the basis for much of her work of the 1870s. Harper's travels in the South added an important dimension to her work; she could combine her interest in moral and social causes with her understanding of the needs of newly freed black people, women in particular. Since Harper had a well-established reputation and firsthand knowledge about the South, she was in a better position than most to speak of the concerns of the Reconstruction period and to advocate civil and equal rights for blacks and women.

Harper's views on women matured during her southern tour. William Grant Still, with whom she corresponded regularly during this period, comments in *The Underground Railroad* (1871) that Harper noted the continuing problems of southern black women: "They have had, some of them, a terribly hard time in Slavery and their subjugation has not ceased in freedom. One man said of some women, that a man must leave them or whip them." Particularly sensitive to the role of working women, Harper was known for refusing payment for lectures attended by women.

Harper's first tour of the South concluded in 1867. She returned to Philadelphia but was there less than a year before returning to the South, where she traveled widely between 1868 and 1871. The years spent touring the South not only inspired her interest in southern black rural women but proved to be Harper's most productive as well. Of the three works written in this period—*Moses: A Story of the Nile* (later enlarged as *Idylls of the Bible*, 1901), *Poems* (1871), and *Sketches of Southern Life* (1872)—*Moses* is considered by critics to be Harper's best work. A dramatic biblical allegory without overt racial references, the forty-page, blank verse poem nevertheless prophesies the rise of a racial leader analogous to Moses. Possibly inspired by Abraham Lincoln, whom she had previously compared to Moses, Harper narrates the familiar biblical story to symbolize the hope and aspirations of black people; she urges moral uprightness and articulates the need for physical and spiritual freedom. She admonishes her black audience to avoid the fate of the Israelites: "If slavery only laid its weight of chains/Upon the weary, aching limbs, e'en then/It were a curse; but when it frets through nerve/And flesh and eats into the weary soul,/Oh then it is a thing for every human/Heart to loathe, and this was Israel's fate,/They failed to strike the impress from their souls." Harper's other themes—the importance of motherhood, the example of history—are also present in the work. Moses' mother is depicted as a woman who never gives up hope, even when her son is about to be named the future heir to the throne of Egypt. When he decides to return to help his people, she is his mainstay and is credited with instilling in him a sense of racial pride. Moses is quite aware of the choice he has to make; the pleasures of a full life must be weighed against lofty purposes and earnest faith. The moral of the story was that the fate of Israel might be the fate of American blacks. The message was that the struggle for freedom was as yet incomplete; although the Civil War had brought physical freedom, Reconstruction through domestic morality, suffrage, and temperance would have to bring spiritual freedom.

Shortly after Harper returned permanently to Philadelphia with her daughter Mary, who never married, she published the two volumes, *Poems*

Mary E. Harper (courtesy of Schomburg Center for Research in Black Culture, the New York Public Library, Astor, Lenox and Tilden Foundations)

(1871) and *Sketches of Southern Life* (1872). Together, the volumes represent the multifaceted, and sometimes contradictory, aspects of Reconstruction.

Sketches of Southern Life is a series of connected verse narratives written in a black vernacular speech, but not in the highly stylized, exaggerated black dialect so common in the regionalists of the late nineteenth century. The narrators are former slaves who, on the surface, closely resemble the cunning and deceptive folk narrators of antebellum literature such as Uncle Remus in the tales of Joel Chandler Harris. *Sketches of Southern Life*, however, differs from this older tradition, for narrators Aunt Chloe and Uncle Jacob, although combining the wisdom of their long years with a characteristic mysticism, have a high degree of political consciousness. They discuss the condition of blacks and the role of education, politics, and religion in uplifting the race. In their innovative style and theme, these narratives provide a dynamic portrait of slave and rural life: the attitudes of slave masters at the advent of the Civil War; the selling of children and eventual reunion of families; the church as the guardian of the social, spiritual, and moral life of black people; and the hopes and failures of Reconstruction.

Aunt Chloe is especially effective in expressing Watkins's attitude toward the need for literacy among black people, especially black women. In "Learning to Read," Chloe relates the persistence and tremendous risks involved in learning to read during slavery.

Very soon the Yankee teachers
  Came down and set up school;
But, oh! how the Rebs did hate it,—
  It was agin' their rule.

Our masters always tried to hide
  Book learning from our eyes;
Knowledge didn't agree with slavery—
  'Twould make us all too wise.

But some of us would try to steal
  A little from the book,
And put the words together,
  And learn by hook or crook.

For Chloe, as for Harper, the acquisition of literacy is clearly related to economic independence, an attitude Melba Boyd calls one of the more independent, black feminist ideas of the period. Yet such radical ideas are tempered in the narrator's last words, couched in a tone of mild humor and pride.

And I longed to read my Bible,
  For precious words it said;
But when I begun to learn it,
  Folks just shook their heads.

And said there is no use trying,
  Oh! Chloe, you're too late;
But I was rising sixty,
  I had no time to wait.

So I got a pair of glasses,
  And straight to work I went'
And never stopped till I could read
  The hymns and Testament.

Then I got a little cabin,
  A place to call my own—
And I felt as independent
  As the queen upon her throne.

Political reform, civil rights, Christian humanism, and human perfection represented various dimensions of political activism for Harper that are comfortably merged in her public speeches and in her poetry. In a letter quoted by Still in *Underground Railroad*, she expressed her belief in a common ground between the races. She cautions whites, however, that devotion to the welfare of the state "does not consist in increasing the privileges of one class and curtailing the rights of the other." In her view the devastation wrought by the American caste system leads into the heart of the black family and reverberates on every level of an individual's life. She says, "While I am in favor of universal suffrage, yet I know that the colored man needs something more than a vote in his hand; he needs to know the value of a home-life; to rightly appreciate and value the marriage relation; to know how to be incited to leave behind him the old shards and shells of slavery . . . like Nautilus, outgrowing his home to build for himself more stately temples of social condition. A man landless, ignorant and poor may use the vote against his own interests, but with intelligence and land he holds in his hand the basis of power and elements of strength."

Once in Philadelphia, Harper began to involve herself in social and reform organizations which would claim her as their spokesperson for forty years. In 1872 she organized and became an assistant superintendent of a YMCA Sabbath School. Several years later, she worked with the American Association of Education of Colored

Youth, becoming its director in 1894. Maintaining her relationship with the AME church, Harper became involved in many of their activities and her writings frequently appeared in their denominational publications.

Harper's activities with the women's movement of the late nineteenth century have become legendary. She was one of the first black women associated with three predominately white and well-established women's organizations, the Women's Christian Temperance Union, the American Woman Suffrage Association, and the National Council of Women. In political philosophy, Harper shared the views of the temperance movement activists, who considered social and moral issues of prime importance. Like many of these women, Harper campaigned fervently against lynching and against sexism in the education of women. As early as 1867, Harper had become a leader in the American Equal Rights Association along with Frederick Douglass, Susan B. Anthony, and Elizabeth Cady Stanton. She was the only black person to serve on the Executive Committee of the segregated Women's Christian Temperance Union, and in that position she fought hard to change the policy on organizational segregation. Between 1875 and 1882, she was superintendent of the Philadelphia and Pennsylvania chapters of the National Women's Christian Temperance Union, Colored Branch, and continued to be active with the organization as head of the Northern United States WCTU from 1883 to 1893. Although she frequently spoke out against the racism in this organization, she consistently represented the views of those who considered universal suffrage too radical a demand for the day. Her work with the WCTU was recognized by that organization when she was placed on the Red Letter Calendar of the World WCTU in 1922.

Between 1875 and 1892, Harper apparently divided her time between the temperance movement, her Sunday school work, the National Council of Women, woman suffrage organizations, and her writing. There is no consistent record of her activities during these years. She attended at least two conventions of the American Woman Suffrage Association (1875 and 1887), and she delivered speeches at the International Council of Women in Washington in 1888 and the National Council of Women in 1891. Harper must have been thinking about her forthcoming novel *Iola Leroy; or, Shadows Uplifted* (1892) when she spoke on the "Duty to Dependent Races" at the National Council. Not only was this speech one of her most comprehensive and persuasive, according to her contemporaries, but it also encompassed all the ideas expressed in her novel. In the address, Harper urged women to work on behalf of equal rights and improved social conditions for blacks and women; the heroine of *Iola Leroy* personifies the ideal that Harper had in mind when she spoke.

Critic Louis Filler has mistakenly suggested that *Iola Leroy* seemed to have been written for the "edification of Negro Sunday school youth." Filler and other scholars missed the significance of the publication of this book about a committed young black woman, steeped in her own contradictory racial heritage, who defies convention. Published when Harper was sixty-seven, *Iola Leroy,* in some ways an unconventional story, was the first widely distributed novel by a black woman in America.

Iola Leroy is written in the tradition of the sentimental novel and displays many of the genteel characteristics of black fiction written after the Civil War. Set on the eve of the war, the study describes the search for a lost family. A somewhat detached, participant-observer, Iola Leroy travels through the South listening to the narrative histories of former slaves who have become successful merchants and landowners. Iola's mother, Marie, and her brother Harry are looking for Iola; Robert Johnson, Iola's uncle, is looking for his sister Marie and his mother, Mrs. Johnson. Robert represents the earlier generation and the intensity of slave degradation. Robert, Marie, and Mrs. Johnson are victims of the slave trade in which families were separated. Marie is bought by a kindly master who frees, educates, and marries her. Iola Leroy is born from this union. It is only after the death of the master father, while Iola is away at a northern school, that Marie is forced back into slavery. Iola, too, becomes a house slave, but she is released to serve as an army nurse. Harper then sets up a triangle between Iola, a white physician who loves her, and a black physician, whom Iola is destined to marry.

As in many typical sentimental novels, *Iola Leroy* has a heroine with flowing, blonde hair and blue eyes who is pursued by an unsuccessful suitor and in her turn pursues another. The novel has Harper's racial and moral concerns, and it presents black characters as idealized types. Here the novel's resemblance to the nineteenth-century stereotype stops, however, for Harper explores nontraditional themes in relation to her women characters, and she does not fall prey to sentimentalizing Iola's discovery of her true identity. There are innovations, as well, in the employment of the mulatto motif.

Iola is not passive, weak, nor simple, as mulattoes of miscegenation novels frequently were. Rather she is fiercely independent, insisting that women must be "self-reliant" and that they should receive educations equal to men. The theme of a commitment to the education of the free black is in keeping with the aims of social reform of the period, but Harper's somewhat unorthodox view of the changing roles of women suggests that she was a bit more racial than her colleagues.

Iola experiences no inner conflict regarding her black racial identity nor is she unable to reconcile her roles as social activist and wife. She remains true to her goals of becoming professionally independent, working in the South, and marrying a black man who shares her commitment to uplift the race.

A sensitivity to the special plight and oppression of black working women and former slave women distinguished Harper from white feminists of the period, many of whom supported the policies of racial segregation in their own organizations. This theme was prominent in her writing and in her public speeches of this period. As early as 1878, she invoked the term "double duty," when she wrote in "The Colored Woman of America," for the *Englishwoman's Review,* that rural women had their housework and also ran the farms on which they lived in the absence of their fathers, husbands, or male companions, working together sometimes with their own children or another female partner.

"Double Standard," one of the poems from *The Sparrow's Fall* (1890?), expresses what might be considered the popular feminist sentiment of the era. The poem is sharply critical of a society that will excuse a man for his sexual improprieties while condemning the woman for hers:

Crime has no sex and yet today
    I wear the brand of shame
Whilst he amid the gay and proud
    Still bears an honored name.

Can you blame me if I've learned to think
    Your hate of vice a shame,
When you so coldly crushed me down,
    And excused the man?

In the final stanzas, the narrator's optimism is restored as she thinks of God's love and justice as opposed to man's.

POEMS

BY

FRANCES E. W. HARPER

PHILADELPHIA:
1006 BAINBRIDGE STREET
1900

Title page for the second enlarged edition of Harper's 1895 collection

No golden weights can turn the scale
    Of justice in His sight;
And what is wrong in woman's life
    In man's cannot be right.

After almost a century of relative critical neglect *Iola Leroy; or, Shadows Uplifted* is slowly being accorded a place in the canon of Afro-American literature. Barbara Christian, in *Black Feminist Criticism: Perspectives on Black Women Writers* (1985), notes that Harper's novel has characteristics, such as the theme of the tragic mulatto, which remain dominant in the fiction of later black women novelists. According to Christian the audience for the novelistic romance was primarily female, and Harper modified the idealized heroine of the novel with some of the features of the late-nineteenth-century black women. By doing so, Harper accomplished her own purpose of writing an inspirational and consciousness-raising work, which would have had a very wide circulation within the growing movement.

Despite the apparent radicalism of *Iola Leroy*, Harper took a somewhat conservative view on suffrage as she spoke before the 1893 World Congress of Representative Women at the Columbian Exposition in Chicago. In her address, "Women's Political Future," she made her now-often-quoted statement opposing unrestricted and universal suffrage for men or women, believing, as she indicated, in moral and educational tests. At the close of this speech she delivered a stirring call to women: "O Women of America! into your hands God has pressed one of the sublimest opportunities that ever came into the hands of the women of any race or people. It is yours to create a healthy public sentiment; to demand justice, simple justice, as the right of every race; to brand with everlasting infamy the lawless and brutal cowardice that lynches, burns, and tortures your own countrymen."

Differences of opinion on universal suffrage or other political issues were normal for the period; yet, they did not prevent black women from organizing. Harper shared many of the ideas about the special needs of black women held by Ida Wells Barnett, Victoria Earle Matthews, Susan McKinney, and Josephine St. Pierre Ruffin, all of whom had been instrumental in forming the black women's club movement, beginning in 1892. These clubs merged to form the National Association of Colored Women, established in Washington, D.C., in 1895, with Harper as one of its founding members.

After *Iola Leroy* Harper published *Atlanta Offering, Poems* (1895), which included the previously published *The Sparrow's Fall and Other Poems* and *The Martyr of Alabama and Other Poems* (1894?), as well as other work. Like most of Harper's writings before the Civil War, the themes in this collected volume were familiar to her audience. There is her characteristic didacticism and morality, especially her pronouncements against racism, illiteracy, and physical abuse, particularly against women and children, and a reliance upon biblical themes and imagery. Many of the poems contained in this volume were inspired by her travels throughout the South, and they reflect her strong optimism and social commitment.

"The Martyr of Alabama," a rather unusual challenge to Harper's hopefulness about social conditions, concerns the murder of a black boy who refuses to entertain whites. The poem is as much a tribute to his Christian martyrdom as it is an indictment of the depravity of whites.

"Come dance for us," the rough men said;
    "I can't," the child replied.
"I cannot for the dear Lord's sake,
    Who for my sins once died."
. . . .
Then recklessly a man arose
    And dealt a fearful blow.
He crushed the portals of that life,
    And laid the brave child low.

And trampled on his prostrate form
    As on a broken toy;
Then danced with careless, brutal feet,
    Upon the murdered boy.

Christians! behold that martyred child!
    His blood cries from the ground;
Before the sleepless eye of God,
    He shows each gaping wound.

Thus despite her praise for "The Present Age," Harper was always prepared to expose the truth. Her poetry registers a constant plea for social, moral, and political reform through Christian unity and an adherence to Christian principles. In all of these collections, Harper continued to portray black people who had been victimized by slavery and who continued to be exploited after emancipation.

Harper's last political and social involvement was her organizing work with the National Association of Colored Women, which represented the struggle for civil rights both for blacks and women. It embodied the very ideals that had been Harper's life's work and it involved such leading black figures as Harriet Tubman, Mary Church Terrell, and Ida Wells Barnett—some of whom she had worked with for more than forty years. Although she had retired from the WCTU, she accepted the vice-presidency of the NACW a year after its founding (1897). In this position, she became even more vocal on the subject of women and equal rights. Thus, Harper, like many of the reformers of the period, is seen as a prototypical feminist; renewed interest in her among twentieth-century feminists is due to this fact. If we accept the view put forward by Paula Giddings in *When and Where I Enter* (1984) that the convictions held by black women leaders such as Harper "inevitably led to feminist ideas," certainly more thoroughgoing criticism of Frances Harper's literary and ideological contribution is long overdue.

After 1901 Harper appeared less and less in public; her health was declining and she was nearly eighty years old. Apparently her daughter died sometime in the first decade of the twentieth century, preceding Harper herself by only a few years. On 22 February 1911 Frances Ellen Watkins Harper died of heart failure. The most significant black woman poet of the nineteenth century, Harper had remained in the forefront of radical black and women's movements, yet her passing went relatively unnoticed. Although few of her books, manuscripts, and correspondence have been preserved, and no full-length biography has yet been written of Harper, studies that critically assess her work and importance as a literary and historical figure are beginning to appear.

References:

Robert Bone, *The Negro Novel in America* (New Haven: Yale University Press, 1965);

Barbara Christian, *Black Feminist Criticism: Perspectives on Black Women Writers* (Elmsford, N.Y.: Pergamon, 1985), pp. 167-172;

Christian, *Black Women Novelists: The Development of a Tradition 1892-1976* (Westport, Conn.: Greenwood, 1980), pp. 3-5, 25-30;

Theodora Williams Daniel, "The Poems of Frances E. W. Harper. Edited with a Biographical and Critical Introduction, and Bibliography," M.A. thesis, Howard University, 1937;

Paula Giddings, *When and Where I Enter . . . The Impact of Black Women on Race and Sex in America* (New York: Morrow, 1984);

Hugh Gloster, *Negro Voices in American Fiction* (Chapel Hill: University of North Carolina Press, 1948);

Maryemma Graham, "The Threefold Cord: Blackness, Womanness and Art, A Study of the Life and Work of Frances Ellen Watkins Harper," M.A. thesis, Cornell University, 1973;

Patricia Liggins Hill, " 'Let Me Make the Songs for the People': A Study of Frances Watkins Harper's Poetry," *Black American Literature Forum*, 15 (Summer 1981): 60-65;

Bert James Loewenberg and Ruth Bogin, *Black Women in Nineteenth Century American Life, Their Words, Their Thoughts, Their Feelings* (University Park: Pennsylvania State University Press, 1976), pp. 243-251;

J. Saunders Redding, *To Make a Poet Black* (Chapel Hill: University of North Carolina Press, 1939), pp. 38-44;

Lawson A. Scruggs, *Women of Distinction* (Raleigh: L. A. Scruggs, 1893);

Joan R. Sherman, *Invisible Poets: Afro-Americans of the Nineteenth Century* (Urbana: University of Illinois, 1974), pp. 62-74;

William Grant Still, *The Underground Railroad* (Philadelphia: Porter & Coates, 1872), pp. 755-780.

Papers:

The largest collections of Harper's books and pamphlets are housed at the Moorland-Spingarn Research Center, Howard University, Washington, D.C., and at the Schomburg Center for Research in Black Culture, the New York Public Library.

Walter Everette Hawkins

(17 November 1883-death date unknown)

Dickson D. Bruce, Jr.
University of California, Irvine

BOOKS: *Chords and Discords* (Washington, D.C.: Murray Brothers, 1909; revised edition, Boston: Richard G. Badger, 1920);

Petals from the Poppies (New York: Fortuny's, 1936).

OTHER: "Thus Speaks Africa" and "To Prometheus," in *Negro Anthology,* edited by Nancy Cunard (London: Wishart, 1934; New York: Negro Universities Press, 1969), p. 426.

PERIODICAL PUBLICATIONS: "Poems of Walter Everette Hawkins," *African Times and Orient Review* (London), 1 (Special Christmas Issue 1912-1913);

"Sayings of Walter Everette Hawkins," *African Times and Orient Review* (London), 1 (1913): 212;

"Ethiopian Maid," *Crisis,* 14 (1917): 130;

"The Poets' Corner," *Messenger,* 1 (November 1917): 27;

"The Voice in the Wilderness," *Messenger,* 2 (January 1918): 18-19;

"The Mob Victim," *Messenger,* 2 (July 1918): 27;

"Credo," Supplement to *Messenger,* 2 (March 1919): 2;

"Where Air of Freedom Is," *Messenger,* 2 (May-June 1919): 30;

"The Mob Victim," *Messenger,* 2 (July 1919): 4;

"Child of the Night," *Crisis,* 27 (1924): 258;

"I Am Africa," *Crisis,* 35 (1928): 232;

"Credo," *Negro History Bulletin,* 31 (April 1968): 9.

Walter Everette Hawkins

Walter Everette Hawkins is one of the more obscure, but one of the more unusual Afro-American poets of the early twentieth century, an important figure in the transition of black literature from the genteel modes of the latter nineteenth century to the flowering of black militancy often identified with the Harlem Renaissance. A poet of strong political convictions, Hawkins produced work that often showed fire and ambition. Such pioneering critics of black literature as Sterling Brown, Benjamin Brawley, and Robert Kerlin singled out Hawkins for both his poetic and thematic boldness.

Hawkins was born in Warrenton, North Carolina, in 1883 (several sources give 1886 as Hawkins's year of birth; however, Hawkins himself, in a 1915 *Who's Who* entry, cited the earlier year). He was the thirteenth child of ex-slave parents who were independent farmers, and the much younger brother of the eminent John R. Hawkins (1862-1939). John R. Hawkins was working for the railway mail service at the time of his younger brother's birth, but later went on to become a teacher and, subsequently, president of Kittrell College in North Carolina. This elder brother eventually moved to Washington, D.C., where he held such prominent offices as financial secretary of the African Methodist Episcopal Church—he was married to a descendant of Richard Allen, founder of the A.M.E. Church—and, from 1921 to 1932, president of the Association for the Study of Negro Life and History. Walter Everette Hawkins himself attended Kittrell, graduating in 1901—although he apparently had difficulty getting along with his teachers and received a few dismissals during the course of his education. (He documented his "wayward" youthful life in an autobiographical poem, "Off to the Fields of Green.") Later, like his more prominent brother, he also left North Carolina for Washington, where he worked as a mail clerk in the post office, and where he wrote much of his poetry. Some time during the late 1920s or early 1930s, he moved to Brooklyn, where he published his final volume.

Hawkins's earliest work as a poet was collected in a volume entitled *Chords and Discords,* the first edition of which appeared in 1909. This work showed his significance as a transitional figure in black literary history. Many of the poems were well within the most conservative outlines of black literary tradition of the late nineteenth and early twentieth centuries. Like virtually all black poets up to his time, Hawkins wrote much on racial questions, arguing, not atypically, that as a black poet he had a special duty to use his gifts to make a statement on behalf of racial justice. In his preface to the collection, he made this obligation clear. His volume was, he said, "an appeal," a work which could persuade "courageous, patriotic men and women" to throw off their prejudices and to come to a better understanding of black people and their character.

Hawkins wrote poems on racial themes that were well within the bounds of turn-of-the-century black writing, formally conservative and employing themes and images recognizable to anyone familiar with black literature from the period. In these poems, Hawkins celebrated what he saw as Ethiopia's coming greatness or proclaimed his own defiance of prejudice and injustice. He praised black heroism and, in a poem entitled "The Mob Victim," condemned both the horror of lynching and the "Christian land" that would allow such a practice to continue. These had all been topics with which black poets had dealt for many years, and they occupied an important place in Hawkins's work.

So, too, did poems based on sentimental themes and images, poems mainly about nature and love. These pieces, which were as formally conservative as his poems on racial themes, also put Hawkins squarely in the dominant black literary tradition of his day, as black writers had long focused their attention on creating a genteel, sentimental poetry—a poetry of fine and cultivated feelings that, one should note, fit in fully with the work dominating the mainstream of American popular writing. Hawkins not only did such work but also offered a sentimental portrayal of himself as a poet. At one point in his preface, he stressed his sensitivity by evoking a picture of himself: when growing up on his parents' farm, he received the poetic muse while "resting on my indulgent hoe or freighted bag between the cotton rows." At another point he gives a verbal self-portrait of a youthful Hawkins "dreaming at my desk above my sister's piano-forte." The image of the poet was fully in keeping with the genteel sentimentality of some of his work.

But what made Hawkins a transitional figure was that he moved, in several pieces, significantly away from such conservative boundaries. Hawkins was, more than many others of his time, a poet of social criticism as well as of racial protest. He used his poetry to assail what he saw as the hypocrisy of contemporary life. One of his targets was religion. In "Too Much Religion," for instance, he wrote, "There is too much talk of Heaven,/Too much talk of golden streets,/When one can't be sympathetic/When a needy neighbor meets." Hawkins also condemned the materialism of the age, as in his poem "Money," an ironic paean to "Gold." And he placed himself squarely in the ideological battle that was sharply dividing black leaders in the early twentieth century, the ideological battle over Booker T. Washington's program, the opposition to which was led most notably by W. E. B. Du Bois. This battle, focusing on Washington's apparent willingness to pursue a strategy of economic development while accommodating with some degree of segregation, aroused strong feelings among prominent black men and women after 1900, and Hawkins made no secret of his own anti-Washington feelings. One of his poems was a tribute to Du Bois as the foremost leader of the race. Another was a virulent attack on Washington, whom Hawkins accused of being a "traitor," of having "sold his race to shame." Such outspokenness and such blunt language were hardly common in black poetry prior to 1909, and they betokened a militancy that made Hawkins more than simply a purveyor of tradition.

And, indeed, *Chords and Discords* was, according to Hawkins, a controversial work. He had himself sponsored its printing by the Murray brothers' company, though the printer, Freeman H. M. Murray—an associate of Du Bois's—who had also written a nice introduction to the volume, was unable to sell many copies. Hawkins felt his language had been too strong and his ideas too bold. Although he had no intention of temporizing, neither his language nor his ideas was, he decided, acceptable in an age of what he saw as "sycophancy." But if the period after the publication of his first book brought some discouragement, it also brought further development in Hawkins's thought and in his poetry.

At the center of Hawkins's developing thought was a concern for freedom and "manhood." In his poem condemning Washington, Hawkins had already shown this concern when, echoing Du Bois's own criticism of Washington's materialism, he asked, "Is wealth supreme, and right and manhood less?" A vision of "right and manhood" played a major role in Hawkins's writings for the rest of his literary career.

One direction in which this vision took Hawkins was toward the development of ideas of black consciousness, toward a celebration of the distinctive characteristics and virtues of black people. This change, too, was in keeping with Hawkins's early admiration for Du Bois, who had done much to promulgate ideas of black distinctiveness in his 1903 book, *The Souls of Black Folk.* Hawkins's own movement in this direction was shown in several ways. One was his early membership in one of the first organizations to be formed around the celebration of a distinctive black culture and heritage, the Negro Society for Historical Research. Founded by Arthur Schomburg in 1912, this organization was devoted to uncovering black history, and it attracted a number of individuals who played a part, in the early years of the twentieth century, in developing and popularizing ideas of black distinctiveness. In addition to Schomburg himself, the society included such other prominent figures as David Bryant Fulton, John E. Bruce (with whom Hawkins corresponded), and William H. Ferris, each of whom did important writing on the beauty and unique virtues of black people. Ferris and Bruce, in particular, extended their own ideals of black distinctiveness into an early Pan-Africanism that stressed the unity of black people throughout the world. Both later became involved in the movement led by Marcus Garvey to recover an African homeland.

It is to the point, along these lines, that Hawkins's next significant publication was a selection of his poems in the 1912-1913 issue of *African Times and Orient Review,* a periodical published in London. Edited by Duse Mohamed, an Egyptian who also gave early encouragement to Garvey, the *Review* focused on people of color throughout the world and took a decidedly Pan-Africanist point of view. It published the works of several American writers, but, in its first "grand Christmas number," the *Review* actually featured a group of poems by Walter Everette Hawkins. Most of these works were taken from *Chords and Discords* and included pieces on both sentimental and racial themes. But one poem was new and made especially clear how Hawkins's thought was developing at the time. "Child of the Night" is a poem that plays on imagery of night and blackness, making a plea for racial justice but also evoking an almost mystical black pride and black heritage. "Child of the Night am I," the poet proclaimed, and, in a recurrent motif, wrote, "I stood arrayed in Night/Ere light was born." "The beginning was blackness and so will the end be;/Black God and black angels, surround and defend me!" It was an unusual poem for 1912, when it first appeared, reminiscent, perhaps, of Du Bois's own 1899 "The Song of the Smoke," but just as clearly it looked forward to some of the key themes and images of the Harlem Renaissance.

In fact, during the Harlem Renaissance, Hawkins published other pieces that showed an interest in ideas of black distinctiveness. Although he was hardly a major figure in that great burst of black literary activity following World War I, he did publish three poems in *Crisis*—an organ of the NAACP important to the Harlem Renaissance and edited for a time by Du Bois—which showed sympathy for the movement's celebration of black culture and a black heritage. One poem was the earlier "Child of the Night," which reappeared in 1924. In 1917, however, and at the very inception of the Harlem Renaissance, he published "Ethiopian Maid," a tribute to the beauty and virtue of black women, albeit a rather conservative, even sentimental tribute. More significant was "I Am Africa," a poem quoted approvingly by Sterling Brown in his classic 1937 study of *Negro Poetry and Drama.* This poem appeared in *Crisis* in 1928, although it had earlier been published in 1927 in an anthology of Washington poets, *Black and White,* edited by J. C. Byars. In this poem, and breaking from his older formal conservatism, Hawkins evoked the history and resources of Africa and directly connected the lives of Afro-Americans with those of their African forebears and contemporaries. Reminiscent of Langston Hughes's "The Negro Speaks of Rivers," Hawkins wrote,

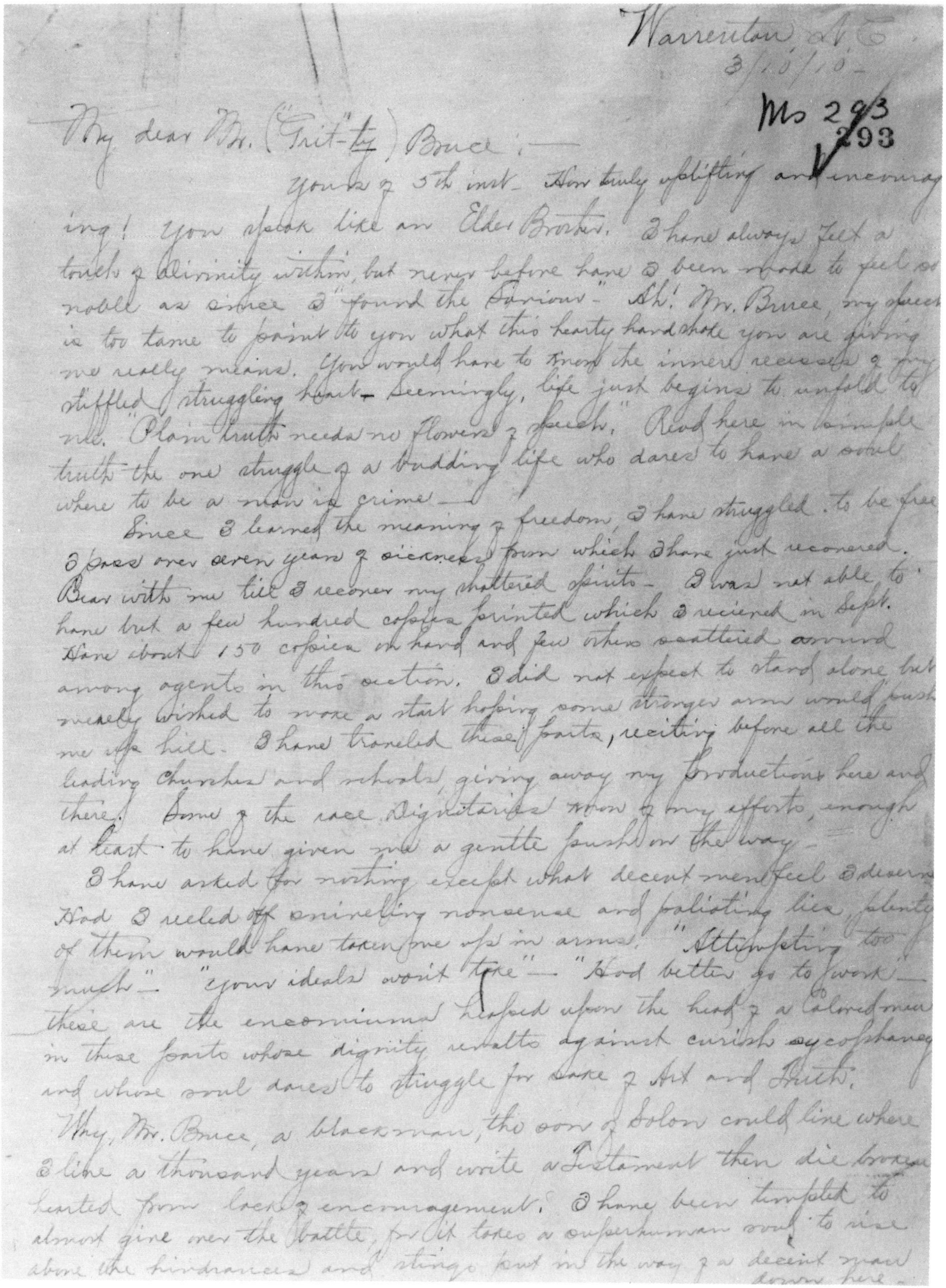

Warrenton N.C.
3/10/10—

My dear Mr. ("Grit-ty") Bruce:—
Yours of 5th inst. How truly uplifting and encouraging! You speak like an Elder Brother. I have always felt a touch of divinity within, but never before have I been made to feel so noble as since I "found the Saviour". Ah! Mr. Bruce, my speech is too tame to paint to you what this hearty handshake you are giving me really means. You would have to know the inner recesses of my stiffled struggling heart. Seemingly, life just begins to unfold to me. "Plain truth needs no flowers of speech." Read here in simple truth the one struggle of a budding life who dares to have a soul where to be a man is crime—

Since I learned the meaning of freedom, I have struggled to be free. I pass over seven years of sickness from which I have just recovered. Bear with me till I recover my shattered spirits. I was not able to have but a few hundred copies printed which I recieved in Sept. Have about 150 copies on hand and few others scattered around among agents in this section. I did not expect to stand alone but merely wished to make a start hoping some stronger arm would push me up hill. I have traveled these parts, reciting before all the leading Churches and schools, giving away my productions here and there. Some of the race Dignitaries know of my efforts, enough at least to have given me a gentle push on the way.

I have asked for nothing except what decent men feel I deserve. Had I reeled off snivelling nonsense and palliating lies, plenty of them would have taken me up in arms. "Attempting too much"— "your ideals won't take"— "Had better go to work"— these are the encomiums heaped upon the head of a colored man in these parts whose dignity revolts against currish sycophancy and whose soul dares to struggle for sake of Art and Truth.

Why, Mr. Bruce, a black man, tho' son of Solon could live where I live a thousand years and write a Testament then die broken hearted from lack of encouragement. I have been tempted to almost give over the battle, for it takes a superhuman soul to rise above the hindrances and stings put in the way of a decent man down here—

First page of a 1910 letter to John E. Bruce written by Hawkins shortly after he "found the Saviour" (courtesy of Schomburg Center for Research in Black Culture, the New York Public Library, Astor, Lenox and Tilden Foundations)

On the fertile banks of the Congo
My sorrow in song I have lifted;
In the cane brakes and cornfields of Texas
My sorrow songs still I am singing.

And, again, he sought to evoke a mystical power in blackness, as well as to protest the violent injustices of American racism. If, by 1927 or 1928, the poem was hardly innovative, it did show a poet who could capture much of the spirit of his age.

But more important for Hawkins's later career as a poet was his brief association with the Harlem magazine, the *Messenger,* edited by A. Philip Randolph and Chandler Owen (the latter a native of Hawkins's own hometown of Warrenton, though six years Hawkins's junior). The *Messenger* was in the center of some of the most significant issues in postwar Harlem political and intellectual life. Seeking to take a socialist perspective on American racial problems, the *Messenger* was the most important black periodical to try to show the strong relationship between racism and capitalism in American life and to explore the relationships between class and race. It was, in addition, a magazine whose editors were unwavering in their opposition to Marcus Garvey's more racially oriented (and economically conservative) Pan-Africanism. Despite Hawkins's own earlier ties with such future Garveyites as John E. Bruce, and despite his efforts to produce poems of black distinctiveness, his work in the *Messenger* shows a powerful attraction to the magazine's ideas.

Hawkins was associated with the *Messenger* during its earliest, and most radical, days. Publishing regularly in the magazine between 1917 and 1919, he was actually listed on two occasions as "The Messenger Poet." Several of Hawkins's *Messenger* contributions were drawn from his earlier work, and even included his more sentimental pieces, as well as such works of social criticism as "Too Much Religion." Among these, too, was the antilynching poem from *Chords and Discords,* "The Mob Victim," published this time without Hawkins's name. Interestingly, though the poem broke no new ground as a work within black literary tradition, it nevertheless attracted the attention of the United States Department of Justice, probably because of its publication in the *Messenger.* In 1919, during America's first great Red Scare, the department printed it as evidence in an investigative report on the *Messenger* and other magazines which were accused of advising sedition. Indeed, Hawkins's poem was printed to prove that the issue of the *Messenger* in which it appeared was "particularly radical." Hawkins had written:

O heathen minds on heathen strand,
What think you of a Christian land,
Where men and boys and women turn
From prayer, to lynch, to rob and burn,
And oft their drowsy minds refresh
Thru sport in burning human flesh?

Black writers had long found white America guilty of violating its own best standards. Thus, Hawkins's poem was far from unique in the form of its indictment of American lynching. That the Justice Department should have singled it out likely had more to do with its ignorance of black thought and rhetoric and with the hysteria of the Red Scare than with anything unusual in the poem itself. Years later, Hawkins sarcastically gave "special thanks" to the Justice Department "for printing voluntarily the poem . . . and distributing same without any expense to me." He added, "This is, to my knowledge, the first instance in the history of the United States in which any poet has had such distinction conferred upon him by any Department of the United States Government."

One of Hawkins's *Messenger* poems was, however, new. Appearing in 1919, this poem was entitled "Credo," and in it Hawkins spoke in a language that broke strikingly from older black literary tradition, carrying his own anger to a new level (even if failing to attract the Justice Department's attention). "I am an Iconoclast," the poet declared,

I break the limbs of idols
And smash the traditions of men.
  I am an Anarchist.
I believe in war and destruction,—
Not in the killing of men, but
The killing of creed and custom.

Calling himself "an Agnostic," as well, Hawkins proclaimed his opposition to all laws, creeds, and "conventionalities" which "obstruct the reign of Right." If it is possible to see how such a poem could have evolved from the work of a writer who, a decade before, had used his work to condemn the hypocrisy of "too much talk of heaven," the poetic freedom of the piece was matched by its message as an effort on Hawkins's part to throw off the past and to develop a radical consciousness as a man and a poet.

Both the black consciousness of Hawkins's *Crisis* poems and the radicalism of his *Messenger* pieces make the 1920 revised edition of *Chords and*

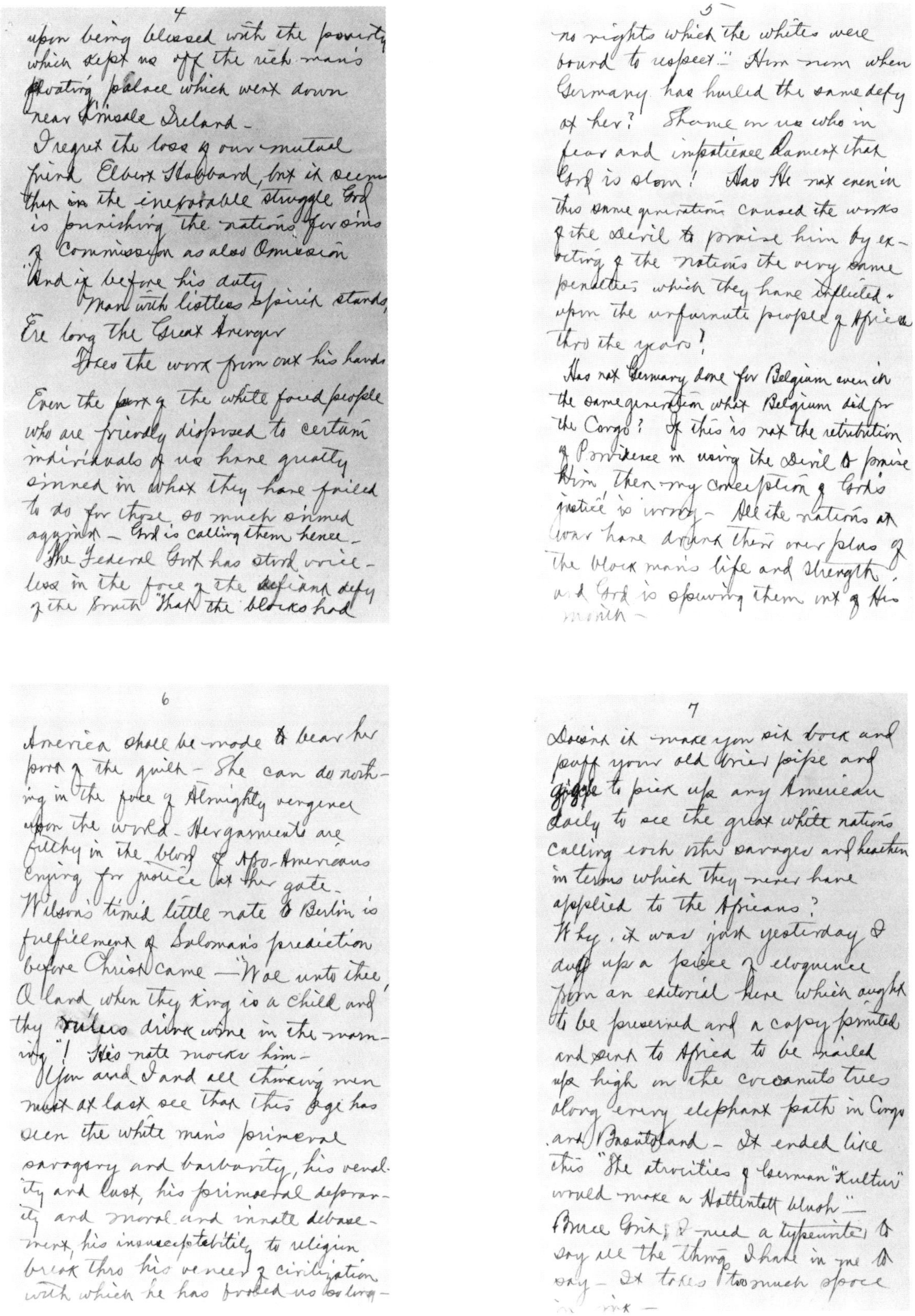

4

upon being blessed with the poverty which kept us off the rich man's floating palace which went down near Kinsale Ireland -
I regret the loss of our mutual friend Elbert Hubbard, but it seems that in the inevitable struggle God is punishing the nations for sins of Commission as also Omission
And if before his duty
Man with listless spirit stands,
Ere long the Great Avenger
Takes the work from out his hands
Even the part of the white faced people who are friendly disposed to certain individuals of us have greatly sinned in what they have failed to do for those so much sinned against - God is calling them hence -
The Federal Govt has stood voiceless in the face of the defiant defy of the South "That the blacks had

5

no rights which the whites were bound to respect." Hum - now when Germany has hurled the same defy at her? Shame on us who in fear and impatience lament that God is slow! Has He not even in this same generation caused the works of the devil to praise him by exacting of the nations the very same penalties which they have inflicted upon the unfortunate people of Africa thro the years?
Has not Germany done for Belgium even in the same generation what Belgium did for the Congo? If this is not the retribution of Providence in using the devil to praise Him, then my conception of God's justice is wrong - All the nations at war have drunk their over plus of the black man's life and strength and God is spewing them out of His mouth -

6

America shall be made to bear her part of the guilt - She can do nothing in the face of Almighty vengeance upon the world - Her garments are filthy in the blood of Afro-Americans crying for justice at her gate.
Wilson's timid little note to Berlin is fulfillment of Solomon's prediction before Christ came - "Woe unto thee, O land when thy king is a child and thy rulers drink wine in the morning"! His note mocks him -
You and I and all thinking men must at last see that this age has seen the white man's primeval savagery and barbarity, his venality and lust, his primordial depravity and moral and innate debasement, his insusceptibility to religion break thro his veneer of civilization with which he has fooled us so long -

7

Doesn't it make you sit back and puff your old briar pipe and giggle to pick up any American daily to see the great white nations calling each other savages and heathen in terms which they never have applied to the Africans?
Why, it was just yesterday I dug up a piece of eloquence from an editorial here which ought to be preserved and a copy printed and sent to Africa to be nailed up high on the cocoanut trees along every elephant path in Congo and Basutoland - It ended like this "The atrocities of German 'Kultur' would make a Hottentott blush" -
Bruce Grit, I need a typewriter to say all the things I have in me to say - It takes too much space in ink -

Pages from Hawkins's 17 May 1913 letter to John E. Bruce in which he details the retribution world war will bring to whites (courtesy of Schomburg Center for Research in Black Culture, the New York Public Library, Astor, Lenox and Tilden Foundations)

Discords all the more interesting. Not surprisingly, it included none of the earlier poems on the Washington-Du Bois debate, since, by 1920, the debate itself was pretty much a dead issue. But it also omitted those poems of black consciousness which Hawkins had published before 1920, "Child of the Night" and "Ethiopian Maid." Indeed, strikingly absent from this second edition of *Chords and Discords* were virtually all those poems from the first edition that had dealt with racial issues. Only "The Mob Victim," retitled "A Festival in Christendom," remained. Instead, the more topical poems appearing in the collection all served to emphasize Hawkins's attachment to the kind of radicalism consistent with his *Messenger* associations. "Credo" appears near the end of the book. So, too, do such poems pointing toward a class-oriented radicalism as "Land of the Living Lie," in which Hawkins condemns "the thieves and lords" who grind men down, who make "grist in the mills" of the "souls of men." The volume also reprints such poems of social criticism as "Too Much Religion."

There is not enough evidence, apart from the poetry itself, to explain why the 1920 *Chords and Discords* should have taken the shape it did, and why, in particular, Hawkins should have omitted those works celebrating blackness. As the *Messenger*'s opposition to Garveyism makes clear, there was a real tension between a socialist radicalism and the racially oriented rhetoric of black consciousness—including that of the Garvey movement. This tension remained strong through the 1920s and even into the 1930s. But there is no clear basis for arguing that in *Chords and Discords* Hawkins was, somehow, choosing sides. He may have been, but the course of his literary career and, particularly, his *Crisis* poems of the mid- to late-1920s make such a view hard to sustain.

But no less striking than the political thrust of the book is that the bulk of its poems are sentimental pieces, focusing on familiar topics of nature and love, treating those topics in familiar, sentimental ways. Some of those poems date back to the first edition of *Chords and Discords*. Others are new.

What one can say with confidence, then, about the character of the 1920 *Chords and Discords* is that taken in light of Hawkins's work, first for the *African Times and Orient Review* and later for the *Messenger* and the *Crisis*, it helps to stress Hawkins's place in black literature as a genuinely transitional figure. Drawn, for a time, to developing ideas of black distinctiveness and, building on the social criticism of his earlier work, to a radicalism that was social as well as political, he also remained tied to the sentimental ideals of his earliest poetry, as Hawkins himself acknowledged in his preface to the book. He wrote, "If I can add to the life of another just a gleam of good cheer, a tint of golden gladness, or a bubble of pure, honest laughter, I shall feel that I am helping to plume the pinions with which we wing ourselves upward. . . . If there be some Discords here which seem harsh to some, know that the harshest note which language owns is mild as childhood's lightest song compared with the pangs of the soul that seeks expression here." Hawkins's understanding of poetry as an expression of feelings, and as an inspiration to feelings, was well in keeping with the sentimental ideals of his earliest work; even his strongest protest poems were justified in terms of those older ideas.

Hawkins's inability to break completely from older sentimental forms was equally apparent in his final volume, *Petals from the Poppies*, published in New York in 1936 following his move to Brooklyn. The book was filled with radical ideas, and Hawkins declared that this was, from his point of view, an important part of its purpose. In his preface he wrote, "Poetry cannot be divorced easily from propaganda, since all Art is to a large extent propaganda. It should, therefore, ally itself with those forces contending mightily for universal justice, freedom and peace; and against all those influences and institutions of evil, oppression and cruelty however ancient and respected they might have become." The words bespeak, as well, Hawkins's continuing attraction to the socialist-inspired radicalism of his *Messenger* days. Indeed, if the poems are any indication, that attraction had become even stronger in the years leading up to 1936.

Several of the poems help to show a clear leftist orientation in Hawkins's point of view. In "My Heart Is a Poppy," for example, Hawkins uses the color of the poppy as a metaphor for his own heart, which is "red as Moscow,—/Crimson as the Kremlin/Where Lenin sleeps." "To Prometheus" begins, "Hail, Prometheus, glad to meet you,/Fellow-radical, I greet you" and concludes:

'Tis my knowledge and belief,
Men don't set a petty thief
Up for worship;
Had you stole a Tea-Pot Dome,
You'd be wined and dined in Rome,
And New York, and Washington;
You would be a favorite son
To be bishop.

This poem, one should note, first appeared in 1934 in Nancy Cunard's left-oriented *Negro Anthology*, perhaps a measure of Hawkins's views, as well. Hawkins even went so far as to drastically revise two of his earlier celebrations of blackness, "I Am Africa" and "Child of the Night," to orient them far less toward a kind of Pan-Africanism and far more toward a proletarian literature of worker solidarity.

Yet he continued to write sentimental poetry, and even, after a fashion, to defend it. If art had to be propaganda, it also had, according to Hawkins, to aim at beauty and truth which, he wrote in a very traditional fashion, portray "the highest and noblest cultures of the mind." His final volume thus held to form, mixing poems of radicalism with the most sentimental verses about nature and love, some of which dated as far back as his 1909 *Chords and Discords*, others of which were new to *Petals from the Poppies*.

Even in the mid-1930s, then, Hawkins remained a transitional figure. Occasionally he attempted to break new poetic ground, and, certainly, he produced political poetry that was as consistent in its leftism as the work of any other black poet of his time. Indeed, his political poems in *Petals from the Poppies* were probably more persistently leftist than the work of any other black poet through the 1930s. But he framed his radicalism in a context that looked steadfastly backward to an earlier time, to a poetry of sentimentality and even gentility. Given the available evidence about Hawkins's life, it is difficult to say why he did this, and, because the evidence is so sparse, one hesitates to speculate. Perhaps it is enough to say that Hawkins's work helps to reveal, more clearly, the forms and questions arising out of black intellectual life in the first third of the twentieth century.

References:

Benjamin Brawley, *The Negro Genius: A New Appraisal of the Achievement of the American Negro in Literature and the Fine Arts* (New York: Dodd, Mead, 1937), pp. 238-239;

Sterling A. Brown, *Negro Poetry and Drama* (Washington, D.C.: Associates in Negro Folk Education, 1937), p. 63;

J. C. Byars, *Black and White* (Washington, D.C.: Crane Press, 1927);

Arthur P. Davis and Michael W. Peplow, *The New Negro Renaissance: An Anthology* (New York: Holt, Rinehart & Winston, 1975), pp. 41, 524;

John William Gibson, *Progress of a Race*, revised and enlarged by J. L. Nichols and William H. Crogman (Naperville, Ill.: J. L. Nichols, 1920), p. 385;

Robert T. Kerlin, *Negro Poets and Their Poems*, revised and enlarged edition (Washington, D.C.: Associated Publishers, 1935), pp. 119-126;

Newman Ivey White and Walter Clinton Jackson, *An Anthology of Verse by Amerian Negroes* (Durham, N.C.: Trinity College Press, 1924), pp. 148-151.

Pauline Elizabeth Hopkins

(1859-13 August 1930)

Jane Campbell
Purdue University, Calumet

BOOKS: *Contending Forces: A Romance Illustrative of Negro Life North and South* (Boston: Colored Co-operative Publishing Company, 1900);
A Primer of Facts Pertaining to the Greatness of Africa (Cambridge: P. E. Hopkins, 1905).

PLAY PRODUCTION: *Slaves' Escape: or the Underground Railroad,* Boston, Oakland Garden, 5 July 1880; edited and revised as *Peculiar Sam, or the Underground Railroad,* n.d.

PERIODICAL PUBLICATIONS:
FICTION
"The Mystery Within Us," *Colored American,* 1 (May 1900): 14-18;
"Talma Gordon," *Colored American,* 1 (October 1900): 271-290;
"George Washington, A Christmas Story," *Colored American,* 2 (December 1900): 95-104;
"Hagar's Daughter, A Story of Southern Caste Prejudice," as Sarah A. Allen, novel serialized in *Colored American,* 2 (March 1901): 337-352; 2 (April 1901): 431-445; 3 (June 1901): 117-128; 3 (July 1901): 185-195; 3 (August 1901): 262-273; 3 (September 1901): 343-353; 3 (October 1901): 425-435; 4 (November 1901): 23-33; 4 (December 1901): 113-124; 4 (January/February 1902): 188-200; 4 (March 1902): 281-291;
"A Dash for Liberty," *Colored American,* 3 (August 1901): 243-247;
"Bro'r Abr'm Jimson's Wedding, A Christmas Story," *Colored American,* 4 (December 1901): 103-112;
"Winona: A Tale of Negro Life in the South and Southwest," novel serialized in *Colored American,* 5 (May 1902): 29-40; 5 (June 1902): 97-110; 5 (July 1902): 177-187; 5 (August 1902): 257-268; 5 (September 1902): 348-358; 5 (October 1902): 422-431;
"Of One Blood; or, The Hidden Self," novel serialized in *Colored American,* 6 (November 1902): 29-40; 6 (December 1902): 102-113; 6 (January 1903): 191-200; 6 (February 1903): 264-272; 6 (March 1903): 339-348; 6 (May/June 1903): 423-432; 6 (July 1903): 492-501; 6 (August 1903): 580-586; 6 (September 1903): 643-647; 6 (October 1903): 726-731; 6 (November 1903): 802-807;
"The Test of Manhood, A Christmas Story," as Sarah A. Allen, *Colored American,* 6 (December 1902): 113-119;
"As the Lord Lives, He is One of Our Mother's Children," *Colored American,* 6 (November 1903): 795-801;
"Topsy Templeton," *New Era* (1916).
NONFICTION
"Toussaint L'Ouverture: His Life and Times," *Colored American,* 2 (November 1900): 9-24;
"Famous Men of the Negro Race," series in *Colored American,* 2 (February 1901)-5 (September 1902); and "Famous Women of the Negro Race," series in *Colored American,* 4 (November 1901)-5 (October 1902);
"The New York Subway," *Voice of the Negro,* 1 (December 1904): 605, 608-612;
"The Dark Races of the Twentieth Century," *Voice of the Negro,* 2 (February 1905): 108-115; 2 (March 1905): 187-191; 2 (May 1905): 330-334; 2 (June 1905): 415-418; 2 (July 1905): 459-463.

Pauline Elizabeth Hopkins, despite an impressive record of productivity and creativity as a novelist, playwright, short fiction writer, editor, actress, and singer, is another Afro-American woman writer who has essentially been consigned to the dustbins of American literary history. Though contemporary with Frances Ellen Watkins Harper, Charles W. Chesnutt, and Paul Laurence Dunbar, Hopkins is only now beginning to receive the kind of critical attention that Harper has enjoyed for a slightly longer period and that Chesnutt and Dunbar have always had. Hopkins had work published in several genres, but her reputation today rests primarily upon *Contending Forces: A Romance Illustrative of Negro Life North and South,* the novel she published in 1900. Although she serialized three

Pauline Elizabeth Hopkins

other novels and published a novella as well as several short stories, the general unavailability of these materials has caused critical appraisal of them to linger behind treatments of the works of her better-known contemporaries.

Hopkins was born in Portland, Maine, in 1859 to Northrup and Sarah Allen Hopkins; the exact date is unknown. Hopkins's father was a Virginian who migrated north. Her mother was a descendant of Nathaniel and Thomas Paul, who founded Baptist churches in Boston. Sarah Hopkins was also the grandniece of poet James Whitfield. Her family moved to Boston early in her life, and the young Pauline attended public schools there; she graduated from Girls High School. Before her graduation, however, her writing ability had already been made clear. When Pauline was fifteen, the eminent William Wells Brown, who had escaped from slavery, completed a narrative of his life in bondage, and traveled extensively as an abolitionist lecturer, lent his name to a contest sponsored by the Congregational Publishing Society of Boston in support of his latest cause: temperance. Pauline submitted an essay to the contest, which had as its general theme the "Evils of Intemperance and Their Remedies"; her entry won the ten-dollar first prize. As Ann Allen Shockley, the source for the most substantive biographical information on Hopkins, has pointed out, the essay reflects a remarkable control of exposition "for one so young."

In 1879 Hopkins saw the first fruits of her desire to become a playwright in the completion of *Slaves' Escape: or the Underground Railroad* (produced in 1880). The musical drama is essentially what the title suggests and reflects one of Hopkins's recurring themes, that of the escape of slaves. Indeed, the word "escape" and the idea of "leaping" or "dashing" into freedom (which would serve as the basis for one of Hopkins's later titles) may reveal Brown's influence upon Hopkins; his play *The Escape; or A Leap for Freedom: A Drama in Five Acts* had been completed in 1858, and certainly Hopkins would have been aware of it (later, when she was on the staff of the *Colored American* magazine and produced a series on "Famous Men of the Negro Race," Brown was one of the men profiled).

The Hopkins' Colored Troubadours performed the drama in Boston at the Oakland Garden on 5 July 1880. Hopkins's mother and stepfather were a part of the cast, and Hopkins herself sang and played a central role. Reviews of the play were generally good. In a revision, Hopkins changed the title of the piece, calling it *Peculiar Sam, or the Underground Railroad,* and she varied the number of acts.

Between the time of the production of her first play and 1892, when Hopkins turned to more realistic ways of making a living, she toured with the family performing group; she was referred to as "Boston's Favorite Soprano" and apparently enjoyed some popularity. She also continued writing plays, completing the unpublished "One Scene from the Drama of Early Days," a dramatization of the story of Daniel in the lion's den; there is no record of the play's production.

Early in the 1890s, Hopkins took a course in stenography and pursued work in that profession for several years, including a four-year stint in the Bureau of Statistics, where she worked on the Massachusetts Decennial Census of 1895. She also became a public lecturer during this period.

Hopkins's publishing career was launched with the founding of the *Colored American* magazine in May 1900. That first issue carried Hopkins's short story "The Mystery Within Us." By the time the journal ceased publication in 1909, Hopkins had published six more short stories in it (one under a pen name), and she had had three novels serialized in its pages. The company producing the magazine, the Colored Co-operative Publishing Company of Boston, also brought out Hopkins's *Contending Forces.*

"The Mystery Within Us" is structured as a conversation between two men who have been separated for five years. The narrator, Jack, visits his friend Tom Underwood, who, formerly destitute, has been transformed into an enviable, prosperous bachelor, physician, and author. The story is Tom's account of what has happened to him; he tells of an evening when he had contemplated suicide as a way of ending his misery, only to have some mysterious Presence appear before him. By sending thought waves to Tom and smiling when his actions agreed with the thoughts, the Presence encouraged Tom to change his mind. Through the auspices of the Presence, Tom is briefly allowed to experience the cognitive essence of a Dr. Thorn, an eminent physician who had died without bringing his many discoveries to the public. Thorn's ideas are reincarnated or manifested in Tom's mind; by using them in altruistic ways, he has been able to attain riches, though the mysterious quality of what has happened to him dictates bachelorhood for him.

The story ends with Tom's account of his transformation, without further commentary from Jack, though Tom ends his tale with a quotation from William Shakespeare's *Hamlet* that Jack has used earlier: "There are more things in heaven and earth than are dreamt of in our philosophy." "The mystical and spiritual phenomena of a higher being," Shockley asserts, are the bases of many of Hopkins's works.

Clearly the story is a deviation from the usual fare produced by black American writers. It is also a departure from what one might expect of a woman writer, especially in the depiction of male narrators and characters without any female presence; indeed, it seems as if Tom's special calling has permanently separated him from female companionship. The story is one of ideas, an opportunity for Hopkins to explore, in expository form, some of her concerns about metaphysics. Slight characterizations and descriptions are subsumed under philosophical ruminations. The suggestion of incompleteness at the story's close perhaps reflects Hopkins's continuing preoccupation with such musings.

In 1900 Hopkins also published her novel, *Contending Forces: A Romance Illustrative of Negro Life North and South,* a story, convoluted by many subplots, of mulatto brother and sister, Will and Dora Smith, and Sappho Clark, a beautiful octoroon, who boards with the Smith family. Will pursues Sappho, loses her when she is compromised by John Langley, another boarder, and is reunited with her by the novel's end. While heir to many of the novelistic features of the day, *Contending Forces* is nonetheless an ambitious endeavor.

The critical neglect of this novel, which was Hopkins's most popular work, can be attributed, in part at least, to the fact that women's writing, in general, has been historically ignored and trivialized. Until recent scholarship by Ann Allen Shockley and Claudia Tate, *Contending Forces* has been all but excluded from the Afro-American literary canon. On the surface, Hopkins's book may strike the reader as a "woman's novel," focusing on domestic issues of marginal concern to the field of Afro-American literature. In fact, *Contending Forces* is a historical romance strategically designed to acquaint a large audience with black women's heroic possibilities and with their significant roles in past events.

Hopkins writes in direct response to the historical conditions and cultural images of her day. She sets as her task the reification of Afro-American humanity, and her exaltation of the ideals pervading the fiction of her male literary counterparts is defined by the exigencies of her time: a Caucasian standard of beauty, high regard for industry, uncritical admiration for Anglo-Saxon "culture" and "refinement," and firm belief that education will allow blacks to surmount prejudice and attain equality. While the novel's major focus tends to be specifically related to women's issues, *Contending Forces* touches on post-Reconstruction problems pertinent to all black Americans: lynching, voting disenfranchisement, educated blacks finding and retaining employment, and expatriation to Africa. Pivotal to Hopkins's romance is her outrage at the victimization of women, and her message is that black women must resist such victimization whenever possible. A reverence for motherhood also informs her romance, and she celebrates the union of families splintered by slavery and underscores the need for the black extended family to value itself.

Hopkins is a pioneer, for *Contending Forces* encourages interest in and respect for investigating personal history, anticipating the works of writers such as Toni Morrison, David Bradley, and Alice Walker. In her novel, Hopkins correlates personal history with public events; providing a glimpse of black women's humiliating experiences during slavery, she warns against sexual exploitation in the present. Denouncing racist myths that erode self-respect and are built on a conception of the moral laxity of black Americans, she challenges her readers to place those myths in a historical context in order to understand their origins. Finally, she urges solidarity among women for the purposes of engendering self-esteem and change.

Contending Forces was meant "to raise the stigma of degradation" from the black race, according to the novel's preface. To accomplish this end Hopkins used the strategies of nineteenth-century women's romances, which surpassed all other fiction in popularity. Hoping to garner the largest possible audience for her political message, Hopkins fashioned a melodrama about a lonely young orphan with a hidden, violent past who must prove her virtue through additional suffering, eventually to be rewarded with an ideal husband.

Contending Forces abounds with trappings of domestic fiction; imperiled heroines, concupiscent villains, and tragic misunderstandings are juxtaposed to serene domestic scenes symbolizing cosmic harmony. At the same time, rhetorical devices with serious political implications permeate the melodrama: the central heroine is predictably beautiful, but her attractiveness suggests the sexual victimization black women have experienced in racist society; villains are not just one-dimensional figures of evil; their individual crimes are emblematic of the social crimes perpetrated against blacks in America. And Hopkins infuses the cult of domesticity with political messages, so that seemingly innocuous gatherings of women proclaim the significance of the black women's club movement, and joyous reunions among kin exemplify the vibrancy of the Afro-American family. Compared with other writers of her day, Hopkins is quite a skillful author, managing an adroit fusion of women's romance and black historical concerns.

Hopkins's feminist perspective is immediately apparent for she has named her heroine for the ancient Greek lyric poet from Lesbos whom other classical writers celebrated as "the tenth muse." The ancient Sappho, who was married and had a daughter, apparently led a group or school of girls who were devotees of poetry and music, and who probably worshipped Aphrodite, the Greek goddess of erotic love and marriage. Extant fragments of Sappho's lyrics express a feminist perspective of human relations and often talk about women's love for women. There is a legend that she killed herself by drowning on learning that her love for the young man Phaon was unrequited. The Sappho of *Contending Forces* functions to acquaint her audience with the grim historical convergence of racism and sexism at the same time she serves as a paradigm of black womanhood.

Hopkins is appalled by the myth that black women invite sexual overtures. No one could imagine a less consciously seductive heroine than Sappho Clark, who views her beauty as a curse rather than an asset, and whose son was the product of Sappho's rape and enforced prostitution when she was only fourteen. Rather than luring men on, Sappho freezes them out when their interests appear to be intrusive or dishonorable. For example, when she discovers that her friend Will Smith has repeatedly entered her room in her absence to light fires in her hearth, she indignantly orders him to cease. Her actions testify to the innate morality of black women who have suffered sexual abuse and social trespass at the hands of a society that has not recognized its victims' humanity.

Sappho's personal history clearly emphasizes the interplay of sexism and racism, and Hopkins demonstrates this convergence of issues by having Sappho stand in counterpoint to the character of Dora. Whereas Dora serves as a mouthpiece for the accommodationist ideas espoused by her fiancé Arthur, a Booker T. Washington-like figure, Sappho denounces Arthur's faith that "industrial education and the exclusion of politics will cure all our race troubles." Dora confesses that the subject is "a little deep" for her and admits that she accepts the values to which men subscribe. This view is a fortunate one for Dora, since Arthur, much to Sappho's disgust, "thinks women should be seen and not heard" with regard to political discussion. The sexual exploitation of women in general, and black women in particular, is further developed through the stock melodramatic device of villains lying in wait for unsuspecting victims. In every case in the novel, the villains are men seeking to exploit black women sexually. Inevitably, these men evince admiration for the victims' charms while harboring violent hatred. Sappho's white uncle, who appears "extremely fond" of her, for example, sells his niece into prostitution and probably rapes her himself. *Contending Forces* decries this exploitation, but it goes a step further to illuminate the companion myth to the sexually available black woman: the black rapist.

Several chapters of *Contending Forces* center on character reaction to the lynching of a black man for a purported rape of a white woman. Will Smith states the truth: "lynching was instituted to crush the manhood of the enfranchised black." The real-

Shall The Race Have a Fair Chance?

Contending Forces.

A Romance of Negro Life

NORTH AND SOUTH

BY

PAULINE E. HOPKINS,

The Popular Colored Writer.

Author of "Talma Gordon," "General Washington," etc.

With original illustrations and cover design by R. Emmett Owen.

Over 400 pages, 8vo. Price, $1.50.

"*The civility of no race can be perfect whilst another race is degraded.*"—EMERSON.

A most fascinating story that is pre-eminently a race-work, dedicated to the best interest of the Negro everywhere. It holds you as by a spell, from start to finish.

A book that will arouse intense interest wherever shown, as it is the most powerful narrative yet published, of the wrongs and injustice perpetrated on the race. Startling in the array of facts shown and logical in the arguments it presents.

The incidents portrayed HAVE ACTUALLY OCCURRED, ample proof of which may be found in the archives of the Court House at Newbern, N. C., and at the seat of government at Washington, D. C.

The author tells an impartial story, leaving it to the reader to draw conclusions. She has presented both sides of the dark picture—lynching and concubinage—truthfully and without vituperation, introducing enough of the exquisitely droll humor peculiar to the Negro to give a bright touch to an otherwise gruesome subject.

It is a book that will not only appeal strongly to the race everywhere, but will have a large sale among the whites. The book mailed postpaid to any address on receipt of $1.50.

AGENTS WANTED EVERYWHERE. LIBERAL COMMISSION.

Many of our Agents are making from $15.00 to $25.00 a week. You can do the same. Address at once for full particulars and special territory,

The Colored Co-operative Publishing Company,

5 Park Square, BOSTON, MASS.

Advertisement for Hopkins's most popular novel

ity of the rapes of black women by white men, dating back to the earliest days of slavery, stands as a bitter reminder that white males have rewritten history for their own benefit. Hopkins insists that black women be wary of white men, for beneath their surface friendliness burns "a living fire of hatred." Such men, Hopkins implies, project their obsession with domination onto black men. For Hopkins, then, black women must refuse to capitulate to the oppressive myths surrounding lynching.

One of the most important chapters in *Contending Forces* fictionalizes the collective efforts of Afro-American women to change history. In this chapter, a large group of women gather to make garments for a church fair. Mrs. Willis, who plays a significant role here, embodies the black women's club movement, which united its participants in the crusades against lynching and Jim Crow laws, and which made significant contributions in the interests of integration. Hopkins charts the black woman's role in changing history through her solidarity with other women, forging a new vision of society that runs counter to the one white culture promulgates. At the same time Hopkins turns to the ideal of domesticity, enshrining the possibilities inherent in the home where a sewing circle can become a political forum.

Suffering under the suffocating mantle of post-Reconstruction, Hopkins crafted a romance that reveals her vital awareness of history, even while she engaged in worship of a domesticity which sanctified motherhood. At the conclusion of *Contending Forces,* for example, Sappho reclaims her son, from whom she has been separated his entire life, and exults in her renewed maternal role. Given the few avenues open to Afro-American females of Hopkins's day, her sanctification of mothers as culture bearers, by whose influence children will gain positive cultural values, is ingenious. For this notion conveyed the message to nineteenth-century black women that childrearing designated them as instrumental in historical process.

Wrestling to abolish dehumanizing stereotypes, Hopkins created a legendary heroine who surmounts historical difficulties without jeopardizing her much-vaunted gentility or femininity. As an orphan victimized by racism, Sappho triumphs over the vicissitudes of personal history through nearly superhuman virtue, offering hope to women who have endured similar fates. Able to pass for white, Sappho decries the need to do so, thereby allying herself with black America (despite Hopkins's occasional lapses into the posture of an Anglophile). Relying on the formula plot of women's fiction that inevitably ended with marriage, Hopkins had *Contending Forces* conclude with Sappho married to a peerless suitor. In the face of mob rule, Jim Crow, and sexual exploitation, black women at the turn of the century were largely barred from the possibilities of heroic roles. Hopkins therefore took refuge in a mythic future, hoping to communicate the transformational possibilities of marriage and motherhood to readers.

Hopkins's literary career became closely bound to the Colored Co-operative Publishing Company, which brought out *Contending Forces,* and the *Colored American* magazine, for which Hopkins would later work. When her novel appeared, the magazine carried advertisements for it; in fact, Hopkins may already have been on the staff when these promotions appeared. Two of her short stories, "Talma Gordon" and "George Washington, A Christmas Story," appeared in the October and December 1900 issues of the journal.

In March 1901 *Colored American* published the first installment of the serialized novel "Hagar's Daughter, A Story of Southern Caste Prejudice," under the pen name Sarah A. Allen. Although authorship of the novel has never been conclusively established, it is probable that Hopkins wrote it, considering the fact that the pseudonym is Hopkins's mother's maiden name. It appears that, in light of the number of pieces she contributed to the journal in 1901, she resorted to a pen name in order not to give the impression that the journal relied so heavily upon her writing talents. She used the pen name again later on for the same reason.

In August 1901 the *Colored American* published Hopkins's "A Dash for Liberty," another story focusing on the theme of escape from slavery. It is the tale of Madison, whose name is surely designed to convey the majestic qualities of his physical stature, for he is "an unmixed African, of grand physique, and one of the handsomest of his race." Madison has escaped from Virginia to Canada and is now working for a kindly white man on that free soil. His greatest desire, however, is to return to Virginia to free his wife Susan, and the story begins with his conveying that wish to his employer, who finally acquiesces to Madison's plan.

In the conversation between Madison and his employer, Hopkins chose striking language for her newly freed slave, which attests to the majesty of his mind. When the kindly Mr. Dickson admonishes Madison to wait for a year or two until they can get his wife to Canada by legal means, Madison responds: "A year or two would mean forever, situated as we are, Mr. Dickson. It is hard for you to understand; you white men are all alike where you are called upon to judge a Negro's heart. . . . Imagine yourself in my place; how would you feel? The relentless heel of oppression in the States will have ground my rights as a husband into the dust, and have driven Susan to despair in that time." Clearly Hopkins identified command of standard English as central to the superior traits she associated with Madison; she later had enslaved black men say things such as "he'll be gone before we git dar" and "turkey was de toughes' meat I eat fer many a day."

Madison pursues his dream of returning to Virginia, where, after hiding out for days, he discovers the location of his wife and makes an attempt to rescue her. Unfortunately, the overseer has somehow learned of the plot and is waiting in Susan's room. Madison is captured and sold into slavery in the Deep South, but not before he has fatally wounded at least three of his captors. The former slave has been prepared for his possible capture, however, and he has sewn small files and saws into his clothing in order to be able to cut through chains, which he promptly proceeds to do as the boat heads further south.

Hopkins then shifted attention from Madison's fate to that of another slave on the ship; she is a beautiful octoroon, "a lady's maid, well-educated," a singer and dancer, who is given a cabin by herself. The reason for this favoritism becomes clear when the captain arrives at her cabin one night ready to seduce her, forcibly if she resists. The night he has chosen is also the night that Madison has completed sawing through his chains, and when she races by the men's cabin, he rescues her by striking the captain dead. In a short time, all the slaves are freed, and a mutiny against the unsuspecting sailors is effected. It is only after all the fighting is over that Madison realizes who he has earlier rescued:

> As the women filed into the captain's cabin where the meal was served, weeping, singing and shouting over their deliverance, the beautiful octoroon with one wild, half-frantic cry of joy sprang towards the gallant leader.
>
> "Madison!"
>
> "My God! Susan! My wife!"
>
> She was locked to his breast; she clung to him convulsively. Unnerved at last by the revulsion to more than relief and ecstasy, she broke into wild sobs, while the astonished company closed around them with loud hurrahs.

The characters all go off to "Nassau, New Providence," presumably to live happily ever after.

The story continues Hopkins's interest in love affairs between people of different colors; indeed, the dark Madison, an "unmixed" African, and the "white" Susan essentially form an interracial couple comparable to those in some of Hopkins's other works. The love interest, along with the melodramatic coincidences, places the story in the vein of many of those at the turn of the century that focused on the plight of the tragic mulatto. The difference is that Madison, a self-determining, *black* man, is assigned the role of bringing about freedom for all, and Susan is clearly devoted to him, so that the potential tragedy is nullified.

Another interesting aspect of the story is Hopkins's use of violence. Madison strikes out against several whites, never with any thought of his personal safety or the retribution involved in violently dispatching white men. Such actions in the novels of Charles Chesnutt or Sutton Griggs would have brought swift retribution from a white community ever looking for fault in black people. Hopkins transcended the vision of her contemporaries by being more hopeful, even if more violent. The last sentence of her story reinforces her philosophy: "Right is a dangerous instrument; woe to us if our enemy wields it." Since the story was written in the post-Reconstruction era, its message was clearly designed to refer to situations more contemporary than slavery.

With the appearance of the second issue of the *Colored American,* Hopkins was listed as editor of the Women's Department. In December 1901 her fifth story, "Bro'r Abr'm Jimson's Wedding, A Christmas Story," appeared in the magazine. In addition to continuing to contribute her own pieces to the journal, she became literary editor in 1903, having apparently proven herself sufficiently cognizant of the literary styles of the day. From May until October of 1902 the journal serialized Hopkins's novel "Winona: A Tale of Negro Life in the South and Southwest," and between November of 1902 and November of 1903 it serialized another of her novels, "Of One Blood; or, The Hidden Self." In December 1902 the journal published "The Test of Manhood, A Christmas Story," by Sarah A. Allen.

The title character of *Winona* is the mixed-blood daughter of a white man who left his own culture, joined an Indian tribe in Buffalo, and became its chief. His wife was a fugitive slave who had married the chief and died while giving birth to Winona. Shockley describes the story as being "sensational and complicated, filled with adventurous escapades, murder, and romance." It concludes with Winona going off to England with her British lover, pursuing life in a territory where she hopes prejudice will not exist. "Of One Blood; or, The Hidden Self" is also a story of interracial romance, equally as complicated as "Winona." In its focus on mystical and mysterious experiences, it echoes "The Mystery Within Us"; in its emphasis upon a common blood that unites all races, it anticipates Hopkins's thesis in her journalistic series on the dark races of the twentieth century.

Also in November of 1903 the *Colored American* published "As the Lord Lives, He is One of Our Mother's Children," the seventh of Hopkins's stories to appear there. She also made other prose contributions to the journal, including a biographical series, "Famous Women of the Negro Race" and "Famous Men of the Negro Race," which included such figures as William Wells Brown, Frederick Douglass, Lewis Hayden, Sen. Blanche K. Bruce, Charles Lenox Remond, Robert Browne Elliott, and John Jasper of Virginia, who was known for the infamous "De Sun Do Move" sermon. Mrs. Jasper was featured in one issue, as were Sojourner Truth, Harriet Tubman, Fanny Jackson Coppin, and Frances E. W. Harper; there were also general pieces on women focusing on such subjects as their involvement in education.

Hopkins was not only involved in the publishing and editing aspects of the *Colored American* but she promoted the magazine as well, in part through the Colored American League in Boston which she founded. Comprised of twenty prominent black citizens, the group was designed to help the magazine through "personal solicitations for subscriptions and business." In 1904 Hopkins also toured the country and gave a series of talks in an effort to garner additional support for the journal.

By September of 1904 Hopkins was apparently too ill to continue her work with the journal. She left the magazine but continued other literary pursuits. She completed a sociocultural survey series called "The Dark Races of the Twentieth Century," which was published in the *Voice of the Negro* in 1905, and her last published work, a novella entitled "Topsy Templeton," appeared in the magazine *New Era* in 1916. In her last years, Hopkins resumed work as a stenographer, holding her final job with the Massachusetts Institute of Technology. She died "on August 13, 1930 when the liniment-saturated red flannel bandages she was wearing to relieve the neuritis she suffered were ignited by an oil stove in her room."

The tragedy of her death is striking, but the consistency of Hopkins's critical neglect is perhaps even more tragic. Except for a few paragraphs by critics Vernon Loggins and Hugh Gloster, both of whom essentially dismissed *Contending Forces* after noting its complicated plotting and patterning in the sentimental genre of the day, Hopkins was virtually ignored in the first few decades following her death. Neither Gloster nor Loggins refers to any of her other work. Shockley's biographical study has provided more information about Hopkins in recent years, and Tate's commentary on the works may be the beginning of new interest.

A pioneer in fiction writing, play production, and editing, Hopkins anticipated such Harlem Renaissance figures as Jessie Redmon Fauset, Charles S. Johnson, and the several young writers who joined together to produce *Fire!!* (1926), Wallace Thurman, Langston Hughes, Zora Neal Hurston, and Bruce Nugent. Her nationalistic interest in famous black people and the "darker races" anticipated the focus of the *Crisis* magazine under the direction of W. E. B. Du Bois. Truly a "literary foremother" to the development of black American literature, Pauline Elizabeth Hopkins will perhaps one day be more widely recognized by her descendants.

References:

Judith R. Berzon, *Neither White nor Black: The Mulatto Character in American Fiction* (New York: New York University Press, 1978);

Robert Bone, *The Negro Novel in America* (New Haven: Yale University Press, 1965);

Hugh M. Gloster, *Negro Voices in American Fiction* (Chapel Hill: University of North Carolina Press, 1948);

Vernon Loggins, *The Negro Author: His Development in America to 1900* (New York: Columbia University Press, 1931);

Ann Allen Shockley, "Pauline Elizabeth Hopkins: A Biographical Excursion into Obscurity," *Phylon*, 33 (1972): 22-26;

Claudia Tate, "Pauline Hopkins: Our Literary Foremother," in *Conjuring: Black Women, Fiction, and Literary Tradition*, edited by Marjorie Pryse and Hortense J. Spillers (Bloomington: Indiana University Press, 1985).

Papers:

The Pauline E. Hopkins papers are in the Fisk University Library in Nashville, Tennessee.

George Moses Horton
(1797?-1883?)

William Carroll
Norfolk State University

BOOKS: *The Hope of Liberty* (Raleigh, N.C.: Gales, 1829); retitled *Poems by a Slave* (Philadelphia: Lewis Gunn, 1837);

The Poetical Works of George M. Horton, The Colored Bard of North Carolina (Hillsborough, N.C.: Heartt, 1845);

Naked Genius (Raleigh, N.C.: Smith, 1865).

George Moses Horton, slave bard of North Carolina, was "the first Negro professional man of letters in America and one of the first professional writers of any race in the South." Horton's three volumes of poetry were published in his lifetime, two of them while he was still legally a slave; one of them was transcribed for him before he had even learned to write. Horton was the first black southerner to have a volume of poetry published. (Phillis Wheatley, a northern slave from Massachusetts, had had volumes of poetry published earlier.)

Despite Horton's impressive list of "firsts," his birth and death dates are not known. George Moses Horton was born as a slave on the farm of William Horton in Northampton County, North Carolina, near the falls of the Roanoke River. The year of his birth is generally believed to be 1797 or 1798, mainly on the strength of a statement in the introduction to his book *The Hope of Liberty* (1829), which says that the author was thirty-two years old in the summer of 1829. Biographer Richard Walser suggests that Horton may have been born before 1797. The birth of a slave child was almost never recorded in the courthouse records and only rarely in the master's family Bible, and, therefore, the exact date of George Moses Horton's birth probably will never be known.

In 1800 William Horton moved his agricultural operations about a hundred miles southwest into the hills of Chatham County to what is now the community of Bynum, less than ten miles from the towns of Chapel Hill and Pittsboro (then Pittsborough), to the north and south respectively. In that setting young Horton's earliest lasting impressions were formed. Horton states explicitly that his mother and all her children were slaves of William Horton. He does not say much about his father except that he was his mother's second husband and that she had left him before George began to show an interest in reading. Horton's mother may have been compelled to leave her husband "behind" in Northampton as the slave of another family when her master relocated in Chatham.

Horton himself was to have a similar experience in his adult life; his own wife and children were the property of a Chatham farmer named Snipes and carried the surname of their slavemaster rather than Horton's. The poet later commented on the forced separation of slave families in such poems as "Division of an Estate," "A Slave's Reflection on the Eve Before His Sale," and "Farewell to Frances."

While growing up on the farm in Chatham County, and between chores, Horton was able to cultivate a love of learning. With the aid of his mother and her Wesley hymnal, some pages of schoolbooks he was able to get from white children, and some friendly competition from his brother, Horton learned to read. He did not learn to write until years later, but his inability to commit his thoughts to paper did not keep him from composing original, mostly religious, verses. Under the influence of the Biblical psalmists, the Wesleys, and possibly some other pious poets whose works he had read, Horton was soon able to fashion such verses as: "Rise up my soul and let us go/Up to the gospel feast;/Gird on the garment white as snow,/ To join and be a guest." Two stanzas of the poem are extant, but he says there were more; they had never been recorded, and it was impossible for him to recall completely his early compositions in later years. Horton said that some of the pieces which subsequently slipped from his memory may have been better than the ones he was able to recall.

Although George Horton's earliest poetic efforts were religiously inspired, his earliest "professional" writings were of a very different nature. In 1814 William Horton's son, James, became George's new master (although William was still alive). Some time between 1814 and 1820, George started taking part in a weekend ritual which evidently was a well-established practice among the black servants within walking distance of the town of Chapel Hill, site of the state university. On Sabbath days (the slaves' traditional "day off"), some servants would take fruits to sell to the students and other possible buyers "on the Hill." George Moses Horton became one of these weekend fruit vendors, and his contacts with Chapel Hill led rather quickly to his literary career.

The students seem to have had a custom of requiring the prospective salespersons to entertain them before they would agree to buy their wares; one fellow reportedly entertained would-be customers by breaking planks over his head. When Horton was called upon to entertain his prospective clients, he burst into streams of oratory. This entertained the audience, but it did not produce the serious effect Horton considered desirable. When he began to recite his poetry, the collegians' reactions ranged from astonishment to incredulity.

THE HOPE

OF

LIBERTY.

CONTAINING

A NUMBER OF POETICAL PIECES.

BY

GEORGE M. HORTON.

RALEIGH:

Printed by J. Gales & Son.

1829.

Title page for Horton's first book of poems

Some of the students were openly skeptical of his ability to compose original verse. However, he gave incontrovertible proof to all the bystanders through what he called "the experiment of acrostics." Horton provides no details regarding the "experiment," but it probably consisted of someone's spelling out a name or some other word upon which basis the slave would compose rhymed acrostical verse.

Horton became a man in demand on the campus. The undergraduates began offering twenty-five cents each for the lyrical productions of "Poet Horton"—a name Horton still liked to use in the 1880s. Some students gave Horton fifty cents or even as much as seventy-five cents to compose a love letter and accompanying poem to be sent to the customer's sweetheart. Horton claims to "have composed love pieces in verse for courtiers from all parts of the state, and acrostics on the names of many of the tip top belles of Virginia, South Carolina, and Georgia."

On weekends, he would go to Chapel Hill, where he would take "orders" for love poems to be delivered the following weekend. During the week, while performing his tasks on the farm, he would compose the commissioned love lyrics (often a dozen or more) and recite them to the respective commissioners on his next trip to the Hill.

Some of his customers gave him books; others gave him clothes; still others gave the slave poet copious drafts of corn whiskey. Horton's experiences with alcohol may have been at least partly responsible for his later composition of a particularly witty poem on the dangers of drinking entitled "The Intemperance Club." Among the books he received were Lindley Murray's *English Grammar*, an abridged version of Samuel Johnson's *Dictionary*, the *Columbian Orator*, and collections of poetry by John Milton, Homer, Virgil, William Shakespeare, George Gordon Byron, Thomas Campbell, and others. Horton reportedly was especially fond of the poetry of Byron. It is also reported that he studied Campbell's poems assiduously, completely memorizing his *Pleasures of Hope*.

Perhaps equally as valuable to Horton's poetic career as any books he might have read was his acquaintance with Caroline Lee Hentz, who was in Chapel Hill from 1826 to 1830. From Lancaster, Massachusetts (although Horton mistakenly reported her hometown as Boston), Hentz was a writer of poetry and of such fiction as *Lovell's Folly* (1833) in which one of the characters was a black slave poet named George. Hentz noted in the novel that the character was based on an actual slave poet that she had known.

Hentz helped Horton with his writing techniques, transcribed some of his work, and assisted him in getting his work into public print in the North as well as in North Carolina. In spring 1828 she sent two of Horton's poems, "Slavery" and "Liberty and Slavery," to her hometown newspaper, the *Lancaster Gazette.* The one entitled "Slavery" was reprinted six years later in William Lloyd Garrison's widely-read *Liberator,* where it served to rekindle the interest of some northern abolitionists in the plight of the poem's author.

However, even before the appearance of Horton's "Slavery" in the *Liberator* in 1834, some northern and southern abolitionists were already aware of his plight, and they had engaged in two unsuccessful attempts to purchase his freedom. The campaigns on Horton's behalf in 1828 and 1829 brought together the efforts of some diverse people and agencies: Hentz; James Henderson, a Chapel Hill physician; English-born newspaper editor Joseph Gales and his son, Weston Raleigh Gales; the native Carolinian polemicist, David Walker, then residing in Boston; and a "philanthropic gentleman" whose identity has never been determined. The North Carolina Colonization Society, the North Carolina Manumission Society, *Freedom's Journal* of New York (the first American newspaper edited by blacks), and the *Raleigh Register,* edited by the Gales family, were active organs in the work for Horton's release.

The first of the two campaigns evidently began with a news story about Horton in the 8 August 1828 edition of *Freedom's Journal.* This campaign lasted three months, but although Horton's master was offered "$100 more than any person of sound judgment should say I was worth," Horton wrote, "To this my master would not accede." Horton characterized his master as "a man who had no regard for liberty, science or genius." In 1829 the North Carolina Colonization Society joined forces with Hentz, the Gales family, and other interested Carolinians in a new project designed to bring about Horton's manumission.

The project involved a plan to publish and sell a book of Horton's poems. It was projected that

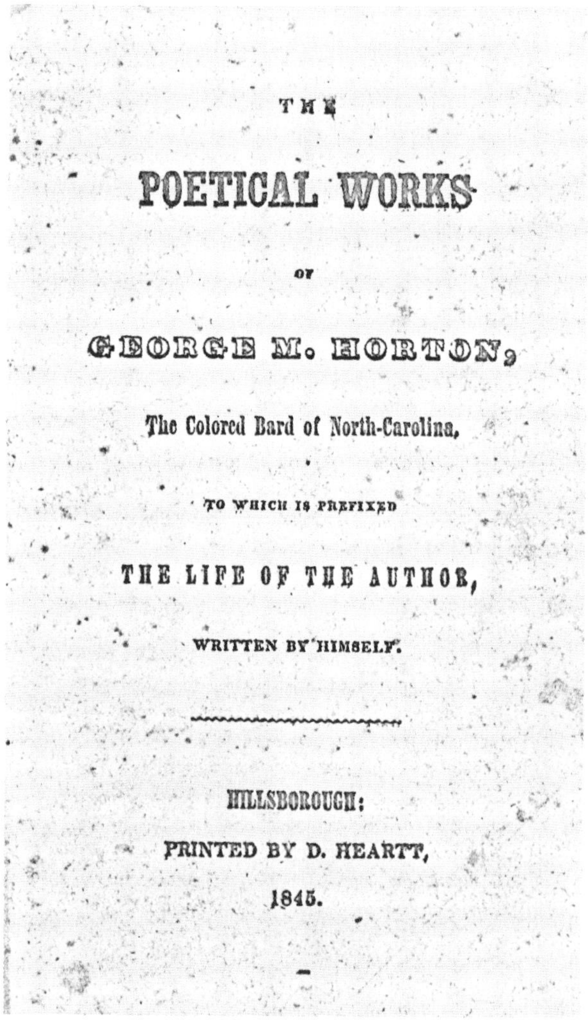
THE

POETICAL WORKS

OF

GEORGE M. HORTON,

The Colored Bard of North-Carolina,

TO WHICH IS PREFIXED

THE LIFE OF THE AUTHOR,

WRITTEN BY HIMSELF.

HILLSBOROUGH:

PRINTED BY D. HEARTT,

1845.

Title page for Horton's second published volume, which sold for fifty cents in 1845 but by 1852 was available for twenty-five cents

the money derived from the sales of the book and from contributions which sympathetic readers would send to Weston Gales would enable the project's sponsors to make James Horton an offer he could not refuse, especially since the Colonization Society stood ready to guarantee the newly-freed bard's speedy departure for Liberia via the earliest available vessel. M. A. Richmond suggests that the proviso that the freed poet emigrate to Liberia constituted the proponents' chief basis for hope that their plan could succeed where the earlier one had failed.

The Hope of Liberty did not fulfill the wish expressed in its title; however, it did accomplish some interesting "firsts," the complex ironies of which cannot possibly be overemphasized: a slave had published a book. The slave's book was published in a slaveholding state, and while teaching a black man to read and write was not yet a crime in North Carolina—it was declared illegal in 1830—it certainly was not a common practice. The book's purpose was to get its author out of slavery, against his master's wish, and people residing in this state were expected to give of their monies in order to get Horton out of the "peculiar institution" which the state's laws declared to be his rightful place. But in order for the slave poet to avail himself of the freedom thus offered, he would have to agree to leave the land of his birth, and the people, black and white, whom he had esteemed during his lifetime, which had spanned nearly a third of a century.

Regardless of the ironies involved in its publication, Horton's *The Hope of Liberty* was the first book of poetry by a black American in more than half a century. It was the first such book of any kind by a black person in the South, and as Horton's biographer states, "It was the first poetic protest by any slave anywhere of his status."

The Hope of Liberty contained twenty-one poems, the subject matter of which was largely confined to love, death, religion, and slavery. Three of the poems were overt antislavery pieces; four were religious lyrics; ten dealt with romantic love in one way or another, including three on the seasons of spring, summer, and winter; two were on death; and the others were philosophical musings set in verse, one entitled "To the Gadfly" and the other "On the Poetic Muse." The collection provided a good sampling of Horton's talents, although the publishers explained that they had excluded a number of the slave poet's offerings in order to keep down printing costs.

Two of the love poems in *The Hope of Liberty* are worthy of note: "Eliza" and "Love." The first of these was probably commissioned by one of Horton's Chapel Hill patrons. The final stanza reads, "Eliza, I shall think of thee—My heart shall ever twine about thee;/Fare thee well—but think of me,/Compell'd to live and die without thee./'Fare thee well!—and if forever,/Still forever fare thee well.' " The quotation marks on the last two lines indicate Horton's conscious borrowing, in this case from Byron. Horton borrowed extensively in many of his poems.

While "Eliza" was evidently written for a particular person, "Love" could have been reworked with slight modifications (and resold) a number of times. The poem begins: "Whilst tracing thy visage I sink in emotion,/For no other damsel so wondrous I see;/Thy looks are so pleasing, thy charms so amazing,/I think of no other, my true-love, but thee."

Both poems are designed to communicate in the language of love. The words are not particularly important; the sentimentality is more valuable than the sentiment, which is a prime consideration for Horton, since the poems were to be sold to people in love.

Horton's antislavery poems had a different audience than did his love lyrics. The poem called "On Hearing of the Intention of a Gentleman to Purchase the Poet's Freedom" is probably the most important work in the volume. The poem's title is a reminder of the mysterious "philanthropic gentleman" who was involved in the project to free Horton in 1828. The poem, fifty-two lines of iambic pentameter couplets arranged in four-line stanzas and one of the longest pieces in the book, recounts some of the emotional vicissitudes experienced by the poet. The lows resulted from his condition of slavery, the highs from the prospect of manumission. The second and third stanzas summarize the contrast:

> Tyrannic storms arose upon my soul,
> And dreadful did their mad'ning thunders roll;
> The pensive muse was shaken from her sphere,
> And hope, it vanish'd in the clouds of fear.
>
> At length a golden sun broke thro' the gloom,
> A calm ensued, and birds began to sing,
> And lo! the sacred muse resumed her wing.

The rhyming iambic pentameter couplets are reminiscent of the heroic couplets of eighteenth-century neoclassicists, but the soaring and singing of the poet's spirit are more in tune with the sentiments of the romanticists.

The influences of the Old and New Testaments and of the Wesley hymnal are apparent in *The Hope of Liberty*. Strains of the hymnal resound loudly in these lines from "On Liberty and Slavery," a protest poem: "Alas! and am I born for this,/To wear the slavish chain?/Deprived of all created bliss,/Through hardship, toil and pain!"

The book that carried Horton's hopes of liberty in 1829 also employed several of the main themes and techniques that would be typical of his work in later years. While Horton would write about new subjects and use more complex verse forms in subsequent volumes, the influences of the Bible, the hymnal, and several British poets would always be part of his poetic repertoire.

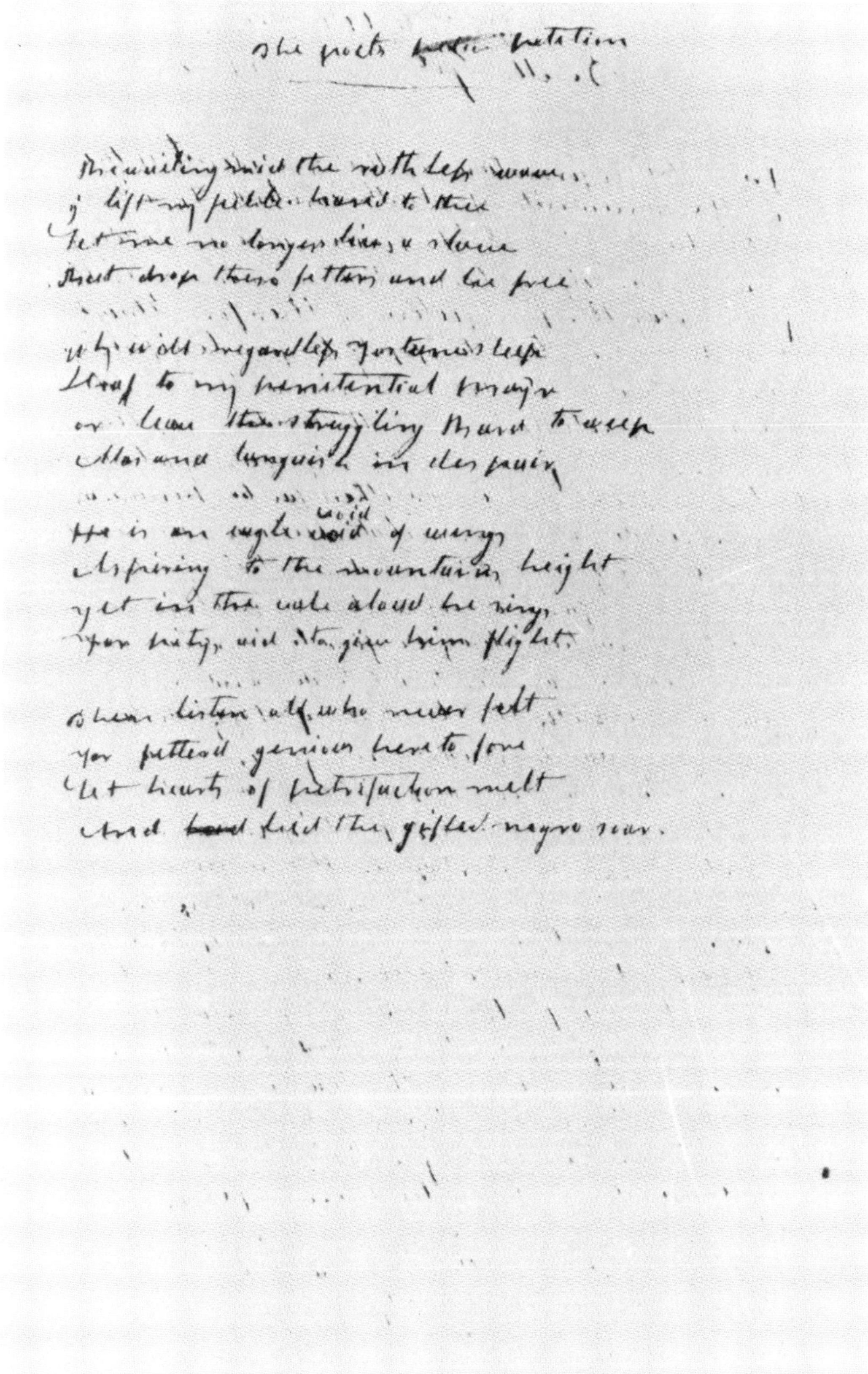
The poets ~~feeble~~ petition

Bewailing mid the ruthless waves
I lift my feeble hand to thee
Let me no longer live a slave
But drop these fetters and be free

Why will regardless fortune sleep
Deaf to my penitential prayer
Or leave the struggling bard to weep
Alas and languish in despair

He is an eagle void of wings
Aspiring to the mountain height
Yet in the vale aloud he sings
For pity's aid to gain his flight

Then listen all who never felt
For fettered genius heretofore
Let hearts of petrifaction melt
And ~~band~~ bid the gifted negro soar.

Poem on the back of a letter to Horace Greeley from Horton (courtesy of Southern Historical Collection, University of North Carolina)

The book's appeal evidently fell upon deaf ears, for it did not achieve the desired result. The book seems to have been largely ignored until 1837 when Philadelphia abolitionist Lewis Gunn had it reprinted with the title *Poems by a Slave.* The following year, *Poems by a Slave* was reprinted in Boston in the same volume with *Memoir and Poems of Phillis Wheatley, a North African and a Slave.* The author probably knew nothing about these northern editions of his book.

In 1830 Hentz left Chapel Hill, and Horton lost a teacher and champion. Another of Horton's champions, David Walker, published his *Appeal in Four Articles, Together with a Preamble, to the Colored Citizens Of the World, but in Particular and Very Expressly to Those of The United States of America.* In his *Appeal,* Walker cited history and scripture in his condemnation of American slavery as unnatural and unlawful. He predicted that practitioners of slavery would feel the wrath of a just and vengeful God. The reactions among slaveholders and proslavery sympathizers ranged from more stringent restrictions on their own slaves to the offering of a $1000 reward for the capture of the renegade Walker, "the amount to be ten times as much if he is taken alive." That same year, the North Carolina legislature enacted a law requiring any slave, upon being freed, to leave the state and never return. The lawmakers also passed a law making it a crime to teach black people to read and write.

The newspapers in Raleigh, Chapel Hill, and other North Carolina cities and towns had made Horton into such a celebrated local figure that the newly imposed strictures on slaves' activities apparently did not seriously impair his business as an author and retailer of love poems. Nevertheless, these strictures must have made his hopes of gaining his freedom seem even more frail than they had seemed in the previous year. Furthermore, outside of the Chapel Hill-Raleigh area, his local celebrity status meant nothing.

The poet's reactions to the events of the 1830s are difficult to assess accurately, since most of the poetry he wrote during those years evidently never got into public print. The work which was preserved (by his customers and by local newspapers and magazines) was the least personal and least critical of his situation. Moreover, Horton's own autobiography, which he wrote in 1845, breaks off at the year 1830 with the departure of Hentz from Chapel Hill. Nowhere in his truncated autobiography does he mention any attempts to gain (or even any strong desire for) his freedom.

Despite the strictures of the time, Horton succeeded, in 1832, in arranging to live in Chapel Hill, where he could be closer to his business interests. James Horton agreed to grant this special kind of quasi freedom for twenty-five cents a week.

As generations of students came and went, the legend of George Moses Horton continued to grow. A Mississippi man named W. H. Thomson wrote a letter to his son, Ruffin Thomson, who was a student at the University of North Carolina in the 1850s. Ruffin had evidently written something to his father regarding the slave poet. The father states that *he* also had known Horton when he had been a student at the university a quarter of a century earlier. One apocryphal story about Norton that evolved was that the first student to purchase a poem from him was James Knox Polk, who later became president of the United States. Another part of the legend was the joke which said that Horton actually owned James Horton and just about owned Dr. Joseph Caldwell, president of the university.

During the time he lived in Chapel Hill, Horton continued his attempts to attain freedom. He tried to enlist the aid of northern abolitionists and liberals, such as William Lloyd Garrison and Horace Greeley. He kept importuning Caldwell and later, Caldwell's successor, ex-governor David Swain, to help him in his freedom-seeking enterprises. And, finally having learned to write, he even wrote letters to James Horton (and later, James's son, Hall Horton) trying to arrange a "deal." Living in Chapel Hill intermittently from the 1830s until the Civil War, Horton became a daily presence on campus instead of a weekly visitor, and he was no longer a novelty. The interest of the situation had worn off for the poet also, and he began to drink.

Sometime in the 1830s or 1840s Horton married a slave woman from the farm of a Chatham County resident named Franklin Snipes. The marriage evidently was not a happy one. It is unlikely that the poet's wife would have shared much of his enthusiasm for literature, history, and other academic subjects. There is no evidence that she had any opportunity to pursue such interests if she had them. Furthermore, with Horton living at Chapel Hill or on the Horton farm, it is hard to imagine how the couple could have spent much time together. Nonetheless the Hortons had a boy and a girl. The children as well as their mother retained the surname of Snipes. According to one source, the son, Free Snipes, died in 1896; the daughter, Rhody Snipes, was living in Raleigh and married to a man named Van Buren Byrum in the early

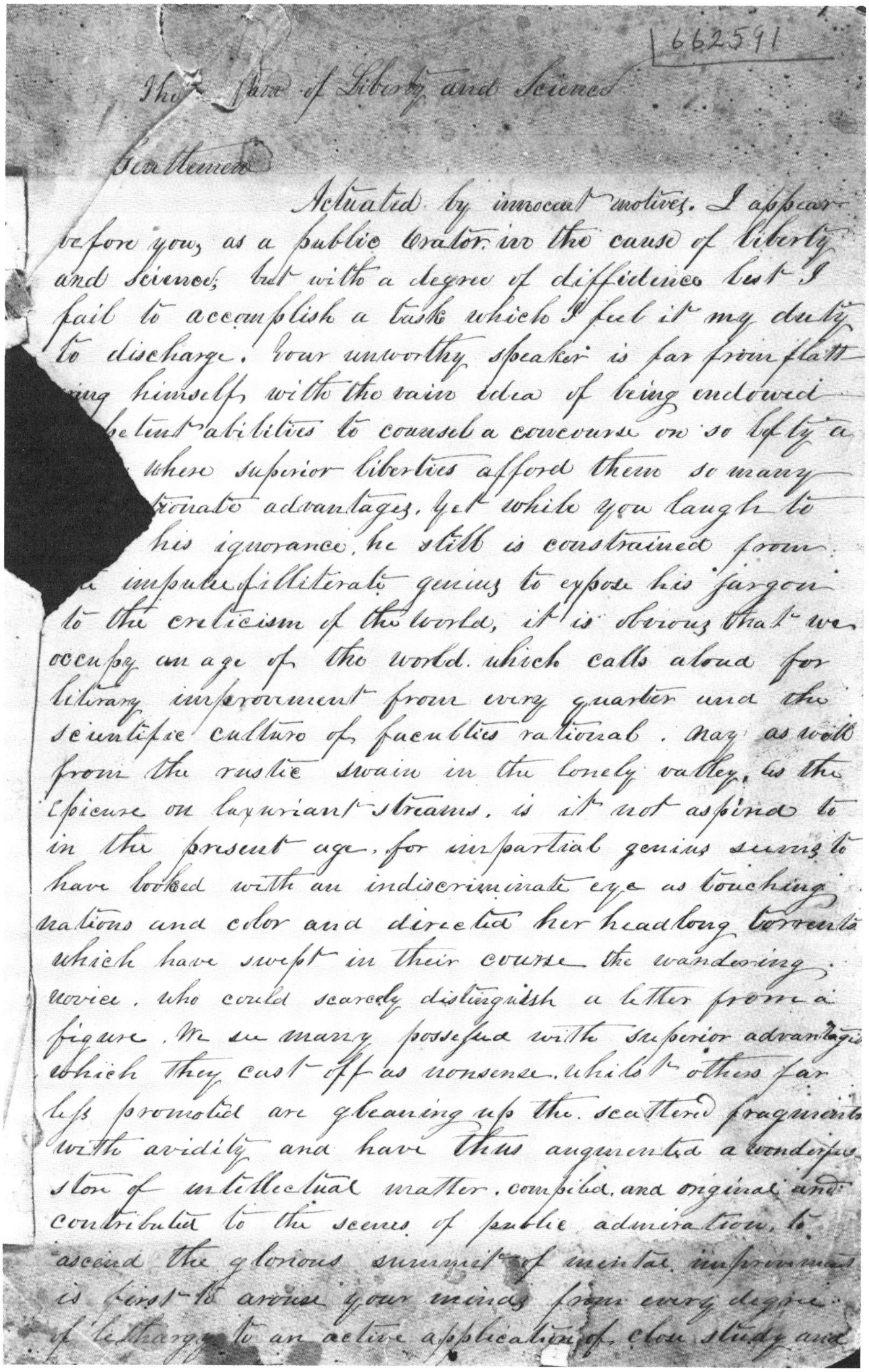

662591

The [illegible]ause of Liberty and Science

Gentlemen

Actuated by innocent motives, I appear before you, as a public Orator in the cause of liberty and science; but with a degree of diffidence lest I fail to accomplish a task which I feel it my duty to discharge. Your unworthy speaker is far from flattering himself, with the vain idea of being endowed [illegible]petent abilities to counsel a concourse on so lofty a [illegible] where superior liberties afford them so many [illegible]tunate advantages, yet while you laugh to [illegible] his ignorance, he still is constrained from [illegible] impulse of illiterate genius to expose his jargon to the criticism of the world, it is obvious that we occupy an age of the world which calls aloud for literary improvement from every quarter and the scientific culture of faculties rational. Nay as well from the rustic swain in the lonely valley, to the epicure on luxuriant streams. is it not aspired to in the present age, for impartial genius seems to have looked with an indiscriminate eye as touching nations and color and directed her headlong torrents which have swept in their course the wandering novice. who could scarcely distinguish a letter from a figure. We see many possessed with superior advantages which they cast off as nonsense. whilst others far less promoted are gleaning up the scattered fragments with avidity and have thus augmented a wonderful store of intellectual matter. compiled and original and contributed to the scenes of public admiration. to ascend the glorious summit of mental improvement is first to arouse your minds from every degree of lethargy to an active application of close study and

Pages from Horton's unpublished 1859 lecture to students at the University of North Carolina (courtesy of North Carolina Collection, Wilson Library, University of North Carolina)

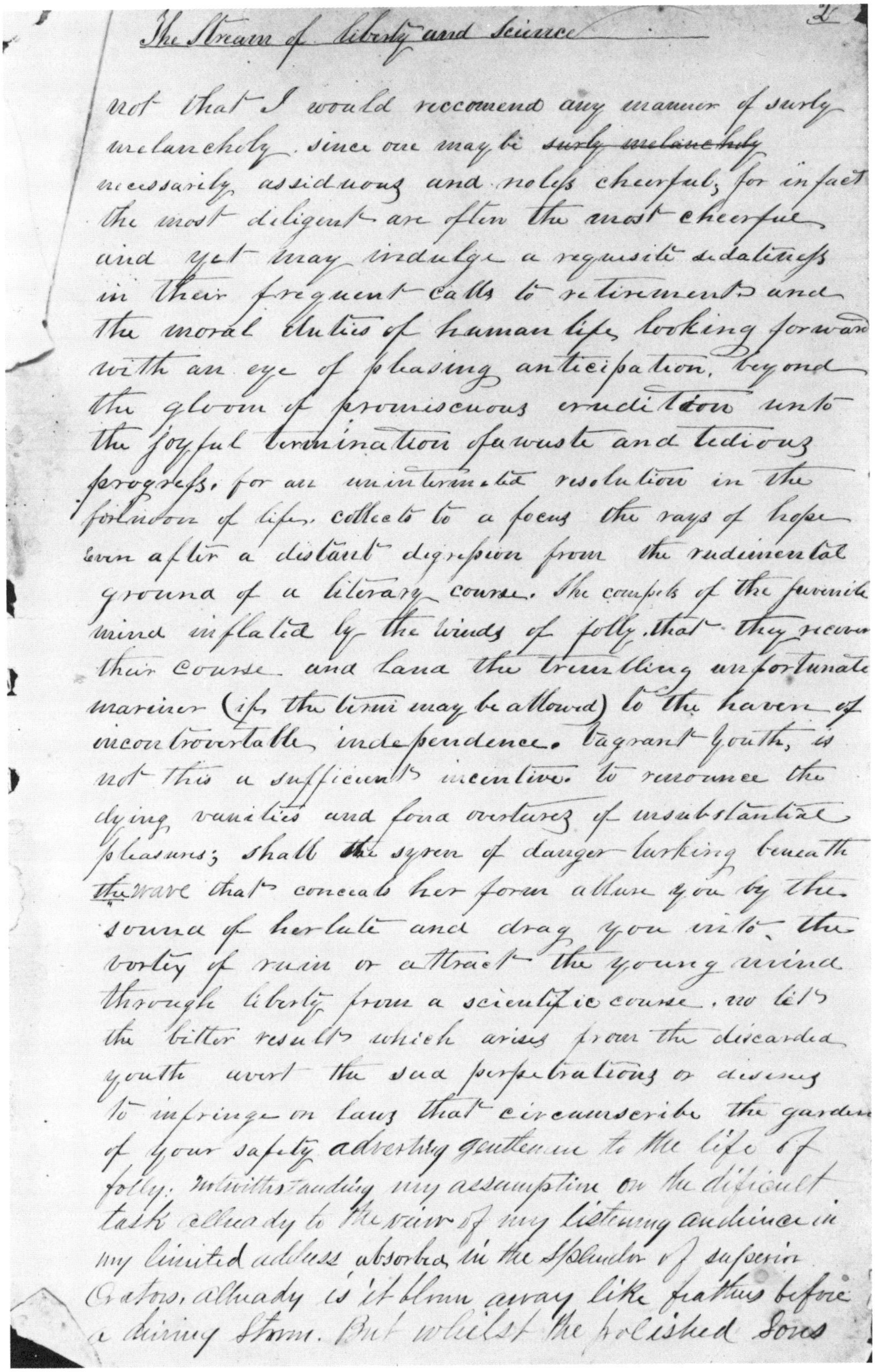

The Stream of liberty and Science 2

not that I would reccomend any manner of surly
melancholy. since one may be ~~surly melancholy~~
necessarily assiduous and noless cheerful, for in fact
the most diligent are often the most cheerful
and yet may indulge a requisite sedativess
in their frequent calls to retirement and
the moral duties of human life looking forward
with an eye of pleasing anticipation, beyond
the gloom of promiscuous erudition unto
the joyful termination of a waste and tedious
progress. for an unintermitted resolution in the
forenoon of life, collects to a focus the rays of hope
even after a distant digression from the rudimental
ground of a literary course. The compass of the juvenile
mind inflated by the winds of folly, that they recover
their course and land the trembling unfortunate
mariner (if the term may be allowed) to the haven of
incontrovertable independence. Vagrant youth, is
not this a sufficient incentive to renounce the
dying vanities and fond overtures of unsubstantial
pleasures; shall the syren of danger lurking beneath
the wave that conceals her form allure you by the
sound of her lute and drag you into the
vortex of ruin or attract the young mind
through liberty from a scientific course. no let
the bitter results which arises from the discarded
youth avert the sad perpetrations or desires
to infringe on laws that circumscribe the garden
of your safety advertising gentlemen to the life of
folly. notwithstanding my assumption on the dificult
task already to the vain of my listening audience in
my limited address absorbed in the splendor of superior
Orators, already is it blown away like feathers before
a driving Storm. But whilst the polished Sons

twentieth century. Horton himself never mentions his wife or his children in any of his writings, unless the verbal barbs he hurls at women in some of his poems published in the 1860s are to be taken as references to his own wife, as one researcher, Mattie Lakin, suggests.

Horton never stopped writing poems; a few even appeared in local periodicals. In 1843 two of his pieces were sent by Professor William Mercer Green to the prestigious *Southern Literary Messenger,* which printed them. They were entitled, "Lines to My . . ." and "Ode to Liberty." The "Ode," ostensibly a paean to the freedom and greatness of "Columbia," actually calls upon "liberty," the "dove of peace," to release Columbia's "pris'ners" and "fan Columbia free." The mention of "pris'ners" provides extra clarity and emphasis for the poem's refrain: "All nations should be free"; Horton was poetically protesting against slavery even though he could no longer be as explicit with his complaints as he had been in *The Hope of Liberty.*

There is no way of estimating how many antislavery poems Horton may have composed after the publication of *The Hope of Liberty.* It is obvious that he could not have expected to find buyers for such poems as readily as he could find buyers for love lyrics and odes to such national figures as Henry Clay and Andrew Jackson. However, it is known that one of the "books" he had in hand before 1840 was a compendious manuscript which he called "The Museum." There is no evidence that "The Museum" was ever published as a book, and no extant copies of the manuscript have ever been located. Nevertheless, printer Dennis Heartt, in the introduction to Horton's *Poetical Works* (1845), refers to "The Museum" as a work with which some readers of Horton's poetry might have had some familiarity. Heartt says of *Poetical Works,* "It is entirely different from his other work entitled *The Museum,* and has been written some time since that, and is not so large."

What Heartt meant when he called *Poetical Works* "entirely different" from "The Museum" is not clear. Perhaps "The Museum" contained antislavery poems which the state authorities would have considered objectionable. If so, this would explain why former governor Swain refused to assist Horton's efforts to publish it. (Swain's name does appear on the subscription list of *Poetical Works.*) Heartt's announcement that this book was "entirely different" from "The Museum" may have served as a tacit signal to readers who had heard of or seen Horton's "Museum" manuscript that *Poetical Works* had been purged of offensive matter. Thus they could lend their names in support of Horton, without any fear of being branded abolitionists or troublemakers.

Perhaps the most amazing thing about *The Poetical Works of George M. Horton, The Colored Bard of North Carolina* (1845) is that it was ever published at all, since the fact that Horton was writing *anything* was a crime for which he could have been publicly flogged. If it was ruled that his writings tended to express or foment dissatisfaction with slavery, then the offense would have been compounded. It is not surprising then that both the poet and his backers were careful about which of the slave's writings were released to public scrutiny during those years.

Significantly, the word "liberty" never appears in the title of any poem in Horton's *Poetical Works.* Neither do the words "slavery," "slave," "free," or "freedom" appear in any of the titles. In view of the frequency with which these words occur in the titles of poems in Horton's other two published volumes, not much imagination is required to infer that a special kind of editing (or censorship) went into the preparation of the *Poetical Works* manuscript.

The poet himself evidently had little or no voice in the decisions regarding what to include in compiling *Poetical Works.* The way Horton's autobiography, which serves as a preface to *Works,* ends in the early 1830s indicates that Horton left some of the most interesting years out of his life story. It is possible that Horton did write more but had it edited out for him before the book was printed.

Although Heartt or someone else may have taken care to see that nothing of Horton's dissatisfaction with slavery was in his autobiography and that no poems with titles suggesting antislavery sentiment got printed in *Works,* some antislavery sentiment within the poems themselves slipped past the editors (or was deliberately allowed to remain). For example, the agony slave families and friends experienced when their relationships were forcefully sundered is suggested in these lines from "Farewell to Frances": "Farewell! alas, the tragic sound/Has many a tender bosom torn;/While desolation spread around,/Deserted friendship left to mourn." The idea of forced separation does not dominate the poem in its entirety; in fact, the idea of the breaking up of a slave family, embedded in this stanza, might escape the notice of the casual reader altogether. Such is not the case in "Division of an Estate," however, the only unquestionably antislavery poem printed in *Poetical Works.*

Although it lacks the forthrightness of many of Horton's protest poems, "Division of an Estate"

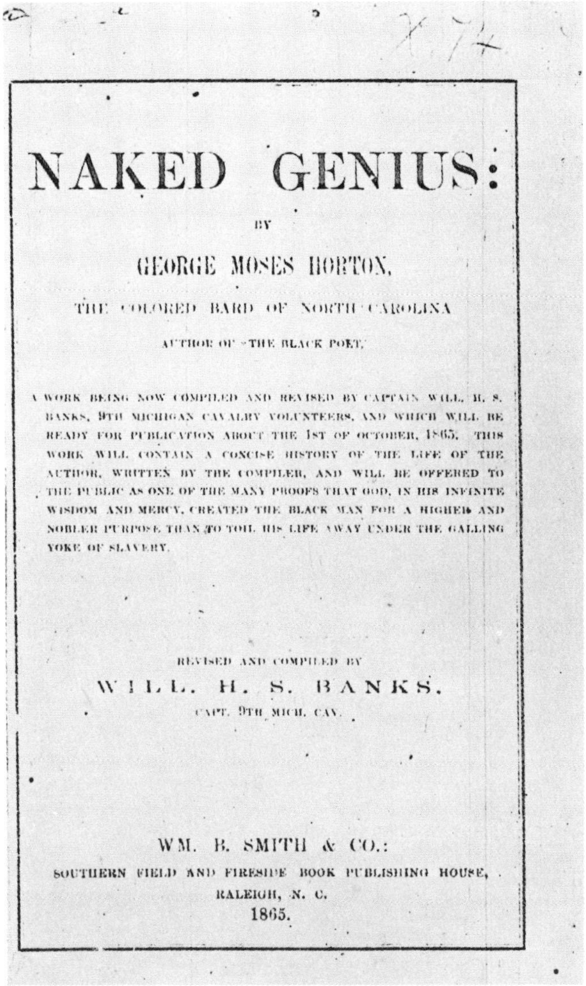
NAKED GENIUS:

BY

GEORGE MOSES HORTON,

THE COLORED BARD OF NORTH CAROLINA

AUTHOR OF "THE BLACK POET,"

A WORK BEING NOW COMPILED AND REVISED BY CAPTAIN WILL. H. S. BANKS, 9TH MICHIGAN CAVALRY VOLUNTEERS, AND WHICH WILL BE READY FOR PUBLICATION ABOUT THE 1ST OF OCTOBER, 1865. THIS WORK WILL CONTAIN A CONCISE HISTORY OF THE LIFE OF THE AUTHOR, WRITTEN BY THE COMPILER, AND WILL BE OFFERED TO THE PUBLIC AS ONE OF THE MANY PROOFS THAT GOD, IN HIS INFINITE WISDOM AND MERCY, CREATED THE BLACK MAN FOR A HIGHER AND NOBLER PURPOSE THAN TO TOIL HIS LIFE AWAY UNDER THE GALLING YOKE OF SLAVERY.

REVISED AND COMPILED BY

WILL. H. S. BANKS.

CAPT. 9TH MICH. CAV.

WM. B. SMITH & CO.:

SOUTHERN FIELD AND FIRESIDE BOOK PUBLISHING HOUSE,

RALEIGH, N. C.

1865.

Title page for Horton's third and final published volume

could be judged Horton's best antislavery poem on the basis of its merits as a work of literary art. Louis D. Rubin says that this poem "embodies a subtlety and a complexity of imagery that are considerably more interesting from a literary standpoint than Horton's hymnal-inspired lyrics most usually found in the anthologies of Black American poetry." The poem certainly deserves more critical attention than it has received. In the first six and a half blank verse lines of the poem, Horton describes a plantation, the master of which is dead or dying, in terms of a human body that has been decapitated:

It well bespeaks a man beheaded, quite
Divested of the laurel robe of life,
When every member struggles for its base,
The head; the power of order now recedes;
Unheeded efforts rise on every side,
With dull emotion rolling through the brain
of apprehending slaves.

Significantly, the first complete sentence of the poem concludes with the word "slaves." They are among the lowest members of the "body" that has lost its "head"; the emotions which roll through the slaves' brains are necessarily "dull" at this point. They become more acutely painful toward the end of the poem.

In the ensuing ten and a half lines, the poet depicts the chaos that reigns on the plantation by describing the disorientation of the farm animals which are either wandering aimlessly or dashing about frantically. In the next fifteen lines, the center of the poem, the heavens seem to be taking part in the proceedings: the expiring master of the estate is portrayed as a setting sun being succeeded by a horde of evening stars (the heirs). The heirs do not seem particularly distressed by the loss of the source of their erstwhile light; they are interested in claiming their respective portions of "the wide empire of fortune."

A very different state of affairs prevails among the slaves, however:

but O, the state,
The dark suspense in which poor vassals stand,
Each mind upon the spire of chance hangs fluctuant;
The day of separation is at hand;
Imagination lifts her gloomy curtains,
Like ev'ning's mantle at the flight of day,
Thro' which the trembling pinnacle we spy,
On which we soon must stand with hopeful smiles
Or apprehending frowns; to tumble on
The right or left forever.

The impending fate of the "poor vassals" is not mirrored in the evening sky with its emerging stars. Rather, it is to be found on the mundane plane in the growing shadows and gloom. If the slaves looked up, they would see only the "spire of chance" or the "trembling pinnacle," symbols of the auction block, on which they must stand to have their futures decided by others who have no regard for their worth as humans.

Only in the last four lines of the poem does Horton make use of the pronoun "we." As the suffering of the slaves becomes more acutely focused, the poet identifies with them more completely. When the slaves' feelings were dull and indeterminate, the persona maintained an aesthetic distance; at the poem's conclusion it has disappeared completely. The irrevocable finality of the word "forever" at the end of "Division of an Estate" sums up and accentuates the despair and anxiety which had been accumulating in the slaves' consciousness from the beginning.

While the slaves share the human emotions and aspirations of the heirs, they are treated like the animals and apportioned or sold with other items of farm property. This poem presents a powerful cry against slavery in a volume which shows strong evidence of having been edited in order to exclude such protest.

Other themes in *Poetical Works* are religion, patriotism, money, drinking, fame, scholarship, poetry itself, and love—the subject that had served Horton so well for nearly a third of a century. The collection even contains an example of a coveted Horton love letter, appropriately titled "A Billet Doux." It consists of a 220-word letter in prose, directed simply to "Dear Miss," and a fifteen-line poem.

Although Horton's *Poetical Works* did not make money for him, the poet continued to write, and in the 1850s and 1860s some of his poems appeared in the campus literary magazine at the university. Some of these poems were signed with Horton's name or initials. Other poems, which looked remarkably like them, bore the names of different authors.

Horton's prospects for freedom did not improve until news of the war reached the central North Carolina area. Students and faculty members left the college to become soldiers, and Horton was forced to return to the Horton farm for lack of patrons. When he heard that a detachment of Union troops was in Raleigh, Horton managed to travel the thirty miles to get there. He also managed to find himself an enthusiastic sponsor, Capt. Will Banks, a cavalry officer from Michigan. The young officer and Horton began making plans for the publication of more books by the poet.

Shortly after the conclusion of the Civil War, in 1865, Banks and Horton did succeed in getting a book of Horton's poems published. The title of the volume was *Naked Genius.* The title page proclaimed its author as the "author of *The Black Poet.*" However, there is no evidence that Horton's "Black Poet" book was ever published. At any rate, the title-page proclamation was patently premature, as Captain Banks placed in the back of *Naked Genius* an advertisement designed to drum up financial support for the publication of *The Black Poet.* Evidently, the advertisement was unsuccessful. *Naked Genius* itself was not successful as a money-making venture for Horton and Banks, possibly because they and William B. Smith and Company, the publishers, were not successful in making *Naked Genius*

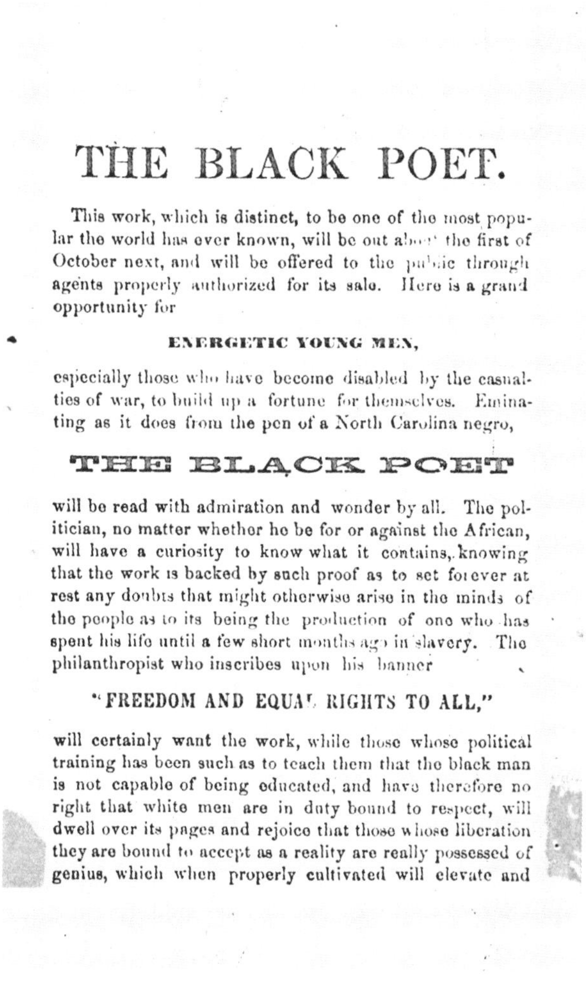
THE BLACK POET.

This work, which is distinct, to be one of the most popular the world has ever known, will be out about the first of October next, and will be offered to the public through agents properly authorized for its sale. Here is a grand opportunity for

ENERGETIC YOUNG MEN,

especially those who have become disabled by the casualties of war, to build up a fortune for themselves. Eminating as it does from the pen of a North Carolina negro,

THE BLACK POET

will be read with admiration and wonder by all. The politician, no matter whether he be for or against the African, will have a curiosity to know what it contains, knowing that the work is backed by such proof as to set forever at rest any doubts that might otherwise arise in the minds of the people as to its being the production of one who has spent his life until a few short months ago in slavery. The philanthropist who inscribes upon his banner

"FREEDOM AND EQUAL RIGHTS TO ALL,"

will certainly want the work, while those whose political training has been such as to teach them that the black man is not capable of being educated, and have therefore no right that white men are in duty bound to respect, will dwell over its pages and rejoice that those whose liberation they are bound to accept as a reality are really possessed of genius, which when properly cultivated will elevate and

Page from a solicitation for investors in a volume of poetry by Horton. "The Black Poet" was never published.

look like a literary work worthy of admiration and support. The book abounds with typographical errors and other evidence of haste.

Despite its flaws, *Naked Genius* is an important work, for it is by far the largest extant collection of Horton's poetry, comprising some 133 pieces, 41 of which had appeared in *Poetical Works* in 1845, a few others in periodicals. Predictably, the book contained poems about love, death, religion, famous people, and the art of poetry. However, there are two innovations in *Naked Genius:* humorous pieces and poems that rail against women.

In a few poems, Horton is able to blend humor into his complaints about women, as in "Snaps for Dinner." The three-stanza piece begins:

Come in to dinner squalls the dame,
  You need it now perhaps;
But hear the husband's loud exclaim,

I do not like your snaps;
'Tis snaps when at your breakfast meal,
And snaps when at your spinning wheel,
Too many by a devilish deal,
For all your words are snaps.

Another poem in which Horton is able to be playful while poking fun at women is entitled "New Fashions." Part of the poem ridicules women who smoke, drink, and curse more than the men.

Most of Horton's antifemale poems, however, are more angry than playful. More than half a dozen poems in *Naked Genius* are misogynistic. One, ironically entitled "Connubial Felicity," says that marriage is a trap, providing only a fleeting illusion of true bliss. Another, "The Treacherous Woman," begins:

Woman, thou bloom of every danger,
From whom all my sorrows rise,
To thee I'd live and die a stranger;
He who shuns thee must be wise.

It is curious that a man whose reputation and livelihood had centered upon the writing of love letters to women should turn against women and marriage in his later days.

Another change in Horton's work in 1865 comes in the tone of his slave protests. His earlier protests had been plaintive, but never really angry or vindictive. In poems like "Slavery" and "The Slave," in *Naked Genius,* Horton referred to the "master class" as thieves and murderers, equated the white man with Cain, and called upon God to smite the "rebels" and set the slaves free. At least two of Horton's angry protest poems were written after the Civil War; the others may well have been written earlier but withheld from public print.

With the war ended and the former slave poet a free man, Horton's literary career did not take the upward flight which might have been expected. Captain Banks went home to Michigan, and George Horton went north to Philadelphia. Nothing is known of Horton's Philadelphia years except that he sought, unsuccessfully, the aid of the Banneker Institute in attempting to get some of his work published.

Collier Cobb, a professor at the University of North Carolina, claimed to have spoken with Horton in Philadelphia in 1883. Cobb said that Horton had been writing short stories based on cleverly adapted plots from Bible stories. No specimens of these stories have been found. Horton is believed to have died in 1883, but the time and place of his death are uncertain.

During Horton's lifetime, several articles were written about him; however, Horton's contemporaries did not make any critical comments on the poetry. It must have seemed to them to be enough that a black slave could write poetry at all. In the 1930s J. Saunders Redding, Benjamin Brawley, and Vernon Loggins wrote critical appraisals commending Horton's work. In 1966 Richard Walser wrote *The Black Poet: The Story of George Moses Horton, A North Carolina Slave,* the first comprehensive critical biography of Horton. Since then other important studies on Horton have been written, including one by William Edward Farrison (*CLA* 1971), and a study by M. A. Richmond in *Bid the Vassal Soar* (1974). George Moses Horton's vanity and arrogance, as well as his wit and intellect, make him a most interesting subject for future critical evaluations.

Biography:

Richard Walser, *The Black Poet: The Story of George Moses Horton, A North Carolina Slave* (New York: Philosophical Library, 1966).

References:

Benjamin G. Brawley, *Early Negro American Writers* (Freeport, N.Y.: Books for Libraries Press, 1968);

Brawley, "Three Negro Poets: Horton, Mrs. Harper, and Whitman," *Journal of Negro History,* 2 (October 1917): 384-392;

Collier Cobb, "An American Man of Letters—George Moses Horton, The Negro Poet," *UNC Magazine* (October 1909);

William Edward Farrison, "George Moses Horton: Poet for Freedom," *CLA Journal,* 14 (March 1971): 227-241;

Blyden Jackson and Louis D. Rubin, Jr., *Black Poetry in America: Two Essays in Historical Interpretation* (Baton Rouge: Louisiana State University Press, 1974);

Vernon Loggins, *The Negro Author in America* (New York: Kennikat Press, 1964);

Merle A. Richmond, *Bid the Vassal Soar: Interpretive Essays on the Life and Poetry of Phillis Wheatley and George Moses Horton* (Washington, D.C.: Howard University Press, 1974).

Papers:

The largest collection of Horton's manuscripts and letters, as well as rare editions of his books, are at the University of North Carolina at Chapel Hill.

Fenton Johnson

(7 May 1888-16 September 1958)

Hammett Worthington-Smith
Albright College

See also the Johnson entry in *DLB 45, American Poets, 1880-1945: First Series.*

BOOKS: *A Little Dreaming* (Chicago: Peterson Linotyping Co., 1913);
Visions of the Dusk (New York: Fenton Johnson, 1915);
Songs of the Soil (New York: Fenton Johnson, 1916);
For the Highest Good (Chicago: Favorite Magazine, 1920);
Tales of Darkest America (Chicago: Favorite Magazine, 1920).

OTHER: "Children of the Sun," "The New Day," "Tired," "The Banjo Player," and "The Scarlet Woman," in *The Book of American Negro Poetry,* edited by James Weldon Johnson (New York: Harcourt, Brace, 1922), pp. 117-123; enlarged edition, adds "Lines from 'The Vision of Lazarus' " (New York: Harcourt, Brace, 1931), pp. 141-146;
"The Lost Love," "How Long, O Lord," and "Who Is That A-Walking in the Corn?," in *The New Poetry: An Anthology of Twentieth-Century Verse in English,* edited by Harriet Monroe and Alice Corbin Henderson (New York: Macmillan, 1923);
"The Banjo Player," "The Drunkard," and "The Minister," in *An Anthology of American Poetry: Lyric America, 1630-1930,* edited by Alfred Kreymborg (New York: Tudor Publishing, 1930), pp. 537-538;
"Rulers," "The Banjo Player," "The Scarlet Woman," "Tired," "Aunt Jane Allen," "When I Die," "The Lonely Mother," and "Who Is That A-Walking in the Corn?," in *The Poetry of the Negro, 1746-1949,* edited by Langston Hughes and Arna Bontemps (Garden City: Doubleday, 1949), pp. 61-64;
"The Daily Grind," "The World Is a Mighty Ogre," "A Negro Peddler's Song," "The Old Repair Man," and "Counting," in *American Negro Poetry,* edited by Bontemps (New York: Hill & Wang, 1963), pp. 25-28.

PERIODICAL PUBLICATIONS: "The Lost Love," "How Long, O Lord," and "Who Is That A-Walking in the Corn?," *Poetry,* 11 (June 1918): 136-137;
"Tired," *Others,* 5 (January 1919): 8;
"Aunt Hannah Jackson," "Aunt Jane Allen," "The Gambler," "The Barber," and "The Drunkard," *Others,* 5 (February 1919): 17-18;
"The Artist" and "Dreams," *Others,* 5 (April-May 1919): 20;
"A Dream" and "The Wonderful Morning," *Poetry,* 19 (December 1921): 128-129.

In his celebration of African and Afro-American life, Fenton Johnson is a forerunner of the Harlem Renaissance. One of the first revolutionary black American poets, Johnson has been hailed as "the foremost African-American pioneer of free verse." His endeavors were not limited to belles lettres. To promote African and Afro-American awareness and to address the crucial issues confronting Afro-Americans he founded and edited the *Champion Magazine* in September 1916, and after it folded in 1917, he started the *Favorite Magazine,* which ceased publication in autumn 1920. In an editorial for the first issue of the *Champion Magazine,* he wrote that his magazine was "Born out of the desire to serve a struggling race impartially," and that it aimed "to make racial life during this twentieth century a life worth living" through bringing about "reconciliation of the races." His magazine, Johnson wrote, would "do all in its power to impress upon the world that it is not a disgrace to be a Negro, but a privilege." Through his efforts for the Reconciliation Movement, he was also active in the Republican party.

Fenton Johnson was one of two sons born in Chicago, Illinois, to Elijah Johnson, a railroad porter, and Jessie Taylor Johnson. Johnson's father, who owned the building on State Street in which the family lived, was one of the wealthiest African-

Fenton Johnson

Americans in Chicago. John "Mushmouth" Johnson, Fenton Johnson's uncle, is reported to have financed the publication of some of Fenton Johnson's volumes of poetry and one of his magazines. Johnson's first published poem, "Absalom's Death," composed of nine eight-line stanzas, appeared in the *Broad Ax,* a Chicago newspaper, on 24 February 1900.

Johnson attended Englewood High School and Wendell Phillips High School in Chicago. Planning to become a clergyman, he was enrolled at Northwestern University in 1908-1909. In February 1910 he attended the University of Chicago as an unclassified student. In his early years he was a messenger for St. James Convent and St. Charles Convent and worked in the U.S. Post Office in Chicago. In 1910-1911 he was an instructor in English at State University in Louisville, Kentucky (now Simmons University). He later worked as a special writer for the Eastern Press Association and acting dramatic editor for the *New York News.* He married Cecelia Rhone.

In his first volume of poetry, *A Little Dreaming* (1913), Johnson explores intricate themes and masters conventional poetic patterns. A sheer lyrical quality pervades even the dialect poems. Poems addressed to poets such as Paul Laurence Dunbar and Algernon Charles Swinburne reveal Johnson's romantic influences, which are also apparent in the metrical patterns and literary devices employed with dexterity throughout the volume.

His themes include reverence for the African past and celebration of the Afro-American. He often employs supernatural motifs from Greek mythology, Islam, and the Judeo-Christian tradition, frequently intertwining all three within a single poem. He celebrates the common man, examining his interaction with nature and society. He looks at love, death, youth, and motherhood.

In "Prelude," the first poem in *Visions of the Dusk* (1915), Fenton Johnson observed:

> And yet some say to me, "O Man of dusk,
> Give us thy songs in broken Afric tongue,—
> The music of the peasant in the peasant in the South—
> The native strain alone in poetry."

These lines may reflect the contemporary reception of Johnson's first book, published at a time when white audiences expected black poets, such as Dunbar, to write in dialect. There is an irony in the expectation that Johnson should write black southern dialect and capture the southern experience: at the time his first volume appeared he had never been farther south than Louisville, Kentucky. In "Prelude," he protests that the source of poetry is in one's experiences and aspirations: " 'tis in living and the wonder Life/We find the soul of Beauty is a God/The vision is the thing and not the word."

When Johnson does write about blacks in the South in *Visions of the Dusk,* he resorts to parody and exaggerated dialect in the tradition of Dunbar. Yet in "The Creed of the Slave"—despite the speaker's exclamation, "Ah lubs de worl' "—there is an underlying bitterness, uncharacteristic of the genre:

> Go crack yo' whups, an' break dis flesh o' mine,
> Ah ain't a-gwine tuh leave dis love behin';
> Ah wu'k an' bleed fu' dose dat hu't me mos',
> But in de mawnin' w'en Ah am a ghos'
> Ah pray de Lawd dat you kin come up daih
> An' play wid me erpon de golden staaih.

Such an outlook may reflect Johnson's growing pessimism, close to the fatalism that would later characterize his work.

In his introduction to *Songs of the Soil* (1916) Johnson comments on the change in his style: "In my previous volumes I devoted myself to attempts at versification in the language of the academies and colleges; now I cast aside the English of the Victorians and assume the language of plantation and levee." Ironically, however, he was turning to dialect poetry at a time when "there is a group within my own race who bitterly oppose the writing of dialect." He justifies his choice of style by explaining, "unless one gains inspiration from the crudest of his fellows, the greatest of his kind cannot be elevated." To use dialect for any other purpose is appalling. "Nothing disgusts me more than to read in a metropolitan newspaper an interview with a colored man in which dialect is employed." He was careful not to use dialect inappropriately, explaining that in Negro spirituals, "the barbaric splendor of those songs are lost in the dialect of the plantation. To clothe a Negro hymn with dialect is like writing an ancient Hebrew psalm in the Yiddish of the Ghetto."

Songs of the Soil was Johnson's last published volume of poetry. Like other Afro-American poets of his time, Johnson felt thwarted in his attempts to be a writer and wondered, "if I should have gone to England or even Paris and cast my lot where I would not have to climb over the barrier of race." Although each of his books received excellent reviews, he was forced to subsidize their publication. As he noted in an interview with the *New York Tribune* (subsequently quoted in the *Brooklyn and Long Island Informer,* 14 May 1921), "And in literature I have published three volumes of verse, two of prose, contributed to Poetry and other magazines, have been in nearly all anthologies and have honorable mention from Poetry for 1918—but no income from literature."

Johnson is now best known for poems that are more experimental than those in his three published collections of poetry. An active participant in the Chicago Renaissance, he had an on-going correspondence with Harriet Monroe and had poems published in *Poetry: A Magazine of Verse.* Several literary critics, including Sterling Brown, have noted the influence of Vachel Lindsay, Edgar Lee Masters, and Carl Sandburg on Johnson's poetry. As Brown observed in *Negro Poetry and Drama* (1937), "Fenton Johnson's works show two extremes of Negro poetry after 1914. Some of his poems are conventional in form and substance; others, patterned upon his fellow Chicagoan, Sandburg, are striking departures in Negro poetry."

Johnson's free-verse poems were included in a collection titled "Arabian Nights." Although this volume was not published, poems from it appear in *Others: A Magazine of Verse* (edited by Alfred Kreymborg), the *Liberator,* and several anthologies. For Brown, these poems—including "Aunt Hannah Jackson," "The Banjo Player," "The Minister," "The Scarlet Woman," and "Tired"—are "snapshots of bitter experience" that combine "Sandburg's technique and Edgar Lee Masters's outlook." These poems introduce the free-verse tendencies that characterize his later verse. He remained concerned about the forces in Afro-American life that prevent a human being from realizing his aspirations—if not denying outright his humanity. He continued to write as one deeply aware of the social deterrents that thwart the individual's determination to succeed. As he becomes an involved observer of society, the lyrical quality of his earlier verse disappears.

Johnson focuses on people within metropolitan settings, interacting with inner city forces. Poems such as "Aunt Hannah Jackson," "Aunt Jane Allen," "The Gambler," "The Drunkard," and "The Barber" focus on a struggle to survive which all too often ends in defeatism. Employing imagistic technique, free verse, stark realism, the language of the common man, and a celebration of technology, this revolutionary poet demonstrates his kinship to the writers of the Chicago Renaissance. In "Aunt Hannah Jackson," for example, the portrait betrays an underlying note of social protest:

> For rubbing on other people's clothes Aunt
> Hannah Jackson gets a dollar and fifty cents a day
> and
> a worn out dress on Christmas.
> For talking to herself Aunt Hannah Jackson gets
> a smile as we call her a good natured fool.

During the 1930s Johnson participated in the "Negro in Illinois" project of the Works Progress Administration. His poems of this period are collected in "42 WPA Poems," an unpublished manuscript that is now at the Fisk University Library. Despite the title, Johnson's WPA experience is the subject for no more than ten of the poems. Other poems celebrate Chicago, technology, love, women, church ritual, spiritual endurance, and the literary artist. Continuing to write in the tradition of the Chicago Renaissance, he demonstrates his mastery of poetic technique. It is, however, the psychological dimension of these poems which enables them to remain provocative. In "The WPA Shovel Man" the speaker explains that he was once a master plumber, but once the Depression came "nobody got up a project for plumbers." The poem ends:

> Of course, shoveling isn't my line

I'm a master plumber;
But I'll never be one again.
I'm getting too old and I've almost forgotten
All I knew when I had my own business.
And nobody ever gets rich shoveling.
It isn't a trade; it's a government job[.]

In 1958, when asked for an update of his biographical data, Fenton Johnson responded that he did not have biographical material "later or since 1930." People who knew him after 1930 remember him as "a man barricaded in an envelope—sending no signals, receiving none." The only literary person with whom he maintained contact was Arna Bontemps.

Fenton Johnson's keen awareness of the Afro-American experience deserves recognition. After publishing his three volumes of so-called "Negro poetry," he began writing portraits that demonstrate his sensitivity to the African-American dilemma in American culture. This later poetry "gave voice in vivid concretized verse sketches to brutal facts—the truth of which could not be evaded."

References:

Sterling Brown, *Negro Poetry and Drama* (Washington, D.C.: Associates in Negro Folk Education, 1937), pp. 61-62;

James P. Hutchinson, "Fenton Johnson: Pilgrim of the Dusk," *Studies in Black Literature,* 7 (Autumn 1976): 14-15;

J. Saunders Redding, *To Make a Poet Black* (Chapel Hill: University of North Carolina Press, 1939), pp. 85-88;

Eugene B. Redmond, *Drumvoices: The Mission of Afro-American Poetry, A Critical History* (Garden City: Anchor/Doubleday, 1976), pp. 165-168;

Jean Wagner, *Black Poets of the United States from Paul Laurence Dunbar to Langston Hughes,* translated by Kenneth Douglas (Urbana, Chicago & London: University of Illinois Press, 1973), pp. 179-183.

Papers:

A typescript for "42 WPA Poems" is in the Special Collections of the Fisk University Library in Nashville. The Cullen-Jackman Collection in the Trevor Arnett Library at Atlanta University has the manuscripts for two poems, "The Cotton Picker" and "The Sunset," and correspondence between Johnson and Arna Bontemps. Correspondence between Johnson and Harriet Monroe is in the Personal Papers of Harriet Monroe at the Joseph Regenstein Library of the University of Chicago. This collection also includes manuscripts for: "The Lost Love," "Who Is That A-Walking in the Corn?," "The Lonely Mother," "A Dream," and "The Wonderful Morning."

George Marion McClellan

(29 September 1860-17 May 1934)

Dickson D. Bruce, Jr.
University of California, Irvine

BOOKS: *Poems* (Nashville: Publishing House, A.M.E. Church Sunday School Union, 1895);
Songs of a Southerner (Boston: Press of Rockwell & Churchill, 1896);
Old Greenbottom Inn and Other Stories (Louisville: N.p., 1906);
The Path of Dreams (Louisville, Ken.: J. P. Morton & Co., 1916).

OTHER: "The Negro as a Writer," in *Twentieth Century Negro Literature; or, a Cyclopedia of Thought on the Vital Topics Relating to the American Negro*, edited by D. W. Culp (Naperville, Ill.: J. L. Nichols, 1902), pp. 275-286.

George Marion McClellan

George Marion McClellan is an unusual figure in the history of black American literature. A poet and short story writer, he began his career on something of a cusp in black American literary history, as the literature itself was becoming increasingly race-conscious and increasingly concerned with the meaning of racial identity. As a poet McClellan showed little interest in such issues, devotedly pursuing a poetry of sentimentalism. As a writer of short stories, however, he displayed a keen awareness of the issues facing black Americans in the years leading up to World War I and a perspective on those issues that was often distinctive.

George Marion McClellan was born in Belfast, Tennessee, in 1860. Little is known of his early life and experiences, but he was, in his adult life and career, typical of the kind of educated, middle-class men and women who comprised the greatest number of black writers in the late nineteenth and early twentieth centuries. He attended Fisk University in Nashville, Tennessee, graduating with an A.B. in 1885, and then he studied at Connecticut's Hartford Theological Seminary from 1885 to 1887. For the next three years he served as a Congregationalist minister in Louisville, Kentucky. In 1888 he married Mariah Augusta Rabb. The couple later returned to Fisk, where Rabb became a member of the faculty and McClellan earned a master's degree in 1890. McClellan commuted from Nashville to Hartford and earned his B.D. in 1891. After reentering the ministry for a year, he served as financial agent for Fisk from 1892 to 1894, and as chaplain of the State Normal School in Normal, Alabama, from 1894 to 1896. The McClellans had two sons, Lochiel, born about 1892, and Theodore, born in 1895. Before the turn of the century McClellan went back to Louisville, where he continued writing, while building a career in the city's public schools, first as a teacher, then as a principal.

Like many black writers of this period, McClellan pursued creative writing as an avocation, and he personally arranged for the publication of his own works. Nevertheless, he was a dedicated writer, as his three major works attest (the fourth, *Songs of a Southerner,* 1896, is really a pamphlet in which pieces from the initial volume of *Poems* are reprinted). As he indicates in several places, he was highly self-conscious as a writer, holding to strong ideas about the special role of the black writer and about the place of black literature in the American tradition.

McClellan revealed much about his own literary career in his first published volume, *Poems,* which appeared in 1895. Although the book was published under the auspices of the A.M.E. Church Sunday School Union, its publication was sponsored by McClellan himself. Despite its title, the book contained not only poetry but also five short prose pieces, two of which appear to be autobiographical: "The Goddess of the Penitentials" and "A Farewell." The short story entitled "Annette" was later slightly expanded and recycled by McClellan for his two subsequent major volumes under the title "For Annison's Sake."

The works themselves in *Poems* reveal the extent to which McClellan was forced to do literary work as an avocation. He produced the book while he was serving as chaplain of the State Normal School. Several of the pieces had been written in New England, and a few went back to the time he had spent as a minister in Nashville. In his introduction to the volume, McClellan apologized for what he saw as a lack of merit in his work which, he felt, grew out of his not having had the leisure that true poetry demanded.

The poetry and prose alike are remarkable for their conservatism. McClellan, like many other writers of this period, black or white, took what was essentially a sentimental approach to literature. He viewed poetry, he wrote in "The Goddess of Penitentials," as essentially a matter of cultivating "exquisite sensibilities," a matter of feeling deeply and of conveying those feelings in words to one's audience. In this sensibility lay the pleasures of poetry, and also its duties, for the black poet, McClellan felt, was able to feel with special keenness the sufferings of the race.

Both his sense of the pleasures of poetry and his sense of its duties informed the kind of work that he did. His poetry was based mainly on the kinds of themes and images that were staples in the popular, genteel verse of the period, which was produced by white and black writers alike. The bulk of it was about nature, love, or religion, and whichever he wrote about, he sought to portray the fine sensibilities he had described in "The Goddess of Penitentials." Thus, he found fit material for poetry in the emotions of hope, beauty, and a kind of serenity evoked by "The June," or "Dogwood Blossoms," or "The March's Promise," which brought "blessed hope of life anew/That comes from death when spring begins" on "March's stormy winds." He found love in the rose, and he felt the pathos of the scene of a maiden's death. His prose was similarly conservative and sentimental. There, McClellan described the sufferings of the drunkard's child and, in an autobiographical piece, the poignancy of a final farewell between friends.

When McClellan turned his pen to racial matters, in keeping with his sense of the sufferings of black Americans, he remained true to his sentimentalist ideal. His poems on racial concerns were all pointed toward protesting injustice, and he couched his protest in wholly romantic terms. A poem entitled "The Octaroon's [*sic*] Farewell" was typical; refined notions of love serve as a background to a genteel but "tainted" young girl's lament that she cannot fulfill her chaste affection for her white lover. A similar effort to portray racism's evils within the framework of a sentimental literary ideal is McClellan's poem entitled "The Color Bane," in which a beautiful, cultured black woman's heart has been filled with hate as a result of her experience with a racist society.

McClellan's earliest work was, thus, strongly based on a literary model of genteel sentimentalism. And, indeed, in only one place did he depart from this approach to literature, and then only slightly. This was in the often-recycled "Annette," a story which relies on folk characters and which uses conjure as a central plot device. McClellan represented conjure as a powerful force in black folklife as he told the story of Annette's efforts to save her lover Annison from approaching death—efforts which are unsuccessful and which lead to her own tragic demise. (McClellan would provide a happy ending for the later version of the tale, which he titled "For Annison's Sake.") But McClellan's departure from gentility was small. He made clear his own rejection of conjure as anything more than superstition, and he focused most of his attention on the decidedly genteel Annette and her perils.

McClellan's sentimentalism did not, in itself, make him an unusual writer for his time. Black literature up to the 1890s was virtually all sentimental and genteel in character. Such divergent strains as realism or the folksy spirit of dialect writing began to take on significance only after the middle of the decade, so that McClellan's work—including his style of protest—looked back faithfully to the main lines of black literary tradition before 1895. There have been a number of explanations offered for this extreme conservatism in black writing before the mid-1890s, explanations generally focusing on assimilationist aspirations. And these explanations have relevance to McClellan himself, whose middle-class origins and experiences are fairly clear.

Genteel black writing in the late nineteenth century has generally been viewed by such literary historians as Robert Bone as an effort on the part of black writers to prove their place in the American mainstream. Middle-class in culture and achievement, these writers used literature to portray a genteel black world that was culturally identical to that of whites. Thus they made the case for their own assimilation into the larger society, indeed, for the transformation of America into a society in which race would become insignificant. McClellan's works fit into this pattern of black, middle-class gentility, and, in an introduction to his volume, he made clear that he, too, wrote with assimilationist purposes in mind.

But McClellan took this approach to literature to a point that was, by his time, unusual. The decade of the 1890s saw a real weakening of assimilationist thought among black Americans, particularly those of the middle class, and a growing interest in the history and experience of black people in the United States. Several writers, notably Paul Laurence Dunbar, had, by McClellan's time, celebrated key aspects of that experience in fiction and poetry. A few black thinkers and writers had even begun to call for the creation of a distinctive black literature. Not only did McClellan's work show no awareness of this but, in his introduction to *Poems,* he actually, if tacitly, denied the validity of these new directions in black literary thought.

For McClellan, the key distinguishing feature of the black American experience was its poverty, and this was, for him, a fact of literary as well as cultural life. Although he argued that true literary genius knew no race, he also asserted that any black writer in the United States operated under a disadvantage. This disadvantage was created by an absence, for blacks, of strong traditions and a "national life" because, according to McClellan, black people in America could claim no real history beyond that of slavery and emancipation. As a result, the black writer was, he felt, necessarily handicapped in the effort to achieve literary excellence and would be until there developed a genuine black historical experience. And this, he said, would not occur for generations.

POEMS.

BY

GEORGE MARION M'CLELLAN.

PRINTED FOR THE AUTHOR.

NASHVILLE, TENN.:
PUBLISHING HOUSE A. M. E. CHURCH SUNDAY SCHOOL UNION.
1895.

Title page for McClellan's first collection of poems

Such a perspective was far from common among black writers of McClellan's day; it is not certain that even writers of the preceding generation would have put their literary ideas quite as he did. Nor is it clear why he should have taken such a strong view of black American history and its meaning. But the strength of his views indicates, above all, the depth of his commitment to the American literary and cultural mainstream, a commitment which, however unusual, would remain a constant in his literary career.

McClellan would never state his sense of the limitations on black writers so strongly as he did in the introduction to his first book. Indeed, by 1902 he began to show not only an awareness of the literature of racial pride and identity but even an appreciation for it, seeking to incorporate that awareness into his own literary perspective. This effort was apparent in his general overview about black literature, "The Negro as a Writer," which appeared in D. W. Culp's 1902 compendium on black life and achievements, *Twentieth Century Negro Literature.* Written at the time McClellan was teaching at Central Colored High School in Louisville, the essay reviewed the state of black writing and offered McClellan's ideas about what black literature should be. In discussing black writers and their works, McClellan ranged widely but showed a consistent interest in ideas of racial pride. He took up the black press and celebrated its unyielding battle for racial justice. He noted George Washington Williams's positive accounts of black American history, and he cited with admiration Anna Cooper's 1892 *A Voice from the South,* an early clarion call for a distinctive black literature. But his focus was mainly on fiction and poetry, and here an increasing breadth in McClellan's literary outlook was no less clear, as he singled out for special praise those black writers who seemed best able to delineate "Negro life and character, thought and feeling." In particular, he identified Paul Laurence Dunbar and Charles Chesnutt (whose name he spelled "Chestnut") as artists of real merit among black writers, in part because of their abilities to render faithfully the black experience.

Still, his was a broadening rather than a changing perspective, for McClellan remained tied to his older, more conservative views of black literature, and of literature in general. He continued to find most black writing mediocre in comparison to that of whites. In singling out Chesnutt and Dunbar for praise, he focused on the only black writers who had a significant white readership, and in discussing Chesnutt's ability to portray Negro character, McClellan looked mainly at those works centered around genteel heroes and heroines—works that betrayed Chesnutt's own assimilationist leanings and that cohered with McClellan's own approach to literary protest. Though he saw special merit in Dunbar's dialect work—and ties between that work and aspects of Negro folk life—he expressed real misgivings about the form itself as a basis for significant work, anticipating James Weldon Johnson's more noted remarks about it. He was, in fact, uncomfortable with the very notion of a distinctive black speech and referred to it as simply "the bad English called Negro dialect." It is significant that his highest tribute to Dunbar took the form of comparing that poet's work to the Scottish dialect poetry of Robert Burns.

Thus, "The Negro as a Writer" marked an important step in McClellan's career insofar as it showed dawning awareness of the possibility of a black American literature based upon black American life. But it was, nonetheless, a testament to McClellan's fundamental literary conservatism and to his continuing to hold to assimilationist literary ideals. However, the essay helps to illuminate what McClellan did, as an author, in his next book, the 1906 *Old Greenbottom Inn,* a collection of stories.

The stories in this collection all focused on black characters and were given settings familiar to McClellan himself: an industrial, normal school much like the one at which McClellan had served as chaplain; Fisk University, the institution from which he had graduated and which he had served as financial agent; and his hometown of Nashville. In a brief "Proem," McClellan clarified the purposes underlying his effort to write about what he earlier called "Negro life and character, thought and feeling." They were the purposes of tragedy. Referring to Shakespeare's *King Lear* and *Hamlet* and to the works of Aeschylus, McClellan defines tragedy as the portrayal of "the unequal struggle of man against fate." But tragedy was not confined to the lives of kings and princes, McClellan added; it was to be found in any setting where one could see "the victim's bitter struggle after the better self amid evil environments, where blind and contradictory forces led the way." The South, he said, was such a setting, especially "among its darker subjects."

These remarks show precisely the position to which McClellan had come by 1906. Prepared to produce a literature based on black life, he still took his literary models from a larger western tradition that harked back to Aeschylus and Shakespeare. Moreover, he did not substantively depart from his earlier, thoroughly assimilationist ideals. Viewing the black experience as, most profoundly, the stuff of tragedy, he saw the origins of tragedy in racism's indifferent hostility to black aspirations, which he conceived of as, above all, making a place in the American mainstream.

McClellan's sense of the tragic meaning of race was especially clear in the title story and centerpiece of *Old Greenbottom Inn.* The story is about interracial love and violence which ultimately lead to the loss of an old southern inn by its white owners and the transformation of the building and its site from a roadhouse to an industrial school for Negroes. Reminiscent of Chesnutt's 1900 *The House Behind the Cedars,* not to mention McClellan's earlier poem "The Octaroon's [*sic*] Farewell," "Old Greenbottom Inn" gives an account of a young, refined woman of mixed race who falls in love with a visiting young white man. The love is real and, overcoming his own racial prejudice, he loves her as

George Marion McClellan

much as she loves him. But race makes the story tragic, nonetheless, since southern society denies the purity of love across racial lines.

In a powerful break from gentility, McClellan's heroine becomes pregnant with the white man's child, not, McClellan stresses, as a result of seduction or rape, but as a result of the two young lovers having been forced to fulfill their love clandestinely and without the possibility of legal or social approval. Only tragedy can result from such a situation, and the young white lover is killed by a jealous black man, who is himself lynched in retribution. The story deals complexly with issues of racial identity and racial unity, but protests, no less strongly, the kind of society that would force the young lovers into a clandestine and, ultimately, tragic relationship. No one, McClellan makes clear, is guilty: rather, all the protagonists are caught up in an environment that, as he said in his proem, makes them subject to the "blind and contradictory forces" of a racism indifferent to human needs and feelings. McClellan produced his strongest, most provocative work in "Old Greenbottom Inn," breaking from gentility enough to explore the meaning and the psychological and emotional implications of the American color line.

The four other stories included in *Old Greenbottom Inn* are not nearly as skillfully executed as the title piece; they lack both its dramatic unity and its power. Only one tale really stands out, and it is a very short story. "The Death of Hanover" is about the death of a noted racehorse, which McClellan uses as a pretext for celebrating what he sees as the native emotionalism of black folk. In this story he captures, for the first and only time in his work, some of the ideas such contemporary thinkers as Anna Cooper and W. E. B. Du Bois had begun to develop about the nature of a black distinctiveness. Of the other stories, "For Annison's Sake" was McClellan's expanded retelling of the earlier "Annette"; "A Creole from Louisiana" used the industrial school and Fisk as settings for a story of love and tragedy complicated by the appearance of a tragic octoroon; and "Essie Dortch" was a tale of seduction and violence, featuring a heroine whose vanity led her into show business but whose genuine pride ultimately took her to a life as a nun. Uniting all the stories in the volume is a sense that blacks were caught up in a world not of their making and powerfully out of their control. Much of the reason for that lay in the realities of American racism. McClellan's was a tragic vision of American race relations, matched among his contemporaries only in the works of Charles Chesnutt and, perhaps, Sutton E. Griggs.

McClellan's final book, *The Path of Dreams*, published in 1916, broke little new thematic ground. The volume was published during a difficult period in McClellan's life. He was achieving some success as an educator, having followed his friend and fellow poet Joseph Seamon Cotter, Sr., as principal of the Paul Dunbar School in Louisville, Kentucky, in 1911. However, his personal life was not so happy. His son Theodore was dying of tuberculosis, and McClellan was having difficulty finding treatment for the young man, clearly because of race. Indeed, during this period McClellan took his son to Los Angeles in quest of treatment, but the effort was in vain. Theodore died in early 1917. *The Path of Dreams* contains a touching tribute from father to son, "To Theodore."

Much of the volume, however, reprints McClellan's earlier work. Only ten of its forty-three poems had not appeared in the earlier *Poems*. Of five stories in the book, only one, "Gabe Yowl," had not appeared in *Old Greenbottom Inn*. Indeed, the 1916 volume virtually reprints that earlier collection, leaving out only "The Death of Hanover."

And yet, the book is not without interest. For one thing, several of the new poems, particularly the title piece, show an increasing technical ability on McClellan's part: "Sweet-scented winds move inward from the shore,/Blithe is the air of June with silken gleams,/My roving fancy treads at will once more,/The golden path of dreams." Among the new poems, too, was McClellan's most ambitious effort as a poet: a lengthy rendition of "The Legend of Tannhauser and Elizabeth." The choice of subject shows the extent to which McClellan had never really abandoned the essentially assimilationist position, and he felt comfortable enough with the subject to take, as he said, some liberty with the ending of the legend.

McClellan based his poem on Richard Wagner's opera *Tannhäuser,* which he cited in his introduction to the poem. Like Wagner, McClellan tells of the knight Tannhauser, who leaves the company of Venus, the goddess of love, in order to seek earthly absolution, which is subsequently denied to him. In Wagner's opera, which deviates from the legend upon which it is based, the disconsolate knight decides to return to his sinful life at "Venusburg," only to be redeemed in death through the intercession of his beloved Elisabeth. McClellan similarly concludes his poem with Tannhauser's death and redemption. More in keeping with late-nineteenth-century, genteel, American notions of sin and salvation, McClellan's Tannhauser gives no thought to going back to his former, sinful ways. As McClellan wrote in the brief introduction, "it seemed to me inconsistent after his chastening to have him consider a return to the Venusburg."

Title page for McClellan's 1916 volume of poetry

The one new short story, "Gabe Yowl," also broke some new ground since, though it deals with the real and potential tragedies of race relations, it does so within the framework of a mystery story. Gabe, framed for the murder of a white man, is at one point threatened with lynching and, at another, with that southern justice which places white retribution above judicial fairness. McClellan is able to use the story to dramatize the harsh realities of southern "law and order" in the early twentieth century. Gabe is freed through a startling series of coincidences that allow McClellan to delineate the same human tragedy he had first set forth in "The Octaroon's [*sic*] Farewell" and "Old Greenbottom Inn," the tragedy of love forbidden by unreasonable racial proscriptions. And in this, perhaps, lies much of McClellan's real significance as an author. As he focused his attention on the tragedies of black American life, he wrote in ways that presented a consistent vision of the emotional and psychological realities of racism, helping to illuminate the impact of prejudice on human lives.

There is little to be said of McClellan's literary career after the publication of *The Path of Dreams.* He continued his work as a teacher for most of his remaining years and studied for a time at the Los Angeles Branch of the University of California. In 1929 he sought to republish *The Path of Dreams* and what must have been an expanded version of "Gabe Yowl" in book form. He also claimed to have done a new work, "The History of American Literature," in which he would discuss the works of black and white American authors in an integrated fashion consistent with his own ideals; but none of it ever appeared. Little is known of his life between his announcement of these plans and his death in 1934.

No one would argue that McClellan was a major writer during his lifetime, nor that he was recognized as such by his contemporaries. He certainly did not receive the acclaim given to Dunbar or

Chesnutt. Nor can it be said that he broke significant new literary ground. Indeed, if anything, his poetry is significant precisely because of its conservatism, however skillful McClellan may have become technically. He was probably more important as a writer of fiction because, working in that form, he helped to reveal the meaning and implications of American racism in the life of an educated, sensitive, and ambitious black man. In this, his works provide an important perspective on the development of black thought and culture at the turn of the century.

References:

Benjamin Brawley, *The Negro Genius: A New Appraisal of the Achievement of the American Negro in Literature and the Fine Arts* (New York: Dodd, Mead, 1937), p. 168;

Arthur P. Davis and Michael W. Peplow, *The New Negro Renaissance: An Anthology* (New York: Holt, Rinehart & Winston, 1975), pp. 13, 528-529;

Robert T. Kerlin, *Negro Poets and Their Poems*, revised and enlarged edition (Washington, D.C.: Associated Publishers, 1935), pp. 173-179;

Richard A. Long and Eugenia W. Collier, *Afro-American Writing: An Anthology of Prose and Poetry*, volume 1 (New York: New York University Press, 1972), pp. 237-241;

Joan R. Sherman, *Invisible Poets: Afro-Americans of the Nineteenth Century* (Urbana: University of Illinois Press, 1974), pp. 154-163;

Sherman, "Tennessee's Black Poet: George Marion McClellan," *Tennessee Studies in Literature*, 18 (1973): 147-162;

Newman Ivey White and Walter Clinton Jackson, *An Anthology of Verse by American Negroes* (Durham, N.C.: Trinity College Press, 1924), pp. 92-97.

Papers:

There is a small collection of McClellan's letters at Case Memorial Library, Hartford Seminary Foundation.

James E. McGirt

(September? 1874-13 June 1930)

Walter C. Daniel
University of Missouri at Columbia

BOOKS: *Avenging the Maine, A Drunken A.B., and Other Poems* (Raleigh, N.C.: Edwards & Broughton, 1899; revised and enlarged edition, 1900); second revised and enlarged edition (Philadelphia: Lasher, 1901);

Some Simple Songs and a Few More Ambitious Attempts (Philadelphia: Lasher, 1901);

For Your Sweet Sake: Poems (Philadelphia: Winston, 1906; enlarged, 1909);

The Triumphs of Ephraim (Philadelphia: McGirt, 1907).

James E. McGirt, poet, songwriter, businessman, and editor, has never been well known in literary circles, but he deserves notice for his efforts to further the cause of Afro-American literature by publishing *McGirt's Magazine*, which regularly reprinted the work of the leading black writers of his day. In his role as *McGirt's* editor he also advanced the causes of black activism, urging his readers toward education and economic autonomy. Through the Constitutional Brotherhood of America, which he founded, and for which his magazine was the "official organ," he promoted voting rights for blacks and encouraged close scrutiny of political candidates. Biographer John W. Parker wrote of McGirt that his vision went beyond the material and social limitations he confronted. Parker suggests that McGirt's "contribution to American letters, by no means pronounced, is perhaps more individual than racial. A dreamer whose dreams never came true, this literary enthusiast nevertheless deserves to be remembered . . . because of his devotion to a worthy ideal and his struggle to reach

James Ephraim McGirt

it in the face of overwhelming odds."

McGirt spent much of his life in Greensboro, having come there from his native Robeson County, North Carolina, during the closing years of Reconstruction. One of four children of sometime farmer Madison McGirt and Ellen Townsend McGirt, an imperious, Bible-toting materfamilias, James Ephraim was probably born in September 1874. He attended Allen Private School in Lumberton, North Carolina, and graduated from public school in Greensboro. In 1891 he entered Bennett College, probably in the secondary school department, from which he graduated with a bachelor's degree in 1895. Aspiring to be a poet, he wrote prodigiously during his college days and sought to bring himself to the attention of white and black literary figures of the time. After college, McGirt supported himself by working as a launderer and a drayman in Greensboro, earning a comparatively comfortable living. In 1899 he published *Avenging the Maine, A Drunken A.B., and Other Poems,* encouraged by the success enjoyed by Paul Laurence Dunbar, William Stanley Braithwaite—whom he had once met—and Charles W. Chesnutt, black writers whose works were published and read by a large public.

McGirt's poems are written in black vernacular and in standard English, in the genteel, sentimental style popular in the nineteenth century. The poems in McGirt's first volume are, for the most part, bucolic pieces, reflecting the poet's early life in rural Robeson County. "The Evening" is about the communal joy neighbors experience after working in the fields, and "The Picnic" is about the sparse, but genuine, pleasures of a people who work hard and participate totally in the leisure available to them. Their lives are hard, but not unhappy.

In general, the verse in *Avenging the Maine* ranges from the patriotic and military to the didactic and race-oriented. One poem, "Memory of Lincoln and the Yankees," praises the "Emancipator" and those who the country folk believe brought freedom to the black slaves. Written primarily in the black dialect style Dunbar had popularized, the poem fails to achieve the unity in structure or the high level of poetic skill that characterize Dunbar's work.

In the second edition of *Avenging the Maine* (1900), McGirt added seventeen poems to the original collection; a third version, in 1901, contained only one new poem. Neither enlargement substantively changed the shape of the volume. *Avenging the Maine* consistently received mixed reviews. In 1901 McGirt published what was essentially a fourth edition of it, *Some Simple Songs and a Few More Ambitious Attempts,* which experienced similarly equivocal success. This group of twenty-one clearly autobiographical poems includes "Avenging the Maine" and six new poems. In its preface, McGirt apologizes for the weak quality of the earlier poems and states that he considers the new ones an improvement. The critics did not agree, pointing out that the poems are largely exercises in imitation of English poets. One piece, for example, "The Century's Prayer," written in the days of the new twentieth century, has been commended by Parker for its "Kiplingesque" characteristics. The poem, three eight-line stanzas, each comprised of sets of rhyming couplets written in iambic tetrameter, seems to borrow elements from Kipling's 1897 hymn for Queen Victoria's Diamond Jubilee, "Recessional," including the address to "Lord God of Hosts." Unlike Kipling, who invokes God's ability to make men remember war, McGirt plaintively asks, "May war and strife and discord cease," and

"May flags of war fore'er be furled."

After several years of seeking to establish his reputation as a poet in Greensboro, McGirt moved to Philadelphia. Before leaving home he had sought patronage from Newman I. White and Walter C. Jackson, faculty members at white colleges in North Carolina, and from the well-respected author Thomas Nelson Page, to whom he wrote, introducing himself as a "would-be-poet (colored)" who, given the strength, would "add a line to American poetry" to be praised. From September 1903 to 1909 McGirt published *McGirt's Magazine* from Philadelphia. Started as a monthly (until August 1908) and later issued as a quarterly, the periodical was used primarily to promote its editor's creative writing. His three volumes of poetry and some of his short stories were carried in the journal. He published his long fictional work "Black Hand" in serial form in the magazine. In addition to his own writing, McGirt included in the magazine an impressive number of reproductions of articles written by black Americans. Among them were pieces by W. E. B. Du Bois, Francis J. Grimké, Kelly Miller, Benjamin T. Tanner, Mary Church Terrell, Richard R. Wright, Jr., Frances E. W. Harper, and Paul Laurence Dunbar. At one time McGirt attempted to induce Charles W. Chesnutt, the most celebrated black fiction writer at the time, to contribute a short story, but Chesnutt declined.

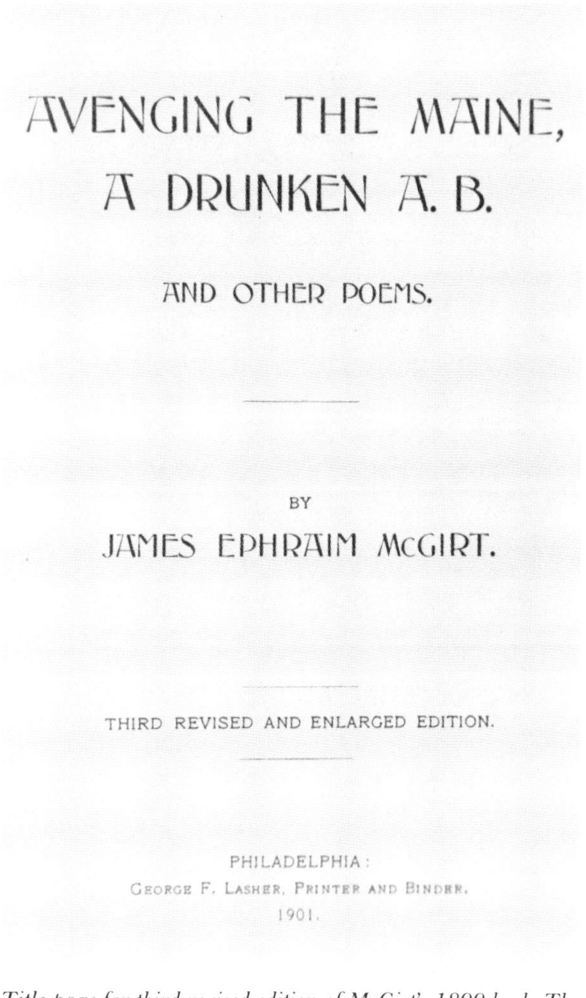
AVENGING THE MAINE,
A DRUNKEN A. B.
AND OTHER POEMS.

BY
JAMES EPHRAIM McGIRT.

THIRD REVISED AND ENLARGED EDITION.

PHILADELPHIA:
GEORGE F. LASHER, PRINTER AND BINDER.
1901.

Title page for third revised edition of McGirt's 1899 book. The second revised edition added seventeen poems; the third revised edition included one additional poem.

Notwithstanding his persistent efforts to become a respected author, McGirt failed to become a leading voice in the black literary movement of the early days of the twentieth century. His editorials in the magazine centered largely around politics and the social tensions found in the nation at the time of the inauguration of Jim Crow practices throughout the South. His editorial voice was less than militant, but it did attract the attention of Du Bois who, perhaps because McGirt seemed to reject "accommodationism" as advocated by Booker T. Washington and his followers, praised *McGirt's Magazine.* He recommended it as one of several periodicals he considered progressive, including the *Boston Guardian,* the *Voice of the Negro,* and *Alexander's Magazine.*

Like Du Bois, McGirt was active in organizations dedicated to improving the lot of black Americans. Never married, McGirt gave his life to such causes. His magazine served as the official journal of the Constitutional Brotherhood of America, a group that sought to organize black voters for balancing power in certain states to insure the effectiveness of the Fourteenth and Fifteenth Amendments to the Constitution, which were endangered by the rise of the Democratic party. The magazine also supported the aims of the National Afro-American Council and lent its voice to Du Bois's Niagara Movement. McGirt constantly reminded the Republican party that it was betraying the Negro, and he told his black following that they could secure rights they had won after emancipation only through strong, intelligent exercise of the ballot. To this extent, he was totally consonant with the philosophy and activities of Du Bois.

McGirt's activities during the time he was in Philadelphia were not limited to his magazine. In 1906 the John C. Winston Company published *For Your Sweet Sake: Poems,* which was released in a new edition in 1909. The second edition contains an "Appreciations" section that includes excerpts from a commendation written by Thomas Nelson Page and a brief letter from Booker T. Washington

Frontispiece and title page for the enlarged edition of McGirt's 1906 volume

which praises "When the Sun Shines Hot," a quasi-dialect poem that urges the wisdom of fishing over working the fields in the heat of the sun. This poem is the type of folksy pastoral that for modern readers may reinforce negative stereotypes: "Des 'bout dark I kum hum, strollin' wid a bunch er lubly trout;/Hannah she c'mmence er grinnin' 'little Rastus 'gin to shout;/Soon de hoe cakes is er bakin', fish er fryin', table sot./No, der ain't no use'n workin' w'en de sun shines hot."

A substantial portion of the poems in *For Your Sweet Sake* are laments for love lost or odes to love. According to critic Joan Sherman, the poem "Some One Some Where," from which the book borrows its title, is addressed to Irene Gallaway, "who married another man when McGirt balked at the altar—he was 'forever confused by his mother's intervention.' " "Two eyes! Two eyes! The hue I cannot tell,/A glance from them, my soul doth ever pine." He continues, "For you! For you! For your sweet sake alone,/I live! I toil. . . ." A startling metaphor in "A Song of Love" demonstrates why McGirt's poems frequently received unenthusiastic reviews: "Just as we bruise a pear to make it sweet,/ So love will bruise her victim with her feet."

In 1909 McGirt's Publishing Company, which funded the magazine and some of his other publishing ventures, failed and, owing to the illness of a sister, McGirt returned to Greensboro in 1910. Living in the ten-room house he bought for his family, McGirt continued to operate some of the businesses he had begun before going to Philadelphia. With his sister Mary Magdalene, he reorganized the Star Hair Grower Manufacturing Company, which became a successful cosmetics manufacturing and distribution enterprise that was

TO THEIR SURPRISE THEY SAW CLEARLY, EPHRAIM STANDING ON A POTATO BARREL

"I AM THINE"

HE SITS ASTRIDE THE WINDOW, THEN AS IF FASCINATED—HALTS

HIS EYES WERE GLARING, HIS LIPS DRAWM BACK, EXPOSING HIS TEETH SHUT TOGETHER, HIS HANDS CLENCHED, ONE ON THE HANDLE OF THE RAZOR, THE OTHER HANGING BY HIS SIDE. ALL THE WHILE HE WAS UTTERING CURSES AND YELLS LIKE A MANIAC

Illustrations for "Hail the King and the Queen" (top left), "The Test that Failed" (top right), "At the Mercy of a Slave" (bottom left), and "From the Clutches of the Devil" (bottom right), published in The Triumphs of Ephraim *(1907)*

one of the leading black businesses in the state. For a while he was even a prominent realtor. McGirt's business ventures brought him visibility and financial success, but his literary career faltered, despite the fact that he had the means and experience to publish his own relatively large output of poems and short fiction.

In disappointment over the negative reaction to his poetry McGirt had turned to writing short stories. Some of them appeared in his magazine from time to time. One of his last literary efforts was *The Triumphs of Ephraim* (1907), a collection of his short fiction. Hugh M. Gloster, in his *Negro Voices in American Fiction* (1948), considers these eight pieces inferior; although they seek to portray the Afro-American advantageously, they also reflect the southern plantation tradition. "At the Mercy of a Slave" fits this literary mode as it praises a black bondsman for his loyalty to the wife and child of his slaveholder, who is fighting in the Civil War. Another, in the same vein, "Lifting the Veil," celebrates a black elderly woman who rears the illegitimate son of a young southern gentleman and a poor white girl. The title story has as its central character a black former coachman whose heroism earns him the hand in marriage of the daughter of the president of a large black college. The bigger-than-life hero is also the central character in "In Love as in War," which shows a black soldier in the Spanish-American War who successfully competes with the son of an aristocratic New Orleans family to become the husband of a Filipino princess.

By the first decade of the twentieth century, the plantation tradition stories were fast losing their appeal, and other black writers associated with literary movements McGirt supported were moving to the depiction of another kind of black man. To a large extent, the new literature was becoming propagandistic, and, later, critics would consider it more sociological than literary. But McGirt's published fiction was incompatible with these new works; his stories did not agree, in philosophy or sentiment, with his editorials in his magazine. His stories were patronizing, overly sentimental, and weak in their outdated genteel technique. McGirt's characters are thinly drawn, leaving the pieces little more than sketches.

McGirt possessed the unusual opportunity to put his works into print, and although his magazine has become primarily an item in histories and encyclopedias of black journals, it is McGirt's most notable accomplishment. It came along at a time when many black Americans were taking to the periodical press to promote black organizations and racial solidarity. In this respect, when he died in Greensboro, North Carolina, on 13 June 1930, his life had been active and effective. His perseverance in writing poetry and short fiction is admirable, but the works themselves represent more ambition than ability.

References:

Penelope L. Bullock, *The Afro-American Periodical Press 1838-1909* (Baton Rouge: Louisiana State University Press, 1981), pp. 79-81;

Hugh M. Gloster, *Negro Voices in American Fiction* (Chapel Hill: University of North Carolina Press, 1948), pp. 70-71;

John W. Parker, "James E. McGirt: Tar Heel Poet," *Crisis,* 60 (May 1953): 287-289;

Parker, "James Ephraim McGirt: Poet of 'Hope Deferred,' " *Negro History Bulletin,* 16 (March 1953): 123-126;

Joan Sherman, *Invisible Poets: Afro-Americans of the Nineteenth Century* (Urbana: University of Illinois Press, 1974), pp. 193-198.

Papers:

A few copies of *McGirt's Magazine* are collected at the Moorland-Spingarn Research Center, Howard University, Washington, D.C.

Oscar Micheaux

(2 January 1884-26 March 1951)

J. Randal Woodland
University of North Carolina at Chapel Hill

BOOKS: *The Conquest: The Story of a Negro Pioneer, by the Pioneer* (Lincoln, Nebr.: Woodruff, 1913);

The Forged Note: A Romance of the Darker Races (Lincoln, Nebr.: Western Book Supply, 1915);

The Homesteader (Sioux City, Iowa: Western Book Supply, 1917);

The Wind From Nowhere (New York: New York Book Supply, 1944);

The Case of Mrs. Wingate (New York: New York Book Supply, 1945);

The Story of Dorothy Stanfield, Based on a Great Insurance Swindle, and a Woman (New York: New York Book Supply, 1946);

The Masquerade: An Historical Novel (New York: New York Book Supply, 1947).

Oscar Micheaux

Oscar Micheaux was a fiercely independent promoter of his own novels and films. He often involved his leading characters in personal and financial struggles for success that mirrored experiences central to his own life. An ardent supporter of the doctrines of Booker T. Washington, who urged that blacks better their own condition through diligence and dedication to practical goals, Micheaux conceived of his work as inspirational as well as entertaining.

Micheaux stands apart from his contemporaries in black letters. In his early books, Micheaux did not write of the rural South, as did Charles W. Chesnutt and Paul Laurence Dunbar, nor of northern ghettos, as did James Weldon Johnson. Nor do his early books focus, as did much black fiction of the period, on the tragic results of slavery and the problems resulting from the powerlessness of blacks in American society. His later novels show that he was but slightly influenced by the Harlem Renaissance; he returns instead to the fictive techniques of his youth.

His style is straightforward, unencumbered by literary pretensions. His aim, in creating novels or films, was to capture his readers' attention with an exciting story and then to provide them with either an uplifting example of the heights to which members of his race might aspire, or a cautionary tale, demonstrating how far individual members of his race were from that lofty goal. Though the melodramatic plots through which his characters achieve success seem dated and contrived today, Micheaux's achievement as a pioneer in exploring the lives of the black middle class marks him as an important literary figure.

The source of most information about Micheaux's early life is his own writing. Although *The Conquest: The Story of a Negro Pioneer, by the Pioneer* (1913) is often referred to as a novel, it is actually autobiography. Micheaux's parents, Calvin and Belle Willingham Michaux (the original spelling), were farmers near Metropolis, Illinois, when Oscar was born, the fifth child in a family of thirteen. The family soon moved to Metropolis to give the children better educational opportunities. Some years later they returned to farming, but Micheaux quickly proved himself better suited to the marketplace than the field.

Discontented in Metropolis where, as he recalled in *The Conquest,* the people "were set in the ways of their localisms, and it was quite useless to talk to them of anything that would better oneself," he left town at age seventeen. Moving through a succession of dead-end positions, he finally settled into a job as a porter on a Pullman car. Disillusioned by the corruption that pervaded the porter system and ever on the lookout for opportunities for advancement, he decided to seek his fortune on the frontier. As the narrator of *The Conquest* recalls it, he "bid farewell to Armour Avenue and Chicago's Black Belt with its beer cans, drunken men and women, and turned [his] face westward with the spirit of Horace Greely [*sic*] before [him,] and his words 'Go west, young man and grow with the country' ringing in [his] ears." He took over a small homestead in Gregory County, South Dakota, worked his claim diligently, and was worth $20,000 by the time he was twenty-four, by his own account.

Micheaux's experience as a homesteader in South Dakota gave him the material for his first book, *The Conquest,* which he called "a true story of a negro who was discontented and the circumstances that were the result of that discontent." The protagonist is named Oscar Devereaux, and although Micheaux has altered place-names throughout, he attempts to make a realistic presentation of events in his own life. Although Micheaux undoubtedly took some artistic license in arranging these events, his narrator intends the reader to accept his successes and failures as actual events and to view his life as a model for others to follow.

The book lacks the unity of focus and purpose that might be expected from a novel, but it works quite well as a loosely structured memoir, showing its main character in his various roles as a homesteader in South Dakota, as an observer of the political intrigue in the small towns in the area, as an apologist for the social doctrines of Booker T. Washington (to whom Micheaux had dedicated his book), and as a lover frustrated by a devious father-in-law and the social conventions that keep him apart from the white woman he loves.

Devereaux's growing prosperity as a farmer, despite hardships and setbacks, is the major concern of the book. Large sections are also given to detailed descriptions of the bureaucratic process of staking a claim and holding it; and of the political rivalry between neighboring towns to influence where the railroad company lays its tracks. In these expository sections the narrator's role narrows to that of a reporter. In the last chapters of the book Devereaux's story again gains prominence as the story becomes a melodramatic romance of thwarted love. The villain is the Reverend N. J. McCraline, father of Oscar's wife, Orlean, and "the biggest old rascal in the Methodist church." The Reverend disapproves of Devereaux and eventually turns his daughter's affections away from him. Devereaux's attempts to regain her fail, and the book ends with his last encounter with Orlean.

The tone of the work is often uneven and the writing awkward, but Micheaux's descriptions of the natural beauty of the wilderness can be striking, and the book gains a kind of unity from the sheer force of the narrator's personality. He is clearly a man who knows what he wants and will endure almost any hardship to get it. Critic Chester Fontenot praises Micheaux's recurring figure of the black pioneer, "an individual able to collapse the distinction between race and class." Such an individual "is freed from the artifices of 'civilization' and is allowed to fulfill his own potential through a process inherent in his cultural history."

Once the book was completed, Micheaux drew on his considerable skills as a promoter to sell copies of it, first to the neighboring white farmers in South Dakota, then on a tour of the South. Meeting with success, he drew on the same sources to form a publishing company, Western Book Supply, to publish his second book, *The Forged Note: A Romance of the Darker Races* (1915).

In *The Forged Note,* Micheaux again drew from events of his own life, but he exercised greater fictional imagination than he had in *The Conquest.* Like Micheaux himself, the protagonist Sidney Wyeth has written a book (entitled *The Tempest*) about his experience as the only black homesteader in a remote region of South Dakota, and like Micheaux, Wyeth sets out on a tour of the South to sell copies of his book door-to-door. A companion plot follows the experiences of Mildred Latham, who is also selling Wyeth's book. The function of the Wyeth sections of the book is to examine the problems of blacks in such cities as Attalia (Atlanta) and Effingham (Birmingham). Wyeth is distressed by the condition of the members of his race there, given as they are to gambling, drinking, and crime. They do not, Wyeth concludes ruefully, "consider feeding the mind an essential to moral welfare," hence they don't buy his books. Black preachers

The Conquest

The Story of a Negro Pioneer

BY THE PIONEER

1913
THE WOODRUFF PRESS
Lincoln, Nebr.

Frontispiece and title page for Micheaux's first novel, which draws heavily on his experiences in Nebraska

are criticized for their failure to provide any relief for the problems of urban blacks. These problems stem, in Wyeth's view, not from the prejudice of whites but from a lack of concern among the black community, who would rather build a new church than a library or a gymnasium to provide healthy alternatives to crime for young people. Wyeth speaks out against such shortsightedness and is criticized "for his method of bringing the truth before eyes which did not wish to see it."

Mirroring Wyeth's story is the melodramatic tale of Mildred Latham, who meets Wyeth in Cincinnati and falls in love with him, but is rejected for reasons that remain mysterious to the reader throughout much of the book. Unable to be with the man she loves, she remains devoted to him and goes south to sell the book on her own. She is followed by a mysterious man with a scar who threatens to expose her past; she finally ends up meeting her long-lost sister, and Wyeth, in New Orleans. Although she has had great success in selling his book, Wyeth rejects her again and flees to the swamps to think, chancing while there to meet an old man who clears up the mystery of Mildred: to protect her father, a minister who had embezzled money from his church in order to be made a bishop, she had agreed to become the mistress of a white man. Wyeth marries Mildred and takes her off to a brighter future in the West.

The Forged Note demonstrates that Micheaux had developed a clearer idea of his intentions for his books. He wanted to provide an inspirational example for others of his race by positing that success comes to the diligent. He intended to criticize those members of his race, be they gamblers or Baptist preachers, who were not contributing to the general welfare. To get his message across to the reading public, he had to produce a good story,

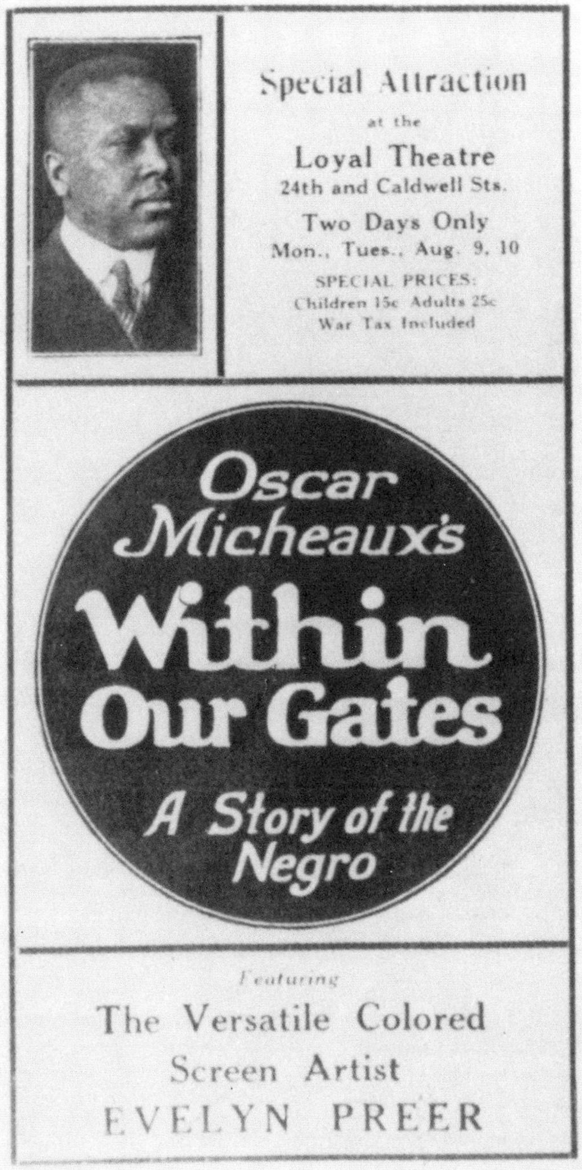

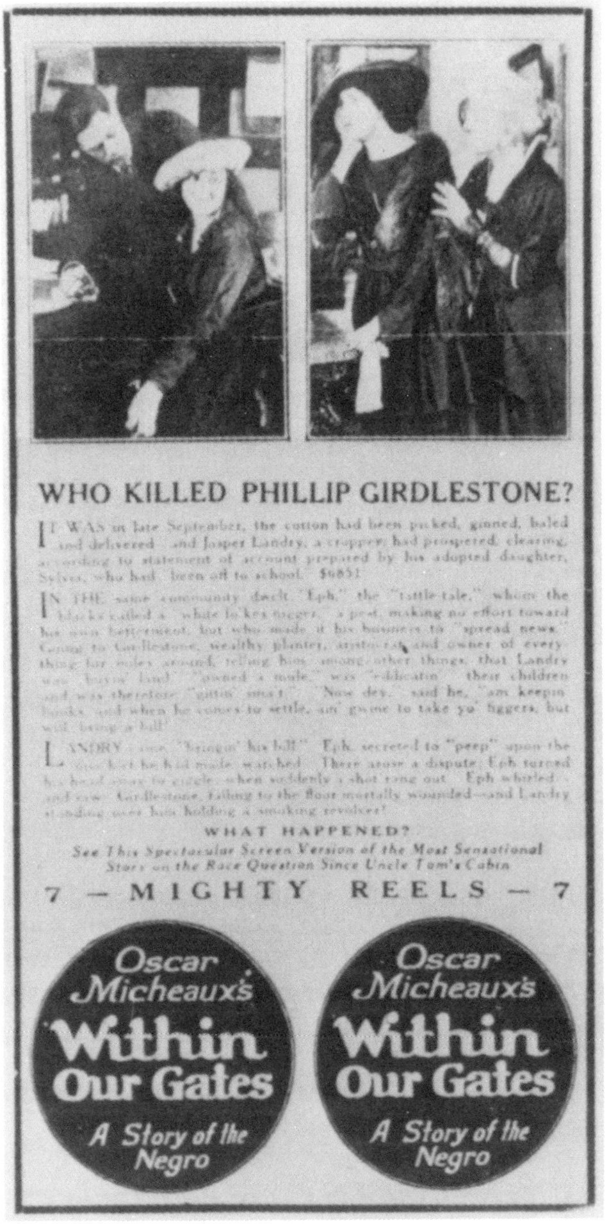

Advertisements for Micheaux's 1920 mystery film, based on the lynching of a black man

full of excitement and romance. In his third book, *The Homesteader* (1917), Micheaux rewrote the story of *The Conquest* with these lessons in mind. Gone are the intricate details of the Homestead Act and the political rivalries and competition for trade. Given more prominence is the romantic side of the story, which undergoes radical expansion and elaboration.

The protagonist of *The Homesteader* is Jean Baptiste, but his early history is quite similar to that of Devereaux. Taking up a claim in South Dakota, Baptiste prospers through hard work. During a snowstorm, he is thrown together with Agnes Stewart, the daughter of a neighboring white farmer, and they fall in love. Yet Baptiste recognizes "the Great fact: *The fact that between him and his dream girl was a chasm so deep socially that bridging was impossible.* Because she was white while he was black, according to *the custom of the country and its law,* she could never be anything to him." Instead Baptiste marries a black woman named Orlean McCarthy, only to be opposed by her father, a minister who breaks up the marriage, brings Orlean back to Chicago, and forces her to sell the property that Baptiste had acquired for her. Tormented by guilt over her father's action, Orlean kills him and herself; Jean is accused of the crimes. Agnes hires a detective who produces evidence that leads to Baptiste's acquittal, and he returns to South Dakota. Agnes then learns that she has black blood, and she and Jean are free to marry, an artificial device that Micheaux employed to mollify reader expectations of the period.

The popularity of *The Homesteader* interested the Lincoln Motion Picture Company, which produced movies starring blacks for black audiences. Unable to agree on contract terms with the company, Micheaux resolved to film it himself, raising money from the same people who had helped to publish his books. Though he had no experience in filmmaking, he taught himself the craft, approaching the project with his typical exuberance. The resulting film, which Daniel J. Leab calls "highly emotional in style if crude in technique," marked a change in Micheaux's career. He used the profits to establish the Micheaux Book and Film Company with offices in New York, Chicago, and Sioux Falls, and he began seeking investors for his next film. He was to write, produce, and direct films for the rest of his life, abandoning the writing of fiction for over twenty years.

The word "producer" best encompasses the contributions Micheaux made to his films. An independent filmmaker, Micheaux was involved in virtually every aspect of production; as film historian Henry T. Sampson reports, Micheaux "did all the work himself. He wrote scenarios, supervised filming, and did the bookkeeping; in short, he did everything." Though it is impossible to identify the specific contributions of Micheaux to each of the films that bear his name, it is clear that they were products of his creative imagination.

Micheaux's most successful films were the silent films he produced in the 1920s. Though they were criticized by some blacks for their depictions of gambling, violence, drinking, and other "objectionable race features," they were a great success at ghetto movie houses. *Body and Soul* (produced in 1924) may be the best of this period. Paul Robeson made his screen debut in this film, a protest against the bootlegging and gambling that, Micheaux felt, hindered the potential of the black community, and against many black preachers who abused the trust their congregations placed in them.

The success of his pictures allowed Micheaux to ignore criticism of their content or lack of polish; he believed that such flaws should be exposed rather than covered up. In an article written for the *Philadelphia Afro-American* in 1925, he explained that his aim in making movies was "to lay before the race a cross section of its own life, to view the colored heart at close range." He continued: "I am too much imbued with the spirit of Booker T. Washington to engraft false virtues upon ourselves, to make ourselves that which we are not."

Critics have not always agreed with Micheaux's opinion of himself. Leab, for example, questions the depth of Micheaux's sincerity: "Despite his public utterances, Micheaux's films were not designed to uplift or to enlighten. They were meant to entertain, to appeal to his concept of black popular taste, and to make money."

Even those limited aims were not always successful. After the bankruptcy of his company in 1928, he had to rely on the backing of white financiers and theater owners to continue production. In 1931 he produced the first all-black talkie, *The Exile,* another reworking of his experiences on the South Dakota frontier. He continued producing the highly melodramatic films that were his trademark, but met increasing opposition from critics in the black community who felt that his films, in addition to their low production quality, merely reinforced the stereotyped and servile image of blacks found in movies produced by the major studios. More recent black critics have faulted him for filling his movies with light-skinned black actors and

Charles Lucas and Evelyn Preer in a scene from Micheaux's 1922 film adaptation of his novel The Homesteader

for focusing on the problem of "passing."

His avowed aim of uplifting his audiences carried him far from a realistic depiction of the problems of inner city or rural blacks. Donald Bogle suggests that the result of such an attempt was often implausibility. "He created a fantasy world where blacks were just as affluent, just as educated, just as 'cultured,'—in short just as white—as white America," concludes Bogle.

Always the tireless promoter, Micheaux employed the same techniques to sell his films to theater owners as he had to promote his books: cross-country tours on which he tried to convince white managements to sponsor special showings of his films for black audiences. Often they agreed, attracted as much by his strong personality as by his talk of the profits to be made from unreached black audiences. Lorenzo Tucker, one of Micheaux's stars, recalled the fervor of Micheaux's personality: "Why he was so impressive and so charming that he could talk the shirt off your back."

Tucker first felt the effects of Micheaux's personality when the filmmaker approached him in the lobby of the Dunbar Hotel in Philadelphia and asked if he were an actor, adding, "You're one of them who *thinks* they are." Tucker later became one of Micheaux's best-known actors (featured as the "black Valentino"), joining other Micheaux stars such as Bee Freeman (called the "sepia Mae West"), Ethel Moses (the "Negro Harlow"), and Slick Chester (the "colored Cagney"). By promising theater owners that future Micheaux productions would feature these actors, Micheaux was often able to convince them to front the money to produce an-

Poster for one of Micheaux's films

other film.

In the 1940s he again returned to writing fiction, but without notable success. He again reworked the story of *The Conquest,* this time as *The Wind From Nowhere* (1944). Drawing on the scenarios of successful films, he wrote *The Case of Mrs. Wingate* (1945), about Nazi spies and a black detective, and *The Story of Dorothy Stanfield* (1946), about "a Great Insurance Swindle—and a Woman!"—as its title page proclaims. His last novel, *The Masquerade* (1947), is a thinly disguised reworking of *The House Behind the Cedars,* by Charles W. Chesnutt.

Micheaux added historical background to his story of a young black woman's attempts to pass as white and replaced the tragic death of Chesnutt's heroine with a happy marriage and escape to the Midwest. While on a promotional tour, Micheaux died in Charlotte, North Carolina, on 26 March 1951.

In a note printed at the front of *The Story of Dorothy Stanfield,* Micheaux defended himself from those who criticized the prevalence of "race-mixing" in his books. "Race-mixing is *not* the theme of Mr. Micheaux's novels by any means," he argues, but its mere presence in the novels has led to the books' rejection by many reviewers, in spite of their popularity. He defends the middle-class setting of his novels by asserting that such images are never found in works by other writers, white or black. Except in his novels, the Negro "is never shown as a contemporary American citizen, talking as most colored people have long been speaking, in plain and simple English. In the matter of romance, he seems presumed not to have any whatsoever."

It is this novel approach to subject matter and theme that marks Micheaux's contribution to American literature. Hugh Gloster notes that his books "introduce characters and settings far removed from the well-trod paths of American Negro fiction." Other critics see this distance as a failing. Robert Bone, for example, links Micheaux with Henry Downing and Mary Etta Spencer as novelists who avoid the "hard fact of caste" and who would rather "indulge in crude success-fantasies," bemoaning the fact that they "appear to have lost all contact with Negro life and culture." Whether or not Micheaux's novels ever gain critical attention proportionate to the popular success they once enjoyed, it is clear that the figure of Micheaux himself, pioneer, promoter, and producer, in his big Western hat, described by Bogle as entering a room as if "he were God about to deliver a sermon," is an important one in American cultural history.

References:

Donald Bogle, *Toms, Coons, Mulattoes, Mammies and Bucks: An Interpretive History of Blacks in American Films* (New York: Viking, 1973), pp. 109-116;

Robert A. Bone, *The Negro Novel in America* (New Haven: Yale University Press, 1958), pp. 49-50;

Thomas Cripps, *Slow Fade to Black: The Negro In American Film, 1900-1942* (New York: Oxford University Press, 1977), pp. 183-193, 342-346;

Chester J. Fontenot, Jr. "Oscar Micheaux, Black Novelist and Film Maker," in *Vision and Refuge: Essays on the Literature of the Great Plains,* edited by Virginia Faulkner (Lincoln: University of Nebraska Press, 1982), pp. 109-125;

Hugh M. Gloster, *Negro Voices in American Fiction* (Chapel Hill: University of North Carolina Press, 1948), pp. 84-89;

Janis Herbert, "Oscar Micheaux: A Black Pioneer," *South Dakota Review,* 11 (Winter 1973): 62-69;

Daniel J. Leab, *From Sambo to Superspade: The Black Experience in Motion Pictures* (Boston: Houghton Mifflin, 1975);

Henry T. Sampson, *Blacks in Black and White: A Source Book on Black Films* (Metuchen, N.J.: Scarecrow Press, 1977), pp. 42-55.

Alice Moore Dunbar Nelson

(19 July 1875-18 September 1935)

Ora Williams

California State University, Long Beach

BOOKS: *Violets and Other Tales* (Boston: Monthly Review Press, 1895);

The Goodness of St. Rocque and Other Stories (New York: Dodd, Mead, 1899);

Give Us Each Day: The Diary of Alice Dunbar-Nelson, edited by Gloria Hull (New York: Norton, 1984).

OTHER: *Masterpieces of Negro Eloquence: The Best Speeches Delivered by the Negro from the Days of Slavery to the Present Time,* edited by Dunbar Nelson (Harrisburg, Pa.: Douglass, 1914);

The Dunbar Speaker and Entertainer, edited, with contributions, by Dunbar Nelson (Naperville, Ill.: J. L. Nichols, 1920);

"I Sit and Sew" and other poems, in *Negro Poets and Their Poems,* edited by Robert T. Kerlin (Washington, D.C.: Associated Publishers, 1923);

"Snow in October," in *Caroling Dusk,* edited by Countee Cullen (New York & London: Harper, 1927).

PERIODICAL PUBLICATIONS:

DRAMA

"The Author's Evening at Home," *Smart Set* (September 1900): 105-106.

FICTION

"The Little Mother," *Standard Union* (Brooklyn), 7 March 1900;

"The Ball Dress," *Leslie's Weekly,* 93 (12 December 1901);

"Science in Frenchtown—A Short Story," *Saturday Evening Mail,* 7 December 1912, magazine section: 8-9, 26, 27;

"Hope Deferred," *Crisis,* 8 (September 1914): 238-242.

NONFICTION

"Appointed, Some Points of View," *Daily Crusader,* 2 July 1894;

"Training of Teachers of English," *Education,* 29 (October 1908): 97-103;

"Wordsworth's Use of Milton's Description of Pandemonium," *Modern Language Notes,* 24 (April 1909): 124-125;

"What Has the Church to Offer the Men of Today?," *A.M.E. Church Review,* 30 (July 1913): 5-13;

"The Poet and His Song," in *Paul Laurence Dunbar: Poet Laureate of the Negro Race,* special issue of the *A. M. E. Church Review* (October 1914): 5-19;

"People of Color in Louisiana," *Journal of Negro History,* 1 (October 1916): 361-376; 2 (January 1917): 51-78;

" 'Hysteria': The Old Time Mass Meeting Is Dead," *Competitor,* 1 (February 1920): 32-33;

"Negro Literature for Negro Pupils," *Southern Workman,* 51 (February 1922): 59-63;

"These 'Colored' United States," *Messenger,* 6 (August 1924): 244-246; 6 (September 1924): 276-279;

"Woman's Most Serious Problem," *Messenger,* 9 (March 1927): 73, 86;

"Textbooks in Public Schools: A Job for the Negro Woman," *Messenger,* 9 (May 1927): 149;

"Facing Life Squarely," *Messenger,* 9 (July 1927): 219;

"The Negro Looks at an Outworn Tradition," *Southern Workman,* 57 (May 1928): 195-200;

"The Big Quarterly In Wilmington," *Journal Every Evening,* (Wilmington, Del.) 27 August 1932, pp. 8, 9.

POEMS

"Rainy Day," *Advertiser,* (Elmira, N.Y.), 18 September 1898;

"Summit and Vale," *Lippincott's* (December 1902): 175;

"Violets" and "Sonnet," *Crisis* (August 1917): 198;

"To Madame Curie," *Public Ledger,* (Philadelphia), 21 August 1921;

"Communion," "Music," and "Of Old St. Augustine," *Oppportunity,* 3 (July 1925): 216;

"Forest Fire," *Harlem: A Forum of Negro Life,* 1 (November 1928): 22;

"Canto—I Sing," *American Interracial Peace Committee Bulletin* (October 1929).

Alice Dunbar Nelson brought to her work a rich cultural legacy. Only one generation removed from slavery and born during the turbulent Reconstruction, periods during which opportunities for black Americans were often deliberately obstructed, Dunbar Nelson defied the stereotype of the ineducable black through her articles, essays, poems, reviews, stories, and anthologies of the works of other Afro-Americans. Her work demonstrates the sense of responsibility she felt toward the generations of Afro-Americans born after her. She wanted to bring to black Americans those works that "might help them with a belief in their possibilities." She made no apology for being highly literate, realizing that sharing her knowledge and experience was her best protest against racism. A writer in the genteel tradition, she did more than provide a good model for black youths; her prolific and extensive writings treat local as well as universal subjects and well-known personalities, and her works are repositories of cultural and social information.

Alice Moore Dunbar Nelson

Alice Ruth Moore was born in New Orleans, Louisiana, to Creole seaman Joseph Moore and seamstress Patricia Wright Moore. The younger of two daughters, Alice would live for many of her adult years with her mother and sister. She spent her first twenty years in New Orleans, where she attended public schools and where, in 1889, she graduated from high school. At the age of fifteen, she entered Straight University in New Orleans for a two-year teacher-training program. Later on she would also study at Cornell University, where she received an M.A., at the Pennsylvania School of Industrial Art, and at the University of Pennsylvania, where she studied psychology and educational testing.

At Straight University, a college sponsored by a number of prominent black politicians, Alice had access to offerings in the normal school, the law school, the printing department, and the classics program in addition to her teacher training. She also took some courses in nursing, trained to become a professional stenographer, and served as editor of the woman's page of the *New Orleans Journal of the Lodge,* the official organ of a black fraternal order. While at school she was a violin-cellist in William Joseph Nickerson's orchestra and a mandolin player in his all-girl mandolin club. Known as "a quick apt scholar," Dunbar Nelson was encouraged to pursue English literature and the classics. As a result of her versatility she had many opportunities for writing, public speaking, and musical performing. All of these early experiences influenced Dunbar Nelson's writings, especially her first volume, *Violets and Other Tales* (1895), a collection of short stories and poems.

One of the most important aspects of Dunbar Nelson's life was her teaching. She became a professional teacher in 1892, when she was slightly more than seventeen years of age, and with few interruptions she taught until 1931. Her first teaching assignment was at the Old Marigny Elementary School in New Orleans. Dunbar Nelson left New Orleans in 1896 and went north with her family to West Medford, Massachusetts. In 1895 poet Paul Laurence Dunbar had initiated an epistolary courtship with Alice, after he fell in love with her from a photograph that appeared in an issue of the *Boston Monthly Review.* Alice did not actually meet her future husband until February 1897 when she went to New York City, where she took a teaching position at Public School 83 in Brooklyn. On the actual eve of Dunbar's departure for a reading tour in England, Alice saw him for the first time, and they became engaged. While Dunbar completed the tour that was a kind of confirmation of his literary reputation, Alice stayed in New York, where she helped to found the White Rose Mission (later the White Rose Home for Girls in Harlem) and then taught at Public School 66. She married Dunbar secretly on 8 March 1898 and left her job to join him in Washington, D.C. In 1902 the Dunbars separated and Alice went to Delaware, where, until 1920, she taught at Howard High School in Wilmington during the academic year and taught at various black colleges during the summer months.

Although she primarily earned her living teaching, Dunbar Nelson devoted an equal amount of time to her writing. During the course of her career, she worked as a journalist, writing for many black newspapers, including the *Pittsburgh Courier,* for which she wrote a column called "Une Femme Dit" (originally called "From the Woman's Point of View") from 2 January to 18 September 1926; and the *Washington Eagle,* for which she wrote the column "As In A Looking Glass" from 1926 to 1930. In addition to *Violets and Other Tales* she wrote a collection of stories, *The Goodness of St. Rocque* (1899), and edited two anthologies, *Masterpieces of Negro Eloquence* (1914) and *The Dunbar Speaker and Entertainer* (1920). In 1920 she founded and coedited the *Wilmington Advocate,* a weekly newspaper. Her two novels, "This Lofty Oak" and "Confessions of a Lazy Woman," are unpublished.

The high quality of Dunbar Nelson's work insured that it was published in all the black and many white publications of her day; hers was one of the most consistent, secure, and independent voices of the black community. She was equally respected for her academic work; her Cornell master's thesis is cited twice in Raymond Dexter Haven's well-known and highly regarded study *The Influence of Milton on English Poets.* Author of stories of Creole life, several historical monographs concerning blacks in Louisiana, and a recognized poet, Dunbar Nelson was also a literary, film, and art critic. Although she is better known as a transitional figure to the writers of the Harlem Renaissance, her work influenced some of the best writers of that period.

In all her writings, from her poetry to her sociological analyses, Dunbar Nelson is always direct, her language is simple and precise. Her concerns about racism, the roles of men and women in society, and the importance of love, war, death, and nature appear as recurring themes across genres.

Dunbar Nelson and Paul Laurence Dunbar were drawn to one another partially because of their mutual love for literature, but their aesthetic values tended to differ, especially when it came to the portrayal of black Americans. Dunbar, who was acclaimed as a dialect poet by William Dean Howells and others, may have valued his standard En-

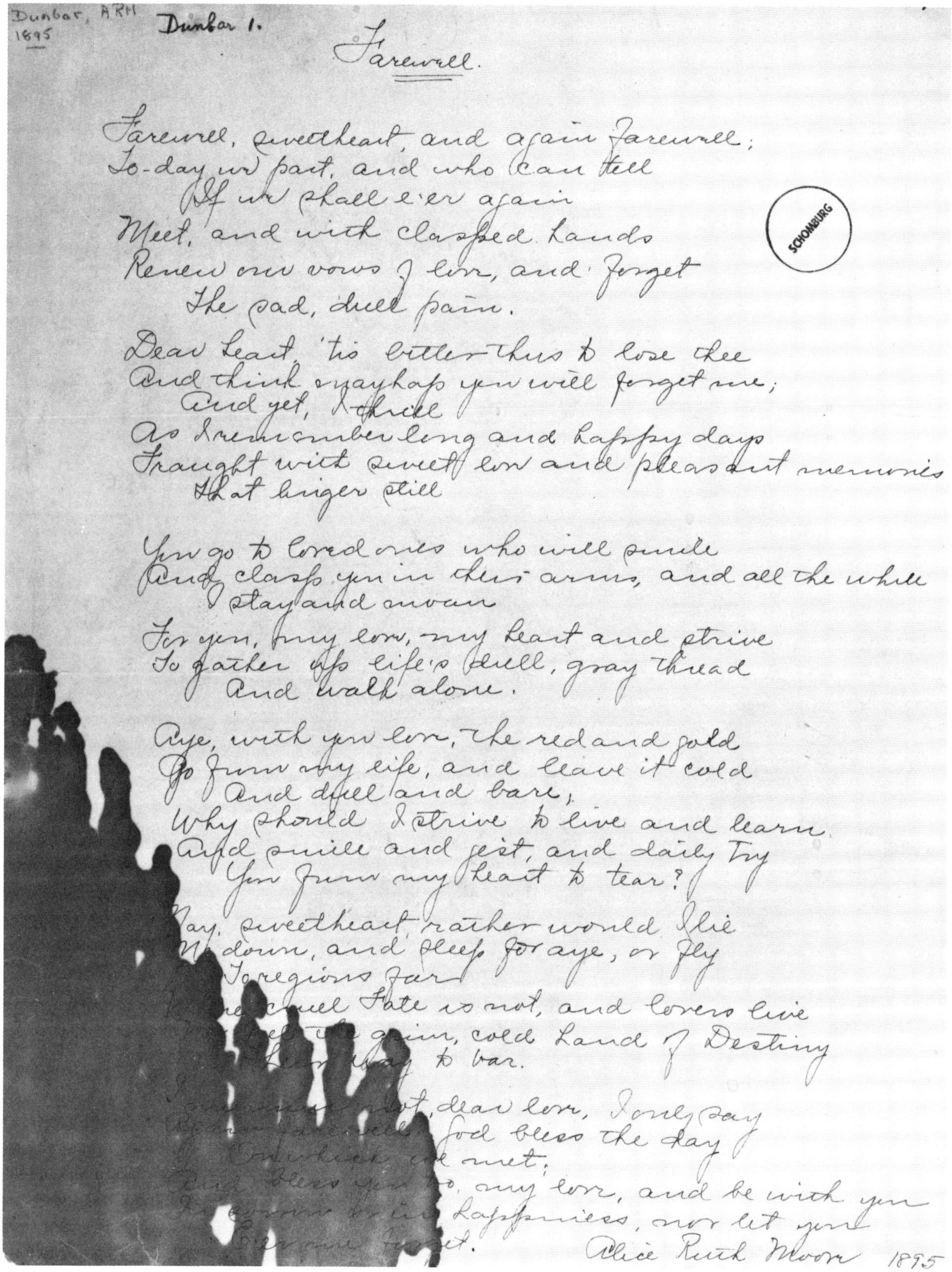

Dunbar, ARM
1895

Dunbar 1.

Farewell.

Farewell, sweetheart, and again farewell;
To-day we part, and who can tell
If we shall e'er again
Meet, and with clasped hands
Renew our vows of love, and forget
The sad, dull pain.

Dear heart, 'tis bitter thus to lose thee
And think mayhap you will forget me;
And yet, I thrill
As I remember long and happy days
Fraught with sweet love and pleasant memories
That linger still.

You go to loved ones who will smile
And clasp you in their arms, and all the while
I stay and moan
For you, my love, my heart and strive
To gather up life's dull, gray thread
And walk alone.

Aye, with you love, the red and gold
Go from my life, and leave it cold
And dull and bare;
Why should I strive to live and learn
And smile and jest, and daily try
You from my heart to tear?

Nay, sweetheart, rather would I lie
Me down, and sleep for aye, or fly
To regions far
Where cruel Fate is not, and lovers live
[illegible] the grim, cold hand of Destiny
[illegible] way to bar.

I murmur not, dear love, I only say
Again farewell. God bless the day
On which we met;
God bless you too, my love, and be with you
In sorrow or in happiness, nor let you
E'er me forget.

Alice Ruth Moore 1895

Manuscript for a poem published in Violets and Other Tales *(courtesy of Schomburg Center for Research in Black Culture, the New York Public Library, Astor, Lenox and Tilden Foundations)*

glish work more, but he could hardly refrain from producing the works that were making him famous. In a letter Dunbar Nelson wrote to Dunbar in May 1895, when they were beginning to know one another through their correspondence, she wrote, "You ask my opinion about the Negro dialect in literature? Well, frankly, I believe in everyone following his own bent. If it be so that one has a special aptitude for dialect work why it is only right that dialect work should be a specialty. But if one should be like me—absolutely devoid of the ability to manage dialect, I don't see the necessity of cramming and forcing oneself into that plane because one is a Negro or a Southerner." In the same letter she voiced her abhorrence of writers who "wedge the Negro problem and social equality and long dissertations on the Negro in general into their stories." This kind of writing she likened to "a quininc pill in jelly." Her dislike for contrived dialect and other stereotypical race materials grew into revulsion months later as she protested to Dunbar: "*don't, don't* write more truck as you've been putting in the *Journal*. . . . To everyone else I champion your taste . . . I agree from all sorts of premises you might do as you please—but to you darling, I must say, *don't*. I know it means money and speeches . . . for us, but sometimes money isn't all. It is not fair to prostitute your art for 'filthy lucre'; is it? It will be such a relief—for every Sunday I find myself asking—'What next?' "

In the very sympathetic, yet insightful article she had been invited to write for the *A.M.E. Church Review*'s special issue devoted to Paul Laurence Dunbar, Dunbar Nelson noted that her late, estranged husband had loved Tennyson and Lowell because "they had expressed yearning for the natural world, and his soul yearned toward their verse." She went on to criticize Howells for advising Dunbar to write in dialect, rather than in the language he felt most comfortable with: "Say what you will, or what Mr. Howells wills, about 'feeling the Negro life esthetically, and expressing it lyrically,' it was in the pure English poems that the poet expressed *himself*." Even years later, in a January 1929 diary entry written after she made an address to a research club, she notes "good crowd—talk on 'Negro's Literary Reaction to American Life,' but of course, they would want to hear Dunbar dialect at the end. Makes me sick." Six months later in her weekly column "As In A Looking Glass," she made an observation about the models white America creates for black Americans: "Certain white writers

Alice Moore Dunbar during her marriage to Paul Laurence Dunbar

have redefined the literature of the Negro people as the 'record of a people's shortcomings and follies.' A black savage dropped bodily into a white culture, a senseless prostitute; Negro primitivism, atavism, reversal to types, to an African . . . a hideously ugly ever-grinned harlot. . . ."

As for herself, she insisted in "The Poet and His Song" that a poet should be a keen observer, have a sense of humor, be close to nature, and dramatize the "delicate perception of the power of suggestion" with the right meter.

Dunbar Nelson's first volume, *Violets and Other Tales,* published in 1895, consists of poetry, essays, and short stories. As many of the titles in this volume suggest, Dunbar Nelson was a romanticist who often mused on death, as in "In Memorium," and who frequently used natural subjects as the focus of her works, for example, "Amid the Roses," "Love and the Butterfly," "At Eventide," and even "Bay St. Louis," which combines topographical detail with local color. The title story of this collection also centers on a romantic image that would become Dunbar Nelson's trademark: violets. Twenty-two years after *Violets and Other Tales* appeared, she wrote a sonnet with the same title, and in her unpublished novel "Confessions of a Lazy Woman," it is a dominant image. (The night she ran away to meet Dunbar before his departure to England, she gave him a bouquet of violets.)

The heroine of the story "Violets" is a maiden in love, who places a bouquet of violets, orange blossoms, pinks, "tube-roses," and evergreens in a letter to her sweetheart. Dunbar Nelson repeats the floral imagery a number of times in this short work. The second section of the sketch is a sentimental treatment of the heroine's death within a year of giving the bouquet; possibly she has died of a broken heart. The action shifts to another city where the suitor, now married to a "regal-looking woman," finds a "faded bunch of flowers tied with a blue ribbon and a lock of hair." He asks, "Wife, did you ever send me these?" She replies that she hates flowers, and she orders him to "Throw them into the fire."

Almost two and a half decades later the poem "Violets" was published; since then it has been set to music by a number of American composers, among them Dorothy Rudd Moore, who has used these lyrics as her lead song in the song cycle *Sonnets of Love, Rosebuds, and Death.*

From the first line the poem seems romantic with its references to "violets of late,/The wild shy kind . . ." and "wistful April days." A close examination reveals a serious well-constructed work, in which the first-person speaker contrasts the natural world of "sweet real things"—including true love—all symbolized by violets, with the artificial, "deadened" man-made world, represented by "garish lights" and "mincing little fops." The unidentified persona establishes a confessional intimacy that draws the reader close; so, it is not surprising to discover in the closing couplet that the sonnet is addressed to a loved one who has jarred the jaded speaker's memory of a more innocent world. The poem itself is a kind of bouquet to the persona's loved one since, in the language of flowers, violets mean "You occupy my thoughts."

Between "Violets" the poem, and "Violets" the sketch, we find more than superficial similarities; the poem appears to be a highly compressed version of the sketch. Dunbar Nelson's alternate title for the poem is "Sonnet to April," and the time of the sketch "Violets" is Easter evening, which often falls in the month of April. In the poem's references to "The perfect loveliness God has made" and "my soul's forgotten gleam" the speaker provides an explicit connection between the violets and a sense of a spirituality. In the sketch, the dawn has "greeted the Savior," while a young girl in love writes her sweetheart telling him that she is sending him a bouquet of flowers as "my Easter token." She also writes that she has worn these flowers to church, suggesting a kind of sanctification of her feelings.

One year later, at Easter time, the heroine is dead, and bells, probably church bells, "Clang out the glad news of the resurrection." In both the poem and the story Dunbar Nelson dramatizes her belief that a true poet is close to "the great Mother-Heart."

Dunbar Nelson's second anthology, *The Goodness of St. Rocque,* was published in 1899 as a companion piece for a special edition of Dunbar's work called *Poems of Cabin and Field.* Her stories focus on the New Orleans Creole culture, while his works are set in a more general southern plantation atmosphere. *The Goodness of St. Rocque,* similar to the Creole studies of George Washington Cable and Kate Chopin, helped to establish Dunbar Nelson as a southern local colorist.

The title work in this anthology is representative of many of Dunbar Nelson's short stories in its mixture of dialect and standard English, blend of Catholic and black magic practices, and balance of realistic and romantic features. The story concerns the efforts and success of Manuela, an exotic Creole girl, in winning back the love of her life. Through voodoo and prayers to the good St. Rocque, Manuela triumphs over her rival, Claralie, and marries Theophile.

Another story in this collection that captures Dunbar Nelson's skill in representing the Creole life is "La Juanita." A "half Spanish and half French" beauty, Juanita loves an "American." Her grandfather, who is her guardian, objects to Mercer, the man of Juanita's choice, because his station is beneath that of Grandpere Colombes's family. Before a special regatta to be held in the treacherous Lake Ponchartrain, Mercer and Juanita promise themselves to each other if Mercer wins the regatta. During the race a fierce storm jeopardizes the fleet. Mercer leads the boats to safety and thus becomes a hero Grandpere Colombes is happy to have in the family. The descriptions of the town, Mandeveille, the regatta, and the specifics about Lake Ponchartrain and the fierce tropical storm that threaten the boats contribute realistic detail and local atmosphere to the action of this essentially romantic story.

The strain of realism in Dunbar Nelson's work is frequently drawn from autobiographical sources. For example, the poem "I Sit and Sew,"

The GOODNESS
OF ST. ROCQUE
AND OTHER STORIES

By
ALICE DUNBAR

New York: DODD, MEAD AND COMPANY *Mdcccxcix*

Title page for Dunbar Nelson's second book

first published in the 1918 *A.M.E. Church Review,* is at once an antiwar piece, a feminist work, a patriotic plea, and a black woman's protest. This three-stanza, twenty-one line poem was inspired by United States involvement in World War I. The poem addresses itself to the fact that the speaker finds she is unable to do anything more than sit and sew, activities she considers idle, because a war, in which men die, rages.

While the work speaks of the plight of women in general, Dunbar Nelson's correspondence and essays suggest that the poem is highly autobiographical. Like scores of other American black women, she struggled to have an active role in World War I, but racial discrimination on all fronts prevented such an involvement. A letter from the National Y.W.C.A. representative of the Department of Method Office delineates the black woman's inability to do "useful things": "I have enquired about colored women being sent to France to work there, taking it for granted you are a colored woman since you have written Miss Bowles, and find that there has been no call for colored workers yet." Then, in a more discouraging vein, the correspondent added, "And if you have knowledge of domestic science and have had experience in the management of a cafeteria you will be much in demand." Dunbar Nelson's frustration at such limitations shows in the poem:

> The little useless seam, the idle patch;
> Why dream I here beneath my homely thatch,
> When there they lie in sodden mud and rain,
> Pitifully calling me, the quick ones and the slain?
> You need me, Christ! It is no roseate dream
> That beckons me—this pretty futile seam,
> It stifles me—God, must I sit and sew?

The activities in which Dunbar Nelson eventually participated reflected her desire to do more than knit or sew. In January 1918 she volunteered her services to the Circle of Negro War Relief, an organization designed to help black soldiers and their families, and in the same year she wrote a patriotic dramatic skit, "Mine Eyes Have Seen the Glory." As the only known black member of the field staff of the Women's Committee on the Council of Defense, she helped organize Southern black women in nine states for the war effort; she planned her own agenda, arranged her own itinerary, found homes in which to stay, and advanced her own expense money for one month.

Dunbar Nelson's subject matter also embraced the universal. The speaker in the 1925 poem "Music," for example, salutes music as an art form. She begins her celebration by forcefully proclaiming the word "Music!" Dunbar Nelson is interested in music in all its diverse forms: "Lilting, soft and languorous,/Crashing, splendid, thunderous." She describes the expressions, effects, and sounds associated with different instruments ("rattle of castanets," "woodwinds in tender frets"), composers ("Symphonic syncopation that Dvorak wove.") and compositions ("Salome's triumph in grunt obscene"). When she proclaims the attributes of music, her expression is, at first, joyous and cheerful. Later, she becomes subdued and sad. This twenty-one line work is a "symphonic poem" that emphasizes the dualities of music: its soothing qualities and its stimulating ones, cacophony versus harmony.

During her career, Dunbar Nelson wrote for a number of newspapers and journals. At one point, she was the editor of a woman's page. Besides the regular columns she wrote in 1926 and in 1930 for the *Pittsburgh Courier,* and from 1926 to 1930 for the *Washington Eagle,* she was also a frequent contributor to such publications as the *Southern Workman,* the *Messenger, Opportunity,* and the *Crisis.*

Many of these contributions were reviews or critiques of novels, poems, movies, plays, and art. The reviews are important because they reflect Dunbar Nelson's aesthetic concepts, the breadth of her knowledge, and her importance to black literature. In *The Big Sea,* Langston Hughes credits Dunbar Nelson with being one of two black critics who gave his *Fine Clothes to the Jew* a favorable review. In "The Young Voices Cry," Mae Crowdery, a young Harlem Renaissance poet, acknowledges the impact Dunbar Nelson's reviews had on younger writers of the Renaissance. The reviews contain invaluable historical information—about racial matters, local events, prominent black artists and leaders, and national situations.

In general, Dunbar Nelson's reviews follow a definite format. She places the work in a literary or historical context by comparing it with a previous work by the subject. Then, she comments on the physical features of the book: its attractiveness, illustrations, or cover design. Next, she examines and evaluates the genre and comments on the unique features of the piece.

Alice Dunbar Nelson

In the article in which Dunbar Nelson reviews Laura Wheeler's *Portrait of the Old Colored Woman* (1926), she gives background information about the exhibit in which the Wheeler painting appears and provides some biographical information about the promoter, Mrs. Carl Diton, who was committed to presenting young black talent to Philadelphians. Dunbar Nelson agrees with critics who assert that Wheeler "excels in portrait painting." She judges Wheeler's portraits and illustrations to be "inimitable." Perhaps Wheeler's greatest strengths are her abilities "to get at the heart of our people." *Portrait of the Old Colored Woman,* whose subject was an elderly black woman who lived near Cheyney University, Dunbar Nelson judged to be "one of the best things that Laura Wheeler ever did" because she finds the old woman to be the "epitome" of the history of black Americans. Dunbar Nelson reviewed the work of some of the most creative artists and writers of the 1920s, including Georgia Douglas Johnson and Langston Hughes, whom she praises because, like Wordsworth and Coleridge, he dared to write about the lowly.

In January 1910 Dunbar Nelson secretly married Henry Arthur Callis, a teacher who returned to school to study medicine. They divorced a year later, and in April 1916 Dunbar Nelson married journalist Robert J. Nelson, with whom she remained for the rest of her busy life. Having had her poetry published in *Crisis, Ebony, Topaz, Lippincott's, Leslie's,* and *Opportunity,* and in anthologies of black writing, Dunbar Nelson became active politically, serving on the State Republican Committee of Delaware and directing the work of black women members in 1920. In 1924 she played a similar role in the New York Democratic campaign. From 1928 to 1931 her political interests took on a broader tone as she worked as executive secretary for the American Friends Interracial Peace Committee. Throughout her literary, teaching, and political activities, starting in 1921, Dunbar Nelson kept a diary, the extant portions of which shed light on this figure whose interests bridge two literary traditions. Alice Moore Dunbar Nelson died on 18 September 1935.

Bibliography:

Ora Williams, "Works by and About Alice Ruth

(Moore) Dunbar-Nelson: A Bibliography," *CLA Journal,* 19 (March 1976): 322-326.

Reference:

Gloria Hull, ed., "A Chronology," in *Give Us Each Day: The Diary of Alice Dunbar-Nelson* (New York: Norton, 1984), pp. 467-469.

Papers:

Microfilm copies of Dunbar Nelson's papers have been placed with the Ohio Historical Society, Columbus, Ohio. Other papers are located in the Morris Library, University of Delaware, Newark, Delaware.

Henrietta Cordelia Ray

(1849-5 January 1916)

Leela Kapai
University of the District of Columbia

BOOKS: *Sketch of the Life of the Rev. Charles B. Ray,* by Ray and Florence T. Ray (New York: Little, 1887);

Lincoln; Written for the Occasion of the Unveiling of the Freedmen's Monument in Memory of Abraham Lincoln, April 14, 1876 (New York: Little, 1893);

Sonnets (New York: Little, 1893);

Poems (New York: Grafton Press, 1910).

PERIODICAL PUBLICATION: "Charles Lamb," *A.M.E. Church Review,* 8 (July 1891): 1-9.

Henrietta Cordelia Ray was a New York schoolteacher and one of the few black women poets in the genteel tradition who achieved a certain amount of local recognition in the nineteenth century. Ray was the youngest of five surviving children born to Charlotte Augusta Burrough, who was from Savannah, Georgia, and Charles Bennett Ray, a one-time blacksmith who became editor of the *Colored American,* the third black-owned newspaper in America. As a journalist, and later as a clergyman serving the Bethesda Congregational Church from 1845 to 1865, Ray's father was actively engaged in lecturing and fund-raising for the causes of abolition, temperance, suffrage, and education. He served the Underground Railroad in arranging the escape of slaves to the North. His work brought him in close contact with well-known leaders, and William Wells Brown observed his importance to the advancement of black causes in *The Rising Son* (1873): "In the multitude of national and state conventions held thirty years ago and thereabouts, the assembly was scarcely considered complete without the presence of Charles Ray."

Ray grew up in a refined environment where she enjoyed the advantages of coming from a prominent black family. The daughters were all college graduates: Florence, with whom Ray lived all her life, earned the master of pedagogy degree from New York University in 1891; Charlotte obtained a law degree from Howard University in 1872 and was the first black woman lawyer admitted to the bar of the Supreme Court. Although details of Ray's early education are not documented, she probably graduated from Sauveneur School of Languages, where she studied Greek, Latin, French, and German, and in 1891 received a master's in pedagogy from New York University, as had her sister. Her education was apparently well rounded, for several contemporary accounts mention that she tutored students in music and mathematics, as well as in languages, Ray, from all accounts, was a shy recluse who opted for a "life of tranquillity." In the words of Hallie Quinn Brown, an early biographer, "Among a generation of brainy New York women, she was probably the most accomplished, yet outside her immediate circle the least known. Her modesty was excessive, she never boasted nor appeared self conscious." Despite her reticent nature, Ray was distinguished by her refinement and manners. According to Brown, "There was a transfiguring light that radiated from her, for she bore herself as one endowed with an innate sense of things divine."

Ray taught in the New York public school system for about thirty years. Records indicate that in 1868 she was teaching in the girl's department of Colored American Grammar School No. 1 on Manhattan's Lower East Side. In the 1890s she taught at School No. 80 under principal Charles Reason, a noted educator and a poet in his own right. Ray never married, although her love poems suggest she may have once experienced unrequited affection. After retiring from the school system, she apparently moved with Florence to Woodside, Long Island, where she gave private lessons.

H. Cordelia Ray, the name by which she preferred to be known, began writing poetry at the age of ten. However, it was not until 1876 that she won public recognition. A public holiday was declared to mark the anniversary of the death of Abraham Lincoln and to commemorate the Emancipation Proclamation. A statue of Lincoln, paid for entirely by contributions from black men and women, was to be unveiled by Pres. Ulysses S. Grant in Lincoln Park in Washington, D.C. Ray had been invited to compose a piece for this event. Her poem *Lincoln; Written for the Occasion of the Unveiling of the Freedmen's Monument in Memory of Abraham Lincoln, April 14, 1876* (1893) was read by William E. Matthews and followed an oration delivered by Frederick Douglass. Ray's poem was circulated extensively but was not printed until 1893.

"Lincoln," a poem in eight stanzas comprised of five rhymed couplets each, pays homage to the man whose lot it was "not worlds to conquer, but men's hearts." Ray extols his qualities and his role in ending the misery of the slaves. The poem concludes with an address: "Emancipator, hero, martyr, friend:/While freedom may her holy sceptre claim/The world shall echo with our Lincoln's name."

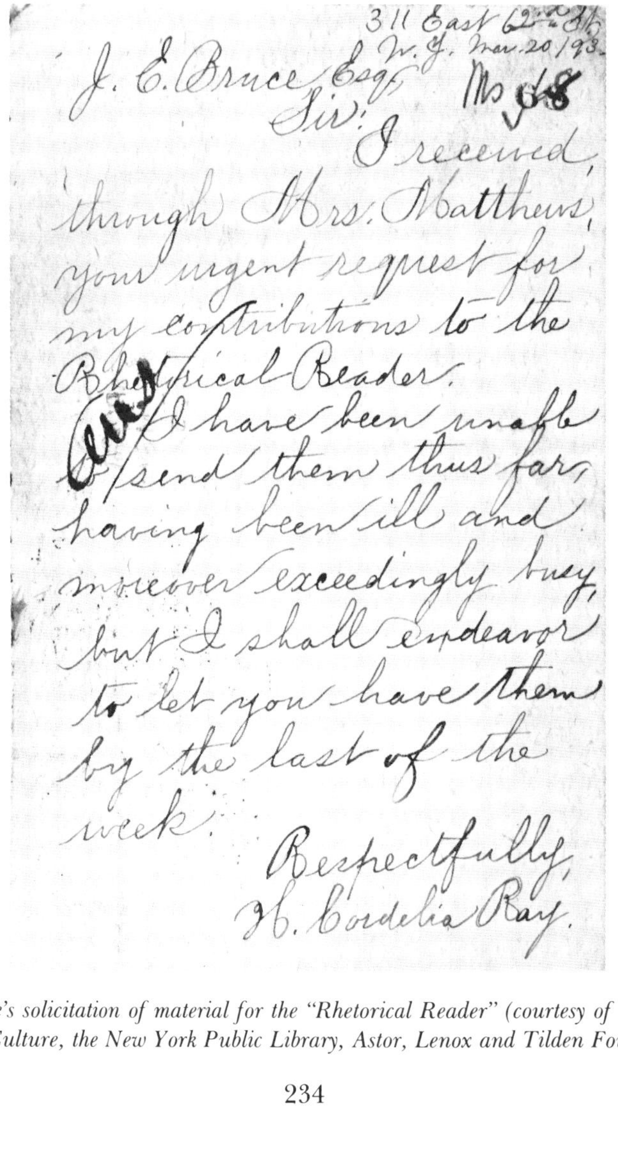

311 East 62nd St.
N.Y. Mar. 20/93.

J. E. Bruce Esq.
Sir:
I received through Mrs. Matthews your urgent request for my contributions to the Rhetorical Reader.
I have been unable to send them thus far, having been ill and moreover exceedingly busy, but I shall endeavor to let you have them by the last of the week.
Respectfully,
H. Cordelia Ray.

Ray's response to John E. Bruce's solicitation of material for the "Rhetorical Reader" (courtesy of Schomburg Center for Research in Black Culture, the New York Public Library, Astor, Lenox and Tilden Foundations)

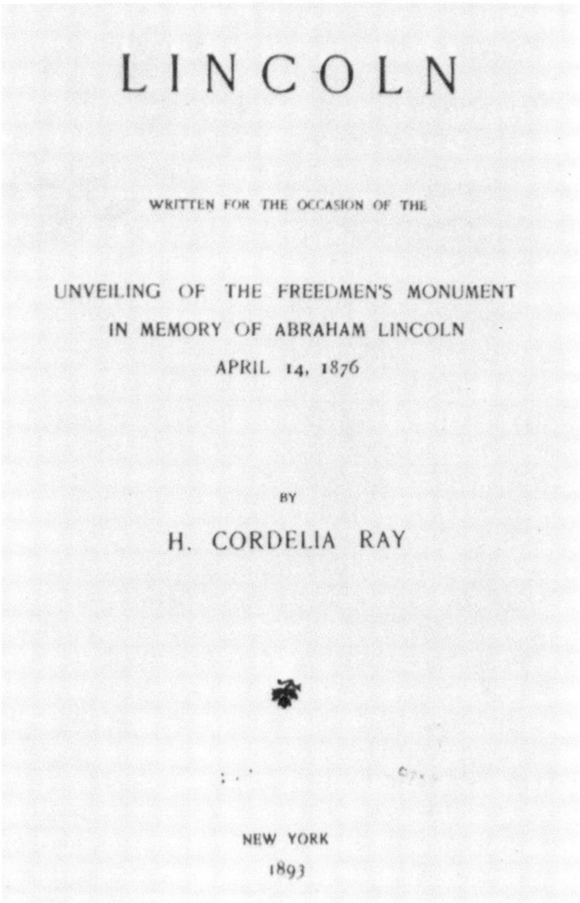

LINCOLN

WRITTEN FOR THE OCCASION OF THE

UNVEILING OF THE FREEDMEN'S MONUMENT
IN MEMORY OF ABRAHAM LINCOLN
APRIL 14, 1876

BY

H. CORDELIA RAY

NEW YORK
1893

Title page for Ray's eighty-line ode which addressed Lincoln as "Emancipator, hero, martyr, friend"

Ray continued to write verses, many of which were published in periodicals. After the death of their father, Ray and Florence wrote a short biography, *Sketch of the Life of the Rev. Charles B. Ray* (1887). "To Our Father," a sonnet written by Ray, preceded the sketch. The poem is a moving tribute to a loving father and a "champion of freedom."

Judged by modern standards, the seventy-nine-page biography lacks distinction and fails to provide any real insight into Charles Ray. Organized into three sections, the sketch covers Charles Ray's parentage, education, and early career; his contributions to the causes of education and abolition, demonstrated in the volume through a compilation of his correspondence and annual reports of societies with which he was associated; and memorials and tributes by friends and associates which comprise the last nineteen pages of the book. Despite its obvious shortcomings, the sketch drew an appreciative notice. The *A.M.E. Church Review* had this diplomatic comment: "In the twenty years of our editorial work we do not remember having received so unique a volume. High judgment, good taste, literary tact and excellence all combine to put it absolutely beyond the range of criticism. As a work of the kind, it is as near perfect as can well be conceived."

Ray's next published volume was *Sonnets* (1893), a collection of twelve poems. The first sonnet, "To My Mother," is Ray's tribute to Charlotte Augusta for filling her life with love, grace, sacrifice, and encouragement. "Niobe" is another sonnet on the theme of motherhood and sacrifice. Four of the sonnets are addressed to men of literature, art, and music—William Shakespeare, John Milton, Ludwig van Beethoven, and the Renaissance artist Raphael. Four other poems present musings on "Life," "Aspiration," "Incompleteness," and "Self-Mastery." All of them lack any philosophical depth or originality. The last two sonnets are "Two Musicians," a fanciful reference to love and thought weaving a tapestry of music, and "The Poet's Ministrants," which recounts how nature ministers to the needs of a poet. All of the sonnets vary in their rhyme schemes, but retain the Petrarchan form. And while some flashes of imagination illuminate a few of the verses, they are largely devoid of depth and complexity.

In 1910 the last of Ray's works, *Poems,* was published. It is a collection of 145 poems, many of them published earlier. Dedicated to Florence and to the memory of "a household made beautiful by the presence of those loved ones who have entered the life immortal," the poems are arranged in ten sections: A Rosary of Fancies, Meditations, Sonnets, Champions of Freedom, Ballads and Other Poems, Chansons D'Amour, Quatrains, The Procession of the Seasons, a trilogy—"The Seer," "The Singer," and "The Sage"—and the Heroic Echoes. Despite the arrangement under different headings, some according to the form and others according to the content, the poems are essentially variations on a few themes: nature, human emotions, piety, duty, and acceptance of life.

Most of Ray's poems are characterized by superb control of form and technique. They reflect the poet's knowledge of classical and historical lore and, invariably, display an element of didacticism. "The Sculptor's Vision," a poem about an artist inspired by the vision of an ideal form, ends on this note: "As in his strife, is it not thus/That we are baffled, all of us,/In seeking clearer, truer light?/Then let us, like the sculptor still/Pursue our toil with deathless will/Advancing toward a glorious height."

When H. Cordelia Ray writes of nature—of the coming of dawn or of the spring, of lakes, forests, clouds, springs, or rills—she sees them as tranquil and inspiring manifestations of divine grace. Several of her poems are meditations on life's intricacies, man's duties and responsibilities, the meaning of success and failure. In an attempt to understand "Failure," she suggests that it may "Sometimes . . . unrest an impulse," and "From the world's dissatisfaction," may come "for us priceless gains."

Poems contains some technically innovative ballads, but Ray's departure from the traditional ballad verse form fails to rescue her work from the genteel sentimentality that pervades her tales of forlorn maidens and jilted and scorned lovers. The collection does contain a few noteworthy lyrics: "Robert G. Shaw," "Toussaint L'Ouverture," and "In Memoriam: Frederick Douglass." Always able to control the rhyme and metrical aspects of her verse, Ray is at her best in these poems when her thoughts and emotions emerge uncluttered by classical and literary allusions. "Shall the race falter in its courage now/That the great chief is fallen?," she asks in her tribute to Frederick Douglass. "Ah, nay!," she answers, "For daring souls are needed e'en today," and "Children unborn will venerate his name."

Poems received favorable comments from contemporary reviewers. Writing in the August 1912 issue of the *Crisis*, Jessie Redmon Fauset expressed her admiration for the themes of images and "versatility of the author." In the January 1913 *A.M.E. Church Review* the work was admired for its idealism. The reviewer, bemoaning the loss of popularity of poetry to novels, found H. Cordelia Ray's book to be a "summons back to idealism." Writing of *Poems*, Hallie Quinn Brown also commented on the poet's "versatility, love of nature, classical knowledge, delicate fancy, and unaffected piety." She compared Cordelia's verse to the "quaint touching music of a shell murmuring of the sea—a faint yet clear note sounding all the pathos and beauty of undying life."

No other work of H. Cordelia Ray was published after *Poems*. She died in New York on 5 January 1916. The obituary in the *Crisis* (April 1916) noted her accomplishments as a teacher and a poet, but laid more emphasis on her personality, which was "pure, gentle, peaceable and easy to be entreated."

The strengths and weaknesses of Ray's works stem from the same source: the sheltered life which provided her an opportunity to nurture her skills,

The bronze Freedmen's Monument commissioned from sculptor Thomas Ball for $17,000

but which blocked the ugly and harsh realities of life outside. The poet who could write movingly of motherhood and depict the sorrows of Niobe had nothing to say of the anguish of slave mothers. No questions of identity plague her work; if she felt conflict, she did not share it with her readers. Except for a few tributes to the leaders who fought for the abolition of slavery her poems reflect no concern with the major issues confronting her race. Writing in the sentimental tradition so popular in the nineteenth century, Ray nevertheless avoided the human concerns of that same tradition. Her genteel upbringing apparently succeeded in imbuing her with a sense of decorum that precluded any discussion of unpleasant and controversial subjects.

It is not surprising, then, that this quiet, unassuming woman who neither sought nor obtained wide acclaim during her lifetime has gradually faded into near oblivion; many recent anthologies of Afro-American literature even fail to mention her. She does, however, deserve to be remembered for her accomplishments as a black woman at a difficult time when just to aspire to be a scholar and a poet was a remarkable achievement.

References:

Hallie Quinn Brown, ed., *Homespun Heroines and Other Women of Distinction* (Xenia, Ohio: Aldine, 1926);

S. Elizabeth Frazier, "Some Afro-American Women of Mark," *A.M.E. Church Review*, 8 (April 1892): 373-386;

William Henry Robinson, Jr., *Early Black American Poets* (Iowa: William C. Brown, 1969), pp. 138-144;

Joan R. Sherman, *Invisible Poets: Afro-Americans of the Nineteenth Century* (Urbana: University of Illinois Press, 1974), pp. 129-135.

Victor Séjour (Juan Victor Séjour Marcou et Ferrand)

(2 June 1817-20 September 1874)

Thomas Bonner, Jr.
Xavier University of Louisiana

BOOKS: *Le Retour de Napoléon* (Paris: Dauvin et Fontaine, 1841);

Diégarias (Paris: C. Tresse, 1844);

La Chute de Séjan (Paris: Michel Lévy Frères, 1849);

Richard III (Paris: Giraud et Dagneau, 1852; New Orleans: Gaux et Dutuit, 1853);

L'Argent du diable, by Séjour and Adolphe Jaime fils (Paris: Michel Lévy Frères, 1854);

Les Noces vénitiennes (Paris: Michel Lévy Frères, 1855); adapted into English as *The Outlaws of the Adriatic,* by Edmund Falconer (London: Thomas Hailes Lacy, 1855);

Le Fils de la nuit (Paris: Michel Lévy Frères, 1856);

André Gérard (Paris: Michel Lévy Frères, 1857);

Le Martyre du coeur (Paris: Michel Lévy Frères, 1858);

Les Grands Vasseaux (Paris: Michel Lévy Frères, 1859);

Le Paletot brun (Paris: Michel Lévy Frères, 1859);

Les Aventuriers (Paris: Michel Lévy Frères, 1860);

Compère Guillery (Paris: Michel Lévy Frères, 1860);

La Tireuse de cartes (Paris: Michel Lévy Frères, 1860); adapted into English as *The Woman in Red,* by Joseph Stirling Coyne (London: Thomas Hailes Lacy, 1868);

Les massacres de la Syrie (Paris: Barbré, 1861);

Les Mystères du Temple (Paris: Michel Lévy Frères, 1862);

Les Volontaires de 1814 (Paris: Michel Lévy Frères, 1862);

Les Fils de Charles-Quint (Paris: Michel Lévy Frères, 1864);

Le Marquis Caporal (Paris: Michel Lévy Frères, 1864);

Les Enfants de la louve, by Séjour and Théodore Barrière (Paris: Michel Lévy Frères, 1865);

La Madone des roses, by Séjour and Barrière (Paris: Michel Lévy Frères, 1869).

OTHER: *Le Retour de Napoléon,* in *Les Cenelles,* edited by Armand Lanusse (New Orleans: Privately printed, 1845); translated by Regine Latortue and Gleason Adams (Boston: G. K. Hall, 1979).

Victor Séjour was one of the few black writers from antebellum New Orleans to lead a distinguished literary career. Twenty of his plays were published in Paris, and still more were produced on the stage in Paris and New Orleans.

According to baptismal records, Victor Séjour was born Juan Victor Séjour Marcou et Ferrand on 2 June 1817 in New Orleans to Juan François Louis Séjour Marcou, a free mulatto from Santo Domingo who operated a cleaning establishment on Chartres Street in the old quarter, and d'Eloisa

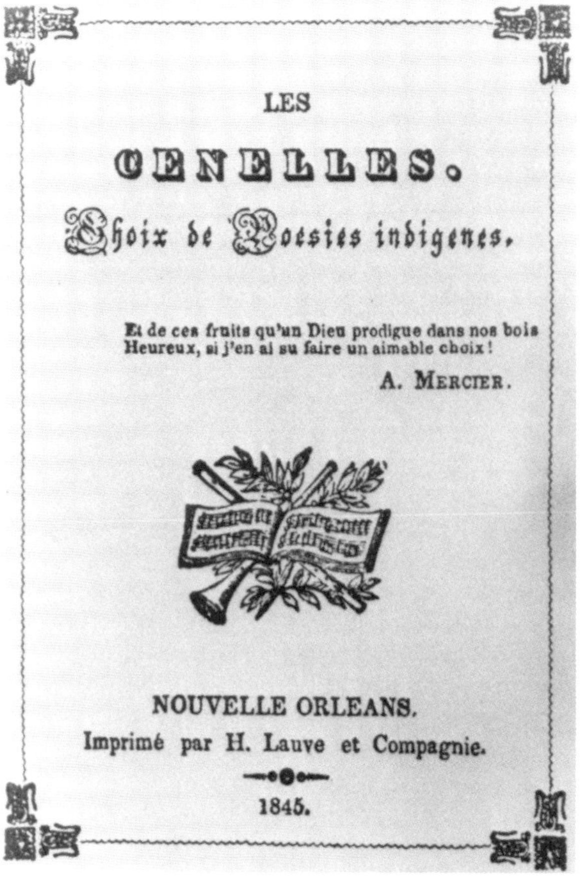

LES

CENELLES.

Choix de Poésies indigènes.

Et de ces fruits qu'un Dieu prodigue dans nos bois
Heureux, si j'en ai su faire un aimable choix!

A. MERCIER.

NOUVELLE ORLEANS.
Imprimé par H. Lauve et Compagnie.

1845.

Title page for the first American anthology of black poetry. Published in French, the volume includes the work of Séjour and sixteen other writers, all of whom were free blacks born in New Orleans.

Phillippe Ferrand, a free octoroon of the city. The free black population of this European city on the North American continent held education in high esteem, and Séjour attended Saint-Barbe Academy, where he proved himself a gifted and determined student and came under the influence of Michel Séligny, a black man who wrote for the local French newspapers. When he was seventeen, Séjour wrote a poem celebrating the anniversary of La Société des Artisans, an association of free black mechanics to which he belonged. Les Artisans greeted the poem with enthusiasm. In 1836, when he was nineteen, his parents—following a practice common among the city's free-black families, especially the Creoles—sent him to Paris to further his education and to begin a career free of the constraints placed upon people of color in the South.

Although there is little evidence that Séjour had any formal training in Paris, his literary life began auspiciously after he met Cyrille Bisette, a mulatto who edited the abolitionist journal *La Revue des Colonies* and who published Séjour's short story "Le Mulâtre" in his magazine in 1837. The narrative of how a slave named Georges kills his master and then discovers that he has murdered his own father, "Le Mulâtre" closes with Georges's suicide. The story is one of the earliest antislavery writings by a black American, and it indicates not only Séjour's continuing concern with matters of race but also, as is evident in Georges's internal dilemma, his interest in moral-psychological relations.

In 1840, inspired by the grand military procession which brought the remains of Napoleon to Les Invalides, Séjour wrote an ode, which was published the following year as *Le Retour de Napoléon.* Its lines are emotional and charged with enthusiasm for France and invective for England, as demonstrated in the following lines, translated by Regine Latortue and Gleason Adams:

> What matters it, he is here! Courage, noble France.
> Your shame, your suffering, cannot long be extended
> For on the marble of the tomb,
> Reviving in our hearts our truncated hatred,
> We will go, young and old, to hone again our swords
> Dulled at Waterloo!!!

Séjour's interest in heroic themes and his enthusiasm for Napoleon continued throughout his life. The success of this poem gained him entrance to Parisian literary circles, where he met Alexandre Dumas and Émile Augier.

Séjour's profession in drama began in 1844 when his five-act play *Diégarias* was performed at the Théâtre-Français (later the Comédie Française). The central character is a minister Castille. Diégarias is a Jew who keeps his name and religion secret from his daughter Inès, who has been seduced by a gentile, Don Juan de Tello. Abdul-Bekri, a Moorish spy, tells Don Juan that Diégarias is a Jew, and the seducer reveals the secret to Henry to save himself from a forced marriage. Stripped of his office by Henry, Diégarias avenges himself against both gentiles—first by demanding that Henry execute Don Juan in return for a much-needed loan and then by engineering a coup d'état. Diégarias triumphs, but the heartbroken Inès poisons herself and dies. The work is characteristic, in its intrigue and romanticism, of his later heroic verse dramas.

From 1844 to 1865 Séjour's plays were regularly staged in Paris. Among his recurring dra-

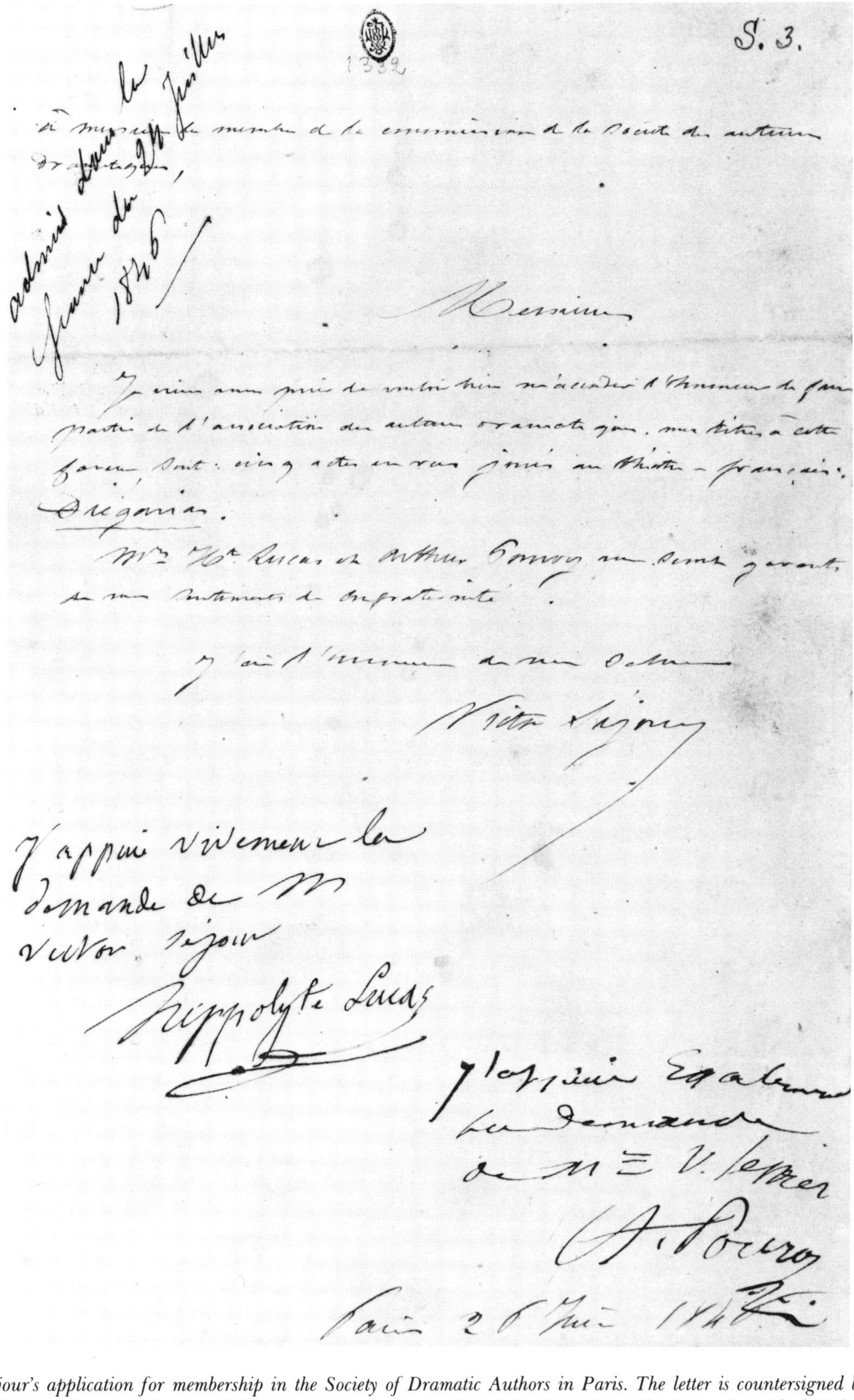

S. 3.

à Messieurs les membres de la commission de la Société des auteurs dramatiques,

Messieurs

Je viens vous prier de vouloir bien m'accorder l'honneur de faire partie de l'association des auteurs dramatiques. mes titres à cette faveur sont: cinq actes en vers joués au théâtre-français: Diégarias.

Mrs Hte Lucas et Arthur Pouray vous seront garants de mes sentiments de confraternité.

J'ai l'honneur de vous saluer

Victor Séjour

J'appuie vivement la demande de M Victor Séjour

Hippolyte Lucas

J'appuie également la demande de Mr V. Séjour

A. Pouray

Paris 26 Juin 1846

Victor Séjour's application for membership in the Society of Dramatic Authors in Paris. The letter is countersigned by Hippolyte Lucas and Arthur Pouray, who seconded his application (courtesy of the Schomburg Center for Research in Black Culture, the New York Public Library, Astor, Lenox and Tilden Foundations).

matic themes are family relationships, nationalism, religion, and social justice—themes that closely represent his own temper and point of view. His plays also reflect the influence of William Shakespeare, whose plays were frequently staged in New Orleans during Séjour's youth, as well as his knowledge of other English renaissance playwrights, such as Ben Jonson, and French writers, including Victor Hugo. Charles Edwards O'Neill, S.J., has observed, "Séjour loved the swirl of passionate feeling. His characters meet head-on in love or in hate. Their debates swell in crescendo of emotion. His plots and dialogue often smack of Shakespeare,—intricately woven, full of dark intrigue and clever interplay. Potions, poisons, and discovery of unknown family relationships also make us think of the Bard of Avon."

After the production of *La Chute de Séjan* at the Théâtre-Français in 1849, Séjour began to move toward melodrama. His plays drew crowds, and he gained recognition. He made several trips to New Orleans during subsequent years—one of them to attend his ailing mother. His reputation in New Orleans spread after the republication of *Le Retour de Napoléon* in Armand Lanusse's *Les Cenelles* (1845), a collection of poems by local black Creoles, and, during the 1850s, at least three of his dramas played in New Orleans. In Paris Séjour became private secretary to Louis Napoleon, a position which assured his artistic success.

During the 1850s his plays were one with popular taste. *Richard III,* produced at the Théâtre du Port-Saint-Martin in 1852, was dedicated to his father in appreciation for his determined parental efforts. A play of great emotional extremes, it focuses on Richard in the context of the War of the Roses and closes with rousing cheers for Elizabeth I and her victorious lover, Richmond. Three years later another play with elements of the heroic tradition and melodrama, *Les Noces vénitiennes,* played in Paris. Amid the hate, jealousy, revenge, and intrigue engendered by the old conflict between the Venetian families of Orséolo and Galiéno, the virtues of love and devotion triumph as the play ends

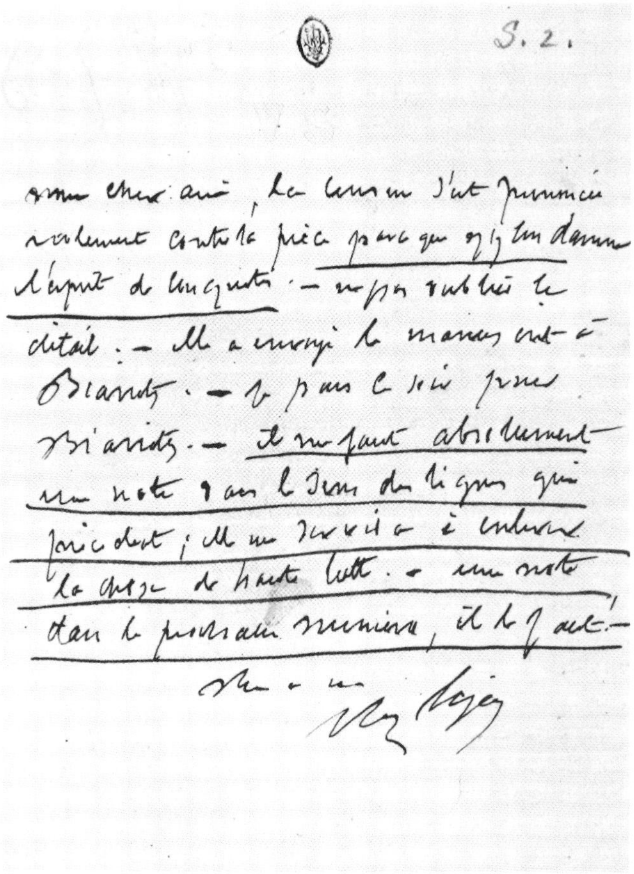

Undated letter to a friend in which Séjour complains about unfair criticism of one of his plays (courtesy of Schomburg Center for Research in Black Culture, the New York Public Library, Astor, Lenox and Tilden Foundations)

with the uniting of Faliero Galiéno and the beautiful Albone Orséolo. His other plays of the period also met with warm receptions as audiences enjoyed the grandiose prose, sumptuous costumes, and spectacular settings. His comedies of the 1850s included *L'Argent du diable* (written in collaboration with Adolphe Jaime fils) and *Le Paletot brun*. Other successes of the period include *Le Fils de la nuit* and *Les Grands Vasseaux.*

In 1860 Séjour was at the height of his stage career. His popularity was enough to bring a new edition of his first play, *Diégarias,* into print seventeen years after its initial production. Of special note is his 1862 drama *Les Volontaires de 1814,* a five-act drama with fourteen tableaux, which focuses on the soldiers of Napoléon I fighting against the Coalition in eastern France and not, as several authors have indicated, on the black and white Louisiana volunteers who fought the British during the Battle of New Orleans.

By 1865 public tastes had shifted and Séjour's popularity had begun to wane. He collaborated on two plays with Théodore Barrière: *Les Enfants de la louve* (1865) and *La Madone des roses* (1869), both five-act dramas, but he was no longer seeing one or two of his plays staged each year, as he had from 1849 through 1864.

Unable to find directors for "Cromwell" and "Le Vampire," he was prevented from having them staged (nor were they published). Within a few years he became destitute and ill. On 20 September 1874 Séjour died from severe tuberculosis, and he was buried at Père Lachaise cemetery.

At his greatest moment, Séjour cut "an impressive figure at Paris" and was described as "Tall, handsome, and distinguished, with sparkling brown eyes" and features that were distinctively those of a black person. His kindness and generosity to his actors earned him their affection, and they graciously received his many revisions. Despite the fact that all of his mature plays, poems, and stories were written in French and in France, his work is American in its energetic and rebellious spirit, and he remains the leading black writer of nineteenth-century Louisiana.

References:

Charles Edwards O'Neill, S.J., "Nineteenth Century Black Artists and Authors," in *Louisiana's Black Heritage,* edited by Robert R. MacDonald and others (New Orleans: Louisiana State Museum, 1979);

O'Neill, "Theatrical Censorship in France, 1844-1875: The Experience of Victor Séjour," *Harvard Library Bulletin,* 26 (1978): 417-441;

John J. Perret, "Victor Séjour, Black French Playwright from Louisiana," *French Review,* 57 (December 1983): 187-193;

Charles B. Roussève, *The Negro in Louisiana* (New Orleans: Xavier University Press, 1937).

Papers:

Collections of Séjour's papers are in the Schomburg Collection at the New York Public Library and in the library of the American Jewish Congress in Great Neck, New York.

Frank J. Webb

(birth and death dates unknown)

Gregory L. Candela
University of New Mexico, Valencia

BOOK: *The Garies and Their Friends* (London: Routledge, 1857).

PERIODICAL PUBLICATIONS: "Two Wolves and A Lamb," *New Era: A Colored American National Journal,* 1 (January-February 1870); "Marvin Hayle," *New Era: A Colored American National Journal,* 1 (March-April, 1870).

Frank J. Webb, the author of one of the earliest novels by a black American, *The Garies and Their Friends* (1857), is a relatively obscure historical figure because his few known literary works—one novel and two novelettes—and Harriet Beecher Stowe's brief preface to *The Garies* provide little biographical information. Stowe, author of *Uncle Tom's Cabin* (1852), describes Frank Webb as "a coloured young man, born and reared in the city of Philadelphia." She introduces him and his book as proof that "the race at present held as slaves [is] capable of freedom, self-government, and progress," and she presents the author as an accurate recorder and representative of "a large class [in Philadelphia that has] increased in numbers, wealth, and standing—they constitute a peculiar society of their own, presenting many social peculiarities worthy of interest and attention."

If Webb were a "young man" in 1857, he was probably born in the late 1820s or the 1830s. Because *The Garies* was published in London and because Webb dedicated the book "most affectionately . . . with profound respect" to his friend Lady Noel Byron, he may have resided in England for a time prior to 1857. Moreover, the fact that Webb knew Harriet Stowe and Lord Brougham, both famous abolitionists who had written prefaces to his novel, suggests that he was involved in the antislavery movement. Although there are no characters in *The Garies* with strong abolitionist views or connections, the novel is full of sympathy for and references to the movement. It is possible that Webb might have toned down any extreme political or ideological stand, in these years directly before the Civil War, to better convey the novel's message about racial oppression to a wider audience. Yet, it is curious that William Wells Brown—abolitionist and author of the first Afro-American novel—does not include Webb among his many biographical sketches in either *The Black Man* (1863) or *The Rising Son* (1873); this omission is particularly perplexing since Brown was very active as a speaker and author for abolitionism in England between 1849 and 1854.

Though Brown's novel *Clotel; or, the President's Daughter* (1853) preceded *The Garies and Their Friends,* the few critics who have commented on Webb's book credit it with several pioneering literary themes and techniques: the novel was, as critic Arthur P. Davis notes, "the first work of fiction to describe the lives and problems of free Northern Negroes; the first to *treat with any appreciable depth* the 'mixed marriage,' the first to emphasize the middle class slant characteristic of Negro novels down to the 1940's; the first to include a lynch mob in a free state; the first to treat ironically . . . the vagaries of the 'color line'; and the first to make 'passing for white' a major theme in a novel."

Another critic notes Webb's comprehension of "the destructive psychology implicit in 'passing' " and comments upon the novel's varied expressions of black militancy. Robert E. Fleming explores the aspects of such militancy in the novel's humor through "a black trickster-figure who perpetrates a joke on the white dupe; thus, the black reader has the dual pleasure of identifying with the player of the joke as well as laughing at the victim." In *The Garies,* characters such as George Winston and Kinch Sanders De Younge play this trickster role.

According to his critics, then, Frank J. Webb's importance for Afro-American literature follows from his realistic and ironic treatment of black themes first introduced in *The Garies and Their Friends.* However, that position of importance is weakened by what those same critics view as Webb's major flaws as a writer: his middle-class formulas for success and his use of melodrama. Yet, a good deal of Webb's black militancy resides in the melodramatic elements of the novel, such as its stereotyped characters and contrived plot, and he spends as much energy questioning the values of white, middle-class Americans as he does presenting them as models for the black community. R. F. Bogardus shows that, though Webb seems "to applaud the seeking of economic success, his acceptance of this [and other] middle class convention is not so worshipful as it is pragmatic." In the novel, such acceptance is also frequently ironic.

The symmetrical plot of the novel reconstructs the history of three families, each of which has its roots in the South and its future determined both by the financial opportunities in the North and the racism they encounter there. The Garie family—composed of a white southern aristocrat, his mulatto wife, and their two children—provides the book's major theme: the destruction of the family and its individual members by racial prejudice. The sole survivor of the Garie family, Emily, marries the only son of the Ellis family, Charlie. The Ellises, a sturdy, middle-class, black family with three children, are the Garies' "friends" of the book's title and represent an alternate thesis: racial identity and pride which insure the physical and spiritual survival of the family against the assaults of bigotry and racial violence. The remaining family, with two offspring, is white and is headed by the melodramatic villain of the novel, "Slippery" George Stevens; except for the daughter, Lizzie, this family is spiritually bankrupt. Each family has one son who symbolizes the continuance of his family's values.

The Garies and Their Friends is carefully structured into three twelve-chapter sections, further divided into four-chapter units, each of which culminates in a significant event. The first twelve chapters bring together the three families in Philadelphia. Mrs. Garie's cousin, George Winston—a black man with an ironical turn of mind, who frequently passes for white—is the direct link between the Garies and the Ellises; yet even though Winston makes fools of the white bigots with whom he associates, he is himself a tortured figure, another of Webb's warnings that living a dual racial life in America is lonely and dangerous.

Winston's glowing stories and letters about Philadelphia do entice the Garies to a move north that ends in tragedy. His sometimes comic "passing" is a manifestation of his racial schizophrenia; like the hypocritical villain of the novel, also named George, Winston is "slippery." He cannot openly associate with whites as a black man, but "he could not bear the isolation and contumely to which [blacks] were subjected. He, therefore, decided on leaving the United States. . . ." Winston is also the butt of Webb's irony when a black servant at a Philadelphia hotel, mistaking him for a white southerner, plays the obsequious "lackey" to secretly solicit funds for the Underground Railroad. George completely misses the point of the hotel man's role playing and becomes self-righteously outraged by his behavior, the cause of which is far nobler than that of his own subterfuge. Except for a brief note in chapter thirty-five, we do not hear from Winston again after chapter four.

The eighth chapter ends on an ominous note; Charlie Ellis breaks his arm and nearly dies from a fall down the stairs. The event foreshadows an incident in which a mob incited by "Slippery" George Stevens chases Charlie's father to the top of a building where a rioter mangles both of Mr. Ellis's hands with a hatchet to force him off the roof. The fall breaks Mr. Ellis's legs and ribs, as

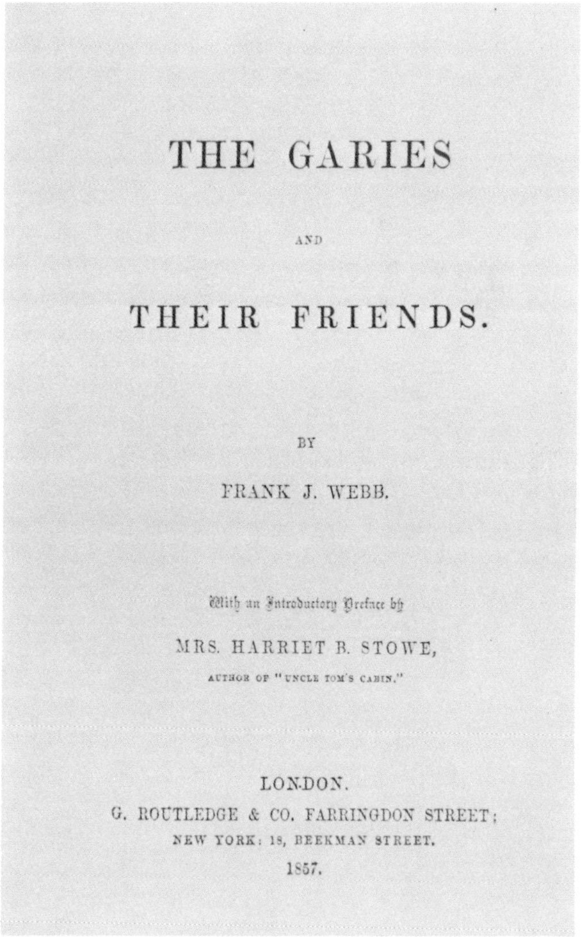

THE GARIES

AND

THEIR FRIENDS.

BY

FRANK J. WEBB.

With an Introductory Preface by

MRS. HARRIET B. STOWE,

AUTHOR OF "UNCLE TOM'S CABIN."

LONDON.

G. ROUTLEDGE & CO. FARRINGDON STREET;

NEW YORK: 18, BEEKMAN STREET.

1857.

Title page for Webb's novel

well as his spirit, disabling him for life. These incidents are also linked to Stevens's later suicidal leap from his balcony, in that all the events are metaphors in the novel for the dismemberment of family due to the internal and external pressures of racism.

We meet George Stevens, a "pettifogging attorney," at the end of the novel's first section. He is a grotesque, villainous caricature and the most melodramatic figure in the novel: "His baldness might have given an air of benevolence to his face, but for the shaggy eyebrows that over-shadowed his cunning-looking grey eyes. His cheek-bones were high, and the cadaverous skin was so tightly drawn across them, as to give it a very parchment-like appearance." His face is "sinister" and his sparse hair forms a "pair of horns" on his head. Stevens's diabolical machinations direct the novel's second, twelve-chapter section, the most gruesome of the book. Stevens's discovery that he is Mr. Garie's cousin and heir leads him to foment a race riot in which he murders Mr. Garie and causes Mrs. Garie's death from exposure and shock. The two Georges, both cousins to the Garies, control the plot of the book's first two sections and cause the family's downfall. Thus, Webb's melodramatic technique functions on a content level as a socially destructive force that crushes virtuous and innocent people. In the novel Stevens, at times, embodies the corrupting force of racism, but the evils heaped on Stevens's head do not disappear with his death as they might have in a more conventional melodrama. In fact, in an ironic parody of the typical villain whose devilish power is often emblemized through his black cape and dark features, Stevens is beaten, tarred to look black, and then abused because he appears to be a "colored." Webb's point, made through a skillful combination of melodrama, irony, and one of the most comedic scenes in the novel, is that, ultimately, the evil of racism cannot be banished from a society by simply reversing the very stereotypes that perpetuate racial prejudice; nor is that evil exclusively located in people labeled as villains—in this case racists. In the novel, Webb depicts racial hatred and fellow feeling in black and white characters. His irony exposes the racism, greed, and deceit on both sides of the color line and in those unfortunate characters split between the two races.

Nowhere are themes more evident than in the final section of *The Garies and Their Friends,* in which the second generation of the novel's three families reaches adulthood, and the sins or graces of the fathers are visited upon the three sons. Webb emphasizes this moral continuity by naming all three men after their fathers. "Slippery" George, the father, had once noted that if he were black "living in a country like this, I'd sacrifice conscience and everything else to the acquisition of wealth." But color has nothing to do with avariciousness, and "Slippery" George sacrifices everything for money "even though" he is white. Like his father, George, Jr. is greedy, and his ill-gotten inheritance, which is eventually taken away from him, only increases his appetite for wealth. His corruptness is not limited to avarice, however, which Webb demonstrates by having George, Jr. maliciously reveal young Garie's racial background to his unsuspecting fiancée. Thus, George destroys "Clary" as certainly as his father shot and murdered Clarence, Sr. Charlie Ellis, a mirror image of his courageous and hardworking father, flourishes in his career as an engraver and marries Emily Garie, incorporating the ill-fated Garie clan into the tenacious Ellis family.

Some critics, pointing to Charlie as a "black Horatio Alger," disparage what they see as Webb's middle-class mentality. However, while Webb endorsed values of initiative and honest gain, in the novel, as the Stevens family bears out, he did not endorse the rapacious acquisition of money by any means possible or for the sake of just having wealth. Through both Charlie and Mr. Walters, the novel's wealthy, black real estate broker, Webb suggests that an honorable path to wealth builds strong character and racial pride; furthermore, he implies that the power of money can ease some of the pain caused by racism. By the same principles, Mr. Garie's aristocratic indolence helps to destroy his family and hastens the death of his only son, Clary, who tries to pass as a white man. For Webb, finally, the color of money is not as powerful as the real or imagined color distinctions of racial prejudice.

Despite Frank Webb's clear disapproval of inherited wealth and the "idle rich," "Two Wolves and A Lamb" and "Marvin Hayle," serialized stories published in 1870, display his attraction to the upper-class society of London, Paris, and Cannes. Although critic Arthur Davis warns that "it is always dangerous to draw biographical data from an author's work. . . . One gathers from reading these novelettes that the author had a better than superficial acquaintance with London and Paris, that he was fairly well-read, and that he appreciated . . . 'cultural' things and experiences." Both stories center upon the pastimes of the European sophisticate, including frequent discourse on the subjects of art and literature.

Although his novelettes are minor works, Frank J. Webb deserves critical attention for *The Garies and Their Friends,* a novel that is structurally sound and realistically details many of the issues confronting Afro-Americans in the 1850s. In particular his skillful handling of the melodramatic elements of the novel deserves more study as a powerful expression of the irony of a black author, rather than being dismissed as simple imitation of second-rate white fiction.

References:

James Barbour and Robert E. Fleming, "Nineteenth Century Black Novelists: A Checklist," *Minority Voices,* 2 (Fall 1969): 27-43;

R. F. Bogardus, "Frank J. Webb's *The Garies and Their Friends:* An Early Black Novelist's Venture into Realism," *Studies in Black Literature,* 5, no. 2 (1974): 15-20;

Arthur P. Davis, "*The Garies and Their Friends:* A Neglected Pioneer Novel," *CLA Journal,* 13, no. 1 (1969): 27-34;

James H. DeVries, "The Tradition of the Sentimental Novel in *The Garies and Their Friends,*" *CLA Journal,* 17, no. 2 (1973): 241-249;

Robert E. Fleming, "Humor in the Early Black Novel," *CLA Journal,* 17, no. 2 (1973): 250-262.

Phillis Wheatley

(circa 1754-5 December 1784)

Kenny J. Williams
Duke University

See also the Wheatley entry in *DLB 31, American Colonial Writers, 1735-1781.*

BOOKS: *An Elegiac Poem, on the Death of that Celebrated Divine, and Eminent Servant of Jesus Christ, the Reverend and Learned George Whitefield . . .* (Boston: Printed & sold by Ezekiel Russell & by John Boyles, 1770); republished in *Heaven the Residence of Saints,* by Ebenezer Pemberton (London: Printed for E. & C. Dilly, 1771);

Poems on Various Subjects, Religious and Moral. By Phillis Wheatley, Negro Servant to Mr. John Wheatley of Boston (London: Printed for Archibald Bell & sold in Boston by Cox & Berry, 1773; Philadelphia: Printed by Joseph Crukshank, 1786);

An Elegy, Sacred to the Memory of that Great Divine, The Reverend and Learned Dr. Samuel Cooper (Boston: Printed & sold by E. Russell, 1784);

Liberty and Peace, A Poem (Boston: Printed by Warden & Russell, 1784).

Collections: *Life and Works of Phillis Wheatley. Containing Her Complete Poetical Works, Numerous Letters and a Complete Biography of This Famous Poet of a Century and a Half Ago,* edited by G. Herbert Renfro (Washington, D.C.: A. Jenkins, 1916);

The Poems of Phillis Wheatley, Edited with an Introduction and Notes, edited by Charlotte Ruth Wright (Philadelphia: The Wrights, 1930);

The Poems of Phillis Wheatley, edited by Julian D. Mason, Jr. (Chapel Hill: University of North Carolina Press, 1966).

Phillis Wheatley's status as a slave has hampered a thorough consideration of her work. While many modern readers—accustomed to placing emphasis upon writers' personal reactions to their subjects—agree that there has been a revolution in poetic taste since the eighteenth century, these same readers are often quick to assume that Phillis Wheatley had little to offer her readers even in her own day. They cite her poetic restraint as evidence of her detachment from the issue of slavery and conclude she should have used her talent to protest prevailing racial attitudes. Critical judgments have ranged from dismissal of her work in the mistaken notion that nothing of artistic merit could emerge from the African mind to paternalistic ecstasy that lacks objectivity. Her race has been a major factor in evaluating her poetry. To regret the absence of

Phillis Wheatley

protest in her poetry is to misunderstand her perceived role, not only in the Wheatley household but also in an eighteenth-century Boston whose loyalty to England was severely tested during her lifetime. Ultimately her responses to her world must be viewed within the context of colonial America.

Carefully executed iambic-pentameter couplets were a commonly used verse form in that era. These often stylized heroic couplets were the means by which poets articulated their faithfulness to such literary models as Alexander Pope, the most revered poet of the eighteenth century. In employing this stanza form colonial poets also reflected their neoclassical view of an ordered life. Even though the latter part of the century was an emotional period which produced numerous documents of freedom, the experimentation, innovation, and personal insights frequently associated with rebellion did not—in the eighteenth century—displace the general notion perpetuated by the Age of Reason that a writer should approach the truth through a conscious and deliberate adherence to the rules of writing established by "the ancients." Viewed in retrospect, even the argumentative prose of that time seems strangely devoid of the intensity of feeling which must have been present in the writers' minds.

Eighteenth-century writing in America was also rooted in New England Puritanism, which emphasized a realistic plain style and was suspicious of any poetry which did not have some didactic purpose. That the Puritans were also wary of poetry which might stimulate the senses at the expense of reason led to their acceptance of neoclassical poetics as a legitimate theory of creativity.

With the exception of the seventeenth-century poets Anne Bradstreet and Edward Taylor (substantially unknown in his own day), the New England Puritans did not produce great poetry. Into the eighteenth century colonial writers continued to be handicapped by a limited view of literature, which engendered a rigid fidelity to form. It was in this environment, barren and sterile though it might appear, that Phillis Wheatley grew to maturity, her fame spreading from New England to Europe. She inherited not only the liabilities but also the assets of her era's prevailing view of literature and life, and her poetry is an important illustration of the eighteenth-century creative mind in New England. Her shortcomings (and they are many) are the weaknesses of an American colonial poetry that was firmly based in an imitative literary tradition and in Christian orthodoxy. Yet, her occasional flashes of insight and her manipulation of the age's popular poetic tradition indicate that she was more than simply an imitator of lifeless literary convention.

It has generally been assumed that she was born sometime around 1753 or 1754—perhaps in Senegal—kidnapped, and brought to New England in 1761. She was purchased by John Wheatley of Boston as a gift for his wife, Susanna Wheatley, who, according to Margaretta Matilda Odell's *Memoir and Poems of Phillis Wheatley* (1834), "visited the slave market" in order "to make a personal selection from the group of unfortunates offered for sale." Though all sources indicate that the child was frail, Benjamin Brawley, in his *Negro Builders and Heroes* (1937), maintains that "her bright eyes attracted the attention of Susanna Wheatley . . . she was purchased, taken home, and given the name of Phillis."

In those early days there was nothing in the delicate child to indicate that she would become a well-known poet, but she learned to read and write quickly. She also became competent in Latin. The legend of her precocity has been aided by her biographers' emphasis on her mastery of English, selected classics, and the Bible within sixteen months. That her education was extremely thorough has generally been accepted; however, whether she was able to read the Bible fluently "in sixteen months"—as ascertained by John Wheatley in a 14 November 1772 letter to an English publisher—has not been proved. It is clear that the Wheatleys took a great interest in the bright youngster. In all probability her education was a fascinating experiment for them, but there is no indication that Susanna Wheatley and her daughter, Mary, were great scholars themselves. Yet, they set about to make the most of the child's inquisitive nature. Odell noted that Phillis "had no brilliant exhibition of feminine genius before her, to excite her emulations," and found the only plausible explanation for her intellectual attainments and poetic gift "in the inspiration of that genius which is the gift of God." Her proficiency in grammar and understanding of style probably resulted initially from her intense interest in Pope's translation of Homer.

Along with a handful of male university graduates, she reached a level of education that was extremely rare in colonial society, especially for females. Undoubtedly one of the community's best-educated young women, she profited intellectually from her association with the elite of Boston, which placed her in a cultural atmosphere denied to most young people growing up in colonial America. The Wheatleys, who were apparently people of taste and refinement, took great delight in showing her off, but inherent in this display was evidence of the ambiguous role she had to play.

Phillis became a devout Christian during the waning days of New England Puritanism, and her commitment to religion, as she understood its principles, cannot be minimized. She became a member of the historic Old South Meeting House in 1771 and accepted the interpretation of Christianity preached there. While she was extremely familiar with biblical literature and took delight in the poetry of Pope, it was the Puritan John Milton—whose great work had set out "to justify the ways of God to man"—who became her favorite. Religion provided her an explanation for her status in life and influenced her writing.

Slavery was not as restrictive for her as for others in bondage. She was free to visit the Wheatleys' friends; Odell, however, observed that when Phillis visited these homes, she requested "that a side-table . . . be laid for her [and] dined modestly apart from the rest of the company," in a position "where she could certainly expect neither to give or receive offense." All of her biographers have noted that her room was well heated and that she had access to lights in the evening. According to Julian Mason, in his introduction to *The Poems of Phillis Wheatley* (1966), "she came to be treated almost as a member of the family and was assigned only very light housekeeping tasks, with permission to ignore even these duties when she felt poetically inclined."

While much has been made of the freedom she enjoyed, little recognition has been given to the psychological toll her situation must have taken upon her. She was indeed a slave and subject to the whims of her owners, no matter how considerate they might have been. That she did not write about her ambiguous position in Boston society may have been due as much to an acceptance of what seemed an inevitability as to her commitment to a literary tradition that prohibited the display of personal concerns and longings.

In *Bid the Vassal Soar* (1974), M. A. Richmond has interpreted an episode reported by Odell in a way which might support the notion that Phillis Wheatley felt isolated. While the young poet was visiting one of the Wheatleys' friends (or, as Richmond claims, she had made "one of her showpiece visits to a distinguished household"), the weather turned cold, and Mrs. Wheatley sent the black coachman, Prince, to bring the young woman home in the family carriage. When they arrived at the Wheatley residence, Phillis was riding up front with Prince. "Do but look at the saucy valet," Mrs. Wheatley allegedly exclaimed, "if he hasn't the impudence to sit upon the same seat as my Phillis," and she harshly scolded him for presuming such familiarity. Richmond has argued that, since Phillis probably chose to sit with Prince, "the explicit reprimand to the coachman contained an implicit rebuke to the poet. In putting Prince in *his* place the mistress was just as surely reminding 'my Phillis' of *hers*." Thus, Richmond concludes, "Hers was a place in which she could not mingle with other black slaves as equals, nor could she encounter whites on terms of equality. She inhabited a strange, ambiguous twilight zone between black society and white society, cut off from any normal contact with either, denied the sustenance of group identity, doomed to a loneliness that, being particular and peculiar, was more tragic than the existentialist generalizations about the human condition. . . . It was white society that designated [her] place."

Various dates have been given for the beginning of her interest in writing. In John Wheatley's 1772 letter to Phillis's English publishers he indicated that she started writing in 1765. It seems likely that she wrote several poems prior to 1767,

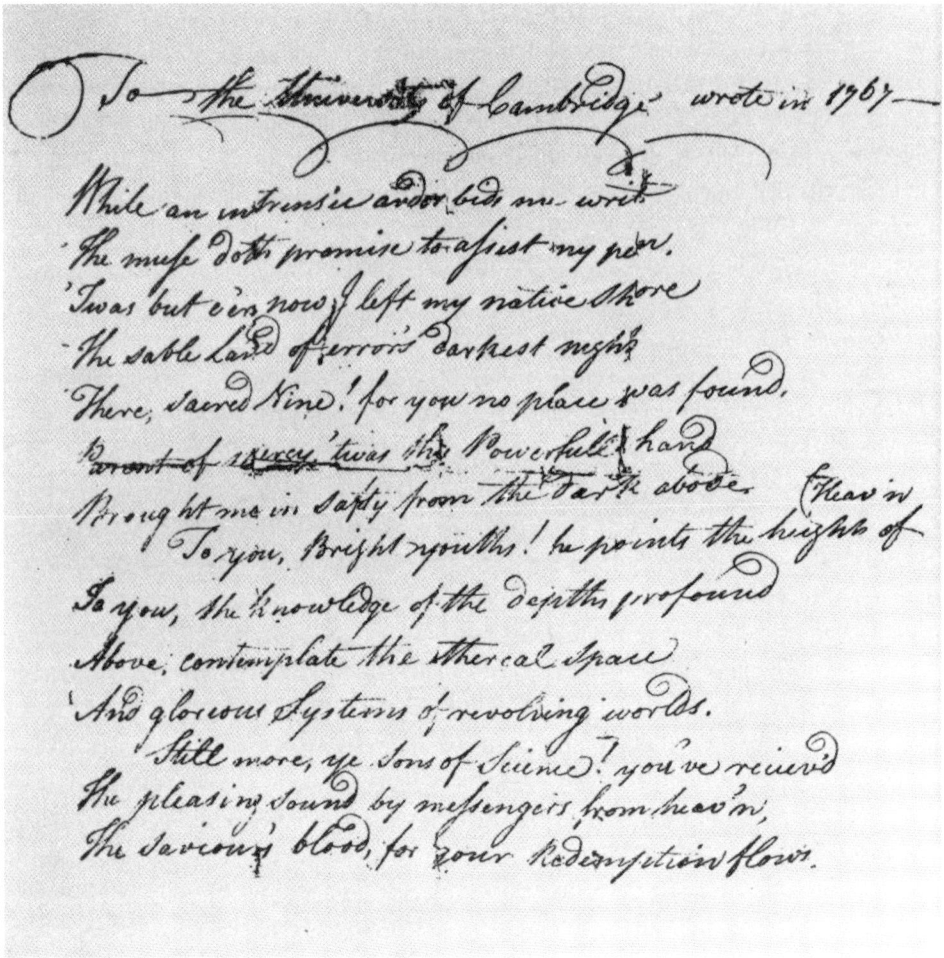
To the University of Cambridge wrote in 1767—
While an intrinsic ardor bids me write
The muse doth promise to assist my pen.
'Twas but e'en now I left my native Shore
The sable Land of error's darkest night
There, sacred Nine! for you no place was found.
Parent of mercy, 'twas thy Powerfull hand
Brought me in safety from the dark abode
To you, Bright youths! he points the heights of Heav'n
To you, the knowledge of the depths profound
Above, contemplate the ethereal space
And glorious Systems of revolving worlds.
Still more, ye Sons of Science! you've receiv'd
The pleasing Sound by messengers from heav'n,
The Saviour's blood, for your Redemption flows.

Manuscript for an early poem (courtesy of American Antiquarian Society)

including such works as "On Being Brought from Africa to America" and "To the University of Cambridge, in New England." Although her 1770 elegy "On the Death of Rev. George Whitefield" was long thought to be her first published work, Carl Bridenbaugh revealed in 1969 that her first poem was "On Messrs. Hussey and Coffin," which appeared in the *Newport Mercury* for 21 December 1767. According to the directions "to the printer" that were published with the poem, Phillis had heard the two men's tale of their narrow escape from drowning during a storm at sea while she was " 'tending Table" during their visit to the Wheatleys. Beginning with typically neoclassical allusions to Boreas and Eolus, she speculates about what would have happened had the men drowned—would they be "With the supreme and independent God," or "down in the Shades below"?—and decides "To Heaven their Souls with eager Raptures soar,/Enjoy the Bliss of him they wou'd adore." The poem ends with an expression of faith:

> *Had I the Tongue of a Seraphim, how would I exalt thy Praise; thy Name as Incense to the Heavens should fly, and the Remembrance of thy Goodness to the shoreless Ocean of Beatitude!—Then should the Earth glow with seraphick Ardour.*
> Blest Soul, which sees the Day while Light doth shine,
> To guide his Steps to trace the Mark divine.

Not Wheatley's most significant poem, "On Messrs. Hussey and Coffin" does illustrate how typically she wrote about an event in a manner that reflected her abiding religious faith. Furthermore, the poem exhibits her use of allusions as well as a maturity not evident in the more popular "To the King's Most Excellent Majesty, 1768," written the following year.

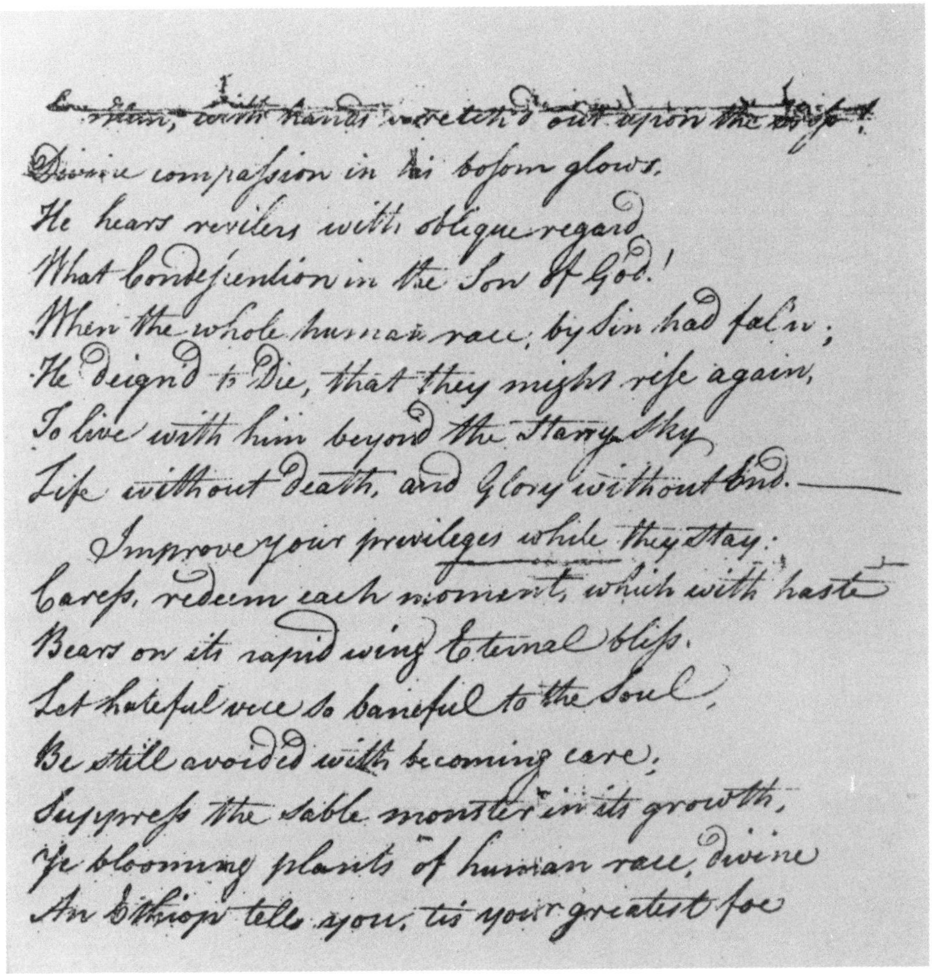

~~... Man, with hands stretch'd out upon the cross.~~
Divine compassion in his bosom glows.
He hears revilers with oblique regard
What Condescention in the Son of God!
When the whole human race, by Sin had fal'n;
He deign'd to Die, that they might rise again,
To live with him beyond the Starry Sky
Life without Death, and Glory without End.—
Improve your privileges while they stay:
Caress, redeem each moment, which with haste
Bears on its rapid wing Eternal bliss.
Let hateful vice so baneful to the Soul,
Be still avoided with becoming care;
Suppress the sable monster in its growth,
Ye blooming plants of human race, divine
An Ethiop tells you, tis your greatest foe

In 1770 Phillis Wheatley's elegy for the Reverend George Whitefield, who had died on 30 September 1770, brought her public recognition. First published in the 11 October issue of the *Massachusetts Spy,* it was published as a broadside and a pamphlet in Boston and was also printed in New York, Newport, and Philadelphia before the end of the year. It first appeared in London the following year, when it was published with Ebenezer Pemberton's funeral sermon for the great evangelist. In these publications she was generally identified as "a Servant Girl of 17 Years of Age, Belonging to Mr. J. Wheatley of Boston:—And has been but 9 years in this Country from Africa."

That she had elected to write of George Whitefield also brought her to the attention of Selina Hastings, Countess of Huntingdon, an avid supporter of humanitarian causes and an important figure in the eighteenth-century revival movement who had helped Whitefield with his American campaign. Her philanthropic activities were well known, as was her aid in the establishment of both Dartmouth College and the College of New Jersey (now Princeton University). That Phillis Wheatley's Whitefield poem enjoyed widespread circulation is perhaps a testimony not only to the greatness of the evangelist and the interest in Phillis Wheatley but also to the influence of the Countess of Huntingdon.

The elegy for Whitefield was followed by two broadsides, *To Mrs. Leonard, on the Death of her Husband* (1771) and *To the Rev. Mr. Pitkin, on the Death of his Lady* (1772), and "Recollection" (later revised as "On Recollection"), which appeared in the March 1772 issue of the *London Magazine.* In a 10 October 1772 letter to the Earl of Dartmouth, whom she considered a "friend" for his opposition to the Stamp Act, Phillis enclosed a poem praising his appointment as Secretary of State for the Colonies.

During 1773 two more elegies appeared as broadsides: *To the Hon'ble Thomas Hubbard, Esq.; On the Death of Mrs. Thankfull Leonard* appeared in January, and was followed in December by *An Elegy to Miss Mary Moorhead on the Death of her Father, the Rev. Mr. John Moorhead.* By far the most important of Phillis Wheatley's 1773 publications was her collection of verse, *Poems on Various Subjects, Religious and Moral,* published in London and dedicated to the Countess of Huntingdon. In his 1966 edition of Wheatley's poems, Mason suggests that the appearance of "Recollection" in the *London Magazine* "either inspired or greatly encouraged the idea of publishing a volume of her poems, for the 1773 volume contains a letter from Wheatley to the publisher of the magazine dated November 14, 1772."

The journey to England that preceded the book's appearance was to provide the high point of her life. The Wheatleys' physician—concerned about her delicate health—had suggested a sea voyage for her, and since Nathaniel Wheatley, Mary Wheatley's twin, was scheduled to go to England on business, it was decided that Phillis would accompany him. The excitement of the impending trip was not without some sadness and apprehension; but in "A Farewell to America," addressed to Mrs. Wheatley, she looks forward to the new experience and indicates "For thee, *Britannia,* I resign/New England's smiling fields." Her status at the time of the trip is not clear. While Brawley asserted in his *Early Negro American Writers* (1935) "that Phillis was manumitted formally before the trip," Odell wrote that she may never have "received any formal manumission," and Vernon Loggins stated, "she was still regarded as a slave" at the time of the trip. More recently Stephanie Ocko, writing in *Early American Life* (August 1980), maintained that she was freed the month after her return from England. It is known, for certain, however, that she had been freed by 1778.

In some respects her status was inconsequential in London, where her African background was considered exotic and contributed to her popularity as well as her reputation as a poet. She was lionized and showered with presents. Brooke Watson, who became Lord Mayor of London, gave her a copy of *Paradise Lost.* The Earl of Dartmouth reportedly gave her money that she spent buying such books as a collection of Alexander Pope's work, John Gay's *Fables,* and Tobias Smollett's translation of *Don Quixote.* Among her visitors was Benjamin Franklin. Though the Countess of Huntingdon was nominally her sponsor, it is doubtful that Phillis ever saw the Countess, who appears not to have been in London when Phillis arrived. Although she requested that the young poet remain in the city until her return, Mrs. Wheatley's illness intervened. On 17 July 1773 Phillis wrote to the Countess expressing sorrow at having missed her "ladiship" and noting: "Am sorry to acquaint your Ladiship that the Ship is certainly to sail next Thursday [on] which I must return to America. I long to see my Friend there, [I am] extremely reluctant to go without having first seen your Ladiship." Although she added a postscript, "my master is yet undetermined about going home," apparently they sailed together a few days later.

In spite of that disappointment, life in England must have been exciting. In a 30 October 1773 letter to Obour Tanner, her friend in Newport, Phillis wrote: "The friends I found there among the nobility and gentry, their benevolent conduct towards me, the unexpected and unmerited civility and complaisance with which I was treated by all, fills me with astonishment. I can scarcely realize it. This I humbly hope has the happy effect of lessening me in my own esteem. . . . The God of the seas and dry land, has graciously brought me home in safety." Speaking of the reason of her return, she merely noted: "My mistress has been very sick above 14 weeks, & confined to her bed the whole time, but is I hope somewhat better, now."

Mrs. Wheatley died on 3 March 1774. Although the young poet did not write an elegy on this occasion, her grief was expressed in another letter to Tanner: "I have lately met with a great trial in the Death of my mistress; let us imagine the loss of a Parent, Sister, or Brother, the tenderness of all these were united in her.—I was a poor little outcast & stranger when she took me in. . . . I was treated by her more like a child than a servant. . . ."

While her productivity may not have lessened after 1773, her work was published infrequently. In a way she was also a casualty of the Revolutionary War. Her book was published at a time when people were more concerned with the political events of the day than with the poetry of a Boston slave. During this period Phillis Wheatley apparently met a "gentleman of the Royal Navy" whose travels had taken him to Africa's "guilded shore." In the *Royal American Magazine* for December 1774, there appeared her enigmatic poem to one of the "blooming sons of Neptune's royal race." His reply in the same issue—to "the lovely daughter of the Affric shore,/. . ./. . .the happy land,/. . ./Where cancers torrid heat the soul inspires"—occasioned her response, published in the January 1775 issue of the magazine. This is one of the few instances in which she emphasized the beauty and the exoticism of Africa rather than its gloom as a non-Christian land.

October 1775 found her in Providence, Rhode Island, where John Wheatley had moved his household in order to avoid the military confusion then existing in Boston. She wrote to George Washington on 26 October and enclosed a poem inspired by his having been "appointed by the Grand Continental Congress to be Generalissimo of the armies of North America." Washington replied to her in a 2 February 1776 letter that concluded, "If you should ever come to Cambridge, or near headquarters, I shall be happy to see a person so favored by the muses, and to whom Nature has been so liberal and beneficent in her dispensation." There are still many unanswered questions concerning the meeting and the relationship between the slave poet and the slaveowner (many of which have been analyzed by M. A. Richmond in *Bid the Vassal Soar*). While the poem which she wrote in his honor may appear to be an overstylized hyperbolic work, it is of considerable interest from a historic point of view. First, given the fact that it was written before Washington's military successes and while the outcome of the war was still in question, it seems strangely prophetic. A result of the patriotic fervor which swept New England, Wheatley's "To His Excellency General Washington" antedates the Washington myth. Her patriotism made her—like others in the colonies—accept George Washington as a contemporary savior in the fight for independence. Furthermore, her reference to the land as "Columbia" is one of the earliest uses of that term to designate the nation. The couplet "Thee, first in place and honours,—we demand/The grace and glory of thy martial band" was misprinted by an early editor to read "first in peace," and the phrase became a popular description of Washington.

Benjamin Quarles, who in *The Negro in the American Revolution* (1961) called Phillis Wheatley "an ardent patriot," thinks she "took a personal role in the agitation." While this information may be questionable, she displayed a great spirit of nationalism on several poetic occasions. In fact, the poem to Washington, which abstractly discusses the importance of freedom, ends with the lines:

Proceed, great chief, with virtue on thy side,
Thy ev'ry action let the goddess guide.
A crown, a mansion, and a throne that shine,
With gold unfading, WASHINGTON! be thine.

Published in the April 1776 issue of the *Pennsylvania Gazette*, edited at the time by Thomas Paine, the poem was one of the earliest poetic encomia to Washington. After the war Washington was the subject of many neoclassical tributes, but it was the slave poet who had led the way.

Life in war-torn New England was far from stable or pleasant. Mr. Wheatley took the family back to Boston after the British had evacuated Boston in March 1776. His death on 12 March 1778, however, effectively broke up the household, and on 1 April 1778 Phillis Wheatley married John Peters, a free black Bostonian. Her marriage may well have been a desire to re-create the security she had experienced with the Wheatley family, which had been damaged first by Mary's marriage to the Reverend Mr. John Lathrop in 1771 and subsequently by the deaths of Susanna and John Wheatley. Mary Wheatley Lathrop died in the same year as her father, and Nathaniel Wheatley, who had gone to live in England, died in 1783.

It has often been said that Peters was "worthless," maintaining that he caused an estrangement between his wife and her white friends, behaved in a superior manner, and lacked the ability to support her and their three children. According to Brawley (in *Negro Builders and Heroes*), Peters has been "variously described as a baker, a grocer, a physician, and a lawyer, but with all of these occupations seems not to have had the ability to earn a living. He wore a wig, sported a cane and generally felt himself superior to labor." Mason refers to Peters as "an enigmatic Negro who seems to have tried his hand" at many jobs "without having much training for them or much success with them. He is reported to have had somewhat grandiose notions. . . ." For reasons not made explicit, Mason asserts that Peters spent part of 1784 in jail. Arthur Schomburg, however, was convinced that Phillis's husband "not only bore a good character, but was in every way a remarkable specimen of his race, being a fluent writer, a ready speaker and an intelligent man." In "An Appreciation" for Charles F. Heartman's first collected edition of Phillis Wheatley's *Poems and Letters* (1915), Schomburg explained that Peters was really "a grocer by trade [but] under the title of 'Doctor' Peters, pleaded the cause of his brethren, the Africans, before the tribunals of the State."

History obviously has not dealt kindly with Peters. It is difficult to determine the validity of the charges made against him for he undoubtedly suffered from the negative attitude toward assertive free blacks in northern cities. His marriage to the "Sable Muse" may have failed because he was unable to assume the responsibilities of family life in a society where free blacks without independent means often had a more difficult time than slaves, or it may have failed because Phillis's classical education had not prepared her for the life of a free black. It seems certain that the people who had lionized her when the Wheatleys lived did little to alleviate her condition after her marriage to Peters. Thus it was that Phillis Wheatley—abandoned, lonely, and destitute—was forced by circumstances to spend her last days as a scullery maid in a rooming house.

She continued to write after her marriage although few of her poems were published. Even her correspondence with Obour Tanner suffered. There was apparently a long silence between the two friends, but in a letter dated 29 May 1778 Phillis summarized the events of the Revolutionary War as well as her life in a cryptic manner: "The vast variety of scenes that have pass'd before us these 3 years past will to a reasonable mind serve to convince us of the uncertain duration of all things temporal, and the proper result of such a consideration is an ardent desire of, & preparation for, a state and enjoyments which are more suitable to the immortal mind." It is strange that she did not specifically mention the death of Mr. Wheatley, her freedom, or her marriage.

When the fighting shifted once again to New England, Phillis Wheatley and her husband sought refuge in Wilmington, Massachusetts. For a period after her marriage, she found a home with one of Mrs. Wheatley's nieces. On 10 May 1779, she once again wrote to Tanner. There is no mention of the fact that her husband had remained in Wilmington nor of the probable birth of a child. In fact, personal references were minimal as she wrote of "a variety of hindrances" that had kept her from writing and expressed the hope that "our correspondence will revive—and revive in better times." Given the conditions that she had faced, to speak of "a variety of hindrances" proves her a master of understatement. Part of her reticence may have been due to her Puritan upbringing or her inability to deal with existing conditions. It is, however, significant that even in her personal letters she revealed little about herself.

Toward the end of 1779 the *Boston Evening Post and General Advertiser* ran in its editions for 30 October, 6 and 27 November, and 4, 11, and 18 December "PROPOSALS, For printing by subscription a volume of Poems & Letters on various subjects, dedicated to the Right Hon. Benjamin Franklin Esq: One of the Ambassadors of the United States at the Court of France, BY PHILLIS PETERS." The author is described as "a *female African,* whose lot it was to fall into the hands of a *generous* master and *great* benefactor." The projected book was to consist of about 300 pages and include thirty-three poems, most of which had not been printed before. In fact, at the time of the proposal only the poems addressed to Washington and "a gentleman of the navy" had been published. Thirteen letters were to be included, of which three were to the Countess of Huntingdon and one to Dr. Benjamin Rush. In spite of the promise that "those who subscribe for six books will have a seventh gratis," there apparently was not enough interest in war-torn Boston to warrant the printing

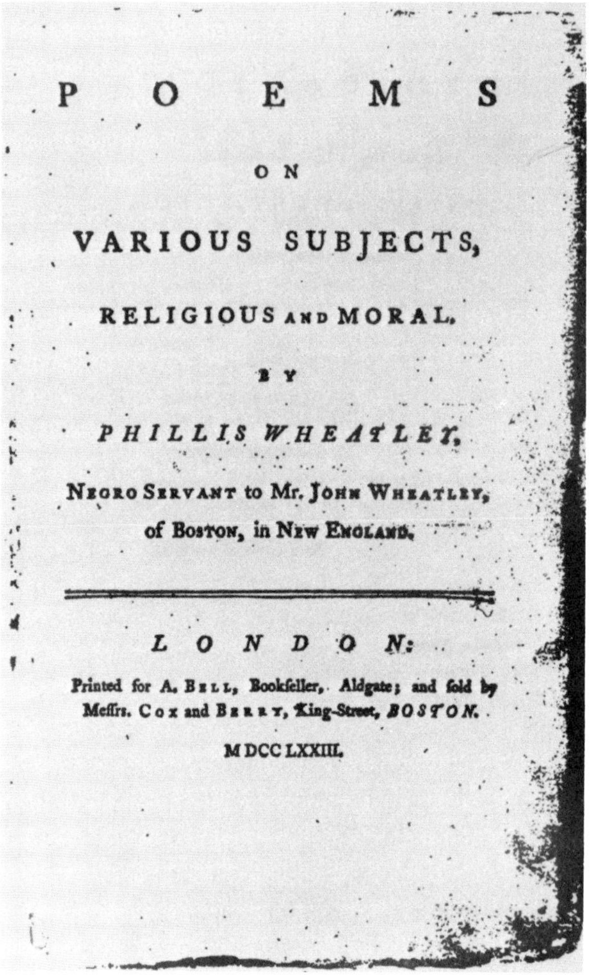

POEMS

ON

VARIOUS SUBJECTS,

RELIGIOUS AND MORAL.

BY

PHILLIS WHEATLEY,

NEGRO SERVANT to Mr. JOHN WHEATLEY, of BOSTON, in NEW ENGLAND.

LONDON:

Printed for A. BELL, Bookseller, Aldgate; and sold by Messrs. COX and BERRY, King-Street, *BOSTON.*

MDCCLXXIII.

Title page for the first collection of poetry by an Afro-American

of the book.

As might be expected, the poems written after her marriage do not allude to her misery. Eight years after her last published poem, "To Mr. and Mrs. ******** on the Death of Their Infant Son" appeared in the September 1784 issue of *Boston Magazine.* Since two of her own children had undoubtedly died by this time, the poem can be viewed as an exercise in control as she maintained the emotional distance demanded by the neoclassical tradition. The poem was accompanied by the notation "selected from a manuscript Volume of Poems, written by PHILLIS PETERS, formerly PHILLIS WHEATLEY—and is inserted as a specimen of her Work: should this gain the Approbation of the Publick, and sufficient encouragement be given, a Volume will be shortly Published, by the printers hereof, who received subscriptions for said Work."

During the same year two other poems were published as pamphlets: *An Elegy, Sacred to the Memory of that Great Divine, The Reverend and Learned Dr. Samuel Cooper* and *Liberty and Peace,* an ode celebrating the end of the Revolutionary War. These were to be the last poems published during her lifetime. She died in Boston on 5 December 1784. Her biographers note that her death was announced in the *Independent Chronicle:* "Last Lord's Day, died Mrs. Phillis Peters (formerly Phillis Wheatley) aged thirty-one, known to the world by her celebrated miscellaneous poems. Her funeral is to be this afternoon, at four o'clock, from the house lately improved by Mr. Todd, nearly opposite Dr. Bullfinch's at West Boston, where her friends and acquaintances are desired to attend."

The life that had dazzled both America and Europe came to a close in the obscurity of a boardinghouse among strangers. It appears that John Peters was absent, and their third child died within a few hours of Phillis. Odell claims that Peters did not "see fit" to tell acquaintances of her death "or to notify them of her interment." It is the supreme irony that freedom for the poet meant a "slavery" which she had never known in the Wheatley household.

In addition to the few poems which appeared separately, the reputation of Phillis Wheatley rests primarily upon *Poems on Various Subjects, Religious and Moral,* published in 1773 when she was nineteen or twenty years old. In order to allay the suspicions of those who might assume that the poetry was a hoax perpetrated by the knowing upon the unsuspecting, a testimony of authenticity opens some copies of the collection. The affidavit was signed by eighteen of "the most respectable characters in Boston, that none might have the least ground for disputing" her work, and included Thomas Hutchinson (the royal governor), John Hancock, James Bowdoin, Samuel Cooper, John Moorhead (the owner of Scipio, the black artist who in all probability did the portrait from which the London engraver drew the likeness of Phillis for the book), John Wheatley, and thirteen other distinguished civic leaders. Also included in the opening pages is the letter from John Wheatley to the English publisher describing Phillis and her progress in educational matters.

While it may be true that her poetry holds little interest for the reader who finds eighteenth-century poetry tedious, her work reflects the strong influences of her early training and reading as well as her fidelity to the prevailing literary tradition of her day. One of the obvious characteristics of any collection of American colonial poetry is the dominance of the heroic couplet. That she adopted Alexander Pope as one of her models is not surprising in an age that often used him as an example of good writing. The fact that her work shows so little emotion must be considered as a further characteristic of a neoclassical aesthetic which did not permit the poet the luxury of displaying great personal feeling. Like most poems in the genre, her many funeral elegies are stilted, sophisticated, and detached. She seldom explored her own thoughts on death, even when she knew the deceased well. Her letters to Obour Tanner demonstrate that she was capable of expressing emotion, but even in these instances it is restraint which seems the paramount characteristic of her writing.

Her poetry is also religious and devout. She knew biblical literature well, and relied heavily upon it. Her constant references to divine providence, mercy, and grace as well as other biblical allusions are more than traditional devices. Her religion—in spite of her interest in Whitefield's Methodism—was strongly conditioned by the fading Puritanism of eighteenth-century Boston and by her membership in the Old South Meeting House. Furthermore, she idolized Milton whom she referred to as "England's Homer," and faint echoes of his work permeate hers.

Much of her poetry was obviously written in response to certain events, and occasional literature tends to lack effectiveness once the event has lost its significance. "To a Lady on Her Coming to North-America with Her Son, for the Recovery of Her Health" and "To a Lady on Her Remarkable Preservation in an Hurricane in North-Carolina," for example, have little relevance for the modern reader and seem inconsequential. Yet, when one considers the type of poetry being produced in America during the latter part of the eighteenth century, one can see that her work exemplifies some of the best as well as the worst features of that era's versification.

While she used primarily the heroic couplet, she experimented with other forms. On at least two occasions she employed six-line stanzas. In "Ode to Neptune" each stanza is composed of four iambic-tetrameter lines followed by a heroic couplet. In "An Hymn to Humanity" each six-line stanza follows an *aabccb* rhyme scheme. The two couplets in each stanza are iambic tetrameter while the third and sixth lines are iambic trimeter. "A Farewell to America" employs a variant of the ballad stanza, while in "To the University of Cambridge, in New England" she attempted blank verse whose success is perhaps marred by two instances of end rhyme in the thirty-line poem.

"On Imagination" reveals Wheatley's awareness of the theories of creativity underlying the poetry of eighteenth-century England. "An Hymn to the Morning" and "An Hymn to the Evening" combine the best of her understanding of Milton with her love of nature. Perhaps nowhere in colonial American literature was the sunset more eloquently described than in the opening lines of "An Hymn to the Evening":

> Soon as the sun forsook the eastern main
> The pealing thunder shook the heav'nly plain;
> Majestic grandeur! From the zephyr's wing,
> Exhales the incense of the blooming spring.

Most of her poems are restrained lyrics, but she did attempt two long narrative poems: "Goliath of Gath" and "Niobe in Distress for her Children Slain by Apollo, from Ovid's *Metamorphoses*, Book VI, and from a View of the Painting of Mr. Richard Wilson." New Englanders displayed a great deal of interest in poetic paraphrases of biblical texts, and "Goliath of Gath" is based upon the seventeenth chapter of First Samuel. In retelling the story of David and Goliath she displayed a control of her subject. Just as this poem illustrates her biblical knowledge, "Niobe in Distress for Her Children" displays her interest in classical literature as well as in landscape painting, and shows her mastery of the epic form. Beginning with the traditional invocation to the Muse, it employs major and minor epic conventions such as the use of the elevated subject, lofty diction, intermingling of natural with supernatural characters, an abundance of classical allusions, and the authorial distance necessary to reinforce the element of grandeur required by the formality of the subject.

Of the thirty-eight poems in Wheatley's collected volume of 1773, fourteen are elegies. As might be expected, they follow rather strictly the neoclassical approach to the genre and demonstrate her sense of evangelical Christianity. In keeping with the neoclassical tradition, her elegies are generally hyperbolic with a great deal of ornamentation. Most of them begin with an invocation to the deceased or to Death and contain numerous classical and biblical allusions which are interspersed throughout the poem without a regard for the shift from the pagan to the Christian concept of God. The excessive personification leads to a stilted diction and exaggerated eloquence. Emotions—where they exist—are presented in an impersonal and artificial manner.

Her use of the elegy was in keeping with the popular New England tradition of employing this poetic form as a means of consolation for a bereaved family. The annals of Puritan literature are filled with poems of this genre, and Wheatley's are far better examples than most of them, which are often simply rhymed doggerel. Among the specific families Wheatley addressed were some of the elite of the community. For example, one elegy was occasioned by the death of the Reverend Dr. Joseph Sewall, pastor of the Old South Meeting House and son of Samuel Sewall, the well-known Puritan diarist and jurist. Phillis Wheatley was a communicant at Sewall's church; her elegy for him contains one of the few personal references in her elegies. Another was occasioned by the death of the wife of Thomas Hubbard, a distinguished citizen of Boston who was associated with Harvard College during most of his public life and was one of the signers of the testimony in Wheatley's 1773 book. Earlier Wheatley had written "To a Lady on the Death of Her Husband," which was a response to the death of the husband of Hubbard's daughter. The death of Boston's eminent physician, Dr. Samuel Marshall, in 1771 motivated still another funeral poem. "To His Honour the Lieutenant-Governor, On the Death of His Lady. March 24, 1773" was addressed to Andrew Oliver, who also signed the 1773 testimony.

In "To a Clergyman on the Death of His Lady" Wheatley's use of parallel construction and an opening periodic sentence demonstrate her ability as an elegist:

Where contemplation finds her sacred spring,
Where heav'nly music makes the arches ring,
Where virtue reigns unsully'd and divine,
Where wisdom thron'd, and all the graces shine,
There sits thy spouse amidst the radiant throng,
While praise eternal warbles from her tongue;
There choirs angelic should her welcome round,
With perfect bliss, and peerless glory crown'd.

Of all of her elegies, however, none contains such simple and effective dialogue as "A Funeral Poem on the Death of C. E. An Infant of Twelve Months." Once again she relies heavily upon parallel construction; and while a modern reader may not be interested in the particular occasion, Wheatley's simple diction seems fitted to her subject. In spite of the restrictions of the heroic-couplet form, the poem conveys strong emotion, perhaps because the combination of the iambic-pentameter couplets with repetitive grammatical patterns creates the feeling of a lullaby. The poem ends with an unpretentious benediction.

While much has been made of the apparent lack of personal references in her work, there are more personal allusions than one might imagine in the 1773 volume. In the opening poem, "To Maecenas," a conventional work expressing gratitude to a patron, there are clear indications regarding her notion of poetry and of herself. As is customary in this type of poem, she bemoans her inability to write the great lines necessary to express the ideas which crowd her imagination and asks for the same kind of power which had been granted to Terence. The poem ends with a clear recognition that her work, produced by a slave, will need support: "Then grant, *Maecenas,* thy paternal rays,/Hear me propitious, and defend my lays." While the identity of her Maecenas may be in doubt, her plea is clear. Of the thirty-eight poems included in the 1773 volume, sixteen other poems contain some personal reference.

Furthermore, her poetry is not as devoid of racial and sociopolitical concerns as has been imagined. On a number of occasions she reminded her audience that she was an African. Terms such as "Afric's muse," "vent'rous Afric," and "an Ethiop" are certainly stilted diction, but they suggest that her problem of identity was not nearly as great as later critics have suggested. Neither was the recognition of racial distinctions in the New World necessarily a suggestion that one group was better than the other. That she was ambivalent about Africa is not as strange as it might appear on the surface. If one is to assume that she indeed was a child of "seven or eight" when she arrived in Boston and that her training there had reinforced the view of Africa as a pagan "dark continent," it should not be surprising that she exhibited no more curiosity than she did. It is interesting, however, to consider two revisions that she made in "To the University of Cambridge, in New England." The fourth line originally referred to Africa as "The sable Land of error's darkest night," and the next line—"There, sacred Nine! for you no place was found"—suggested that the muses could not exist in that pagan land. The twenty-eighth line, referring to sin, requested that the students "Suppress the sable monster in its growth," thus, through the repetition of "sable," associating Africa and sin. In her revision for the 1773 volume, the fourth line was changed to "the land of errors, and Egyptian gloom"; the next line was deleted; and "sable monster" became the "deadly serpent," eliminating the implied comparison while still regretting Africa's paganism. In "To Maecenas" it is also important to recognize the footnote explaining that Terence "was an African by birth" as an apparent attempt to make certain that her readers would understand that the art of poetry was not racially restricted, and her poem to the slave artist Scipio Moorhead reinforces the notion of the universality of art.

Later in her career, it may well be that she viewed Africa in more romantic terms as indicated in her reply to "the gentleman in the navy." Mason, however, has wisely suggested that "one should be cautious in being tempted to use" the lines about the beauty of Africa "and her reference to Gambia as specific evidence for her homeland. It was the 'Gentleman in the Navy' who introduced the topic of Africa. . . . What she says may be a poetic pose in reaction to his poem." Yet, Mason adds, "current events and the recent death of Mrs. Wheatley probably made such reminiscence—even under someone else's instigation—more attractive than it might have been otherwise."

It has also been charged that Phillis Wheatley was oblivious to the conditions of slavery. In "On Being Brought from Africa to America" it is true that she views slavery as a form of mercy which rescued her from a life of paganism, but she seems to understand slavery's damage to human liberty, as indicated in her poetic address to the Earl of Dartmouth, which includes these frequently cited lines:

Should you, my lord, while you peruse my song,
Wonder from whence my love of *Freedom* sprung,
Whence flow these wishes for the common good,

By feeling hearts alone best understood,
I, young in life, by seeming cruel fate
Was snatch'd from *Afric's* fancy'd happy seat:
What pangs excruciating must molest,
What sorrows labour in my parent's breast?
Steel'd was that soul and by no misery mov'd
That from a father seiz'd his babe belov'd:
Such, such my case. And can I then but pray
Others may never feel tyrannic sway?

Wheatley's poetry also reveals her awareness of the events surrounding the American Revolution. Like most colonists she at first hoped for a peaceful solution to the disputes with England, and her poetic appeals to Dartmouth (probably written in 1772) and King George III (dated 1768), her poem on the death of George Whitefield, and her association with the Countess of Huntingdon illustrate her fondness for England. She seemed both intellectually and emotionally tied to England and was willing to assume that men such as the Earl of Dartmouth and George III were concerned about the elimination of tyranny. To Dartmouth she could sing:

HAIL, happy day, when, smiling like the morn,
Fair Freedom rose *New-England* to adorn:
The northern clime beneath her genial ray,
Dartmouth, congratulates thy blissful sway:
. . . .
For favours past, great Sir, our thanks are due,
And thee we ask thy favours to renew,
Since in thy pow'r, as in thy will before,
To soothe thy griefs, which thou did'st once deplore.

And to George III she could write, after the repeal of the Stamp Act:

May *George,* belov'd by all the nations round,
Live with heav'ns choicest constant blessings crown'd!
Great God, direct, and guard him from on high,
And from his head let ev'ry evil fly!
And may each clime with equal gladness see
A monarch's smile can set his subjects free!

Once the war began, however, she was able to express allegiance to the colonial cause, a switch which apparently the Wheatleys' son, Nathaniel, was unable to make. Turning her attention toward the colonies and seeing potential in them as a symbol of political freedom, she accepted without question the values for which the Revolutionary War was being fought. Given the fact that many of her early supporters became Loyalists, her commitment to the goals of the colonists represents a break from the past.

The central issue—as far as she was concerned—was "freedom's cause," which England had violated. Her poem for George Washington was followed by "On the Capture of General Lee," dated 30 December 1776, in which she once again addressed a war issue. The poem, which was not published until October 1863 in the *Proceedings of the Massachusetts Historical Society,* is prefaced by the statement: "The following thoughts on his Excellency Major General Lee being betray'd into the hands of the Enemy by the treachery of a pretended Friend; To the Honourable James Bowdoin Esqr. are most respectfully Inscrib'd, By his most obedient and devoted humble servant, Phillis Wheatley." The content of the poem betrays a degree of political naiveté. She seems to have been unaware that, hoping for personal glory that would lead to his replacement of Washington as commander-in-chief, Gen. Charles Lee had ignored

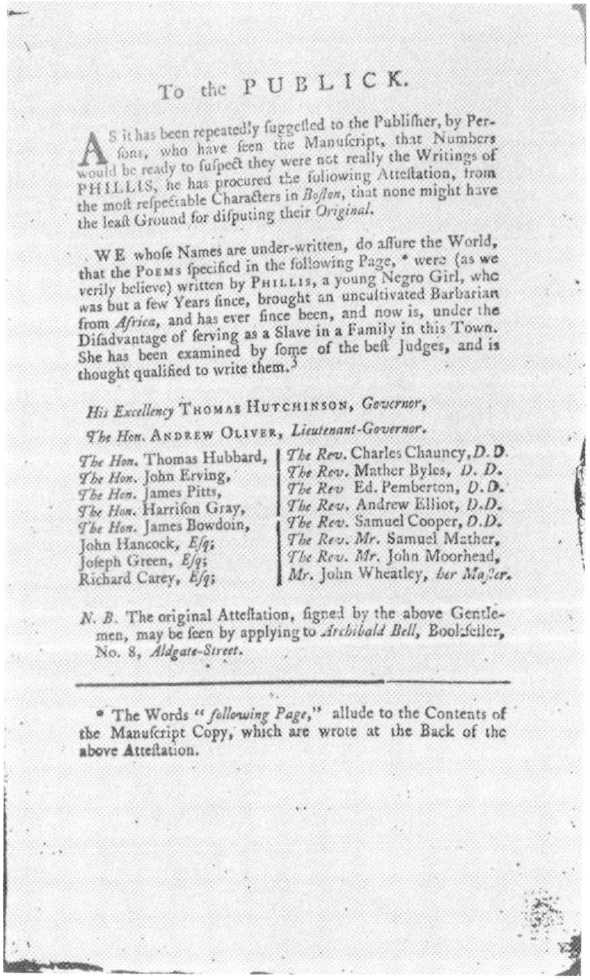

To the PUBLICK.

AS it has been repeatedly ſuggeſted to the Publiſher, by Perſons, who have ſeen the Manuſcript, that Numbers would be ready to ſuſpect they were not really the Writings of PHILLIS, he has procured the following Atteſtation, from the moſt reſpectable Characters in *Boſton*, that none might have the leaſt Ground for diſputing their *Original*.

WE whoſe Names are under-written, do aſſure the World, that the POEMS ſpecified in the following Page, * were (as we verily believe) written by PHILLIS, a young Negro Girl, who was but a few Years ſince, brought an uncultivated Barbarian from *Africa*, and has ever ſince been, and now is, under the Diſadvantage of ſerving as a Slave in a Family in this Town. She has been examined by ſome of the beſt Judges, and is thought qualified to write them.[3]

His Excellency THOMAS HUTCHINSON, *Governor*,
The Hon. ANDREW OLIVER, *Lieutenant-Governor*.

The Hon. Thomas Hubbard,
The Hon. John Erving,
The Hon. James Pitts,
The Hon. Harriſon Gray,
The Hon. James Bowdoin,
John Hancock, *Eſq*;
Joſeph Green, *Eſq*;
Richard Carey, *Eſq*;

The Rev. Charles Chauncy, *D.D.*
The Rev. Mather Byles, *D.D.*
The Rev Ed. Pemberton, *D.D.*
The Rev. Andrew Elliot, *D.D.*
The Rev. Samuel Cooper, *D.D.*
The Rev. Mr. Samuel Mather,
The Rev. Mr. John Moorhead,
Mr. John Wheatley, *her Maſter*.

N. B. The original Atteſtation, ſigned by the above Gentlemen, may be ſeen by applying to *Archibald Bell*, Bookſeller, No. 8, *Aldgate-Street*.

* The Words "*following Page*," allude to the Contents of the Manuſcript Copy, which are wrote at the Back of the above Atteſtation.

Attestation of the authenticity of Wheatley's writings, first published in a 1773 edition of Poems on Various Subjects

Washington's orders to retreat after the battle of White Plains and as a consequence was captured by the British. Mason speculates that the historic inaccuracies prevented Bowdoin from having the poem published, but explains that "Phillis was a civilian far from the place where Lee was captured . . . and was therefore subject to many rumors." Even though she may not have understood fully the political and military situation involving the capture of Lee, the poem reaffirms her strong commitment to a colonial victory and is characterized by a martial strain unique in Wheatley's work.

By the end of the war she was clearly convinced of the justice of the colonial cause. In *Liberty and Peace* (1784) she—like so many others—saw the potential promise of the new country: "E'en great *Britannia* sees with dread Surprize,/And from the dazzl'ing Splendor turns her Eyes!" Yet she also recognized that the colonies had suffered from the ravaging of the countryside:

> *Columbia* mourns, the haughty Foes deride,
> Her treasures plunder'd, and her Towns destroy'd:
> Witness how *Charlestown's* curling Smoaks arise,
> In sable Columns to the clouded Skies!
> The ample Dome, high-wrought with curious Toil,
> In one sad Hour the savage Troops despoil.

But with the war's end came freedom and the promise that "in her train Commerce and Plenty" will return.

Given the brevity of her productive years, it is amazing that Wheatley achieved as much diversity in her work as she did. Despite its shortcomings, *Poems on Various Subjects, Religious and Moral* is a major collection of American colonial poetry. Yet, attitudes toward her work have varied greatly from acceptance of her as a good poet to dismissal of her work as an inadequate imitation of the popular poets of England.

Criticism of her work began before her death, and Mason has included an excellent survey of it in his introduction to *The Poems of Phillis Wheatley* (1966). As early as 1773 English reviewers were citing her work not as good poetry but because it had been produced by an African. The *Monthly Review* (London) for December 1773 took the occasion of its review of *Poems on Various Subjects . . .* to make a political observation: "We are much concerned to find that this ingenious young woman is yet a slave. The people of Boston boast themselves chiefly on their principles of liberty. One such act as the purchase of her freedom would, in our opinion, have done them more honor than hanging a thousand trees with ribbons and emblems." The review also noted, "The poems written by this young negro bear no endemical marks of solar fire or spirit," but, it acknowledged, "She has written many good lines. . . ."

Among eighteenth-century critics perhaps no one was as caustic as Thomas Jefferson, who noted in his *Notes on the State of Virginia* (1785) that even though "misery is often the parent of the most affecting touches in poetry," such was not the case "among the blacks [where there] is misery enough, God knows, but no poetry." Jefferson dismissed Wheatley's work as being "below the dignity of criticism" and concluded "religion, indeed, has produced a Phyllis Whately [*sic*]; but it could not produce a poet." Thomas Jefferson's negative view was taken to task by a number of his contemporaries, who found merit in her work. Both Benjamin Franklin and Benjamin Rush willingly recognized her ability. In *An Essay on the Causes of the Variety of Complexion and Figure in the Human Species* (1787), Samuel Stanhope Smith questioned Jefferson's doubts about Phillis Wheatley and wondered how many American slave "masters could have written poems equal to those" produced by Wheatley. Thomas Clarkson, a noted English abolitionist, observed in his *An Essay on the Slavery and Commerce of the Human Species, Particularly the Africans* (1785) that the enslavement of Phillis Wheatley was an irony of human existence, and, if this servitude were ordained in heaven, then "the greater part of the inhabitants of Britain must lose their claim to freedom."

Throughout the remainder of the century and into the next there were sporadic references to her both among those who argued that blacks could be taught the higher arts and among those who supported the notion of the intellectual inferiority of blacks. Perhaps her strongest advocate was Henri Grégoire, the French critic who did much toward presenting a balanced portrait of Afro-American literature in his *De la littérature des Nègres* (1808), which was translated by D. B. Warden as *An Enquiry Concerning the Intellectual and Moral Faculties, and Literature of Negroes* and published in Brooklyn in 1810. Grégoire argued in his scientific treatise that racial designations tend to be insignificant in the development of moral and artistic individuals.

During the 1830s, the *Liberator* republished much of her work in its pages. Later in the century John R. Slattery wrote an excellent summary for the *Catholic World* (July 1884) in which he noted that one had to consider that "a slave-girl should write so many poems from the fifteenth to the twentieth year of her age—a time of life when most girls are given to all giddiness" in order to discover the magnitude of her work. Furthermore, he added, "the lofty sentiments of her mind are still more wonderful when Phillis' race is remembered." Nineteenth-century literary critics such as Rufus Griswold, Clarence Stedman, Charles Richardson, and Evert and George Duyckinck tended to rank her as one of the best colonial American poets. Certainly she had the ability to reproduce the rhythmic structure of Pope with greater fidelity than Trumbull, Dwight, and Barlow, who also wrote poems in the neoclassical mode. Missing from her poetry, however, was Pope's great gift of satire, which undoubtedly was partially due to her serious evangelical nature.

Among twentieth-century critics it has been customary to recognize her as one of the first Afro-American poets, but increasingly—with the exception of Newman Ivey White in *An Anthology of Verse by American Negroes* (1924)—there has been little interest in her accomplishments as a poet. Her work has been criticized as devoid of any racial significance. In *Negro Poets and Their Poems* (1923) Robert Kerlin called her "the slave-girl rhymer of Boston," and Loggins asserted that "the facility and thoroughness with which she, a slave transported from Africa, imitated the artful idiom of Pope and his meticulous school while she was scarcely more than a child present one of those marvels of precocity which baffle psychological explanation." He continued with the observation that her work is "noteworthy as an accomplishment in imitation" and noted: "Her work is sophisticated rather than primitive, artificial rather than spontaneous, polished rather than crude. With the exception of certain specific passages in which the author identified herself, it contains nothing which marks it as the work of a member of the African race." Apparently unwilling to acknowledge that neoclassical is by its very nature "sophisticated, artificial, and polished," Loggins disposed of her work with the judgment: "Her power to attain this place of eminence must be pronounced as due to her instinct for hearing the music of words, an instinct which was possibly racial."

In spite of James Weldon Johnson's assertion in *The Book of American Negro Poetry* (1922) that she was an "important American poet," critics have generally accepted the observations of J. Saunders Redding, who in *To Make a Poet Black* (1939) emphasized that she seemed strangely unmoved by slavery, even though it must have been discussed in the circles which she frequented. Noting the religious nature of her work—Redding asserted, "The Wheatleys had adopted her, but she adopted their terrific New England conscience." He then questioned the effectiveness of her poetry by pointing out that "first and last, she was the fragile product of three related forces—the age, the Wheatley household, and New England America. Her works lack spontaneity because of the first, enthusiasm because of the second, and because of the third it lacks an unselfish purpose that drives to some ultimate goal of expression." He also questioned whether or not she understood "the full significance" of being a Negro poet and singled out the absence of "a straightforward word for the freedom of the Negro" (in spite of the references she made in her poem addressed to the Earl of Dartmouth). Even Julian Mason, who has done more than anyone else in recent years to place her work in a proper perspective, has concluded, "It is quite clear that Phillis Wheatley was not a great poet. She was not a poet in the classical Greek sense of maker, seer, creator, nor were her concerns really with Emerson's meter making argument or Poe's rhythmical creation of beauty."

The faults of Phillis Wheatley's work are largely the faults of her models. To expect her work to differ appreciably from that of her contemporaries is to expect more of her than of other poets of her time and place. She must be judged in the context of eighteenth-century Boston rather than on the basis of what might have been, and ultimately any complete study of colonial American poetry must include Phillis Wheatley.

Letters:

Charles Deane, ed., *Letters of Phillis Wheatley, The Negro Slave-Poet of Boston* (Boston: Privately printed, 1864);

Charles Frederick Heartman, ed., *Phillis Wheatley (Phillis Peters), Poems and Letters,* with an appreciation by Arthur A. Schomburg, Heartman's Historical Series, no. 8 (New York: Printed for the author, 1915).

Bibliography:

William H. Robinson, *Phillis Wheatley: A Bio-Bibliography* (Boston: G. K. Hall, 1981).

Biographies:

Margaretta Matilda Odell, *Memoir and Poems of Phillis Wheatley* (Boston: Light, 1834);

Benjamin Brawley, Note on Wheatley, in *Early Negro American Writers: Selections with Biographical and Critical Introductions,* edited by Brawley (Chapel Hill: University of North Carolina Press, 1935);

Brawley, *Negro Builders and Heroes* (Chapel Hill: University of North Carolina Press, 1937);

Merle A. Richmond, *Bid the Vassal Soar: Interpretive Essays on the Life and Poetry of Phillis Wheatley (ca. 1753-1784) and George Moses Horton (ca. 1799-1883)* (Washington, D.C.: Howard University Press, 1974).

References:

Benjamin Brawley, *The Negro Genius: A New Appraisal of the Achievement of the American Negro in Literature and the Fine Arts* (New York: Dodd, Mead, 1937);

Carl Bridenbaugh, "The Earliest-Published Poem of Phillis Wheatley," *New England Quarterly,* 42 (December 1969): 583-584;

Charles Frederick Heartman, *Phillis Wheatley (Phillis Peters): A Critical Attempt and Bibliography of Her Writings,* Heartman's Historical Series, no. 7 (New York: Printed for the author, 1915);

Sara Dunlap Jackson, "Letters of Phillis Wheatley and Susanna Wheatley," *Journal of Negro History,* 57 (April 1972): 211-215;

Robert Kerlin, *Negro Poets and Their Poems* (Washington, D.C.: Associated Publishers, 1923; revised and enlarged, 1935);

Vernon Loggins, *The Negro Author: His Development in America to 1900* (New York: Columbia University Press, 1931);

Stephanie Ocko, "Phillis Wheatley," *Early American Life,* 11 (August 1980): 44;

Benjamin Quarles, *The Negro in the American Revolution* (Chapel Hill: University of North Carolina Press, 1961);

J. Saunders Redding, *To Make a Poet Black* (Chapel Hill: University of North Carolina Press, 1939);

Herbert Renfro, "A Discourse on the Life and Poetry of Phillis Wheatley," *African Methodist Episcopal Church Review,* 7 (July 1891): 76-109;

J. R. Slattery, "Phillis Wheatley, The Negro Poetess," *Catholic World,* 39 (July 1884): 484-498;

William H. Yeocum, "Phillis Wheatley—The First African Poetess," *African Methodist Episcopal Church Review,* 6 (January 1890): 329-333.

Papers:

The following libraries hold documents, letters, manuscripts, and memorabilia pertaining to Phillis Wheatley: American Antiquarian Society, Boston Public Library, Bowdoin College, Connecticut Historical Society, Dartmouth College, Duke University, Harvard University, Haverford College, Historical Society of Pennsylvania, Library of Congress, Massachusetts Historical Society, Moorland-Spingarn Research Center of Howard University, and the Schomburg Collection of the New York Public Library.

James Monroe Whitfield

(10 April 1822-23 April 1871)

Doris Lucas Laryea
North Carolina State University

BOOK: *America and Other Poems* (Buffalo: James S. Leavitt, 1853).

OTHER: *Emancipation Oration by Dr. Ezra R. Johnson, and Poem, by James M. Whitfield, Delivered at Platt's Hall, January 1, 1867, In Honor of the Fourth Anniversary of President Lincoln's Proclamation of Emancipation* (San Francisco: Elevator Office, 1867).

A gifted poet, who was encouraged by William Wells Brown, Frederick Douglass, and Martin R. Delany to develop what Douglass called his "rare, poetic powers," James Monroe Whitfield was unable to reach his full potential as a writer because he lacked the financial support he needed to leave his work as a barber. One of the most talented and forceful black poets of the nineteenth century, he aligned himself with the black separatism movement in the 1850s and vigorously advocated the immigration of blacks to South and Central America.

The poet was born in Exeter, New Hampshire, to free blacks whose names are unknown. It is believed that he was a descendant of Ann Paul, sister of Rev. Thomas Paul of Exeter. Whitfield's sister was Mrs. Elizabeth P. Allen, whose daughter Annie Pauline Lindell became a well-known singer. Whitfield attended his neighborhood elementary school, but whether he entered high school or not is uncertain.

While a young man, Whitfield left Exeter for a short stay in Boston, and later he settled in Buffalo, New York, which in the 1850s was the center of the abolition movement. Sometime thereafter he married a local woman who bore him two sons and a daughter.

He probably learned his barber's trade before he left Exeter or shortly after his arrival in Buffalo. He became skilled at this work and prosperous enough to open his own barbershop in 1858. Located at 30 East Seneca Street, it attracted the most sophisticated and refined black gentlemen of the city. The poet himself was of gentlemanly deportment, and his conversations stirred the interest of those who visited his shop. Possessed of strong racial pride, Whitfield was deeply interested in bringing an end to the institution of slavery.

He contributed poems to various newspapers and magazines, including such abolitionist publications as the *Liberator,* the *North Star,* and *Frederick Douglass's Paper.* From 1849 to 1852 his poems appeared regularly in the *North Star* and *Frederick Douglass's Paper,* and from 1867 to 1870 they appeared in the *San Francisco Elevator.*

In 1853 Whitfield negotiated with the James S. Leavitt Company in Buffalo to publish *America and Other Poems,* which he dedicated to his friend Martin R. Delany, a colonizationist who for a time was coeditor of *Frederick Douglass's Paper.* The anonymous writer of the introduction, perhaps Whitfield himself, appealed to the public for funds to help the poet receive "the aid of intellectual culture" so that he might "cultivate, improve, and fully develop the talent which God hath given him." The writer went on to say that "we do not claim that the poetry is of the highest order; but we do claim that it would be creditable to authors of greater pretensions than the humble colored man, who hath wrought it out amid the daily and incessant toil necessary for the maintenance of family, who are dependent upon the labor of his hands for support. There is in it the fire of a genius which, under more favored circumstances, would have soared high and obtained no mean place in the world's estimation." Although the volume was well received, it failed to earn Whitfield sufficient money to support his family and devote full time "to the cultivation of his mind, and to writing."

The book clearly displays Whitfield's talent and accomplishments, especially in his smooth handling of metrics and rhythm and in his powerful and precise use of classical imagery. Stylistically, *America and Other Poems* resembles in theme, diction, structure, and patterns the work of Byron, his model. Byron's sense of alienation, deprivation, and despair are unmistakably evident in poems such as "Self-Reliance," "Delusive Hope," and "The

Misanthropist."

The strongest and most controversial works in the collection are the antislavery poems "America," "Lines on the Death of John Quincy Adams," and "How Long?" Displaying both Whitfield's intellect and poetic skills, the title poem was inspired by the abolitionist spirit that had gained strength after the passage of the Fugitive Slave Law in 1850. "America" poignantly compares the struggle of Americans to be free and independent from Great Britain and the struggles of blacks to be free from slavery. In the opening lines of the poem Whitfield points out the actuality of America's racism in contrast to its stated principles: "America, it is to thee,/Thou boasted land of liberty,—/It is to thee I raise my song,/Thou land of blood, and crime, and wrong."

Whitfield dwells at length on the irony of the American Revolution, explaining how black soldiers shared the pain of war and the joy of victory in the belief that after the war slavery would be abolished and the freedmen's natural rights granted to them. He attacks the cruelty of slavery—including the separation of families, sexual exploitation of black women and men, and floggings—and argues that the slave would be justified to overthrow slavery by buying his freedom with his life: "And with stout heart and weapon strong,/Pay back the tyrant wrong for wrong. . . ." He touches on the religious discrepancies in America under the slave system and affirms that all men are made in God's image, even though white Christian ministers preach that the holding of another man in bondage had been sanctioned by God. After 133 lines full of pessimism and resentment, the poem ends in pure Garrisonian style, not with a challenge for the slaves to take up arms and fight for their freedom, as David Walker and Nat Turner had suggested, but with a twenty-seven-line prayer of hope that God will avenge the wrongs done the slaves and that America will recognize and act upon the discrepancies between its ideals and actualities.

One of the longest poems in the collection is "How Long?" Written in iambic tetrameter like "America" with varying rhyme schemes, the 238-line poem is full of vivid metaphors. In "How Long?" the poet questions God, as he does in other poems, about why, despite the slaves' prayers for deliverance, he allows them to be trampled and dehumanized by white slaveholders who call themselves Christians: "How Long shall Afric' raise to thee/Her fettered hand, O Lord! in vain,/And plead in fearful agony/For vengeance for her children slain?" The oppressed are treated like criminals, the poet charges, while clergymen and politicians—calling right anything that brings them wealth, rank, and power—combine their forces to keep the blacks enslaved. The poet reminds slaveholding Christians that Christ died for *all* mankind, but, he asserts, they have shut their minds and hearts to this fact by sanctioning the institution of slavery and treating slaves as though they are less than human. Whitfield argues not only for the emancipation of American slaves but for universal freedom of all oppressed people and in favor of all natural God-given rights—"The right to speak, and think, and feel." Yet, although he acknowledges the existence of oppression in Africa and Europe, no other country, he charges, has "worse scenes of rapine, lust, and shame" as America, the land "which claims, par excellence, to be/The refuge of the brave and true,/The strongest bulwark of the free/The grand asylum for the poor/And trodden down of every land,/Where they may rest in peace, secure,/Nor fear the oppressor's iron hand. . . ." As in "America" Whitfield summons the wrathful and vengeful God of the Old Testament to hasten and set "the trembling captive free."

Aside from racial protest poems, *America and Other Poems* includes occasional verses for Christmas and New Year's, several hymns and verses on church dedications, and four love poems. The rich allusions in these poems reveal Whitfield's wide reading in the classics, mythology, religion, and history. Other poems, such as "Self-Reliance," "Delusive Hope," "Yes, Strike Again That Sounding String," and "The Misanthropist," focus on themes of alienation, despair, fatalism, and death. The speaker in the poems is undoubtedly the poet, and according to Joan Sherman, the order of their composition may possibly be discerned from the speaker's progressively darker pessimism and despair. For example, "Self-Reliance," with its youthful speaker, seems to be a fairly early poem while "Delusive Hope," concentrating on life's miseries and hypocrisies, seems to have been written later. Despairing poems such as "Yes, Strike Again That Sounding String" and "The Misanthropist" probably also date from later in the poet's career.

"The Misanthropist," one of the earliest attempts by a black writer to portray the pathos of the black man's social isolation, describes the black poet's spirit as blighted by his position as a black and a poet in America—the double-consciousness which was later described in W. E. B. Du Bois's *The Souls of Black Folk* (1903) and Countee Cullen's "Yet Do I Marvel" (1925). In "The Misanthropist" the poet presents himself as another Childe Harold filled with melancholy and gloom. Life is arid and barren; no ray of hopeful light pierces the poet's throbbing, burning, and seething brain. The poet finds no healing power in nature, literature, love, or religion, having learned from study that the history of religion is a chronicle of greed, warfare, and ultimately death. Thus his poetic inspiration has reached its nadir, and his every thought "Is from its first conception fraught/With gloom and darkness, woe, and pain." In this abysmal state not even "Virtue's self can bring,/Unto my moody spirit, rest." The poet can sing only a dirge of despondency, estrangement, and futile aspiration.

Whitfield never published another collection of verse and apparently wrote fewer poems after 1854, when he became actively involved in the American Colonization Society. One of his later poems is the 400-line "Poem" which he read at Platt's Hall in San Francisco on 1 January 1867, in celebration of the fourth anniversary of the Emancipation Proclamation. An account of 200 years of American history, it employs an extended farm metaphor of planting, growing, harvesting, and blighting.

Whitfield's interest in the black colonization movement reaches back to an address he prepared, when he was only sixteen years old, for a Cleveland convention, which convened for the purpose of planning the immigration of blacks to the borders of California. In the 1850s he joined Martin R. Delany and Rev. James Theodore Holly as one of the major advocates and organizers of the emigration movement. He supported the proposal for a National Emigration Convention in August 1854, at which proponents of emigration could devise the best means for carrying out the colonizing of free blacks in the West Indies and Central and South America.

The appeal met with staunch opposition from many black leaders, who had no sympathy for emigrationists' positions. In the *North Star* for 25 July 1853 Frederick Douglass wrote that whites would interpret this meeting as "a cause of rejoicing. . . . and discover in this movement a division of opinion amongst us upon a vital point." This statement prompted an exchange of letters in the paper among Whitfield, Douglass, and William J. Watkins.

In response to Douglass's criticism, Whitfield wrote letters that were published in the *North Star* on 25 September, 15 November, and 30 December 1853. He vigorously defended emigrationist goals on the grounds that blacks must establish themselves politically, socially, economically, and educationally. Emigration was to be restricted to those blacks who refused to "lick the dirt from the foot that kicks" them or to work for the economic and political advancement of whites. They must become self-reliant, he wrote, and chart their own destiny; they must help shape "the policy of the American Continent," and secure a "proper field for the full development of their power and resources." He believed it was the "destiny of the Negro, to develop a higher order of civilization and Christianity than the world has yet seen" and "to possess all the tropical regions of this continent." By establishing politically powerful black nations as models, they could demonstrate the race's "physical, moral, and mental" superiority. Such nations would proclaim the doctrines of Pan-Africanism and would eventually demand the freedom of all oppressed black people around the globe. The letters clearly revealed Whitfield's impatience with America and his loss of faith in God's divine justice.

At the Cleveland Convention, Whitfield and others urged the founding of a quarterly newspaper to publicize the emigration cause as well as "all questions" connected with the "welfare, progress and development of the Negro race." The first issue of the *Afric-American Repository,* with Whitfield as editor, was due to appear in Buffalo in July 1858, but there is no evidence that it was ever published. Whitfield's activities during 1859-1861 are likewise uncertain, but it is thought that he may have been traveling in the "tropical regions" of the Americas in search of land for a black nation.

Sometime in 1861, he arrived in San Francisco, still an advocate of separation. His anger at America had mellowed since 1853. Writing to the *Pacific Appeal,* 9 August 1862, Whitfield urged Americans "of the loyal states" to stop the rebellion, for the American government must make "an alliance with . . . the people of color." The government, he wrote, must "abrogate or nullify the odious Dred Scott decision, which takes from every colored man his rights as a man and a citizen."

After 1862 he did not speak out publicly for emigration. He worked as a barber and wrote poetry when he had time. From June 1863 until some time in 1865 he lived and worked as a barber in Portland, Oregon, and in Placerville and Centerville, Idaho. Apparently he returned to San Francisco in 1865 and opened a barbershop at 916 Kearny Street. In May 1869 he moved to Elko, Nevada, where he became a member of the Elko Republican Club and participated in political activities. Sometime after July 1870 the poet returned to San Francisco, and on 23 April 1871 he died of heart disease and was buried in the Masonic Cemetery.

Whitfield's last poem was probably "Poem by J. M. Whitfield," which he read in April 1870 in Virginia City, Nevada, and which was published in the *San Francisco Elevator* on 22 April 1870. Its 152 lines, addressed to "order, law and liberty," have an antislavery message, but the poem praises America, calling it the world's leader in the arts, wealth, commerce, and freedom for all.

James Monroe Whitfield was not a prolific writer; yet his contributions to American letters demonstrated his natural poetic talent. His poems and his prose portray a sensitive soul keenly aware of and wrestling with the inhumanity of man in the quest for power and personal gratification.

Letters:

Carter G. Woodson, ed., *The Mind of the Negro as Reflected in Letters Written during the Crisis, 1800-1860* (Washington, D.C.: Association for the Study of Negro Life and History, 1926).

References:

Benjamin Brawley, ed., *Early Negro American Writers: Selections with Biographical and Critical Introductions* (Chapel Hill: University of North Carolina Press, 1935);

Vernon Loggins, *The Negro Author, His Development in America to 1900* (New York: Columbia University Press, 1931);

William Robinson, ed., *Early Black American Poets: Selections with Biographical and Critical Introductions* (Dubuque: William C. Brown, 1969);

Joan Sherman, *Invisible Poets: Afro-Americans of the Nineteenth Century* (Urbana, Chicago & London: University of Illinois Press, 1974).

Papers:

Copies of *America and Other Poems* and some of Whitfield's letters and speeches are located in the Moorland-Spingarn Collection at Howard University, at the Library of Congress, and in the Schomburg Collection at the New York Public Library.

Albery Allson Whitman

(30 May 1851-29 June 1901)

Blyden Jackson
University of North Carolina at Chapel Hill

BOOKS: *Essay on the Ten Plagues and Miscellaneous Poems* (1871?);

Leelah Misled (Elizabethtown, Ky.: Richard LaRue, 1873);

Not a Man and Yet a Man, with Miscellaneous Poems (Springfield, Ohio: Republican Printing, 1877);

The Rape of Florida (St. Louis: Nixon, Jones Printing, 1884); revised as *Twasinta's Seminoles; or, Rape of Florida* (St. Louis: Nixon, Jones Printing, 1885);

Twasinta's Seminoles/Not a Man and Yet a Man/Drifted Leaves: A Collection of Poems (St. Louis: Nixon, Jones Printing, 1890);

The World's Fair Poem (Atlanta: Holsey Job Print, 1893);

An Idyl of the South, An Epic Poem in Two Parts (New York: Metaphysical Publishing, 1901).

An impressive number of respected critics of Afro-American literature—including D. W. Culp, Benjamin Brawley, Sterling A. Brown, Joan R. Sherman, and Louis Rubin—rank Albery Allson Whitman as one of the most important black poets between Phillis Wheatley and Paul Laurence Dunbar. Of the black poets who were his near contemporaries, only Frances Ellen Watkins Harper approached him in productivity. In the second half of the nineteenth century Harper had the larger audience, principally because Harper, an accomplished and peripatetic elocutionist and lecturer, declaimed her poetry from hundreds of platforms throughout the eastern and southern United States. Whitman also recited his own poetry before numerous audiences. Neither Harper nor any other black poet before Dunbar, unless it was

Albery Allson Whitman

George Moses Horton, seems to have been so much a born poet as Whitman. His verse tends toward the sensuous in sound and imagery, and Whitman resembles Edgar Allen Poe, rather than Walt Whitman, in his allegiance to traditional aesthetics and in his philosophy of composition. Like Poe, he largely eschewed overt political or social messages.

For Whitman life began near Munfordville, Kentucky, and the Green River on a white Kentuckian's small Hart County estate, which was much more a family farm than the stereotypical plantation of the legendary antebellum South. The son of slaves, Whitman was orphaned after the deaths of his mother in 1862 and his father in 1863. As their slave child he was early set to work in the fields. Yet he was never to speak bitterly of his experience of bondage, and he seemed always to have remembered with genuine affection the locality of his birth. In the years after emancipation and the end of the Civil War Whitman took to the road. After living in Louisville and Cincinnati, he went to Troy, Ohio, where he worked first in a shop where plows were made and then as a laborer in a railroad-construction gang. He also went to school for a total of seven months. Armed with this exposure to learning, he taught in Carysville, Ohio, and then in Kentucky, near his first home. No later than 1870 he resumed his formal education at Wilberforce University, although apparently for a period of only six months. It was at this time that he met Daniel Alexander Payne, a bishop of the African Methodist Episcopal (A.M.E.) church, who, as president of Wilberforce, was instrumental in the school's success. Small of stature and fragile of physique, Payne exerted a tremendous influence upon many, not the least of whom was Whitman. Whitman, who considered himself for all of his life Bishop Payne's protégé, almost a son, was later a pastor for A.M.E. churches in Ohio, Kansas, Texas, and Georgia, founding some of them as well. He was also officially connected with Wilberforce University for a number of years. By 1877 he was the school's general financial agent, an elder in the A.M.E. church, and pastor of a church in Springfield, Ohio. Whitman married a woman named Caddie, with whom he had two daughters. He drank excessively, and while alcoholism may well have shortened his life, it never occasioned his abandonment by his denomination or his wife, although it surely destroyed any hopes he may have had for a bishopric (he was known as a fine pulpiteer). His last ministerial charges were St. Phillips in Savannah, which a storm destroyed, and Allen Temple in Atlanta. On a visit to Anniston, Alabama, in 1901 he contracted pneumonia. Borne home to Atlanta, he survived only a week and was buried in Atlanta.

No copies of *Essay on the Ten Plagues and Miscellaneous Poems,* Whitman's first book, are known to exist today. His second, *Leelah Misled* (1873), is a distressful tale of a young, blond and blue-eyed girl's betrayal by McLambert, a rich profligate and philanderer to whom she has surrendered her virginity. The "noble" six-foot-three-inch Rodney, hero of the epic title poem in *Not a Man and Yet a Man, with Miscellaneous Poems* (1877), is considered black even though he is "eighty-five per cent Anglo-Saxon." The epic begins when Rodney is barely twenty years old and continues, past Rodney's prime, for approximately 5,000 lines. For many years it was commonly reputed to be the longest poem ever written by an Afro-American and it held that distinction until the publication in 1903 of the Reverend Robert E. Ford's *Brown Chapel, a Story in Verse,* a poem of some 8,600 lines.

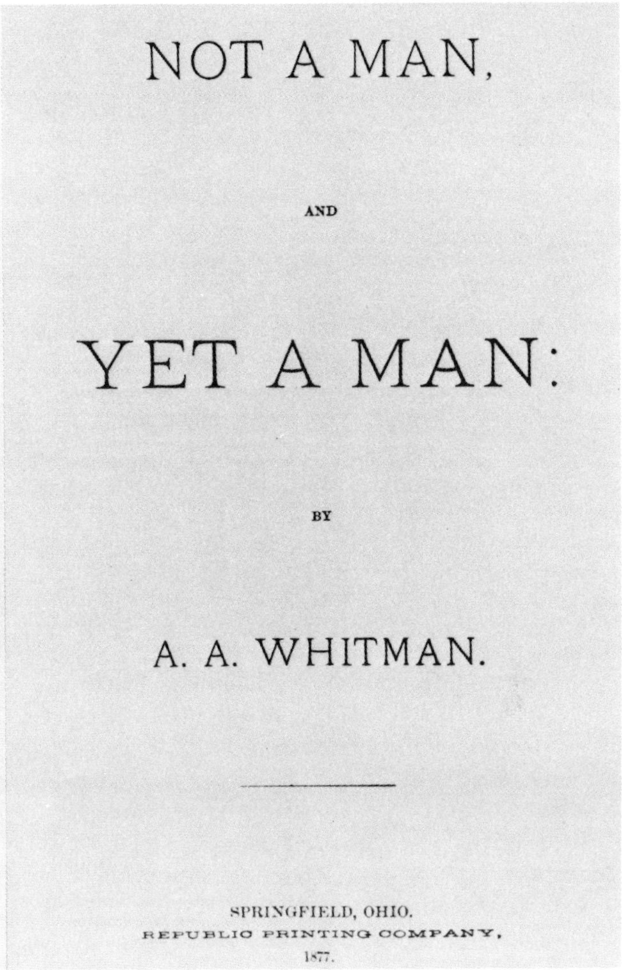

NOT A MAN,

AND

YET A MAN:

BY

A. A. WHITMAN.

SPRINGFIELD, OHIO.
REPUBLIC PRINTING COMPANY,
1877.

Frontispiece and title page for Whitman's epic poem

Rodney, a slave, lives in the frontier settlement of Saville, Illinois. After the whites of Saville, led by the sadistic and racist Sir Maxey, attack a nearby tribe of Sac Indians and murder the beautiful Indian princess Nanawawa, the Indians capture Dora, Sir Maxey's daughter. Singlehandedly, against appalling odds, Rodney rescues Dora, but his reward for his heroism is his sale into further, and worse, slavery in the Deep South. In Florida he falls in love with the light-skinned Creole Leeona. After Leeona has been ravished and left with child by her master, she and Rodney escape. When they finally reach Canada, they are befriended by Dora, who has become a sister of mercy. With the coming of the Civil War Rodney and his sons by Leeona fight for the Union cause and witness the death of Leeona's former master.

Less than half the length of *Not a Man and Yet a Man,* Whitman's second major work, *The Rape of Florida* (1884; revised as *Twasinta's Seminoles,* 1885), focuses on two Seminole chieftains, the aging Palmecho and the young Atlassa, lover of Palmecho's beautiful daughter, Ewald, who has some Negro blood but is otherwise Indian and Spanish. Despite Palmecho's wisdom and Atlassa's heroism, the Seminoles suffer from the duplicity of American whites. Atlassa and Ewald are temporarily separated but are reunited when they, with other Seminoles, including Palmecho, are exiled to Mexico.

The two poems in *The World's Fair Poem* (1893) are among Whitman's least successful works. "The Veteran," a poem of nine six-line stanzas, rehearses patriotic banalities, while "The Freedman's Triumphant Song," about five times longer and one of Whitman's few overt social-protest poems, concentrates on a defense—based on their previous actions in America and their intentions for the future—of Whitman's fellow blacks in their role as American citizens.

An Idyl of the South (1901) consists of "The Southland's Charms and Freedom's Magnitude" and "The Octoroon," both composed entirely in ottava rima. "The Southland's Charms" ranges, not too coherently, over Whitman's widely varied impressions and opinions about the South. "The Octoroon," a narrative of 161 stanzas, may be Whitman's best poem. It recounts the tragedy of a white man, Sheldon Maury, as handsome as a Norse god or Viking hero, and a beautiful octoroon slave, Lena. The two fall deeply in love, and Maury plans a permanent liaison with Lena that will dishonor neither her nor him. But Maury's father, who owns Lena, becomes aware of his son's attachment to Lena and considers intolerable his son's concept of the possible relations between whites and blacks of different sexes. He sells Lena to a master who employs his rights of chattel over Lena to serve his own lustful ends. Young Maury tracks Lena to this new master, only to find her dying in a woodsman's cottage.

Though Whitman was mainly a narrative poet, he did write some lyrics, including the eighteen lyric poems appended to *Not a Man and Yet a Man.* One of these poems, "Ye Bards of England," eulogizes Chaucer, Shakespeare, Byron, and other British poets while another eulogizes the black American poet Joshua McCarter Simpson. "The Great Strike," another of Whitman's overt social commentaries, is decidedly unflattering to organized labor. Twenty-three lyric poems appear in the "Drifted Leaves" section of the 1890 volume that also included new editions of *Twasinta's Seminoles* and *Not a Man and Yet a Man.* In addition to eulogies for Stonewall Jackson, General Custer, and General Grant, the book also includes Whitman's only dialect poems.

In *The Negro Author, His Development in America* (1931) Vernon Loggins describes Whitman as a "mockingbird" poet, and it is true that Whitman's imitation of other poets is easily discernible. In *The Rape of Florida,* he was the first black to employ the Spenserian stanza in a poem of epic length, imitating the Spenserian stanza as used by Byron rather than Spenser's original use of the form in *The Faerie Queen.* In *Not a Man and Yet a Man,* Whitman employed a number of forms, imitating poets such as Longfellow. Indeed, the sections in *Not a Man and Yet a Man* which deal with Nanawawa and her Indian compatriots are unmistakably close imitations of Longfellow's *Hiawatha.* Whitman seems also to have been particularly fond of Whittier and William Cullen Bryant. Almost nowhere in Whitman's poetry does he seem unaware of some poet whose ways of writing poetry have affected him. Yet Whitman repeatedly displays excellences of his own. In *The Rape of Florida,* for instance, neither Byron nor Spenser is nearly totally responsible for the beauty of the section Whitman called "The Boatman's Song":

> "Come now, my love, the moon is on the lake,
> Upon the water is my light canoe;
> Come with me, love and gladsome oars shall make
> A music on the parting waves for you,—
> Come o'er the waters deep and dark and blue;
> Come where the lilies in the marge have sprung,
> Come with me, love, for Oh, my love is true!"
> This is the song that on the lake was sung,
> The boatman sang it over when his heart was young.

Similarly, no mere imitator could have written of Lena, in "The Octoroon," as does Whitman in the following lines:

> Just in the dawn of blushing womanhood
> Her swan-neck glimpsed through shocks of wavy hair;
> A hint of olives in her gentle blood,
> Suggesting passion in a rosy lair;
> This shapely Venus of the cabins stood,
> In all but birth a princess, tall and fair;
> And is it any wonder that this brave
> And proud young master came to love this slave?

To some extent Whitman was a mockingbird, but his original genius must be recognized.

In physical appearance, Whitman was light skinned enough to have passed for white (it has been conjectured that his wife was legally white), and, except for his championing of his race, he responded to the America of his days in ways reflective of the values of middle-class whites. Throughout *Not a Man and Yet a Man* Whitman pursued the theme of the supreme value to every human individual of freedom. Thinking of freedom in Emersonian terms, he constantly preached self-reliance and self-improvement. Not an emigrationist, he was satisfied to be self-reliant and to improve himself in America. Though his values were conservative he was hardly an accommodationist like Booker T. Washington. He followed in the tradition of Frederick Douglass.

Above all, Whitman was a writer for whom self-expression was a supreme condition of his existence. His verse was often too long, too digressive, and shallowly facile. Yet his poetry should be read for the many lines that display his original genius.

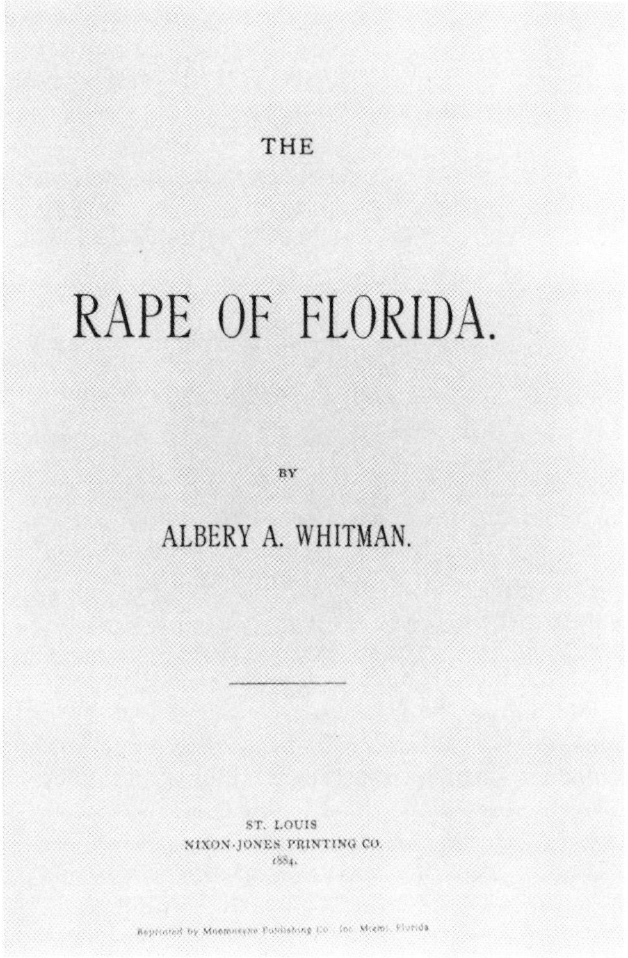
THE

RAPE OF FLORIDA.

BY

ALBERY A. WHITMAN.

ST. LOUIS
NIXON-JONES PRINTING CO.
1884.

Reprinted by Mnemosyne Publishing Co. Inc. Miami, Florida

Frontispiece and title page for Whitman's work about the persecution of Seminole Indians by whites

References:

Benjamin Brawley, *The Negro Genius: A New Appraisal of the Achievement of the American Negro in Literature and the Fine Arts* (New York: Dodd, Mead, 1937);

Sterling A. Brown, *Negro Poetry and Drama* (Washington, D.C.: Associates in Negro Folk Education, 1937);

D. W. Culp, ed., *Twentieth Century Negro Literature* (Naperville, Ill. & Toronto: J. L. Nichols, 1902);

Blyden Jackson and Louis D. Rubin, Jr., *Black Poetry in America: Two Essays in Historical Interpretation* (Baton Rouge: Louisiana State University Press, 1974);

Vernon Loggins, *The Negro Author, His Development in America* (New York: Columbia University Press, 1931);

Eugene B. Redmond, *Drumvoices: The Mission of Afro-American Poetry, A Critical History* (Garden City: Anchor/Doubleday, 1976);

Joan R. Sherman, "Albery Allson Whitman: Poet of Beauty and Manliness," *CLA Journal*, 15 (1971): 126-143;

Sherman, *Invisible Poets: Afro-Americans of the Nineteenth Century* (Urbana, Chicago & London: University of Illinois Press, 1974);

Kenny J. Williams, *They Also Spoke: An Essay on Negro Literature in America, 1787-1930* (Nashville: Townsend Press, 1970).

Harriet E. Adams Wilson

(1828?-1863?)

Henry Louis Gates, Jr.
Cornell University

BOOK: *Our Nig; or, Sketches from the Life of a Free Black, in a Two-Story White House, North. Showing that Slavery's Shadows Fall Even There. By "Our Nig."* (Boston: Printed by Geo. C. Rand & Avery, 1859).

Harriet E. Adams Wilson is thought to be the very first Afro-American woman to have published a novel in English. In a period in which racial "firsts" have been heralded loudly and widely, as talismans drawn out to counter racist aspersions cast upon Afro-American culture as a whole, the rediscovery of Harriet Wilson's text and the authentication of her gender and racial identity have pushed back the starting point for fiction by Afro-American women from 1892 to 1859. *Our Nig; or, Sketches from the Life of a Free Black, in a Two-Story White House, North. Showing that Slavery's Shadows Fall Even There. By "Our Nig."* (1859) is a major example of genre fusion created by the writer's appropriation of a black, masculine, literary model (the slave narrative) and a white, female one (the sentimental novel). The result is a synthesis at once peculiarly black and female. The originality Wilson displays in fashioning a novelistic romance out of her autobiography insures her place not only as the first black woman novelist but also as one of the first major innovators of American fictional narrative form.

There is little actual detail available about this newly rediscovered author whose text began enjoying its fullest readership a century and a quarter after its initial printing. We know with certainty only a few facts concerning her life between 1850 and 1860, the decade she represents in her autobiographical novel, *Our Nig*. It was the verification of these biographical details of her life that allowed for the positive identification of Wilson as both the text's thinly veiled subject and its author.

Harriet E. Adams was probably born in New Hampshire in 1827 or 1828, according to the 24 August 1850 New Hampshire federal census in which she is listed as being a twenty-two-year-old black female. Her marriage license of 1852 lists Milford, New Hampshire, as her birthplace. However, the 1860 Boston federal census lists a Mrs. Harriet E. Wilson, born in Fredericksburg, Virginia, in 1807 or 1808, and the internal evidence of *Our Nig* suggests that Wilson was living in Massachusetts in 1859 when she wrote the novel. Not much is known about her life until 1850, after which time a number of details about her which are depicted in *Our Nig* are verified in various public documents.

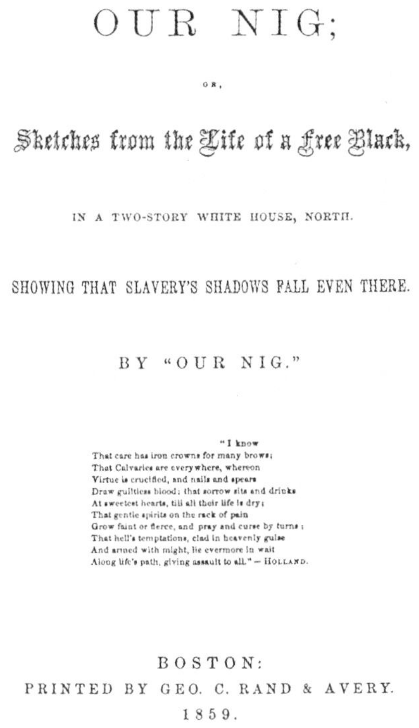
OUR NIG;

OR,

Sketches from the Life of a Free Black,

IN A TWO-STORY WHITE HOUSE, NORTH.

SHOWING THAT SLAVERY'S SHADOWS FALL EVEN THERE.

BY "OUR NIG."

"I know
That care has iron crowns for many brows;
That Calvaries are everywhere, whereon
Virtue is crucified, and nails and spears
Draw guiltless blood; that sorrow sits and drinks
At sweetest hearts, till all their life is dry;
That gentle spirits on the rack of pain
Grow faint or fierce, and pray and curse by turns;
That hell's temptations, clad in heavenly guise
And armed with might, lie evermore in wait
Along life's path, giving assault to all." — HOLLAND.

BOSTON:
PRINTED BY GEO. C. RAND & AVERY.
1859.

Title page for Wilson's novel, which she wrote in the hope of making enough money to retrieve her son from foster care

In 1850 Adams was living with the white family of Samuel Boyles in Milford. Boyles was a married, middle-aged carpenter and the father of a seventeen-year-old son. It is possible that Adams was the Boyles's indentured servant who based her fictional account of protagonist Alfrado's barbarous treatment as a servant upon her experiences with Mary Louisa Boyles, Samuel's wife.

According to a letter appended to *Our Nig*, by "Allida," an unknown friend of Wilson's, shortly after the 1850 census was taken, Harriet Adams moved to "W———, Massachusetts," taken there by "an itinerant colored lecturer." She went to live with a Mrs. Walker and became a "straw-sewer." Soon, however, because her "constitution was greatly impaired," Adams became Mrs. Walker's domestic servant and put aside her career as a milliner.

Early in the spring of 1851 the "itinerant colored lecturer" returned to town, accompanied by a fugitive slave. This slave, who claimed that he had once been a house servant, was named Thomas Wilson. Adams married Wilson on 6 October 1851 at Milford, then moved with him to New Hampshire. George Mason Wilson, the only issue of this marriage, was born in late May or early June of 1852, approximately nine months after his parents' marriage. Shortly before the birth of this child, Thomas Wilson had run away to sea. George was born in the "County House" (Hillsborough County Farm) at Goffstown, New Hampshire, where the destitute of various sorts were herded.

Thomas Wilson returned to his family as mysteriously, apparently, as he had disappeared, and Wilson was able to keep her son at home. Once more, however, her husband deserted them, and Wilson was forced to return her son to the County Farm, where he was eventually to be rescued by "a kindly gentleman and lady" who took him as a foster child. Harriet Wilson's health had apparently deteriorated, forcing her to relinquish her son because she could not "pay his board every week."

While George remained in a white foster home in New Hampshire, Harriet moved to Boston in 1855, where she was a dressmaker. She remained in Boston at least until 1863. While in Boston, she wrote *Our Nig* and had it published on 5 September 1859. (The novel was copyrighted on 18 August 1859.) She wrote the novel, as she tells her readers in her preface, so that she might retrieve her son from his foster home. Six months later, however, on 15 February 1860, George Mason Wilson died of "fever." After a final listing in the *Boston City Directory* of 1863, Harriet E. Adams Wilson disappears from public record.

If Wilson's personal life is obscure, the life of her text is equally so. Printed by George C. Rand and Avery Company in what must have been a small run, the novel received almost no commentary between 1859 and 1983. Nevertheless, the novel is a remarkable document of the consciousness of a black woman indentured in the North, a consciousness shaped by a racist bondage as brutal, psychologically, as any rendered in the body of black slave literature.

In *Our Nig* a white orphan, Mag Smith, is seduced and abandoned by a wealthy gentleman, then scorned by her neighbors. She gives birth to a child who dies within weeks of its birth. Ostracized, Mag Smith removes herself to the margins of her society, living alone for years in her hut. "A kind hearted African," named Jim, is the only soul bold enough to disturb Mag Smith's isolation. He proposes. She is shocked and disgusted, initially, but assesses the degree of her desolation and decides that miscegenation is a better choice than isolated poverty. Within a week, they marry.

A few years later, having fathered "two pretty mulatto" children with Mag, Jim succumbs to consumption, leaving Mag in poverty once again. Jim's partner, Seth Shipley, and Mag return to her previous home, "the hut," determined to abandon her six-year-old daughter, Frado, and to flee town. They leave the child at the home of a middle-class white family, the Bellmonts, and depart, never to be heard from again.

At age seven, Frado becomes an indentured servant, feeding the hens, driving the cows, retrieving wood, washing dishes, cleaning the house, and suffering much abuse. She is beaten regularly by the relentlessly evil Mrs. Bellmont. For two years she attends elementary school, only to be withdrawn by her mistress who fears the effects an education might have upon her servant.

For years Frado suffers at the hands of Mrs. Bellmont and her daughter Mary, a miniature counterpart in evil. Frado's plight is relieved only by her relationship with the male members of the Bellmont family, particularly the older son, James, who is married and living in Baltimore. James returns Frado's affections and plans to take her to Baltimore as his servant. Illness, however, forces him to return to Massachusetts to his parents' home, where both James's and Frado's health decline.

In chapter ten Wilson reverses the action of the plot by having Frado prevent Mrs. Bellmont from beating her, threatening not to work if she is struck again. Frado, the narrator informs us, "stood like one who feels the stirring of free and independent thoughts." James dies, as does Mrs. Bellmont's daughter. Frado turns to books for relief and comfort.

In the spring of her eighteenth year Frado at last is free, although she has a lame leg, and only "one decent dress, and a Bible." She works as a servant until her ill health prevents physical labor. A series of generally horrendous working experiences ensue during the next few years, interrupted only by a warm relationship with an employer named Mrs. Moore. Frado's health waxes and wanes, forcing her on and off public charity. Gradually, however, she perfects her talents at needlework, and her mastery of this skill leads to one of her new forms of freedom; Frado soon leaves New Hampshire for Massachusetts, where she sews straw hats and lives with a kind white woman who teaches her more about the art of sewing and who gives her books to read.

Frado's brief but blissful period of freedom is interrupted, and eventually ended, by a black man who comes to town as part of the fugitive slave lecture circuit. He sees Frado, proposes, and marries her, all on one page of the text. The two move back to the New Hampshire town in which Frado was raised. Samuel, earning a living as a lecturer, leaves his wife for weeks on end, finally running away to the sea. Abandoned, Frado becomes ill, accepts public charity, and gives birth to a son. Samuel returns, rescues his family from the county farm, only to abandon them once again. He dies of fever in New Orleans. Wilson, in this part of her text, writes close to her own experiences of love and betrayal.

The novel ends with a hurried and abbreviated account of Frado's adventures in New Hampshire and Massachusetts, fleeing slave-catchers and "kidnappers," receiving abuse from "professed abolitionists" who "didn't want slaves at the South, nor niggers in their houses, North." She learns, as did Harriet Wilson, how to dye gray hair back to its original color, and maintains herself in this way. The text ends in Harriet Wilson's own voice, in a direct appeal to her readers to purchase her book so that she might retrieve her son. Six months later, we know, her son was dead.

Until the Random House republication of *Our Nig* in 1983, there existed almost no critical commentary on this novel, except for a brief mention by Herbert Ross Brown in *The Sentimental Novel in America* (1940), who marvels at Wilson's relatively balanced depiction of an interracial marriage. James Joseph Kinney's superb dissertation, "The Theme of Miscegenation in the American Novel to World War II" (1972), also analyzes the novel, asserting along the way that the fiction is autobiographical. Perhaps the fullest reference to the novel is found in a letter that Lydia Maria Child, the well-known abolitionist, author, and editor of Harriet Jacobs's slave narrative, sent on 9 July 1878 to her friend and confidante Sarah Shaw. The relevant passage reads as follows:

> Poor Mag! She was one of that host of forlorn beings, who go through life with souls gasping and perishing, for want of somebody to love them, and somebody to love. It is so hard to tell what to *do* with characters so blighted by neglect, and hardened by harshness! Every kind person is willing to make efforts to redeem them; but where to place them, after the process of redemption is begun,—that is the puzzling question. Compassion is not enough for them; they need the consciousness of being loved by somebody, and of being essential to the comfort of some one. Dear Bessie Green's rule never to separate a mother from her illegitimate child was a wise provision for this craving of human nature. How to find a *home* for such outcasts as poor Mag is a very difficult problem.

It seems likely that Child here refers to "lonely Mag Smith." She is struck by Mag's seduction and subsequent abandonment, and the desperate behavior that this abandonment engenders. It seems curious that Mag Smith's condition assumes precedence over Frado's, until we recall that the action of the plot is set in motion by Mag's unmarried pregnancy.

Our Nig, as Prof. Martin Price argues in unpublished comments, recalls other sentimental novels, such as those of Daniel Defoe or Sir Walter Scott. Although it was not written in the first-person, as Defoe's novels were and the slave narratives were, it cultivates a remarkable documentary authority, not the least of which is in that final appeal to the reader, which can be read as an assertion of the tale's subjective authenticity. The elements that further suggest Defoe, apart from the strict attention to narrative, is the openness of *motives* of various kinds. Frado acts out her dreams of independence or superiority, however unguardedly and humorously; she is not shorn of all aggression or self-esteem, as is generally the case for the protagonist in the sentimental novel. The reader is drawn to her all the more because of this charmingly assertive trait and finds her more impressive as an *individual* for her capacity to resent and especially to hate. The characterization of Frado in all her complexity and Wilson's abstention from making moralistic simplifications make *Our Nig* attractive in the way Defoe made a book such as *Moll Flanders* attractive; that is, by allowing the protagonist to be human. This approach is not found in any other black novel published before the turn of the century.

Had Wilson lived, had she possessed, as Alice Walker, echoing Virginia Woolf, has written of her, "a body of her own, a room of her own, and a love of her own," it is difficult to imagine the degree of artistic attainment that the black novel might have realized before the advent of Paul Laurence Dunbar and Charles Chesnutt.

References:

Leslie Bennetts, "An 1859 Black Literary Landmark is Uncovered," *New York Times,* 8 November 1982;

Ira Berlin, "America's First Black Novel," *Washington Post Book World,* 3 July 1983;

Henry Louis Gates, Jr., Introduction and notes to *Our Nig; or, Sketches from the Life of a Free Black* (New York: Random House, 1983), pp. xi-lix;

Margo Jefferson, "Down & Out & Black in Boston," *Nation,* 28 May 1983;

Milton Meltzer and Patricia G. Holland, eds., *Lydia Maria Child: Selected Letters, 1817-1880* (Amherst: University of Massachusetts Press, 1982), pp. 552-553;

Review of *Our Nig, New Yorker* (20 June 1983);

Marilyn Richardson, "The Shadow of Slavery," *Women's Review of Books* (October 1983);

Michele Slung, Review of *Our Nig, Washington Post Book World,* 8 May 1983.

Appendices

Charlotte Forten

Pages from her Diary

Charlotte Forten, daughter of one of the most prominent free black families in the Northeast, was the only Afro-American among the teachers sent to South Carolina in 1862 to participate in an experiment at Port Royal that was of national interest. On 7 November 1861, in response to Abraham Lincoln's directive to close the southern coasts, the Union Army mounted a sea attack against its first targets: the sea island plantations off the South Carolina coast. Once the Port Royal area was in the possession of the North, progressive abolitionists, educators, and students of culture mounted a massive campaign to teach academic and vocational skills to the newly freed slaves of the region, while recording the unique character of island life. The following pages from Forten's diary preserve a segment of the Port Royal experiment through Forten's impressions and experiences among the southern blacks whose culture was sometimes as alien to her as it was to the northern whites with whom she taught. The portion of the diary reproduced here dates from 27 October to 16 November 1862 and is reproduced courtesy of the Moorland-Spingarn Research Center at Howard University.

—Editor's Note

(?)

Steamer "United States."

At Sea, Monday, Oct. 27, 1862.

Have been in no condition for writing until to-day. And now, being in a somewhat bewildered state, scarcely know where to commence. It was on Friday, the 24th, that we left N.Y. Enjoyed the sail down the harbor perfectly. The shipping is a noble sight. The sky was blue, the sea calm, the sunlight bright and joyous. Was in good spirits. The sadness that I had felt the night before at leaving some who are very dear, was quite gone. One long-cherished wish of my heart was fulfilled at last.— I was southward bound, on the mission to which I have long felt called. Had no symp-~~toms of sea-sickness until night, when, being seated~~ at the supper-table, an inexpressibly singular sensation caused me to make a hasty retreat to the deck, where, seated on a coil of ropes, and keeping perfectly still, managed to spend several hours quite comfortably. My first night at sea. I shall not forget it; the starlight, the solemn stillness, broken only by the sound of the waves, and here and there a solitary lighthouse gleaming through the darkness— for it was very dark although the stars were shining. There was something very wild and strange in it all to me. And I enjoyed it. It gave me a sense of deep, sweet rest and peace, such as I had never felt before. Went below, with into the

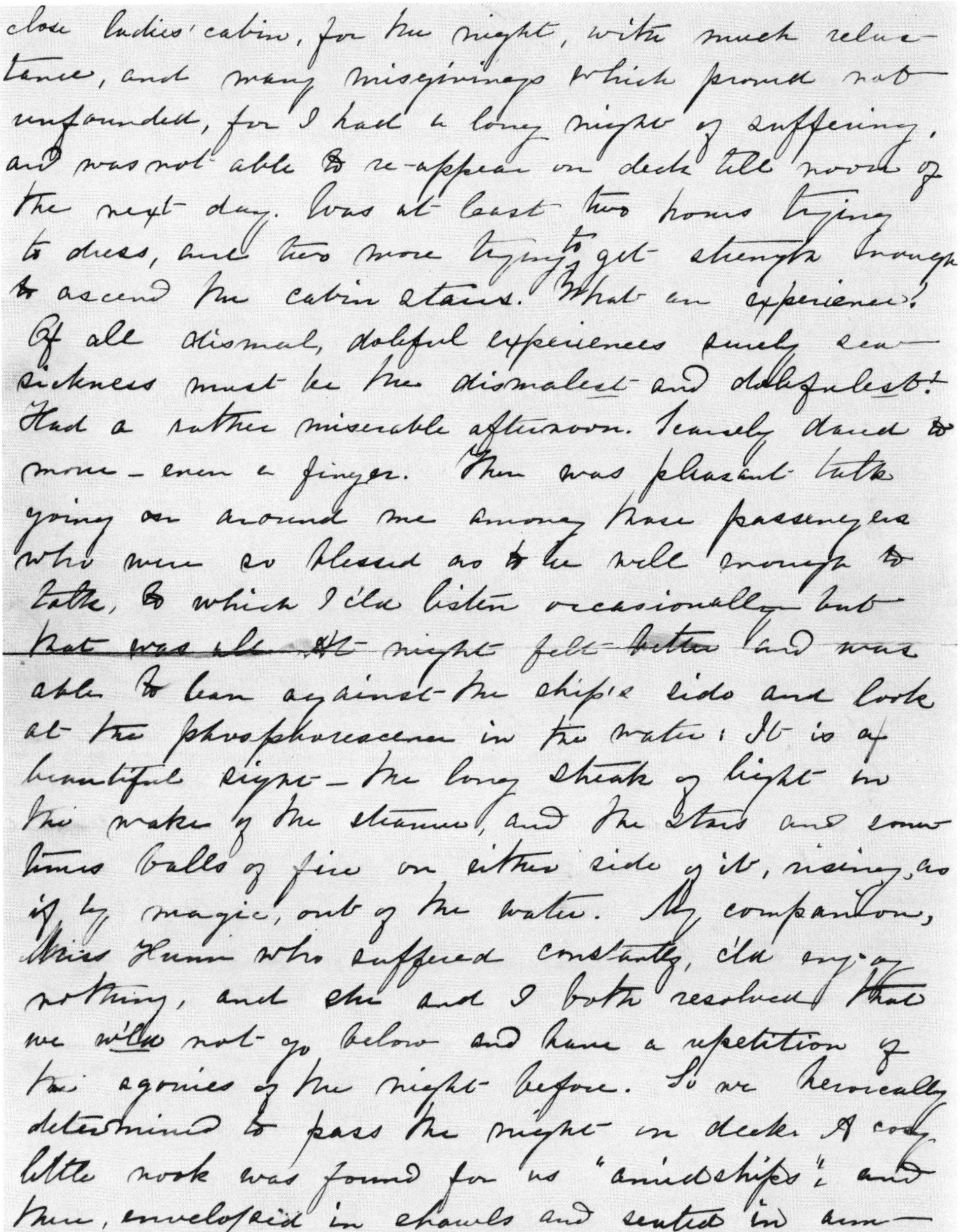
close ladies' cabin, for the night, with much reluc-
tance, and many misgivings which proved not
unfounded, for I had a long night of suffering,
and was not able to re-appear on deck till noon of
the next day. Was at least two hours trying
to dress, and two more trying to get strength enough
to ascend the cabin stairs. What an experience!
Of all dismal, doleful experiences surely sea-
sickness must be the dismalest and dolefulest!
Had a rather miserable afternoon. Scarcely dared to
move—even a finger. There was pleasant talk
going on around me among those passengers
who were so blessed as to be well enough to
talk, to which I c'ld listen occasionally but
that was all. At night felt better and was
able to lean against the ship's side and look
at the phosphorescence in the water. It is a
beautiful sight—the long streak of light in
the wake of the steamer, and the stars and some-
times balls of fire on either side of it, rising, as
if by magic, out of the water. My companion,
Miss Hunn who suffered constantly, c'ld enjoy
nothing, and she and I both resolved that
we will not go below and have a repetition of
the agonies of the night before. So we heroically
determined to pass the night on deck. A cozy
little nook was found for us "amidships"; and
there, enveloped in shawls and seated in arm-
chairs, we were very comfortably established for

the night. Two of the passengers entertained us for a time with some beautiful singing. Then they retired, and we passed the rest of the night in the society of Old Ocean alone. It was very dark. The sea was high. How very strange it seemed there, on the deck, in the dark night,—only the dim outlines of sea and sky to be seen, only the roar of the waves to be heard. I enjoyed it very much. The thought that we were far away from land was a pleasant one to me. It gave me a sense of freedom—this being out on the wide sea—almost alone—in the solemn stillness of the night. The next day, Sunday, was emphatically a <u>dismal</u> day. It rained almost ceaselessly. As soon as we, deceived by a momentary brightening of the sky, would get ourselves comfortably seated on deck, down came the rain, and we were obliged to take refuge in the upper cabin, which was almost as close and uncomfortable as the lower one—for the propeller "United States" has <u>not</u> the most delightful accommodations in the world.

Tried to read in my French bible, but in vain. The day was mostly spent in the very interesting occupation of trying to keep well by keeping perfectly and painfully quiet. Towards night a violent storm arose. The ship rocked so much that it was impossible to sit up. So we had mattresses and blankets arranged for us in the

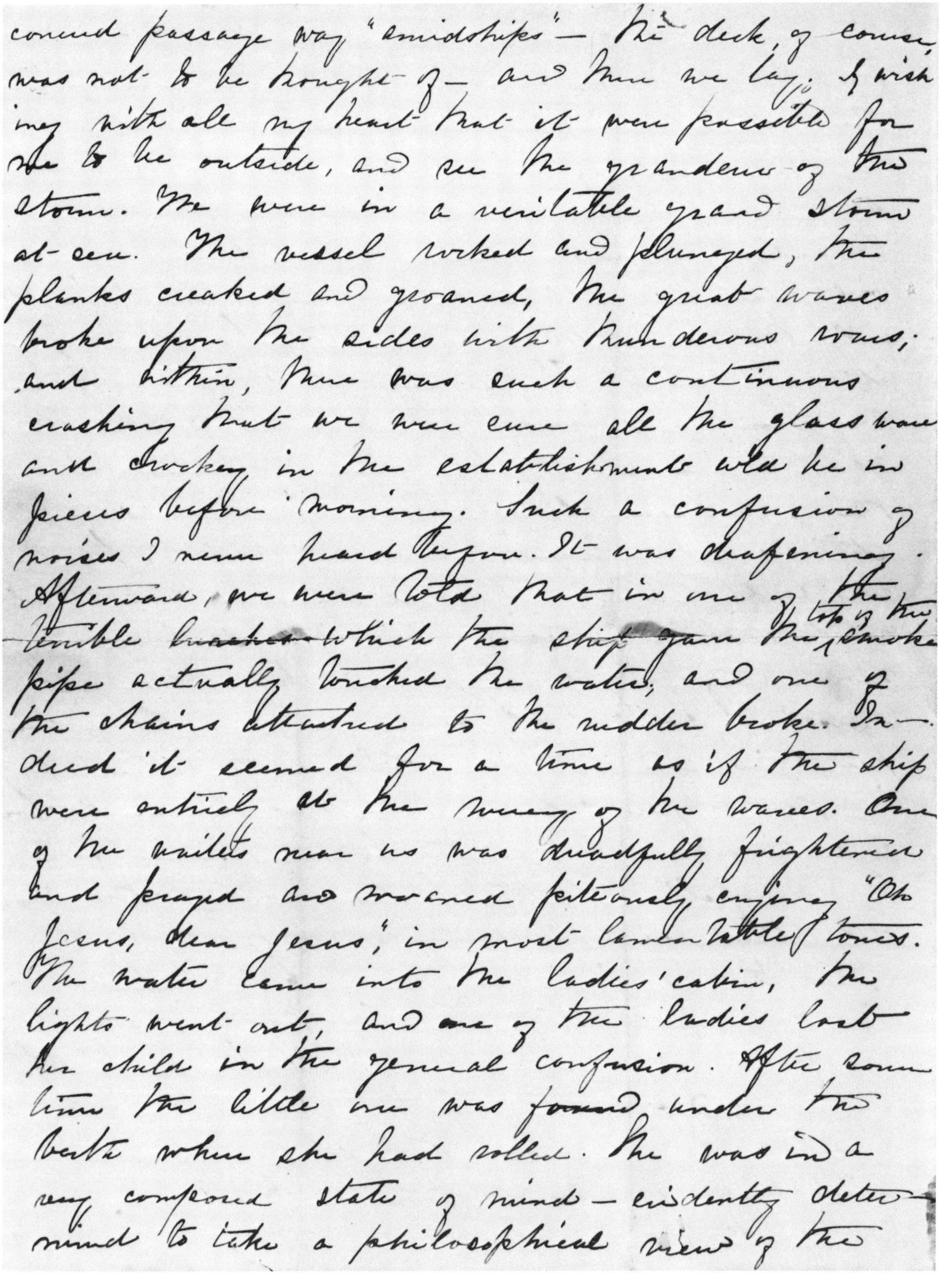
covered passage way "amidships"— The deck, of course,
was not to be thought of— and there we lay, I wish-
ing with all my heart that it were possible for
me to be outside, and see the grandeur of the
storm. We were in a veritable grand storm
at sea. The vessel rocked and plunged, the
planks creaked and groaned, the great waves
broke upon the sides with thunderous roars;
and within, there was such a continuous
crashing that we were sure all the glass ware
and crockery in the establishment w'ld be in
pieces before morning. Such a confusion of
noises I never heard before. It was deafening.
Afterward, we were told that in one of the
terrible lurches which the ship gave the top of the smoke
pipe actually touched the water, and one of
the chains attached to the rudder broke. In-
deed it seemed for a time as if the ship
were entirely at the mercy of the waves. One
of the waiters near us was dreadfully frightened
and prayed and moaned piteously crying "Oh
Jesus, dear Jesus," in most lamentable tones.
The water came into the ladies' cabin, the
lights went out, and one of the ladies lost
her child in the general confusion. After some
time the little one was found under the
berth where she had rolled. She was in a
very composed state of mind— evidently deter-
mined to take a philosophical view of the

5 matter, and not at all alarmed at her sudden and involuntary journey. During all the storm which lasted the whole night, I felt no fear, even when I believed that we were in danger. I do not know why it was. I felt strangely calm. And now I am glad to have experienced what I have so longed for—a grand storm at sea. This morn. (Monday) the sea was still very rough, but with much difficulty I made my way on deck, for I wanted to see what I could of the effects of the storm. The sky was still overcast, the great, white-capped waves were rising high and breaking with fury against the sides of the ship. Clinging to the sides I stood and watched them. How wild, how untamed, how glorious they were. The sky has quite cleared off now, and the day is lovely. The sea is calmer. I am feeling well, and luxuriating in the perfect beauty of sea and sky. The sea is grand. It far more than realizes all my expectations. The sky too is beautiful—a deep, delicious blue, with soft white clouds floating over it. People talk of the "monotony" of the sea. I don't think it could ever be monotonous to me. There is "infinite variety," constant enjoyment in it. We have seen several sails to-day, in the distance, but still no land, whereat I greatly rejoice.

As to the passengers, there's not much to be said about them. There are about a dozen beside

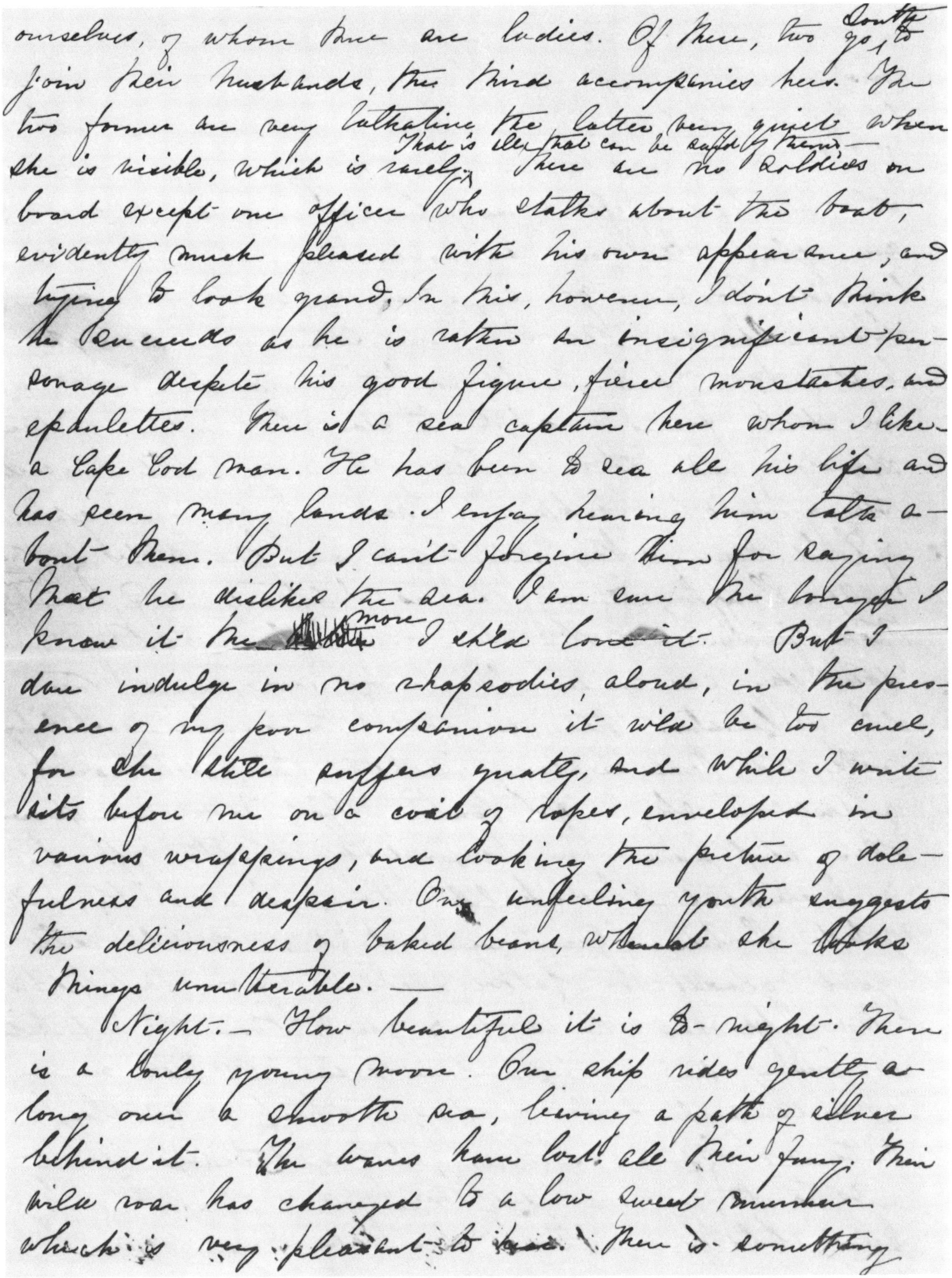
ourselves, of whom three are ladies. Of these, two go South to join their husbands, the third accompanies hers. The two former are very talkative, the latter very quiet when she is visible, which is rarely. That is all that can be said of them.— There are no soldiers on board except one officer who stalks about the boat, evidently much pleased with his own appearance, and trying to look grand. In this, however, I don't think he succeeds as he is rather an insignificant personage despite his good figure, fierce moustaches, and epaulettes. There is a sea captain here whom I like— a Cape Cod man. He has been to sea all his life and has seen many lands. I enjoy hearing him talk about them. But I can't forgive him for saying that he dislikes the sea. I am sure the longer I know it the more I shld love it. But I dare indulge in no rhapsodies, aloud, in the presence of my poor companion it wld be too cruel, for she still suffers greatly, and while I write sits before me on a coil of ropes, enveloped in various wrappings, and looking the picture of dolefulness and despair. One unfeeling youth suggests the deliciousness of baked beans, whereat she looks things unutterable.—

Night.— How beautiful it is to-night. There is a lovely young moon. Our ship rides gently along over a smooth sea, leaving a path of silver behind it. The waves have lost all their fury. Their wild roar has changed to a low sweet murmur which is very pleasant to hear. There is something very soothing in this soft moonlight, and perfect, perfect quiet. Perfect, save for that sweet music of the waves.

Tuesday, Oct. 28. Early this morning some one came to our door to tell us that we were in sight of the blockading fleet off Charleston harbor. Of course we sprang from our berths and hastened to the window. Thence we saw the masts of the vessels looking like a grove in the distance. We were not near enough to see the city—were fifteen or twenty miles from it. I did not realize that we were so near that barbarous little place—that strong-hold of Secession. We are again in sight of land. Have passed Edisto and several other islands and are approaching Hilton Head—our first stopping place. ~~The~~ S.C. shore is low and sandy, bordered by scanty trees. It looks very uninviting. A gentleman tells us that the oranges are ripe now, and that in every respect this is the pleasantest season to go South, which is encouraging. Our ship has been boarded by Health Officer and Provost Marshal. We pass some formidable looking gunboats. Officers and sailors greet gladly the latest arrival from the North. We approach the landing at Hilton Head. All is hurry and confusion on board. What a crowd awaits us on the wharf—a motley throng—officers, soldiers, and "contrabands" great and small, of every hue, the predominant one being black. I must lay thee aside, friend

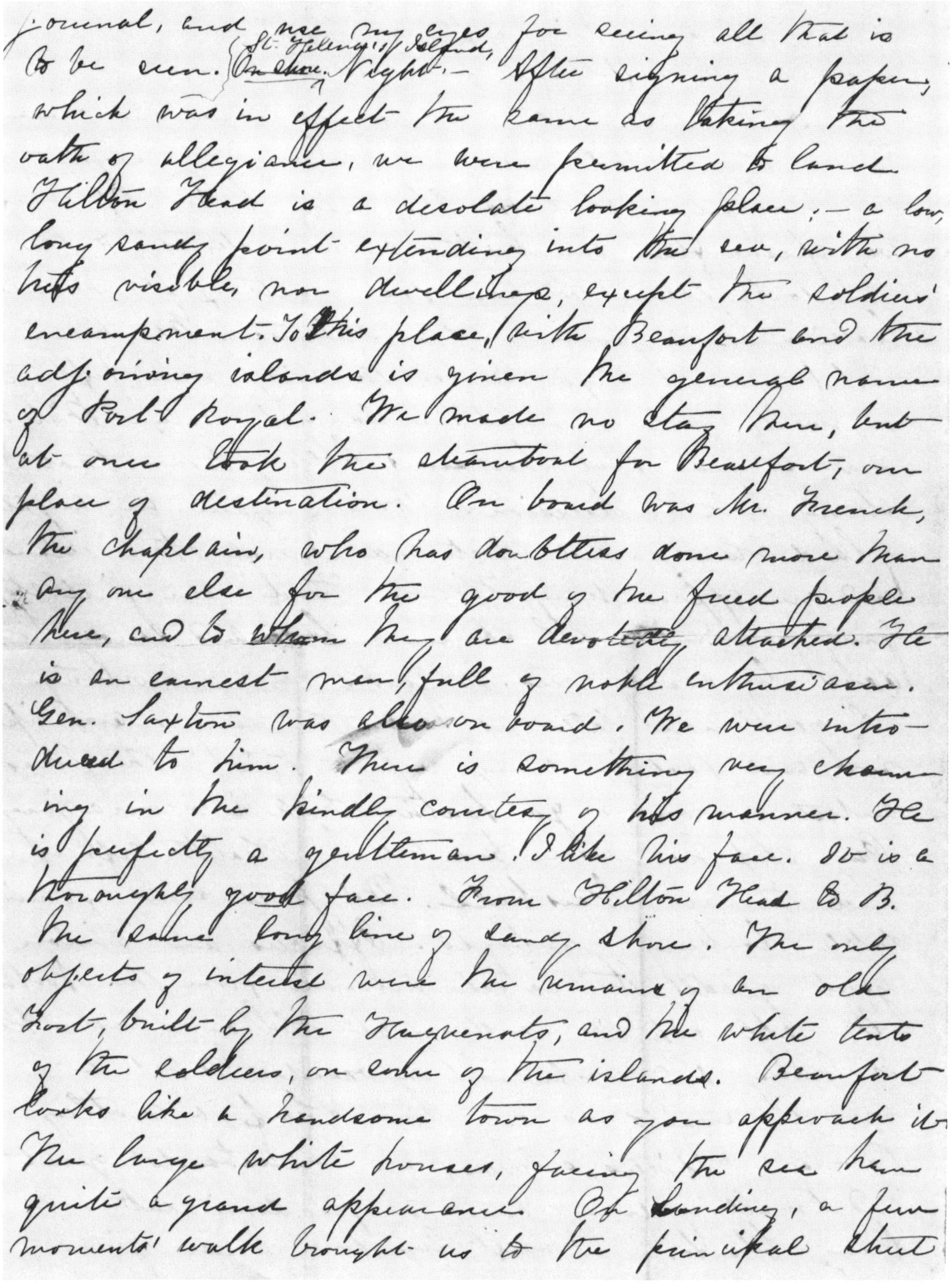
journal, and use my eyes for seeing all that is
to be seen. ~~On shore~~ St. Helena's Island, Night.— After signing a paper,
which was in effect the same as taking the
oath of allegiance, we were permitted to land.
Hilton Head is a desolate looking place;— a low,
long sandy point extending into the sea, with no
hills visible, nor dwellings, except the soldiers'
encampment. To this place, with Beaufort and the
adjoining islands is given the general name
of Port Royal. We made no stay there, but
at once took the steamboat for Beaufort, our
place of destination. On board was Mr. French,
the chaplain, who has doubtless done more than
any one else for the good of the freed people
here, and to whom they are devotedly attached. He
is an earnest man, full of noble enthusiasm.
Gen. Saxton was also on board. We were intro-
duced to him. There is something very charm-
ing in the kindly courtesy of his manner. He
is perfectly a gentleman. I like his face. It is a
thoroughly good face. From Hilton Head to B.
the same long line of sandy shore. The only
objects of interest were the remains of an old
fort, built by the Huguenots, and the white tents
of the soldiers, on some of the islands. Beaufort
looks like a handsome town as you approach it.
The large white houses, facing the sea have
quite a grand appearance. On landing, a few
moments' walk brought us to the principal street

9. of the town. The houses are of wood, painted white and built in the usual Southern style with verandahs around them, and surrounded by gardens which must once have been beautiful, and are still rich in oleanders and orange trees. I noticed one magnificent magnolia tree,—the leaf is beautiful, a rich dark glossy green—the tree itself as large as some of our largest shade trees. They tell me that when these trees are in blossom their fragrance is almost overpowering in its sweetness. Houses and gardens are now in rather a decayed and dilapidated condition, as might be expected of a place where soldiers have taken up their abode. This was a favorite watering place with the rebels,—the Newport of S. C.—and these almost deserted streets, through which only a few soldiers and some light-hearted "contrabands" are idly strolling, were but a little while ago alive with the gay equipages of the elegant dames and the redoubtable "Chivalry" of this most chivalrous "Palmetto State." The freed people tell us with delight how "Missus and massa hab to run when day hear de Yankees comin'." Arrived at Beaufort we found we had not yet quite reached our home—St Helena's Island, which is about six miles from the main land of Beaufort. It is here that the large school is established in which I am to teach, and where Mr. Hunn—the Quaker gentleman under whose protection I came—is to keep

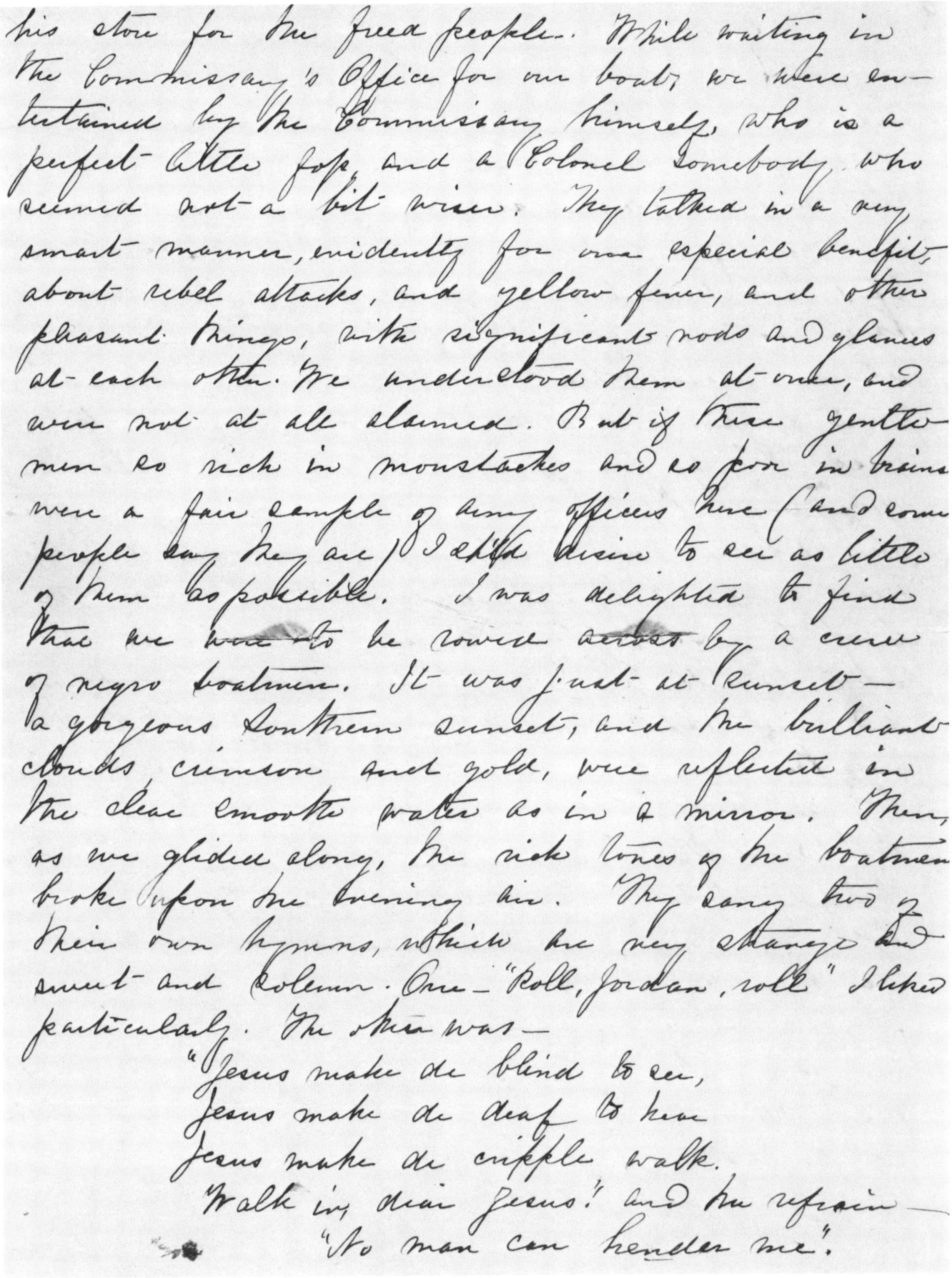

his store for the freed people. While waiting in the Commissary's Office for our boat, we were entertained by the Commissary himself, who is a perfect little fop, and a Colonel Somebody, who seemed not a bit wiser. They talked in a very smart manner, evidently for our especial benefit, about rebel attacks, and yellow fever, and other pleasant things, with significant nods and glances at each other. We understood them at once, and were not at all alarmed. But if these gentlemen so rich in moustaches and so poor in brains were a fair sample of army officers here (and some people say they are) I sh'd desire to see as little of them as possible. I was delighted to find that we were to be rowed across by a crew of negro boatmen. It was just at sunset— a gorgeous Southern sunset, and the brilliant clouds, crimson and gold, were reflected in the clear smooth water as in a mirror. Then, as we glided along, the rich tones of the boatmen broke upon the evening air. They sang two of their own hymns, which are very strange and sweet and solemn. One—"Roll, Jordan, roll" I liked particularly. The other was—

"Jesus make de blind to see,
Jesus make de deaf to hear
Jesus make de cripple walk.
Walk in, dear Jesus!" and the refrain—
"No man can hender me".

Then they improvised a song in our honor — so a gentleman told us, who acted as interpreter, for they speak a tongue which is yet unknown to us. I want to hear these men sing Whittier's "Song of the Negro Boatman". I shall see if it cannot be taught them. I think he wld like that. They have certainly a great deal of musical talent. Their singing impressed me much. It is very, very beautiful, and accompanied by a peculiar, swaying motion of the body which makes it more effective. They sing with the greatest enthusiasm. After reaching the island we had a three miles drive through the loneliest roads in the dark night. How easy it wld have been for a band of guerillas had any chanced that way — to capture and hang us. But we feared nothing of the kind, supposing that the islands was well protected by gunboats and negro pickets. There are no white soldiers on it. We were in quite a jubilant state of mind, and sang the John Brown song with spirit, as we drove through the pines and palmettos. It was good, it was glorious to be privileged to sing the praises of that grand old man, here, in the very heart of Rebeldom. Arrived at the Superintendent's house we were cordially greeted by New England people (with one exception) and shown into the parlor, where a cheerful wood fire glowed in the

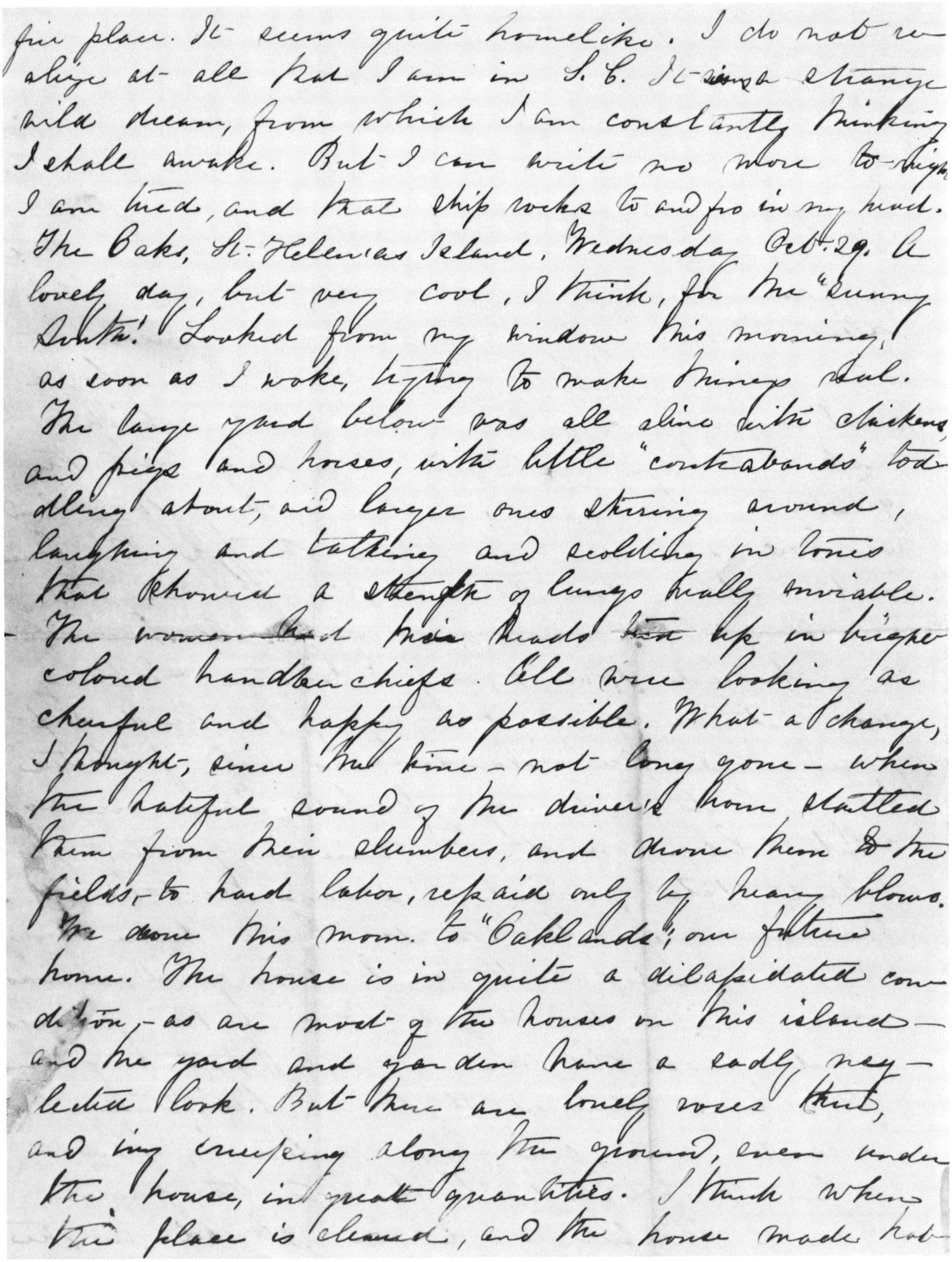
fine place. It seems quite homelike. I do not re-
alize at all that I am in S.C. It seems a strange
wild dream, from which I am constantly thinking
I shall awake. But I can write no more to-night.
I am tired, and that ship rocks to and fro in my head.
The Oaks, St. Helena's Island, Wednesday Oct. 29. A
lovely day, but very cool, I think, for the "sunny
South." Looked from my window this morning,
as soon as I woke, trying to make things real.
The large yard below was all alive with chickens
and pigs and horses, with little "contrabands" tod-
dling about, and larger ones stirring around,
laughing and talking and scolding in tones
that showed a strength of lungs really enviable.
The women had their heads tied up in bright
colored handkerchiefs. All were looking as
cheerful and happy as possible. What a change,
I thought, since the time—not long gone—when
the hateful sound of the driver's horn startled
them from their slumbers, and drove them to the
fields,—to hard labor, repaid only by many blows.
We drove this morn. to "Oaklands", our future
home. The house is in quite a dilapidated con-
dition,—as are most of the houses on this island—
and the yard and garden have a sadly neg-
lected look. But there are lovely roses there,
and ivy creeping along the ground, even under
the house, in great quantities. I think when
the place is cleaned, and the house made hab-

13 -table it will be a pleasant place. The negro
"quarters" are not very far off,— a row of humble
little cabins. The negroes seem very kind and po-
lite. I think we shall get on admirably with them.
They work for the government and are paid in
rations and money, but they still consider
themselves somewhat under the protection of the
people who live in "the house", as they always
call the planter's residence. After talking
with them for some time, and making arrange-
ments for having the house repaired we left
"Oaklands", and drove to the little Baptist
Church where the school is kept. The teachers
are Miss Murray, and Miss Towne. Miss M.
is of English parentage, born in the Provinces
but whose home is now in Newport, R.I. She is
a very charming person; a whole-souled, warm-
hearted woman. I felt drawn to her from the first.
Miss T. is a Philadelphia lady. She — like Miss
Murray — is a very refined and intellectual woman
full of life and energy. She is teacher, nurse, house-
keeper, physician, everything at "The Oaks," and
indeed everywhere,— the most indispensable
person here. She knows a great deal of about
medicine, and has a large homeopathic practice
on the plantations. The people are warmly at-
tached to her, and look upon her as a kind of
ministering angel. These ladies teach with en-
thusiasm. The little Church is beautifully sit-

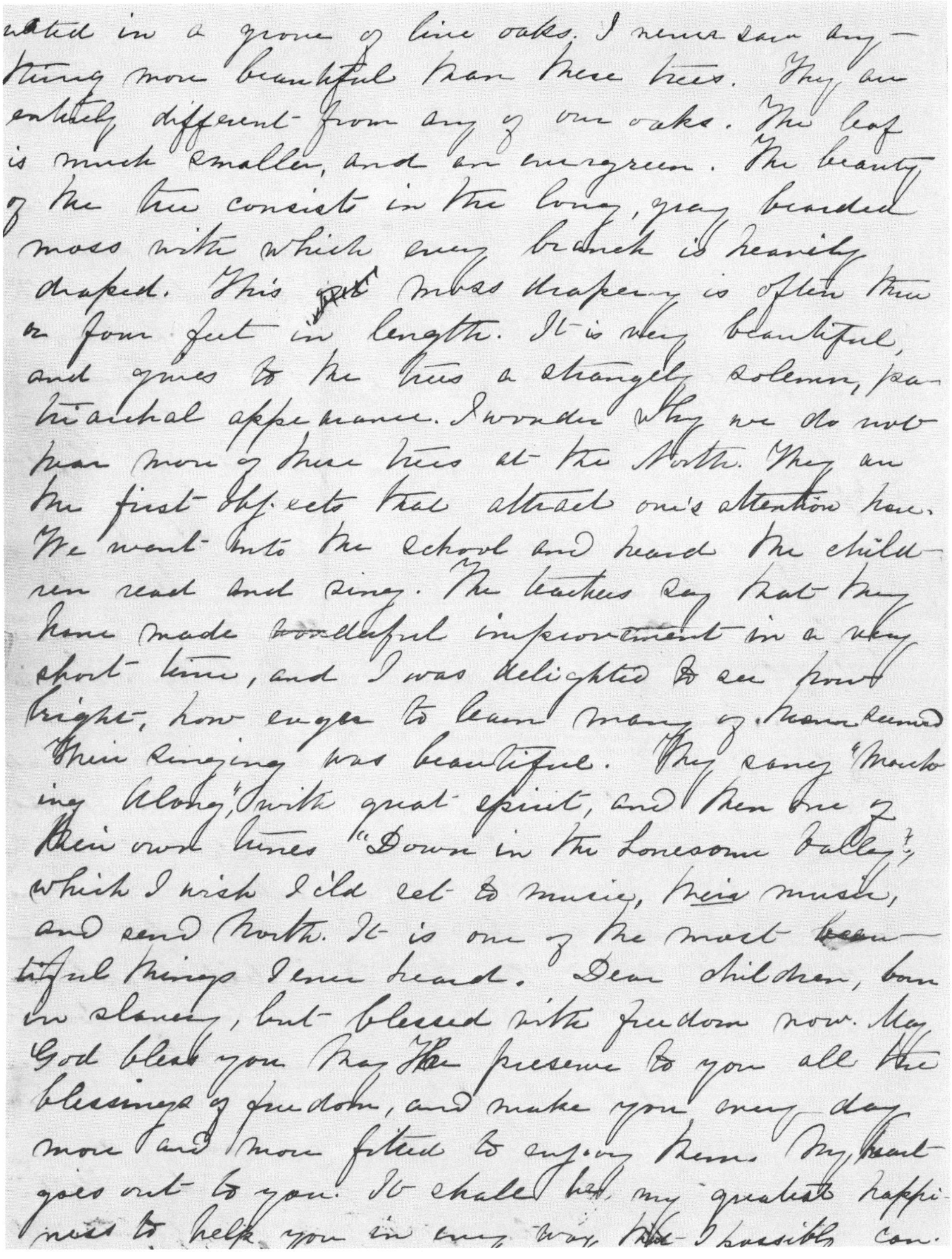
uated in a grove of live oaks. I never saw anything more beautiful than these trees. They are entirely different from any of our oaks. The leaf is much smaller, and an evergreen. The beauty of the tree consists in the long, gray bearded moss with which every branch is heavily draped. This moss drapery is often three or four feet in length. It is very beautiful, and gives to the trees a strangely solemn, patriarchal appearance. I wonder why we do not hear more of these trees at the North. They are the first objects that attract one's attention here. We went into the school and heard the children read and sing. The teachers say that they have made wonderful improvement in a very short time, and I was delighted to see how bright, how eager to learn many of them seemed. Their singing was beautiful. They sang "Marching Along," with great spirit, and then one of their own hymns "Down in the Lonesome Valley," which I wish I cld set to music, their music, and send North. It is one of the most beautiful things I ever heard. Dear children, born in slavery, but blessed with freedom now. May God bless you. May He preserve to you all the blessings of freedom, and make you every day more and more fitted to enjoy them. My heart goes out to you. It shall be my greatest happiness to help you in every way that I possibly can.

As we drove homeward I noticed that the leaves are just beginning to turn. But the trees are not so brilliant as with us. Quantities of beautiful scarlet berries were growing by the roadside, and everywhere the live oak with its graceful moss drapery. The palmettos disappoint me. They are generally stiff and ungraceful and their foliage has a very jagged appearance. The cotton fields disappoint me, too. The plants grow in a straggling fashion, and the pods are small and inferior looking; not at all the snowballs I had imagined. The country is very level—not a hill to be seen—and it w'ld be rather dreary were it not for the beautiful woods.—The fields have all a desolate look.

Sunday Nov. 2. Attended church to-day, the Baptist Church in which the school is held. The church was full. Old and young were there in their Sunday attire,—clean gowns, clean head-handkerchiefs, bright-colored, of course. I noticed that some had reached the dignity of straw hats with bright feathers. But the handkerchiefs are much more becoming. The minister, Mr. Phillips, is an earnest N. E. man, who is much beloved by the people. The sermon was very good, and was listened to with the greatest attention. The congregation was composed of negroes with the exception of fourteen or fifteen—superintendents of the different plantations, and teachers. The

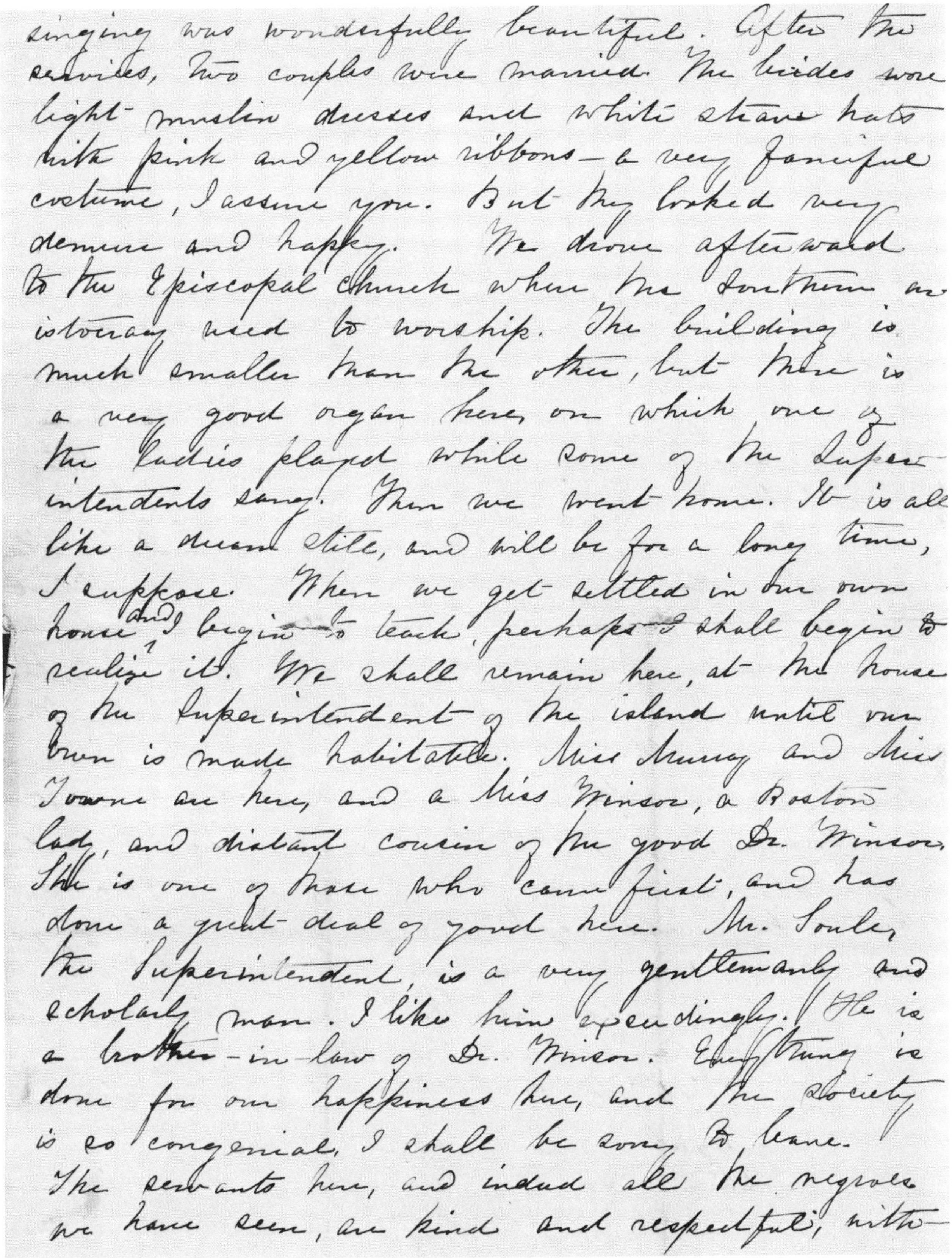
singing was wonderfully beautiful. After the
services, two couples were married. The brides wore
light muslin dresses and white straw hats
with pink and yellow ribbons—a very fanciful
costume, I assure you. But they looked very
demure and happy. We drove afterward
to the Episcopal Church where the Southern ar-
istocracy used to worship. The building is
much smaller than the other, but there is
a very good organ here, on which one of
the ladies played while some of the Super-
intendents sang. Then we went home. It is all
like a dream still, and will be for a long time,
I suppose. When we get settled in our own
house and I begin to teach, perhaps I shall begin to
realize it. We shall remain here, at the house
of the Superintendent of the island until our
own is made habitable. Miss Murray and Miss
Towne are here, and a Miss Winsor, a Boston
lady, and distant cousin of the good Dr. Winsor.
She is one of those who came first, and has
done a great deal of good here. Mr. Soule,
the Superintendent, is a very gentlemanly and
scholarly man. I like him exceedingly. He is
a brother-in-law of Dr. Winsor. Everything is
done for our happiness here, and the society
is so congenial, I shall be sorry to leave.
The servants here, and indeed all the negroes
we have seen, are kind and respectful; with-

17 —out anything cringing about them. They have what Emerson calls "fine manners"— that natural courtesy that comes from the heart. I notice it in their behavior to each other as well as to the whites. And it is a very pleasant thing to see. They are all jubilant over the arrival of the "Unions" as they call them. Some of them have said to me "We bress de Lord, missus, we bress de Lord ebery day fa sendin de Unions here to make us free. Nobody to strike us, nobody to whip us now. We suffered long time. But de Lord, de Lord, he bring it all right at las'."

Oaklands, Tuesday, Nov. 4.— Came to our new home to day. This house and indeed all the houses on the island, after the flight of the rebels, were quite stripped of their furniture, which was either destroyed by the soldiers or taken possession of by the negroes. So our house is in a desolate condition; the only furniture consisting of two bureaus, one bedstead, three small pine tables and two chairs, one of which has a broken back. We intended to get mattresses in N.Y. but had no time to do so. What we are to do for beds I know not. Must content ourselves with blanket substitutes until we can do better. I do not care. I don't mean to be discouraged at anything. Have never felt more hopeful and cheerful than I do now. My companion, Lizzie Hunn, and I have manufactured a tolerable druggett

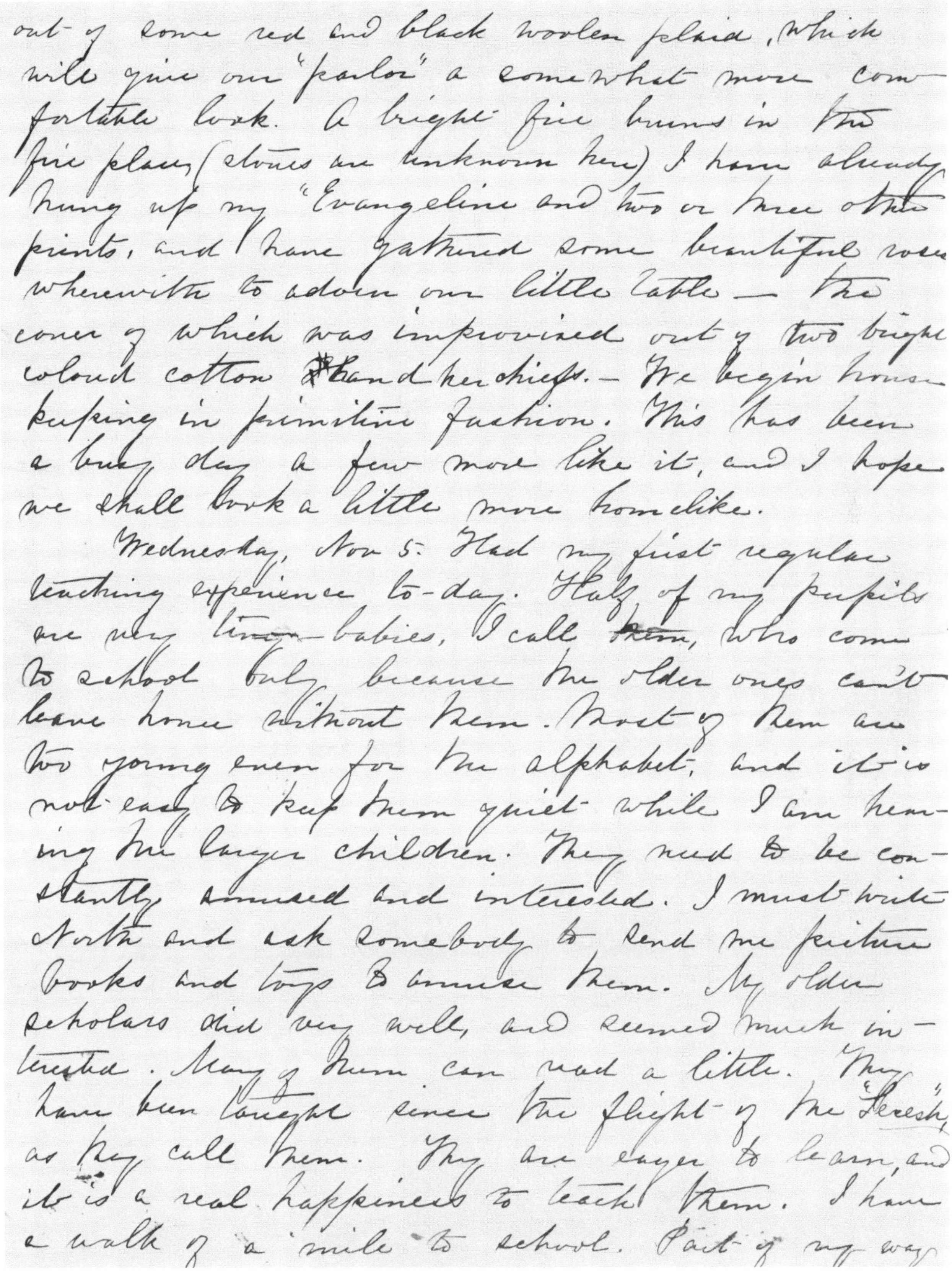
out of some red and black woolen plaid, which will give our "parlor" a somewhat more comfortable look. A bright fire burns in the fire place (stoves are unknown here) I have already hung up my "Evangeline" and two or three other prints, and have gathered some beautiful roses wherewith to adorn our little table — the cover of which was improvised out of two bright colored cotton handkerchiefs. — We begin housekeeping in primitive fashion. This has been a busy day a few more like it, and I hope we shall look a little more homelike.

Wednesday, Nov 5: Had my first regular teaching experience to-day. Half of my pupils are very tiny babies, I call them, who come to school only because the older ones can't leave home without them. Most of them are too young even for the alphabet, and it is not easy to keep them quiet while I am hearing the larger children. They need to be constantly amused and interested. I must write North and ask somebody to send me picture books and toys to amuse them. My older scholars did very well, and seemed much interested. Many of them can read a little. They have been taught since the flight of the "Secesh," as they call them. They are eager to learn, and it is a real happiness to teach them. I have a walk of a mile to school. Part of my way lies along a delightful road with woods on either side, just brightening to scarlet now. Mocking birds are singing in the trees. The ground is carpeted with those brown, odorous pine leaves which I love so well, for there are many pines among the other trees. The store has been crowded all day. It is such a delightful novelty to these people to have money of their own to buy clothing with like other people. The head handkerchiefs—imitation Madras—are an especial attraction. We've established our household on a firm basis—as we hope. We have Rose for our maid of all work, Amaretta for cook, washer, and ironer, ~~and~~ Cupid, yes, Cupid himself for major domo, oysterman, and coachman in prospectus. These are all very black, very good natured and obliging, and I think even Miss Ophelia w'ld acknowledge that they are not so "shiftless" as Southern servants usually are. For a reasonable compensation one can obtain much more "help" than one wants here. I must inform thee, friend journal, that we have made for ourselves a bed, whereon we hope to rest to-night, for rest I certainly did not, last night despite innumerable blankets designed to cover and conceal the bones (alias slats) of our bedstead. But said bones did so protrude, that sleep was an impossibility to

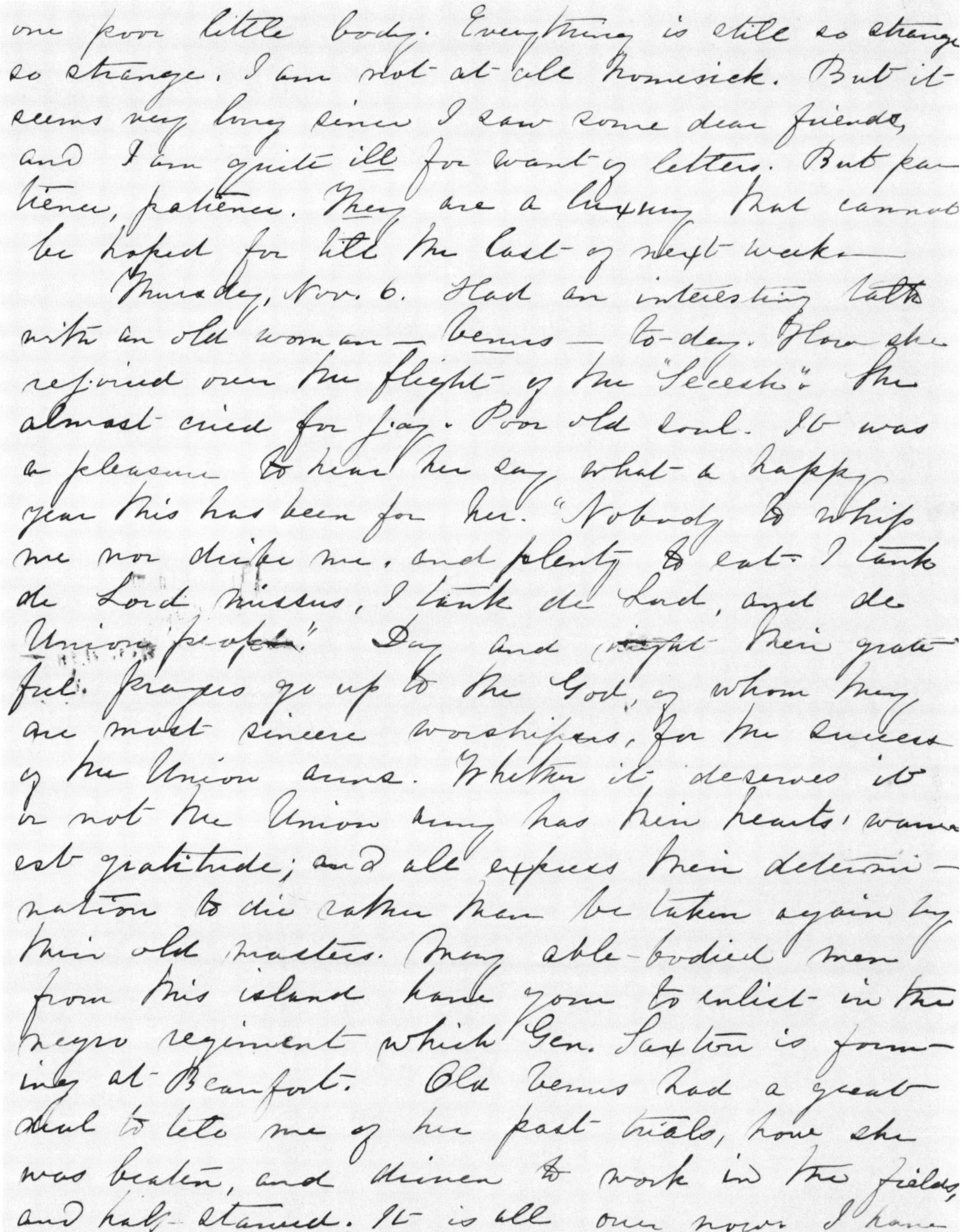
one poor little body. Everything is still so strange
so strange. I am not at all homesick. But it
seems very long since I saw some dear friends,
and I am quite ill for want of letters. But pa-
tience, patience. They are a luxury that cannot
be hoped for till the last of next week.—
Thursday, Nov. 6. Had an interesting talk
with an old woman—Venus—to-day. How she
rejoiced over the flight of the "Secesh." She
almost cried for joy. Poor old soul. It was
a pleasure to hear her say what a happy
year this has been for her. "Nobody to whip
me nor drive me, and plenty to eat. I tank
de Lord, missus, I tank de Lord, and de
Union people." Day and night their grate-
ful prayers go up to the God, of whom they
are most sincere worshippers, for the success
of the Union arms. Whether it deserves it
or not the Union army has their hearts' warm-
est gratitude; and all express their determi-
nation to die rather than be taken again by
their old masters. Many able-bodied men
from this island have gone to enlist in the
negro regiment which Gen. Saxton is form-
ing at Beaufort. Old Venus had a great
deal to tell me of her past trials, how she
was beaten, and driven to work in the fields,
and half-starved. It is all over now. I have
promised to make a dress for her great

21 grand child which is only two weeks old. It shall be a bright pink calico, such as will delight the little freeborn baby's eyes when it shall be old enough to appreciate it. I enjoy going to the cabins and talking with the people. The sadness of their past lot only makes the present contrast the brighter. I have not had time yet to see nearly so much of them as I want to see. At school we are teaching the children the "John Brown Song." They will soon learn it. Singing comes as natural to them as talking.

Thursday, Nov. 13. Yesterday Miss T. told the children about John Brown — the brave old man who died for their race. And then they sang the song, and sang it beautifully. To-day I told them a little about Toussaint. They listened very attentively. It is well that they should know what one of their own color did for his race. I long to inspire them with courage and ambition (of a noble sort) and high purposes. It is noticeable how few mulattoes there are here. In our school, which has until recently averaged eighty or ninety, the children are, with two or three exceptions, black. A little mulatto child strayed into the school house yesterday — a pretty little thing, with large black eyes shaded by beautiful long lashes. But so dirty! I longed to seize her and put her in a bath.

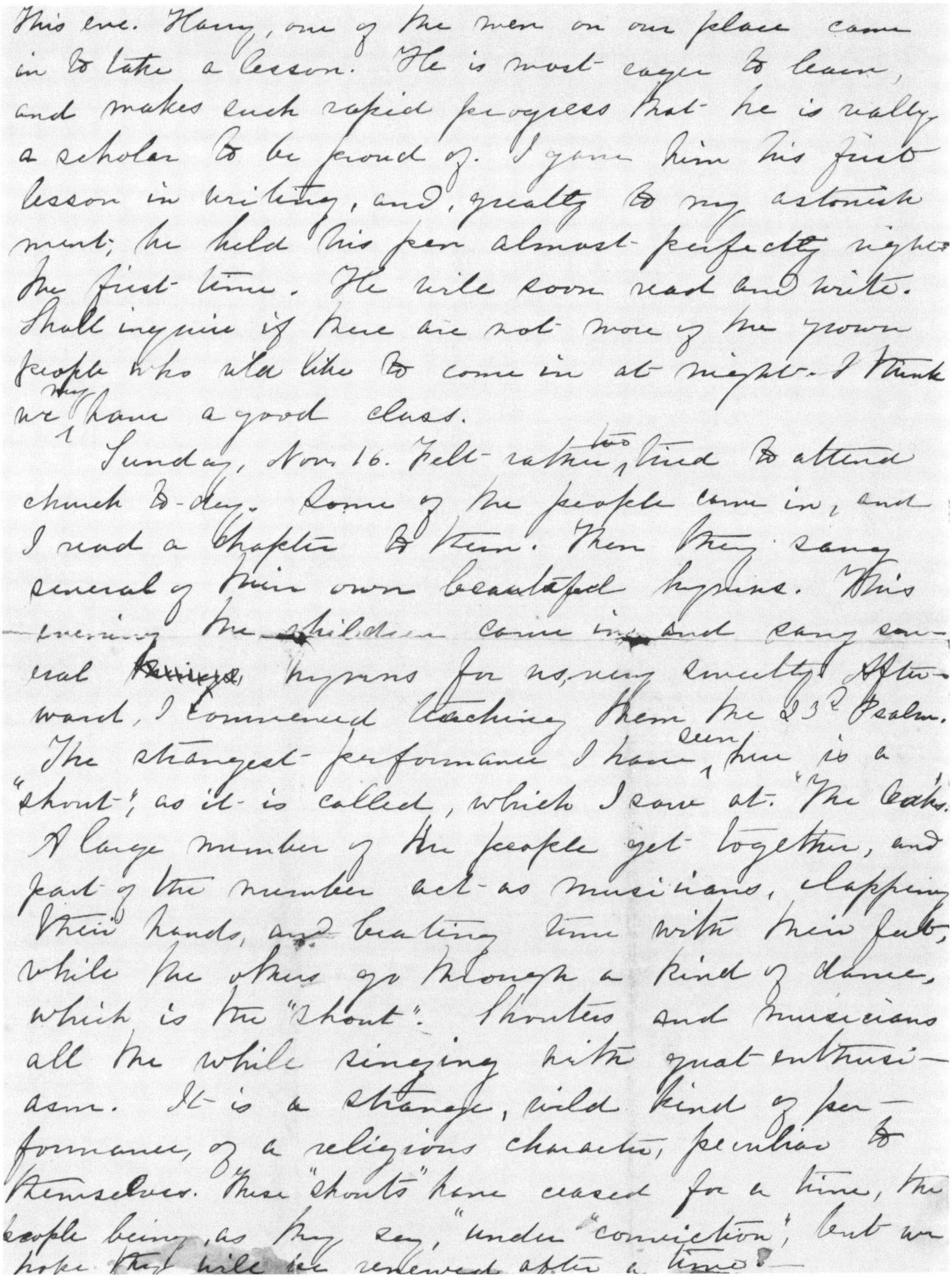

this eve. Harry, one of the men on our place came in to take a lesson. He is most eager to learn, and makes such rapid progress that he is really a scholar to be proud of. I gave him his first lesson in writing, and, greatly to my astonishment, he held his pen almost perfectly right the first time. He will soon read and write. Shall inquire if there are not more of the grown people who wd like to come in at night. I think we may have a good class.

Sunday, Nov. 16. Felt rather too tired to attend church to-day. Some of the people came in, and I read a chapter to them. Then they sang several of their own beautiful hymns. This evening the children came in and sang several hymns for us, very sweetly. Afterward, I commenced teaching them the 23d Psalm.

The strangest performance I have seen here is a "shout," as it is called, which I saw at "The Oaks." A large number of the people get together, and part of the number act as musicians, clapping their hands, and beating time with their feet, while the others go through a kind of dance, which is the "shout". Shouters and musicians all the while singing with great enthusiasm. It is a strange, wild kind of performance, of a religious character, peculiar to themselves. These "shouts" have ceased for a time, the people being, as they say, "under conviction," but we hope they will be renewed after a time.

John Edward Bruce

Three Documents

Standing behind the great and remembered writers of any age in any culture are usually found the mentors and bibliophiles, the business folk, and social facilitators whose behind-the-scenes work on behalf of the literary arts often goes unrecorded. Newspaperman John Edward Bruce, himself an author of fiction, plays, poetry, and music, pamphlet disquisitions, political tracts, profiles, and histories of the people and events of Afro-American culture, was just such a pivotal figure. His wide-ranging influence touched the careers of many black writers working in the late nineteenth and early twentieth centuries. A slave in childhood who devoted his adult life to the advocacy of the interests of blacks in every sphere of American life, Bruce typifies, in his own writing and in his activism on behalf of others, the committed black journalist at the turn of the century.

Born on 22 February 1856, in Piscataway, Maryland, Bruce was raised solely by his mother, Martha Allen Clark Bruce, from the time his father, Robert Bruce, was "sold south" in 1859. According to a scant, unpublished autobiographical sketch, when "the first regiment of Union soldiers passed through Maryland on their way to Washington," Bruce and his mother simply joined their march and took up lives as free people in Washington, D.C.

Largely self-educated, Bruce began his career as a journalist sometime in the 1870s. He once worked as a "helper" in the *New York Times* office for the Washington correspondent; he went on to become a contributor to the *Times*, as well as to the *Boston Transcript*, *Buffalo Gazette*, *Washington Evening Star*, *New York Herald*, *St. Louis Globe-Democrat*, and other papers. He was the American correspondent for the *London African Times and Orient Review* and was widely published in Jamaican newspapers. Termed by nineteenth-century social historian Alexander Crummell "the Negro satirist of the times," Bruce lent his vituperative pen to public cause and private concern through his articles, editorials, and copious personal correspondence with and about everybody who was anybody in the power spheres of nineteenth-century America.

Founder of a succession of his own newspapers—including the *Washington Argus* and *Sunday Item* (1880), the *New York Grit* (with politician Charles William Anderson, in 1884), *Chronicle*, and *Weekly Standard* (1908)—he came to be called Bruce Grit, through identification with his outspoken periodical and for his frank voicing of his sometimes unpopular opinions. He was equally fearless in attacking prejudiced white politicians like Coleman Blease and Tom Dixon whom he once called "microcephalous lizzards," and prominent black figures like the "slick" Booker T. Washington, whose program at Tuskegee Institute Bruce described in outrage as "hog and hominy."

A Mason and a Republican, member of the Order of African Redemption, London's Africa Society, and the A.M.E. Episcopal Zion Church, Bruce was strategically placed to give and take information. In 1897 New York governor Levi P. Morton appointed Bruce representative of the state's interests at a Tennessee exposition. He was in contact with "everybody, [he] read everything" and always had something to say about it. Only a few years later he became one of Marcus Garvey's lieutenants in the "Back to Africa" movement; and as "late as January 2, 1929, Bruce wrote the rough draft of a cable for Garvey which stated: 'Du Bois—*Crisis*—on trip to Africa, bent on mischief . . . watch him. . . .' " In private he was devastatingly blunt. A letter Robert Harris received from G. W. Jewett euphemistically explained that Charles Chesnutt's application for an Annapolis cadetship was dismissed because Chesnutt's "talents would find better outlet as . . . [a] teacher." Harris passed the letter on to Bruce, who penned on it: "He took the flattery route & eliminated the Nigger 'thout battin a eyelash."

With Arthur Alfonso Schomburg, Bruce and others established a cultural league in 1911 modeled on Crummell's American Negro Academy. The Negro Society for Historical Research was dedicated to promoting research and collecting material by and about black thinkers. Bruce served the society as its first president, and the Schomburg Collection—as the society's library came to be known—houses some of Bruce's papers. Among these holdings are the following manuscript and typescript items which, while they attest to Bruce's interest in promoting black literature, barely reveal the huge machinery of personal interest and involvement he brought to bear on this subject throughout his life.

The first item is a manuscript draft for an undated editorial that surveys the beginnings of Afro-American poetry by focusing on three slave writers—Jupiter Hammon, Phillis Wheatley, and George Moses Horton. The second item is scholar Moses Da Rocha's typescript introduction, written 30 October 1902, in response to Bruce's proposed anthology of black American literature, which, as Bruce wrote at the end of the entry, he "Couldn't make . . . go." The last manuscript item, probably dating from 1913, is an editorial ostensibly about the need for Negro literature. In fact, Bruce used the editorial to promote Fred W. Hooke's study of Edward Wilmot Blyden, which Bruce proposed to publish with C. C. Hunt. The book was never published.

The three documents reproduced here represent the spirit of active self-promotion and revivification of critical and popular interest in black American literature advanced through public forum and private interest at the century's turn. The journalistic and entrepreneurial efforts of John Edward Bruce, and others like him, helped to lay the foundation for twentieth-century interest in the Afro-American literary past as well as its aesthetic and pragmatic present and future.

—Editor's Note

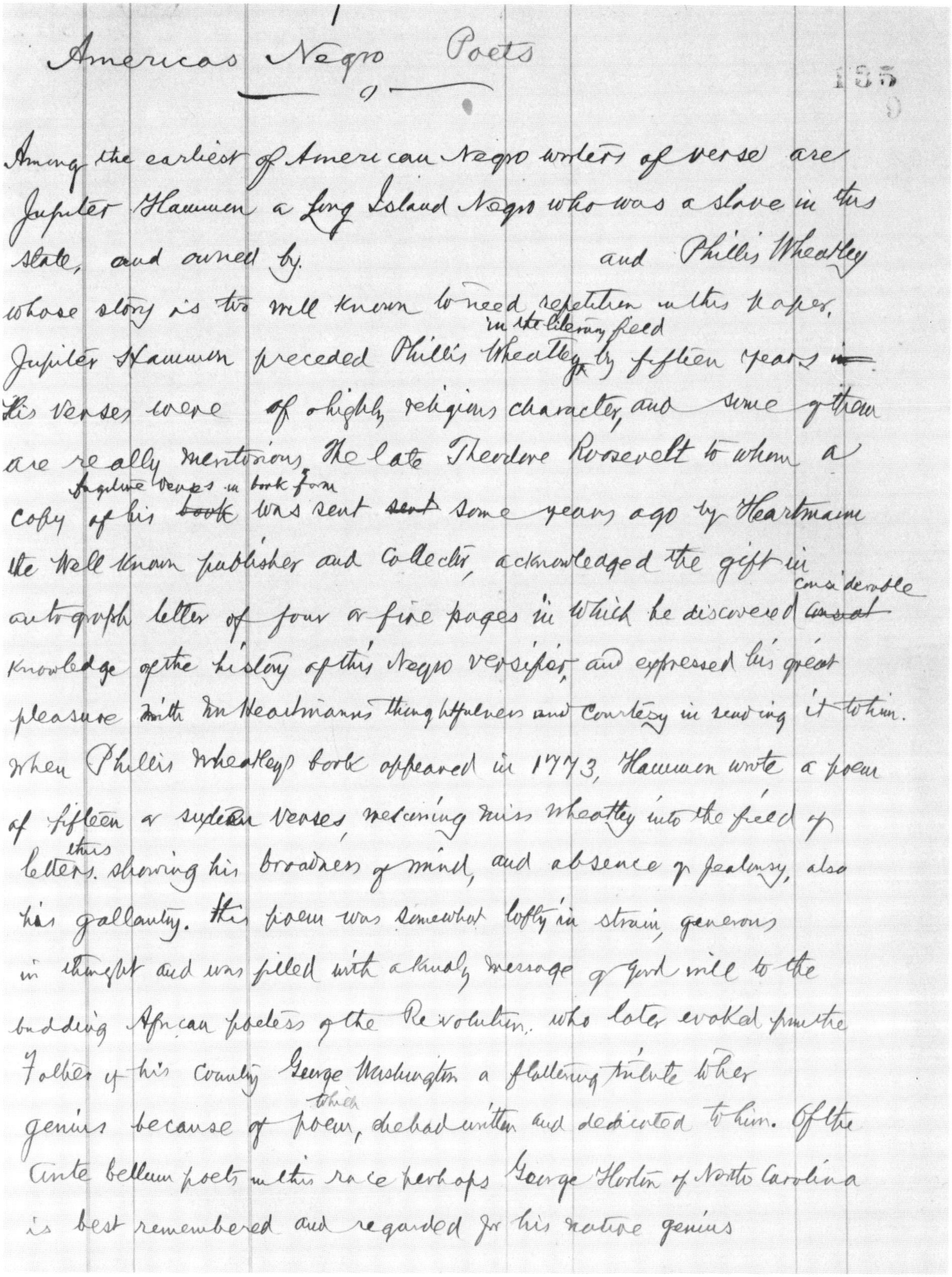

1

Americas Negro Poets

155

Among the earliest of American Negro writers of verse are Jupiter Hammon a Long Island Negro who was a slave in this state, and owned by   and Phillis Wheatley whose story is too well known to need repetition in this paper. Jupiter Hammon preceded Phillis Wheatley in the literary field by fifteen years. His verses were of a highly religious character, and some of them are really meritorious. The late Theodore Roosevelt to whom a copy of his fugitive verses in book form ~~book~~ was sent ~~sent~~ some years ago by Heartmann the well known publisher and collector, acknowledged the gift in autograph letter of four or five pages in which he discovered considerable ~~great~~ knowledge of the history of this Negro versifier, and expressed his great pleasure with Mr Heartmann's thoughtfulness and courtesy in sending it to him. When Phillis Wheatley's book appeared in 1773, Hammon wrote a poem of fifteen or sixteen verses, welcoming Miss Wheatley into the field of letters. thus showing his broadness of mind, and absence of jealousy, also his gallantry. This poem was somewhat lofty in strain, generous in thought and was filled with a kindly message of good will to the budding African poetess of the Revolution, who later evoked from the Father of his Country George Washington a flattering tribute to her genius because of poem, which she had written and dedicated to him. Of the ante bellum poets of this race perhaps George Horton of North Carolina is best remembered and regarded for his native genius

Manuscript draft for Bruce's undated editorial celebrating black poets (courtesy of Schomburg Center for Research in Black Culture, the New York Public Library, Astor, Lenox and Tilden Foundations)

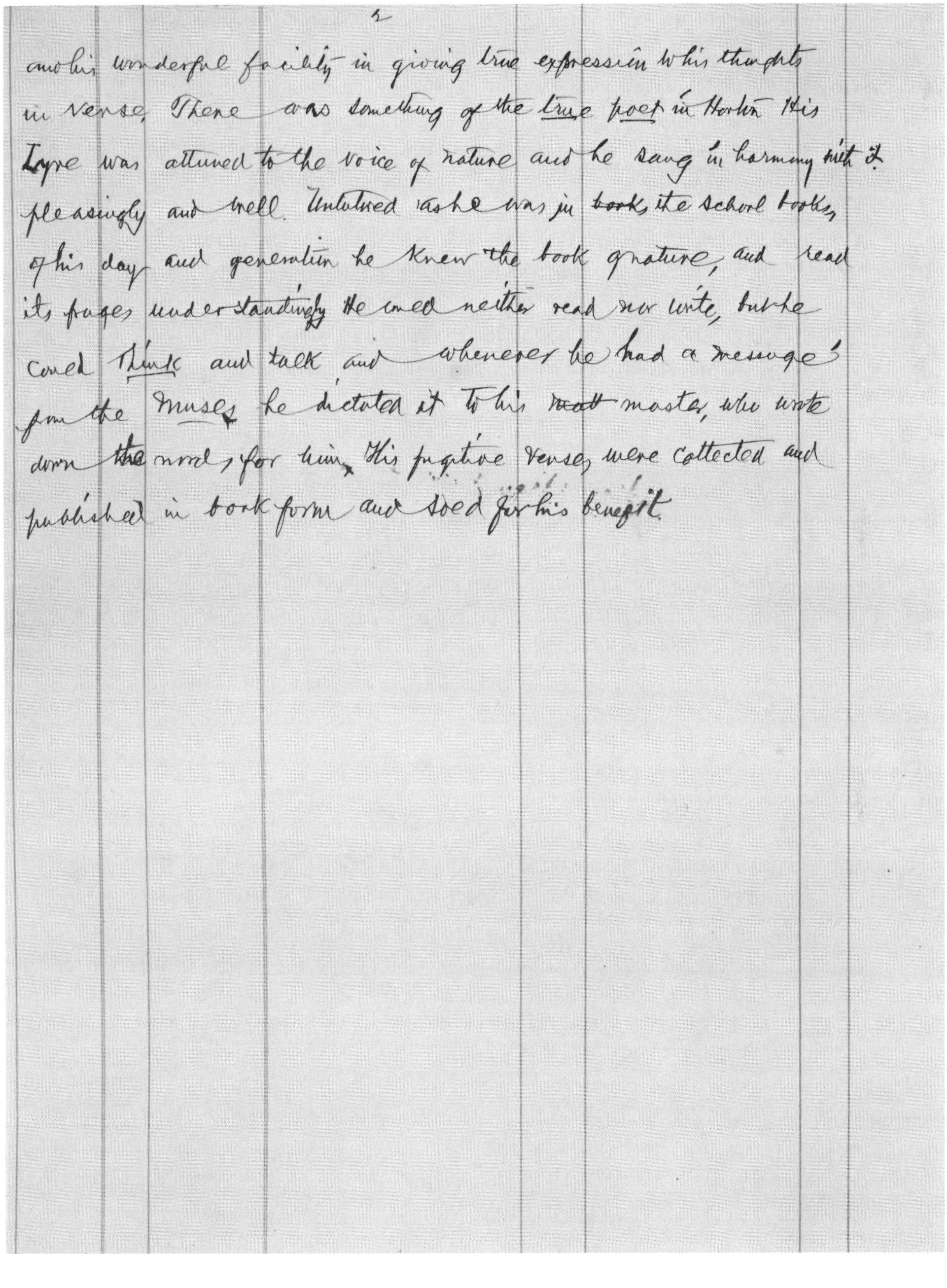
2

and his wonderful facility in giving true expression to his thoughts
in verse. There was something of the true poet in Horton. His
Lyre was attuned to the voice of nature and he sang in harmony with it
pleasingly and well. Untutored as he was in ~~book~~ the school books,
of his day and generation he knew the book of nature, and read
its pages understandingly. He could neither read nor write, but he
could think and talk and whenever he had a message
from the Muses he dictated it to his ~~mast~~ master, who wrote
down the words for him. His fugitive verses were collected and
published in book form and sold for his benefit.

7

INTRODUCTION.

Mr. John E. Bruce has done me a great honour in asking me to write the introduction to his book. My friend, as is well known, has won considerable distinction in Journalism. He is one of the best living Negro writers. His able articles have been quoted, and his pamphlets commented upon, in the English Press.

The custom now-a-days is to deplore the intellectual poverty of the Negro, to under-rate his achievements. It is too often forgotten that the race has produced such men as Frederick Douglass, Edward Blyden, Booker T. Washington, Samuel Crowther, Alexander Crummell, James Johnson, Tengo Jabavu, and John Edward Bruce.

The Crummell Historical Society, of Albany, New York, by-the-way, owes its name to the late Alexander Crummell. In 1848, there was published in London a remarkable book by Wilson Armistead, entitled "A Tribute for the Negro." This was "respectfully inscribed to James W. C. Pennington, Frederick Douglass, and Alexander Crummell. " Mr. Armistead had been so favourably impressed with "the moral, intellectual, and religious capabilities of the coloured portion of Mankind," that he conceived the idea of writing a book in their defence.

The latest production from Mr. Bruce's pen covers a very wide field. It literally ranges "from China to Peru. " It is no less than a compilation of Negro Literature published from 1800 down to 1902. The collection consists of speeches, orations, magazine, articles, and poems.

Typescript for Moses Da Rocha's introduction to Bruce's proposed anthology of Afro-American literature, which would have been the first collection of its kind in English (courtesy of Schomburg Center for Research in Black Culture, the New York Public Library, Astor, Lenox and Tilden Foundations)

-2-

by, among others, Hilary Teague(a famous Liberian statesman), Alexander Crummell, J. W. E. Bowen, Frederick Douglass(the great American Negro statesman), E. W. Blyden (the foremost Negro scholar in the world), and J. Robert Love(the Editor of the "Jamaica Advocate). These names alone are of especial signifance. Moreover, the author gives us the cream of the poetical works of Phyllis Wheatley, Mrs. Grimke, Mrs. Harper, D. W. Davis, Paul Lawrence Dunbar(the foremost Negro poet), Alexander Poushkin (" Russia's Black Byron"), Placido, D. W. Williams, George Horton, and T. Thomas Fortune (the brillaint Editor of the "New York Age"). His pride of race forbade the inclusion of a single line that was not elevat-ed in tone or worthy of serious reflection.

This purely Negro enterprise cannot be too warmly com-mended. It is at once novel and interesting. No such book has ever been published by a Negro. It is really a cabinet of choice Negro Literature, selected with great care, designed for the home, the library, and the desk. As a birthday gift or Christmas present, nothing could be more acceptable.

The debt we owe to Mr. Bruce is incalculable. He has won our eternal gratitude by his brilliant vindication of the race. No one can read his book without realizing that the Negro can think, and does think well, on many subjects which the proud Caucasian imagines he alone can grapple with.

Moses Da. Rocha
(of Edinburgh University).

Edinburgh,
October 30, 1902.

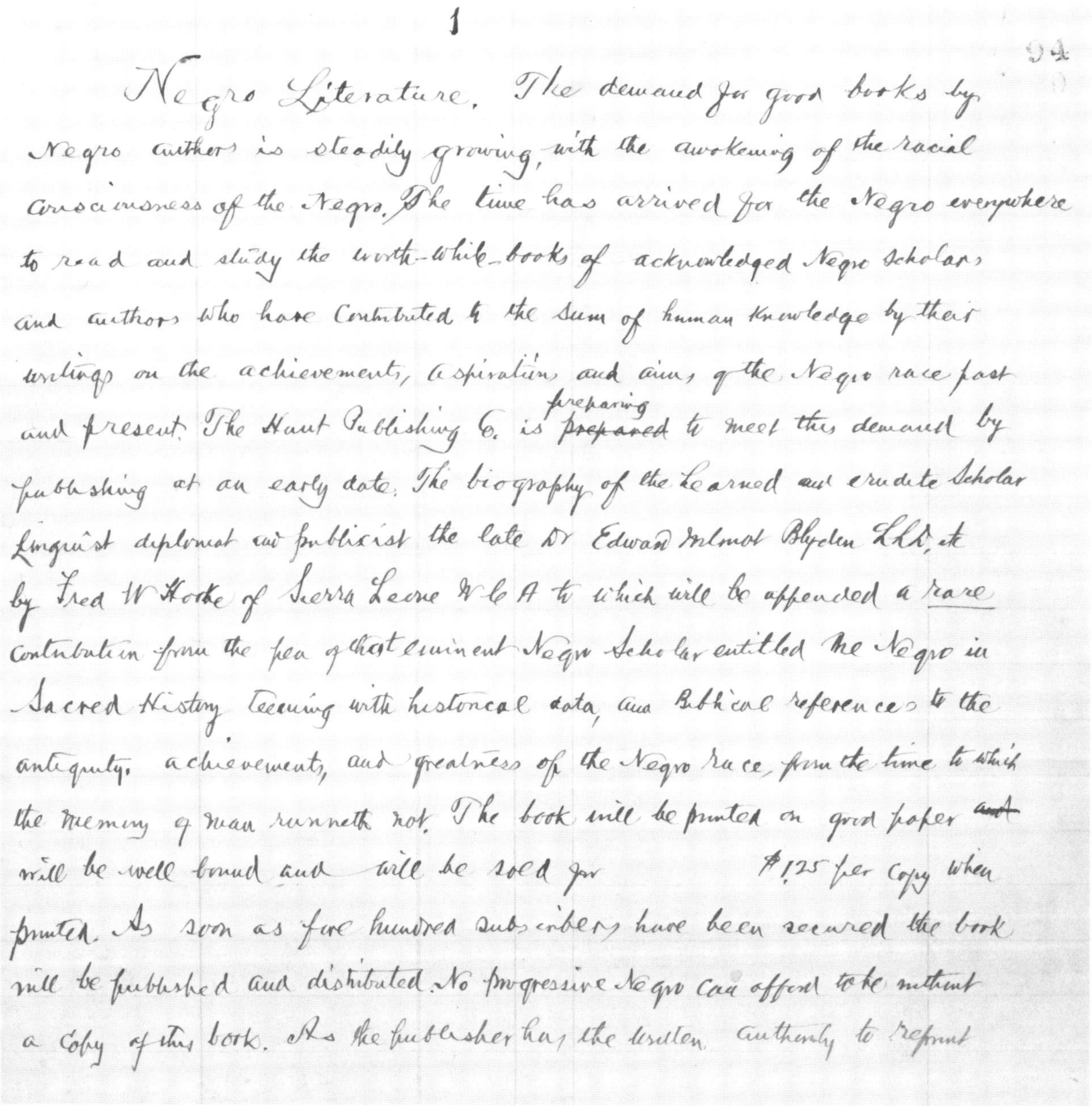

1

94

Negro Literature. The demand for good books by Negro authors is steadily growing, with the awakening of the racial consciousness of the Negro. The time has arrived for the Negro everywhere to read and study the worth-while books of acknowledged Negro scholars and authors who have contributed to the sum of human knowledge by their writings on the achievements, aspiration and aims of the Negro race past and present. The Hunt Publishing Co. is ~~prepared~~ preparing to meet this demand by publishing at an early date. The biography of the learned and erudite scholar linguist diplomat and publicist the late Dr Edward Wilmot Blyden LLD, etc by Fred W Hooke of Sierra Leone W C A to which will be appended a rare contribution from the pen of that eminent Negro scholar entitled The Negro in Sacred History teeming with historical data and Biblical references to the antiquity, achievements, and greatness of the Negro race, from the time to which the memory of man runneth not. The book will be printed on good paper ~~and~~ will be well bound and will be sold for $1.25 per copy when printed. As soon as five hundred subscribers have been secured the book will be published and distributed. No progressive Negro can afford to be without a copy of this book. As the publisher has the written authority to reprint

Manuscript for editorial soliciting subscribers to enable Bruce to publish Fred W. Hooke's study of black scholar and diplomat Edward Wilmot Blyden (courtesy of Schomburg Center for Research in Black Culture, the New York Public Library, Astor, Lenox and Tilden Foundations)

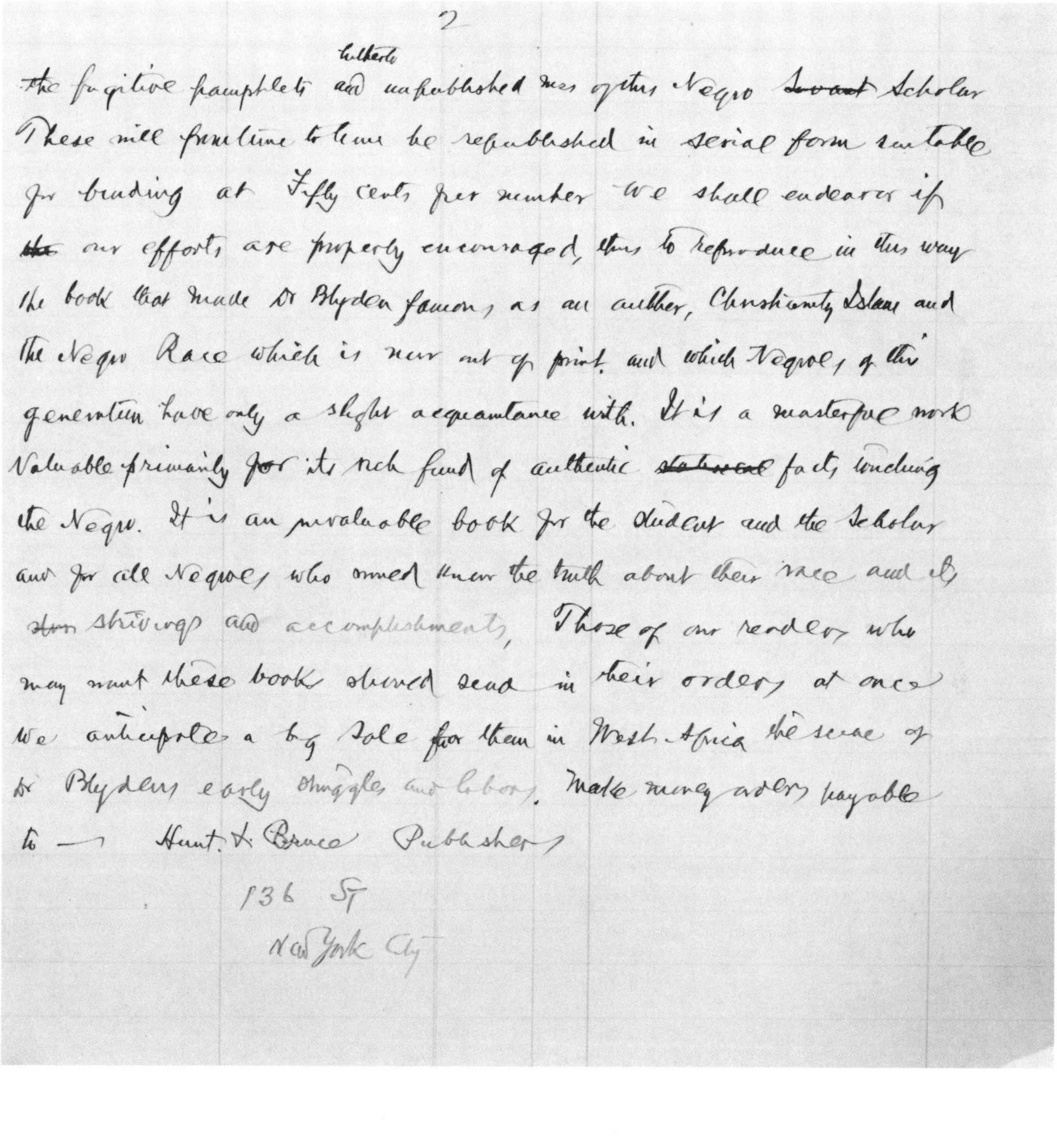

2

the fugitive pamphlets and [hitherto] unpublished mss of this Negro ~~Savant~~ Scholar
These will from time to time be republished in serial form suitable
for binding at Fifty cents per number. We shall endeavor if
~~the~~ our efforts are properly encouraged, thus to reproduce in this way
the book that made Dr Blyden famous as an author, Christianity Islam and
the Negro Race which is now out of print. and which Negroes of this
generation have only a slight acquaintance with. It is a masterful work
Valuable primarily for its rich fund of authentic ~~statement~~ facts touching
the Negro. It is an invaluable book for the student and the Scholar
and for all Negroes who would know the truth about their race and its
~~strn~~ strivings and accomplishments. Those of our readers who
may want these books should send in their orders at once
We anticipate a big sale for them in West Africa the scene of
Dr Blydens early struggles and labors. Make money orders payable
to — Hunt & Bruce Publishers

136 St

New York City

William Dean Howells

Introduction to Paul Laurence Dunbar, *Lyrics of Lowly Life* (1896)

William Dean Howells, an author and perhaps the most prominent literary critic in America in the late nineteenth and early twentieth centuries, was powerful enough to influence the reputation of a writer and the direction his career would take. He chose to make Paul Laurence Dunbar a celebrity. In a 27 June 1896 *Harper's Weekly* review of Dunbar's second volume, *Majors and Minors* (1896), Howells praised the dialect poems as Dunbar's original contribution to American literature; he thereby inadvertently narrowed the future critical response to Dunbar. Although he was as adept in standard English as in black vernacular and as conversant in traditional literary forms as in black folk forms, Dunbar was never able to overcome the public view of him as a dialect poet. In the following introduction to *Lyrics of Lowly Life* (1896), Howells reworks his earlier review. The dominance of the pronoun "I" reveals the perch from which the white critic pronounced his lofty judgments on the work of the black poet whose literary status was almost exclusively dependent upon white reception.

—*Editor's Note*

I think I should scarcely trouble the reader with a special appeal in behalf of this book, if it had not specially appealed to me for reasons apart from the author's race, origin, and condition. The world is too old now, and I find myself too much of its mood, to care for the work of a poet because he is black, because his father and mother were slaves, because he was, before and after he began to write poems, an elevator-boy. These facts would certainly attract me to him as a man, if I knew him to have a literary ambition, but when it came to his literary art, I must judge it irrespective of these facts, and enjoy or endure it for what it was in itself.

It seems to me that this was my experience with the poetry of Paul Laurence Dunbar when I found it in another form, and in justice to him I cannot wish that it should be otherwise with his readers here. Still, it will legitimately interest those who like to know the causes, or, if these may not be known, the sources, of things, to learn that the father and mother of the first poet of his race in our language were negroes without admixture of white blood. The father escaped from slavery in Kentucky to freedom in Canada, while there was still no hope of freedom otherwise; but the mother was freed by the events of the civil war, and came North to Ohio, where their son was born at Dayton, and grew up with such chances and mischances for mental training as everywhere befall the children of the poor. He has told me that his father picked up the trade of a plasterer, and when he had taught himself to read, loved chiefly to read history. The boy's mother shared his passion for literature, with a special love of poetry, and after the father died she struggled on in more than the poverty she had shared with him. She could value the faculty which her son showed first in prose sketches and attempts at fiction, and she was proud of the praise and kindness they won him among the people of the town, where he has never been without the warmest and kindest friends.

In fact, from every part of Ohio and from several cities of the adjoining States, there came letters in cordial appreciation of the critical recognition which it was my pleasure no less than my duty to offer Paul Dunbar's work in another place. It seemed to me a happy omen for him that so many people who had known him, or known of him, were glad of a stranger's good word; and it was gratifying to see that at home he was esteemed for the things he had done rather than because as the son of negro slaves he had done them. If a prophet is often without honor in his own country, it surely is nothing against him when he has it. In this case it deprived me of the glory of a discoverer; but that is sometimes a barren joy, and I am always willing to forego it.

What struck me in reading Mr. Dunbar's poetry was what had already struck his friends in Ohio and Indiana, in Kentucky and Illinois. They had felt, as I felt, that however gifted his race had proven itself in music, in oratory, in several of the other arts, here was the first instance of an American negro who had evinced innate distinction in literature. In my criticism of his book I had alleged Dumas in France, and I had forgetfully failed to allege the far greater Pushkin in Russia; but these were both mulattoes, who might have been supposed to derive their qualities from white blood vastly more artistic than ours, and who were the creatures of an environment more favorable to their literary development. So far as I could remember, Paul Dunbar was the only man of pure African blood and of American civilization to feel the negro life æsthetically and express it lyrically. It seemed to me that this had come to its most modern consciousness in him, and that his brilliant and unique achievement was to have studied the American negro objectively, and to have represented him as he found him to be, with humor, with sympathy, and yet with what the reader must instinctively feel to be entire truthfulness. I said that a race which had come to this effect in any member of it, had attained civilization in him, and I permitted myself the imaginative prophecy that the hostilities and the prejudices which had so long constrained his race were destined to vanish in the arts; that these were to be the final proof that God had made of one blood all nations of men. I thought his merits positive and not comparative; and I held that if his black poems had been written by a white man, I should not have found them less admirable. I accepted them as an evidence of the essential unity of the human race, which does not think or feel black in one and white in another, but humanly in all.

Yet it appeared to me then, and it appears to me now, that there is a precious difference of temperament between the races which it would be a great pity ever to lose, and that this is best preserved and most charmingly suggested by Mr. Dunbar in those pieces of his where he studies the moods and traits of his race in its own accent of our English. We call such pieces dialect pieces for want of some closer phrase, but they are really not dialect so much as delightful personal attempts and failures for the written and spoken language. In nothing is his essentially refined and delicate art so well shown as in these pieces, which, as I ventured to say, describe the range between appetite and emotion, with certain lifts far beyond and above it, which is the range of the race. He reveals in these a finely ironical perception of the negro's limitations, with a tenderness for them which I think so very rare as to be almost quite new. I should say, perhaps, that it was this humorous quality which Mr. Dunbar had added to our literature, and it would be this which would most distinguish him, now and hereafter. It is something that one feels in nearly all the dialect pieces; and I hope that in the present collection he has kept all of these in his earlier volume, and added others to them. But the contents of this book are wholly of his own choosing, and I do not know how much or little he may have preferred the poems in literary English. Some of these I thought very good, and even more than very good, but not distinctively his contribution to the body of American poetry. What I mean is that several people might have written them; but I do not know any one else at present who could quite have written the dialect pieces. These are divinations and reports of what passes in the hearts and minds of a lowly people whose poetry had hitherto been inarticulately expressed in music, but now finds, for the first time in our tongue, literary interpretation of a very artistic completeness.

I say the event is interesting, but how important it shall be can be determined only by Mr. Dunbar's future performance. I cannot undertake to prophesy concerning this; but if he should do nothing more than he has done, I should feel that he had made the strongest claim for the negro in English literature that the negro has yet made. He has at least produced something that, however we may critically disagree about it, we cannot well refuse to enjoy; in more than one piece he has produced a work of art.

Reprinted from Paul Laurence Dunbar, *Lyrics of Lowly Life* (New York: Dodd, Mead, 1896).

G. M. McClellan

"The Negro as a Writer"

George Marion McClellan, a black poet contemporary with Paul Laurence Dunbar, published throughout the Harlem Renaissance. He is not well known as a poet or critic. Among his works are *Poems* (1895), *Songs of a Southerner* (1896), and *Path of Dreams* (1916), the latter two privately published. In the following survey, McClellan, in contrast to Wallace Thurman, attempts to provide an inside view of some of the achievements of black Americans early in their literary history. McClellan recognizes the integral influence of politics on art by discussing newspaper writing and publication as well as poetry and fiction. His own politics are unclearly articulated attempts to offer uncensored critical evaluations while trying not to offend, a stance he also recognizes as prevalent in many of the writers and works he reviews. More descriptive than critical—but striking in the few truly evaluative comments offered—McClellan's piece is valuable as an early assessment of the literary accomplishments of black Americans. McClellan referred to Charles Chesnutt as "Chestnut," a common error that has been corrected in the following essay.

—Editor's Note

"The pen is mightier than the sword." It would have seemed idle to have said this at the mouth of the mountain pass at Thermopylæ with Leonidas and his immortal Spartan heroes all lying dead amid the wreck made by the mighty host of Xerxes. A century afterward, at Cannæ, one sixth of the whole population of Rome lay dead on the battlefield by the sword thrust. Where was the might of the pen to compare with this? The might of the sword at Thermopylæ, together with the concluding events at Salamis, turned back the Persian hordes and thereby saved the Greek civilization for Europe. Again, after the blood of Cannæ, at Zama, Hannibal was utterly broken and Carthage, with her attending civilization, was doomed to everlasting death, while Rome, her mighty adversary, with her eagles and short sword, carried her dominion and her splendid civilization from England to India. One more great movement in the world illustrating the power of the sword is too tempting to pass by in this connection. From the deserts of Arabia a fanatical dreamer came forth claiming a new revelation from God and as a chosen prophet to give the world a new religion. His pretensions at first caused his expulsion from Mecca, together with a small and insignificant band of followers. Yet because of these it was not long until there came from out of the desert the sound of the marching of a mighty host, heralding the approach of the Arab, the despising and despised. Before these barbarous hordes the principalities of the East were doomed to crumble and yield up their accumulated treasures of the ages, and so triumphant were these invaders from the desert they decided to appropriate for themselves the whole world, and from this they were not *dissuaded* until Charles Martel sent them back from Tours and out of Europe, together with their hateful civilization. So it would seem from these and all other mighty movements of races and tribes, men and nations, the sword has ever been the arbiter. Yet over all the mighty sweep of events and the *stupendous* results of the sword-thrust throughout the ages, comes this insinuating claim, "The pen is mightier than the sword." And when we consider the whole of accumulated philosophy, the onward march of science and human thought, and the consequent development of the human race, the comparative might of the sword becomes insignificant before the less demonstrative power of the conquering pen. And here comes the question, which in some phase or other comes up in all great questions of America, "What part has the Negro in the might of the pen?" Nobody doubts that the great movements of the world at present, let their primary manifestations be military or political, scientific or industrial, have any other great lever than knowledge and sentiment brought into notice and activity by writers.

The chief agencies for the dissemination of thought and discoveries are the newspapers, magazines, literary journals and books of fiction. The newspapers have the most immediate and controlling influence over the action of men in the business and political world. To undertake to estimate with anything like exactness the part the Negro has in molding sentiment through the press and giving the consequent direction to the action of men would be a task impossible in the very nature of the case.

It shall be, then, the purpose of this article to discuss in a general way the Negro as a writer in all lines in which he has essayed to express thought. It would be easy to dispose of the question in two ways. One would be to separate all that he has done as far as that would be possible, and put it over against the production of the white race and thus so minimize it by comparison that its power would likely to be *underrated.* Another way would be to magnify all that has been done as especially praiseworthy, because the production comes from the Negro, thus overrating its significance, forgetting that whatever power any writing can have can only be in proportion to its real merit in the thought-world, regardless of all source from which it came. Overrating the Negro as a writer is more likely to be done in passing on his attempts in *literary* art than in any other field. But in literary lines the number who can command attention and be worthy of notice is very small. One does not have to go far to see that the most effective work, so far as creating sentiment is concerned, and thereby *wielding* power in the great moving forces of this age, the Negro as a writer is best evinced by the Negro press. We have many newspapers, and after thirty years we have not been able to produce one single great newspaper, nor for many good reasons one single great editor who is a power in the land. Indeed, the most of the many papers of ours that come from the press have but little in them that can attract the intelligent minds of the race. There is, however, among us too great a tendency to ridicule the Negro press unreservedly, and though much of the ridicule may be deserved it remains true that the accumulative power of the Negro press is hardly appreciated as it deserves to be. They who write for us and fight our battles are essentially our only spokesmen, and as ignored as our articles and editorials would seem to be by the white press, it is true nevertheless that the white newspapers take close notice of what the Negro writers have to say. They may not ordinarily deign to appear to take notice, but let any publication be made in our most humble sheets that seems to them to be dangerous or too presumptuous to let pass, and it will be seen then that the white press takes notice and the power of the colored press will become apparent. I have said that we have not yet produced one single great paper, nor one great editor, as white papers and editors are great, and to this I think there can be justly no exceptions taken, for we are lacking in nearly all the accessories to make such greatness possible, but we do have a few papers and editors of marked power. The two most exceptional papers of power that have come under my notice are the New York Age, edited by Mr. T. Thomas Fortune, and the Richmond Planet, edited by Mr. Mitchell. These two papers and their editors have been, and are yet, valiant warriors for the race and of incalculable benefit to the race. As a terse, caustic and biting editorial writer Mr. Fortune is hardly surpassed by anyone, and his paper for years has been uncompromising in fighting all adverse issues in the race question. Almost the same thing can be said of the Richmond Planet, and more than any other, perhaps, has this paper been valiant in waging war against lynching. These two papers, together with a host of others, have set forth the power of the pen and have accomplished far more to offset the adverse sentiment created by the white press than can ever be fully determined. There is another class of Negro writers than those I have mentioned that gets an occasional hearing in the white papers of the South and is of great value to the race. Anyone familiar with the strictures of the South, knows that the Negroes themselves have essentially no chance to discuss through the white newspapers the great questions which are ever to the front concerning them, and their position in the South, and also but very little more in the newspapers of the North, unless in the South the Negroes write some articles to say amen, and highly sanction the white man's dictums and positions on the Negro questions that happen to be up. But there are a few who are able to write on some questions in our defense without compromise, and yet so skillfully as not to offend. In speaking of the attitude of the white press, and its representations, it is not assumed that there is no disposition of fairness on the part of the writers of the white press. Many of the great editors mean to be fair from their standpoint. The Southern white people are prejudiced and supersensitive on some points beyond all reason, and in all questions between the Negro and the white man, as man to man, the assumptions, without an exception, are arrogant beyond all naming, so that it comes about at any point of issue, where men differing, usually would permit the opponent his views as fitting from his side of the question, what the Negro has to say, if he is emphatic and decided, is called impudence. The writer must be skillful, then, to write uncompromisingly and yet not be of the "impudent." There are a few men among us who are able to write for the Southern white papers with reserve, yet without compromise, greatly to our advantage. Among those few, prominent are Prof. G. W. Henderson, of Straight University, New Orleans, and President W. H. Councill, of the College, Normal and Industrial School at Normal, Alabama. Prof. Henderson is a graduate of Middlebury College, Vermont, and Yale Theological Seminary, having taken the fellowship from that institution and studied in Germany two years. His writings show his scholarship and refinement. He has been persistent and valiant in all race matters, especially in educational lines in Louisiana, and his articles, though uncompromising, have from time to time found a hearing and forced respect from the great dailies of New Orleans. President Councill is the most widely accepted in the Southern white press of all Negroes. On some points of disagreement between the Negroes and the white people he concedes more to some of the white man's claims than any other Negro who writes. Secondly, he is truly a great man, and has gained his right to a hearing in intelligent sources. As a writer, pure and simple, he is forcible; and while the whole of his attitude may not be accepted generally by his own race, there is no doubt about his uncompromising attitude and loyalty to his own race first and last, and anyone who has followed his articles in newspapers and leading magazines have surely seen that the apparently sometimes too generous bouquet throwing to the white brother is fully offset by the terrible blows given that same white brother for his sins against the Negro race. This is especially seen in his symposium article in the April number of the Arena, 1899. It would be impossible in the limitation of this article to mention the many Negro writers who are acceptable in leading magazines, and to a greater extent in the great weekly journals of this country. Only one or two can be mentioned: Rev. H. H. Proctor, pastor of the First Congregational Church at Atlanta, Ga., is a graduate of Fisk University and Yale Theological Seminary, and he is a young man of exceptional ability as a writer on timely questions, but as an article writer is often seen in the Outlook, the New York Independent, and such papers. Above them all is Bishop Tanner, of Philadelphia. For diction, fine style, conciseness and logical conclusions, one must go far to find his superior. In the way of history, textbooks on various subjects, and scientific presentation, not much has yet been done among us. Mr. Geo. W. Williams, the Negro historian, has done more in that field than any other. Dr. D. W. Culp has written a treatise on consumption and other medical subjects that have attracted attention and favorable criticism.

It now remains to speak of the writers in literary art. In this field there are many who have certainly made praiseworthy attempts, and of the ladies who cannot be classed with those who have truly made a place among successful literary artists, but whose writing has attracted attention and in character is literary, most complimentary things can be said of Mrs. Frances E. W. Harper, of Philadelphia; of Mrs. Fanny Barrier Williams, of Chicago; of Miss Edna Matthews, of New York, and of Mrs. Cooper, Washington, D.C. Mrs. Cooper's book, "A Voice from the South," is a work in purpose and execution of decided merit. In real literary art, perhaps there are only two in the whole race who have reached a place of genuine high rank among the critics, namely, Dunbar and Chesnutt. There are four poets, however, who have attracted much attention and favorable criticism, and of these I will speak in turn. It is in order to speak of Mr. A. A. Whitman first, because he appeared first of all and in one particular of excellency he is first of all four. His "Rape of Florida" is truly poetry and as a *sustained effort,* as an attempt *in great lines,* it surpasses in true merit anything yet done by a Negro, and this assertion without one qualifying word. He failed as a poet? Certainly. Mr. Whitman made attempts in lines in which Shelley, Keats and Spenser triumphed, and with such mediocrity only possible to him in such a highway, what else could follow beyond a passing notice, though his "Rape of Florida" is a production of much more than passing merit. Aside from the mediocrity of the work attempted in Spenserian lines the man himself in his lack of learning, in his expressible egotism, was derogatory to his ultimate success, and his styling himself as the William Cullen Bryant of the Negro race was sickening in the extreme. Mr. Whitman died recently, but not before he had done all in literary excellence that could be hoped from him. It remains true, however, that he was worthy of a much better place than is accorded him as a Negro poet, and it is to be regretted that his work is so little known among us.

Ten years after Mr. Whitman, Paul Dunbar came forth as a new singer, and got the first real recognition as a poet. As a poet, pure and simple, as a refined verse maker in all directions, Mr. Dunbar surpasses Mr. Whitman by far in the truest significance in the term poet, and he is justly assigned the first place among Negro poets. For many reasons Mr. Dunbar is famous, and to enter into any extended discussion of his work in this connection is needless. Mr. Dunbar is the first Negro to attempt poetic art in Negro dialect. To speak the truth, however, it must be said that there is no such thing as a Negro dialect, but in the bad English called Negro dialect Mr. Dunbar has in verse chosen to interpret the Negro in his general character, in his philosophy of life, in his rich humor and good nature, and the world knows how well he has succeeded. Robert Burns has shown how the immortal life of all beautiful things can be handed down for all time in dialect, but it can scarcely be believed by anyone that great poetry can ever be clothed in the garb known as Negro dialect. But for some pathos and to put the Negro forward at his best in his humorous and good-natured characteristics the so-called dialect is the best vehicle, and in these lines, and these lines only, is Mr. Dunbar by far greater than all others. Out of those lines he is still the first poet, Whitman not excepted, but he is first with nothing like the difference in real merit and the fame he has above all others. But in passing from him, here is Dunbar at his best, dialectic and otherwise:

"When de co'n pone's hot—
Dey is a time in life when nature
  Seems to slip a cog an' go,
Jes' a-rattling down creation,
Lak an ocean's overflow;
When de worl' jes' stahts a-spinnin'
  Lak a pickaninny's top,
An' you feel jes' lak a racah,
  Dat is trainin' fu' to trot—
When yo' mammy says de blessin'
  An' de co'n pone's hot.

"When you set down at de table,
  Kin' o' weary lak an' sad,
An' you's jes' a little tiwhed
  An' purhaps a little mad;
How yo' gloom tu'ns into gladness,
  How yo' joy drives out de doubt,
When de oven do' is opened,
  An' de smell comes po'in out;
Why, de 'lectric light o' Heaven
  Seems to settle on de spot,
When yo' mammy says de blessin'
  An' de co'n pone's hot.

"When de cabbage pot is steamin'
  An' de bacon good an' fat,
When de chittlins is a-spuller'n'
  So's to show you whah dey's at;
Tek away yo' sody biscut,
  Tek away yo' cake an' pie,
Fu' de glory time is comin',
  An' it's 'proachin' mighty nigh,
An' yo' want to jump an' hollah,
  Dough you know you'd bettah not
When yo' mammy says de blessin',
  An' de co'n pone's hot.

"I have hyeahd o' lots o' sermons,
  An' I've hyeahd o' lots o' prayers,
An' I've listened to some singin'
  Dat has tuck me up de stairs
Of de Glory-lan' an' set me
  Jes' below de mahstah's th'one,
An' lef' my hea't a-singin'
  In a happy aftah tone;
But dem wu'ds so sweetly murmured
  Seemed to tech de softes' spot,
When my mammy says de blessin',
  An' de co'n pone's hot."

This is not so great a poem as the "Cotter's Saturday Night" by Burns, because the spiritual element and the whole scope of the tenderest concerns of the family and of life in that poem are left out of this. But in Dunbar's poem, where only the festival is pictured, the scene is so intensified that one feels the warmth and sees the glow of the evening fire and inhales the appetizing odors of the coming homely cheer, and can see back of these the tender care and ineffable love of the "Mammy," who puts the crowning touch upon her love with the blessing. As far as it goes, "When the co'n pone's hot" is great precisely in the same lines that the "Cotter's Saturday Night" is great.

Mr. Dunbar has also written a number of novels and short stories. It has not been my good fortune to see "The Stories from Dixie"; but the novels I have bought and read. If there were not Charles Chesnutt, Mr. Dunbar's novels would have to be discussed in this connection, and he would have to be put down as the very first Negro novel writer, mainly, however, because there would be no other; but with Mr. Chesnutt in the field, no true admirer of Mr. Dunbar will ever discuss the prolific diffusions of his, bearing the name novels, in any connection with Dunbar, the poet. There is only enough space left in this article for the poets, to barely mention the names of Mr. Daniel Webster Davis, of Manchester, Virginia, and Mr. James D. Corrothers of Red Bank, New Jersey, and to give a selection from each and let their poems speak for them as writers. Both of them have received notice in the best magazines and favorable criticism elsewhere. Both owe their distinction mainly to their work in dialectic verse which, I fear, is too much like the "ragtime" music, considered quite the proper dressing for Negro distinction in the poetic art.

Here is to "De Biggis' Piece ub Pie," by Mr. Davis:

"When I was a little boy
I set me down to cry,
Bekase my little brudder
Had de biggis' piece ub pie.
But when I had become a man
I made my min' to try
An' hustle roun' to git myself
De biggis' piece ub pie.

"An' like in bygone chil'ish days,
De worl' is hustlin' roun'
To git darselbes de biggis' slice
Ub honor an' renown;
An' ef I fails to do my bes',
But stan' aroun' an' cry,
Dis ol' worl' will git away
Wid bof de plate an' pie.

"An' eben should I git a slice
I mus' not cease to try,
But keep a-movin' fas' es life
To hol' my piece ub pie.
Dis ruff ol' worl' has little use
Fur dem dat chance to fall,
An' while youze gittin' up ag'in
'Twill take de plate an' all."

The one more selection from Mr. Davis will show him as a poet outside of dialect:

A ROSE

"The rose of the garden is given to me,
And, to double its value, 'twas given by thee;
Its lovely bright tints to my eyesight is borne,
Like the kiss of a fairy or blush of morn.

"Too soon must this scent-laden flower decay,
Its bright leaves will wither, its bloom die away;
But in memory 'twill linger; the joy that it bore
Will live with me still, tho' the flower's no more."

Mr. James D. Corrothers writes:

A THANKSGIVIN' TURKEY

"Cindy, reach dah 'hine yo' back
'N han' me dat ah Almanac;
W'y, land! t'morrer's Thanksgivin'!
Got to git out an' make hay—
Don't keer whut de preachah say—
We mus' eat Thanksgivin' day,
Uz sho' uz you's a-libbin.

"You know whah Mahs Hudson libs?
Dey's a turkey dah dat gibs
Me a heap o' trouble.
Some day Hudson g'ine to miss
Dat owdashus fowl o' his;
I's g'ine ober dah an' twis'
'At gobbler's nake plumb double.

"Goin' pas' dah t' othah day,
Turkey strutted up an' say,
'A-gobble, gobble, gobble,'
Much uz ef he mout remahk,
'Don' you wish 'at it wuz dahk?
Ain't I temptin'?' S' I, 'you hah'k,
Er else dey'll be a squabble.

" 'Take an' wring yo' nake righ' quick,
Light on yo' lak a thousan' brick,
'N you won't know whut befell you.'
'N I went on. Yet evah day
When I goes by that a-way,
'At fowl has too much to say;
'N I'm tiahd uv it, I tell you.

"G'ine to go dis bressed night
An' put out dat turkey's light,
'N I'll nail him lak a cobblah.
Take keer, 'Cindy, lemme pass,
Ain't a-g'ine to take no sass
Off no man's turkey gobblah."

And now for the last and the greatest Roman of them all in literary art—Mr. Charles W. Chesnutt, of Cleveland, Ohio. I have never seen him, and at present the only personal acquaintance I have with him, is a brief letter of a dozen or more lines; but Mr. Chesnutt, revealed by his novels, I know well. The chief distinction one finds in reading Mr. Chesnutt from all other Negro story-writers, so far as there are such, is that he is truly an artist and that his art is fine art. Secondly, and this is of the greatest concern to Negroes in any thought of the Negro as a writer, he is the best delineator of Negro life and character, thought and feeling, of any who has attracted notice by writing. It is not possible to give in this connection any quotations from Mr. Chesnutt's work that may speak for him, but it is fitting in this article to speak of the character of some of Mr. Chesnutt's stories, and, as far as possible, suggest the ground and purpose of his fiction. Perhaps, to mention the stories, "The Wife of His Youth," "The Wheel of Progress," and "The

House Behind the Cedars," would serve best for this occasion. There are some situations of the Negroes too full of ineffable pity for utterance. Who has not sat at some time in a Negro church and heard read the pitiful inquiry for a mother, or a child, or a father, husband or wife, all lost in the sales and separations of slavery times—loved ones as completely swallowed up in the past (yet in this life they still live) as if the grave had received them. At such a reading, though it was given with unconcern, one heard the faithful cry of faithful love coming out of the dark on its sorrowful mission.

And in this realm Mr. Chesnutt tells us of a mulatto boy who marries a woman of Negro type, and who was old enough for the boy's mother, but had, at that time, youth enough left to make the disparity of age at the time of little objection, especially in the times and situation where there was little objection to marriages of any sort. But the youth escapes from slavery and in the far North receives education, development and culture, and in time earns a competence that makes life desirable and opens up vistas to new happiness, for the old life is now only a memory of what the new man once was, and the new man is on the borderland of new love and marriage befitting all his advancements, while the mulatto slave boy, the slave girl, the black slave-wife and the slave connections are left forever behind. But in all these twenty-five years the black slave wife is still living, still ignorant and yielding all the while to age until she is an old woman. But there was one thing that did not yield to age and time, and that was her love for her boy husband, and, what was more, her sublime and unwavering faith in the constancy of her "Yaller Sam," after whom she sends inquiry after inquiry, and year after year tramps from place to place in her search, with faith and love divine ever leading her on, until one day in a Northern city, to which place she had finally traced him, she stopped at his very door to humbly inquire of the strange gentleman she saw for her "Yaller Sam," never dreaming that it was he to whom she spoke, though he knew her and had to face the bitter tragedy of it all. But Mr. Chesnutt's art enables him to take care of so sorrowful a case satisfactorily.

"The Wheel of Progress" touches another phase of pathetic situations arising out of the mixture of people and sentiments in the South. The story tells of an ostracized Northern white teacher who, from young womanhood, labors away her life for the Negroes, until her age and health reach that degree of disadvantage that her position as teacher, once her medium of charity, becomes her only means for a living. In the meantime the Negroes whom she and others helped to uplift and develop, and to whom, because of race distinction, most all avenues outside of menial labor are closed, except preaching and teaching, had become her competitors. In the conflict that arose over the reappointment of the white missionary teacher and a young Negro to the place the pitiful situation is again taken care of by Mr. Chesnutt's fine art. "The House Behind the Cedars," until his latest, "The Marrow of Tradition," was his most ambitious attempt. In this book the story of an Octoroon family is put forth in all the pathos and tragedy that is the lot of so many Negroes who belong wholly to neither race.

Mr. Chesnutt's latest book, "The Marrow of Tradition," is a strong and vigorous presentation of the colored man's case against the South in the form of a dramatic novel. This book especially deserves a wide reading among the Negroes, who have none too many friends to plead their cause. Mr. Chesnutt, as one truly high-rank novelist among us, ought to have such a hearing among the eight millions that would give him all the advantages of a successful novelist from a financial standpoint as a return for his labor, which is by no means for himself alone.

In closing, it is but fair to say, while the artists of high rank among us are few in number, in an article discussing the Negro as a writer, in mentioning names at all, it must necessarily follow that there are very many names not here mentioned that would deserve to be if in such an article as this there were any intention or necessity to mention the whole list of Negro writers who write well and with power in every department of letters.

Reprinted from *Twentieth Century Negro Literature; or, a Cyclopedia of Thought on the Vital Topics Relating to the American Negro* (Naperville, Ill.: J. L. Nichols, 1902).

Wallace Thurman

"Negro Poets and Their Poetry"

Wallace Thurman, commonly identified with the writers of the Harlem Renaissance, is best known for his novels *The Blacker the Berry* . . . (1929), one of the few literary works featuring a dark-skinned heroine, and *Infants of the Spring* (1932), a bitterly satiric account of events and writers associated with the Renaissance. In the following piece, which appeared in the July 1928 issue of *Bookman,* he turns his satiric skills to an evaluation of black American poetry. Representative of one kind of thinking among Harlem Renaissance writers looking back at their literary forebears he finds no black poet worthy of unqualified praise and few poems worthy of merit. Assuming a mantle of critical objectivity, if not emotional detachment, Thurman rejects consideration of any extenuating circumstances relevant to the creation or publication of poetry by black Americans; a black aesthetic is an inconceivable concept to him. Exacting in his standards, to the point of seeming unsympathetic to the efforts of individuals who produced under constraining circumstances, Thurman nonetheless provides valuable commentary because he was one of the few Afro-Americans who tried, in the first decades of the twentieth century, to assess in any critical sense the work of other blacks. Because the tone is as much a part of the essay as the critical judgments, the piece reveals as much about Thurman as it does about the nature of Afro-American creativity.

—*Editor's Note*

Jupiter Hammon, the first Negro in this country to write and publish poetry, was a slave owned by a Mr. Joseph Lloyd of Queens Village, Long Island. Hammon had been converted to the religion of Jesus Christ and all of his poems are religious exhortations, incoherent in thought and crudely executed. His first poem was published in 1761, his second, entitled "An Address to Miss Phillis Wheatley, Ethiopian Poetess in Boston, who came from Africa at eight years of age and soon became acquainted with the Gospel of Jesus Christ," in 1768.

This Miss Phillis Wheatley, who had been bought from a slave-ship by a family named Wheatley in Boston Harbor and educated by them, wrote better doggerel than her older contemporary Hammon. She knew Alexander Pope and she knew Ovid—Hammon only knew the Bible—and she knew Pope so well that she could write like a third-rate imitator of him. Phillis in her day was a museum figure who would have caused more of a sensation if some contemporary Barnum had exploited her. As it was she attracted so much attention that many soft hearted (and, in some cases, soft headed) whites and blacks have been lead to believe that her poetry deserves to be considered as something more than a mere historical relic. This is an excerpt from her best poem:

Imagination! who can sing thy force?
Or who describe the swiftness of thy
    course?
Soaring through the air to find the bright
    abode,
The empyreal palace of the thundering
    God,
We on thy pinions can surpass the wind,
And leave the rolling universe behind,
From star to star the mental optics rove,
Measure the skies, and range the realms
    above,
There in one view we grasp the mighty
    whole,
Or with new worlds amaze the unbounded
    soul.

She never again equalled the above, far less surpassed it. And most of the time she wrote as in the following excerpt from "On Major General Lee." (This poem would warm the heart of "Big Bill" Thompson of Chicago; he really should know about it.) A captured colonial soldier is addressing a British general:

O Arrogance of tongue!
And wild ambition, ever prone to wrong!
Believ'st thou, chief, that armies such as
    thine
Can stretch in dust that heaven defended
    line?

In vain allies may swarm from distant
lands,
And demons aid in formidable bands,
Great as thou art, thou shun'st the field of fame,
Disgrace to Britain and the British name.

She continues in this vein, damning the British and enshrining the Americans until she reaches a climax in the following priceless lines:

Find in your train of boasted heroes, one
To match the praise of Godlike Wash-
ington.
Thrice happy chief in whom the virtues
join,
And heaven taught prudence speaks the
man divine.

Thomas Jefferson is quoted as saying that "Religion has produced a Phillis Wheatley, but it could not produce a poet. Her poems are beneath contempt." Nevertheless, Phillis had an interesting and exciting career. The Wheatleys carried her to London, where her first volume was published in 1773. She was exhibited at the Court of George III, and in the homes of the nobility much as the Negro poets of today are exhibited in New York drawing-rooms. She wrote little about slavery, which is not surprising considering that save for her epic trip across the Atlantic in a slave-ship, she had never known slavery in any form. She often mentioned her homeland and once spoke of herself as "Afric's muse," but she was more interested in the religion of Jesus Christ and in the spreading of piety than in any more worldly items, save perhaps in her patriotic interest for the cause of the American colonists.

Heretofore every commentator, whether white or black, when speaking of Phillis Wheatley, has sought to make excuses for her bad poetry. They have all pointed out that Phillis lived and wrote during the eighteenth century, when, to quote from the introduction of White and Jackson's "Poetry of American Negro Poets," "the great body of contemporary poetry was turgid in the style of debased Pope." It would be too much, they continue, to expect "a poet of Phillis Wheatley's rather conventional personality to rise above this influence." In his preface to "The Book of American Negro Poetry," James Weldon Johnson contends that "had she come under the influence of Wordsworth, Byron, Keats or Shelley, she would have done greater work." Does it smack too much of lese-majesty to suggest that perhaps Phillis wrote the best poetry she could have written under any influence, and that a mediocre imitation of Shelley would have been none the less mediocre than a mediocre imitation of Pope? Phillis was also influenced by the Bible, but her paraphrases of the scripture are just as poor as her paraphrases of "debased Pope."

Phillis died in 1784 and until Paul Laurence Dunbar published his "Oak and Ivy," in 1892, American Negro poetry stayed at the level at which she had left it, although there must have been over one hundred Negroes who wrote and published poetry during this period. Most of them came into prominence during and after the Civil War, and were encouraged by abolitionists to write of their race and their race's trials. Frances Ellen Harper is probably the best of this period. One volume, "On Miscellaneous Subjects," was published with an introduction by William Lloyd Garrison. Over ten thousand copies were circulated. Mrs. Harper also wrote and published "Moses, a Story of the Nile," in verse covering fifty-two closely printed pages. Many of her contemporaries were equally ambitious. Length was a major poetic virtue to them.

It seems highly probable that these people wrote in verse because neither their minds nor their literary tools and backgrounds were adequate for the task of writing readable and intelligent prose. They could be verbose and emotional in verse, and yet attain a degree of coherence not attainable when they wrote in prose. George M. Horton is a good illustration. He was born a slave in Chatham County, North Carolina, in 1797. It is said that he "was not a good farm worker, on account of devoting too much time to fishing, hunting and attending religious meetings." He taught himself to read with the aid of a Methodist hymn-book and a red-backed speller. In 1830 he secured work as a janitor at Chapel Hill, the seat of the University of South Carolina. [*sic*] Here he made extra money writing love poems for amorous students. Desiring to obtain his freedom and migrate to Liberia, Horton, aided by some of his white friends, published a volume of verse entitled "The Hope of Liberty," but the returns from the sale of this volume were not sufficient for his purpose. But he remained more or less a free agent, and was allowed to hire himself out instead of having to remain on his master's plantation. In 1865, a troop of Federal soldiers, who had been quartered in Chapel Hill, were ordered north. Horton left with them and went to Philadelphia where he eventually died.

Here is a sample of his prose: "By close application to my book and at night my visage became considerably emaciated by extreme perspiration, having no lucubratory apparatus, no candle, no lamp, not even lightweed, being chiefly raised in oaky woods." And here is a sample of his verse:

> Come liberty. Thou cheerful sound
> Roll through my ravished ears;
> Come, let my griefs in joy be drowned
> And drive away my fears.

Further comment would be superfluous.

After the Civil War, the Negro found himself in a dilemma. He was supposed to be free, yet his condition was little changed. He was worse off in some respects than he had been before. It can be understood, then, that the more articulate Negroes of the day spent most of their time speculating upon this thing called freedom, both as it had been imagined and as it was in actuality.

However, none of the poetry written at this time is worthy of serious critical consideration. It was not even a poetry of protest. Although Negro poets objected to the mistreatment of their people, they did not formulate these objections in strong, biting language, but rather sought sympathy and pled for pity. They wept copiously but seldom manifested a fighting spirit. The truth is, only one American Negro poet has been a fighting poet, only one has really written revolutionary-protest poetry, and that is Claude McKay, who will be considered later.

Paul Laurence Dunbar was the first American Negro poet whose work really merited critical attention. Dunbar was the son of two ex-slaves, both supposedly full-blooded Negroes, a fact flagrantly paraded by race purists, to controvert the prevalent Nordic theory that only Negroes with Caucasian blood in their veins ever accomplish anything. He was born in Dayton, Ohio, June 27th, 1872. His father had escaped from his master and fled to Canada, but later returned to the States and enlisted for military service during the Civil War in a Massachusetts regiment. Dunbar may have inherited his love for letters and writing from his mother, whose master had often read aloud in her presence.

Dunbar attended the public schools in his home town, and was graduated from the local high-school, where he had edited the school paper. Then he found employment as an elevator operator. In 1892 he delivered an address in verse to the Western Association of Writers, and shortly afterwards he published his first volume, "Oak and Ivy." In 1896, through the subscription method, he was able to publish another volume entitled, "Majors and Minors." William Dean Howells wrote a most favorable review of this volume and later paved the way for Dodd, Mead and Company to publish "Lyrics of Lowly Life," for which he wrote an introduction. Meanwhile Dunbar had visited England, and had become a great friend with Coleridge-Taylor, the Negro composer, with whom he collaborated on many songs. On his return to the United States, another friend, Robert G. Ingersoll, helped him to get a position in the Library of Congress. He was only able to keep this job two years, for meanwhile he had developed pulmonary tuberculosis, and despite pilgrimages to such lung-soothing climates as the Adirondacks, the Rockies, and Florida, he finally succumbed to the disease and died in Dayton, Ohio, on February 9, 1908.

From 1892 until the time of his death Dunbar published five volumes of verse, four volumes of collected short stories, and four novels. Not only was he the first Negro to write poetry which had real merit and could be considered as having more than merely sentimental or historical value, but he was also the first Negro poet to be emancipated from Methodism, the first American Negro poet who did not depend on a Wesleyan hymn-book for inspiration and vocabulary. Most of the poets preceding him were paragons of piety. They had all been seized upon by assiduous missionaries and put through the paces of Christianity, and their verses were full of puerile apostrophizing of the Almighty, and leaden allusions to Scriptural passages.

Yet Dunbar was far from being a great poet. First of all, he was a rank sentimentalist, and was content to let surface values hold his interest. He attempted to interpret the soul of his people, but as William Stanley Braithwaite has said, he succeeded "only in interpreting a folk temperament." And although he was, as William Dean Howells affirmed, the first "man of pure African blood of American civilization to feel Negro life aesthetically and express it lyrically," neither his aesthetic feeling nor his expression ever attained enough depth to be of permanent value.

Dunbar is famous chiefly for his dialect poetry. Yet he often regretted that the world turned to praise "a jingle in a broken tongue." He was ambitious to experiment in more classical forms, and to deal with something less concrete than the "smile through your tears" plantation-darky of reconstruction times. Here perhaps was his greatest limitation. Being anxious to explore the skies, he merely skimmed over the surface of the earth.

After Dunbar, there was a whole horde of Negro poets, who like him, wrote in dialect. The sum total of their achievement is zero, but happily, in addition to these parasitic tyros there were also two new poets who had more originality and more talent than their contemporaries. And though neither of these men produced anything out of the ordinary, they did go beyond the minstrel humor and peasant pathos of Dunbar, and beyond the religious cant and doggerel jeremiads of Dunbar's predecessors. One of these men, William Stanley Braithwaite, is best known as a student and friend of poets and poetry rather than as a poet. He has yearly, since 1913, issued an anthology of American magazine verse, and has also published some academic studies of English literature.

The second, James Weldon Johnson, achieved little as a poet until recently, when he published "God's Trombones," a volume of Negro sermons done in verse. His first volume, "Fifty Years And Other Poems," contains little of merit. The title poem, which recounts in verse the progress of the race from 1863 to 1913, has, because of its propagandist content, been acclaimed as a great poem. No comment or criticism is necessary of this opinion when part of the poem itself can be quoted:

Far, far, the way that we have trod
From heathen trails and jungle dens
To freedmen, freedmen, sons of God,
Americans and citizens.

Mr. Johnson, it seems, has also been fairly intimate with Methodist hymn books.

His sermon poems, while at times awkward and faulty in technique, have an ecstatic eloquence and an individual rhythm which immediately place them among the best things any Negro has ever done in poetry. Although his may not be saying much, and although, as a poet Mr. Johnson may not be adequate to the task of fully realizing the promise of these sermon poems, he has at least laid a foundation upon which a new generation of Negro poets can build. He will have to be remembered as something more than just a historical or sentimental figure. He, like Dunbar, is an important, if a minor bard; and if the Negro poet of the future is to make any individual contribution to American literature he must derive almost as much from the former's "God's Trombones" as from the latter's "Lyrics of Lowly Life."

To consider all the Negro poets who since 1913 have lifted up their voices in song would necessitate using an entire issue of any journal. It is not only an impossible task but one not worth the time and space it would require. For our present study we will touch only the high spots, passing over such people as Fenton Johnson, whose early promise has never been fulfilled; Joseph Cotter, Jr., who, it is alleged by most critics in this field, would have been a great poet had he lived but whose extant work belies this judgment; Georgia Douglas Johnson, whose highly sentimental and feminine lyrics have found favor; Arna Bontemps, who specializes in monotonous and wordy mystic evocations which lack fire and conviction, and Helene Johnson, who alone of all the younger group seems to have the "makings" of a poet.

But taking up the contemporary triumvirate—McKay, Cullen, and Hughes—all of whom have had volumes published by reputable houses and are fairly well known to the poetry-reading public, we have poets of another type. Each one of them represents a different trend in Negro literature and life.

Claude McKay was born in Jamaica, British West Indies, where he received his elementary education, served a while in the constabulary, and wrote his first poems. A friend financed his journey to America to finish his scholastic work, but McKay found himself at odds with the second-rate schools he attended here, and finally fled to New York City where he became a member of the old *Masses, Seven Arts, Liberator* group of radicals and artists. During this period he received a legacy which, he tells us, was spent in riotous living. Broke, he attempted to make a living by washing dishes, operating elevators, doing porter work—the usual occupations engaged in by Negro artists and intellectuals.

McKay's first volume was published while he was still in Jamaica, a compilation of folk-verse done in the native dialect. The Institute of Arts and Science of Jamaica gave him a medal in recognition of this first book. It is in many ways remarkable, and in it the poet gives us a more substantial portrait and delves far deeper into the soul of the Jamaican than Dunbar was ever able to in the soul of the southern Negro in America.

McKay's latter poetry is often marred by bombast. He is such an intense person that one can often hear the furnace-like fire within him roaring in his poems. He seems to have more emotional depth and spiritual fire than any of his forerunners or contemporaries. It might be added that he also seems to have considerably more mental depth too. His love poems are not as musical or as haunting as Mr. Cullen's, but neither are they as stereotyped. His sonnet to a Harlem dancer may not be as deft or as free from sentiment as "Midnight Nan" by Langston Hughes, but it is far more mature and moving. All of which leads us to say that a study of Claude McKay's and of the other better Negro poetry convinces us that he, more than the rest, has really had something to say. It is his tragedy that his message was too alive and too big for the form he chose. His poems are for the most part either stilted, choked, or overzealous. He could never shape the flames from the fire that blazed within him. But he is the only Negro poet who ever wrote revolutionary or protest poetry. Hence:

If we must die, let it be not like hogs
Hunted and penned in an inglorious spot,
. . . .
Oh, Kinsman! We must meet the common
foe;
Though far outnumbered, let us still be brave,
And for their thousand blows, deal one
death blow!
What though before us lies the open grave?
Like men we'll face the murderous pack,
Pressed to the wall, dying—but fighting
back.

There is no impotent whining here, no mercy-seeking prayer to the white man's God, no mournful jeremiad, no "ain't it hard to be a nigger," no lamenting of or apologizing for the fact that he is a member of a dark-skinned minority group. Rather he boasts:

Be not deceived, for every deed you do,
I could match—out match; Am I not
Africa's son,
Black of that black land where black deeds
are done?

This is propaganda poetry of the highest order although it is crude and inexpert. Contrast it with these lines from Countee Cullen's sonnet "From The Dark Tower":

We shall not always plant while others reap
The golden increment of bursting fruit,
Nor always countenance abject and mute
That lesser men should hold their brothers
cheap.

Countee Cullen is the symbol of a fast disappearing generation of Negro writers. In him it reaches its literary apogee. On the other hand Langston Hughes announces the entrance of a new generation, while Claude McKay, glorious revolutionary that he is, remains uncatalogued. For two generations Negro poets have been trying to do what Mr. Cullen has succeeded in doing. First, trying to translate into lyric form the highly poetic urge to escape from the blatant realities of life in America into a vivid past, and second, fleeing from the stigma of being called a *Negro* poet, by, as Dunbar so desired to do, ignoring folk-material and writing of such abstractions as love and death.

There is hardly anyone writing poetry in America today who can make the banal sound as beautiful as does Mr. Cullen. He has an extraordinary ear for music, a most extensive and dexterous knowledge of words and their values, and an enviable understanding of conventional poetic forms. Technically, he is almost precocious, and never, it may be added, far from the academic; but he is also too steeped in tradition, too influenced mentally by certain conventions and taboos. When he does forget these things as in his greatest poem, "Heritage":

What is Africa to me:
Copper sun or scarlet sea,
Jungle star or jungle track,
Strong bronzed men, or regal black
Women from whose loins I sprang
When the birds of Eden sang?
One three centuries removed
From the scenes his fathers loved,
Spicy grove, cinnamon tree,
What is Africa to me?

and the unforgettable:

All day long and all night through,
One thing only must I do:
Quench my pride and cool my blood,
Lest I perish in the flood,
Lest a hidden ember set
Timber that I thought was wet
Burning like the dryest flax,
Melting like the merest wax,
Lest the grave restore its dead,
Not yet has my heart and head
In the least way realized
They and I are civilized.

or his (to illustrate another tendency):

I climb, but time's
Abreast with me;
I sing, but he climbs
With my highest C.

And in other far too few instances he reaches heights no other Negro poet has ever reached, placing himself high among his contemporaries, both black or white. But he has not gone far enough. His second volume is not as lush with promise or as spontaneously moving as his first. There has been a marking time or side-stepping rather than a marching forward. If it seems we expect too much from this poet, we can only defend ourselves by saying that we expect no more than the poet's earlier work promises.

Mr. Cullen's love poems are too much made to order. His race poems, when he attempts to paint a moral, are inclined to be sentimental and stereotyped. It is when he gives vent to the pagan spirit and lets it inspire and dominate a poem's form and context that he does his most impressive work. His cleverly turned rebellious poems are also above the ordinary. But there are not enough of these in comparison to those poems which are banal, though beautiful.

Langston Hughes has often been compared to Dunbar. At first this comparison seems far-fetched and foolish, but on closer examination one finds that the two have much in common, only that where Dunbar failed Langston Hughes succeeds. Both set out to interpret "the soul of his race"; one failed; the other, just at the beginning of his career, has in some measure already succeeded.

The younger man has not been content to assemble a supply of stock types who give expression to stock emotions which may be either slightly amusing or slightly tragic but which are never either movingly tragic or convincingly comic. When Langston Hughes writes of specific Negro types he manages to make them more than just ordinary Negro types. They are actually dark-skinned symbols of universal characters. One never feels this way about the people in Dunbar's poetry. For he never heightens them above their own particular sphere. There is never anything of the universal element in his poems that motivates Mr. Hughes.

Moreover, Langston Hughes has gone much farther in another direction than any other Negro poet, much farther even than James Weldon Johnson went along the same road in "God's Trombones." He has appropriated certain dialects and rhythms characteristically Negroid as his poetic properties. He has borrowed the lingo and locutions of migratory workers, chamber-maids, porters, boot-blacks, and others, and woven them into rhythmic schemes borrowed from the blues songs, spirituals and jazz and with them created a poetic diction and a poetic form all his own. There is danger in this, of course, for the poet may and often does consider these things as an end in themselves rather than as a means to an end. A blues poem such as:

I'm a bad, bad man
'Cause everybody tells me so.
I'm a bad, bad man,
Everybody tells me so.
I takes ma meaness and ma licker
Everywhere I go.

or:

Ma sweet good man has
Packed his trunk and left,
Ma sweet good man has
Packed his trunk and left.
Nobody to love me:
I'm gonna kill ma self.

may be poignant and colorful but the form is too strait-laced to allow much variety of emotion or context. The poems produced are apt to prove modish and ephemeral. But when this blues form is expanded, as in:

Drowning a drowsy syncopated tune,
Racking back and forth to a mellow croon,
    I heard a Negro play.
Down on Lenox Avenue the other night
By the pale dull pallor of an old gas light
    He did a lazy sway
    He did a lazy sway
To the tune o' those Weary Blues.
With his ebony hands on each ivory key
He made that poor piano moan with melody.
O Blues!
Swaying to and fro on his rickety stool
He played that sad raggy tune like a musical
        fool.
    Sweet Blues!
Coming from a black man's soul.

the poet justifies his experiment, and finds at the same time the most felicitous and fruitful outlet for his talent.

Mr. Hughes, where his race is concerned, is perfectly objective. He is one of them so completely that he, more than any other Negro poet, realizes that after all they are human beings; usually the articulate Negro either regards them as sociological problems or as debased monstrosities. To Mr. Hughes, certain types of Negroes and their experiences are of permanent value. He is not afraid of, nor does he ignore, them. He can calmly say:

Put on yo' red silk stockings,

Black gal.
Go an' let de white boys
Look at yo' legs.
. . . .
An' tomorrow's chile'll
Be a high yaller.

or:

My old man's a white old man
And my old mother's black
. . . .
My old man died in fine big house.
My ma died in a shack.
I wonder where I'm gonna die,
Being neither white nor black?

and reach the heights of his achievement in "Mulatto," one of the finest and most vivid poems written in the past few years. But Mr. Hughes has also written some of the most banal poetry of the age, which has not, as in the case of Mr. Cullen, even sounded beautiful.

The future of Negro poetry is an unknown quantity, principally because those on whom its future depends are also unknown quantities. There is nothing in the past to crow about, and we are too close to the present to judge it more than tentatively. McKay is exiled in France, an alien and a communist, barred from returning to this country. Once in a while a poem of his appears, but the period of his best work in this field seems to be at an end. Langston Hughes and Countee Cullen are both quite young, as poets and as individuals. Neither can be placed yet, nor can their contributions be any more than just intelligently commented upon. Whether they are going or will continue to go in the right direction is no more than a matter of individual opinion. All of us do know that as yet the American Negro has not produced a great poet. Whether he will or not is really not at all important. What does matter is that those who are now trying to be great should get intelligent guidance and appreciation. They seem to have everything else except perhaps the necessary genius.

Reprinted from *Bookman,* 67 (July 1928): 555-561.

Contributors

William L. Andrews .... *University of Wisconsin-Madison*
Thomas Bonner, Jr. .... *Xavier University of Louisiana*
A. Russell Brooks .... *Frankfort, Kentucky*
Dickson D. Bruce, Jr. .... *University of California, Irvine*
Keith E. Byerman .... *University of Texas*
Jane Campbell .... *Purdue University, Calumet*
Gregory L. Candela .... *University of New Mexico, Valencia*
William Carroll .... *Norfolk State University*
Walter C. Daniel .... *University of Missouri at Columbia*
Henry Louis Gates, Jr. .... *Cornell University*
Addison Gayle, Jr. .... *Bernard M. Baruch College of the City University of New York*
Maryemma Graham .... *University of Mississippi*
Michael Greene .... *North Carolina A&T State University*
Trudier Harris .... *University of North Carolina at Chapel Hill*
Russell K. Hively .... *Neosho, Missouri*
Blyden Jackson .... *University of North Carolina at Chapel Hill*
Leela Kapai .... *University of the District of Columbia*
Doris Lucas Laryea .... *North Carolina State University*
Carol P. Marsh-Lockett .... *Georgia State University*
Sondra A. O'Neale .... *Emory University*
James Robert Payne .... *New Mexico State University*
Wilfred D. Samuels .... *Prairie View A&M University*
Lorenzo Thomas .... *University of Houston/Downtown College*
Betty E. Taylor Thompson .... *Texas Southern University*
Kenny J. Williams .... *Duke University*
Ora Williams .... *California State University, Long Beach*
J. Randal Woodland .... *University of North Carolina at Chapel Hill*
Hammett Worthington-Smith .... *Albright College*
Richard Yarborough .... *University of California, Los Angeles*

Cumulative Index

Dictionary of Literary Biography, Volumes 1-50
Dictionary of Literary Biography Yearbook, 1980-1985
Dictionary of Literary Biography Documentary Series, Volumes 1-4

Cumulative Index

DLB before number: *Dictionary of Literary Biography,* Volumes 1-50
Y before number: *Dictionary of Literary Biography Yearbook,* 1980-1985
DS before number: *Dictionary of Literary Biography Documentary Series,* Volumes 1-4

A

B

C

D

G

H

I

J

K

L

M

Cumulative Index

O

P

Q

R

S

T

U

V

W

Y

Z